European Union Politics

Palgrave Foundations

A series of introductory texts across a wide range of subject areas to meet the needs of today's lecturers and students

Foundations texts provide complete yet concise coverage of core topics and skills based on detailed research of course requirements suitable for both independent study and class use – the firm foundations for future study.

Published

A History of English Literature (second edition)
Biology
British Politics (second edition)
Chemistry (fourth edition)
Communication Studies
Contemporary Europe (third edition)
Economics
Economics for Business
European Union Politics
Foundations of Marketing
Global Politics
Modern British History
Nineteenth-Century Britain
Philosophy
Physics (third edition)
Politics (third edition)
Theatre Studies

European Union Politics

JOHN McCORMICK

palgrave
macmillan

First published 2011 by
PALGRAVE MACMILLAN

Palgrave Macmillan in the UK is an imprint of Macmillan Publishers Limited, registered in England, company number 785998, of Houndmills, Basingstoke, Hampshire RG21 6XS.

Palgrave Macmillan in the US is a division of St Martin's Press LLC, 175 Fifth Avenue, New York, NY 10010.

Palgrave Macmillan is the global academic imprint of the above companies and has companies and representatives throughout the world.

Palgrave® and Macmillan® are registered trademarks in the United States, the United Kingdom, Europe and other countries.

ISBN 978–0–230–557706–0   hardback
ISBN 978–0–230–557707–7   paperback

This book is printed on paper suitable for recycling and made from fully managed and sustained forest sources. Logging, pulping and manufacturing processes are expected to conform to the environmental regulations of the country of origin.

A catalogue record for this book is available from the British Library.

Library of Congress Cataloging-in-Publication Data
McCormick, John, 1954-
European Union politics / John McCormick.
p. cm.
Includes index.
ISBN 978-0-230-57707-7 (pbk.)
1. European Union. 2. European Union countries–Politics and government. I. Title.
JN30.M375 2011
341.242'2–dc22

10 9 8 7 6 5 4 3 2 1
20 19 18 17 16 15 14 13 12 11

Printed in China

Brief Contents

v

Full Contents

Illustrations and Features

Figures

Tables

Maps

Illustrations

Documents

Debates

Focus on

Profiles

Timelines

Acronyms and Abbreviations

ACP — African Caribbean Pacific programme
ALDE — Alliance of Liberals and Democrats for Europe
CAP — Common Agricultural Policy
CCP — Common Commercial Policy
CFP — Common Fisheries Policy
CFSP — Common Foreign and Security Policy
CoR — Committee of the Regions
DG — directorate-general
EADS — European Aeronautic Defence and Space Company
EAP — Environment Action Programme
EBRD — European Bank for Reconstruction and Development
EC — European Community
ECB — European Central Bank
ECSC — European Coal and Steel Community
ECHR — European Convention on/Court of Human Rights
ECJ — European Court of Justice
EDC — European Defence Community
ECU — European Currency Unit
EEA — European Economic Area/European Environment Agency
EEAS — European External Action Service
EEC — European Economic Community
EESC — European Economic and Social Committee
EFTA — European Free Trade Association
EIB — European Investment Bank
EMI — European Monetary Institute
EMS — European Monetary System
ENP — European Neighbourhood Policy
EMU — economic and monetary union
EP — European Parliament
EPC — European Political Community/European Political Cooperation
EPP — European People's Party
ERDF — European Regional Development Fund
ERM — Exchange Rate Mechanism
ESDP — European Security and Defence Policy
ESM — European Social Model
EU — European Union
EU-12 — the 12 pre-1995 member states of the EU
EU-15 — the 15 pre-2004 member states of the EU
Eurojust — Judicial Cooperation Unit
Europol — European Police Office
GATT — General Agreement on Tariffs and Trade
GDP — gross domestic product
HR — High Representative for the CFSP
IGC — intergovernmental conference
IGO — intergovernmental organization
IMF — International Monetary Fund
IO — international organization
IR — international relations
JHA — justice and home affairs
MEP — Member of the European Parliament
MLG — multilevel governance
NATO — North Atlantic Treaty Organization
NGO — non-governmental organization
OECD — Organisation for Economic Co-operation and Development
OEEC — Organization for European Economic Cooperation
PASD — Progressive Alliance of Socialists and Democrats
PR — proportional representation
QMV — qualified majority vote
RIA — regional integration association
SAA — Stabilization and Accession Agreement
SEA — Single European Act
SMP — single-member plurality
TEC — Treaty Establishing the European Community

TEEC	Treaty Establishing the European Economic Community
TEN	trans-European network
TFEU	Treaty on the Functioning of the European Union
UN	United Nations
VAT	value added tax
WEU	Western European Union
WTO	World Trade Organization

EU member states

AT	Austria
BE	Belgium
BG	Bulgaria
CY	Cyprus
CZ	Czech Republic
DE	Germany
DK	Denmark
EE	Estonia
EL	Greece
ES	Spain
FI	Finland
FR	France
HU	Hungary
IE	Ireland
IT	Italy
LT	Lithuania
LU	Luxembourg
LV	Latvia
MT	Malta
NL	Netherlands
PL	Poland
PT	Portugal
RO	Romania
SE	Sweden
SI	Slovenia
SK	Slovakia
UK	United Kingdom

Preface

This is a book about the politics and policies of the European Union, written for anyone who wants to better understand this critically important – and yet at times frustratingly opaque and peculiar – phenomenon. It is designed mainly for students taking courses or modules on the European Union, but will hopefully interest anyone who wants to find out more about how the EU works, and what difference it makes. Its impact on Europe has been nothing short of revolutionary; it has changed how we understand Europe, how Europeans relate to each other, how Europe fits into the global political and economic system, and even how we think about government and politics more generally. But explaining it is not easy, because it is so unusual, because it is constantly evolving, and because opinion on its significance is divided.

My approach in the chapters that follow is guided by four main goals. First and foremost, I have tried to write a book that is informative and challenging while also being readable and relevant. The best textbooks are written to meet the needs of students rather than to reflect the preoccupations of their authors, and are substantial without being esoteric. No less an authority than Albert Einstein once argued that if you cannot explain a topic simply, you probably don't understand it well enough. Along the same lines, if you cannot explain a topic simply, you are going to make life unnecessarily difficult for those who seek to understand.

The EU has long suffered from an image of impenetrability. It was barely up and running before the British politician Kenneth Younger was complaining that 'European unity is a subject which defies all attempts to make it exciting' (Younger, 1959, p. 92). More recently, the British journalist Emma Hartley (2006, pp. ix, 31), reflecting on a university course she once took on Europe, used terms such as *baffling*, *jargon-filled* and *mind-numbing* to describe its content, and remembers it being heavy on treaty articles but light on 'big ideas with which to grapple'. Later, as a journalist, she wanted to understand how the EU worked but found it 'too large a subject' and too far abstracted from reality. The media, she argues, have compounded the problem by making the EU seem technical and bureaucratic, and for having 'a special gift for making things seem boring'.

European Union Politics sets out to release the EU from the too-often abstract and abstruse world of academic analysis and to make it real, alive and approachable. Every field of academic enquiry has its own specialist vocabulary that describes often complex ideas and concepts, but while often essential it can also sometimes mystify the uninitiated. This book recognizes the importance of understanding that vocabulary, but tries to cut through the jargon and dense conceptualization that is too often a feature of academic writing, and to bring out the drama, intrigue, crises, triumphs, heroes and villains that can be found sprinkled through the long and fascinating history of European integration.

Second, I have tried to write a book that will engage students with different levels of interest in the EU. For some, this will probably be their only formal exposure to the politics of European integration; others, meanwhile, will want to take their studies to another level and will be looking for the foundation that helps make that possible. I also recognize that this book will be used in courses in several different countries, and that instructors will have different ideas about the amount of attention that should be paid to different topics. The contrasts were clear even among the reviewers who read this book in draft manuscript form; they advised me to provide both more and less coverage of theory, both more and less coverage of history, and both more and less coverage of different policy areas. Several asked me to keep the book short, but then suggested additions that would have made it much longer.

Books like this one cannot cover everything in depth; it is first and foremost a survey, setting out to provide an overview of all the most important ideas, facts and principles of the EU, and to offer a taste of the current debates about European integration (influenced, of course, by my own take on what it all means). My hope is that students who read this book will become well-informed observers of the EU, and that it will give them all the tools they need to take their studies to a deeper level, if that is what they have in mind. Above all, I hope that no one reading this book will have to re-live Emma Hartley's frustrations.

Third, where much of the academic work on the EU approaches it as an international organization writ large, reflecting the influence long exerted on EU studies by the writings and theories of scholars of International Relations (IR), *European Union Politics* treats it as a political system in its own right. I come out of the sub-discipline of comparative politics, and believe that the EU should be approached and understood as a self-contained political unit, and should be compared with government and politics in states. For that reason, the chapter structure and general approach used in this book reflects those typically found in textbooks about national politics in Britain, the United States and other countries. I also make comparisons between the way that government and politics works in the EU and in states, reviewing both the similarities and the differences.

There is nothing quite like the EU anywhere else, which limits the number of analogies we can use to compare its institutions and processes. It has been made up mainly on the fly, with differences of opinion about its final destination and about how to get there. Its rules are constantly changing, making new treatments of the EU not only essential but quite a challenge – ordinary Europeans find the EU hard enough to understand, but even those of us who study it and write about it for a living often struggle to keep up: even between the first draft and copy-editing stages of this book, for example, there were important institutional changes in the European Commission and with the creation of the new European External Action Service, and the effects on the euro of the Greek debt crisis were still playing themselves out.

Fourth, my perspective on the EU is driven by my mobile transatlantic existence. I have lived in the United States since 1986 but I am still a British citizen and travel to Europe (which, unlike many Britons, I define as including Britain) several times each year. This allows me to see how integration has evolved in both Europe and the United States (which, after all, began life as 13 separate and mutually suspicious states), and to see how the EU is regarded both by Europeans and non-Europeans. I also tend to see the EU from the perspective of how political business is conducted in the United States; the particular style and culture of American politics gives me insights into politics and policies in the EU that only living outside Europe can offer. My periodic trips to the EU also give me snapshots of its evolution, the changes presenting themselves forcibly every time I step off the plane.

I am particularly struck by how often the EU (and the EEC before it) has been declared dead, dying or comatose over the decades, and yet somehow manages to survive. As I was writing early drafts of this book in February 2010, Commission president José Manuel Barroso was giving a speech at the European Parliament in which he appealed for Europeans to deny the 'intellectual glamour of pessimism and constant denigration' that was doing so much harm to the EU and to Europe's image. As my drafts progressed, the Greek debt crisis began to pick up speed, and it was impossible to ignore the talk of a crisis of European leadership and even the possible collapse of the euro. Every week, another gloomy issue of *The Economist* arrived in the mail with grim declarations of Europe's crisis spinning 'out of control', dark talk of the 'end of progress' in its 'decades-long advance towards an ever-more civilized society', and warnings that the EU had three years to 'save the euro', which the magazine's editors considered 'cursed from birth'. (But then *The Economist* has been warning of the imminent death of the EU almost since the Treaty of Rome.)

It is interesting how often the failures of the EU are contrasted with the stability and dynamism of the United States, and yet the US has many problems too, as most Americans would readily admit. (So did *The Economist*, which in February 2010 described American democracy as 'a study in paralysis'.) In May 2010 a new public opinion poll revealed that 56 per cent of Americans believed their country to be heading in the wrong direction, that just 21 per cent approved of the job being done by the US Congress, that only one-third of voters had positive views about either of the major political parties, and that nearly one-third of Americans 'almost never' trusted the federal government to do what was right (*Wall Street Journal*/NBC News poll, 13 May 2010). It may be unscientific, but a Google search for *Europe* and *crisis* in July 2010 generated about 39 million results, while a similar search for *United States* and *crisis* yielded about 32 million, really not that big a difference.

The chapters that follow are divided into three sections, the first dealing with the ideas and history that are essential to an understanding of the EU, the second covering the major institutions and the key political processes that drive EU politics and governance, and the third covering the major policy areas in which the EU is active. At first glance this looks like a fairly conventional approach, but *European Union Politics* also includes material found in no other comparable texts: there are separate chapters, for example, on the defining qualities of Europe and the Europeans, and on public opinion in the EU and how it relates to European integration. There is also more detailed coverage of the specialized agencies of the EU (such as the European Central Bank), as well as of environmental policy, justice and home affairs, trade policy, and the different facets of external relations.

In terms of presentation, the overall design follows that of others in the Palgrave *Foundations* series, but while I have borrowed some of their features I have introduced many of my own, the overall goal being to present all the material as clearly and as compellingly as possible.

Chapter summaries Every chapter begins with a preview of what the chapter will be about and how it is structured, and ends with a summary that recaps the major topics covered and the major arguments made in each chapter.

Key issues Every chapter also begins with a brief set of open-ended and occasionally provocative questions designed to help students think about some of the critical issues raised in the book, to inspire more thought about those issues, and to suggest subjects for further research.

Terms and concepts Key terms in the text (nearly 200 in all) are given short marginal definitions (all of which are listed at the end of each chapter), while short paragraphs go into more depth on key concepts such as the state, enlargement, Europeanization, euroscepticism, and soft power.

Debates Several chapters include debates that put the case for and against a proposition, such as whether or not the state is dying, whether or not Turkey should be allowed to join the EU, and whether or not the euro might replace the US dollar as the world's major international currency. The goal of these debates is to encourage students to think about some of the more critical disagreements in the saga of European integration, and more actively to think about the different sides of each debate.

Focus The debates are complemented by boxes that go into more depth on topics related to the material in the body of the text. These include details on the origins of the EU flag, the European response to the 2007–10 global recession, and how meetings of the key EU institutions work.

Profiles Where helpful, there are profiles of key European personalities, some of them figures from the history of the EU, and others holders of the key offices in today's EU institutions. The goal here is to put a human face on the EU, and to offer insight into some of the characters that have taken their turn on the European stage.

Tables and figures The text is dotted with tables and figures that present key data on the EU or that try to express some of the more complex ideas in visual form. Most are based on the latest data available from the web sites of key EU and international organizations. Using the URLs to visit those web sites will provide the most recent data.

Timelines and documents The history chapters include timelines that list key events, and also have quotations from selected documents of key historical significance, such as treaties, speeches and declarations.

Further reading Every chapter ends with a short list of books that will provide useful further information, with a focus on the most recent, important and/or helpful sources.

Websites A companion website for this text can be found at www.palgrave.com/politics/mccormick. It contains links to key EU institutions and key sources of news and information on EU affairs, sites contained within figures and tables in the book, updates on key developments in the EU, a searchable glossary, chapter outlines, a full (and searchable) chronology, test banks and additional discussion questions.

Writing this book took me the best part of 2010, and as with all such projects demanded the support and encouragement of a team of dedicated professionals. I particularly want to thank my publisher Steven Kennedy, whose idea it was that I write the book, and who provided his hallmark support and gentle nudging as the work progressed. He is without question a paragon among publishers. I would also like to thank Helen Caunce and Stephen Wenham at Palgrave Macmillan for their work on the book, and Keith Povey Editorial Services Ltd and Ian Wileman for their usual quick and efficient work on the editing, design and production. The book was sent out in manuscript form to seven reviewers, whose suggestions and responses helped guide the final redrafting of the book, and added to it in several important ways. Martí Grau, a former MEP, also read through the chapters on the European Parliament and elections, and made several helpful suggestions. Finally, my thanks and love to Leanne, Ian and Stuart for everything they bring into my life.

JOHN MCCORMICK

About the author

John McCormick is Jean Monnet Professor of European Union Politics at the Indianapolis campus of Indiana University in the United States. He has held visiting positions at the University of Exeter and the University of Sussex in Britain, and at the College of Europe in Belgium, and has been involved since 2007 with a multi-national European consortium that offers a master's degree on European culture. His teaching and research interests lie in comparative politics and public policy, with particular interests in the politics of the EU, British politics, environmental policy and transatlantic relations. His other publications include *Environmental Policy in the European Union* (Palgrave Macmillan, 2001), *The European Superpower* (Palgrave Macmillan, 2007), *Europeanism* (Oxford University Press, 2010), *Understanding the European Union* (Palgrave Macmillan, fifth edition forthcoming 2011), and *Comparative Politics in Transition* (Wadsworth, seventh edition forthcoming 2012).

Photo Credits

The author and publishers would like to thank the following who have kindly given permission for the use of pictorial copyright material:

John McCormick, pp. 17, 302, 406; European Union, 2010, pp. 20, 29, 47, 55, 68, 70, 72, 73, 80, 81, 87, 89, 99, 101, 105, 116, 134, 139, 149, 154, 172, 175, 206, 207, 210, 214, 224, 226, 235, 240, 248, 256, 265, 279, 315, 323, 333, 346, 372, 381, 389, 397, 399, 420, 430, 438; Press Association, pp. 118, 120, 140, 169, 239, 284, 293, 337, 353, 363; Peter Haas, p. 22; Photographic Service of the Council of the EU © European Union, pp. 24, 40, 125, 160, 176, 189, 195, 198, 201, 416, 417; Court of Justice of the European Union, pp. 227, 232; Picture Alliance, p. 62.

Introduction

In March 2007, the Berlin Declaration was published to mark the fiftieth anniversary of the European Union. It claimed that the centuries-old dream of European peace and understanding had been fulfilled, made possible by European unification. It celebrated the end of the 'unnatural division' of Cold War Europe, noted the new strengths of democracy and the rule of law, hailed the 'democratic interaction' of the EU member states and the European institutions, claimed that the EU was 'founded on equal rights and mutually supportive co-operation', and spoke of a European model that combined economic success and social responsibility. 'We, the citizens of the European Union,' it concluded, 'have united for the better'.

Stirring words, to be sure, and yet they were born out of one crisis, and preceded yet more. It was an attempt to jump-start European integration following the shock of negative votes in France and the Netherlands in 2005 on a proposed European constitution, an event greeted by many commentators as representing the death of the European dream. Within a year of Berlin the world entered its worst economic downturn since the 1930s, sparking new doubts about the quality of European global leadership. A year later, following a new all-time low for turnout at elections to the European Parliament, news broke of an economic crisis in Greece that would shake the foundations of the euro, spawning another round of speculation that the European experiment was on the rocks.

This ongoing tension between success and failure, between swagger and humility, and between optimism and pessimism, has been part of the story of European integration since the beginning, and is the core theme of this book. On the one hand, supporters credit the European experiment with bringing lasting peace to Europe, revitalizing the European marketplace, changing the definition of Europe and altering the global balance of power. Its regional economic character has been transformed under the guidance of integration, and while the EU continues to wrestle with unemployment, problems with productivity, labour market restrictions, and a declining and aging population, Europeans are wealthier and healthier than they have been at any time in their history. The EU has redefined both the way in which Europeans see themselves and the way the world sees Europe, and the building of a common body of laws and policies has brought Europeans closer together to their mutual advantage. Some even look forward to the day when Europeans can become citizens of a United States of Europe.

1

Not so fast, respond the detractors. The European experiment has undermined the sovereignty of European states, has sullied the quality of European democracy, has been foisted on unwilling Europeans by political elites, takes too little account of national differences, and makes it more difficult for European states to address economic problems that could once be contained by national governments responding to local circumstances. The EU constitutes a new level of European 'government' that lacks adequate transparency or accountability, and its member states have suffered rather than benefited from the effects of integration, losing their identity and some of their freedom as faceless bureaucrats in Brussels write new laws that seem to be driven by the goal of creating a bland and homogenized Europe.

Meanwhile, both within Europe and internationally the EU continues to generate much bafflement. It is not a conventional state, and non-Europeans often scratch their heads over the distinction between the EU and its member states, undecided over whether to treat the EU as a single entity or simply as a club to which its member states happen to belong. As a global actor, the EU is routinely criticized for punching below its weight, while much of the speculation about the changing balance of power in the international system has bypassed the EU, leapfrogging instead to China, India and even sometimes to Brazil. The euro has quickly become the most recognized symbol of European integration, but in 2010 suffered the shock of the Greek debt crisis, raising questions about its long-term viability.

But whatever we think of the EU, and however we understand its core personality, it is hard to ignore. On the global stage, the EU is the world's wealthiest marketplace, the world's biggest trading power, the world's biggest market for corporate mergers and acquisitions, the world's biggest source of and target for foreign direct investment, and plays a role in international relations unlike that of any other major actor in world history in that it relies on civilian and peaceful means to project itself, rather than military means. From the modest first step taken with the signature of the Treaty of Paris in April 1951, creating the European Coal and Steel Community, we now have today's European Union: 27 member states containing nearly 500 million people, with almost every other European state actively seeking membership of the club, or certainly pondering the possibility. The Cold War political and economic divisions of Europe have gone, and it is now less realistic to think of European states in isolation than as partners in an ever closer European Union. It may not be a United States of Europe, but it is hard to imagine a future without some form of European political union.

In short, Europeans and non-Europeans alike need to better understand how the EU works and what difference it makes. Hence this book, which sets out to provide a survey of the principles, history, politics, policies, and effects of European integration. It asks six core questions:

- What is the European Union?
- Where did it come from and how has it evolved?
- What is the context within which it has functioned?
- How is it governed?
- What are the results of its work?
- How has it changed Europe?

Map I.1 The European Union

EU states

It addresses these questions by dividing the story of integration into three parts. **Part One** (Chapters 1 to 9) sets the scene by reviewing the history and the core principles of European integration. It begins with two chapters that look at the theoretical debates over how and why the EU evolved, and then over what it has become. These chapters make clear that although many explanations have been proposed, there is almost no agreement among scholars of the EU, and we have not yet even agreed an easy answer to the simple question 'What is the EU?' Chapter 1 reviews key theories coming out of the study of international relations, including functionalism, intergovernmentalism, supranationalism,

Table 0.1 The EU in figures

	Area ('000 square km)	Population (millions)	Gross domestic product ($ billion)	Per capita gross national income ($)
European Union				
Germany*	357	82.1	3,649	42,710
France*	547	62.0	2,857	42,000
United Kingdom	245	61.4	2,803	46,040
Italy*	301	59.9	2,303	35,460
Spain*	505	45.6	1,604	31,930
Netherlands*	42	16.4	871	49,340
Poland	313	38.1	528	11,730
Belgium*	31	10.7	504	44,570
Sweden	450	9.2	479	50,910
Austria*	84	8.3	414	45,900
Greece*	132	11.2	356	28,400
Denmark	43	5.5	341	58,800
Finland*	337	5.3	273	47,600
Ireland*	70	4.5	268	49,770
Portugal*	92	10.6	243	20,680
Czech Republic	79	10.4	216	16,650
Romania	238	21.5	200	8,280
Hungary	93	10.0	155	12,810
Slovakia*	49	5.4	98	16,590
Slovenia*	20	2.0	55	24,230
Luxembourg*	3	0.5	53	69,390
Bulgaria	111	7.6	50	5,490
Lithuania	65	3.4	47	11,870
Latvia	65	2.3	34	11,860
Cyprus*	9	0.9	25	26,940
Estonia*	45	1.3	23	14,570
Malta*	0.3	0.4	7	16,690
TOTAL	1,498	496.5	18,456	

* Eurozone

Table 0.1 The EU in figures   (*continued*)

	Area ('000 square km)	Population (millions)	Gross domestic product ($ billion)	Per capita gross national income ($)
Non-EU Europe				
Switzerland	41	7.6	492	55,510
Norway	324	4.8	452	87,340
Ukraine	604	46.2	180	3,210
Croatia	57	4.4	69	13,580
Belarus	208	9.7	60	5,360
Serbia	102	7.3	50	5,590
Bosnia & Herzegovina	51	3.8	19	4,520
Iceland	103	0.3	17	40,450
Albania	29	3.1	12	3,840
Macedonia	25	2.0	9	4,130
Moldova	34	3.6	6	1,500
Montenegro	14	0.6	5	6,660
Kosovo	11	1.8	5	2,300
TOTAL	1,603	95.2	1,376	
Marginal Europe				
Armenia	30	3.1	12	3,350
Azerbaijan	87	8.7	46	3,830
Georgia	70	4.3	13	2,500
Turkey	781	73.9	735	9,020
TOTAL	968	90.0	806	
Other				
United States	9,629	304.1	14,093	47,930
Japan	378	127.7	4,911	38,130
China	9,597	1,325.6	4,327	2,940
Russia	17,075	141.8	1,679	9,660
Canada	9,976	33.3	1,501	43,640
India	3,288	1,139.9	1,159	1,040
World	57,309	6,692.0	60,587	8,613

Source: Population and economic figures from World Bank at http://www.worldbank.org (retrieved June 2010). All figures are for 2008.

realism, and spillover. Chapter 2 switches the focus to comparative politics, considering the qualities of the EU as a political system, and comparing the explanatory value of federalism and confederalism.

Chapter 3 tries to come to grips with the parameters of Europe, reviews the troubling questions about identity in Europe, and then looks at some of its critical demographic trends. The next four chapters provide a survey of the history of the EU, beginning with an explanation of the challenges facing postwar Europe and then tracing integration through the development of treaties, the different stages in enlargement, key policy developments, and the international environment within which integration proceeded. Today's European Union can be traced back to the signature of the 1951 Treaty of Paris, which created the European Coal and Steel Community. Although a useful start, the ECSC was limited in its aims and in 1957 the Treaty of Rome was signed, creating the European Economic Community, the core goal of which was the creation of a European single market. Only six states initially took part, but the first of several waves of enlargement occurred in 1973, moving through stages to 2007 when the accession of Bulgaria and Romania took membership to 27. Along the way, new treaties expanded the reach of integration into new areas of policy, a landmark change coming with the creation of the European Union as a result of the 1992 Treaty on European Union, and another coming in 1999 with the launch of the euro. Chapters 8 and 9 round out the first part of the book by looking in turn at the nature of the agreements reached among Europeans, and at the impact these have had on the relations between EU institutions and the member states.

Part Two (Chapters 10 to 17) focuses on politics and governance by looking at the work and structure of the major EU institutions.

- The *European Commission* is the administrative and executive arm of the EU, promoting European interests and being responsible for drafting new laws and overseeing their execution once they have been adopted, for managing the EU budget, and playing a key role in the EU's external relations, most notably its common trade interests. Headquartered in Brussels, it is overseen by an appointed president who chairs a 27-member College of Commissioners and several thousand career bureaucrats.
- The *Council of Ministers* is an intergovernmental body consisting of ministers from each of the member states, and shares powers with the European Parliament over the adoption of new EU laws. Headquartered in Brussels, it is steered by a presidency, held in a rotation of six months each by the governments of the member states. It is closely related to the *European Council*, consisting of the heads of government of the member states, chaired by an appointed president, and which is responsible for making key strategic decisions.
- The *European Parliament* is the only directly elected European institution, represents the interests of European voters, and shares powers with the Council of Ministers over the adoption of new EU laws. Split between Brussels, Luxembourg, and Strasbourg in France, it has 736 members divided up among the member states on the basis of population, and elected for fixed five-year renewable terms. Members organize themselves into cross-national party groups, and the EP is chaired by a president elected from among its members.

- The *European Court of Justice* is the EU's constitutional court, charged with interpreting the treaties and issuing judgements on cases involving parties in a dispute over EU law, and for issuing rulings in cases in national courts where an EU law is at stake. Based in Luxembourg, it is headed by a president, has one judge for each member state, and is supported by a General Court (dealing mainly with less complex cases) and a Civil Service Tribunal (dealing with EU staff matters).
- A growing network of more specialized agencies deal with specific aspects of EU policy. They include financial bodies such as the European Central Bank, regulatory agencies such as the European Aviation Safety Agency and the European Police Office (Europol), temporary executive agencies that manage specific EU programmes, advisory bodies such as the Committee of the Regions, and independent bodies such as the European Space Agency.

Each chapter begins with some brief historical background, then focuses on the structure and powers of the institutions, showing what each of them does and how they relate to the others. The section ends with Chapters 15 to 17, which focus on the ways in which Europeans engage with these institutions through the work of political parties and interest groups, look at the mechanics and impact of European elections and national referendums, and review public opinion in the EU, both about integration itself and a range of broader issues.

Part Three (Chapters 18 to 25) asks what difference the EU has made by focusing on its policy outputs. Chapter 18 sets the scene with a survey of the policy process and the qualities of public policy in the EU, and is followed by separate chapters dealing with the key policy areas in which the EU has been most active: economic, monetary, agricultural, environmental, cohesion, and justice and home affairs, ending with two chapters that look first at the underlying principles and general policies of the EU as a global actor, and then at the nature of its relationship with specific parts of the world, focusing on the United States, its most immediate neighbours, China, and the developing world.

Throughout this survey of the EU, the tensions between success and failure will be clearly on show. Advances will be contrasted with retreats, achievements will be reviewed along with failures, and hopefully the immensity of the task of moving independent states into the unexplored territory of integration will become clear. At the same time, the chapters that follow will also ask why Barroso's 'intellectual glamour of pessimism and constant denigration' is so prevalent in assessments of European integration, when it is so patently missing from reviews of politics and policy in the EU member states and other liberal democracies. What is it about the EU that invites so much scepticism and doubt? Is it that we do not fully understand the EU or where it is headed, or that we have not yet understood how it compares with conventional state political systems, or is it simply that the exercise is genuinely flawed? These and other questions will be addressed in the chapters that follow.

PART 1 History and Ideas

CHAPTER 1

Understanding Integration

PREVIEW
Today's European Union traces its roots to the creation in 1952 of the European Coal and Steel Community. With this event began a long and complex process by which national interests came to be overlaid with collective European interests. How and why this happened has been the subject of much debate. Multiple theories have been proposed and fine-tuned, but while they offer many valuable insights, no grand theory of European integration has yet been proposed, nor would one likely win general agreement.

The earliest explanations came mainly out of International Relations (IR), and represented the European Community first as a process with its own internal logic, and then as an international organization driven by decisions taken by the governments of the member states. These theories are reviewed in this opening chapter. But as the reach and the powers of the EC and then of the EU expanded, so the focus switched to explanations coming out of comparative politics and public policy, which argued that the EU was a political system in its own right, and that we should pay more attention to the character of its institutions, processes, and policy dynamics. These theories are reviewed in Chapter 2.

How we think about the EU depends mainly on how we understand the changing role of states. Once clearly the dominant actors on the European political stage, states have undergone much change. Inter-state cooperation has grown, and global political and economic forces have encouraged states to work more closely together. In few parts of the world has this been more true than in Europe, where some argue that the EU has developed many of the features of a European super-state, or a new level of government and authority working above the level of the traditional state.

KEY ISSUES

- Is the state dying? If so, are European states dying more rapidly than those in other parts of the world?

- How far can we still think of the EU as an international organization, and how far has it developed the features of a state?

- What role does theory play in understanding the EU, and should theories be primarily explanatory, predictive, or a combination of the two?

- Is realist theory still a useful way of thinking about how states function in the international system?

- Are intergovernmentalist arguments still helpful?

The Westphalian system

The international state system is often known as the Westphalian system after the 1648 Peace of Westphalia. Actually, states had begun to emerge well before 1648, and the worldwide expansion of the state system did not accelerate until after 1945 with the break-up of European empires, but the agreement reached at Westphalia gave that system impetus. Many now question the health of the system, arguing that the state is dying, and point to the European Union and other examples of regional integration as proof of how government and authority are being redefined.

● **The state**: A legal and political arrangement through which all large-scale political communities are organized, combining territory with sovereignty, independence and legitimacy.

● **Sovereignty**: The authority to rule, control, and/or make laws, usually associated with states and incorporating territorial integrity and political independence.

States and nations

In order to understand the context in which the EU has emerged, we first need to understand the qualities of states and nations. For the last three to four hundred years, the **state** has been the usual means for organizing large-scale political communities. The modern state was born in Europe some time in the Middle Ages as competition for power and influence among empires, kingdoms, duchies and the Catholic Church changed territorial boundaries. By the seventeenth century the outlines of today's European state system had become more clear, the defining event being the 1648 Peace of Westphalia. This brought an end to the Eighty Years' War and the Thirty Years' War, adjusted the boundaries of Sweden, France, and the German states, and confirmed the independence of the Netherlands, Switzerland, and the northern Italian states. Borders and **sovereignty** achieved a new prominence, and the term **Westphalian system** is today often used as shorthand for the resulting international order. (For examples of some of the debates involved in the emergence of the state, see Caporaso, 2000.)

Few concepts in political science have since been so hotly debated or contested as the state. There is little agreement on its exact definition, but most scholars would agree that a state is a legal and political entity that has four key qualities: territory, sovereignty, independence, and legitimacy (see Figure 1.1). None of these qualities has ever been static or absolute, because the boundaries of states change, the authority of state institutions is not equally recognized by everyone, no states are truly independent because none is self-sufficient, and there are many states whose international legal standing is either disputed (including Taiwan, Northern Cyprus, and Kosovo) or ambiguous (including the micro-states of Europe, such as Andorra, Monaco, and the Vatican City).

Within these general conditions, however, states have proliferated in recent centuries; in 1800 there were barely two dozen, and only 45 more had been created by the time of the outbreak of the Second World War. With decolonization and the break up of European empires after the war, there was an explosion of newly independent states (80 were created in the period 1950–79 alone,

Figure 1.1 The qualities of a state

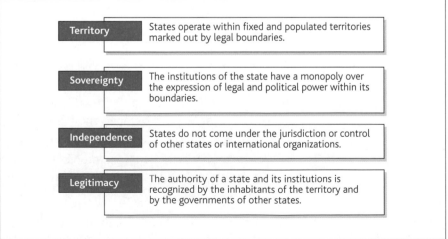

mainly in Africa), and more than 20 were added to the list in the 1990s with the break-up of the Soviet Union and Yugoslavia. Today there are nearly 200 states in the world, with more in the pipeline as pressures for independence, secession or dissolution in Western Sahara, Kosovo, Palestine, Somalia, Sudan, Scotland, Belgium, Dagestan, Corsica, and the Basque Country play themselves out.

Alongside states, we must also understand – particularly in the European context – the sometimes competing claims of nations. If a state is a legal and political entity, then a **nation** is primarily a cultural entity: a group of people who identify with one another on the basis of a mix of real and mythical qualities, which include language, ancestry, history, culture, territory, religion, and symbols. National identity entered its era of rapid growth at about the time of the French Revolution, quickly becoming the main source of political legitimacy in Europe (Dunkerley *et al.*, 2002, p. 44), and the glue that many governments used to extend and define their power. It was also used by minorities to claim their right to self-determination and independence. But, like the state, the nation is a difficult concept to pin down. The nineteenth century French philosopher Ernest Renan described nations as 'a soul, a spiritual principle' driven by a legacy of memories and sustained by the willingness of individuals to live together and to continue to value their heritage (Renan, 1882). More recently, Benedict Anderson has strikingly described them as 'imagined communities' (Anderson, 2006, p. 6).

Pushed far enough, identification with nations may spawn **nationalism**, a belief in the value of preserving the identifying qualities of a nation, and in promoting and protecting its interests. (For a useful reader on the history and meaning of nationalism, see Smith, 2001.) Nationalists may argue that every nation should have its own state and that this goal is worth struggling for through political action. Because few states coincide with nations – particularly in Europe, where almost every state has its national minorities (see Chapter 3) – nationalism has often sparked inter-community conflict and political instability. In extreme cases, it has spilled over into ethnocentrism, racism, ethnic cleansing, genocide, civil war, and inter-state war. It was at the heart of many of the disputes that destabilized Europe during the nineteenth century, and was at the heart of the pressures that led to the outbreak of the First World War. In the inter-war years it plumbed new depths with the Nazi interpretation of history as a racial struggle, and Hitler's belief in racial purity, in extending the *Lebensraum* (living space) of Germans, and in persecuting the Jews and the Roma. As late as the 1990s, nationalist violence tore apart Yugoslavia, and even today national minorities in Britain, Spain, and other European states continue to campaign for self-government or even independence.

In spite of the number of national minorities who would like their own states, and in spite of the large role of European states in running public programmes such as welfare and social security, there are many doubts today about the health of the state. It has always had its critics, who accuse states of creating unnecessary divisions among humans, of often being the major protagonists in war and conflict, of often failing to deal with other states without building antagonistic alliances and using the threat of violence, and of doing a poor job of working with other states to address shared problems such as terrorism, transboundary pollution, illegal immigration, and the spread of disease. Some now argue that states have lost so much of their power and credibility that the

● **Nation**: A community whose members identify with each other on the basis of a shared history, language and culture.

● **Nationalism**: A belief in the primary interests of nations and in the promotion of nation-states founded on national self-determination.

Westphalian system may be on its way out (see, for example, Camilleri and Falk, 1992; Ohmae, 2005).

Van Creveld (1999) argues that after reaching their 'commanding heights' between 1945 and 1975, states have gone into decline, either combining themselves into larger communities or falling apart altogether, many of their functions being assumed by non-state actors. Strange argues that the state has become just one source of authority among several, and that the forces of world markets 'are now more powerful than the states to whom ultimate political authority over society and economy is supposed to belong' (Strange, 1996, p. 4, 73). All states, argues former US Secretary of State Strobe Talbot, are 'social arrangements' that in spite of their seeming permanence and sacredness are in fact 'artificial and temporary'. Within the next hundred years, he suggests, states will be obsolete and we will instead 'recognize a single, global authority', giving the phrase 'citizen of the world' a new meaning (Talbot, 1992).

Others are not prepared to go so far, and argue that the state is not declining so much as being transformed. States still have a monopoly over the control and use of militaries, they are still the major players in the management of economic production and international trade networks, their citizens still identify mainly with states and are subject to the authority and rules of the state, and the ability of states to respond to new challenges has grown thanks to technological innovation. Rather than the state being on its way out, perhaps its role is simply changing as globalization, trade, international law, changes in national identity, and modernization have changed the nature of state power, the relationship among states, and the relationship between states and citizens. (For a survey of the debate, see Sørensen, 2004 and 2006.)

These debates matter in the European context, where the focus of people's allegiance is now divided between states, nations, and Europe. The implications are discussed in more depth in Chapter 3, but the rise of the European Union must be seen not only as a reaction to the historical tensions created by states and nations, but also as a challenge to conventional ideas about political organization. Where once almost every European associated with a state or a nation, what many observers see happening today is the construction of Europe as a new kind of political organization, a revival of identification with nations, and the relative decline of state power. Not everyone is pleased with the results.

International organizations

If one of the defining features of world politics since the end of the Second World War has been a growth in the number of states, another has been the growth of inter-state cooperation. This has spawned thousands of **international organizations** (IOs) through which states or groups of citizens in different states work together on common or shared interests. The underlying motives have varied: states cooperate in the interests of promoting peace, encouraging trade, sharing ideas and resources, reducing duplication, and addressing shared problems such as illegal immigration, environmental decline, cross-border crime, and financial regulation. Most of their efforts have been channelled through bilateral and multilateral contacts between and among governments, but states have also sometimes found it more efficient to create international organizations within which their representatives can work together, and which can employ

● **International organization**: A body that functions in two or more states, or that is set up to promote cooperation among states, based on the principles of voluntary cooperation, communal management, and shared interests.

Debating...
Is the state dying?

YES	NO
States are not the most efficient and peaceful means for ordering human society, because they create avoidable tensions and divisions.	The reach and powers of wealthy states have been growing as they provide more public programmes (such as welfare and social security) and as they control more information about their citizens.
The rise of the global marketplace has meant increased power for multinational corporations, the growth of complex new trade regimes, changes in technology and communications, and new patterns of migration. This has pushed states into complex new patterns of interdependence, reducing the independent powers of state governments.	The rise of international organizations and new levels of supranational authority is not so much evidence of the retreat of states as it is a means of complementing the administrative powers of the state.
Many of the most urgent international problems cannot be solved by states acting alone, because they need to cooperate and place shared interests above state interests. As this happens, their independence of action declines.	Challenges to state sovereignty today are no stronger than they have ever been, and states have adapted to their past problems, learning from their mistakes.
States are being threatened from within as national minorities assert themselves and demand greater self-determination, and even sometimes their own states.	States still have the trump card of controlling militaries and being able to decide when and where to use them. Whatever changes are taking place in the global economy, military force is still the major defining quality of power.
	Citizens still identify mainly with states, and many of their economic and political choices are still limited by state boundaries.

staff to manage joint programmes, gather data, and monitor the progress of international agreements. This kind of cooperation moves us into the realm of supranationalism (see later in this chapter).

The oldest IOs predate the First World War, but the real era of growth in international cooperation has only been since the Second World War. By one estimate, there were less than 220 IOs in existence in 1909, about 1,000 in 1951, and still only about 4,000 as late as 1972. By 1989 the number had risen to nearly 25,000, and today there may be as many as 62,000 (Union of International Associations, 2009). Most IOs fall into one of two major categories:

- International nongovernmental organizations (INGOs) whose members are individuals or the representatives of private associations. They include interest groups such as Amnesty International, Greenpeace, and the International Red Cross, and multinational corporations such as Ford, Toyota, Royal Dutch Shell, ING, and HSBC.
- Intergovernmental organizations (IGOs) whose members are states and whose goal is to promote cooperation among state governments. They include the United Nations, the World Trade Organization, NATO, the OECD, and Interpol.

CONCEPT

Regionalism

The promotion of cooperation and collective action among a group of states based on the identification of shared interests, common goals, the promotion of efficiency, the pooling of resources, and the creation of opportunity. Although states may be motivated by broad philosophical goals such as peace and unity, regionalism is usually focused on economic cooperation, including the promotion of trade and investment. The arrangements made to achieve this vary, but they usually include treaties outlining goals and terms, and the creation of new regional institutions charged with working towards those goals.

Unlike states, IGOs do not usually have control over – or association with – any territory, unless part of their mission is to own and manage land for one purpose or another. Nor do they have much opportunity for independent action, since they are based on the voluntary cooperation of their members, nor do they usually have much authority beyond the requirements of the terms of membership, which rarely provides them with independent powers or the ability to impose their rulings on their members. (The World Trade Organization is one notable exception; its dispute resolution procedure allows states to use the WTO to help resolve trade disputes between members.) But they do have legitimacy, at least among their members, because they are created through the free will of their members (see Figure 1.2).

Taken far enough, international cooperation can evolve into support for **regionalism**. This usually happens when a group of states forms a **regional integration association** (RIA) designed to encourage collective action and develop common rules on shared interests (usually economic cooperation). (This use of the term *regional* should not be confused with cooperation among local communities *within* states.) Regional integration usually goes beyond cooperation, and involves the transfer, sharing, or pooling of sovereignty. Integration involves the creation of regional institutions that have the authority (or 'competence', as it is known in EU terminology) to oversee the making of new rules and regulations in areas where their members have agreed to cooperate. But the institutions are usually set up in such a way that the member states have the final say on the adoption of those rules and regulations, and the regional institutions are mainly denied direct powers of execution, which are left to the governments of the member states.

Regionalism is nothing new, and traces its roots back to the alliances that were once made among monarchs and imperial leaders. In the modern era, the first major exercises in regional integration date from the nineteenth century, and include the *Zollverein* (customs union) among German states dating from the 1820s that laid the foundations for the eventual unification of Germany, the Moldovian-Wallachian customs union of 1847 that was a key step on the road to

Figure 1.2 The qualities of an international organization

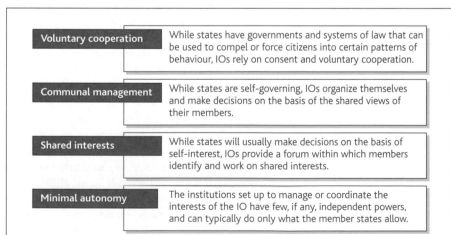

● **Regional integration association**: An organization within which independent states work to encourage cooperation and the pooling of authority and resources for the mutual benefit of its members.

Illustration 1.1
The Council of Europe

The Council of Europe in Strasbourg is one of Europe's oldest international organizations, its achievements in fields such as human rights often overlooked in the attention focused on the European Union.

the creation of Romania in 1878, and the 1848 constitution that formed the basis of the Swiss Confederation (Mattli, 1999, pp. 1–5).

The motives behind regionalism vary by time and place, but in most cases states have been interested in economic cooperation, which – depending on political and economic circumstances – can lead to progressively deeper degrees of integration (see Figure 1.3). Although regionalism was rare before the Second World War, there are today few countries in the world that are not members of one RIA or another (see Table 1.1). Their prospects for success vary (see discussion

Figure 1.3 Stages in the process of integration

Integration is not necessarily a linear process, and different groups of states will have different motives and unique thoughts about the appropriate steps to take, but if there was a European model of integration, it would appear as follows:

Agreement of **free trade area** with the removal of internal barriers to trade (such as tariffs and border restrictions) while maintaining a common external tariff against non-member states.

The creation of a **single market**, meaning the removal of barriers to the free movement of people, money, goods and services.

Efforts to promote **monetary union**, where smaller currencies are tied to a leading currency (as with the Common Monetary Area of southern Africa which links several countries to the South African rand, but has not yet achieved a single currency) or efforts are made to agree a single currency (as with the euro).

RIAs often talk in general terms about the value of peace and political cooperation, and even of political 'unity', but so far the idea of **political union** has been too controversial to be anything more than a theoretical goal.

Table 1.1 Major regional integration associations

Year of founding	Name	Membership in 2010
1952	European Union	27
1957	Council of Arab Economic Unity (Greater Arab Free Trade Area 2005)	18
1960	Latin American Free Trade Association (superseded 1980 by Latin American Integration Association)	
1960	Central American Integration System (suspended 1973-91)	8
1966	Economic Community of Central African States	6
1967	Association of Southeast Asian Nations	10
1967	East African Community (defunct 1977–99)	5
1969	Andean Group	4
1973	Caribbean Community (Caricom)	15
1975	Economic Community of West African States (West African Economic and Monetary Union 1994)	15
1980	Latin American Integration Association	12
1980	Southern African Development Community	15
1981	Gulf Cooperation Council	6
1985	South Asian Association for Regional Cooperation (South Asia Free Trade Agreement 2006)	7
1989	Arab Maghreb Union	5
1989	Asia-Pacific Economic Cooperation	21
1991	Southern Common Market (Mercosur)	4
1991	Commonwealth of Independent States	9
1994	North American Free Trade Agreement	3
2000	Eurasian Economic Community	5
2001	African Union	53

later in this chapter about integrative potential), and the implications of states forming themselves into regional blocs are debatable. But there is no question that political support for regionalism has been growing, and as the number of RIAs has increased, so has scholarly interest in trying to understand them. The study of regional integration is still dominated by the European case, and by academics from Europe and the United States (Breslin *et al.*, 2002), and the broader implications of integration – and its sometimes different motives outside Europe – are not yet fully understood. But this has not prevented some scholars from pointing to integration as more evidence of the declining power of states (Ohmae, 1995).

From federalism to neofunctionalism

Just as international cooperation began to enter its most active phase of growth after the First World War, so the new academic discipline of **International Relations** (IR) began to take its first tentative steps. Scholars of IR began to

● **International Relations**:
The study of relations among states, focusing on alliances, diplomacy, and the dynamics of decisions reached by states working together or in competition with each other.

study the dynamics of relations among states, including alliances, diplomacy, conflict, war, the balance of power, and dependency, and their work was reflected in the growth after the Second World War (particularly in the United States) of the theory of **realism**. Realists argue that because humans are by nature self-centred and competitive, rational self-interest and conflicting objectives encourage states to protect their interests relative to other states and not to trust long-term cooperation and alliances. Realists talk of an anarchic global system in which there is no authority above the level of states that is capable of helping them manage their interactions with one another, and believe that states must use both conflict and cooperation to ensure their security through a balance of power among states. (Neorealism later changed the focus by arguing that the most powerful states acted as poles in the system, driving the actions of themselves and others and creating a system that could be described as unipolar, bipolar, or multipolar.)

A contrasting philosophy was offered, in Europe at least, by supporters of **federalism**. Surveying the ruins created by the Second World War, they argued that states had lost their credibility and their political rights because they could not guarantee the safety of their citizens (Spinelli, 1972). Left to their own devices, elites would rebuild the state system after the war, raising the danger of a revival of inter-state tensions and so of conflict and war. The answer was to replace the European state system with a European federation, and federalists hoped to capitalize on the disruption caused by war to build on this idea. Seeking particularly to address the perennial problem of tensions between France and Germany, members of the wartime resistance movements championed federalist ideas, and in 1946 created the European Union of Federalists (EUF). But by the time the first Congress of the EUF met in The Hague in 1948, national political systems were already being rebuilt, and its moment was largely past (although federalism still remains an important point of reference for understanding integration).

Among the ranks of federalists was Jean Monnet, a French bureaucrat who went on to become one of the founding fathers of European integration (see Chapter 4). Although a supporter of federalism, he thought it would be an end-state that could only be reached gradually: a federal Europe would not be created as a result of 'some great political mutation', he argued (Monnet, 1978, p. 367), but the creation of the European Coal and Steel Community (ECSC) in 1952 would instead be the first small step, and the ECSC experience would spread via osmosis to other areas of policy, with the eventual achievement of a European federation. Looking beyond the state to solve common problems could encourage new cooperative links and new habits of working together, the commitment to which would be strengthened as results started to be felt.

This so-called 'Monnet method' of 'federalism by instalments' was criticized by Altiero Spinelli, an Italian politician who later served as a European Commissioner and a Member of the European Parliament. Spinelli argued that Monnet's proposal suffered from the lack of a political centre, or the leadership to push the process along. Strong and independent institutions were needed, otherwise the process of integration would be run by state governments (see Burgess, 2009). But the idea of transferring power to such institutions has always been anathema to state governments, and even today there remains much resistance to federalist ideas among European leaders and citizens. Under the circum-

● **Realism**: A theory of international relations which argues that we live in an anarchic global system (one without rules or an authority above the level of the state), and that states relate to-and compete with-each other according to their self-interest.

● **Federalism**: Promotion of, or support for, the idea of federation. For European federalists this means a belief in the merits of replacing the European state system with a new European federation, or a United States of Europe.

Jean Monnet (1888–1979)

Jean Monnet is often regarded as the founding father of Europe, his main contribution being the ideas that lay behind the European Coal and Steel Community. A committed internationalist, he was born in Cognac in western France, working for his family business before becoming an advisor to the French government during the First World War, then being named first secretary-general of the League of Nations. He later worked as a financier, advising eastern European governments and living and working in the United States and China. He was behind a proposal for an Anglo-French union in 1940, then served as a representative for the British government in Washington DC. He headed France's postwar planning commission, and oversaw the discussions that led to the creation of the ECSC, becoming first president of its High Authority.

stances, Monnet's federalism by stages was always going to be the more practicable alternative.

Another critic of federalism was David Mitrany, a Romanian-born British social scientist whose treatise *A Working Peace System* became the basis of **functionalism**. Criticizing the 'fixation' with states that had become central to studies of IR (Rosamond, 2000, p. 34), Mitrany argued that the key challenge was 'to weld together the common interests of all without interfering unduly with the particular ways of each'. He claimed that federalism was too rigid in its framework, in its constitution, and in the limits it placed on action, and that it would be difficult to maintain against a background of political nationalism (Mitrany, 1966, pp. 68, 155–6). The best way to bring about peace was not through alliances and agreements among governments, but by setting up a network of functionally specific international institutions dealing with relatively non-controversial matters such as postal services or the harmonization of weights and measures, and managed by bureaucrats.

Within their separate areas, Mitrany argued, these agencies would find themselves coordinating their functions across state lines, then coordinating with other groups of functional agencies, then working together with international planning agencies. Success in one area would encourage cooperation in others, building a network of cooperation that would result in the decline of national sovereignty and its replacement by a new international community. In time, the economic and functional ties built among states would lead to political ties, because governments would find themselves living in a web of international agencies, leaving them less capable of independent action. In short, peace was more likely to be achieved through stealth by 'doing things together in workshop and marketplace than by signing pacts in chancelleries', and this web of cooperation would result not in a 'protected peace' but in a 'working peace' (Mitrany, 1966, pp. 25, 27–31, 92, 163).

Mitrany was interested in how to achieve world peace, not just European peace, and in fact worried that regional integration would reproduce inter-state tensions at a higher level while preserving the decision-making structures of states (Rosamond, 2000, pp. 36–8). His arguments were not so much a theory as a suggested course of action, spelling out what should be done to achieve peace rather than explaining the conditions needed to make his scheme succeed (Mattli,

● **Functionalism**: The idea that if states cooperate and create new functionally specific interstate institutions and agencies, regional integration will develop its own internal dynamic, and peace can be achieved through the creation of a web of interstate ties without the need for grand intergovernmental agreements.

CONCEPT

Spillover

A phenomenon through which cooperation among states in one area of policy will lead to pressures to cooperate in other areas. On the economic front, the connections created by trade and investment would encourage integration in one sector to lead to integration in others, requiring the creation of functional IGOs to manage the process, leading to a decline in the powers of national government institutions. As the power and reach of the new functional agencies grew, so political actors would be encouraged to switch their loyalties towards a new centre, whose institutions would demand greater powers (Haas, 1958, p. 16).

● **Neofunctionalism**: The theory that integration in one area of activity will lead to pressures and political support for integration in other related areas.

David Mitrany (1888–1975)

David Mitrany was a historian and political theorist best known today as the pioneer of integration theory. Born in Romania, he studied sociology at the London School of Economics before serving in British government intelligence during the First World War, and then working as a journalist on *The Guardian* and on the faculty of several British and American universities. He also became a naturalized British citizen. At the core of his scholarly interests was the question of how states could work together to address transboundary problems, and the approach he adopted became known as functionalism. This argued that humans could be encouraged away from their loyalty to nations and states by learning the benefits of international cooperation (Griffiths, 1999). His best-known publication was *A Working Peace System*, first published in 1943.

1999, p. 23). This perceived shortcoming was addressed in 1958 by the American political scientist Ernst Haas in his book *The Uniting of Europe*, which set out to understand European integration on its own terms with a study of the still new European Coal and Steel Community. Haas's work (which made no mention of Mitrany) tried to generalize 'the processes by which political communities are formed among sovereign States', and gave birth to the theory of **neofunctionalism**.

Haas was among the first to realize that reducing the barriers to the cross-border flow of money and people might transform the European state system. Questioning the core ideas of realism, he wanted to understand how and why states voluntarily cooperated with their neighbours while acquiring new techniques for resolving conflict (Haas, 1970). He concluded that in addition to the cooperation that would automatically arise from functional links, integration would need to be deliberately encouraged by political and economic actors pursuing self-interest. These actors worked mainly at the sub-national level (including interest groups and political parties) and at the supranational level (the new regional institutions). The role of state governments was only to respond to these developments, by accepting, ignoring, sidestepping, or trying to sabotage the efforts of the regional institutions (Mattli, 1999, p. 24).

Haas argued that if two or more states agreed to cooperate in a particular area of activity, and created a new regional organization to oversee that cooperation, the full benefits of integration would not be felt until there was cooperation in other, related, areas of activity (Haas, 1958, p. 29). Governments would soon find themselves subjected to growing regional pressures, and obliged to give more authority to regional organizations. The expectations of citizens would shift increasingly to the region, and satisfying those expectations would increase the likelihood of economic and social integration evolving into political integration (Ruggie *et al.*, 2005). Integration would take on a life of its own (an 'expansive logic') through the phenomenon of **spillover**, described by Lindberg as a process by which 'a given action, related to a specific goal, creates a situation in which the original goal can be assured only by taking further actions, which in turn create a further condition and a need for more action' (Lindberg, 1963, p. 10).

Both Haas and Philippe Schmitter had begun to wonder how far theories of European integration could be applied elsewhere in the world (Haas and

Ernst Haas (1924–2003)

Ernst Haas was a leading theorist of international relations and founder of the theory of neofunctionalism. Born in Germany, he emigrated to the United States with his family in 1938, and studied at Columbia University before joining the faculty of the University of California at Berkeley in 1951. He has been credited with helping 'invent' the study of European integration, mainly through his development of neofunctionalism (which he insisted was not a theory). He also began a tradition in which most of the cutting-edge debates on integration theory have been generated by American scholars or European scholars based in the United States. The best-known of Haas's many publications was *The Uniting of Europe*, published in 1958 and later chosen by the journal *Foreign Affairs* as one of the fifty most important books on international relations of the twentieth century (see Ruggie *et al.*, 2005).

Schmitter, 1964). This encouraged Joseph Nye in 1971 to argue that attempts to understand neofunctionalism were too driven by the European case, and that it could stand to be used comparatively and applied also to non-European cases. Building on Haas, Nye argued that regional integration involved an **integrative potential** that determined the extent to which different groups of states were likely to succeed in their efforts, and that this depended on several conditions:

● The economic equality and compatibility of the states involved.
● Complementarity among elites, or the extent to which the elite groups that controlled economic policy in the member states thought alike and held the same values.
● The presence and the extent of interest group activity, the absence of which made integration more difficult.
● The capacity of the member states to adapt and respond to public demands, which depended in turn on levels of domestic stability and the capacity – or desire – of decision makers to respond (Nye, 1970).

On almost all of these counts, the EU has a relatively high integrative potential, in contrast, for example, to the African Union. The latter was created in 2001 to replace the Organization of African Unity, and is an almost exact copy – institutionally speaking – of the EU. But it has 53 members that vary enormously in their economic wealth and potential, that are divided by race and religion, that include authoritarian regimes in which no formal opposition or independent group activity is allowed, and where public opinion is often heavily controlled. Where western Europe had, early on, many of the necessary pre-conditions for successful integration, Africa faces a longer uphill struggle.

● **Integrative potential**: A measure of the extent to which states will be able to integrate successfully, based on a combination of economic and political factors.

The spotlight moves to governments

Neofunctionalism dominated early studies of European integration but by the 1970s was beginning to fall out of favour, thanks in part to Haas's own loss of faith in his creation, which he felt lacked strong predictive abilities (Haas, 1975).

Neofunctionalism failed, among other things, to adequately explain the role of governments in the process of integration, or to show how the preferences of sub-national and supranational actors would translate into political action. There also seemed to be little prospect of the western European experience being replicated anywhere else in the world, and the process of European integration itself – after early optimism – had entered stormy waters, exemplified by disputes centred on President Charles de Gaulle of France. As part of his ongoing defence of French influence in the new European Economic Community (EEC), he unilaterally vetoed two applications for British membership of the EEC, then objected to attempts to strengthen the powers of the European Commission and the European Parliament (see Chapter 5 for more details). This seemed to suggest that the role of national governments in the process of integration had been underestimated.

Prompted by these developments, the French-American political scientist Stanley Hoffmann argued that neofunctionalism concentrated too much on the internal dynamics of integration without paying enough attention to the global context. Hoffmann also questioned the automatic nature of spillover, and argued that the importance of state actors and the persistence of nationalism had been overlooked by neofunctionalists; the European nation-state may have been transformed, he argued, but it still existed. He and others argued that national interests still played an important role in European politics, and that while spillover had worked in some areas, in others it had slowed to a trickle. It had become easier for the EEC to agree negative measures (such as eliminating tariffs and quotas) than positive measures that required a more painful transformation of existing practices; the first integrative steps had been easiest, but as more vital interests began to be at stake, so the process became more difficult (Hoffmann, 1965).

Hoffmann focused on the idea of **intergovernmentalism**. This is an arrangement under which an IGO has no independent powers or authority, and is instead the meeting place of representatives from state governments who pursue state interests while paying less attention to the broader interests of the community of states represented. This philosophy sees the EU primarily as a forum within which member states negotiate in an attempt to achieve a consensus, and where all decisions are taken by the representatives of the member states. Hoffmann argued that while non-state actors played an important role in the process of integration, state governments alone had legal sovereignty, the political legitimacy that came from being elected, and the authority to decide the pace of integration (Hoffmann, 1966). Alan Milward (1984) later agreed, his study of the early years of integration leading him to the conclusion that national governments and bureaucracies were the key actors in the process of integration, the extent of integration being determined by national self-interest.

Intergovernmental ideas stand in contrast to **supranationalism**, an arrangement in which an IO is still the meeting place of the representatives of state governments, but those governments will compromise state interests in the common good, and agree to transfer authority to institutions that function above the level of states and promote the common interests of those states. We find supranationalism at work in the EU when its administrative bodies are given the power and authority to make decisions above the level of the member states, and in the interests of the EU as a whole. But – as we will see in Chapters 10 to 13 – while the European interest tends to dominate in the work of the

● **Intergovernmentalism**: A political dynamic in which key decisions are made as a result of negotiations among representatives of the member states of an IGO.

● **Supranationalism**: A political dynamic by which IGOs become the forum for the promotion of the joint interests of state members, which involves the transfer of authority to joint institutions functioning above the states.

**Illustration 1.3
Intergovernmentalism
meets supranationalism**

Intergovernmentalism and
supranationalism meet at a
2010 summit of the
European Council; French
President Nikolas Sarkozy
(*left*) and Italian Prime
Minister Silvio Berlusconi
(*right*) discuss matters with
European Commission
President José Manuel
Barroso.

European Commission and the European Court of Justice, it has to be seen in the context of the defence of government interests, which dominate the work of the Council of Ministers and the European Council.

As with all theories of regional integration, intergovernmentalism has its critics. The main problem is that decisions among governments cannot be treated in isolation, and governments are subject to economic and social forces that either encourage them to cooperate, or discourage them from cooperating. The motives behind cooperation also vary; governments may be responsible for making key decisions, but they are often forced into making those decisions by circumstances, the Greek debt crisis of 2009–10 being a prime example. And the history of the EU throws up numerous cases where governments have been pushed into cooperating by the external logic of economics and efficiency. Spillover, for example, has been at the core of the construction of the European single market, where many unanticipated hurdles to the free movement of people, money, goods and services have had to be cleared. These include different environmental standards, different educational systems, different technical standards, and the pressures created by different levels of unemployment and different sets of working conditions.

Logically, then, the key to understanding how the EU evolved is probably to combine intergovernmentalism and supranationalism, seeing them not as two points on a spectrum of cooperation but as complementary aspects of the process of integration. David Mitrany argued that cooperation among governments was 'not a matter of surrendering sovereignty, but merely of pooling as much of it as may be needed for the joint performance of the particular task' (Mitrany, 1970). As outlined in the Schuman Declaration, the creation of the ECSC was all about the pooling of decisions over coal and steel production. Keohane and Hoffmann (1990, p. 277) agreed that the European Community could be seen as 'an experiment in pooling sovereignty, not in transferring it from states to supranational institutions'. For his part, Haas argued that supranationalism did not mean that Community institutions exercised authority over national governments but rather that it was a style of decision-making in which 'the participants refrain from unconditionally vetoing proposals and instead seek to attain agreement by means of compromises upgrading common interests' (Haas, 1964, p. 66).

Another attempt to combine the two approaches led to development of the theory of **liberal intergovernmentalism**, associated mainly with the American political scientist Andrew Moravcsik. Emerging in the 1980s and 1990s, it combines the neofunctionalist view of the importance of domestic politics with the role of the governments of the EU member states in making major political choices. At one level, the choices made by state governments are determined by the limitations and opportunities created by economic interdependence, and by domestic political pressures and demands. Governments want to keep themselves in office, which means they need the support of voters, parties, interest groups, and bureaucracies at home. The pressures created show themselves at a second level, by determining the positions that governments take in international negotiations. Governments have the advantage of having more information available to them in EU-level negotiations, and they can use this information to reach agreements which they can then sell to domestic audiences. In other words, the positions of the governments of the member states are decided at the domestic level, and European integration then moves forward as a result of bargains reached among those governments negotiating at the European level (Moravcsik, 1993 and 1998).

At the end of the day, there is no grand theory of European (or even of regional) integration, and it can sometimes seem as though European integration has happened in spite of the considerable intellectual energy that has been devoted to the development of theories of the process. Michael Burgess neatly summarizes the situation when he notes that 'the EU works in practice but not in theory' (Burgess, 2006, p. 245). The EU, he argues, is a conceptual enigma and an intellectual puzzle, an outcome that he ascribes to a combination of the novel manner in which European integration was originally planned and built, and to the inadequacies of the existing mainstream theories of IR and European integration. But however the history of the EU is best understood, more important now is to understand what the EU has become.

● **Liberal intergovernmentalism**: A theory combining elements of neofunctionalism and intergovernmentalism, arguing that intergovernmental bargains are driven by pressures coming from the domestic level.

SUMMARY

● Academic debates about the origins and history of the EU have been dominated by theories of international relations, which portray the EU as an international organization driven by decisions taken by the governments of the member states.

● How we think about the EU depends in large part on how we think about states and their changing role and powers in the world since 1945.

● Our understanding of European states also demands an understanding of nations, which have played a key role in determining political and social relations among Europeans since at least the French Revolution.

● Since the Second World War there has been a marked growth in the number of international organizations, set up to promote cooperation among states, and based on the principles of communal management, shared interests, and voluntary cooperation.

● Functionalists such as David Mitrany argued that the best way to achieve global peace was through the creation of functionally specific interstate institutions, which would bind states into a web of cooperation.

● Neofunctionalists such as Ernst Haas argued that integration had its own internal expansive logic. Pressures to integrate would grow through a process of spillover, so that governments would find themselves cooperating in a growing range of additional and related areas.

● Intergovernmentalists took the focus back to the deliberate and conscious decisions of governments, and argued that the pace and nature of integration has been ultimately driven by state governments pursuing state interests.

KEY TERMS AND CONCEPTS

Federalism

Functionalism

Integrative potential

Intergovernmentalism

International organization

International Relations

Liberal intergovernmentalism

Nation

Nationalism

Neofunctionalism

Realism

Regional integration association

Regionalism

Sovereignty

Spillover

The state

Supranationalism

Westphalian system

FURTHER READING

Haas, Ernst B. (1958), *The Uniting of Europe: Political, Social, and Economic Forces, 1950–1957* (Stanford: Stanford University Press). The first systematic study of the process of European integration.

Mitrany, David (1966), *A Working Peace System* (Chicago: Quadrangle). Even though Mitrany was more interested in world peace than in European integration, this is the usual starting point for studies of the theory of European integration.

Rosamond, Ben (2000), *Theories of European Integration* (Basingstoke: Macmillan); Antje Wiener and Thomas Diez (eds) (2009), *European Integration Theory*, 2nd edn (Oxford: Oxford University Press). Two surveys of theories of European integration, outlining all the major theories and the responses to them.

CHAPTER 2

What is the European Union?

PREVIEW

The beginning of wisdom, runs a Chinese proverb, is to call things by their right names. But this is no easy task with the EU, which fits few of the conventional models of the way in which politics and government function. In our attempts to understand how large-scale political communities are organized, we have only two mainstream points of reference: states and international organizations. But while the EU has some of the qualities of both, it is not entirely either.

As we saw in Chapter 1, attempts to agree how it evolved have spawned lengthy theoretical debates, but few agreements. There has been a similar problem with the debates over what the EU has become. Scholars have suggested concepts such as multi-level governance, consociationalism and quasi-federal polity, but none has yet won general acclaim. Others have applied older and more well-worn terms such as federal and confederal, but the former is not a neutral idea for many Europeans, and (for reasons that are not entirely clear) few scholars or politicians are willing to think of the EU as a confederation. Yet others have opted for describing the EU as an actor, or as sui generis (unique), before quickly moving on. For Jacques Delors, former president of the European Commission, the EU was simply an 'unidentified political object'.

Chapter 1 focused on theories developed by scholars of International Relations, who mainly see the European Community/Union as a cooperative arrangement among governments. This chapter, by contrast, focuses on the European Union as a political system in its own right, and reviews the arguments made by scholars of comparative politics and public policy. After asking where the discussion starts, it reviews the comparative method, and then goes into detail on the contrasting features of federations and confederations.

KEY ISSUES

- What are the relative costs and benefits of using IR and comparative approaches to understanding the EU?
- What is the difference between multi-level governance and federalism?
- Is the EU more federal than confederal, or vice versa?
- When some Europeans worry about a federal Europe, what exactly are they worrying about?
- Why have confederalist ideas been so marginal to attempts to understand the character of today's EU?
- What exactly is the EU?

Where to start?

There are at least five possible approaches that we could use in our attempts to pin down the character of the EU (see Figure 2.1), but each presents its own problems. To begin with, thinking of the EU as an international organization (IO) will not take us far because almost everyone now agrees that while the European Economic Community in its early years was a fairly conventional IO, the EU today is much more: It has many clear supranational qualities, it has long had much bigger ambitions than any other IO, and is today far more than an IO in terms of its reach, powers, and the obligations of membership. At the same time, Moravcsik (2007, p. 47) warns that 'we learn far more by viewing the EU as the most advanced model for international cooperation . . . rather than as a nation-state in the making, which encourages cycles of overambition and disappointment'.

Attempts to understand it as a regional integration association (RIA) would allow us to apply theories developed by comparative studies of regionalism (see Farrell *et al.*, 2005; Fawcett and Hurrell, 1992; Laursen, 2003; Rüland *et al.*, 2008), but since RIAs have most of the same core features as IOs, the focus would still be on intergovernmentalism with its limitations as an explanatory theory. And in terms of the reach of its institutions, policies, and laws, the EU has moved far beyond most other examples of regional integration, which have more to learn from the EU than the EU has to learn from them.

The third option – admitting that the EU is unique – has its merits, but if the EU is neither a state nor an international organization, then what is it? People like labels, and they like to know what those labels mean. The terms *actor* and *entity* are often applied to the EU, but they are vague and clumsy, which leaves

Figure 2.1 Five approaches to understanding the EU

APPROACH	ASSUMPTION
International organization	Its institutions have little or no autonomy, and the EU makes its most important decisions through negotiations and bargains among governments. Best understood using theories of international relations.
Regional integration association (RIA)	It is comparable with other regional blocs such as the Association of Southeast Asian Nations (ASEAN) or the African Union, again using IR approaches.
Unique (*sui generis*)	It emerged out of a unique set of circumstances, that has unique qualities and goals, and that might never be replicated elsewhere – and might not even have emerged in Europe if the process of integration had started much later than it did.
Political system in its own right	It is a European superstate, and its structure and operating principles can be compared with conventional states. Best understood using approaches of comparative politics, with a particular focus on federalism and confederalism.
Combination	It is a mix of elements of all the above.

Source: Inspired by, but different from, the listing in Rosamond, 2000, pp. 14–16.

Illustration 2.1
The European Quarter

Institutions are the most visible indicators of the existence of a political system, or polity. The growth of the EU is reflected in this design for the European Quarter in Brussels, developed by French architect and urban planner Christian de Portzamparc.

us with the more general term **polity**, referring to an organized system of government and administration. At the same time, enough scholars of the EU have identified enough points of comparison or similarity between the EU and other kinds of political organization to suggest that the EU may not be unique at all, but just a reconfiguration of our conventional understandings about political structures and institutions.

The fourth option, where we think of the EU as a political system in its own right, has gained traction since the 1990s as the authority and independent powers of the EU have grown. It is also the approach taken in this book. One problem is that most of our understandings of political systems are based on how they work in relation to states, and as we saw in Chapter 1, the EU lacks many of the defining qualities of a state. At the same time, if the term *system* is understood to imply coordination, organization and order, there is no denying that the EU is a political system with its own institutions, laws, procedures, responsibilities, and policies, even in some ways looking much like a state: it has territory, a large degree of authority (if not necessarily sovereignty), a lesser degree of independence, and legitimacy.

Given the disputes among scholars about how the EU evolved, a final option is to combine elements of the first four into attempts to explain the EU as a hybrid or a compound. This is the approach that has underwritten some of the debates reviewed in Chapter 1, and it continues to be part of the debate about what the EU has become. And yet the EU reflects ever fewer of the features of a conventional IO or RIA, and ever more of the features of a conventional state, raising questions even about the balance of its composite qualities. So, having argued that it is difficult to know where to start, what are the explanatory concepts available to us?

● **Polity**: An organized and structured system for the government and administration of a political unit, such as a state or a city.

Figure 2.2 The dimensions of the EU

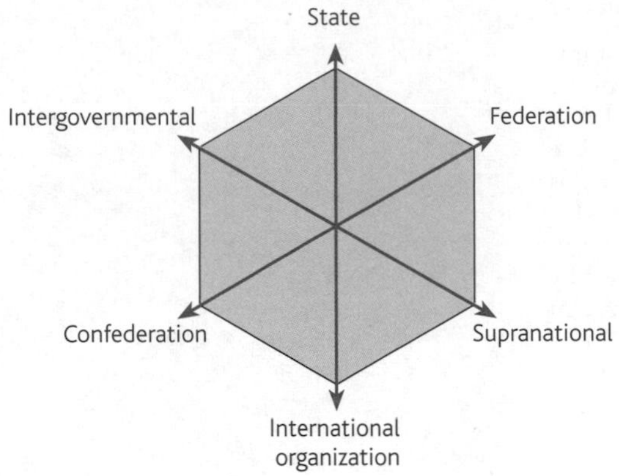

The three main competing sets of views about the personality of the EU, which lies somewhere within the area indicated by the hexagon-but just where is a matter of debate.

The comparative approach

As we saw in Chapter 1, the debates over how the EU evolved have been dominated by scholars of International Relations (IR), but the conclusions they have reached have been conditional at best. And while the European Economic Community might reasonably have been studied as an IO until the passage of the 1986 Single European Act, much has since changed: the process of integration has accelerated, the relationship between EU institutions and the member states has changed, and the reach of EU institutions, law and policy has expanded. This has led some to conclude that we should consider the EU a political system in its own right, using the methods and principles of **comparative politics**.

Arguably the oldest and the most fundamental of all approaches to understanding politics and government, comparative politics involves the study of different political systems or different elements of those systems with the goal of using an understanding of each to shed light on the others. We can study political systems in isolation, but the picture we paint will always be incomplete until we appreciate their differences and similarities with others. The **comparative method** helps us describe political systems, it gives us the context we need to decide what is important or unusual or missing in different systems, it gives us points of reference to help us better understand the significance of what we are studying, and it helps us draw up rules about politics and government by helping us develop and test hypotheses, explain trends, and better understand, explain, and predict political change (see discussion in Landman, 2003, pp. 6–10).

IR scholars, being more interested in process rather than system, did not see the EEC as a new form of government; hence their focus on supranationalism and intergovernmentalism. An early hint of a shift came in a 1975 article written by Donald Puchala, in which he noted how often he had heard the complaint from officials in the EEC that political scientists, in their search for

● **Comparative politics**: The study of different political systems, usually based on cases, and aimed at drawing up general rules about how those systems function.

● **Comparative method**: One of the core methods for all research (the others being the experimental, the statistical, and the case study methods), based on drawing conclusions from the study of a small number of samples.

Focus on . . .
The comparative method

At the heart of political comparison is the comparative method, by which different cases or samples are systematically studied in order to establish empirical relationships among two or more variables while the others are held constant (Lijphart, 1971). It has been argued that to talk of an independent comparative method is redundant, because the scientific method is 'unavoidably comparative' (Lasswell, 1968), and that if political science is a science, then it goes without saying that it is comparative in its approach (Almond, 1966). Most comparison is based on the study of a few carefully selected cases using a middle level of analysis, rather than the more intensive analysis possible with a few cases, or the more abstract analysis necessary with many cases (Landman, 2003, p. 29.). The two most common approaches to comparative study are based on levels of similarity (see Lim, 2006, pp. 34–44):

- The *most similar systems* (MSS) approach is based on the idea that the greater the similarities among cases, the easier it should be to isolate the factors responsible for their differences (Lipset, 1990, xiii). So, for example, we can look at levels of secularism in the generally similar cases of western Europe and the United States and perhaps isolate the factors that explain why religion is growing in the United States but declining in Europe.

- The *most different systems* (MDS) approach uses cases that are different in almost every respect except for the variable under investigation. So if we want to understand why people migrate within Europe, we can compare it with Asia, Africa, and Latin America, which are different in many respects apart from the fact that they too have large numbers of migrants. By ignoring the differences as an explanatory factor, we can try to isolate the particular quality or factor that explains why Europeans move across borders.

models of the Community, were 'working at levels of theoretical abstraction too far removed from day-to-day political behaviour' and were painting 'elaborate and sophisticated pictures of phenomena that are simply not happening'. One official bluntly told him that when he read the results, 'you tell me that I am working to cause spillover, or that I am making a new nationality from old ones, or that I am challenging national sovereignty. This is nonsense. I and my colleagues are working to harmonize economic, social and legal practices in several countries so that the Common Market can function effectively for the benefit of all' (Puchala, 1975).

A chastened Puchala decided to take a comparative case study approach in order to better understand the effects of the decisions taken at the Community level, a move that hinted at new thinking about the Community as an international **regime** within which member state governments cooperated on the basis of rules, norms, and decision-making procedures (Hoffmann, 1982). Studying it as such meant that it could be compared with other exercises in economic integration, and even with federations such as the United States, Canada, or Germany. But then the passage of the 1986 Single European Act (SEA) paved the way for a transformation of scholarly perspectives:

- European integration entered a period of furious activity, with five more treaties signed after the SEA, membership of the Community (later EU)

● **Regime**: The rules and norms that lie at the basis of a system of government. Can also be used to describe (sometimes with negative implications) the holders of office within a government.

growing from 10 to 27, integration reaching into new policy areas, and the euro replacing national currencies in more than a dozen countries. These changes dramatically altered perceptions about the personality of the EU.

- It has become clear that the EU is more powerful – and has involved greater commitments on the part of its members – than any international organization that has ever existed. This has made it a more likely candidate for comparison with federal states, and even to some extent with non-federal (that is, unitary) states such as France and Poland.

- The growth in the number of RIAs has opened up new comparative possibilities. Even if the EU is clearly the most highly evolved of all RIAs, the experience of the others could be used with the MDS approach to argue that the EU is more like a conventional state than a conventional regional association.

More hints of a change in scholarly interest followed. In 1983, William Wallace – noting the disagreements that the governments of the member states were having over rules, powers, and objectives – argued that the Community's capacity for handling complex issues and for promoting discussion, bargaining, and decision-making on them was 'extremely limited', and concluded that the Community was 'more than an international regime, but less than a fully-developed political system' (Wallace, 1983, p. 409). And yet with further enlargement and agreement on the Single European Act and on the first steps along the path to the euro, the Community's decision-making capacity was clearly growing.

In 1992, Alberta Sbragia identified two views of the Community among American scholars: one that it was mainly a free trade area whose institutions were marginal to economic forces, and whose dynamics were thus frequently overlooked, and another that the Community and its member states were governed in roughly the same way, and that the Community was an emerging superstate. She suggested that comparative federalism in particular had much to offer as a way of understanding the Community, and that perhaps the study of the Community could be incorporated into and contribute to the study of comparative politics rather than being isolated (Sbragia, 1992).

In 1994, Simon Hix argued that while the political system of the Community might only be part-formed, the practice of politics in the EC was not so different from that in any democratic system. While international relations theories had been helpful to an understanding of European integration, he suggested, the Community was now more than an international organization, and comparative politics approaches were more appropriate to understanding Community politics; they could help us understand how power was exercised in the Community, how Europeans related to Community institutions, and how European 'government' was influenced by political parties, elections, and interest groups (Hix, 1994).

There is a political element to this debate: the suggestion that the EU is anything more than an international organization (even one with unusual powers) has long been resisted by scholars, political leaders, and even ordinary Europeans, because to admit as much would be to acknowledge that significant power and sovereignty has been transferred from the member states to the EU, and that national governments are weaker as a result. There are many who do not like this idea. To speak of a European **government** is particularly troubling, because the term typically applies to the institutions and officials (elected or appointed) that make up the formal governing structure of a state, the clear understanding being that they have powers to make laws and drive the political agenda.

Although the EU clearly has a group of 'governing' institutions staffed by several thousand full-time employees, few scholars would agree that there is a European government as there are national or local governments in the member states. Many instead prefer the looser term **governance**, describing an arrangement in which laws and policies are made and implemented not by a formally constituted set of governing institutions with the power to make and execute laws and policies, but as a result of interactions among a complex variety of actors, including member state governments, EU institutions, interest groups, and other sources of influence. Put another way, governance means that decisions are made and implemented without the existence of a government in the conventional sense of the term.

Taking this idea a step further, the term **multilevel governance** (MLG) has become popular in academic circles since the early 1990s as a way of explaining the character of the EU. This describes a system in which power is shared among the supranational, national, sub-national, and local levels of government, with a high degree of interaction among these levels (see Marks, 1993; Hooghe and Marks, 2001). But like so many 'new' ideas in the social sciences, it is not all that new, and is reflected, for example, in Donald Puchala's suggestion in 1975 that the Community could be seen as 'a multileveled system arranged in political layers from the local to the supranational', with complex organizational linkages binding centre and peripheries, going upwards and downwards, and inwards and outwards (Puchala, 1975). Peters and Pierre (2004) describe the main features of MLG as follows:

- It is about governance, not government.
- It 'refers to a particular kind of relationship, both vertically and horizontally, between several institutional levels', that is not hierarchically ordered.
- It applies to 'a negotiated order rather than an order defined by formalized legal frameworks'.
- It is often conceived as a political game.

For some, MLG is no more than a variation on the theme of federalism, for which – as we will see later in this chapter – there is no fixed model. For others, it adds a valuable new element to the debate over the EU, notably with its focus on horizontal relationships and cross-border initiatives. Meanwhile, several other concepts have been developed or adopted that are of potential interest to understanding the European Union, including the following:

- *Cooperative federalism* describes an arrangement in which national, state, and local governments work together to address and solve common problems, rather then working separately on policy. No level has exclusive competence in any policy area, and decisions are made as a result of cooperation among the parts.

● **Government**: The institutions and officials that make up the formal structure by which states or other administrative units (counties, regions, provinces, cities, towns, and even universities) are managed and directed.

● **Governance**: An arrangement by which decisions, laws and policies are made without the existence of formal institutions of government.

● **Multilevel governance**: An administrative system in which power is distributed and shared horizontally and vertically among many different levels of government, from the supranational to the local, with considerable interaction among the parts.

Federation

An administrative system in which authority is divided between two or more levels of government, each with independent powers and responsibilities. Although there are about two dozen federations in the world, the relationship between national and local governments varies from one to another, and has evolved in each over time. In Switzerland, for example, the federal government is much weaker relative to local government (the cantons) than is the case in Russia, where the federal government dominates Russia's local governments. As for the European Union, it is considered quasi-federal at best.

- *Consociationalism* is an idea associated with the Dutch-American political scientist Arend Lijphart, and describes an arrangement in which power is shared among groups in divided societies, with representation based on the population of each group, government through a grand coalition of elites from each group, and the encouragement of consensus decision-making through mutual veto (Lijphart, 1977 and 1999). While it has been suggested as a way of understanding the EU (Gabel, 1998), it has failed to exert much of a grip on the mainstream debate.

The invention and adoption of new conceptual terms reflects how little agreement there has been on how best to understand the EU. The failure to agree on any of them suggests, in turn, that the debate still has some way to go, with more terms being added to the lexicon before it runs its course. But as is so often true in life, the best options may be the simplest, and here we might focus on two older and better-developed concepts to offer us guidance through the maze. One of these is *federalism*, which has already been much discussed in relation to how the EU evolved. The other – *confederalism* – languishes on the margins of the debate in spite of how much it promises as a path to understanding the EU.

Federalism

Federalist ideas have played a key role in the political and theoretical debates about how European integration has evolved, and yet they have been given surprisingly short shrift as a possible means of understanding what the EU has become. Rosamond (2000, p. 23) points out that there are no famous names in the academic debate about federalism to compare with Mitrany and Haas, and that there is no clear-cut academic school of European federalism. Part of the explanation may lie in the political nature of the federalist debate; because it is not seen as a neutral concept, but is instead the dream of those who hope for a United States of Europe, it is avoided as a possible analytical tool.

The more technical part of the explanation lies in the difficulty of pinning down what federalism actually means (see Burgess, 2005, Chapter 1). At first glance it might appear fairly straightforward: a **federation** is a system of administration involving two or more levels of government with autonomous powers and responsibilities (see Figure 2.3), while the term *federalism* refers either to the principles involved in federal government, or to advocacy for the idea of federation. The federal approach contrasts with the unitary systems we find in states such as France and Sweden, where the balance and focus of power lies with the national government.

There are about two dozen formally-declared federations in the world (see Table 2.1). But as Birch (1966, p. 15) long ago remarked, federalism is a concept with 'no fixed meaning', and more recently Watts (2008, p. 1) has warned that 'there is no single pure model of federalism' and that we cannot 'just pick models off a shelf'. On the contrary, federations come in many different forms, the specifics changing according to the relationship between the whole and the parts. This means that federalism runs the danger of being whatever we want it to be, and the definition and presence of federalism will be decided by the biases and preferences of the observer rather than by objective measures of how power is divided and shared. In turn, this means that the existence of federalism (as in the EU) can be denied simply because we have no fixed agreement on what a federation should look like. How, then, can anyone warn of the dangers of a federal Europe when no-one can agree on what a federal system looks like? (see discussion in Börzel, 2005)

Even in the United States, the benchmark for all federal systems because it was the world's first modern federation, there has been an ongoing debate about how federalism works in practice. The states were originally powerful, with their own independent arenas of power, but since the 1930s there has been a shift towards the federal government in Washington DC, as a result both of historical trends toward greater national unity and of the growth of federal government programmes that have reduced state powers. Americans constantly debate the appropriate role of the federal government in national life, and debate how the American federation works, with at least three possibilities:

- Layer cake federalism (or dual federalism) where national and local levels of government are distinct from each other, with separate responsibilities.
- Marble cake federalism (or cooperative federalism) where the layers are intermingled and it is difficult to see who has ultimate responsibility.
- Picket fence federalism, where national and local government share powers. (There is an extensive literature on American federalism; for surveys, see Morgan and Davies, 2008; Zimmerman, 2008.)

The waters of the debate have been muddied by developments in several other countries that have never formally described themselves as federations, but where the transfer of powers to local units of government has resulted in a process of federalization. In Britain, for example, the creation in the 1990s of regional assemblies in Scotland, Wales and Northern Ireland made all three more like states within a federal United Kingdom; all it would take to finish the job would be to create an English regional assembly. In Argentina, Spain and South Africa, too, powers have devolved to provinces and local communities without the formal creation of a federation, creating *de facto* federations or **quasi-federations**.

What of the European Union as a federation? Predictably, opinion ranges widely. William Wallace (1983) described the European Community as 'less than a federation, more than a regime'. David McKay (2001, pp. 8–10) argues that we can think of the EU as 'a species of federal state', with some clear federal qualities and a trend over time to greater federalism. Andrew Moravcsik (2001, p. 186) has described the EU as 'an exceptionally weak federation' because of its modest budget and bureaucracy, its lack of coercive force, the constraints on its decision-making rules, and its powerful competitors; in fact, he argues, its federal qualities are so weak that the difference between the EU and national federations is not one of degree but one of kind. (Does that mean, then, that it is a confederation? See arguments later in this chapter.)

Few have expended more effort on reviewing the EU's federal qualities than Michael Burgess, who argues that 'until recently it was possible to describe the EU as a classic example of federalism without federation'. In other words, it has always been a repository of federal ideas and influences without becoming a formal federation. But he goes on to argue that the main reason why it has been so hard to pin down is 'precisely because it is a new kind of federal model the like of which has never before been seen', which was born out of a slow, incremental and piece-

● **Quasi-federation**: An arrangement by which powers are divided between central and regional government, resulting in some of the features of federalism without the creation of a formal federal structure.

CONCEPT

Confederation

An administrative system in which independent states come together for reasons of security, efficiency, or mutual convenience, retaining the powers that they consider best reserved to themselves , and working together through joint institutions on matters best dealt with together, such as foreign, trade and security policy. Put another way, a confederation is a looser form of a federation, a union of states with more powers left in the hands of the constituent members.

Table 2.1 The World's federations

Federations	Transitional or quasi-federations
Australia	Argentina
Austria	Comoros
Belgium	Democratic Republic of the Congo
Bosnia and Herzegovina	Iraq
Brazil	Malaysia
Canada	Russia
Ethiopia	South Africa
Germany	Spain
India	Sudan
Mexico	Venezuela
Micronesia	
Nigeria	
Pakistan	
Palau	
St Kitts and Nevis	
Switzerland	
United Arab Emirates	
United States	

Source: Based on Watts (2008).

meal metamorphosis (Burgess, 2005, p. 226; see also Burgess, 1996 and 2000).

Although the EU is not a *de jure* federation with statehood, and its member states still have far more power and authority than the local units of government in a formal federation such as Australia or Canada, federalism is still very much a part of the analytical debate about the EU. That debate, however, has so far been limited to discussions about tendencies in the EU rather than absolutes. Burgess (2000, p. 273) sees a continuity of federal ideas, influences and strategies in the evolution of the European idea, argues that federal ideas have seeped into all the central institutions of the EU, and describes federalism as 'a constant reminder of a conception of Europe going well beyond mere intergovernmental cooperation'. But its application continues to be limited both by the dominance of international relations theory in understanding the EU, and by the political resistance in Europe to the idea of a federal EU.

Confederalism

If the EU is not a federation, then perhaps it is a **confederation**. This is a conceptual cousin of federalism, describing a looser form of association among states. Where a federation is a unified state, within which power is divided between national and local levels of government, and there is a direct link between government and citizens (government exercises authority over citizens, and is answerable directly to the citizens), a confederation is a group of sovereign states with a central authority deriving its authority from those states, and citizens linked to the central authority through the states in which they live. As Lister

Figure 2.3 Comparing federations and confederations

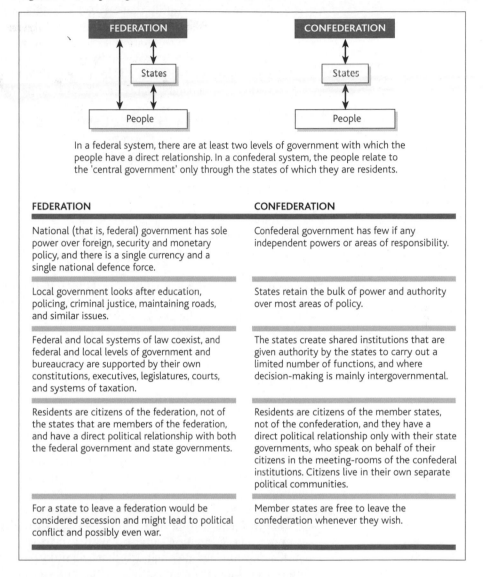

In a federal system, there are at least two levels of government with which the people have a direct relationship. In a confederal system, the people relate to the 'central government' only through the states of which they are residents.

FEDERATION	CONFEDERATION
National (that is, federal) government has sole power over foreign, security and monetary policy, and there is a single currency and a single national defence force.	Confederal government has few if any independent powers or areas of responsibility.
Local government looks after education, policing, criminal justice, maintaining roads, and similar issues.	States retain the bulk of power and authority over most areas of policy.
Federal and local systems of law coexist, and federal and local levels of government and bureaucracy are supported by their own constitutions, executives, legislatures, courts, and systems of taxation.	The states create shared institutions that are given authority by the states to carry out a limited number of functions, and where decision-making is mainly intergovernmental.
Residents are citizens of the federation, not of the states that are members of the federation, and have a direct political relationship with both the federal government and state governments.	Residents are citizens of the member states, not of the confederation, and they have a direct political relationship only with their state governments, who speak on behalf of their citizens in the meeting-rooms of the confederal institutions. Citizens live in their own separate political communities.
For a state to leave a federation would be considered secession and might lead to political conflict and possibly even war.	Member states are free to leave the confederation whenever they wish.

puts it, if a federation is a union of peoples living within a single state, then a confederation is a union of states (Lister, 1996, p. 106).

While the number of federations has been growing, there have been few examples in history of confederations, and none have lasted.

- **Switzerland** was confederal from the medieval era until 1789, and then again from 1815 to 1848, when it tightened its internal political links and became a federation. But the Swiss brand of federalism emphasizes the parts at the expense of the whole; direct democracy through referendums is encouraged, and the governing Federal Council is elected by the directly elected Federal Assembly. One of the members of the Council serves a one-year term as head of state and head of government.

- **The United States** was a confederation from 1781 to 1789, operating under Articles of Confederation that created a 'league of friendship'. This could declare war and conclude treaties but could not levy taxes or regulate commerce, there was no national executive or judiciary, Congress met rarely, and defence was provided by state militias. How far the Confederate States of America that seceded from the United States in 1861–65 were truly confederate is debatable, since the states won new powers in some areas but lost them in others, and the constitution of the confederacy was copied almost directly from the federal US constitution.
- **Germany** was a confederation from 1815 to 1866 when several central European states came together as successors to the Holy Roman Empire. There was only one shared political institution, a Federal Assembly made up of ambassadors from the different parts of the confederation, and it met rarely. The states agreed not to make war with one another, they were allowed to make external alliances, they contributed to a common army, and most were brought closer together in 1834 under the *Zollverein* (the customs union) (see Forsyth, 1981, pp. 43–53).

What of the European Union as a confederation? Curiously, there is almost no debate on the matter, for four possible reasons. First, confederalism has been all but ignored by scholars of politics – in general terms as well as in its application to the EU (for exceptions, see Forsyth, 1981; Lister, 1996). Any entity that looked like a confederation could simply be described as a weak form of federation, a concept that has attracted far more study and attention. Second, it pleases neither European federalists, who want much more, nor eurosceptics, for whom history shows that confederations always evolve into federations or new states. Third, as with federalism there is no standard, uniform, or simple model of confederalism. Indeed, while there are plenty of federations in existence today with which comparisons can be made, there are no formal confederations. Finally, there is a strong statist tradition in Europe; Europeans have lived with states since Westphalia, and a confederation is not a state (Majone, 2006).

At the same time, the EU is often described as a confederation in everything but name. Commenting on the final passage of the Lisbon treaty in 2009, for example, *The Economist* came up with a neat (if unconscious) definition of confederalism when it concluded that 'the union will thus continue as a mainly intergovernmental organization with supranational attributes' ('Wake up Europe!' in *The Economist*, 10–16 October 2009). And confederalism does have its small band of academic proponents. Forsyth argued in 1981 that the study of confederations in history revealed that the EEC was clearly an economic confederation in both content and form (Forsyth, 1981, p. 183). Lister later agreed, describing the EU as a 'jumbo confederation' whose member states and governments continue to dominate the EU's institutions (Lister, 1996, Chapter 2). For Moravcsik (quoted above as describing the EU as 'an exceptionally weak federation'), the EU is, 'despite a few federal elements, essentially a confederation of member-states' (Moravcsik, 2007, p. 25). Majone agrees, arguing that the confederal model describes 'precisely' the arrangement found in the EU, and bemoaning the fact that confederalism has been 'practically banned from the discourse about the future and finality of the Union' (Majone, 2006, p. 136).

Table 2.2 The federal and confederal features of the EU

Federalism	Confederalism
• The EU has several levels of administration (European, state, provincial, urban, and local), and each has some autonomy in different areas of policy.	• While the minimum necessary two levels of administration needed for a federal system both exist, the EU institutions are weaker relative to national institutions than is the case in a 'conventional' federal system.
• It has treaties that are the functional equivalent of a constitution and that allow for administrative institutions that function above the level of the member states, and that distribute powers between the European institutions and the member states.	• Although the EU has treaties and administrative institutions, the interests of the member states play a greater role in the relationship between the whole and the parts than is the case in federations.
• One of the core treaty principles is subsidiarity, or the idea that policy responsibilities should be transferred to the EU institutions only where they are more efficiently dealt with at the European level rather than the state level (see Chapter 9). This seems to confirm the existence of two levels of government.	• There is no European constitution adopted by the member states and capable of being amended and developed by proposals from the EU institutions and the approval of a majority of member states. Instead the EU is based on a series of treaties that each had to be accepted by all member states before they were adopted.
• The European Court of Justice acts as an umpire that works independently of the member states and rules on disputes about the distribution of power within the EU.	• One of the key qualities of a confederation is indirect representation in the joint government through state governments. Although EU voters are directly represented through the European Parliament (a federal quality), much power still lies in the hands of the European Council and the Council of Ministers, which are more clearly confederal in character.
• There is direct representation of the views of the member states within the EU institutions, notably in the European Council and the Council of Ministers.	• The member states are still distinct units with separate identities, they have their own national defence forces and policies, they can still sign bilateral treaties with non-EU states, and the governments of the EU states can still argue that the EU institutions exist at their discretion.
• There is a separate executive/bureaucracy (the European Commission), a separate legislature (the European Parliament), and a separate court (the European Court of Justice), that coexist and share powers with their national equivalents. The existence of the European Parliament takes the EU beyond a confederation.	• Unlike federations, the EU is a voluntary association, so its members are free to leave if they wish.
• There are at least two systems of law: European and national (and sub-national systems of law in federations such as Austria, Belgium and Germany).	• Although the EU has leaders and institutions that look much like a European government, they have fewer powers than their national counterparts.
• The member states of the EU are increasingly defined not by themselves but in relation to their EU partners, and Europeans increasingly identify with Europe and with European priorities (see Chapter 3 for more discussion).	• The EU may have its own flag and anthem, but most of the citizens of the member states still have a higher sense of allegiance towards national flags, and anthems and they cannot surrender their state citizenships and become citizens of the European Union.

**Illustration 2.2
The confederal Council**

As a central institution deriving its powers from the EU member states, the Council of Ministers in Brussels fits the definition of a confederal institution.

Perhaps it is time to consider lifting that ban. At the very least, and going back to the point made earlier in this chapter about combining one or more competing approaches to understanding what the EU has become, perhaps we should consider combining federal and confederal explanations. Several scholars have suggested that the EU is a hybrid, containing features of both. For example, McKay (2001) argues that depending upon how we understand federalism, it may be best to think of the EU as quasi-federal or as a hybrid. Burgess (2005, p. 239) concedes that the EU is not a federation in the conventional sense, but that it is 'a political union with strong federal and confederal elements .... [or] a new kind of federal-confederal union that we can classify as a "new confederation" or a new federal model'. Blankart (2007) argues that the EU is neither a confederation nor a federation, but is instead an 'association of compound states', some policies being dealt with in a federal manner and others in a confederal manner. And Watts (2008, pp. 56–8) describes the EU as a 'hybrid confederation-federation', and sees its confederal roots in the powers of the Council of Ministers, its small budget, its legal basis in a series of treaties, and the policy powers kept by the member states. He sees its federal qualities in the work of the European Commission and the European Court of Justice.

While the concept of confederalism has something to offer our understanding of what the EU has become, so do federalism, multi-level governance, and – to a lesser degree – consociationalism. But just as there is no general agreement on how and why the EU evolved the way it did, so there is no general agreement on what it has become. Most of us are still locked in to the idea of states, and we look at the EU in terms of how far (or not) it has travelled along the road to becoming a European superstate. This is a loaded concept, though, because there are many Europeans who fear and resist such an outcome. But until we can think outside the box of the state, it is unlikely that we will be able to agree on the character of the EU. At the end of the day, perhaps Monnet was right when he argued that the EU would become a federation by osmosis.

SUMMARY

- There are at least five possible approaches to understanding the EU today: we could think of it as an international organization, as a regional integration association, as a unique organization with unique qualities, as a political system in its own right, or as a combination of all four.
- While the debates over how the EU evolved were dominated by scholars of international relations, the debate over what the EU has become have been increasingly dominated by scholars of comparative politics, who approach the EU as a political system with its own institutions, processes, procedures, and policies.
- There is a debate over whether we should approach the EU as a government, or use the looser term *governance* to understand its procedures. The term *multi-level governance* has won some support.
- Federalism has been given short shrift as a means of understanding the EU. This is partly because there is so much resistance to the idea of a federal Europe, and also because there is no standard model of federalism.
- Even less attention has been paid to confederalism as a means of understanding the EU, in part because there are few historical examples of confederalism at work (and no contemporary examples), and in part because it falls short of the hopes of European federalists.
- One compromise may be to think of the EU as a unique hybrid federal-confederal system of administration.

KEY TERMS AND CONCEPTS

Comparative method
Comparative politics
Confederation
Federation
Governance
Government
Multilevel governance
Polity
Quasi-federation
Regime

FURTHER READING

Burgess, Michael (2000 and 2006), *Federalism and European Union: The Building of Europe, 1950-2000* (London: Routledge), and *Comparative Federalism: Theory and Practice* (London: Routledge). Two books from the most prolific scholar of the EU as a federation, the former a revisionist history of the evolution of the EU.

Forsyth, Murray (1981), *Unions of States: The Theory and Practice of Confederation* (Leicester: Leicester University Press); Frederick K. Lister (1996), *The European Union, the United Nations, and the Revival of Confederal Governance* (Westport, CT: Greenwood). Two of the few full-length studies of confederalism, both prompted by the case of the EU.

Hix, Simon, and Bjørn Hoyland (2011), *The Political System of the European Union*, 3rd edn (Basingstoke: Palgrave Macmillan). The paradigm text of the argument that the EU should be approached as a political system in its own right.

CHAPTER 3

Who are the Europeans?

PREVIEW   Getting to grips with the European Union is only partly a question of understanding its political character. We must also understand its people: who they are, how they think of themselves in relation to others, and how they perceive the European Union. Most Europeans still regard themselves as citizens of the states in which they live, or as members of a national group, and only a few have taken to the idea that they are also Europeans.

Europe has a population of nearly 600 million, divided among 40 sovereign states (44 if the definition of 'Europe' is expanded), speaking more than 60 major languages, and belonging to several hundred different national groups. Because the lines of states and nations do not always coincide, most European states are multinational, and many of the larger national groups are divided among two or more states. The exercise of European integration – although it was designed to help Europeans move past their historical suspicions of one another – has made only limited progress in helping build a sense of European identity.

This chapter begins with an attempt to pin down where Europe begins and ends. It then reviews questions of identity in Europe, looking at what divides Europeans while also explaining how the sense of association with Europe and the EU is changing. It finishes with a review of some of the the key demographic trends in Europe, including its declining and aging population, the impact of immigration, and changes in the definition of the European family. It argues that Europe is undergoing a fundamental change of identity and demographic structure, but that while current trends are becoming more clear, the end result is still open to debate.

KEY ISSUES
- Where should the lines of Europe be drawn? Should Turkey or Russia be included?
- What does it mean to be European, and how does allegiance to Europe differ from allegiance to states or nations?
- What matters most in defining identity: culture, place, history, language, ethnicity, religion, ideology, philosophy, or aesthetics?
- Should citizens of EU member states be offered the alternative of citizenship of the EU? If so, what would that citizenship mean in practical terms?
- Is Europe's declining population the problem that many make it out to be, or an opportunity to rethink political, economic and social priorities?

Where is Europe?

Europe is often described as a continent, but geographers define continents as large, unbroken, and discrete landmasses almost entirely surrounded by water. On that basis, only North and South America, Asia, Africa, Australia, and Antarctica wholly fit the bill. Strictly speaking, Europe is part of the Asian continent (or the supercontinent of Eurasia, as it is sometimes called), and so is more properly described as a sub-continent. But Europeans are racially, culturally, and linguistically distinct from Asians, and vice versa, and although they share the same landmass, geography is less a defining feature of Europe than culture and history. (The same is true of Africa, with its division between Arabs and black Africans.)

On three sides, Europe's limits are reasonably clear. To the south it ends with the Mediterranean, to the west it ends with the Atlantic, to the north it ends with the Arctic Ocean, and in all three directions it includes islands with political and cultural links to Europe, such as Greenland, Iceland, Svalbaard, Crete, Sicily, and Malta. But to the east and the southeast there are still many unresolved questions. The border with Asia is particularly problematic, the conventional view being that it is marked by the Ural Mountains in Russia. But this is convention only because of a decision by the eighteenth-century Russian historian Vasily Tatishchev, who thought that nominating the Urals would allow Russia to claim to be an Asian as well as a European power. All well and good, but the Urals are more than a thousand kilometres inside Russia, and they are a natural feature rather than a cultural or political boundary.

Russians themselves are undecided: some see themselves as part of Europe and the West, others distrust the West and see their state as distinct from both Europe and Asia, and yet others see Russia as a bridge between the two (Smith, 1999, p. 50). Ethnic Russians make up about 80 per cent of the population of Russia, and there are also large Russian minorities living in EU member states such as Estonia, Latvia and Lithuania. While the case could be made that they and the Slavic and Caucasian minorities of western Russia (including Ukrainians, Belorussians, and Ossetians) are European, three-quarters of the land area of Russia lies east of the Urals (territory which is clearly in Asia, not in Europe) and is home to numerous ethnic minorities – including Tatars, Kazakhs, Uzbeks, and the Siberian minorities of Buryatia, Evenki, Khakassia, and Selkup – that are unquestionably Asian. For practical political purposes, then, the border between Europe and Asia is best taken as the western frontier of Russia.

To the southeast, meanwhile, the lines are even fuzzier. The easy option is to connect the Russian-Ukrainian border to the Bosporus Strait between Turkey and the Balkans, but many of the 16 million residents of Armenia, Azerbaijan and Georgia might protest. Ethnographers consider them European, all three states have been members of the Council of Europe since 2001, and – as we will see in Chapter 9 – there have been hints in the cases of all three (as with Ukraine) of future EU and NATO membership. But all three also have close political and economic ties with Russia, and unless Turkey also joined, they would be physically isolated from the rest of the EU.

Without question the most troubling debate about the limits of Europe relates to Turkey. Geographically, only the four per cent of its land area west of the Bosporus is European, but Turkey's historical ties with Europe are strong, not least because it is the successor to the Ottoman Empire that once covered most of the Balkans, including Bulgaria, Hungary, and Romania. The question of Turkey's European credentials has been growing since 1963 when Turkey became an associate member of the Community, which agreed at the time that eventual full membership was possible. Turkey has been a member of NATO since 1952, and has been lobbying for membership of the EU since 1987, but although it is now recognized as a candidate country, opinion on its prospects (see Chapter 9) remains deeply divided, and questions about its claims to be European remain unanswered.

One final but much less seriously considered candidate for inclusion in Europe is Israel. Its creation was accelerated by a European event (the Holocaust), many of its Jewish residents have European roots, and its strained relations with many of its Middle Eastern neighbours have encouraged Israel to build stronger ties with Europe. Several Israeli government ministers have broached the idea of EU membership, as have the leaders of several eastern European states and prime minister Silvio Berlusconi of Italy. But the political relationship between Israel and the EU is a troubled one (see Chapter 25), Israel has a large Arab minority, and in geographical terms it is not a European state.

Map 3.1 The borders of Europe

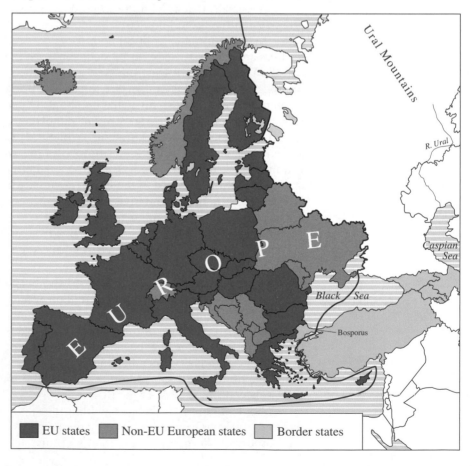

Identity

A term used in the social sciences to describe how people understand or see themselves, either as individuals or as part of a group. Individual identity is driven by psychological questions such as role, gender, image and self-esteem, but group identity is driven by a wider range of factors such as culture, place, history, language, ethnicity, religion, ideology, philosophy, and aesthetics. Europeans today find themselves faced by the sometimes competing options of local, national, state and European identity.

Although Israel and the EU have agreements that establish limited free trade and allow for discussions on political and economic questions, the prospects of Israeli membership of the EU have never been seriously discussed.

Where, then, is Europe? If its eastern limits are its borders with Turkey and Russia, then it consists today of 40 states: the 27 members of the EU, three other western European states (Iceland, Norway and Switzerland), and ten eastern/central European states. (Strictly speaking, there are also five micro-states that might be included in the list: Andorra, Liechtenstein, Monaco, San Marino and Vatican City. These are legally independent, and all except the Vatican City are members of both the Council of Europe and the United Nations, but none has separate membership of the EU, and none is convention-ally listed among the major states of Europe.) If a broader definition of Europe is accepted, then it includes four more states (Armenia, Azerbaijan, Georgia, and Turkey) for a total of 44 (or 49 if the micro-states are counted seperately) (see Table 3.1).

Understanding European identity

If geography is inconclusive as an indicator of Europe, even more problematic is the question of **identity**, or how Europeans define themselves relative to others.

Table 3.1 The states of Europe

Albania	(Georgia)	Netherlands
(Armenia)	Germany	Norway
(Azerbaijan)	Greece	Poland
Austria	Hungary	Portugal
Belarus	Iceland	Romania
Belgium	Ireland	Serbia
Bosnia and Herzegovina	Italy	Slovakia
Bulgaria	Kosovo	Slovenia
Croatia	Latvia	Spain
Cyprus	Lithuania	Sweden
Czech Republic	Luxembourg	Switzerland
Denmark	Macedonia	(Turkey)
Estonia	Malta	Ukraine
Finland	Moldova	United Kingdom
France	Montenegro	

Micro-states: Andorra, Liechtenstein, Monaco, San Marino, Vatican City.

Blue: Member states of the EU

Note: All except Belarus, Kosovo, and Vatican City were members of the Council of Europe in 2010, along with Russia.

This is a topic that has been the subject of an increasingly animated and complex debate, the questions about how identity is formed and changed typically outnumbering the answers (see Fligstein, 2008; Robyn, 2005; Cerutti and Lucarelli, 2008). The most immediate sense of identity comes from place, or the community to which people feel the greatest sense of affinity. But this has different meanings for Europeans:

- It may be the village, town or city in which they live.
- It can be the local administrative units under whose jurisdiction they fall, whether they are counties, provinces, departments, or regions.
- It may be the part of the state in which they live. The English and the Italians, for example, make broad distinctions between northerners and southerners, and ascribe many different characteristics – both real and mythical – to the two groups.
- National identity remains alive and well, such that – for example – many Scots feel more Scottish than British, and many Basques place national feelings above association with Spain or France.
- It may be the state of which they are a citizen or a legal resident.
- To all of these sets of association has been added in the last few decades the notion of identity with the European Union and with Europe more generally.

Attempts to pin down what it means to be European are most immediately complicated by cultural associations with nations. As noted in Chapter 1, a nation is a group of people who identify with one another on the basis of a mixture of real and mythical qualities, typically including language, history, culture, and a variety of symbols that tie them together. One of the most telling – and sometimes most troubling – of political and societal pressures in Europe since at least the late eighteenth century has been the push among nations to have their own states. But while the borders of nations and states have increasingly coincided, no European state is entirely homogeneous in national terms, and Europeans have long lived in states divided by culture, nation, and language. In most, a workable balance has been achieved, but in others the nationalist tensions remain: Belgium, for example, is divided between the Dutch-speaking Flemish, French-speaking Walloons, and a small German-speaking minority in the east.

There are numerous national groups in Europe, although estimates of the number vary according to how a nation is defined: Minahan (2000) lists 143 nations, or 106 if European Russia is excluded, while Pan and Pfeil (2004) list 160 nations in the 27-member EU alone. These range in size from the Germans, Italians, French, English, Polish, and Spanish – who together account for nearly two-thirds of the population of the EU-27 – to national minorities each numbering in the tens or hundreds of thousands, including Maltese, Luxembourgers, Montenegrins, and Estonians (see Table 3.2). To further complicate the picture, few European states are culturally homogeneous; while almost all have a single dominant national group, all but the smallest have at least three indigenous national minorities, and in most cases many more (Pan and Pfeil, 2004; see also Panayi, 2000). This diversity is the heritage of the repeated reordering of territorial lines in Europe over the centuries, with new patterns of immigration since 1945 adding more variety. The result has been the creation of at least six groups of minorities within Europe:

- National minorities related to national majorities in neighbouring states, such as Germans living in Romania, Albanians in Kosovo, Greeks in Cyprus, Poles in the Ukraine, Czechs in Slovakia, and Ukrainians in Poland. Talk in 2010 of offering Hungarian citizenship to the estimated 2.5 million Magyars living in Slovakia, Ukraine, Romania, and Serbia raised the spectre of a revival of Hungarian nationalism and territorial claims on Slovakia.
- Transnational minorities that live in two or more states but do not form a majority anywhere. These include the Basques and Catalans of Spain and France, and the Frisians of Germany and the Netherlands.
- Indigenous minorities living within a single state, including the Scots and the Welsh of Britain, the Corsicans and Bretons of France, and the Galicians of Spain.
- Foreigners legally resident in Europe, including citizens of one European state living in another. According to Eurostat, there were about 32 million foreigners legally resident in the EU member states in 2008, accounting for more than 6 per cent of the population (Eurostat web site, April 2010).
- New racial and religious minorities arriving from outside Europe. In spite of the attention drawn to them by the media, these minorities actually make up only a small part of the bigger picture: only about 25 million of the EU's legal residents (5 per cent of the population) belong to a racial minority, a proportion far smaller than the United States (23 per cent) or Canada (16 per cent).
- Foreigners illegally resident in Europe. It is impossible to know exact numbers, but estimates place the total at between 4 and 8 million, with perhaps as many as 400,000 more arriving each year.

The clearest indicator of national differences is language, the preservation of which has been at the heart of many struggles by minorities to assert their separate identity. Language is also the most effective barrier to the development of a

Illustration 3.1
Multilingual Europe

The winning design (by Polish graphic designer Szymon Skrzypczak) for the logo commissioned to mark the 50th anniversary of the treaties of Rome in 2007, reproduced here in all 23 official languages of the EU

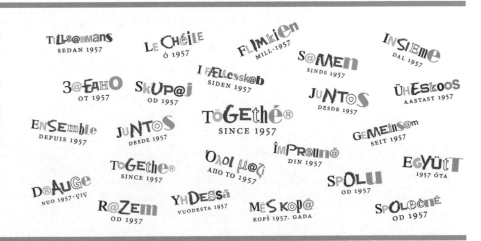

Table 3.2 The nations of Europe

Nationality	Population (millions)	States of major concentration
Large (20–85 million)		
German	83.8	Germany, Belgium, Poland
Italian	57.1	Italy, France, Croatia
French	52.1	France
Ukrainian	51.7	Ukraine, Poland, Belarus
English	47.6	UK, Ireland
Polish	44.9	Poland, Ukraine, Belarus, Lithuania, Germany
Spanish	36.2	Spain
Romanian	23.7	Romania, Ukraine, Russia, Hungary, Moldova
Medium (5–15 million)		
Dutch	14.1	Netherlands, Germany, Belgium
Rhinelander	13.8	Germany
Magyar	12.9	Hungary, Romania, Slovakia, Serbia, Ukraine
Occitan	12.2	France, Spain, Italy
Portuguese	11.9	Portugal, France
Belarussian	11.7	Belarus, Ukraine, Poland
Greek	11.6	Greece, Cyprus, Germany
Czech	10.6	Czech Republic, Slovakia
Bavarian	10.5	Germany
Catalan	9.8	Spain, France
Turk	9.6	European Turkey, Bulgaria, Cyprus, Greece
Andalusian	9.5	Spain
Roma	8.0 –10.0	Multiple states. Biggest groups in Romania, Bulgaria, Spain, Hungary, Slovakia,
Swabian	8.8	Germany
Lombard	8.7	Italy, Switzerland
Serb	8.7	Serbia
Bulgarian	8.5	Bulgaria, Romania, Moldova
Swede	8.5	Sweden, Finland
Saxon	7.8	Germany
Sicilian	7.8	Italy
Austrian	6.9	Austria
Albanian	6.2	Albania, Serbia, Macedonia, Greece
Flemish	6.1	Belgium, France
Irish	5.9	Ireland, UK
Scottish	5.8	UK
Slovak	5.6	Slovakia
Croat	5.5	Croatia, Bosnia
Dane	5.1	Denmark
Finn	5.1	Finland, Sweden

Small (less than 5 million)

Swiss German	4.8	Switzerland
Norwegian	4.4	Norway
Georgian	4.2	Georgia
Walloon	4.1	Belgium
Norman	4.0	France
Moldovan	3.8	Moldova
Piedmontese	3.8	Italy
Venetian	3.7	Italy
Galician	3.6	Spain
Northumbrian	3.5	UK
Lithuanian	3.3	Lithuania, Russia, Latvia
Welsh	3.1	UK
Breton	2.8	France
Burgundian	2.6	France
Basque	2.4	Spain, France
Macedonian	2.2	Macedonia, Bulgaria, Greece
Sard	2.2	Italy (Sardinia)
Alsatian	2.1	France
Slovene	2.0	Slovenia
Bosnian	1.9	Bosnia and Herzegovina
Ligurian	1.9	Italy
Canarian	1.8	Canary Islands
Szeklar	1.8	Romania
Scanian	1.7	Sweden
Latvian	1.6	Latvia, Russia
Moravian	1.5	Czech Republic
Romand	1.4	Switzerland
Tyrolean	1.4	Austria, Italy
Savoyard	1.1	France, Italy
Estonian	1.0	Estonia, Russia
Frisian	0.9	Netherlands, Denmark, Germany
Fruili	0.8	Italy
Cornish	0.6	UK
Montenegrin	0.6	Montenegro
Sorb	0.6	Germany, Poland
Sanjaki	0.5	Serbia
Corsican	0.4	France
Istrian	0.4	Croatia
Madeiran	0.4	Madeira
Maltese	0.4	Malta
Azorean	0.3	Azores
Icelander	0.3	Iceland
Kashub	0.3	Poland
Luxembourger	0.3	Luxembourg
Vorarlberger	0.3	Austria

Note: Does not include groups with homelands in Russia, or groups with less than 250,000 members.
Source: Based on Minahan (2000).

Citizenship

A complex notion tied to the idea of belonging to a political community (normally a state). At its most basic, citizenship of a state means the right to live in that state, to hold a passport of that state, to take part in the political life of a state, and to enjoy freedom of speech and a minimum standard of economic and social welfare. But legal residents of a state of which they are not citizens have almost all the same rights and duties as citizens. Ultimately, an individual could declare that – like the Greek philosopher Diogenes – they were a citizen of the world, but this is an attitude or a philosophy, not a legal reality.

true sense of European identity; in spite of the growth of language education, the majority of Europeans speak only their native language, creating a barrier to cross-cultural communication and making it difficult for Europeans to better understand each other. Natives of the EU alone speak more than forty different languages, of which 23 are currently recognized as official (see Table 3.3). This designation means that that all EU documents must be translated into those languages, that simultaneous translation must be offered if requested at EU meetings, and that EU citizens have the right to be heard by EU institutions in those languages.

But English, thanks in part to its growth as the language of commerce, technology, and diplomacy, and in part to the spread of Western (mainly American) culture, is rapidly becoming the common language of Europe, not to mention a global language (Crystal, 2003). The work of EU institutions is increasingly conducted in English (and to a lesser extent French), European corporate executives are increasingly expected to be able to speak English, it is used more often in higher education, and it has become the lingua franca of European tourism. Its spread worries the French in particular and other Europeans to some extent, but it offers the advantage of giving Europeans a way of talking to each other, and helping reduce the cultural differences that divide them.

Citizenship and patriotism

If cultural associations with nations complicate attempts to pin down what it means to be European, they are further complicated by legal associations with states. As noted in Chapter 1, a state is a legal and political entity marked by territory, with a government that has sovereignty within that territory, and whose independence and legitimacy is recognized in law. European state lines have changed constantly, but in addition to the existing sovereign states of Europe, new potential states lie waiting in the wings as pressures grow for the independence of Scotland and the Basque Country, and for the break-up of Belgium. Although many Europeans owe their cultural allegiance to nations, they owe their legal allegiance to states through the ties of **citizenship**.

The debate over the meaning of this term has been long and complex, ranging over the centuries across its social, moral, legal and political qualities, touching along the way on ideas about identity, and being divided by philosophical arguments about duties (the civic republican strain) and rights (the liberal strain). Although duties such as civic engagement and military service are

Table 3.3 The official languages of the EU

Bulgarian	German	Polish
Czech	Greek	Portuguese
Danish	Hungarian	Romanian
Dutch	Irish	Slovak
English	Italian	Slovene
Estonian	Latvian	Spanish
Finnish	Lithuanian	Swedish
French	Maltese	

still relevant to an understanding of citizenship, it is the liberal strain that has the most real and immediate meaning to most people. Tracing its roots to the transition in Britain from a monarch–subject relationship to a state–citizen relationship, it ties citizenship to the right to vote, the right to just treatment under the law, and the right to own property (Heater, 2004).

For most of us, citizenship comes down to a series of legal qualities: being a citizen of a state means having the right to live and work in that state (although this right is also given to legal residents), to vote and run for elective office, to be protected against forcible removal from that state to another without the agreement of the governments involved, to hold (or claim) a passport of that state, and to receive protection from the home state when outside its borders. A citizen is regarded as a subject of his/her home state by other governments, and must usually obtain the permission of other governments to travel through or live in their territory. Reduced to its most basic, about the only difference between a citizen and a legal resident of a given state is that the citizen has the right to vote and run for office, while the non-citizen does not. Otherwise the two have more or less all the same rights and responsibilities.

The EU has developed its own concept of **European citizenship**, but it is less than it seems. While Lisbon says that 'every person holding the nationality of a Member State shall be a citizen of the Union', it also goes on to note that 'citizenship of the Union shall be additional to and not replace national citizenship' (Article 20). Symbolically, all passports of EU member states are printed in the same burgundy colour and list 'European Union' alongside the name and symbol of the member state. Citizens of EU member states also have the additional benefit of going through the same lines when entering the EU from abroad, while travellers from non-EU states go through different and sometimes slower-moving lines with sometimes different documentary requirements. Beyond that, citizens of the EU have since the 1992 Maastricht Treaty on European Union (see Chapter 6) had the following rights:

- To move and live freely within the territory of member states (although this is not an unconditional right, and is available also to almost anyone who is a legal resident of an EU member state).
- To vote and stand as a candidate in local and European Parliament elections in whichever state they are legally resident.
- To seek the help of any EU embassy if they run into difficulties in a foreign country where their state has no representation.
- To address EU institutions in any of the 23 official languages of the EU, and to receive a reply in the same language.

● **European citizenship**: A concept developed by the EU in order to provide its citizens with more of a transnational sense of belonging, but falling short of conventional ideas of citizenship.

Ward (1996, p. 40) describes these qualities as 'a pleasant touch, but of limited practical value', while Guild (1997, p. 30) sees them as no more than 'some fancy words on a piece of paper' that fail to confer on the holder 'any rights which he or she did not already have'. What they ultimately fail to offer is an alternative to state citizenship; in other words, citizens of an EU state cannot turn in their national passports and have them replaced with EU passports, and EU citizens still do not have the option of what Maas (2007, p. 95) describes as 'supranational political membership', or what Balibar (2004) describes as 'transnational citizenship' (although it is more accurately 'trans-state' citizenship, since citizenship is not tied to nations). This has not happened for the simple reason that there is no European state, government or authority that would be responsible for protecting the rights of European citizens, and to which these citizens might appeal if they had problems with any of the member states of the EU.

Against the background of this discussion about the role of nations and states in identity, how do we approach the meaning of identity with Europe? Who are those people who take a European view of themselves and the world around them? Who are the 'Eurostars', as Favell (2008) labels them: the people who have taken up, physically or culturally, the new opportunities for mobility offered by integration? Residents of the EU do not have the option of cultural association with the EU (as they do with nations) or legal association (as they do with states), so where, then, must we look for indications of European identity? The results of opinion polls give us some sense of what is happening. For example, when respondents in the then EU-15 member states were asked by the Eurobarometer polling service in 2004 how they would conceive of themselves in the near future in terms of identity, only 4 per cent considered themselves European. But only 41 per cent identified exclusively with their home states, meaning that a clear majority had at least some sense of identity with Europe (see Figure 3.1).

Fligstein puts it slightly differently when he divides Europe into three camps: one (including about 10–15 per cent of the population) is connected by deep economic and social ties, and benefits materially and culturally from Europe; a second (40–50 per cent) has a more shallow relationship with Europe, aware of what is going on across borders but still wedded to national language, culture and politics; the third (40–50 per cent), which tends to be older, poorer, and less educated, does not travel or consume culture from other societies, is more wedded to home, and is more fearful of European integration (Fligstein, 2008, p. 250).

Eurobarometer also periodically asks Europeans if they feel a sense of attachment to the EU (but does not explain what 'attachment' means). The 2007 poll revealed that only about half of respondents had such a feeling (see Figure 3.2), a figure that correlates closely with the number of Europeans who agree that membership of the EU has been a good thing for their country (see Chapter 17). As in most such polls, however, the range among states was wide, and few strong patterns emerged from the results. Most of the founder states of the EEC were at

Figure 3.1 What Europeans think: identification with Europe

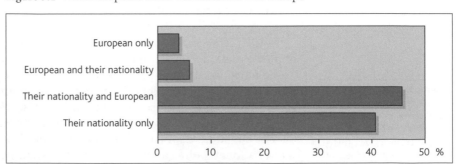

Source: European Commission, *Eurobarometer* 61, Spring 2004.

Figure 3.2 What Europeans think: identification with the EU

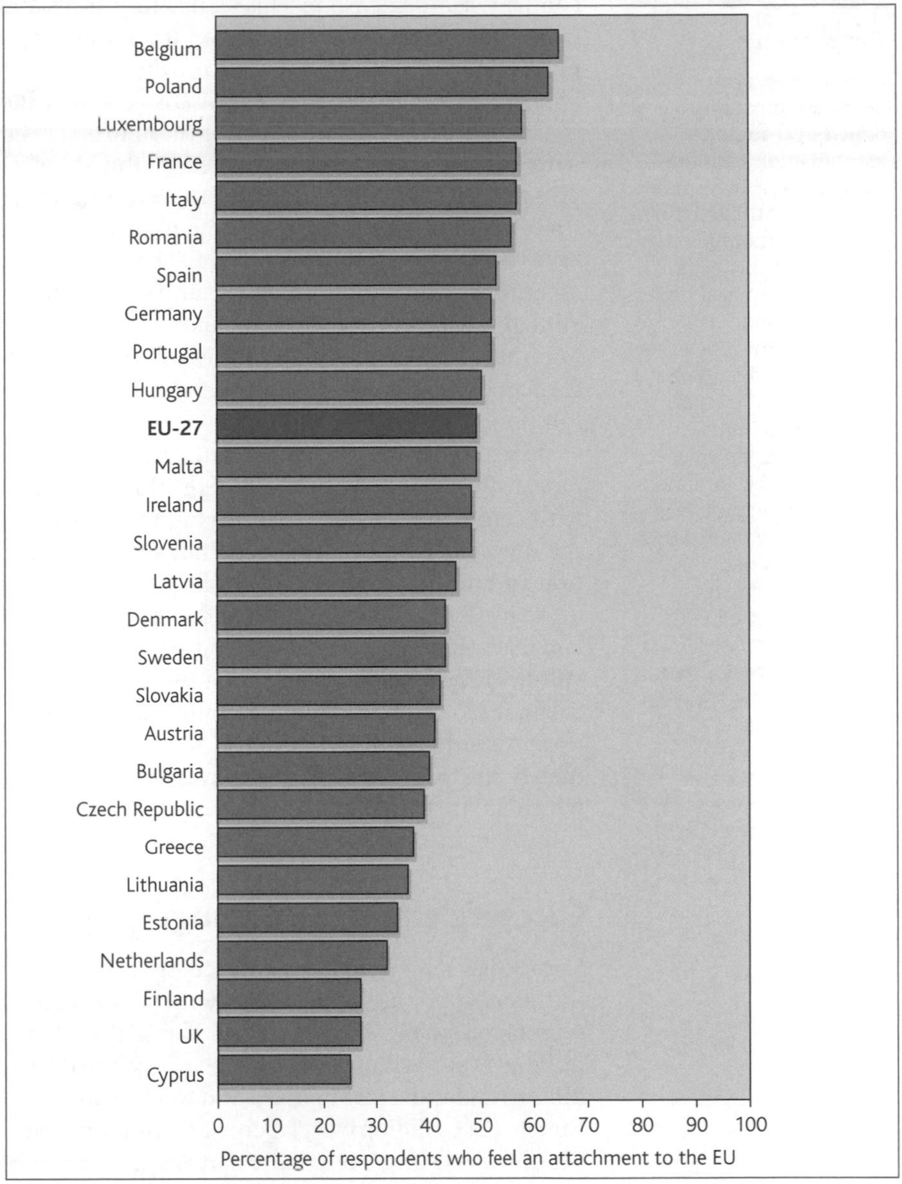

Source: European Commission, *Eurobarometer* 68, Spring 2007.

the higher end of the range (the Netherlands being a notable exception), several Scandinavian states were at the lower end of the range, and Britain took its accustomed place at the lowest end of the range. Interestingly, eastern European states had a wide range of levels of attachment (from a high of 63 per cent in Poland to lows of 34–45 per cent in the Baltic states), and there was no obvious correlation between wealth and identity.

But what does 'attachment' or 'identification' mean? Most of us feel attached to (or identify with) the states of which we are citizens either because we take comfort in our familiarity with their character, history, and customs, or because

CONCEPT

Patriotism

Pride in, love of, or devotion to country, driven by a sense of identification with the history and achievements of that country. Although usually associated with positive support for a country, it can spill over into hostility or superiority towards other countries, and the belief that criticisms of the home country are somehow unpatriotic. For some it can be conflated with nationalism, which may mean the pursuit of the interests of a national group over others that stand in its way or pose some kind of real or imaginery threat. While some take pride in the achievements of the EU, it has not yet achieved the place in public consciousness that makes it the object of patriotism.

we have a legal association through a passport or some other document that confirms our citizenship. This association translates for many into **patriotism**, or a sense of pride in the state or the nation to which we belong. But many Europeans are wary of patriotism, which has earned a bad name through its long-time association with nationalism, which has in turn often been at the root of conflict and war. The idea that Europeans might identify more actively with Europe is further complicated by the absence of all the usual factors that give people a sense of belonging to a community; there is no single European state, nation, language, government, people, religion, citizenship, passport, army, police force, or culture. The EU has worked to produce a series of symbols of Europe – including a flag, an anthem, a motto ('United in Diversity'), an annual Day of Europe (9 May), and there are claims also that the euro and the burgundy EU passport are symbols of Europe – but these have not yet attracted the same sense of association with Europe or the EU as national and state symbols.

Icons are an important element of 'belonging', to be sure, but Europeans are repeatedly reminded of their differences: language is the most telling reminder, with culture and history also playing their part. The EU has tried to overcome the divisions by promoting activities since Maastricht aimed at drawing attention to Europe's common cultural heritage while at the same time preserving diversity. It provides funding and other support for the arts, education, and language training, selects one or two cities each year as European capitals of culture (examples have included Bruges, Cork, Istanbul, Lisbon, Liverpool, Salamanca, and Stockholm), and the Commission gives annual awards for the preservation of cultural heritage. But while such projects have value, it is ultimately up to Europeans themselves to develop a sense of European identity, which in turn means that they must better understand what they have in common (see discussion in Chapter 17).

Europe's changing demography

Europe has long been a dynamic centre of population growth, and is today one of the most populous and most densely-populated regions of the world: with a population of nearly 500 million if just the EU is counted, or more than 590 million if all 44 European states are included, it ranks third after China (1.3 billion) and India (1.1 billion), and well ahead of the United States (305 million), Russia (142 million) or Japan (128 million). But recent trends suggest that Europe faces some potentially damaging demographic trends: fewer Europeans are having children, more of them are living longer, and the balance between workers and retirees is changing. These trends promise in turn to lead to social and economic difficulties: rising costs for health care and social security that must be met out of a shrinking tax base, and concerns about everything from declining economic productivity to reduced standards of living, inter-generational tensions, changes to the way that businesses operate and work is organized, and new approaches to the planning of urban development, transport, and infrastructure.

An allied issue is that of immigration, which is a world-wide phenomenon but has been particularly important in Europe, where even countries that were long sources of emigration (such as Ireland and Italy) have been magnets for

Focus on . . .
The European flag

Without question the most ubiquitous and immediately recognizable symbol of European integration is the flag of the EU, its twelve gold stars on a blue background found everywhere from government buildings and hotels to vehicle licence plates, driving licences, identity cards, passports, and euro banknotes. And yet despite how common the flag has become, little is known about how it evolved or what – if anything – its design represents. The story is a curious one.

Soon after its creation in 1949, the Council of Europe appointed a committee to design a flag. Although no public competition was announced, the Council received more than 120 prospective designs, ranging from the dull to the strange and the outright bizarre. Among the early suggestions: the flag of the Pan-European Movement (a red cross on a yellow circle on a blue background); the flag of the European Movement (a large green E on a white background); a single yellow star on a blue background; a constellation of 35 yellow stars on a blue background, laid out to indicate Europe's capital cities; a leaping tiger (*sic*); and a circle of 15 yellow stars on a blue background, each star representing a member state of the Council of Europe. The design eventually chosen was the circle of stars, but with the number reduced to 12 because of various objections to the numbers 15, 14, and 13.

The flag was approved and unveiled in 1955, the Council encouraging other European organizations to adopt it so that it could become the symbol of Europe more generally. It was adopted by the European Parliament in 1983, and then by the European Council (for use by the European Community) in 1985, and finally for use by the European Union from 1993. It is now controlled jointly by the EU and the Council of Europe.

When membership of the Community was 12, many thought that the 12 stars each represented a Community member state, but the number was not increased after enlargement in 1995, leading to a number of entertaining speculations about what the stars represented. Suggestions have ranged from the months in the year to the number of apostles, the signs of the zodiac, the labours of Hercules, and the tribes of Israel. There has also been speculation, mainly in Catholic countries like Poland, that the stars were inspired by those sometimes found in the halo surrounding the head of the Madonna in church paintings. But the 12 stars were chosen simply because all members of the design committee could live with that number. The number has no political, religious, social, or cultural significance or symbolism whatsoever. (Information in this box comes mainly from Kowalski, 2009.)

immigration (see Parsons and Smeeding, 2006). While natural increase accounted for almost all population growth in Europe in the 1960s, growth in numbers is now almost entirely generated by net immigration. But this has not been big enough to make up for population decline, and even if it helps add to overall European population numbers it brings with it the promise of increased social, economic and political tensions, since many of the newcomers will be Arabs, Africans, and/or Muslims. Immigration has grown since the 1950s and

1960s, but efforts by European governments to protect jobs by limiting the entry of foreign workers have not only contributed to an influx of unskilled illegal workers, but these workers have long been marginalized, with few efforts made to integrate them into mainstream society. Racism and religious bigotry have worsened, and support for right-wing anti-immigrant parties has grown, while infrastructure and social institutions have come under greater pressure. (See Chapter 23 for more details.)

The numbers are clear. Where Europe in 1900 accounted for about a quarter of the world's population, today it accounts for one-ninth, and UN projections suggest that it could account for just one-fourteenth by 2050. This is in part due to rapidly growing populations in other parts of the world, but also to slowing growth in Europe. Fertility rates in the EU fell by 45 per cent between 1960 and 2004 (Pearce and Bovagnet, 2005), and today stand at well below the replacement level of 2.1. No EU state has a rate higher than 1.7, while in Italy and Spain it is as low as 1.2, and the EU average is 1.5. As a result, the European population is projected to fall by six per cent between 2015 and 2050, while that of India will grow by 25 per cent, the United States by 22 per cent, and Brazil by 8 per cent. China will grow by 5 per cent by 2035, after which it will start to fall (see Figure 3.3). While numbers in most smaller European countries are climbing, in the bigger states the story is quite different: the populations of Germany and Poland are already falling, that of Italy is expected to fall after 2020, and that of France will level out after 2045, leaving only Britain among the big EU states with a growing population, thanks mainly to immigration.

Figure 3.3 Population change compared

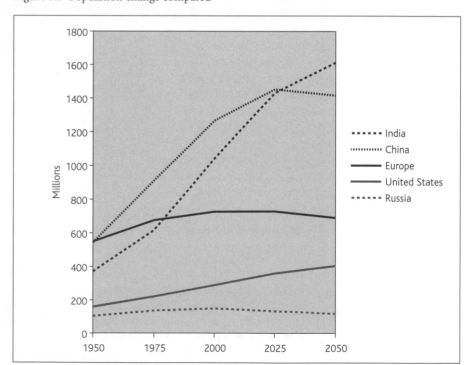

Source: United Nations Population Division, http://esa.un.org/unpp (retrieved August 2010).

Meanwhile, there has been an aging of the population. Between 1960 and 2006, the number of western Europeans aged 65 and older rose in most countries from about 9–12 to about 15–18 per cent of the population, leaving the region with more retirees than any other part of the world except Japan (see Figure 3.4). While the median age for the world's population in 2010 was just over 29, in Europe it was 40.2 and rising (United Nations Department of Economic and Social Affairs, 2009). The ratio of pensionable people to people of working age in Europe in 2005 was 35:100, and that figure is expected to rise to 75:100 by 2050, coming close to parity in some countries. Some European governments have become so worried about these trends that they have adopted policies aimed at encouraging people to have more children, including increased job security, extended parental leave, expanded child care and after-school programmes, free or subsidized education and health care, and flexible work schedules. But while the decision to have a child is a deeply personal one, it has long been influenced by economic pressures: where once children were a source of labour and then of support for aging parents, today the decision to have children is delayed by the number of women pursuing careers and by medical advances that make it possible to have children later in life. Government policies, no matter how generous, are not going to have much impact on these trends.

Figure 3.4 Comparing aging populations

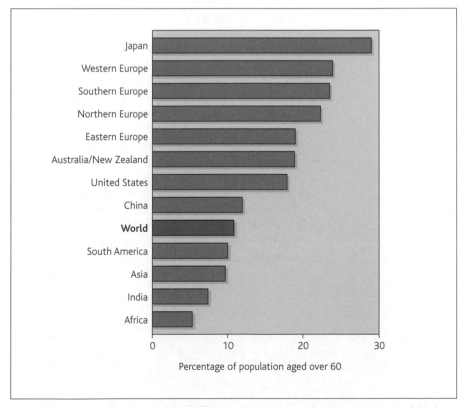

Source: UN Department of Economic and Social Affairs, Population Division, at http://esa.un.org (retrieved October 2010). Figures are for 2009.

Birth patterns in Europe have also been influenced by developments in the structure of the family. The notion of the 'standard' family unit (one in which a parent or two married parents live together with their children in what sociologists call a nuclear or conjugal arrangement) has long been something of a myth, but certainly nowhere is this more true today than in Europe, where the nuclear family is becoming a thing of rarity, impacted by three key trends.

- Fewer Europeans are marrying, and they are delaying the age at which they marry. Where once it was usual for people to marry in their early twenties, and often even in the late teens, the average age for first marriages in the EU-27 in 2006 ranged between 27 and 34 (Eurostat press release 32/2008, 6 March 2008). This is explained mainly by the desire of more women to start careers, but also by the decision of more Europeans not to marry.
- More children are being born outside marriage, the figure in western Europe rising from between two and five per cent in 1960 to nearly 33 per cent in 2000, rising as high as 40– 45 per cent in Denmark, Latvia, France, Britain and Finland, and 55 per cent in Sweden (Eurostat press release STAT/06/59, 15 May 2006). Birth outside marriage, once associated mainly with poverty, is increasingly a deliberate choice for European parents.
- Single-parent households and households without children have become more usual. The former accounted in 2005 for 13 per cent of all those households with children, while two-thirds of households in the EU-25 had no children at all, and only 17 per cent had two children or more (Eurostat press release STAT/06/59, 15 May 2006).

Although similar trends are under way in other industrialized countries, nowhere have they gone so far as in Europe, and nowhere has the debate about the possible implications been more vocal. Those who doubt the wisdom of European integration wonder if the European Union can sustain its political influence and economic growth so long as its population is declining. But quality is arguably more important than quantity; it is not how many people we have so much as how well they live. China and India may be the world's population superpowers, but many of their people live in abject poverty with minimal access to basic services. We have also been warned for decades of the dangers of a rising global population, and its growing pressures on finite natural resources. While the changing balance between workers and retirees in Europe will inevitably lead to reforms of welfare and social security, declining population numbers will also mean less pressure on resources and less over-crowding. Is this a crisis, then, or an opportunity?

SUMMARY

- The geographical, political and ethnic borders of Europe are debatable. To the south, west and north they are marked by coastlines, but there is no obvious border to the east.
- If the external limits of Europe are contested, so is its internal identity. Nations offer Europeans the most obvious reminder of their differences, with language, culture, history and symbols preventing a broader sense of European identity.
- Europe is divided into at least 40 different states and 160 different nationalities, with natives of the EU speaking more than 40 different languages, of which 23 are currently recognized as official. English, though, is rapidly becoming the common language of Europe.
- Although the EU has promoted an EU 'citizenship' (giving EU citizens the right to live in different EU states, and to run and vote in local and European Parliament elections, for example), this is not the same as providing Europeans with the same rights and legal status as those who are citizens of a member state.
- Polls suggest that only about 4 per cent of Europeans consider themselves as such, while about 41 per cent identify exclusively with the states of which they are citizens, and about 55 per cent have some mixture of European and state identity. Only about half of EU residents feel a sense of attachment to the EU.
- A combination of declining fertility and improved life expectancy means that the population of Europe is both shrinking and becoming older. This is leading to concerns about the region's economic productivity and about the growing costs of supporting an aging population.
- Europe's population growth is now almost entirely accounted for by net immigration, which presents a host of troubling political and social challenegs.

KEY TERMS AND CONCEPTS

Citizenship
European citizenship
Identity
Patriotism

FURTHER READING

Checkel, Jeffrey T., and Peter J. Katzenstein (eds) (2009), *European Identity* (Cambridge: Cambridge University Press). A study of the idea of European identities and of how they might be better understood from political, historical, sociological and anthropological perspectives.

Favell, Adrian (2008), *Eurostars and Eurocities: Free Movement and Mobility in an Integrating Europe* (Oxford: Blackwell). A study of the human face of integration, looking at what mobility has meant to individual Europeans.

Fligstein, Neil (2008), *Euroclash: The EU, European Identity, and the Future of Europe* (Oxford: Oxford University Press). Argues that changes in European business, trade, popular culture, and social interaction have helped promote a transnational European identity.

CHAPTER 4

Organizing Postwar Europe

PREVIEW War and conflict have for centuries been part of the fabric of Europe, prompting philosophers to develop numerous plans for bringing peace to the region, but finding their suggestions falling mainly on deaf ears. The tensions among Europeans deepened during the nineteenth century as nationalism burgeoned and great power competition paved the way for two world wars. Before those wars, all the great world powers had been European: their empires circled the globe, they dominated global trade, and their banks, financial institutions, armies and navies faced few serious challenges. But their power and influence now suffered a shattering blow.

Europe embarked on peace in 1945 with most of its economies devastated, its political systems destabilized, its colonies agitating for independence, and its states distrustful of each other and threatened by a new kind of Cold War between two external powers: the United States and the Soviet Union. Europeans had tired of violence, and sought ways to make future conflict impossible, but while there was support for the idea of European cooperation, governments and elites were divided over what this meant, and how to proceed.

A start was made with the creation in 1949 of the Council of Europe, but this was not enough for federalists, who focused instead on the development of supra-national institutions; a new approach was taken in 1952 with the founding of the European Coal and Steel Community. Tracing the story from Bretton Woods to the Marshall Plan and the start of the Cold War, this chapter attempts to capture the spirit of the postwar debate, and to understand the confluence of circumstances that came together to make the first steps in the process of integration possible.

KEY ISSUES

- What were the major historical causes of European conflict and war?
- What had changed by 1945 to make Europeans more receptive to the idea of cooperation?
- Why were France and Germany so central to the interests of European integration?
- How important was the Marshall Plan to the postwar recovery of Europe?
- Does Winston Churchill deserve more credit as one of the founders of the European Union?
- Was focusing on coal and steel a wise move, or a distraction?

Europe before the war

Societies are always changing, but in few parts of the world have the changes been so dramatic – or had such wide-ranging effects – as in Europe. The advent of the European Union is just the latest (and perhaps most revolutionary) development in the search for an answer to the question of how politics and economies should be ordered in one of the world's most heavily populated, politically competitive, and culturally complex regions. That Europeans have lived in relative harmony since 1945 is remarkable given the long history of violence in the region. That history runs from the wars of antiquity through to the invasions of the Early Middle Ages, the Crusades, wider European conflicts such as the Hundred Years' War (1337–1453) or the Eighty Years' War (1568–1648), attempts to fend off foreign invaders such as the Arabs and the Ottoman Turks, civil wars, wars of independence, and the two world wars of the twentieth century.

The causes of Europe's conflicts have varied, the focus shifting from wars over land and between competing dynastic houses to wars of religion in the Middle Ages as first the Latin and Orthodox churches struggled with each other, then Catholics and Protestants fought for influence, then monarchs challenged the authority of the papacy. Through the sixteenth and seventeenth centuries much of Europe was in a state of almost constant religious warfare. A milestone was reached in 1648 when the Peace of Westphalia brought an end to more than a century of war, and confirmed the emergence of the modern state system. Political boundaries in Europe began to achieve a new clarity, but so did the power and reach of governments, which established standing armies to protect their interests, creating new tensions and possibilities for conflict.

A dangerous new quality was added by the mismatch between states and nations: people speaking different languages and with separate cultural and sometimes religious identities were brought together under common governments, whose rule they often resented. As Enlightenment ideas led to the rejection of claims by monarchs that their powers were based on God's authority, and support for the idea that sovereignty lay with the people, so the struggles for national self-determination grew. Another combustible element was added to the mix when European states began to build overseas empires, bringing a new global dimension to competition for power within Europe.

Frustrated by what they saw, idealists explored ways in which Europeans might cooperate through regional associations. Suggestions ranged from assemblies of princes to courts that might adjudicate disputes, a European parliament, and a European federation (see de Rougemont, 1966; Heater, 1992; Urwin, 1995; Salmon and Nicoll, 1997). The philosophical benchmark for the debate was laid down in 1795 when the German philosopher Immanuel Kant published his thoughts on the conditions needed for mankind to achieve a state of perpetual peace, including the abolition of standing armies and a federation of free states. Europe's achievements in maintaining peace since 1945 have often earned the region the epithet *Kantian* (see Chapter 24).

The Napoleonic wars (1803–5) were generated at least in part by the resistance of nationalists to Napoleon's plans to build a European empire, and although Europe as a whole was mainly at peace between the 1815 Congress of Vienna and the outbreak of the Great War in 1914, nationalism was generating dangerous new pressures. Governments asserted their authority as minorities struggled for independence, the goal for many being the creation of nation-states: a state for every nation. This meant resistance to foreign rule and demands for independence in Belgium, Bulgaria, Greece, Hungary, Ireland, Italy, Poland, and Romania, and efforts to unify Germany and Italy. Nationalism and imperialism came together in a volatile combination , and it took only one small spark – the assassination in June 1914 of the heir to the Austro-Hungarian throne by a Slav nationalist – to set off the series of events that would lead within two months to the outbreak of the Great War.

The war resolved little, and did so at staggering cost: an estimated 15 million people died, including unprecedented numbers of civilians. If there was anything positive to come out of the carnage it was the birth of a new audience – particularly in smaller states tired of being caught in the crossfire of big power rivalry – more amenable to notions of inter-state cooperation. But although several modest attempts were made to put ideas into practice – Belgium and Luxembourg, for example, created a limited economic union in 1922 – most Europeans remained doggedly attached to their national and state identities.

In 1922, the Austrian diplomat Count Richard Coudenhove-Kalergi wrote an article (turned into a book titled *Pan-Europa* in 1923) in which he warned that Europe was 'a powder keg of international conflicts' whose atmosphere was poisoned by 'the mutual hatred of Europeans for each other'. Its problems would be 'resolved only by the union of the peoples of Europe', to which the greatest obstacle, in his view, was the 'thousand-year rivalry' between Germany and France (Coudenhove-Kalergi, 1926). His ideas found a receptive audience in several current and future political leaders, including French Prime Minister Édouard Herriot (in office 1924–25), who suggested the creation of a United States of Europe founded on the postwar cooperation being promoted by the new League of Nations. His colleague Aristide Briand followed up in 1930 by suggest-ing a European federation working within the League of Nations, using in his proposal such terms as *common market* and *European Union* (Briand, 1997).

But the 1919 Treaty of Versailles, by punishing Germany and demanding reparations, had already laid the foundations for more conflict. The rise of

Richard Coudenhove-Kalergi

Richard Coudenhove-Kalergi (1894–1972) was the son of an Austro-Hungarian diplo-mat and his Japanese wife. Born in Tokyo, he was raised mainly in what is now the Czech Republic, and educated in Vienna. He was author of the pamphlet *Pan-Europa*, creator in 1923 of the Pan-European Union, and editor of its journal *Paneuropa* until 1938. He proposed dividing the world into five power groups: Paneuropa (including all European states except Britain), the British empire, a Pan-American Union in North and South America, the Soviet Union in Eurasia, and a Pan-Asian Union centred on Japan and China. He spent the Second World War in exile, mainly in the United States, inspiring the character Victor Laszlo in the film *Casablanca*. He continued to promote his ideas of European unity after the war.

Nazism squashed all ideas of peaceful cooperation, and the outbreak of another European war in 1939 suggested that the region was incapable of finding the formula for a lasting peace (Marks, 2003). The Second World War brought new levels of death and destruction, cost millions of civilian and military lives, left cities in ruins, cut agricultural production by half, created an estimated 13 million refugees by the war's end, destroyed essential infrastructure, and brought political and economic dislocation to winners and losers alike.

The troubled state of postwar Europe

Relief at the end of the war was reflected in the rejoicing and celebration that broke out on VE Day, 8 May 1945. But it was also clear that Europeans now faced the sobering and monumental task of rebuilding not just the infrastructure

Map 4.1 Europe after the Second World War

destroyed by war but often entire political, economic and social systems. They had suffered physically and psychologically, and now cast anxious eyes at the challenges that lay ahead, some more apparent than others.

- **France** had suffered a wartime division between collaborators and the Resistance, and while it now worried about how to modernize its economy and extend welfare provisions, its international standing was unclear. It acted like a great power, but the constitution of the Fourth Republic (adopted in 1946) was flawed, and France was to suffer blows to its military pride in Indochina in 1954 and again at Suez in 1956 (see Chapter 5). Charles de Gaulle would come out of retirement in 1958 to head the new Fifth Republic, and to reorder France's place in Europe and the world.
- **Britain** had seen its finest hour during the war, but while it was politically stable and enjoyed rapid economic recovery after the war, bolstered by nationalization and welfare reform, its international role had changed. The beginning of the end of its great power status came in August 1947 with independence for India and Pakistan, but many Britons still held on to their national pride and their interests outside Europe, valued close cooperation with the United States, and paid little attention to developments on the continent. Suez was to force a reappraisal, but even today most Britons remain reluctant Europeans.
- **West Germany** was focused on economic reconstruction and the challenge of dealing with a national sense of shame. Germany as a whole was under four-way foreign occupation, and by 1948 was divided into socialist eastern and capitalist western sectors. The Federal Republic of Germany (or West Germany) was founded in May 1949, and the Christian Democrats won the August elections. The popular chancellor Konrad Adenauer (in office 1949–63) worked to side his new state with the Atlantic Alliance and to rebuild German respectability, goals which inevitably made it a champion of regional integration.
- **Italy** was less successful than West Germany in achieving postwar economic and political stability. Christian Democrats dominated the new Italian republic created in June 1946, but there were frequent changes of government, systematic corruption, and bureaucratic incompetence. For Prime Minister Alcide de Gasperi (in office 1945–53) integration with Europe was a means of encouraging peace while helping Italy deal with its economic problems. But the country has never lived up to its potential as a leading European power.
- The **Nordic states** had different wartime experiences: Sweden remained neutral, Finland became neutral after going to war with the USSR, Denmark and Norway were both invaded by Germany, and a newly-independent Iceland was wary of international cooperation (there were street riots when it became a founding member of NATO in 1949). But the five had political stability, homogeneous populations, and few internal social problems. They harmonized national laws, agreed common foreign policy positions, and launched joint ventures such as the airline SAS (created in 1946). In 1952 the Nordic Council was formed to promote the abolition of passport controls, the free movement of workers, and more joint ventures.

- The **Benelux states** (Belgium, the Netherlands, and Luxembourg) had all been occupied by the Germans, and were interested in economic cooperation. In 1948 the Benelux customs union was created, paving the way for the 1960 Benelux Economic Union (BEU), which proved to be a landmark experiment in European integration.
- In **Greece, Portugal** and **Spain**, the road to democracy and economic growth was rocky. Greece enjoyed postwar economic growth, but political tensions would lead to a military dictatorship in 1967–74. Portugal had been under the authoritarian government of Antonio Salazar since 1928, and Spain under the dictatorship of Francisco Franco since 1939. Surrounded by efforts to encourage postwar international cooperation, all three remained isolated.
- **Ireland** had been officially neutral during the war but with its economy bound to that of Britain, its postwar approach to Europe was subject to the British lead. It joined the Community in 1973 with Britain, after which it maintained its neutrality while enjoying economic growth.
- **Austria** had had been left relatively unscathed by war, and although it was divided like Germany into separate postwar zones of occupation, it returned quickly to its 1920 constitution and held democratic elections. It declared itself neutral in 1955, but economic ties pulled it into the western European orbit.
- Prospects of **eastern Europe** taking part in broader regional cooperation were trampled by its postwar absorption into the Soviet sphere, and its obligation to follow the Soviet lead on foreign policy, which meant no cooperative deals with the West. Only after the end of the Cold War in 1991 would eastern Europe emerge from its shell and begin working with the West.

In addition to its effects on individual states, the Second World War also resulted in a reordering of the international system. Until 1939, the world's great powers were mainly European, their influence based on their large militaries and economies, their strong positions in international trade, and their financial investments around the world (Levy, 1983, pp. 16–18). But while Britain and France continued to act like great powers after the war, it soon became clear that there was a new international order in place, dominated by the United States and the Soviet Union. Their power was so great and their reach so far that they earned the new label *superpower* (Fox, 1944, pp. 20–1) (see Chapter 24 for further discussion). Europe's fall was soon confirmed by the region's division in an ideological cold war between the superpowers in which Europeans were to play only a supporting role.

Three urgent priorities now faced European states:

- Economic reconstruction was needed if Europe was to recover and regroup, but it was clear that the region was too tired and drained to be able to manage this alone.
- Europeans not only continued to be suspicious of each other, but now faced the prospect of being a battlefield in a war between the Americans and the Soviets, overlaid by the threat of the ultimate form of destruction: nuclear annihilation.

TIMELINE

Organizing postwar Europe

1914–18		First World War
1919	June	Signature of Treaty of Versailles
1923		Creation of Pan-European Union
1939–45		Second World War
1944	July	Bretton Woods conference
1945	May	End of the war in Europe
1946	March	Churchill's 'iron curtain' speech
	June	Creation of Italian republic
	September	Churchill's 'United States of Europe' speech
	October	Creation of French Fourth Republic
1947	March	Announcement of Truman Doctrine
	June	George Marshall's speech at Harvard
	August	Independence of India and Pakistan
1948	January	Benelux customs union enters into force
	March	Brussels Treaty creates Western Union

1948	April	Launch of the Marshall Plan; first meeting of OEEC
	May	Congress of Europe meets in The Hague
	June	Start of Berlin blockade
	October	Creation of European Movement
1949	April	Signature of North Atlantic Treaty, and creation of NATO
	May	Creation of Council of Europe; end of Berlin blockade; creation of Federal Republic of Germany
1950	May	Schuman Declaration
	June	Negotiations begin on coal and steel agreement
1951	April	Signature of Treaty of Paris
1952	March	Creation of Nordic Council
	July	Treaty of Paris enters into force
	August	European Coal and Steel Community begins work
1955	May	Creation of Warsaw Pact

● Nationalism had been the main cause of both world wars, and Europeans could not hope to live in peace unless it was channelled in a more benign direction.

Looking back today with the benefit of hindsight, it is remarkable how much Europe has since been able to achieve: after centuries of bloodshed, the region has become the poster child for peace, diplomacy, and the resolution of conflict.

CONCEPT

Bretton Woods system

The arrangement agreed at Bretton Woods in 1944, by which it was hoped that the economic and financial mistakes of the mid-war years would be avoided, and a new and more sustainable international commercial and financial system created. The key goal of the system was exchange rate stability, using gold as the reference point, and a free convertibility of currencies that would encourage trade. The system ended in August 1971 when the United States unilaterally ended the convertibility of gold and the US dollar, sparking exchange rate volatility and helping encourage Europe to take the first steps in what would eventually lead to the creation of the euro.

● **Marshall Plan:** A programme under which the United States offered financial assistance to encourage postwar recovery in Europe. Often credited with providing the investments needed to pave the way to regional integration.

But achieving this has not been easy, and it happened only because of a fortuitous coincidence of circumstances, without which the history of postwar Europe might have taken a very different turn.

Rebuilding economies (1945–51)

The structure of the postwar international economic system was mapped out at a landmark meeting in July 1944, when economists and government leaders from both sides of the Atlantic gathered at the Mount Washington Hotel, set in the forested hills of Bretton Woods, New Hampshire. There they laid down the principles of what became known as the **Bretton Woods system**: the convertibility of currencies, free trade, non-discrimination, and stable rates of exchange, underpinned by the new strength of the US dollar, and by the creation of two new international organizations: the International Monetary Fund (IMF) would encourage exchange rate stability in the interests of promoting international trade, and the World Bank would lend to European countries affected by war (van Dormael, 1978). A third body, the International Trade Organization, failed to win support in the US Congress and it was instead agreed to set up the General Agreement on Tariffs and Trade (GATT) as a temporary measure to oversee negotiations aimed at the progressive reduction of barriers to trade.

Noble as these goals may have been, it soon became clear that the economic costs of conflict had been underestimated: there was a brief postwar boom, but growth was not sustained, food was still being rationed, and western Europeans were using up their dollar reserves buying essential imports. Large amounts of capital investment were needed, and the only ready source was the United States. Its wartime economy had prospered, and although it had provided more than $10 billion in loans and aid to Europe between 1945 and 1947 (Milward, 1984, pp. 46–8), a more structured approach was needed. In a speech at Harvard University in June 1947, US Secretary of State George Marshall announced that the US would do whatever it could to help encourage Europe's economic revival. His motives were clearly political (a strong Europe would help prevent Soviet expansionism and create a new market for US exports), but he couched his arguments in humanitarian terms, arguing that US policy was directed 'against hunger, poverty, desperation and chaos' and that 'its purpose should be the revival of a working economy in the world so as to permit the emergence of political and social conditions in which free institutions can exist'.

Within weeks, representatives of 16 western European governments had met in Paris to begin listing needs. (The Soviets also attended, but left when they decided that US goals were incompatible with their own.) Between 1948 and 1951 the European Recovery Programme (otherwise known as the **Marshall Plan**) was to provide $12.5 billion in aid (Milward, 1948, p. 94) (about $115 billion in 2010 terms, adjusted for inflation). But while Marshall was awarded the 1953 Nobel Peace Prize for his efforts, the long-term role and significance of Marshall aid remains contested. Hitchcock (2004, pp. 134–8) points out that economic recovery was already under way before the aid arrived, with most western European countries already back up to, or close to, pre-war levels of production. Furthermore, the aid itself was only a small fraction of the gross national product of the recipient states. On the other hand, it had much psychological value: it reassured an economically nervous western Europe, helped bind

Illustration 4.1
The Marshall Plan

Marshall Plan assistance begins to arrive in Europe, providing devastated postwar economies with an essential boost to their plans for reconstruction.

together transatlantic economic interests, and helped offset communist influence in western Europe. In short, contends Judt (2005, p. 97), it 'helped Europeans feel better about themselves'.

The Marshall Plan also helped lay critical foundations for European integration. The United States wanted a single market in the interests of economic recovery, and insisted upon the creation of a new international body, the **Organisation for European Economic Co-operation** (OEEC), to coordinate the distribution of aid. Meeting for the first time in April 1948, its goals included reduced tariffs and other barriers to trade, and a free trade area or customs union among its members (Articles 4–6 of the Convention for European Economic Cooperation, quoted in Palmer *et al*, 1968, p. 81). Critics have dismissed it as clumsy and inadequate, and as nothing more than a clearing-house for economic information (Milward, 1984, p. 208; Wexler, 1983, p. 209; Dinan, 2004, p. 28). But it was western Europe's first permanent organization for economic cooperation, it encouraged inter-state cooperation, and it helped reveal the degree of economic interdependence among its members (Urwin, 1995, 20–2). (In December 1960 the OEEC was reorganized as the Organisation for Economic Co-operation and Development (OECD).)

● **Organisation for European Economic Co-operation**: An international body set up to coordinate and manage Marshall aid, and that some see as the first significant step in the process of postwar European integration.

Addressing external threats (1946–49)

Economic reconstruction was their most immediate priority, but western Europeans also worried about threats to their security, now more external than internal. The United States had pulled most of its military out of Europe soon after the war, encouraged by public opinion at home that favoured leaving future peacekeeping efforts to the new United Nations. But it soon became clear that Stalin had plans to spread Soviet influence in Europe, replacing the old Nazi threat with a new communist threat. Winston Churchill drew public attention to the dilemma with his famous March 1946 speech in Fulton, Missouri, in which he warned of the descent of an 'iron curtain' across Europe. He also observed that from what he had seen of the Russians during the war, there was nothing they admired so much as strength, 'and there is nothing for which they have less respect than for weakness, especially military weakness'.

The Americans expected that responsibility for European security would be shared with the British and the French, but neither had the resources to keep up their end of the bargain. Britain had provided financial aid and military security in Greece (which Churchill had established as a British sphere of influence in return for giving the Soviets control over Romania), but it soon had to withdraw, raising concerns about communist influence in the region. In March 1947, US President Harry S. Truman concluded that the United States should step into the breach, and announced what was to become known as the Truman Doctrine: it would now be US policy, he declared, 'to support free peoples who are resisting attempted subjugation by armed minorities or by outside pressures'. The new insecurities of Europe were quickly illustrated by events in Germany.

While the western Allies favoured German self-sufficiency, the Soviets first wanted reparations and a guarantee of security from German aggression. Prompted by Soviet belligerence, Britain, France, and the Benelux states in March 1948 signed the Brussels Treaty, creating a Western Union (renamed Western European Union in 1954 – see Chapter 5) whose members pledged to provide 'all the military and other aid and assistance in their power' in the event of attack. The Allies also began discussions aimed at building a new West German government and tying West Germany into the western alliance. When they announced their plans in June 1948 (which included the creation of a new currency, the deutschmark), the Soviets responded by setting up a blockade of West Berlin, obliging the British and the Americans to organize an 11-month airlift of supplies to the beleaguered city.

With the twin need of protecting western Europe and also sharing the burden, the Americans and their western European allies in April 1949 signed the North Atlantic Treaty, under which the idea of mutual protection was expanded to include the United States, Britain, France, Canada, Italy, the Benelux countries, Denmark, Iceland, Norway and Portugal. The treaty was given institutional substance with the creation of the **North Atlantic Treaty Organization** (NATO).

● **North Atlantic Treaty Organization:** A defensive alliance created in 1949 between the United States, Canada, and most major western European states, and designed to send a security warning to the Soviet Union.

As with the Marshall Plan, opinion on the significance of NATO has been divided. On the one hand, the treaty stated that 'an armed attack against one or more of [the members]… shall be considered an attack against them all', but it obliged each member to respond only with 'such action as it deems necessary, including the use of armed force'. In other words, there was no firm commitment to a combined military response. On the other hand, the creation of NATO sent a clear message to the Soviets, who countered in 1955 with the creation of their own defensive agreement, the Warsaw Pact. NATO also represented the first peacetime military agreement ever made by the United States, and set up the first ever peacetime integrated military command.

Winston Churchill

Winston Churchill (1874–1965) (*second from right*) was prime minister of Britain between 1940 and 1945, and again between 1951 and 1955. Although he was the great symbol of British resistance to the Nazi threat during the Second World War, he is a controversial figure in the gallery of Europeanists. On the one hand, he inspired many of the ideas that defined Europe's postwar condition and that set the tone for discussions about cooperation, including his suggestion for a United States of Europe, his role in the creation of the Council of Europe, and his warning of the 'iron curtain' that had descended across the continent. On the other hand, he was clearly a champion of Britain's association with the English-speaking peoples of the world, and equivocated on the precise role that Britain might play in Europe. He has never quite been elevated to the same ranks in the European debate as the other 'founding fathers', such as Paul-Henri Spaak of Belgium (*left*), Paul Reynaud of France (*second from left*) and Robert Schuman (*right*).

The Council of Europe (1946–49)

Within a few years of the end of the Second World War, then, and encouraged mainly by the United States, there was a new atmosphere of receptivity to cooperation in western Europe. Several pro-European groups were founded or revived, but what was still lacking was a strong political lead, which could come only from Britain, still the major power in Europe. During the war, Winston Churchill had suggested the creation of 'a United States of Europe' operating under 'a Council of Europe' with reduced trade barriers, free movement of people, a common military, and a High Court to adjudicate disputes (Palmer *et al.*, 1968, p. 111). He repeated the suggestion in a speech co-drafted by Coudenhove-Kalergi (Salmon and Nicoll, 1997, p. 6) and given in Zurich in September 1946 (see Document 4.1). But Britain still had too many interests outside Europe, including its empire and its links with the United States, and Churchill neatly summed up British attitudes when he proclaimed that Britain was 'with Europe but not of it. We are interested and associated, but not absorbed' (Zurcher, 1958, p. 6).

Undeterred, pro-European groups organized the Congress of Europe in The Hague in May 1948, presided over by Churchill and attended by more than 600 delegates from 16 states and observers from Canada and the United States. But opinion differed on the meaning of European unity (Dinan, 2004, p. 23). While federalists hoped for a wholesale redrawing of the map of Europe, with the replacement of individual states by a United States of Europe, others still believed in the state and were interested only in cooperation. In October the **European Movement** was created with a view to moving the debate along, and there was talk of creating a European Assembly. The eventual compromise was the signing on 5 May 1949 of a statute in London creating the **Council of Europe.**

● **European Movement**: An organization created in 1948 to champion the cause of European integration. It was behind the setting up of the Council of Europe and continues today to lobby for a federal Europe.

● **Council of Europe**: An organization founded in 1949 at the suggestion of Winston Churchill, and which has gone on to promote European unity with a focus on issues relating to democracy and human rights.

DOCUMENT 4.1

Churchill's Zurich speech, 19 September 1946 (excerpts)

I wish to speak to you today about the tragedy of Europe. This noble continent . . . is the home of all the great parent races of the western world. It is the fountain of Christian faith and Christian ethics. It is the origin of most of the culture, arts, philosophy and science both of ancient and modern times.

If Europe were once united in the sharing of its common inheritance, there would be no limit to the happiness, to the prosperity and glory which its . . . people would enjoy. Yet it is from Europe that have sprung that series of frightful nationalistic quarrels, originated by the Teutonic nations, which we have seen even in this twentieth century and in our own lifetime, wreck the peace and mar the prospects of all mankind . . .

Some of the smaller states have indeed made a good recovery, but over wide areas a vast quivering mass of tormented, hungry, care-worn and bewildered human beings gape at the ruins of their cities and homes, and scan the dark horizons for the approach of some new peril, tyranny or terror. Among the victors there is a babble of jarring voices; among the vanquished a sullen silence of despair.

Yet all the while there is a remedy . . . It is to re-create the European Family, or as much of it as we can, and provide it with a structure under which it can dwell in peace, in safety and in freedom. We must build a kind of United States of Europe . . .

If Europe is to be saved from infinite misery, and indeed from final doom, there must be an act of faith in the European family and an act of oblivion against all the crimes and follies of the past . . . The first step in the re-creation of the European family must be a partnership between France and Germany . . .

If we are to form the United States of Europe or whatever name or form it may take, we must begin now . . . The first step is to form a Council of Europe. If at first all the states of Europe are not willing or able to join the union, we must nevertheless proceed to assemble and combine those who will and those who can.

Source: James (1974).

The goal of the new body was to achieve 'a greater unity between its Members . . . by discussion of questions of common concern and by agreements and common action in economic, social, cultural, scientific, legal and administrative matters'. Its most lasting contribution was the drafting in 1950 and the subsequent management of the European Convention on Human Rights, which today plays a key role in the European legal structure (see Chapter 8). But as for the broader issue of European integration, the Council was too limited in its goals for the tastes of federalists. Jean Monnet described it as 'entirely useless', and later French president Charles de Gaulle regarded it as 'simply ridiculous' (Simpson, 2001, p. 646).

Monnet, who had made his name as a civil servant and French government planner, had loftier ambitions, and recruited to his cause the incumbent foreign minister of France, Robert Schuman. Both were committed integrationists, both felt that the noble statements of the unity lobby needed to be translated into practical action, and both agreed with Churchill that the logical focus should be on the Franco-German problem. Schuman was instinctively suspicious of Germany, but was encouraged by US Secretary of State Dean Acheson to give it political credit, and to provide French leadership on the tricky question of bringing West Germany back into the western community. (The division of Germany had been confirmed by the founding in May 1949 of the western Federal Republic of Germany, followed three months later by the eastern German Democratic Republic.) An opportunity was created by US and British interest in West German rearmament; this ran the danger of tilting the European balance of power (Hitchcock, 2004, pp. 151–2), but not if West Germany was allowed to rebuild under the auspices of a new supranational organization that would bind it into the wider process of European reconstruction.

The European Coal and Steel Community (1949–52)

At early meetings of the European Movement, the suggestion had been made that coal and steel offered strong potential for cooperation. They were the building blocks of industry as well as the raw materials for weapons of war, and cooperation might eliminate waste and duplication, boost industrial development, and make sure that West Germany became reliant on trade with the rest of western Europe (Milward, 1984, p. 394). It would also allow France to exert some control over production in the German industrial heartland of the Ruhr. As to how to proceed, Monnet's experience with government bureaucracies told him that a new supranational organization with powers and a life of its own was needed. He discussed this with Schuman and with Konrad Adenauer, and they agreed on the creation of a new body within which responsibility for coal and steel production could be pooled in the hope of laying the foundations for what might eventually become a European federation. Their proposal was announced by Schuman at a press conference held on 9 May 1950 – five years almost to day after the end of the war in Europe – at the French Foreign Ministry in Paris (see Document 4.2).

Illustration 4.2
The Schuman Declaration

Robert Schuman addresses a press conference in the salon de l'Horloge at the Quai d'Orsay in Paris on 9 May 1950, and announces the plan to set up a European Coal and Steel Community.

Robert Schuman

Robert Schuman (1886–1963) was the quintessential European: born to French parents in Luxembourg, he was brought up in then German-ruled Lorraine, attended university in Germany, and served in the German army during the First World War. Elected after the war to the French parliament, he refused to serve in the French Vichy government during the Second World War, and was imprisoned by the Gestapo for his criticism of German policy. He escaped, joined the French Resistance, and was re-elected to the French legislature in 1945. He served as France's finance minister and briefly as prime minister before serving as foreign minister from 1948 to 1952. Although the May 1950 declaration of the ECSC bears his name, it was the brainchild of Jean Monnet, and Monnet later claimed that Schuman 'didn't really understand' the plan (Jenkins, 1989, p. 220). Nonetheless, Schuman has won a permanent place in the pantheon of the pioneers of integration.

The Schuman Plan was revolutionary in the sense that France was offering to surrender a measure of national sovereignty in the interests of building a new supranational authority that might help build a new European peace (Gillingham, 1991, p. 231). But few other governments shared Monnet's enthusiasm, and only four agreed to sign up: Italy sought respectability and stability, and the three Benelux countries were small and vulnerable, had twice been invaded by Germany, were heavily reliant on exports, and felt that the only way they could have a voice in world affairs and guarantee their security was to be part of a bigger unit. As for the others:

- Britain trusted neither the French nor the Germans, still had too many political and economic interests outside Europe, exported little of its steel to Europe (Milward, 1984, p. 402), and had recently nationalized its coal and steel industries. Prime Minister Clement Attlee argued that he was 'not prepared to accept the principle that the most vital economic forces of this country should be handed over to an authority that is utterly undemocratic and is responsible to nobody' (Black, 2000, p. 303). He, like his social democratic peers in the Scandinavian countries, was also wary of the role being played by continental Christian Democrats in early initiatives on integration.
- Because Ireland's economy was predominantly agricultural, it had little to gain from the proposal. It also had to follow the British lead because of its economic ties with Britain.
- For Denmark and Norway, memories of the German occupation were still too fresh, while Austria, Finland, and Sweden valued their neutrality.
- Portugal and Spain were dictatorships with only limited interest in international cooperation.
- Eastern Europe was out of the picture thanks to Soviet control.

Against this less than encouraging background, the governments of the Six opened negotiations in June 1950. There was resistance to Monnet's plans to

DOCUMENT 4.2

The Schuman Declaration, 9 May 1950 (excerpts)

World peace cannot be safeguarded without the making of creative efforts proportionate to the dangers which threaten it. The contribution which an organized and living Europe can bring to civilization is indispensable to the maintenance of peaceful relations . . .

Europe will not be made all at once, or according to a single plan. It will be built through concrete achievements which first create a *de facto* solidarity. The coming together of the nations of Europe requires the elimination of the age-old opposition of France and Germany . . .

With this aim in view, the French Government proposes that action be taken immediately on one limited but decisive point. It proposes that Franco-German production of coal and steel as a whole be placed under a common High Authority, within the framework of an organization open to the participa-

tion of the other countries of Europe. The pooling of coal and steel production should immediately provide for the setting up of common foundations for economic development as a first step in the federation of Europe, and will change the destinies of those regions which have long been devoted to the manufacture of munitions of war, of which they have been the most constant victims.

The solidarity in production thus established will make it plain that any war between France and Germany becomes not merely unthinkable, but materially impossible. The setting up of this powerful productive unit, open to all countries willing to take part and bound ultimately to provide all the member countries with the basic elements of industrial production on the same terms, will lay a true foundation for their economic unification.

Source: Europa website at http://europa.eu/abc/symbols/9-may/decl_en.htm (retrieved July 2010).

break down coal and steel cartels, and the negotiations – notes Gillingham (2003, p. 25) – were 'often tough and even brutal', several times standing on the verge of collapse. Disagreement centred on the break-up of the German coal and steel industries, the role of the ECSC High Authority, the weighting of votes in its Council of Ministers, and even which languages should be used and where the ECSC institutions should be based (Dinan, 2004, pp. 51–4). But Monnet prevailed and on 18 April 1951 the Treaty of Paris was signed, creating the **European Coal and Steel Community** (ECSC). It was charged with building a common market in coal and steel by eliminating import and export duties, discriminatory measures among producers and consumers, subsidies and state assistance, and restrictive practices. The treaty entered into force in July 1952 and the new organization began work in August, managed by four institutions (see Figure 4.1).

The birth of today's European Union is usually dated to the later creation of the European Economic Community (EEC), and yet the process of integration needed this smaller preparatory step, representing as it did the first time that European governments had transferred authority to a supranational organization. The ECSC faced some political resistance, and although it initially benefited from rising demand for coal and steel on the back of the Korean War, it ultimately failed to achieve its core goal of a single market for coal and steel (Gillingham, 1991, p. 319). But like the Marshall Plan and NATO, it had an

● **European Coal and Steel Community**: The first organization set up to encourage regional integration in Europe, with qualities that were both supranational and intergovernmental.

Figure 4.1 Structure of the European Coal and Steel Community

INSTITUTION	MEMBERSHIP	FUNCTION
High Authority	Nine members (two each from the larger states, and one each from the smaller states) appointed for six-year terms	To remove barriers to the free movement of coal and steel. Represented joint interests of the ECSC
Special Council of Ministers	Relevant government ministers from each member state. Presidency held by each member state in rotation for periods of three months	To make decisions on proposals from the High Authority
Common Assembly	78 members chosen by national legislatures, and divided among member states on the basis of population	Advisory
Court of Justice	Seven members: six judges and a trade union representative	Settled conflicts between states and ruled on legality of High Authority decisions

important psychological effect, obliging the governments of the Six to work together and to learn new ways of doing business. It functioned independently until 1965, when the High Authority and the Special Council of Ministers were merged with their counterparts in the EEC and Euratom (see Chapter 5). The Treaty of Paris expired in July 2002, fifty years after it came into force.

SUMMARY

- Europe had long been divided by conflict as one power invaded or tried to dominate another, or as religious disputes spilled over into violence, and then as states began to emerge and national minorities struggled for independence.
- Numerous suggestions had been made for ways in which Europeans might cooperate, but it took the traumas of two world wars to bring these ideas to a wider audience.
- The Franco-German question dominated many of the discussions, but while Italy and the Benelux countries were keen on cooperation, Britain kept its distance, others were wary of international efforts, and eastern Europe was under Soviet control.
- Europe in 1945 had three critical needs: to rebuild war-ravaged economies, to ensure security from one another and from external threats, and to limit the dangers of nationalism.
- Economic reconstruction was given a boost by the United States, which provided assistance through the Marshall Plan. Security assurances were also provided by the United States through the new North Atlantic Treaty Organization.
- The problem of nationalism was addressed by new initiatives to promote regional unity, beginning in 1949 with the creation of the Council of Europe. But its goals were too limited for the tastes of Europeanists such as Jean Monnet and Robert Schuman.
- The signature of the 1951 Treaty of Paris led to the creation in 1952 of the European Coal and Steel Community, a first step in the process of building European economic ties. But only France, West Germany, Italy and the three Benelux countries joined.

KEY TERMS AND CONCEPTS

Bretton Woods system
Council of Europe
European Coal and Steel Community
European Movement
Marshall Plan
North Atlantic Treaty Organization
Organisation for European Economic Co-operation

FURTHER READING

Dinan, Desmond (2004), *Europe Recast: A History of European Union* (Basingstoke: Palgrave Macmillan). The best general history of European integration, and essential reading before moving on to more detailed or revisionist studies.

Gilbert, Mark (2003), *Surpassing Realism: The Politics of European Integration Since 1945* (Lanham, MD: Rowman and Littlefield), and John Gillingham (2003), *European Integration, 1950–2003: Superstate or New Market Economy?* (Cambridge: Cambridge University Press). Two more opinionated histories of European integration; Gillingham is particularly critical, writing of missed opportunities and bad decisions.

Hitchcock, William I. (2004), *The Struggle for Europe: The Turbulent History of a Divided Continent* (New York: Anchor Books). This does for Europe what Dinan does for the EU: a readable survey of postwar European history that helps place more detailed studies in perspective. For a more detailed treatment, see Tony Judt (2005), *Postwar: A History of Europe since 1945* (New York: Penguin).

CHAPTER 5

Building a Single Market

The creation of the European Coal and Steel Community was a critical first step along the path to European integration, but its possibilities were always bound to be limited. So, after failing with two far more ambitious initiatives – the creation of European defence and political communities – the six ECSC members switched their focus to the building of a single market. The 1957 Treaties of Rome created the European Economic Community (EEC) and the European Atomic Energy Community (Euratom), the former setting the goal of creating a European market within which there would be free movement of people, money, goods and services. But this was no easy target, and the EEC would see only mixed progress during the 1960s as its member states failed to remove all the barriers to the single market, and failed to exploit its possibilities.

This was also a troubling time in international relations, with the Berlin and Cuban missile crises, escalation of the war in Vietnam, and the Soviet crackdown on reform in Czechoslovakia, in all of which the critical players were the Americans and/or the Soviets. Meanwhile, the EEC was to be troubled by political disagreements over the powers and reach of its institutions and over enlargement, French president Charles de Gaulle twice vetoing British applications for membership.

In 1973 the Community welcomed its first new members (Britain, Ireland and Denmark), followed in the 1980s by more (Greece, Spain and Portugal). The main effect of enlargement was to change the political balance of integration as France and Germany found their previously dominant roles challenged. The EEC faced many hurdles, some of its own making and others created by the ebbs and flows of the Cold War and the transatlantic relationship. At heart, it was – in its early years – an elitist project that had little impact on European public opinion.

KEY ISSUES
- Were the European Defence Community and the European Political Community doomed to failure?
- How important was the Suez crisis to the history of European integration?
- What does de Gaulle's role in the early years of the EEC say about the problems and possibilities of strong leadership in European affairs?
- What impact did Vietnam have on European integration?
- Could the EEC have managed without Britain as a member?

Internal and external shocks (1950–58)

Opinion on the long-term significance of the ECSC is divided. For Dinan (2004, p. 55, 64), it was 'politically important and institutionally innovative but economically insignificant', and he doubts that it contributed much to Europe's economic growth. For Gillingham (2003, pp. 22–23), while it may not have operated either as intended or 'even satisfactorily', and the strategic importance of European coal and steel may have been overstated, it was an essential first step to Franco-German reconciliation. But its achievements were more symbolic than substantive, and something more ambitious was needed if integration was to have the kind of reach and effects that its most committed supporters hoped for. The focus now shifted from the modest to the wildly over-optimistic as discussions were held on two new initiatives on a grand scale.

The first was the **European Defence Community** (EDC). It had first been proposed in 1949 by West German Chancellor Konrad Adenauer, seeking West German remilitarization in the interests of self-defence, and had been given a decisive push by US support for rearming West Germany in the wake of the June 1950 outbreak of the Korean War (Dinan, 2004, pp. 57–9). With the underlying goal of encouraging western European defence cooperation while also binding West Germany into a regional security system, and echoing ideas outlined by Winston Churchill in a speech to the Council of Europe in August, a draft plan was published in October 1950 (Eden, 1960, p. 32). Although named for incumbent French Prime Minister René Pleven, it was – like the Schuman Plan – mainly the work of Jean Monnet (Gillingham, 2003, p. 29). It spoke of the need for a common defence and for a European Army made up of units from different countries coming under the control of a European Minister of Defence, responsible in turn to a Council of Ministers and a European Assembly (Pleven Plan, in Stirk and Weigall, 1999, pp. 108–9).

Although a draft EDC treaty was signed in May 1952 by the six members of the ECSC, and quickly ratified by all but France, it immediately faced two critical handicaps: it lacked support from Britain, the only remaining large military power in Europe, and its core goal of building a Franco-German military force could not be achieved without the full remilitarization of West Germany, which was unlikely to happen for several more years. Then in May 1954 came a humiliating blow to French national pride and global influence: the surrender of 12,000 French forces besieged by communists at Dien Bien Phu in French Indochina (for details, see Windrow, 2004). In a sombre mood, and following a debate in which deep concerns were expressed about the potential loss of French sovereignty and national standing, the French National Assembly rejected the EDC treaty in August.

Eager to encourage some kind of military cooperation that went beyond the loose obligations of NATO, Britain now used the occasion of West Germany and Italy joining the Western Union to propose its transformation into the **Western European Union** (WEU) (Urwin, 1995, pp. 68–71). This was to be intergovernmental (in contrast to the supranational EDC), and reiterated the commitment made in the 1948 Treaty of Brussels that, in the event of an attack on one of its members, the others would respond with 'all the military and other aid and assistance in their power' (a commitment that contrasted with the NATO obligation on a member to respond only with 'such action as it deems necessary').

● **European Defence Community**: A stillborn plan to create a common European military as a means of binding a rearmed West Germany into western Europe.

● **Western European Union**: A defensive alliance (created in 1948 as the Western Union) that was always to be overshadowed by NATO, and in spite of being given a potential new role in EU defence in the 1990s eventually became dormant.

WEU was also more than a security agreement: modifications to the Treaty of Brussels signed by its seven founding members in Paris in October 1954 included agreement to 'promote the unity and to encourage the progressive integration of Europe.' The creation of the WEU also helped give new clarity to the lines of the Cold War: it began work in May 1955, just as West Germany became a member of NATO, and within days the Soviet bloc had created its own defensive alliance in the form of the Treaty of Friendship, Cooperation and Mutual Assistance (the Warsaw Pact).

The second major initiative of the early 1950s was the **European Political Community** (EPC). Prompted by the hopes of Italian Prime Minister Alcide de Gasperi to develop a fast-track to a European federation, but driven mainly by the need to create a political control mechanism to oversee both the EDC and the ECSC (Gillingham, 2003, p. 30; Dinan, 2004, p. 62), a draft plan had been agreed in 1953. Since described as Europe's 'first constitution' (Griffiths, 2000), it included proposals for a European Executive Council, a Council of Ministers, a Court of Justice, and an elected bicameral Parliament. All these ideas would resurface in the European Community and today's European Union, but it was too soon to be thinking so ambitiously, and the collapse of the EDC meant the end also of the EPC. Their failure gave the year 1954 a pivotal quality, but for Dinan it was 'a turning point at which Europe failed to turn' (Dinan, 2004, p. 63). The shockwaves were felt in the ECSC, where Monnet left the presidency of the High Authority in 1955, disillusioned by political resistance to its work (Monnet, 1978, pp. 398–404).

Another shock was to follow, with the unfolding of the 1956 **Suez crisis**. Seeking funds to build a new dam on the Nile, Egyptian leader Gamal Abdel Nasser nationalized the British-run Suez Canal in July 1956. The canal's strategic value was declining, and the nationalization had no impact on British access, but because Nasser was considered a threat to western interests, the governments of Britain, France and Israel entered into a conspiracy by which Israel attacked Egypt in October, providing the British and the French with an excuse to step in and 'restore' peace in the canal zone. Coincidentally, the Soviets were cracking down on attempts by the Hungarian government to introduce democracy and withdraw from the Warsaw Pact, putting the United States in the invidious position of not being able to criticize the USSR without also criticizing British and French action at Suez. In the face of US demands, Britain and France withdrew from Suez with their tails between their legs.

The reverberations of Suez were to be felt for many years (see Hourani, 1989). The dominant role of the United States in the Atlantic Alliance was confirmed, but the French and the British disagreed on what this meant. The French were left more doubtful than ever about American trustworthiness, and more convinced of the importance of European policy independence (Lundestad, 2003, p. 115). For Britain, there was new recognition that it was no longer a world power capable of significant independent action. Until Suez it had been more interested in its historical links with Australia, Canada and New Zealand, but now it was encouraged to accelerate the process of dismantling its empire, and also to look more towards Europe (Gorst and Johnman, 1997, p. 151, 160). British leaders concluded that they could never again so openly disagree with the US on matters of foreign policy, but while the United States might have been an indispensable ally, notes Judt (2005, p. 302), Britain's

● **European Political Community**: An attempt to create a political community to oversee the ECSC and the European Defence Community, but which collapsed with the demise of the latter.

● **Suez crisis**: An attempt made by Britain, France and Israel to reverse Egypt's nationalization of the Suez Canal, leading to an international outcry, the humiliation of Britain and France, and a change in British attitudes towards European integration

Paul-Henri Spaak

Paul-Henri Spaak (1899–1972) was a Belgian politician who played a central role in the early years of European integration, and was a champion of a supranational Europe. He was prime minister of Belgium at the outbreak of the Second World War, and was part of the Belgian government-in-exile in London during the war. He served briefly as the first elected chair of the UN General Assembly in 1946, and then served three terms as Belgian foreign minister, two terms as prime minister (1946 and 1947–49), one term as president of the Common Assembly of the ECSC (1952–54), and one term as secretary-general of NATO (1957–61). He was involved in the creation of the Benelux customs union, and was chair of the committee whose report formed the basis of the discussions leading to the creation of the EEC.

dependence on the US illustrated its weakness and isolation, and it had nowhere else to look but Europe to recover its international standing. It had shunned the ECSC, but within five years of Suez it had applied for membership of the European Economic Community.

The European Economic Community (1955–58)

The failures of the European defence and political communities had left supporters of integration chastened, and yet they also contributed to an improvement in Franco-German relations. When ECSC foreign ministers met in June 1955 in Messina, Sicily, to appoint a successor to Jean Monnet as president of the High Authority, they soon found their discussions turning to proposals for further economic integration, including a customs union. They agreed a resolution to consider working 'for the establishment of a united Europe by the development of common institutions, the progressive fusion of national economies, the creation of a single market, and the progressive harmonization of their social policies' (Messina Resolution, in Weigall and Stirk, 1992, p. 94). A committee chaired by Belgian foreign minister Paul-Henri Spaak developed what Spaak himself admitted was a plan motivated less by economic cooperation than by a desire to take another step towards political union (Urwin, 1995, p. 76). In retrospect, Messina was the event that marked the 'relaunching' of Europe.

● **European Economic Community**: An international organization created in 1957 with the core goal of establishing a single (or common) market among its member states.

● **European Atomic Energy Community**: An international organization created in 1957 to coordinate research in its member states on the peaceful use of nuclear energy.

The Spaak report (focusing mainly on the idea of a European single market) was issued in April 1956 and followed by a new round of negotiations among the six ECSC members. These began in Venice in May 1956, and paved the way for the signing on 25 March 1957 of the two Treaties of Rome, one creating the **European Economic Community** (EEC) and the other the **European Atomic Energy Community** (Euratom). Following ratification by member state parliaments during 1957, both treaties entered into force in January 1958. Euratom was of more interest to the French than to others, and was quickly relegated to focusing on research. The EEC was by far the more substantial experiment, and although Judt (2005, p. 303) considers the Treaty of Rome little more than 'a declaration of good intentions', the EEC is today widely considered the starting

CONCEPT

Single market

A multi-state economic area (otherwise known as a common or internal market) in which there is free movement of people, money, goods and services (the so-called 'four freedoms'). Although the main goal of the EEC was the creation of a single market, progress was halting until the passage of the 1986 Single European Act. Even critics of European integration agree that the single market was a noble goal, and complain that integration has since far overstepped this basic idea. But a truly open market does not yet exist in the EU, because there are still restrictions on the movement of workers.

point for what has evolved into the European Union. It committed its six members to the following goals:

- The completion within 12 years of a **single market** in which there would be free movement of people, money, and services. Movement of workers was 'subject to limitations justified on grounds of public policy, public security or public health'.
- The elimination of customs duties between member states, and agreement of a common external customs tariff.
- The establishment of common policies on agriculture, trade, transport and competition.
- The creation of a European Social Fund and a European Investment Bank.

The EEC inherited the same core institutional framework as the ECSC, with some changes (see Figure 5.1, p. 85). By 1958, then, there were three communities in place that were moving their member states along the road to integration. But the political dynamics of the relationship among the leaders of the Six remained complicated, and most western European states remained outside the fold. The problems faced by the EEC were perhaps inevitable: it was sailing through uncharted territory, and had set course for an unknown destination. It would only be in retrospect, notes Gillingham, that the 'strange tale' of its early years would make sense (Gillingham, 2003, p. 53).

The single market takes shape (1958–68)

In its early years, European integration was very much an intergovernmental process, the Community institutions having little independent authority. It was

Illustration 5.1
The Treaty of Rome

Delegates from six western European states gather in the Palazzo dei Conservatori on Capitoline Hall in Rome on 25 March 1957 to sign the Treaty of Rome.

Building a single market

1952	May	Signature of the European Defence Community treaty
1953	March	Plans announced for European Political Community
1954	May	French defeat in Indochina
	August	Collapse of plans for European Defence Community and European Political Community
	October	Creation of Western European Union
1955	May	Creation of Warsaw Pact
	June	Opening of Messina conference
1956	May	Opening of discussions on what would become the EEC
	Oct–Dec	Suez crisis
1957	March	Signature of Treaties of Rome
1958	January	Treaties of Rome come into force
1960	January	Signature of Stockholm Convention creating European Free Trade Association
1961	August	Work begins on construction of the Berlin wall; Britain applies for EEC membership

1962	October	Cuban missile crisis
1963	January	De Gaulle vetoes British membership of EEC
	July	Signature of Yaoundé Convention
1965	April	Signature of Merger treaty
	July	Empty chair crisis begins
1966	January	Empty chair crisis ends with Luxembourg Compromise
1967	May	Second British application for EEC membership
	November	Second veto by de Gaulle of British membership of EEC
1968	April	Beginning of Prague Spring
	July	Agreement of EEC's common external tariff
1972	September	Norwegian referendum goes against EEC membership
1973	January	Britain, Denmark, and Ireland join EEC
1981	January	Greece joins Community
1986	January	Portugal and Spain join Community

also elitist, key decisions being made by government ministers and the staff of the European institutions with little reference to public opinion. Eichengreen (2007, p. 198) considers this 'a golden age of growth' for the EEC, but progress was mixed. Internal tariffs and trade quotas were brought down, clearing the way for agreement in July 1968 of a common external tariff and an industrial customs union. This helped encourage accelerated economic growth, a halving

Map 5.1 The European Economic Community, 1958

of the contribution of agriculture to economic output (Ionescu, 1975, pp. 150–4), and a growth in trade between the EEC partners at a rate three times faster between 1958 and 1965 than that with third countries (Urwin, 1995, p. 130). But non-tariff barriers to trade remained, mainly in the form of different national product standards, and there was slow progress on the development of a common transport policy, and on addressing regional economic disparities.

After much debate, a Common Agricultural Policy (CAP) was agreed in 1968 with the acceptance of a watered-down version of a plan drawn up by agriculture commissioner Sicco Mansholt (Pinder, 1991, pp. 78–86; Urwin, 1995, pp. 132–5). Very much reflecting French national interests (specifically, how to manage its agricultural overproduction), CAP created a single market for agricultural products and guaranteed prices to EEC farmers for everything they produced. But it did this at the expense of encouraging over-production, bene-

Opening articles of the Treaty of Rome, 25 March 1957

Article 1

By this Treaty, the HIGH CONTRACTING PARTIES establish among themselves a EUROPEAN ECONOMIC COMMUNITY.

Article 2

The Community shall have as its task, by establishing a common market and progressively approximating the economic policies of Member States, to promote throughout the Community a harmonious development of economic activities, a continuous and balanced expansion, an increase in stability, an accelerated raising of the standard of living and closer relations between the States belonging to it.

Article 3

For the purposes set out in Article 2, the activities of the Community shall include . . .

(a) the elimination . . . of customs duties and of quantitative restrictions on the import and export of goods, and of all other measures having equivalent effect;

(b) the establishment of a common customs tariff and of a common commercial policy towards third countries;

(c) the abolition . . . of obstacles to freedom of movement for persons, services and capital;

(d) the adoption of a common policy in the sphere of agriculture;

(e) the adoption of a common policy in the sphere of transport;

(f) the institution of a system ensuring that competition in the common market is not distorted;

(g) the application of procedures by which the economic policies of Member States can be coordinated and disequilibria in their balances of payments remedied;

(h) the approximation of the laws of Member States to the extent required for the proper functioning of the common market;

(i) the creation of a European Social Fund in order to improve employment opportunities for workers and to contribute to the raising of their standard of living;

(j) the establishment of a European Investment Bank to facilitate the economic expansion of the Community by opening up fresh resources;

(k) the association of the overseas countries and territories in order to increase trade and to promote jointly economic and social development.

Article 4

The tasks entrusted to the Community shall be carried out by the following institutions:

an ASSEMBLY,
a COUNCIL,
a COMMISSION,
a COURT OF JUSTICE.

Each institution shall act within the limits of the powers conferred upon it by this Treaty.

Source: Europa web site at http://eur-lex.europa.eu/en/treaties/index.htm#founding (retrieved July 2010).

fiting large-scale commercial farmers at the expense of small farmers, ignoring the environmental consequences of greater use of chemical fertilizers and pesticides, and making CAP the largest item in the Community budget, which in turn diverted spending from other areas.

Under their Common Commercial Policy, the Six worked as one in international trade negotiations, exploiting the new power of the single market. They together negotiated the 1963 Yaoundé Convention, an association agreement with 18 former African colonies, and they formed a united bloc in the Kennedy Round of GATT talks that closed in 1967. Meanwhile, the institutional identity of the

Figure 5.1 Structure of the European Economic Community

INSTITUTION	MEMBERSHIP	FUNCTION
Commission	Nine members (two each from the larger states, and one each from the smaller states) appointed for six-year terms	Less power than the HA to impose decisions on member states. Charged with initiating policy and overseeing implementation
Council of Ministers	Government ministers sharing 17 votes. Some decisions had to be unanimous, and some could be taken by a simple majority, the rest required a qualified majority of 12 votes from four states	To make decisions on proposals from the Commission
Parliamentary Assembly (renamed European Parliament in 1962)	142 appointed members (elected from 1979)	Could question or censure the Commission, but had little legislative authority
Court of Justice	Seven judges appointed for renewable six-year terms	Responsible for interpreting the treaties and for ensuring that the EEC institutions and the member states fulfilled their treaty obligations

European Commission was fleshed out under the leadership of its first president, Walter Hallstein, and decision making was streamlined in April 1965 with the signature of the Merger treaty, which created a single institutional structure for all three communities. The European Parliament had also shrewdly exploited its moral advantage as a 'representative' body to win more legislative authority (it would be transformed by the institution of direct elections in 1979), and the European Court of Justice contributed quietly but vitally by issuing judgements that changed the personality and the legal reach of the Community.

But not all in the garden was roses, and two major crises were sparked by Charles de Gaulle's preference for protecting French interests at the expense of moving along the debate on Europe. The first came in January 1963 when he unilaterally vetoed Britain's application to join the EEC (see details later in this chapter). The second came in July 1965 with the **empty chair crisis**, at the heart of which lay the question of the relative power of EEC institutions and EEC member states. Several factors came together to spark the crisis:

- Walter Hallstein was an ardent federalist whose attempts to build the Commission were undermined by the fact that he had never been elected to office (he had spent much of his career as a professor of law).
- Decision making by qualified majority vote (a weighted voting system – see Chapter 11) was scheduled to come into force in the Council of Ministers in January 1966 on several new issues, including agriculture and trade. This would restrict use of the national veto (even though it was understood that decision making in the EEC was by consensus).

● **Empty chair crisis**: A dispute in 1965 over the relative powers of EEC institutions and the governments of EEC member states, which encouraged France to boycott meetings of the Council of Ministers.

- During discussions over CAP, Hallstein suggested that EEC funding should be changed from national contributions to an independent source (otherwise known as 'own resources') coming out of revenues from external tariffs and levies on agricultural imports. At the same time, he suggested that the European Parliament should be given the power to scrutinize and vote on the budget.

This was all too much for de Gaulle, who – to complicate matters – faced a new national election in late 1965, at which the Community for the first time became a central issue (Dinan, 2004, p. 107). Although Hallstein backed down in the face of pressure from West German Chancellor Ludwig Erhard, de Gaulle had already decided to use the issue to express some of his frustrations with the direction being taken by the EEC, and directed his representatives to boycott meetings of the Council of Ministers, making it impossible for any decisions on new laws and policies to be taken. The crisis ended only with agreement of the January 1966 **Luxembourg Compromise** by which it was agreed that the qualified majority vote would not be used when member states felt that 'important interests' were at stake. While preserving the informal norm of consensus, the 'compromise' had the effect also of preserving the national veto. Institutionally, the result was a deceleration in the growth of Commission powers and the placing of more power into the hands of the Council of Ministers (see Palayret *et al.*, 2006).

International developments: The nervous 1960s

Developments within the EEC took place against a troubled international background, where critical salvoes were being fired in the Cold War that would have long-term implications for the tripartite relationship between the United States, the Soviet Union, and Europe. The anti-communist witch-hunts of the 1950s had caused some nervousness and bemusement in western Europe, but then came the Berlin crisis of 1961. The Western occupying powers refused to withdraw from West Berlin, a move which combined with concerns that the rapid redevelopment of the west was casting a bad light on the stagnation of the east (and encouraging many easterners to leave for the west) to encourage Soviet leader Nikita Khrushchev to acquiesce in the building first of a barbed wire fence between East and West Berlin, and then of a concrete wall.

In 1962, Khrushchev's erratic leadership style resulted in the stationing of nuclear missiles in Cuba. Concerned that this was part of a Soviet ploy to get its way on Berlin (Judt, 2005, p. 254), President John F. Kennedy put his foot down, and for ten days in October the world teetered on the brink of nuclear war. Western Europeans were unsettled as much by the event as by how it seemed to make clear that western European opinion had been marginalized in US calculations. For de Gaulle, it meant that Europeans might now face 'annihilation without representation' (quoted in Bernstein, 1980). Transatlantic tensions grew over US policy in Vietnam, where the despatch of military advisors in 1962–63 heralded an escalation into a full-fledged war in 1965. This was met with deep political misgivings and growing public hostility in western Europe, where the war revealed the extent to which transatlantic divisions on critical security problems differed. Anti-war demonstrations were held in many countries, and a 1967 poll found 80 per cent of western Europeans critical of US policy (Barnet, 1983, p. 264).

- **Luxembourg Compromise**: A 1966 agreement ending the empty chair crisis, and making consensus the informal norm in Council of Ministers decisions. The effect was to slow down the process of European integration.

Enlargement

The process of expanding membership of the European Community/Union. While it had many potential benefits, it also had political costs: France and Germany in particular have worried about how it has reduced their dominating role in European decision making, and with more members there has been a greater variety of interests to be heard and disagreements to be resolved. With expansion from 6 to 9 to 12 to 15 to 27 members (with more waiting in the wings), the personality, goals, values and internal political and economic dynamics of the EU have never stopped changing.

At the close of the 1960s, the focus shifted to a seeming thaw in relations between western and eastern Europe. First came the Prague Spring in Czechoslovakia, when the reformist Alexander Dubček came to power in 1968 and instituted a series of political and economic reforms that prompted an invasion by Soviet and other Warsaw Pact troops in August. Then came the initiative by Willy Brandt, elected West Germany's first social democratic chancellor in October 1969, to reach out to East Germany and then to Poland and other eastern European countries through his *Ostpolitik* (Eastern policy).

Although the Soviet crackdown on Czechoslovakia reminded western Europeans of the fragility of the international situation in which they found themselves, *Ostpolitik* showed what was possible in bringing east and west together. But part of the bargain involved acknowledgment that the postwar division of Europe was permanent. Although Brandt's policies caused some initial divisions within western Europe, with France and Britain in particular worrying that it might result in West Germany being pulled into the Soviet orbit (Lundestad, 2003, pp. 172–3), Hitchcock (2004, p. 300) sees the changes as replacing the Cold War with a 'cold peace', and argues that by normalizing that division, 'Brandt may have been the first European statesman to swing a pickaxe at the Iron Curtain'.

Enlargement tops the agenda (1960–86)

There was only so much that the EEC could achieve with just six members. Together they had a population of about 180 million, or about 56 per cent of the western European total, along with a 56 per cent share of western Europe's economic wealth. But if regional peace and economic prosperity were the two underlying purposes of integration, then other European states had to be brought into the fold through **enlargement.** While the EEC treaty (Article 237) stated that 'any European State may apply to become a member of the Community', the number of realistic potential new members was limited; all of eastern Europe was excluded, the Scandinavians were wary of supranationalism

Charles de Gaulle

Charles de Gaulle (1890–1970) was the pre-eminent statesman of France in the twentieth century, and a man known for his charisma, his defence of French national interests, and his efforts to promote a global role for Europe in the face of US dominance. He served in the First World War and then in the opening battles of the Second World War, escaping after the fall of France in 1940 to Britain, from where he organized the Free French forces. Upon his return in 1944 he briefly became prime minister before retiring in 1946. Political crisis led to his return to power as the principal author of the new constitution of the Fifth Republic, and as the first president under the new constitution in 1958. De Gaulle's European policies focused on the Franco-German axis, resistance to the supranationalism of Community institutions, and efforts to reduce British influence (and, by extension, American influence). His heavy-handed leadership led to worker and student riots at home in 1968, and to his resignation as president in April 1969.

and had their own internal ties, and Greece, Portugal and Spain were either too poor and/or not sufficiently democratic.

The most obvious absentee was Britain, still the biggest national economy and largest military power in Europe, and a critical bridge between western Europe and the United States. Until Suez, at least, Britain still saw itself as a great power, and one with global political and economic interests that might be compromised by closer association with the rest of Europe. For Dean Acheson, US Secretary of State during the Truman administration, Britain's decision not to negotiate on membership of the ECSC had been its 'great mistake of the postwar period' (Acheson, 1969, p. 385). As for the EEC, few in the British government felt that it had much potential, the official view – according to Prime Minister Harold Macmillan – being 'a confident expectation that nothing would come out of Messina' (Macmillan, 1971, p. 73). Its concerns about supra-nationalism were understandable, but it could have used its power to negotiate the terms of the EEC in its favour (just as France had done), so its lukewarm attitude to Europe was a missed opportunity. In the event, argues Dell (1995), its posture amounted to an 'abdication of leadership in Europe'.

Britain's initial strategy was to champion the development of an alternative to the EEC, in the form of the looser and less ambitious **European Free Trade Association** (EFTA). It tried to lure West Germany and the Netherlands into EFTA, and then proposed that the new EEC join as a bloc (Dinan, 2004, p. 90). When this failed, it invited six non-EC states to join, and EFTA was founded in January 1960 with the signing of the Stockholm Convention by Austria, Britain, Denmark, Norway, Portugal, Sweden, and Switzerland. It had the same core goal as the EEC of promoting free trade, but unlike the EEC it involved no contractual arrangements, it had no political goals, it did not plan to agree a common external customs tariff, and its only institutions were a Council of Ministers that met infrequently and a group of permanent representatives serviced by a small secretariat in Geneva. It helped cut tariffs and promoted trade among its members, but several of them did more trade with the EEC than with each other, and it had been created as an attempt to pull EEC states into a broader free trade area; once this failed it ceased to have much purpose.

Even before the signing of the Stockholm Convention, Britain's attitude to the EEC had begun to change. Not only had Suez shattered the nostalgic idea that Britain was still a great power, but it had also rattled the 'special relationship' with the United States. Key world issues were now being discussed by the US and the Soviet Union bilaterally, and it had become clear that political influence in Europe lay with the EEC, which was making strong economic progress, and that Britain would risk political isolation and economic disadvantage if it stayed out. So, in August 1961, barely 15 months after the creation of EFTA, Britain applied to join the EEC. Denmark also applied, prompted by the importance of Britain as its main food export market, and by the view that the EEC was both a big new market for Danish agricultural surpluses and a possible boost to Danish industrial development. Ireland also applied, obliged as it was to follow the British lead but also hoping that the EEC would reduce its reliance both on agriculture and on Britain. They were joined in 1962 by Norway, which saw the new importance of EEC markets. Britain was clearly the elephant at the negotiating table, however, accounting for about 85 per cent of the population and GDP of the four applicant countries.

● **European Free Trade Association (EFTA):** A free trade grouping championed by Britain and founded in 1960, with more modest goals and looser organization than the EEC.

All might have proceeded smoothly but for Charles de Gaulle, who resented Britain's lukewarm attitude towards integration and its creation of EFTA, was concerned that Britain might want to redefine some of the goals of the Community at the expense of French interests (particularly on agriculture), and regarded Britain both as a rival to French influence in the EEC and as a back door to US influence in Europe. This last concern seemed to be confirmed in December 1962 when Britain – just as it was negotiating EEC membership terms – accepted the US offer of Polaris missiles as delivery vehicles for Britain's nuclear warheads. But the smaller Community states were supportive of British membership as a means of offsetting French influence, and the British application had the support of the United States, of West Germany, and of Jean Monnet.

De Gaulle's views prevailed, however, and in the space of just ten days in January 1963, he vetoed the British application and signed a Franco-German Friendship Treaty. He added insult to injury by referring his decision to none of his EEC partners except West Germany, and by making the announcement as an answer to a pre-arranged question posed by a journalist at a press conference in Paris. He couched his reasons mainly in terms of agricultural policy, arguing that integrating the British economy into the EEC would be too difficult, and that allowing Britain in would mean having to allow other countries in, and would complicate the EEC's relations with other parts of the world (see Document 5.2). But Paul-Henri Spaak dismissed de Gaulle's actions as reflecting 'a lack of consideration unexampled in the history of the EEC, showing utter contempt for his negotiating partners, allies and opponents alike' (Spaak, 1971, p. 375). And since Britain's application was part of a four-state package, Denmark, Ireland and Norway, too, were denied entry.

Britain applied again in 1967 and was again unilaterally vetoed by de Gaulle, still trying to protect French interests in CAP and still seeing Britain as a Trojan

**Illustration 5.2
Britain joins the
Community**

British Prime Minister Edward Heath signs the UK treaty of accession on 22 January 1972, paving the way for his country to be part of the first enlargement of the EEC in January 1973.

DOCUMENT 5.2

De Gaulle says 'Non' to Britain, 14 January 1963 (excerpts)

The Treaty of Rome was concluded between six continental States . . . which are, economically speaking . . . of the same nature . . ., whether it be a matter of their industrial or agricultural production, their external exchanges, their habits or their commercial clientele, [or] their living or working conditions . . . It so happens, too, that there is between them no kind of political grievance, no frontier question, no rivalry in domination or power . . .

Great Britain posed her candidature to the Common Market . . . after having earlier refused to participate in the communities we are now building, as well as after creating a free trade area with six other States, and, finally, after having . . . put some pressure on the Six to prevent a real beginning being made in the application of the Common Market . . .

England in effect is insular, she is maritime, she is linked through her exchanges, her markets, her supply lines to the most diverse and often the most distant countries; she pursues essentially industrial and commercial activities, and only slight agricultural ones.

She has in all her doings very marked and very original habits and traditions . . .

[Allowing entry to Britain and the other applicants] will completely change the whole of the actions, the agreements, the compensation, the rules which have already been established between the Six . . .

Further, this community, increasing in such fashion, would see itself faced with problems of economic relations with all kinds of other States, and first with the United States. [The] cohesion of its members . . . would not endure for long, and . . . ultimately it would appear as a colossal Atlantic community under American dependence and direction, and which would quickly have absorbed the community of Europe . . .

[It] is possible that one day England might manage to transform herself sufficiently to become part of the European community, without restriction, without reserve and preference for anything whatsoever; and in this case the Six would open the door to her and France would raise no obstacle.

Source: European Navigator web site at http://www.ena.lu (retrieved July 2010).

horse for the Americans; letting Britain and the other countries in at this point, he claimed, 'would lead to the destruction of the European Community' (quoted in Dinan, 2004, p. 110). Britain and the others now had to bide their time until de Gaulle's resignation as president of France in 1969, when a third application was lodged and this time accepted. Following remarkably rapid membership negotiations in 1970–71 (several later entrants to the EU would have to wait between 8 and 14 years between first application and admission – see Chapter 6), Britain, Denmark, Ireland and Norway were all cleared for EEC membership. Norway opted to hold a national referendum on the issue in September 1972, resulting in a narrow majority against membership (thanks mainly to the concerns of farmers and fishing communities). So it was with Britain, Denmark and Ireland that the EEC entered its first enlargement on 1 January 1973. The Six had now become the Nine.

Interest in the Community was also emerging elsewhere. Greece had made its first overtures in the late 1950s but had an underdeveloped and mainly agricultural economy, so was given only associate membership in 1961 with a plan for a customs union with the EEC within twelve years. Full membership might have

Map 5.2 The first two rounds of enlargement, 1973–86

come much sooner had it not been for the military coup of April 1967, following which even its association agreement was suspended. With its return to civilian government in 1974, it applied almost immediately for full Community membership. Portugal and Spain had also shown early interest in associate membership, but both were still dictatorships with underdeveloped and mainly agricultural economies. Preferential trade agreements were signed with Spain in 1970 and with Portugal in 1973, but it was only with the overthrow of the Caetano regime in Portugal in 1974 and the death of Franco in Spain in 1975 that full EEC membership for the two states was taken seriously.

Despite the relative poverty of all three states, and concerns in Portugal and Spain over fishing rights and over workers moving north in search of work, the EEC felt that welcoming the three countries would strengthen their democracies and help link them more closely to NATO and western Europe. Negotiations opened with Greece in 1976, leading to membership in January 1981, and with Portugal and Spain in 1978–9. The fragility of Spain's new democracy was illustrated with an attempted military coup in January 1981, but both Spain and the membership negotiations survived, and Spain and Portugal joined the EEC in January 1986. The Nine had now become the Twelve.

The doubling of the membership of the EEC between 1973 and 1986 had several consequences. It changed the economic balance among the member states, by bringing in first the poorer British economy and then the even poorer Mediterranean states, which in turn meant a redistribution of EEC spending. It also increased the international influence of the EEC, which was now the largest economic bloc in the world. At the same time, it complicated the Community's decision-making processes by requiring that a wider range of opinions and interests be considered, among the more troublesome being the repeated resistance to Community initiatives offered by Britain. Although membership applications were received also from Turkey in 1987, from Austria in 1989, and from Cyprus and Malta in 1990, there was now to be a focus on deepening rather than widening. East Germany was to enter the Community through the back door with the reunification of Germany in October 1990, but there would be no further enlargement until 1995.

SUMMARY

- Attempts to clear the way to West German remilitarization, while tying it closely into western Europe, led to the signature in May 1952 of a treaty setting up a European Defence Community (EDC), and to the creation in 1954 of a Western European Union.
- There were hopes, too, of creating a European Political Community (EPC), but political opposition within France to the EDC led to its collapse in August 1954, along with plans for the EPC.
- Economic cooperation was behind the signature in 1957 of the Treaties of Rome, creating the European Economic Community (EEC) and the European Atomic Energy Community.
- The goals of the EEC included a single market, a common external customs tariff, and common policies on agriculture, trade, transport, and competition.
- Progress on the single market was mixed, with many barriers coming down but many non-tariff barriers remaining, and slow progress on the development of a common transport policy, and on addressing regional economic disparities.
- The 1960s were a time of Cold War nervousness, opening with the Berlin and Cuban missile crises and closing with an escalation of the war in Vietnam. These events impacted the tripartite relationship between Europe, the US, and the USSR.
- Enlargement of the EEC moved up the agenda, but British applications were twice vetoed by Charles de Gaulle.
- Britain, Denmark and Ireland joined the EEC in 1973, followed in 1981 by Greece and in 1986 by Spain and Portugal. The political and economic personality of the EEC changed as a result.

KEY TERMS AND CONCEPTS

Empty chair crisis

Enlargement

European Atomic Energy Community

European Defence Community

European Economic Community

European Free Trade Association

European Political Community

Luxembourg Compromise

Single market

Suez crisis

Western European Union

FURTHER READING

Gorst, Anthony, and Lewis Johnman (1997), *The Suez Crisis* (Abingdon: Routledge); Keith Kyle (2003), *Suez: Britain's End of Empire in the Middle East* (London: I. B. Taurus). Two studies of the landmark events of 1956.

Griffiths, Richard T. (2000), *Europe's First Constitution: The European Political Community, 1952–1954* (London: Kogan Page). A study of the draft EPC treaty, drawing parallels between the political situation in the 1950s and that in the early years of the EU.

Mangold, Peter (2006), *The Almost Impossible Ally: Harold Macmillan and Charles de Gaulle* (London: I. B. Taurus); Jonathan Fenby (2010), *The General: Charles de Gaulle and the France he Saved* (London: Simon & Schuster). Two studies of Charles de Gaulle, the former focusing on his critical relationship with British Prime Minister Harold Macmillan.

CHAPTER 6

Paving the Way to European Union

PREVIEW

The building of the single market was at the core of European integration in the 1960s, but there had been only slow progress. Continued efforts to achieve exchange rate stability pushed monetary union up the agenda, leading to the launch in 1979 of the European Monetary System. With worries about rising international competition and inflexible European labour markets, there was a renewed effort in the 1980s to complete the single market, resulting in agreement on the first new treaty since Rome, the 1986 Single European Act (SEA). This gave the European Economic Community – now more often known as the European Community, or simply 'the Community' – a new sense of mission and identity.

Meanwhile, the collapse of the Berlin Wall in 1989 symbolized the end of the Cold War division of the continent, and emphasized the urgent need for the Community to assert itself on the global stage. But serial embarrassments followed as the Community failed to agree on what action to take in the 1990–91 Gulf War or in the crisis in the Balkans. New leadership brought new ideas, leading to the agreement in 1992 of the Maastricht treaty. This confirmed plans for the creation of a single European currency, gave new emphasis to building a common foreign policy, and brought a change of name: the Community would now be part of a broader-based European Union.

There was also a new focus on enlargement, with EFTA members given access to the single market through a new European Economic Area in 1994, followed in 1995 by the accession of Austria, Finland and Sweden. But there was also a backlash against integration, and signs that many Europeans had increasing doubts about the decisions being taken in their name by their leaders.

KEY ISSUES

- What were the pressures that pushed economic and monetary union up the agenda of integration?
- How revolutionary was the Single European Act?
- Were the Community's failures in the Gulf and the Balkans inevitable?
- What were the relative roles of political leadership and international
- circumstances in pushing forward the process of European integration?
- Why was Maastricht more controversial than the Single European Act?
- Should the backlash against integration have been foreseen?

First steps to monetary union (1969–92)

One of the goals of the Bretton Woods system had been exchange rate stability as a means of avoiding the economic problems of the mid-war years (see Hosli, 2005, pp. 17–19), and there were several institutional developments in this direction. The International Monetary Fund (IMF) was charged with helping maintain that stability, based on the convertibility of the world's major currencies with gold and the US dollar. In 1950 the European Payments Union was set up to help encourage the convertibility of European currencies by setting realistic exchange rates (see Chang, 2009, p. 17). In 1958 it was replaced by the European Monetary Agreement, under which EEC members (along with Britain, Ireland and Sweden) worked to keep exchange rates within 0.75 per cent either way of the US dollar. In 1964 a Committee of Central Bank Governors began meeting to coordinate monetary policy, becoming the forerunner of today's European Central Bank.

While monetary cooperation was one thing, monetary union was quite another, with its troubling implications for loss of national sovereignty; a state that gave up its national currency would lose control over much of its economic independence. But political resistance to the idea began to decline in 1969 with changes of leadership in France and West Germany, where Georges Pompidou and Willy Brandt brought new ideas and fresh perspectives. At a summit of Community leaders in The Hague in December, the main items on the agenda were enlargement, agriculture, and **economic and monetary union** (EMU) (Dinan, 2004, p. 129). A year later, a committee headed by Luxembourg Prime Minister Pierre Werner came down in favour of parallel efforts to coordinate national economic policies while also working to hold exchange rates steady (Commission of the European Communities, 1970).

Then came the shock end of the Bretton Woods system. This had been based on confidence in the US dollar, which in turn depended on the strength of the US economy and the convertibility of US dollars and gold (Spero and Hart, 2003, p. 17). But the rapid growth of western European economies in the 1960s combined with a focus by the United States on domestic policy and the rising costs of fighting the war in Vietnam to cause inflation in the US and to reduce international confidence in the dollar. The Nixon administration tried to deflect some of the blame onto the Community, charging it with protectionism and an unwillingness to take more responsibility for the costs of defence (Judt, 2005, p. 454). It then unilaterally took the decision in August 1971 to end the convertibility of the US dollar with gold, ending Bretton Woods and ushering in an era of international monetary turbulence. This was made worse by an international energy crisis set off by the October 1973 Yom Kippur war between Israel and the Arabs, which resulted in Arab oil producers quadrupling the price of oil.

In a frantic attempt to control the threat that floating exchange rates posed to the Common Agricultural Policy, Community leaders agreed in February 1972 to a structure known as the 'snake in the tunnel', within which EEC member states would work to hold the value of their national currencies within 2.25 per cent either way of the US dollar, preparing the way for monetary union by 1980. The snake was launched in April 1972, with all six EEC member states participating, along with Britain, Denmark, and Norway. But exchange rate volatility quickly forced Britain, Denmark and Italy out. France left in 1974, rejoined in 1975, then left again in 1976 (Eichengreen, 2007, pp. 248–9).

● **Economic and monetary union**: A programme agreed by the EEC in 1969 to coordinate economic policy in preparation for the switch to a single currency.

Meanwhile, enlargement was creating new pressures. Economic disparities among the six founding members had been relatively manageable (per capita GDP in the Community's ten richest regions was about four times greater than that in its ten poorest regions), but the gap widened with the accession of Britain and Ireland. In 1973, the Commission-sponsored Thomson report concluded that the disparities were big enough to be an obstacle to a 'balanced expansion' in economic activity and to EMU (Commission of the European Communities, 1973). With France and West Germany supporting Community spending as a means of helping Britain integrate into the Community, and the government of Prime Minister Edward Heath seeing it as a way of making EEC membership more palatable to British voters (Dinan, 2004, p. 149), a decision was taken in 1973 to launch the European Regional Development Fund (ERDF). This would match existing national development spending, with an emphasis on improving infrastructure and creating new jobs in industry and services.

A new boost to monetary union was provided in 1977 by incoming European Commission president Roy Jenkins (Gilbert, 2003, p. 138ff.), with French and West German support. In March 1979 the snake was replaced by a **European Monetary System** (EMS), using an Exchange Rate Mechanism (ERM) based on the European Currency Unit (ecu). This was a unit of account whose value was determined by a basket of the EC's national currencies, each weighted according to their relative strengths (see Figure 6.1). Participants undertook to work to keep their currencies within 2.25 per cent either way of the ecu (or 6 per cent in the case of Italy). In addition to creating a zone of monetary stability, the hope was that the ecu would become the normal means of settling debts between EC members, and that it would psychologically prepare Europeans for the idea of a single currency. Since *ecu* also happened to be the name of an ancient French coin, there was speculation that it might become the name of the new single currency.

But while the Commission argued that EMU was helping encourage more economic efficiency and allowing the EEC to take a stronger role in the interna-

Figure 6.1 Composition of the ecu basket

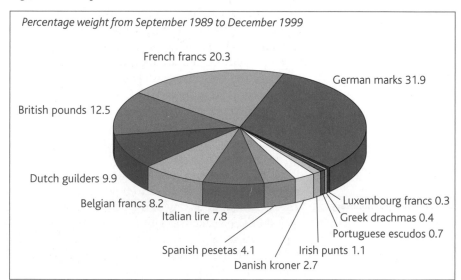

Percentage weight from September 1989 to December 1999

French francs 20.3
German marks 31.9
British pounds 12.5
Dutch guilders 9.9
Belgian francs 8.2
Italian lire 7.8
Spanish pesetas 4.1
Danish kroner 2.7
Irish punts 1.1
Portuguese escudos 0.7
Greek drachmas 0.4
Luxembourg francs 0.3

tional economy, several member states found it difficult to control exchange rates. The problems worsened in the early 1990s with turbulence in world money markets, Germany had problems trying to adjust to its 1990 reunification (Gilbert, 2003, p. 227ff.), and Britain found the demands of staying in the ERM too much to bear. It had delayed joining until 1990, by when inflation and interest rates were high, and its efforts to keep the pound stable were undermined by speculation on international currency markets; the investor George Soros famously made an estimated $1 billion profit by short selling (profiting from a decline in the price of assets between their sale and repurchase) his holdings of sterling. After furiously trying to prop up the pound, mainly by raising interest rates in order to encourage investors to buy sterling, Britain withdrew from the ERM on 16 September 1992, a date that became known as Black Wednesday.

The Single European Act (1983–93)

While there had been progress during the 1960s on building the single market, many non-tariff barriers persisted, including different technical standards, quality controls, health and safety standards, and levels of indirect taxation. Travellers still had to go through customs and immigration checks at borders, and anyone planning to move permanently to another state still came up against efforts to protect jobs and home industries (see Armstrong and Bulmer, 1998, Chapter 1; Gilbert, 2003, Chapter 6).

Meanwhile, European corporations were not taking much advantage of the single market, still looked outside Europe for merger and joint venture opportunities, and had lost market share to competition first from the United States and then from Japan. By the early 1980s there was worried speculation about the effects of what was later described as **Eurosclerosis** (Giersch, 1985): the role of excessive regulation and generous welfare systems in contributing to high unemployment and slow job creation in western Europe, the inflexibility of whose labour market was contrasted – and continues to be contrasted even today – with the more dynamic and open market of the United States (the slowdown brought by the global economic crisis of 2007–10 notwithstanding).

Pulling the Community out of its lethargy and responding to the accelerating effects of globalization and technological change were priorities for the new president of the Commission, Jacques Delors, who took office in January 1985. A committee chaired by Irish politician Jim Dooge identified the need for a new focus on the single market, and an intergovernmental conference was quickly convened to discuss the necessary steps. A Commission White Paper – named for its primary author, internal market commissioner Lord Cockfield – was published within months, listing 282 pieces of legislation that would need to be agreed and implemented in order to remove all remaining non-tariff barriers and create a truly open market (Commission of the European Communities, 1985). The result was the signature in February 1986 of the **Single European Act** (SEA), the first substantial expansion of Community powers since the Treaty of Rome.

Compared to later treaty changes, the SEA was not particularly controversial; it had mainly economic goals, few Europeans had yet fully grasped the implications of integration, and the treaty was not so much a new project as the relaunching of an old one. (By contrast, the 1992 Maastricht treaty would move Europe in a different direction, and so would face stiffer resistance; see later in

● **Eurosclerosis**: A term coined in 1985 to describe the inflexibility of the western European labour market, and its failure to create new jobs quickly enough to meet demand.

● **Single European Act**: The first major change to the treaties, signed in 1986 with the goal of reviving plans to complete the single European market.

Paving the way to European Union

1969	December	EEC leaders agree principle of economic and monetary union
1971	August	US abandons dollar/gold convertibility; end of Bretton Woods system
1972	April	Launch of 'snake in the tunnel'
1973	October	Yom Kippur War
1975	January	Launch of European Regional Development Fund
	March	First meeting of European Council
1979	March	Launch of the European Monetary System
	June	First direct elections to European Parliament
1985	January	Jacques Delors takes over as president of the Commission; first burgundy European passports issued
	June	Signature of Schengen Agreement
1986	February	Signature of Single European Act (SEA); Danish referendum supports SEA
1987	May	Irish referendum supports SEA
	July	Single European Act comes into force
1989	April	Announcement of Delors three-stage plan to monetary union
	Sept–Dec	Collapse of communist governments in eastern Europe; fall of Berlin Wall
1990	August	Iraqi invasion of Kuwait
	October	German reunification
1991	February	Ground war in Kuwait/Iraq
	June	Slovenia and Croatia declare independence; outbreak of war in Yugoslavia
1992	February	Signature of Treaty on European Union
	June	Danish referendum rejects Maastricht; Schengen Agreement comes into force
	September 16	Black Wednesday
1993	January	Single European market enters into force; break-up of Czechoslovakia
	May	Second Danish referendum on Maastricht
	June	Agreement of Copenhagen conditions
	November	Treaty on European Union enters into force
1994	January	Creation of European Economic Area
1995	January	Austria, Finland and Sweden join the EU
	March	Schengen Agreement comes into force
	September	Dayton peace accords end war in Yugoslavia

Jacques Delors

Delors (born 1925) was arguably the most influential and dynamic of all presidents of the European Commission. He made his mark on European integration during two terms in office (1985–95) by overseeing the negotiation and signature of the Single European Act and the Maastricht treaty, more enlargement, reforms to the Community budget, the creation of the European Economic Area, and laying the groundwork for the later adoption of the euro, as well as witnessing the end of the Cold War and the outbreak of civil war in the Balkans. Born in Paris, he trained as an economist and worked in the banking industry before briefly serving as a Member of the European Parliament (1979–81), and as French economics and finance minister between 1981 and 1984. As president of the Commission he was known for his ambitious plans and assertive style of management, and for capturing the headlines more than any of his predecessors. He stepped down in 1995, resisting suggestions that he run as the socialist candidate in that year's French presidential election.

this chapter.) The biggest misgivings were in Denmark, where parliament (the Folketing) failed to approve the draft treaty for fear of its implications for national sovereignty. When other member states refused to make changes to meet its objections, Denmark in February 1986 became the first Community state to put a treaty to a national referendum, resulting in 56.2 per cent of votes in favour, with a healthy 74 per cent turnout. In Ireland, too, there were problems, this time of a constitutional nature (see Chapter 8 for details), but the issue was resolved by a May 1987 referendum that came down heavily in favour of the SEA, clearing the way for its entry into force two months later.

The passage of the SEA was made possible by a combination of economic and political factors: member states were increasingly dependent on intra-EC trade, they were experiencing reduced growth and worsening unemployment, the EMS was off the ground, and European business strongly favoured the single market. The SEA also had political support: Jacques Delors had built a strong case for the single market, and there was (for once) a congruence of opinion among the leaders of Britain, France and West Germany (Eichengreen, 2007, pp. 338–41). Even British Prime Minister Margaret Thatcher was supportive: 'At last, I felt, we were going to get the Community back on course, concentrating on its role as a huge market, with all the opportunities that would bring to our industries' (Thatcher, 1993, p. 556).

But for some the goals of the SEA were not sufficiently ambitious, and several states had already gone ahead with a side agreement on a border-free Europe. In June 1985, representatives of France, West Germany, and the Benelux countries met on a river boat moored near the village of Schengen in Luxembourg, which symbolically lay at the confluence of the borders of France, Luxembourg and West Germany. There they signed the **Schengen Agreement** providing for the fast-track removal of border controls. A second agreement was signed in June 1990, and 'Schengenland' finally came into being in March 1995. It was incorporated into the EU treaties by the 1997 Treaty of Amsterdam, and all EU member states except Britain and Ireland have since signed Schengen and implemented its terms, along with Iceland, Norway and Switzerland. (Britain has stayed out because it claims

● **Schengen Agreement**: A fast-track agreement to set up a border-free Europe, signed in 1985 among five Community states, and which has since expanded to 28 states.

that island states face more difficulties in controlling illegal immigration, while Ireland has stayed out mainly because it has a passport union with Britain.)

Meanwhile, ordinary Europeans were starting to feel the effects of integration for themselves. Cross-border travel was becoming easier, foreign corporations were becoming more visible as they merged with (or bought up) businesses in other EU states, and two important new symbols of European integration were adopted in 1985. The first of these was a passport with a standard design, first proposed in 1974 and issued for the first time in January 1985. Holders were still citizens of their home states, but all Community passports were now the same burgundy colour and bore the words 'European Community' alongside the state coat of arms. The second was the Community flag (12 gold stars on a blue background), adopted from the Council of Europe in June 1985 and soon to become a common sight throughout the Community.

The SEA came into force amid great fanfare in July 1987, setting midnight on 31 December 1992 as the target date for completion of 'an area without internal frontiers in which the free movement of goods, persons, services and capital is ensured'. As well as relaunching 'Europe' as the biggest market and trading bloc in the world, the SEA brought other changes:

- Legal status was given to meetings of the heads of government within the European Council, and to Community foreign policy coordination.
- New powers were given to the European Court of Justice, and a new Court of First Instance was created to help deal with the growing legal caseload.
- The European Parliament (EP) was given more power relative to the Council of Ministers through the introduction of a new cooperation procedure and a new assent procedure (see Chapter 12 for details).
- Many internal passport and customs controls were eased or lifted.
- The Community was given more responsibility over environmental policy, research and development, and regional policy.
- Banks and companies could now do business and sell their products and services throughout the Community.

New prominence was also given on the Community agenda to 'cohesion' (balanced economic and social development), and the target was set of creating a European social area in which there were equal employment opportunities and working conditions. There was to be new spending under the so-called structural funds of the Community, including the ERDF, the European Social Fund, and the Cohesion Fund, and another boost for social policy came in 1989 with the Charter of Fundamental Social Rights for Workers (the Social Charter). This was designed to encourage free movement of workers, fair pay, better living and working conditions, freedom of association, and protection of children and adolescents (see Chapter 22).

International developments: the end of the Cold War (1989–99)

Changes in the Community were taking place against a background of dramatic political events that would redefine the meaning of Europe and fundamentally

Illustration 6.1
The end of the Berlin Wall

Berliners clamber over the Berlin Wall, whose dramatic opening in 1989 symbolized the end of the Cold War division of Europe.

alter its place in the world. The first hint of an impending new order had come in March 1985 when Mikhail Gorbachev was appointed general secretary of the Soviet communist party, and quickly made clear that it would not be business as usual in the USSR. He set out to restructure the Soviet economic and political system, and to encourage more public discussion about the problems that the USSR faced and how they might be addressed. But he quickly lost control of his own agenda, which was hijacked by a struggle for power between conservatives opposed to change and progressives seeking its acceleration. The new openness in the USSR was interpreted in eastern Europe as an opportunity to press for long wished-for democratic and free-market changes, which soon followed:

- In East Germany, rigged elections in May 1989 sparked anger, and when Hungary opened its borders with Austria in September, several thousand East Germans fled to the west via Hungary. Demonstrations broke out in October in East Berlin, and in November access was made available to West Berlin through the Berlin Wall, which began to be dismantled. In place since 1961, one of the most potent symbols of Cold War division was removed on 3 October 1990 with the reunification of Germany.
- In Czechoslovakia, the anti-communist Velvet Revolution broke out in November 1989, leading to the end of the one-party state and the holding of democratic elections in June 1990. Economic and nationalist tensions fed into demands for a looser political association between Czechs and Slovaks, who had lived together in an uneasy arrangement since the creation of Czechoslovakia in 1917. These demands led eventually to the 'velvet divorce', and in January 1993 the Czech Republic and Slovakia came into being as independent states.

● In Romania, the most Stalinist of eastern European states, the authoritarian Nicolae Ceauşescu (in power since 1965) was re-elected as leader of the Romanian communist party in November 1989 and indicated no change in direction. Years of resentment immediately boiled over, and when the military took the side of demonstrators, Ceauşescu and his wife were taken into detention, summarily tried, and eventually executed.
● Democracy also came to Albania, Bulgaria, Hungary, and Poland, and – with the dissolution of the Soviet Union on Christmas Day, 1991 – independence came to Belarus, Estonia, Latvia, Lithuania, Moldova, and Ukraine.

Meanwhile, the Middle East entered the equation once again when Iraq invaded Kuwait in August 1990. The United States quickly orchestrated the formation of a multinational coalition and the launching of an air war against Iraq, followed by a four-day ground war in February 1991. But the Community dithered (see van Eekelen, 1990; Anderson, 1992). Britain fell in with the Americans and placed more than 40,000 troops under US operational command, while France committed 18,000 troops but emphasized a diplomatic resolution in order to maintain good relations with Arab oil producers and protect its weapons markets. Germany could do little, constrained as it was by a postwar tradition of pacifism and constitutional limits on the deployment of German troops outside the NATO area. Fearing retribution, Belgium refused to sell ammunition to Britain and, along with Portugal and Spain, refused to allow its naval vessels to be involved in anything more than minesweeping or enforcing the blockade of Iraq. Meanwhile, Ireland remained neutral.

A frustrated Luxembourg foreign minister Jacques Poos bemoaned the 'political insignificance' of the Community, dismissed by Belgian foreign minister Mark Eyskens as 'an economic giant, a political dwarf, and a military worm' (*New York Times*, 25 January 1991). Jacques Delors summed up the implications of the problem when he mused that while the member states had taken a firm line against Iraq on sanctions, once force entered the equation it was clear that the Community had neither the institutional machinery nor the military force to allow it to act in concert (Delors, 1991).

Worse was to follow in the Balkans, where nationalist tensions had been building since the death of Josep Broz Tito in 1980, the eventual break-up of Yugoslavia beginning in June 1991 when Slovenia and Croatia declared independence, followed in September by Macedonia. There followed a bloody melange of war, sieges, massacres, genocide, and ethnic cleansing, and once again the response of the Community was to dither. When it tried to broker a peace conference, a confident Jacques Poos was moved to declare 'This is the hour of Europe, not of the United States' (*The Economist*, 'War in Europe', 6 July 1991). But when the Community recognized Croatia and Slovenia in January 1992, its credibility as a neutral arbiter collapsed. The EU monitors sent to Bosnia – dressed all in white and disparagingly referred to as 'ice-cream men' – were powerless to stop the slaughter, and it was left to the United States to lead the way to the September 1995 Dayton peace accords. Later, when ethnic Albanians in Kosovo tried to break away from Yugoslavia in 1997–98, it was left to NATO – again under US leadership – to organize a bombing campaign against Serbia between March and June 1999. The Community was clearly failing to match its economic power with an international political presence.

CONCEPT

European
Political
Cooperation

The process by which
Community foreign
ministers met on a
regular basis with the
goal of agreeing common
foreign policy positions.
Foreign ministers learned
the value of multilateral
discussions, national
diplomats set up
networks of
communication, and EPC
became 'a working model
of intergovernmental
cooperation without
formal integration'
(Wallace, 2005, p. 435).
But while it encouraged
helpful new habits, it had
little impact on public
opinion, and did little to
bring national policies in
the EEC into closer
convergence.

The Community becomes a Union (1990–93)

In spite of resistance to the surrender of national sovereignty, the demands of economic integration had always ensured pressure for wider political coordination in the Community. The occasional summits among EEC leaders in the 1960s led to new thinking about imposing some order on the process, and a 1970 report authored by Belgian diplomat Etienne Davignon identified foreign policy coordination as a potentially useful first step. The report recommended quarterly meetings of the six foreign ministers, liaison among EC ambassadors in foreign capitals, and common EC instructions on certain matters for those ambassadors (Urwin, 1995, p. 148).

Thus had been born **European Political Cooperation** (EPC), a process of foreign policy coordination that while modest in its details at least encouraged new habits and focused political minds. Among its early results were a 1970 joint EC policy declaration on the Middle East, the signing of the 1975 Lomé Convention on aid to poorer countries, and joint Community responses during the 1980s to the Anglo-Argentinean war in the Falklands, developments in Poland and Iran, and apartheid in South Africa (White, 2001, Chapter 4). But EPC was more reactive than proactive; far more substantial as a step towards greater political coordination among Community leaders was the creation in December 1974 of the European Council, which formalized the periodic summits among heads of government. Less an institution in the mould of the European Commission than a forum within which heads of government could regularly convene, the Council reached decisions on strategy without becoming bogged down in detailed administrative issues. It met for the first time in March 1975 and went on to launch some of the defining initiatives in the process of integration (as well as being the site of some of its most bitter political squabbles).

Another attempt was made to move forward in 1975 when the report of a committee headed by Belgian Prime Minister Leo Tindemans described European union as the next logical step in the journey from the EEC to an eventual European federation. It recommended institutional changes, including a stronger Commission and Parliament, and greater use of qualified majority voting in the Council of Ministers, and also recommended further movement on EMU, foreign and security policy, and social and regional policy. These suggestions were too radical for the 1970s (Dinan, 2004, pp. 162–3), but their time would come.

For EMU, that time eventually came in 1989–90 with a favourable alignment of circumstances. First, France, West Germany and Spain had new leaders (François Mitterrand, Helmut Kohl, and Felipe González) who had won office in part on the strength of their support for integration, and the European Commission was still being run by the dynamic and ambitious Jacques Delors. Second, when the 1989 revolutions in eastern Europe helped pave the way to German reunification, France expected a reaffirmation of Germany's commitment to Europe so that German and European unification could move ahead in parallel (Dyson and Featherstone, 1999, p. 4). Finally, in spite of problems with the European Monetary System, there was widening political agreement to move ahead with the single currency. Delors now headed a committee that reviewed the necessary steps, and its April 1989 report (Commission of the European Communities, 1989) suggested a three-stage process:

- Stage I, to begin by July 1990, was to be based on free use of the ecu, increased cooperation between central banks, and free capital movement.
- Stage II would involve new independence for national central banks, increased coordination of monetary policies, and the establishment of a European Monetary Institute (EMI) as a precursor to a European central bank.
- Stage III, to be achieved by January 1997, would involve a single monetary policy under the control of the European System of Central Banks, the introduction of the single currency, and the permanent fixing of exchange rates.

Most Community leaders were supportive, so the June 1990 European Council decided to open a new intergovernmental conference (IGC) on economic and monetary union, and later a second IGC to discuss political union. This latter notion was less than it sounded: it involved not so much the laying of foundations for a federal Europe as the transfer of more policy responsibilities to the European level, giving more powers to the Commission and Parliament, and extending the use of qualified majority voting in the Council of Ministers (Dinan, 2004, p. 246).

Negotiations in 1990–91 resulted in the **Treaty on European Union**, signed in February 1992 in Maastricht in the Netherlands. The original draft had included mention of a 'federal goal' for Europe, but this was firmly opposed by Britain, so the wording reverted to that found in the preamble to the Treaty of Rome, which spoke of 'an ever closer union' among the peoples of Europe. A cumbersome agreement was also reached by which a new European Union would be created, resting on three organizational 'pillars': the renamed European Community, foreign and security policy, and justice and home affairs (see Chapter 8 for details). There was also agreement to begin work on a new Common Foreign and Security Policy (CFSP), confirmation of the three-stage plan to monetary union, and several other changes:

- New powers were given to the European Parliament relative to the Council of Ministers, and a new Committee of the Regions was created to represent local interests.
- The EU was given new responsibility in policy areas such as consumer protection, industrial policy, education, and social policy, and there would be more cooperation on immigration and asylum, including the creation of a European police intelligence agency (Europol) to combat organized crime and drug trafficking.
- More regional funds would be set aside for poorer member states.
- There were new rights for European citizens and the creation of an ambiguous European Union 'citizenship' allowing Europeans to live wherever they liked in the EU and to stand and vote in local and European elections.

● **Treaty on European Union**: A treaty signed in February 1992 and that came into force in November 1993, creating the European Union and outlining a commitment to a single European currency and a common foreign policy.

Where the Single European Act had been approved without much debate, Maastricht represented a significant change of direction, was more political in its intent, and so was always going to be more controversial. Denmark once again opted for a national referendum, and in June 1992 sent shockwaves through the Community by becoming the first member state ever to reject a European treaty in a national referendum (albeit by the narrow margin of just 50,000 votes; 50.7 per cent of voters were opposed, with 83 per cent turnout). There was also a

Illustration 6.2
The Maastricht Treaty

The signing ceremony for
the Treaty on European
Union, held in Maastricht
on 7 February 1992.

DOCUMENT 6.1

Opening articles of the Treaty on European Union, 7 February 1992

Article A

By this Treaty, the High Contracting Parties establish among themselves a European Union, hereinafter called 'the Union'.

This Treaty marks a new stage in the process of creating an ever closer union among the peoples of Europe, in which decisions are taken as closely as possible to the citizen.

. . . Its task shall be to organize, in a manner demonstrating consistency and solidarity, relations between the Member States and between their peoples.

Article B

The Union shall set itself the following objectives:

– to promote economic and social progress which is balanced and sustainable, in particular through the creation of an area without internal frontiers, through the strengthening of economic and social cohesion and through the establishment of economic and monetary union, ultimately including a single currency in accordance with the provisions of this Treaty;

– to assert its identity on the international scene, in particular through the implementation of a common foreign and security policy including the eventual framing of a common defence policy, which might in time lead to a common defence;

– to strengthen the protection of the rights and interests of the nationals of its Member States through the introduction of a citizenship of the Union;

– to develop close cooperation on justice and home affairs;

– to maintain in full the 'acquis communautaire'.

Source: Europa web site at http://europa.eu/abc/treaties (retrieved July 2010).

Map 6.1 The European Economic Area, 1994

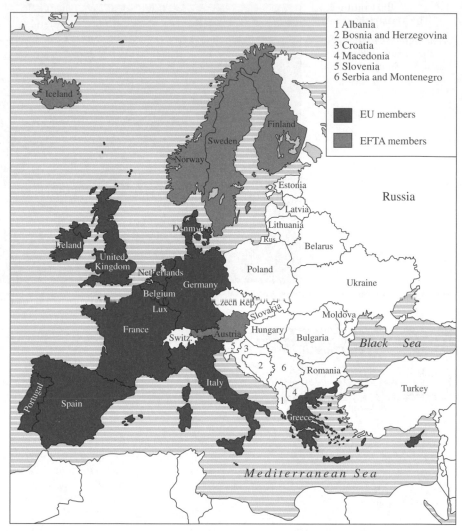

debate about the treaty in Ireland, where, after agreement of a protocol guaranteeing that the Irish ban on abortion would not be impacted, it was passed by a majority of nearly 69 per cent in favour in a June 1992 referendum, This was followed by a *petit oui* (literally, 'small yes') in France in September, when Maastricht was approved by just 51.04 per cent of voters, with 70 per cent turnout (an outcome explained at least in part by the declining popularity of French President François Mitterrand (Criddle, 1993)).

Once the dust had settled, a compromise was arranged by which Denmark was given opt-outs from the clauses dealing with the single currency, defence, citizenship, and justice and home affairs. A second Danish referendum was then organized in May 1993, in which the treaty was approved by 56.8 per cent of voters. With all other member states also on board, Maastricht entered into force in November 1993, nearly a year late.

More enlargement (1990–95)

As noted in Chapter 5, the doubling of Community membership between 1973 and 1986 had brought key changes to the relationship among the member states, to the institutional character and policy agenda of the Community, and to its international role and standing. But enlargement had been a piecemeal affair, lacking either a grand plan or specific rules on the credentials that states should have in order to qualify for membership. There was an understanding that they should be European (so there was little question about rejecting an application from Morocco in 1987), but beyond that the rules were vague. By the early 1990s the question of clarity was pressing for attention, because applications for membership had been lodged by Turkey (1987), Austria (1989), Cyprus and Malta (1990), Sweden (1991), and Finland, Norway and Switzerland (1992), and the end of the Cold War had raised the prospect of enlargement to the east.

By way of preparation (or, in the view of Dinan (2004, p. 268), to fob off the new aspirant members), negotiations began in 1990 on the creation of a **European Economic Area** (EEA) under which the terms of the SEA would be extended to the seven members of the European Free Trade Association (Austria, Finland, Iceland, Liechtenstein, Norway, Sweden, and Switzerland). They, in return, would accept the rules of the single market. Negotiations were completed in February 1992, but the Swiss turned down membership in a December 1992 referendum, so only six EFTA states joined when the EEA came into force in January 1994. Even as the EEA was being negotiated, however, agreement was

Figure 6.2 Growth of the European Union

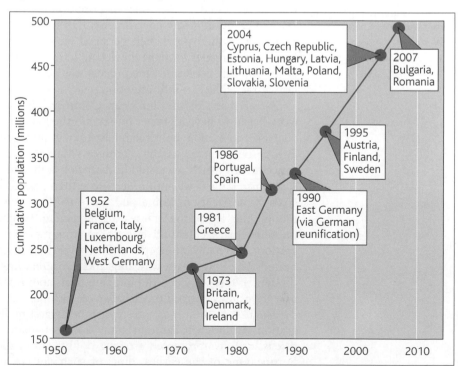

● **European Economic Area**: An agreement under which EFTA member states were given access to the single European market without full EU membership.

CONCEPT

Acquis communautaire

The body of treaties, laws and regulations adopted by the EU. Derived from the French *acquis* (meaning *accepted* or *acquired*) and *communautaire* (of the community), the term is most often used in the context of the obligations of aspirant new members of the EU. Negotiations on membership split the *acquis* into multiple chapters that are used as the basis of discussions, and new members must agree to transpose the *acquis* into national law and to implement it upon accession. Transitional periods and temporary derogations (a loosening or weakening of obligations) are sometimes agreed, but no permanent derogation is allowed (see Chapter 18).

reached to open talks on Community membership for Austria, Finland, Norway, and Sweden, and in June 1993 the first set of formal requirements for EU membership was agreed at the Copenhagen European Council. Henceforth, the 'Copenhagen conditions' would require that applicant states should be democratic, should have functioning free markets, and should be able to take on the obligations of the **acquis communautaire** (the body of laws and regulations already adopted by the EU).

With membership terms agreed in March 1994, referendums were held in Austria, Finland, Norway and Sweden, and majorities came down in favour in all but Norway. Austria, Finland and Sweden joined the EU in January 1995, pushing membership to 15, increasing the land area of the EU by one-third, and for the first time giving it a shared border with Russia. Although there was to be a break of nine years before the next round of enlargement, the wheels had already been set in motion with the 1990 applications from Cyprus and Malta, followed in 1994 by those from Poland and Hungary, and in 1995–96 by those from Bulgaria, the Czech Republic, Estonia, Latvia, Lithuania, and Slovenia. A taste of the implications of eastern enlargement had been offered by German reunification in October 1990; although this was the result of a domestic German decision (and not one that was entirely popular in other Community states), it gave some insight into the problems and promises involved in trying to integrate communist states into the capitalist European Union.

Growing signs of a backlash

In its early years, the speed and content of integration was set by bureaucrats and government ministers meeting in closed session, emerging with agreements that were never tested in the court of public opinion. These agreements were not reached easily, and saw governments fighting to protect state interests, leaders imposing on their peers their personal views about the process of integration, and bitter struggles to move the debate in new directions. But the issues at stake were primarily economic, the process was elitist and technocratic, and integration attracted little public attention.

As the reach of the European Community expanded, however, and as its work began to have a greater impact on the lives of ordinary Europeans and to take on more of a political quality, so it drew new public attention. Most Europeans knew it as the Common Market, a relatively benign economic concept with which few could find serious fault. And when the Single European Act came along, it was not much more than an affirmation of the original core goals of the Treaty of Rome, and generated little controversy. At the same time, though, the '1992 programme' (a reference to the target date for completion of the single market) had the effect of making more Europeans familiar with integration. Inevitably, then, the debate over Maastricht was going to be more heated. The new treaty was long and dense, its implications demanded more thought, it raised more troubling questions about national sovereignty, and two new terms now entered the debate over Europe.

The first of these was *euroscepticism*, suggesting hostility to the idea of integration. Although it came in many different shades (see Chapter 17 for more discussion), it represented growing doubts about the direction being taken by Europe. One of the earliest hints of such doubts had come in 1972 with the

Map 6.2 Third enlargement, 1995

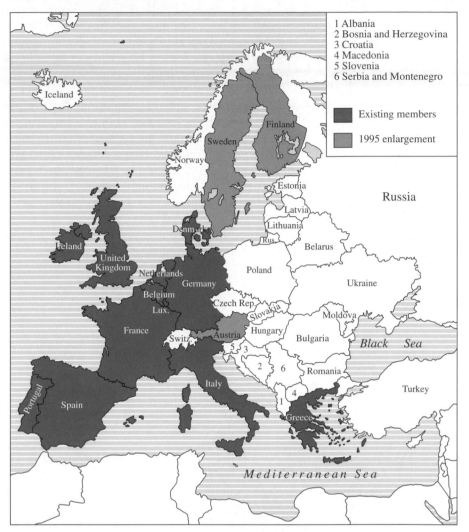

Norwegian vote against membership of the EEC. Much later, when the Single European Act was being ratified, Denmark in 1986 became the first country to put a European treaty to a national referendum. Six years later, far greater public attention was generated by the June 1992 Danish rejection of Maastricht, the near miss in France three months later, and the rejection by the Swiss in December of membership of the European Economic Area.

The second new term was *democratic deficit*, referring to the growing gap between the powers and authority of EU institutions and the ability of EU citizens to impact their work (see Chapter 18 for more discussion). Ironically, the concerns over this deficit grew even as European public opinion played a greater role in the decisions over Europe. National government leaders and ministers considered that opinion as they deliberated in the Council of Ministers, and later in the European Council. Meanwhile, EU voters had been given the opportunity since 1979 to take part in direct elections to the European Parliament, and

Parliament's powers over the legislative process had been growing. But most voters still understood little of the manner in which decisions were taken at the Community level (see discussion in Chapter 18 about the knowledge deficit), and they turned out at EP elections in declining numbers: from a high of 63 per cent at the first elections in 1979, turnout by 1999 was down to 49 per cent (and has continued falling since).

The three 1992 votes were symptomatic of an increasingly heated public debate about the merits of integration which showed that even though many Europeans were still confused about its implications, and so were more easily swayed in their opinions by supporters and critics of integration, they cared much more than they had even a decade before. Where decisions about Europe in the 1950s and 1960s could be taken by bureaucrats meeting in closed session, by the 1990s this was no longer possible, and the dynamics of the debate over Europe had taken on an entirely new character.

SUMMARY

- Exchange rate stability had been central to western economic and monetary policy since Bretton Woods. The first attempt to pave the way to a single currency – the 1972 'snake in the tunnel' – failed mainly because of bad timing, and it was replaced by the 1979 European Monetary System.

- In the mid-1980s an attempt was made to refocus attention on completion of a European single market. The result was the signature in 1986 of the Single European Act, the first major amendment to the founding treaties of the European Community. Its key goal was a single market by the end of 1992.

- Concerned about the slowness with which borders were being opened within the EEC, several member states signed the Schengen Agreement in 1985, aimed at a fast-track lifting of customs and immigration checks.

- The political revolutions of 1989 brought an end to the Cold War and began lifting the divisions between western and eastern Europe.

- The signature of the 1992 Treaty on European Union confirmed the three stages to the achievement of a single currency, expanded the policy reach of integration (notably into foreign and security policy), and created a new three-pillar European Union. The treaty proved controversial, and was delayed by a negative vote (later reversed) in a Danish national referendum.

- With more countries hoping for EU membership, the European Economic Area was created in 1994 to give EFTA members access to the single market, and 1995 saw the entry of Austria, Finland and Sweden.

- The process of integration had at first attracted little public attention. But the passage of the Single European Act made the headlines, paving the way for a heated debate over Maastricht that changed the nature of the debate. Supporters and opponents of integration became more vocal, and national governments had no choice but to pay more attention to public opinion.

KEY TERMS AND CONCEPTS

Acquis communautaire

Economic and monetary union (EMU)

European Economic Area

European Monetary System (EMS)

European Political Cooperation

Eurosclerosis

Schengen Agreement

Single European Act

Treaty on European Union

FURTHER READING

Drake, Helen (2000), *Jacques Delors: Perspectives on a European Leader* (Abingdon: Routledge). A profile of the most influential and controversial president of the European Commission to date, which sets out to pin down the 'Delors factor' in politics.

Gros, Daniel, and Niels Thygsen (1998), *European Monetary Integration: From the European Monetary System to Economic and Monetary Union* (New York: Prentice-Hall). A review of the history and effects of the European Monetary System.

Padoa-Schioppa, Tommaso (2000), *The Road to Monetary Union in Europe: The Emperor, the Kings, and the Genies* (Oxford: Oxford University Press). A review of the background to the *Single European Act and Maastricht*, written by an Italian banker who later became Italy's minister of finance.

CHAPTER 7

To Lisbon and Beyond

PREVIEW Maastricht had brought a change of name, the European Community becoming part of the new European Union, but it was not clear what 'union' meant in this context. And much pressing business remained unfinished: the single market had been given a boost, and preparations had been made for a single European currency, but there had been less progress on foreign policy, and the EU institutions were being stretched by the prospects of eastern enlargement.

Two more treaties – Amsterdam in 1997 and Nice in 2001 – did little more than amend some institutional rules and confirm new policy responsibilities, the real focus of political attention at the time being the single currency, by now named the euro. Exchange rates in participating member states were locked in place in 1999, and three years later euro banknotes and coins began circulating. World events impinged again when several EU governments, led by Germany and France, publicly fell out with the United States over the 2003 invasion of Iraq. Once again the failures of these governments to agree on a critical policy issue were brought into the harsh light of day.

An attempt was made in 2002–03 to agree a draft constitutional treaty for the EU, but while it was approved by 17 member states, the treaty was turned down by French and Dutch voters in 2005. This happened as the EU was again moving ahead with enlargement, bringing 12 new mainly eastern European states into the fold in 2005–07, and thereby comprehensively bringing an end to the Cold War division of Europe. The failed constitution was reinvented as the Treaty of Lisbon, which came into force in 2009, its advent capping more than 25 years of active and sometimes controversial treaty-building by EU states.

KEY ISSUES

- Given the history of postwar transatlantic relations, what was the significance of the dispute over Iraq?
- How much did the negative votes against the treaties or the euro in Denmark, France, Ireland, the Netherlands and Sweden reflect on the direction being taken by European integration, and how much did they reflect on domestic political dissatisfaction in these countries?
- How politically significant was the EU enlargement to eastern Europe?
- Was the Treaty of Lisbon a constitution by another name?
- What role have crises played in the history of European integration?

From Amsterdam to Nice (1997–2002)

Because the Maastricht treaty had left a number of items of business unfinished, another IGC was convened in 1996–97 that resulted in agreement of the **Treaty of Amsterdam**. Signed in October 1997, and coming into force in May 1999, it was less important than either the SEA or Maastricht, and focused on consolidation rather than innovation. It was designed mainly to make some of the institutional and political changes needed to deal with enlargement, and to help the EU better address issues such as globalization, terrorism, and international crime. It also confirmed plans for eastern enlargement and for the launch of the single currency, along with more specific changes:

- It confirmed plans to implement a Common Foreign and Security Policy (CFSP) along with 'the progressive framing of a common defence policy'. Decisions on the CFSP were to remain intergovernmental and unanimous, but the European Council was given the power to agree common strategies and positions, and a new office of High Representative for the CFSP was created.
- EU policy responsibilities were extended to health and consumer protection.
- The Schengen Agreement was incorporated into the treaties.
- The principle of '**enhanced cooperation**' was established, allowing member states to work more closely together in selected areas without harming the overall process of integration.
- The powers of the European Parliament were expanded, and it was given the power of approval over appointments to the College of Commissioners.

But Amsterdam fell short of requirements, so yet another IGC was convened to look at institutional change in anticipation of enlargement. 'Rarely', concludes Dinan (2004, p. 288), 'did an intergovernmental conference devote so much time to so few issues with so few consequential results.' Many items of business were left for discussion at the European Council meeting in Nice, France, in December 2000, and even then the resulting **Treaty of Nice** did little more than make minor changes to the structure of the Commission, to the terms of qualified majority voting in the Council of Ministers, to the European Parliament, and to the court system.

Nice was signed in February 2001 with the expectation that it would be quickly ratified by member states. But another referendum surprise came in June, this time in Ireland, which until then had a reputation as a relatively contented member of the EU. A surfeit of confidence had led the Irish government to make little effort to educate voters on Nice, creating an information breach into which stepped an unlikely coalition of environmentalists, religious conservatives, and those concerned about preserving Ireland's neutrality (Costello, 2005). On referendum day, barely one-third of voters turned out, and 54 per cent of those rejected the treaty. EU leaders refused to renegotiate the terms of the treaty, but the European Council did confirm that Ireland would not have to be party to any mutual defence obligations. A second Irish referendum was scheduled for October 2002, and this time a spirited information campaign was organized and the issues were more actively debated. The new

● **Treaty of Amsterdam**: A set of relatively limited changes to the treaties, signed in 1997 and taking force in 1999.

● **Treaty of Nice**: Another set of relatively limited changes to the treaties, signed in 2001 and taking force – after unexpected delays – in 2003.

vote resulted in nearly 63 per cent approval with a 50 per cent turnout, and Nice finally came into force in February 2003.

While public attention was focused on Amsterdam and Nice, another initiative with important implications for the political lives of Europeans was completed with much less fanfare in the form of the Charter of Fundamental Rights of the European Union. Sparked by a 1996 decision by the European Court of Justice that its treaties did not allow the EU to accede to the 1950 European Convention on Human Rights, the charter was discussed and approved during 2000, and 'proclaimed' at the Nice European Council in December. Reaffirming a selection of rights with which no European could really take much issue, the Charter came into force with the Treaty of Lisbon in 2009 (see later in this chapter), since when it has been part of the legal structure of the EU (see Chapter 8 for more details).

Meanwhile, there were new initiatives on the economic front. In spite of progress on the single market and preparations for the single currency, many still worried that the EU was not fulfilling its potential as the largest marketplace in the world. Planners contemplated lagging productivity rates, high unemployment in parts of the EU, an inflexible labour market, and continued economic disparities among member states. In order to set new targets, the Lisbon European Council in March 2000 agreed the **Lisbon strategy**, which set the ambitious goal of making the EU – within ten years – 'the most dynamic and competitive knowledge-based economy in the world capable of sustainable economic growth with more and better jobs and greater social cohesion, and respect for the environment'. To do this, employment rates would be raised, more women would be brought into the workplace, telecommunications and energy markets would be liberalized, transport would be improved, and labour markets opened up (Wallace, 2004). Sceptics doubted that this was possible, and were to be proved correct.

Arrival of the euro (1995–2002)

● **Lisbon Strategy**: An attempt made in 2000 to set economic modernization targets for the EU, with the goal of making it the world's most dynamic marketplace within ten years.

● **Convergence criteria**: Standards that EU member states must achieve before being allowed to adopt the European single currency, including low national budget deficits and inflation, and controls on public debt and interest rates.

Stage I on the road to monetary union (new levels of cooperation among banks) had been in place since 1990, and Stage II had been launched in January 1994. This led to the establishment of the European Monetary Institute, designed to oversee preparations for Stage III, the creation of a European single currency, which in 1995 was named the euro. Maastricht had set five **convergence criteria** that states would have to meet in order to qualify to adopt the planned new currency (see Table 7.1). Because several states had trouble achieving the criteria, the target date for Stage III was postponed from January 1997 to January 1999. When EU leaders met in 1998 to decide which states qualified to make the switch, they found varied levels of readiness; all had met the budget deficit goal, for example, but only seven had met the debt target. Since Maastricht allowed member states to qualify if their debt-to-GDP ratio was 'sufficiently diminishing and approaching the reference value at a satisfactory pace', strict adherence to the criteria was set aside, immediately raising questions about how seriously they were being taken. The decision to bring Greece into the eurozone, for example, would later come home to roost with a vengeance (see later in this chapter).

In June 1998 the new European Central Bank (ECB) replaced the European Monetary Institute and became responsible for monetary policy in the eurozone.

Table 7.1 The convergence criteria

Budget deficit	Less than 3 per cent of GDP
Public debt	Less than 60 per cent of GDP
Inflation	Within 1.5 per cent of the average in the three countries with the lowest rates
Interest rates	Within 2 per cent of the average in the three countries with the lowest rates
Exchange rates	Kept within ERM fluctuation margins for two years

On 1 January 1999 the euro was officially launched, becoming available as an electronic currency (but not yet a physical currency) and participating countries permanently fixed the exchange rates of their national currencies against one another and against the euro. All dealings of the ECB with commercial banks and all its foreign exchange activities were now transacted in euros, which began to be quoted against the yen and the US dollar in international financial markets. The euro started out at a healthy $1.18, fell to a low of 82 cents in late 2000 (sparking claims of crisis), climbed back up to reach parity in mid-2002, and was to reach a high of nearly $1.60 in mid-2008 before falling again (see Chapter 20).

Discussion about the design of the new euro banknotes and coins had been resolved fairly easily. In the case of the banknotes, the designs could not be tied to any one country but instead had to capture general European themes, so it was decided to use designs based on styles of European architecture. As for the coins, one side had a common design including a map of Europe (without Turkey, it is interesting to note), while the other had designs peculiar to the participating states: Belgium, Luxembourg, the Netherlands, and Spain chose images of their monarchs, Ireland opted for the Celtic harp, France included images of Marianne (a mythical icon of liberty), and Germany used oak twigs, the Brandenburg Gate, and the German eagle.

But even as political leaders and bankers made their preparations, ordinary Europeans had many doubts about the euro. Opinion polls found support across the EU-12 and then the EU-15 between 1993 and 1996 running at about 51–54 per cent, with 36–37 per cent opposed (*Eurobarometer 49*, September 1998). Opposition in 1998 was greatest in Denmark, Sweden, and Britain, but even among member states planning to adopt there were mixed opinions; enthusiasm was highest in Ireland, Luxembourg, the Netherlands and Spain, and lowest in Finland, Germany and Portugal. The German figure was particularly worrying given that Germany was critical to the exercise of monetary union: in the end, suggests Tsoukalis (2003, pp. 34–5), most Germans ultimately signed on only because they saw a need to reaffirm their commitment to Europe in the wake of German reunification.

In January 2002 euro coins and notes began circulating in all EU-15 member states except Britain, Denmark, and Sweden. This final launch of the physical euro was a monumental task, involving the challenge of preparing consumers and businesses, of making sure that enough coins and notes were available to meet demand (14 billion banknotes were printed and 56 billion coins minted), and of converting ATMs, cash registers and vending machines throughout the

Illustration 7.1
Launch of the euro

Commission President Jacques Santer (*right*) and economics and financial affairs commissioner Yves-Thibault de Silguy (*left*) pose with a reproduction of the new 1 euro coin, May 1998.

eurozone. It had been assumed that the transition would be expensive and complicated, so national currencies were to be allowed to circulate alongside the euro for six months. But the problems proved unfounded, within a month euros were accounting for 95 per cent of cash payments in the eurozone, and the transition was over by the end of February. For the first time since the Roman era much of Europe had a single currency.

Shockwaves from Iraq (2003–05)

The United States has always played a critical role in the process of European integration, both intentionally and unintentionally. Intentionally, it provided the political and economic support needed to help get the process off the ground in the late 1940s and early 1950s, it provided security guarantees through NATO, and it provided economic leadership and opportunity through the Bretton Woods system and the Marshall Plan. Unintentionally, it helped bring western Europeans together by pursuing policies during the Cold War that both alarmed and repelled. Starting with Korea, and moving through Suez, the Cuban missile crisis, Vietnam, the Middle East, central America and beyond, western Europeans regularly found themselves at odds with US policy. But while public opinion was often openly hostile, governments rarely made their disquiet public. All now changed with the controversy over Iraq, which not only brought transatlantic political tensions into the open, but had consequences for Europe that are still not fully understood.

As we saw in Chapter 6, the 1990s were not good years for the EC/EU on the foreign policy front. The goal of developing a Common Foreign and Security Policy had been agreed, and the EU had moved quickly to capitalize on the changes brought by the end of the Cold War, investing heavily in eastern Europe and opening the prospect of enlargement. It had also flexed its muscles on the

To Lisbon and beyond

1997	October	Signature of Treaty of Amsterdam
1998	June	Creation of European Central Bank
1999	January	Launch of the euro
	May	Treaty of Amsterdam enters into force
2000	December	Proclamation of Charter of Fundamental Rights of the EU
	March	Agreement of the Lisbon Strategy
2001	February	Signature of Treaty of Nice
	June	Irish referendum rejects Nice
	September	Terrorist attacks in the United States
2002	January	Euro coins and banknotes begin circulating
	March	Opening meetings of Convention on the Future of Europe
	October	Second Irish referendum accepts Nice
2003	February	Treaty of Nice comes into force; large anti-war demonstrations in major European cities

2003	March	Launch of US-led invasion of Iraq
2004	March	Terrorist bombings in Madrid
	May	Ten mainly eastern European states join the EU
	October	Signature of Treaty on the European Constitution
2005	May–June	French and Dutch voters reject the constitutional treaty
	July	Terrorist bombings in London
2007	January	Bulgaria and Romania join the EU
	December	Signature of Treaty of Lisbon
2008	June	Irish referendum rejects Lisbon
2009	January	Slovakia becomes 13th EU member state to adopt the euro
	October	Second Irish referendum accepts Lisbon
	November	Treaty of Lisbon comes into force
2011	January	Estonia becomes 17th EU member state to adopt the euro

trade front, agreeing common positions and pursuing its interests aggressively through the dispute resolution system made available when GATT was replaced in 1995 by the World Trade Organization. But the weak and divided European response to the Gulf War and to crises in the Balkans showed that much work still remained.

The September 2001 terrorist attacks on New York and Washington DC at first generated an unprecedented degree of transatlantic solidarity, suggesting that international terrorism might be a new challenge around which a new Atlantic Alliance might be forged. Many Europeans died in the twin towers, the EU expressed its moral outrage, its foreign ministers described the attack as an assault 'against humanity itself', and the French newspaper *Le Monde* famously declaring '*Nous sommes tous Americains*' (We are all Americans). EU leaders were also generally in support of the US case for quick action to be taken against the Taliban in Afghanistan, a haven for terrorists. But when the administration of George W. Bush began preparing for a pre-emptive invasion of Iraq, claiming that its leader Saddam Hussein possessed weapons of mass destruction and thus posed a threat to neighbouring states and to US interests, everything changed.

In notable contrast with earlier such crises, where EU leaders would have chosen among open support, qualified support or diplomatic silence, several were now openly critical of US policy. Supporters included the governments of Britain, Denmark, Italy, the Netherlands, Spain, and many of those in eastern Europe, while the opposition – which included Austria, Belgium, and Greece – was led vocally and openly by President Jacques Chirac of France and Chancellor Gerhard Schroeder of Germany. US defence secretary Donald Rumsfeld caused some head-scratching at a press conference in January 2003 when he improvised an answer to a question by dismissing France and Germany as 'old Europe' and as 'problems' in the Iraqi question, contrasting them with the eastern European governments that supported US policy.

Largely overlooked in the mix was the deep and near uniform public hostility across the EU to the invasion. This was reflected in opinion polls that found majorities of between 70 and 90 per cent opposed in Britain, Denmark, France, Germany, and even in 'new' European countries such as the Czech Republic and

Illustration 7.2
Londoners protest Iraq

Coordinated demonstrations on 15 February 2003 against the invasion of Iraq – such as this one held in London – sent a powerful message about the new willingness of many Europeans to question US foreign policy.

Hungary (see Figure 7.1). It was also reflected in the massive and coordinated anti-war demonstrations held in EU capitals on 15 February, and in the unpopularity of several pro-war governments; these included Spain – where government support for the war was a factor in the unexpected loss of the April 2004 election by the ruling conservative government of José Maria Aznar – and Britain, where Tony Blair was never able to recover politically from the domestic unpopularity of his decision to support the invasion, struggling on in office until stepping down in June 2007.

Showing just how much transatlantic relations had suffered, a remarkable October 2003 survey found that 53 per cent of Europeans viewed the United States as a threat to world peace on a par with North Korea and Iran (Eurobarometer poll, October 2003). This was more than just a dispute over Iraq, however, or even an EU response to George W. Bush, clearly among the most reviled (in Europe) of all US presidents. Instead, the breach over the invasion could be seen as symptomatic of the new willingness of the EU to assert itself in its relations with the United States. The transatlantic relationship since 1945 had always been more nervous than many had realized, but while western European governments had occasionally resisted American leadership and criticized US policy, they had always done so privately; now the split was out in the open. The end of the Cold War had removed much of the glue that had kept the

Figure 7.1 What Europeans think: the invasion of Iraq, 2003

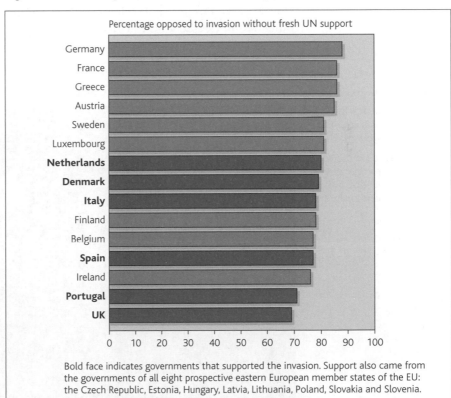

Bold face indicates governments that supported the invasion. Support also came from the governments of all eight prospective eastern European member states of the EU: the Czech Republic, Estonia, Hungary, Latvia, Lithuania, Poland, Slovakia and Slovenia.

Source: EOS Gallup poll, January 2003.

Americans and the western Europeans on the same page, and the division over Iraq showed how much postwar Europe had grown, and how much it now sought to express its independence. This would be a theme that continued in discussions about transatlantic relations even after the election of Barack Obama in 2008.

The EU looks east (1994–2007)

The 1995 enlargement of the EU to Austria, Finland and Sweden had gone relatively easily. Far more challenging – and also politically significant – was the prospect of enlargement to the east. While it would put the final cap on the end of the Cold War division of Europe, it also meant bringing in states that had long been guided by communism, and were far poorer than any western states had been when they had joined the EC/EU. By way of preparation, the Commission had agreed to take responsibility for coordinating western European aid to the east following the end of the Cold War. To this end, the European Bank for Reconstruction and Development was founded in 1991 to provide loans, encourage capital investment, and promote trade; Europe Agreements were signed with several eastern countries to allow for progress on free trade; and in 1997 the EU launched Agenda 2000, listing the changes needed to prepare ten eastern European states for EU membership.

Negotiations opened between 1998 and 2000 with Bulgaria, Cyprus, the Czech Republic, Estonia, Hungary, Latvia, Lithuania, Malta, Poland, Romania, Slovakia and Slovenia. Following their completion in December 2002, all but Bulgaria and Romania were invited to join in an initial wave of enlargement. All accepted, all but Cyprus held referendums that confirmed support for membership, and in May 2004 the biggest round of enlargement to date was completed

**Illustration 7.3
Romanians celebrate
joining the EU**

Romanians see in the new year of 2007, celebrating the accession of their country to the European Union.

when ten new states joined the EU. Membership of the EU was now up to 25, and for the first time former Soviet republics (Estonia, Latvia, and Lithuania) were members of the club. But while the population of the EU grew by more than 23 per cent (from nearly 380 million people to 467 million), its economic wealth grew by just 5 per cent (less than the GDP of the Netherlands). In a second phase of eastern enlargement, Bulgaria and Romania joined in January 2007, pushing the EU population up to just short of half a billion.

The symbolism of this latest round of enlargement was unmistakable: as well as sealing the end of the Cold War division of Europe, it was a dramatic step in the transformation of former Soviet bloc states from communism to liberal democracy, and gave new meaning to the word *European*. Until 2004 the 'European' Union had ultimately been a western European league, and the absence of its eastern neighbours reflected the political, economic and social

Map 7.1 Eastern enlargement, 2004–07

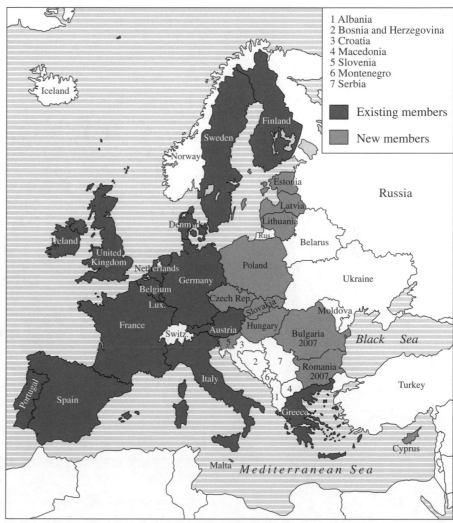

divisions of the continent. By 2007, 27 of the 40 sovereign states of Europe – containing 84 per cent of the population of Europe – had been brought together under the aegis of the European Union.

The process was by no means simple or trouble-free, to be sure. Neither was it quick – see Figure 7.2. There were arguments over the terms of entry, including questions about how much access workers from the new member states would have to free movement and residence, Turkey objected not just to claims that the government of Cyprus represented the whole of the divided island but also to the fact that Cyprus had slipped past Turkey in the queue to join the EU, and there was much political resistance in Malta to joining. There was also a new sense of 'enlargement fatigue' in some of the existing member states, which contributed in turn to new levels of support for far right political parties in Austria, Belgium, and the Netherlands. And yet the queue of prospective members has never stopped growing.

As this book went to press, Croatia, Iceland, Macedonia, Montenegro and Turkey had been accepted as 'candidate countries', meaning that membership

Figure 7.2 The long road to enlargement

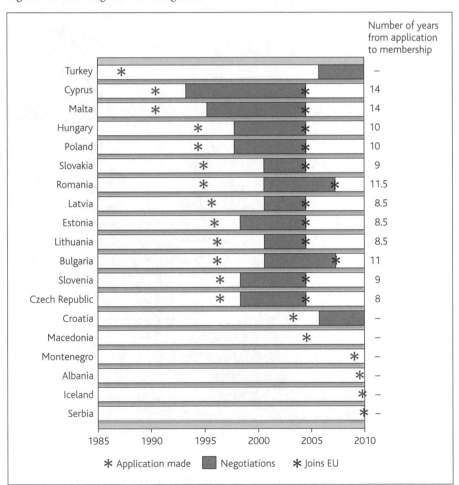

has been agreed in principle for all five, and negotiations on terms had begun with all but Macedonia. Croatia and Iceland are likely to join soonest, but with Turkey the problems are much more substantial, based on a combination of its size, poverty, religion, mixed political record, as well as concerns over its attitude towards Cyprus and questions about whether it is truly a European country (see Chapter 9 for more discussion). Two more countries – Albania and Serbia – have applied for membership, and along with Bosnia and Kosovo are now considered potential candidate countries.

The failed constitutional treaty (2001–05)

Although Amsterdam and Nice took care of most of the immediate institutional needs of the expanding EU, there was support for the idea of taking a broader approach to planning the future of the EU. Nothing could be broader than the idea of a constitution for Europe, and it was with this in mind that the Laeken European Council in December 2001 decided to set up a Convention on the Future of Europe (or the **European Convention**). This met for the first time in March 2002, with former French President Valéry Giscard d'Estaing in the chair, and former Italian Prime Minister Giuliano Amato and former Belgian Prime Minister Jean-Luc Dehaene as vice-chairs. It brought together 105 delegates drawn carefully from a variety of sources and designed to make sure that a wide range of opinions were heard:

- Representatives from each of the 15 member states.
- Representatives from 13 potential member states.
- Two members from each of the 28 national legislatures.
- 16 members of the European Parliament.
- Two representatives of the European Commission.

Several guiding questions dominated the thinking of the Convention: how the EU might play a more effective role in the world, how ordinary Europeans could connect more fully and effectively with the EU, how the division of responsibilities between the EU and the member states could be more clearly explained, how the organizational rules of the EU could be simplified, what arrangements needed to be made to pave the way for more enlargement of the EU, and how the EU could achieve greater democracy, transparency and efficiency. Public plenary sessions were held monthly, the Convention breaking out between those sessions into working groups to discuss particular issues in more detail.

● **European Convention**: A series of meetings held during 2002–03 to draft a constitution for the EU.

● **Treaty Establishing a Constitution for Europe**: A treaty signed in 2004 that was intended to replace the process of developing new treaties with a constitution for the EU. It failed when rejected by French and Dutch voters in 2005.

After months of debate, focusing often on the minutae of how to reform EU institutions and to structure the decision-making process, the convention agreed a draft **Treaty Establishing a Constitution for Europe**. This was designed to combine all the rules and principles established by past treaties and the growing body of European case law, and to bring an end to the process of treaty amendment. A final draft was published in July 2003, was further discussed at an IGC beginning in October and at the European Council in June 2004, and the treaty was signed in October (for details, see Dinan, 2004a). Some of its provisions were new, bringing changes to the institutional structure of the EU, while others simply confirmed established habits.

As usual, ratification was needed by all EU member states, but it was also agreed for the first time that a negative vote by even one state would be enough to terminate the treaty. It was widely assumed that Britain would be the spoiler – the Blair administration was in favour but public opinion was not – but it was spared that embarrassment by surprising events elsewhere. Lithuania became the first member state to ratify in November 2004 with a parliamentary vote, followed by Hungary, Slovenia, and Italy. The treaty then passed its first national referendum in Spain in February 2005, when 77 per cent voted in favour with a lethargic turnout of only 42 per cent. More parliamentary votes followed in Greece, Austria, Belgium, Estonia, Slovakia and Germany, at which point – with 11 positive votes in the bag – the spotlight shifted to France, which had made arrangements for a referendum in late May.

Both the governing conservatives and the opposition socialists campaigned in favour of the treaty, and opinion polls suggested that it would be approved by a healthy majority. But opposition began to build around concerns on the left that the treaty would force a neoliberal economic model on France, and on the right that it would entail too great a loss of national sovereignty. Matters were complicated by the unpopularity of President Jacques Chirac and his prime minister Jean-Pierre Raffarin, both champions of the constitution (*The Economist*, 'France After the Referendum', 2 June 2005). There was high turnout (69 per cent) on polling day on 29 May, but nearly 55 per cent of voters rejected the constitution. For the first time in the history of the EU, one of its two major founding powers had voted against the process of European integration, and there was no possibility of the treaty being renegotiated or of opt-outs and guarantees being provided. In spite of this, the Netherlands went ahead with a planned referendum three days later, and any doubts about the future of the constitution were laid to rest with its rejection there by 62 per cent of voters, with turnout of more than 63 per cent.

All major Dutch political parties had campaigned in favour of the treaty, but polls showed a split in public opinion, with about half the voting population admitting to knowing almost nothing about its content. In the end, the result was explained by a combination of the unpopularity of the Dutch government, a perception that the European project was one generated by elites with too little reference to ordinary Europeans, public resentment that the Netherlands had never before been given the opportunity of a referendum (notably on adoption of the euro), concerns about immigration from Turkey and eastern Europe, concerns that the treaty would mean reduced influence for the Netherlands in Europe, and the negative vote in France. Luxembourg went ahead with a planned referendum in July, at which 56 per cent voted in favour of the treaty, and there were successful legislative votes in Latvia, Cyprus, Malta, Bulgaria and Romania. But in spite of the fact that a total of 17 member states eventually ratified the treaty, the French and Dutch results made the matter moot; the constitution was dead.

The Treaty of Lisbon

Writing in his memoirs in 1978, Jean Monnet had warned that Europe would be 'established through crises and . . . the outcome will be the sum of the outcomes of those crises' (Monnet, 1978, p. 518). The tale of integration can indeed seem

Illustration 7.4
The Treaty of Lisbon

The ceremony for the signature of the Treaty of Lisbon in December 2007. It may be many years before another effort is made to agree a new European treaty.

one of crisis following crisis, and the process has been declared dead or dying more times than can be counted. In this time-honoured tradition, the collapse of the constitutional treaty in 2005 was greeted as yet another blow to Europe, and one that clouded the entire direction being taken by European integration. Britain's *Independent* newspaper (30 May 2005) believed that the result 'could destroy Europe's ambitions to speak with one political voice', Spain's *El Pais* concluded that the EU was now 'a ship without any clearly defined course', and German foreign minister Frank-Walter Steinmeier described it as 'the writing on the wall' for Europe (both quoted in *The Guardian*, Press Review, 1 June 2005). Cafruny and Ryner (2007, pp. 2–3) described the votes as 'a rebuke to Europe's discredited technocratic elite' that signified 'a systemic crisis of European political representation'.

But just as with all earlier cries of 'wolf!', the EU continued to function, even if its institutions were becoming increasingly creaky; it was even able to absorb Bulgaria and Romania when they joined in January 2007 (albeit by sweeping many of the most serious problems under the carpet). After a 'period of reflection', European leaders regrouped to pick up the pieces, and did so in what was widely criticized as a devious manner. The German presidency of the EU declared in January 2007 that a new treaty was needed in order to take care of outstanding organizational needs, and used the occasion of the fiftieth anniversary of the Treaty of Rome in March 2007 to issue the Berlin Declaration, which hinted at the hope that there would be a new agreement in place before the June 2009 European Parliament elections. A draft of what was initially known as the Reform Treaty was duly discussed at an IGC in Lisbon in July 2007, and signed there the following December.

It quickly became clear that the content of what eventually became the **Treaty of Lisbon** was almost exactly the same as that of the constitutional treaty; it was 'different in approach but not in content', noted Valéry Giscard d'Estaing.

● **Treaty of Lisbon**: The most recent change to the EU treaties, signed in 2007 and entering into force in 2009. It makes most of the changes that had been intended by the stillborn constitutional treaty.

It was another amendment to the treaties rather than a reformulation of the treaties as a constitution, to be sure, but beyond that the differences were marginal, and most of the key changes intended by the constitution survived:

- A new president for the European Council, appointed by its members for a two-and-a-half-year term (renewable once) and approved by Parliament.
- A High Representative of the Union for Foreign Affairs and Security Policy, appointed by the European Council to five-year terms, charged with conducting the CFSP, and backed up by a new European External Action Service.
- Abolition of the pillar system introduced by Maastricht, and of the European Community.
- Equal powers for the European Parliament and the Council of Ministers over proposals for almost all EU legislation.
- Recognition of the rights laid out in the Charter of Fundamental Rights, and accession to the European Convention on Human Rights.
- More powers for the EU in the areas of energy policy, public health, climate change, crime and terrorism, commercial policy, humanitarian aid, sport, tourism, research and space.
- A new formula for qualified majority voting in the Council of Ministers from 2014: at least 55 per cent of member states must be in favour representing at least 65 percent of the population of the EU, with at least four states needed for a blocking minority.
- Expansion of the use of qualified majority voting, but the national veto to be retained for foreign and defence policy and taxation.
- A single legal personality for the EU, designed to strengthen its negotiating powers on the international stage.
- Formal recognition, for the first time, of the freedom of a member state to leave the EU.

With the exception of Ireland, all member states argued that Lisbon was an amendment to past treaties and so did not require national referendums, a position that was criticized by Lisbon's opponents as a ploy to push through the constitution by other means and with a different name. In spite of this, it was widely assumed that it would go through with few difficulties, and could come into force by January 2009. However, Ireland was once again required to organize a referendum to change its constitution, and once again played the role of spoiler when – on 12 June 2008 – 53 per cent of Irish voters rejected the treaty (with 53 per cent turnout).

Few Irish voters had taken the time to read the treaty or to understand its critical components, creating a breach into which supporters and opponents stepped with alacrity. Opponents wrongly claimed that Lisbon would mean legalized abortion in Ireland, compromised Irish neutrality, and a change to tax policy. A protocol for Ireland was negotiated and agreed in June 2009, including confirmation of neutrality and guarantees that Lisbon did not provide for the creation of a European army, that the powers of member states on tax issues remained unchanged, that the number of European commissioners would not be reduced as planned, and that Ireland's constitutional provisions for the right to life, family and education would not be impacted. Against this background, a second Irish referendum was held in October 2009, resulting in a 67 per cent majority in favour, with 59 per cent turnout. In spite of the unpopularity of the Irish government, the Yes campaign was helped by fallout from the global economic crisis that had broken in 2007, which made many in Ireland realize that EU membership had alleviated its effects.

Apart from putting an end to the clumsy three-pillar arrangement intro-duced by Maastricht, the most significant institutional change to come out of Lisbon was the creation of two key new positions in the EU hierarchy: a presi-dent of the European Council, and a new foreign minister for the EU. Their creation was seen as an opportunity to give the EU new direction and to make it a more effective player in the international system, the hope among some being that the new president would be someone with a strong international profile and a proven leadership style, rather than one of the lesser political leaders rather

Focus on . . .
The EU and the global economic crisis

In late 2007 a global economic crisis broke whose long-term implications for the international financial system are still not fully understood, but which prompted some deep reflections on the effects of European economic integration. The crisis had its origins in the sub-prime mortgage industry in the United States: seeking new profits, and encouraged by weak financial regulations, banks and financial companies lent to low-income home-buyers, encouraged by growing home prices. These loans could be turned into securities and sold off, earning large profits while also passing on the risk. When the US housing bubble burst in 2007, the value of assets held by banks and financial institutions fell. With few reserves to back them up, many either went bankrupt or turned to the government for help, stock prices plummeted, many people lost their jobs, and shrinking consumer demand led to financial woes for business. Given the interconnectedness of the global trading, financial and investments system, the crisis quickly went global.

Europeans initially blamed the crisis on the United States, pointing to its emphasis on corporate profits and its disdain for regulation, and arguing that the correct response was not government bail-outs but stronger regulation. But critics argued that the EU had weakened itself with excessive debt and too little financial regulation, and EU leaders were divided over how to respond to the crisis; it revealed the rifts between those wanting more regulation and those wanting bail-outs, between euro and non-euro states, and between eastern and western states (the latter generally experiencing more serious problems than the former). While the European economy had been healthy, there had been progress on regional integra-tion, but once the crisis broke EU governments found that they had neither the institutions nor the processes nor the political agreement to respond.

In fact there was significant cooperation among EU leaders, who raised guarantees for individual bank deposits, and did not allow any bank whose failure might pose systemic risks to the EU financial system to fail. The Commission issued guidelines on bank recapi-talization, and announced a stimulus package to which EU leaders quickly agreed. Assistance was also offered to non-euro eastern European states and to any euro-zone state facing a balance of payments crisis. These responses showed how much the structure of European economies had been homogenized by the single market, increased intra-European trade and investment, corporate mergers and acquisitions, and common poli-cies on competition.

unkindly described by *The Economist* as 'Europygmies' (*The Economist*, 'Wake up Europe!', 10–16 October 2009). British foreign secretary David Miliband put it succinctly when he said that the Council needed some who could 'do more than simply run through the agenda', who was guaranteed access to political leaders at the highest level, and who could bring traffic to a halt when they landed in Beijing or Washington or Moscow (quoted in *The Guardian*, 25 October 2009).

Early speculation focused on former British Prime Minister Tony Blair, who had the necessary credentials and reputation but whose candidacy was sullied by his support of the US-led invasion of Iraq in 2003, and by Britain's refusal to adopt the euro or to sign on to the Schengen Agreement. There was also a preference among the leaders of smaller countries for the job to go to one of their own, hence early frontrunners included former Finnish Prime Minister Paavo Lipponen, Dutch Prime Minister Jan Peter Balkenende, and Luxembourg Prime Minister Jean-Claude Juncker. In the event, the Council opted for the little-known Belgian Prime Minister Herman van Rompuy, apparently preferring someone who would not upstage national leaders, who had a reputation as a consensus-builder, and who – like most of those on the Council – was a moderate conservative. The choice was widely derided by many as a missed opportunity and as the triumph of politics over ambition; Europe's leaders, railed *The Economist*, had 'made their union look ridiculous' ('Behold, two mediocre mice', 28 November 2009).

Those leaders also reached into the ranks of the obscure in their choice for the new EU foreign minister, appointing the incumbent trade commissioner from Britain, Catherine Ashton. Never elected to public office, and all but unknown outside her home state, she had been nominated to the Commission in 2008 to replace Peter Mandelson, who returned to national government in Britain. She had no foreign policy experience, but was well regarded by Commission president José Manuel Barroso, was championed by British Prime Minister Gordon Brown, and by coming from the ideological left gave political balance to the two positions. Given the staff and the resources that Ashton would have at her disposal, it was widely thought that her position might end up being the more significant of the two. But little traffic would have to be halted to allow for the foreign visits of either van Rompuy or Ashton.

As if enough stress had not been created by the crisis over the death of the constitutional treaty, followed by the cynical manner in which the Treaty of Lisbon was pushed through, followed by the global economic downturn, a home-grown economic crisis broke in late 2009 when it became clear that Greece had lied about its levels of economic growth and had accumulated a budget deficit far above that set for participants in the euro. The Greek government had to impose unpopular austerity measures, EU leaders bickered over how to respond, there was speculation that economic collapse in Greece could expose weaknesses in other EU states (notably Spain and Portugal), that the euro might be irrevocably harmed, and that even the United States and Japan would feel the effects. The reverberations were still being felt as this book went to press, making it difficult to speculate on the consequences, but once again the cracks in the edifice of European integration had been laid bare, and once again EU leaders were being severely tested by the depth and the strength of their response.

SUMMARY

- Unfinished organizational business from Maastricht was addressed in the treaties of Amsterdam (1999) and Nice (2003), but only limited changes were agreed.
- The new single currency was named the euro in 1995, it was launched as an electronic currency in January 1999, and the final switch was made in 12 EU countries in early 2002 when national currencies were abolished.
- The 2001 terrorist attacks on the United States were condemned by all EU governments, but when the US made plans to attack Iraq on what were widely regarded as spurious grounds, a split emerged among EU leaders; public opinion in the EU, however, was overwhelmingly opposed to the invasion.
- In May 2004, eight eastern European states, together with Cyprus and Malta, joined the EU. They were followed in January 2007 by Bulgaria and Romania. The new round of enlargement confirmed the end of the Cold War, and the EU was now truly European rather than a club of western states.
- The Convention on the Future of Europe in 2002–03 resulted in the drafting of a constitutional treaty for the EU. But its passage required ratification by all EU member states, and when French and Dutch voters rejected the treaty in 2005, plans for the constitution died.
- The constitution was reinvented as the Treaty of Lisbon, which – following a delay after a negative vote in Ireland, followed by a second positive vote – came into force in 2009.
- Following hard on the heels of the global economic downturn that began in 2007, a more localized crisis broke in 2010 in Greece, and the EU was given insight into the consequences of not respecting its own rules. Some spoke of the possible collapse of the euro.
- In spite of the EU's economic and political problems, the line of states hoping to join remained long.

KEY TERMS AND CONCEPTS

Convergence criteria
Enhanced cooperation
European Convention
Lisbon Strategy
Treaty Establishing a Constitution for Europe

Treaty of Amsterdam
Treaty of Lisbon
Treaty of Nice

FURTHER READING

Hix, Simon (2008) , *What's Wrong with the European Union and How to Fix It* (Cambridge: Polity Press). Argues that the EU needs more political competition in order to encourage policy innovation and to address public apathy.

Meunier, Sophie, and Kathleen R. McNamara (eds) (2007), *Making History: European Integration and Institutional Change at Fifty* (Oxford: Oxford University Press). The most recent in a series of periodic reviews of the state of the EU.

Peterson, John, and Mark A. Pollack (eds) (2003), *Europe, America, Bush: Transatlantic Relations in the Twenty-First Century* (London: Routledge); Thomas A. Mowle (2004), *Allies at Odds? The United States and the European Union* (New York: Palgrave Macmillan). Two studies of transatlantic relations written just before Iraq and still interesting for what they have to say.

CHAPTER 8

The Treaties

Almost all democratic bodies – whether states, international organizations, corporations, or some other kind of institution with members and a governing structure – are based on constitutions. These are documents that outline the purposes and rules of the body, and provide it with its legal authority. While the EU has no formal constitution as such, it has agreed a series of treaties – ranging from Paris in 1951 to Lisbon in 2009 – that have played almost the same role: they include declarations about the purposes and powers of the EU, and rules on the functioning of its institutions and on the obligations of its members. The attempt to agree a constitutional treaty in 2002–05 may have failed, but the remaining treaties have provided the necessary order and direction.

But just as many Europeans shy away from the term federalism for what it implies about loss of state sovereignty, so they shy away from the term constitution out of concern that it will confirm and make permanent that loss. It could be argued that the EU cannot establish real permanence until it agrees and governs itself on the basis of a constitution, and the difficulties of agreeing new treaties over the years have sparked regular cries of woe and warning of impending chaos. But the EU has managed regardless, Lisbon achieved most of what the constitutional treaty was designed to achieve, and it has been argued that a kind of constitutional equilibrium has now been achieved in Europe. It is unlikely that public or political opinion could stomach more changes any time soon, meaning that Lisbon may be the last treaty for many years to come.

- What are the differences between the EU treaties and a constitution?
- Are the EU treaties the functional equivalent of a constitution?
- Have changes in the way the treaties have been negotiated and confirmed reflected well or badly on the nature of European democracy?
- Since it is not a full-fledged state, does the EU need a formal constitution, or can it continue to rely on the treaties?
- What are the likely long-term effects on human rights of the EU having its own legal personality?

Understanding the treaties

A **constitution** is a document (or a set of documents) that sets out the general rules by which a state (or almost any formally constituted body) is governed. At its most basic, argues Raz (1998, p. 153), a constitution is 'the law that establishes and regulates the main organs of government ... [and] that establishes the general principles under which [a] country is governed'. In the case of a state constitution, it will usually include the following:

- A listing of the general goals and values of the state (such as democracy, equal rights, and the rule of law).
- An outline of the powers and responsibilities of its governing bodies.
- An outline of the procedures used in electing or appointing government leaders, and of the limits on their powers.
- A listing of the rights of its citizens.
- The steps needed to change or amend the constitution.

Constitutions are the source of legal authority for the work of states, and most are both written and codified (that is, arranged as an organized legal code in a single document; Britain is one of the exceptions to this rule). They are typically supported by a constitutional court whose job is to protect and interpret the constitution, and to issue judgements when questions are asked about whether or not the actions of government fit with the goals and principles of the constitution. The level of detail contained in a constitution varies; some lay out only the core rules and the general aspirations of government, while others (particularly in younger and more politically divided states) go into greater detail. Some reflect the realities of the state they are intended to guide, while others will try to change political behaviour, in a process known as constitutional engineering.

The constitution of the United States is often taken as the benchmark for all others, because it was the first modern document of its kind. It was drawn up in 1787 when delegates from 12 of the 13 states met at a Constitutional Convention in Philadelphia to replace the flawed Articles of Confederation adopted in 1781. In spite of much drama and disagreement, they spent just two months on the task, producing a document that remains the legal foundation of one of the world's most successful democratic societies (and a template for many others). Their task was made easier by the small number of people involved (the 13 states had a population of less than four million), by the homogeneity of the states, and by the concentration of voting power in the hands of a few educated white men. There have since been numerous disputes over the meaning of the details contained in the US constitution, to be sure, and it has had to be clarified and expanded by amendments, new laws, and by the judgements of a federal judicial system topped by the US Supreme Court. Like all human constructs it has its problems and imperfections, but it has, overall, proved stable and durable.

The EU experience has been rather different. To begin with, the EU is not a state, but began life as an international organization whose qualities it has never fully shaken off, and is still very much influenced by the views of Jean Monnet, who avoided the goal of achieving a final constitution in favour of 'integration by stealth' through a step-by-step process. Its population has always been large and diverse, and the national interests of its member states have become more

● **Constitution**: A document, usually codified, that spells out the principles and powers of government, limits on the powers of government, and the rights of citizens.

CONCEPT

Constitutional-ization

The process by which rules and treaties have been agreed that have conferred a constitutional status on the EU without the agreement of a formal constitution. Although the treaties have outlined rules and responsibilities in much the same way as a constitution, they have been legal agreements among member states rather than a finished constitution. The EU has been moving along the road to agreeing a constitution without so far taking that last, critical step.

diverse and complex as it has grown; a population of nearly half a billion people living in a cluster of vibrant democracies is bound to generate a wide range of opinions that elected officials ignore at their peril. And while the US constitution was designed for a group of states that declared themselves to be the United States of America, the EU has always been a club of independent states. The relative tidiness of the American constitutional convention of 1787 stands in contrast to the variety of opinions and interests represented at the European constitutional convention of 2002–03.

European integration began with a **treaty**, and has since proceeded with the agreement of more treaties and side agreements that have added to and amended those that came before. Unlike constitutions, which are typically holistic in the sense that they deal with entire systems of government, treaties are agreements reached among the constituent parts of those systems, meaning – in the case of the EU – the member states. This reliance on treaties has meant in turn that Europeans have had to live with a process of **constitutionalization** by which a constitutional status has been conferred on the treaties that make up the basic legal framework of the EU (Snyder, 2003). This process is described by Haltern (2003) as having taken the EU from being an international organization based on a set of legal agreements binding together sovereign states to a polity with 'a vertically integrated legal regime conferring judicially enforceable rights and obligations on all legal persons and entities' within its sphere.

Put another way, where the typical experience with states has been to intentionally design and agree a (hopefully finished and final) constitution, and then to fine-tune it and help it evolve through amendments and judicial interpretation, the EU has been retroactively and incrementally constitutionalizing its legal order through a process that is formal and informal, explicit and implicit, and that connects each of the steps in the process of constitutional change (Christiansen and Reh, 2009, pp. 4–5). As to whether the EU now has a *de facto* constitution, opinion is divided. EU leaders apparently felt that it did not, which is why they tried to win agreement in 2002–04 on a constitutional treaty. Brunkhorst (2004, p. 89) has 'no doubt' that the EU has a constitution, while Keleman (2006) argues that the treaties are a constitution in all but name. At the very least, the EU has what might be called a material constitution in the sense that the treaties are legally binding, the EU institutions amount to a political community that is separate from the member states, and EU law amounts to a constitutional legal order (Eriksen *et al.*, 2004, pp. 4–5). This order has several key elements, ranging from treaty articles to judgements of the European Court of Justice and the obligations of international law (see Figure 8.1).

One way of coming to grips with the EU experience is to consider the differences between **'thin' and 'thick' constitutions**. Tushnet (2000, pp. 9–17) describes the former as aspirational, mainly philosophical, and focused more on rights than on rules, and the latter as functional and as containing detailed provisions about how government should be organized. Raz (1998, pp. 153–4) describes a thin constitution as one that establishes and regulates the main bodies of government, and the general principles under which a state is governed, while a thick constitution has seven key qualities:

- It outlines the structure and powers of the main institutions of government.

● **Treaty**: An agreement under international law entered into between sovereign states and/or international organizations, committing all parties to shared obligations, with any failure to meet them being considered a breach of the agreement.

● **Thin and thick constitutions**: Constitutions that differ in both their intent and their character, the latter being more detailed, consistent and permanent than the former.

- It is stable, and intended to be durable.
- It is contained in one or a small number of written documents (hence references to *the* constitution).
- It is superior, meaning that it invalidates conflicting ordinary laws.
- It is justiciable, meaning that there are procedures in place by which its superiority can be implemented.
- It is entrenched, meaning that amending the constitution is more difficult than passing ordinary laws.
- It relies on common ideological principles such as democracy and individual rights, which reflect the beliefs of a population about the way in which their society should be governed.

Christiansen and Reh (2009, p. 42) argue that while the EU treaties have many of the same qualities as a constitution (they are written, codified, hold up to Raz's principle of superiority, are binding and justiciable, constitute a supranational political order with a single institutional framework, and are concluded for an unlimited duration) they are also missing many critical constitutional functions. For example, their supremacy is not accepted unconditionally, the EU institutions lack the power to make decisions on the definition of their tasks and authority, and the treaties have always been unstable: rather than there being a single codified document that can be amended, amendments are made with every new treaty. The treaties also lack the necessary levels of public knowledge and acceptance. The result is that just as the EU itself is described as more than an international organization but less than a European superstate, or more than a regime but less than a federation, so what we have here is more than a treaty

Figure 8.1 Sources of constitutional norms in the EU

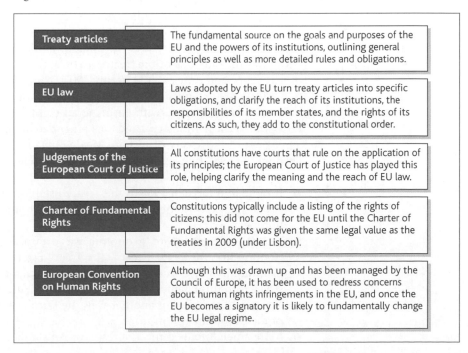

Illustration 8.1
The constitutional treaty

EU heads of government and their foreign ministers gather in Rome in November 2004 to sign the new constitutional treaty. Comparisons with the American constitutional convention nearly 220 years earlier ended abruptly when the treaty was rejected by French and Dutch voters.

but less than a constitution. In short, the treaties are neither thin nor thick, but somewhere in between.

Coming to grips with the treaties can be confusing, even for experts. It does not help that most have had both formal and informal names: hence the Merger treaty of 1965 is formally the Treaty of Brussels, and the Maastricht treaty of 1992 is formally the Treaty on European Union. More troublesome by far is the curious use of the plural. Although there have been eight major treaties dating back to the 1951 Treaty of Paris, they do not continue to exist today as a set of eight. The 1951 Treaty of Paris was an anomaly, because it was never amended, and it was the only one of the treaties to be agreed with a time limit: it had a life of fifty years, and duly expired in July 2002. The 1957 Euratom treaty continues to exist today (it resulted in the creation in 1960 of the Euratom Supply Agency in Luxembourg, charged with ensuring an equitable supply of materials to the European nuclear industry), and was amended significantly in 2007 following agreement of the Treaty of Lisbon. Meanwhile, the focus of treaty-building has been on the 1957 EEC treaty, which has undergone several changes of identity:

- It came into force in 1958 as the Treaty Establishing the European Economic Community (TEEC), and was later amended by the Single European Act.
- In 1992, when the word 'Economic' was dropped from 'European Economic Community', the TEEC became the Treaty Establishing the European Community (TEC) and was subsumed (through the three-pillar system – see later in this chapter) under the Treaty on European Union (TEU, or the Maastricht treaty). Put another way, the European Community became part of the European Union.
- More amendments came as a result of Amsterdam and Nice.

- The formal name of the Treaty of Lisbon was 'The Treaty of Lisbon amending the Treaty on European Union and the Treaty Establishing the European Community'. One of its effects was to finally abolish the European Community, so the TEC became the Treaty on the Functioning of the European Union (TFEU), and the current source of legal authority in the EU is the consolidated version of the TEU and the TFEU. (In reading the treaties, a careful distinction must be made between each individual treaty – indicated from the SEA onwards by tell-tale phrases such as 'Article I will be amended as follows' – and the single consolidated treaty, of which there is only ever one, incorporating all the amendments agreed to that point.)

As if all this is not confusing enough, more potential confusion is added by the distinction between the Big Eight major treaties – Paris, the two Rome treaties, the Single European Act, Maastricht, Amsterdam, Nice, and Lisbon – and a cluster of mini-treaties and side agreements that have had constitutional implications in the sense that they have changed the rules of the game (see Figure 8.2). There have, for example, been several housekeeping treaties focused on making the Community or EU decision-making process more efficient, and there have been several agreements outside the treaties that were eventually integrated into the treaties (the Schengen Agreement on internal borders being a prime example). Added to this, every time a new member state has joined the EU there has been a new agreement signed that has changed, albeit marginally, some of the details of how the EU has functioned (see later in this chapter). Under the circumstances, it is hardly surprising that so many Europeans find the structure and powers of the EU difficult to understand.

The treaty-building epic

The process by which Europeans have planned, discussed and adopted their guiding treaties has gone through two distinct phases. In brief, Phase I lasted from 1951 to 1987, from Paris to the Single European Act, and was characterized by debates behind closed doors involving technocrats and government representatives, attracting little public interest or attention and the resulting treaties being relatively quickly approved. Phase II lasted from 1992 to 2009, from Maastricht to Lisbon, and was characterized by far more substantial changes to the direction of European integration, far more public and political interest, and treaties being put to both legislative and public votes.

Phase I included not just the treaties of Paris and Rome but also three housekeeping agreements that drew little public attention. The first of these was the 1965 Treaty of Brussels (the Merger treaty), which tidied up the structure of the three Communities by combining the separate Councils of Ministers and Commissions/High Authority of the three Communities into a single Council of Ministers and European Commission. Then in 1970 came an agreement to change the source of funds for the Community budget from contributions by member states to 'own resources' such as customs duties and agricultural levies (and also creating a single budget for the three Communities). This was followed in 1975 by an agreement to give Parliament the power to reject the Community budget.

The lack of more ambitious goals and the absence of greater political rancour during Phase I can be ascribed to five main causes:

Figure 8.2 A summary of the treaties

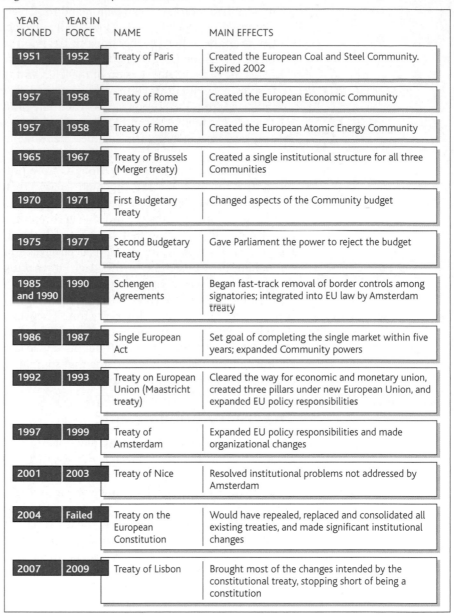

YEAR SIGNED	YEAR IN FORCE	NAME	MAIN EFFECTS
1951	1952	Treaty of Paris	Created the European Coal and Steel Community. Expired 2002
1957	1958	Treaty of Rome	Created the European Economic Community
1957	1958	Treaty of Rome	Created the European Atomic Energy Community
1965	1967	Treaty of Brussels (Merger treaty)	Created a single institutional structure for all three Communities
1970	1971	First Budgetary Treaty	Changed aspects of the Community budget
1975	1977	Second Budgetary Treaty	Gave Parliament the power to reject the budget
1985 and 1990	1990	Schengen Agreements	Began fast-track removal of border controls among signatories; integrated into EU law by Amsterdam treaty
1986	1987	Single European Act	Set goal of completing the single market within five years; expanded Community powers
1992	1993	Treaty on European Union (Maastricht treaty)	Cleared the way for economic and monetary union, created three pillars under new European Union, and expanded EU policy responsibilities
1997	1999	Treaty of Amsterdam	Expanded EU policy responsibilities and made organizational changes
2001	2003	Treaty of Nice	Resolved institutional problems not addressed by Amsterdam
2004	Failed	Treaty on the European Constitution	Would have repealed, replaced and consolidated all existing treaties, and made significant institutional changes
2007	2009	Treaty of Lisbon	Brought most of the changes intended by the constitutional treaty, stopping short of being a constitution

- The member states were too focused on implementing the terms of the first three treaties to consider a major expansion of objectives, and had learned the dangers of being too ambitious from the failures of the European defence and political communities.
- There were only six member states, and their governments were mainly agreed on the goals and purposes of integration. The states also had similar political and economic personalities, in contrast to the greater variety of political, economic and social features and opinions that came with the later and bigger EU.

- There was an absence of the kind of political leadership and initiative that would spark more ambitious amendments to the treaties in the 1980s and 1990s.
- The early years of the EC were ones of economic growth and relative political harmony (Dinan 2005, pp. 47–8), and it would not be until much later that concerns about Europe's declining place in the world would become more clear, helping prompt new treaty initiatives.
- Several later treaties were drawn up to account for enlargement, a process that would not begin to significantly alter the character of the EU until the 1990s.

Compared to what would follow, even the SEA went through a relatively easy approval process, the only serious misgivings being (as we saw) in Denmark and Ireland. The Danish situation was resolved by the February 1986 referendum, but in Ireland there was a more complex problem: an historian named Raymond Crotty – concerned about the implications of the foreign policy provisions of the SEA for Irish neutrality – took legal action against the Irish government, which led to an Irish Supreme Court decision that the state did not have the authority to ratify the SEA because it would mean a reduction of government control over foreign policy. As a result, a public referendum had to be held in May 1987 on an amendment to the constitution allowing the government of Ireland to ratify the SEA. Nearly 70 per cent voted in favour, clearing the way for the SEA to come into force in July 1987.

Phase II was an animal of a very different stripe. It began with the controversies over the 1992 Treaty on European Union, which marked the beginning of nearly two decades of intensive treaty-drafting, accompanied by often strident political and public debate. This was a result partly of the growing stakes in each new treaty, and partly of the better organization of movements of supporters and opponents of integration. The meetings organized to draft and amend the treaties in this phase were often long and contentious, political agreement was sometimes reached only as a result of bad-tempered eleventh hour compromises, treaties were occasionally voted down or only narrowly approved in national referendums, and cynics greeted each successive failure as a crisis, calling into question the very nature and future of European integration.

The content of Maastricht was impacted by concerns (mainly from Britain) about the growth of Community powers, resulting in a peculiar compromise in which **three pillars** were created (see Figure 8.3). This allowed the supranational qualities of the European Community to be preserved while making provision for intergovernmental decision making on matters related to foreign and secu-

Figure 8.3 The three pillars

● **Three pillars**: A compromise reached in the Maastricht treaty by which intergovernmental decision making for foreign and security policy and for justice and home affairs was preserved by making them legally separate from the European Community.

THE EUROPEAN UNION		
Supranational Existing procedures and powers of the European Communities. Covered economic, agricultural, environmental, social, and immigration policy	**Intergovernmental** Cooperation on foreign and security policy	**Intergovernmental** Cooperation in the field of justice and home affairs (including issues such as customs, immigration, asylum, and cross-border crime)

Focus on . . .
Intergovernmental conferences

The meetings at which leaders of the member states sign new treaties attract considerable media attention, but they are only the final and usually brief step in a process that may have lasted as long as several years and have involved intensive negotiations among national government ministers and permanent representatives of the member states. These representatives meet at intergovernmental conferences (IGCs) which take place outside the decision-making framework of the EU, and may last days, weeks, or even months. (For a detailed analysis of the dynamics of the IGCs, see Christiansen and Reh, 2009, Chapters 6–8). Their use emphasizes the extent to which decision making on the major initiatives of the EU still rests with the member states.

Depending on how they are defined, there have been as many as a dozen IGCs since 1950:

- The first (1950–51), chaired by Jean Monnet, discussed plans for the European Coal and Steel Community and resulted in the Treaty of Paris.

- The second (1955–56) resulted in the two Treaties of Rome.
- Several more in the 1960s and 1970s dealt with more limited issues: a one-day IGC in April 1965 led to the Merger treaty, another in 1970 discussed budgetary issues, and another in 1975 discussed the terms of the European Investment Bank (Pijpers, 1998, p. 294).
- The third major IGC (1985–86) developed the framework for the Single European Act.
- Two more IGCs (1991) separately discussed political and monetary union, resulting in the signature in 1992 of the Treaty on European Union.
- IGCs in 1996, 1997 and 2000 focused on institutional reform and preparations for eastward enlargement, drafting the treaties of Amsterdam and Nice.
- Undoubtedly the grandest of all IGCs was the Convention on the Future of Europe, which met in 2002–03 to draft the constitutional treaty.
- A 2007 IGC drafted the Treaty of Lisbon, which was signed in December 2007.

rity policy, and to justice and home affairs. The whole edifice was to support a new European Union; although the European Community still existed in law, and all European law was technically Community law rather than EU law, it now became more usual to use the label European Union. (The pillars were thankfully abolished under the terms of Lisbon.)

As we saw in Chapter 6, adoption of Maastricht was slowed down by the negative vote in June 1992 in Denmark, by a barely affirmative vote in France, by doubts in Ireland, and by negotiations leading to the second (and affirmative) vote in Denmark in May 1993. There were two major reasons for Maastricht's problems. First, the political environment in which it was launched was not a good one, with a slowdown in economic growth, rising unemployment, and emerging security problems in the Balkans. Second, the treaty itself was dense and complex, meaning that few Europeans read or understood it, giving opponents more leeway to manipulate public opinion by making the case that it involved the surrender of too much national sovereignty.

While Maastricht eventually went through, the Danish No vote and the French *petit oui* changed the political environment in which future treaties would be reviewed. Before Maastricht there had been an atmosphere of **'permissive consensus'** in which political leaders had been able to exploit the

● **Intergovernmental conferences**: Conferences convened among representatives of the governments of the EU member states to discuss and agree amendments to the treaties.

(see Chapter 16)

lack of public interest in European integration to move ahead at their own pace, and to assume that national votes were not needed (see discussion in Carubba, 2001). But after Maastricht all new treaties were subjected to much closer public scrutiny and generated more intense political debates. More national governments felt obliged to hold referendums (see Chapter 16), the arguments of pro- and anti-Europeans became louder, and a renegotiation of the terms of the treaties – or, at least, the provision of opt-outs or assurances for states where votes went against a treaty – became more usual.

The Treaty of Amsterdam dealt with relatively non-controversial issues, so it was quickly ratified by all the member states, even passing national referendums in Denmark and Ireland. The Treaty of Nice should also have been adopted fairly easily, but as we saw in Chapter 7 it was unexpectedly turned down in a June 2001 Irish referendum (then later accepted). As we also saw in Chapter 7, the next step was the ambitious but ultimately failed attempt by European leaders in 2002–03 to end the process of constantly updating the treaties, and to agree a constitution (actually, a constitutional treaty) for the EU. In the public debates over the draft it became clear that bigger states were more comfortable than smaller states, which were concerned that their voices would not be heard. But for Moravcsik (2007, p. 23, 24) the treaty (like Amsterdam and Nice before it) was less than it was made out to be by critics. It was, in his view, 'a conservative document that consolidated rather than transcended the constitutional status quo' and that 'reaffirmed rather than fundamentally reformed the existing scope of European integration'. In the midst of the confusion, some states opted to put the issue to a national referendum (in some cases because they were required to by national law), while others opted – often controversially – for ratification in a legislative vote. In the event, the treaty was terminated by negative votes in the summer of 2005 in France and the Netherlands.

Once again undeterred, and after taking a break of about 18 months, EU leaders revisited the questions and problems left unanswered by the failure of the constitutional treaty, and 2007 saw the draft of what was to become the Treaty of

CONCEPT

Permissive consensus

This refers to the idea that political elites could pursue their own plans for European integration, given the widespread lack of public interest in what they were doing. How far this has been a problem depends on whether we think of the EU as an international organization or as a proto-state, on how confident we are about the extent to which elected leaders take account of public opinion, and how much faith we have in the European public to make informed decisions about the process of integration (see discussion in Chapter 17 about the knowledge deficit).

**Illustration 8.2
The Treaty of Amsterdam**

The signature of the Treaty of Amsterdam in October 1997 represents – in hindsight – the calm before the storms that were to confirm the end of the permissive consensus in European treaty-making.

Lisbon. Following another No vote in Ireland, followed by a Yes vote, Lisbon came into force in December 2009. After nearly twenty years of often heated constitutional activity (running from the start of the 1991 IGC that led to the Maastricht treaty to the second Irish vote on Lisbon in 2009), it seemed unlikely that European leaders or publics would any time soon want to consider another new treaty, for three main reasons:

- Almost all the changes planned by the stillborn constitution were put in place by Lisbon, so there was no longer a pressing need to change the treaties to keep up with the needs of the growing membership of the EU.
- The political challenges of drafting and agreeing new treaties had become increasingly difficult to address the criticism directed at the ways in which national leaders work their way around the democratic process has done the EU no good, each new controversy has served to undermine the credibility of the European project, and few Europeans could likely stomach the idea of more national referendums and the risk of more division and rejection.
- Europeans needed time to recover from their 'reform fatigue'.

It has also been argued that a political and constitutional plateau has been reached. For Moravcsik (2007, pp. 23, 24, 47), the process of integration has achieved 'a stable constitutional equilibrium' that is 'likely to endure, with incremental changes, for the foreseeable future', and while the EU may enlarge, may continue to reform, and may deepen its reach, the time has come to acknowledge a 'European constitutional settlement'. It is no longer necessary, he argues, for the EU to move forward to consolidate its achievements: 'When a constitutional system no longer needs to expand and deepen in order to assure its own continued existence, it is truly stable. It is a mark of constitutional maturity'. Duff (2008, p. 13) makes similar arguments, suggesting that while some additional rationalization and simplification may be needed, the system achieved by Lisbon should be 'strong and durable', and it is unlikely that there will be any more treaties.

**Illustration 8.3
Ireland rejects Lisbon**

Members of an Irish anti-Lisbon treaty group celebrate the result of the June 2008 national referendum in which a majority of voters rejected the new treaty. The result would be reversed in a second vote 16 months later.

Debating . . .
Does the EU need a constitution?

YES	NO
Understanding how the EU works is difficult enough without additional complications being created by the absence of a succinct (ideally) set of rules and guiding principles to which Europeans can refer for clarification, and by the political stresses and confusion surrounding the writing and adopting of new treaties.	It already has one in the form of the treaties, and the passage of the Treaty of Lisbon provided all the remaining changes needed to allow the EU to work efficiently. As Moravcsik puts it, the EU now has a stable constitutional settlement.
The lack of a constitution undermines the legitimacy of the EU by raising questions about the significance and openness of the process by which decisions are taken at the EU level.	The British case – where there is no single, codified constitution, but a large body of laws, commentaries, and traditions – shows that it is possible for a political entity to function well without a finished constitution.
The lack of a constitution makes it harder for governments and courts to settle questions over the jurisdiction and authority of the EU, particularly if its reach is constantly changing.	The debates over the writing and adoption of new treaties have been increasingly harmful to the process of integration, because they have been dominated by supporters and detractors who manipulate the argument to their own ends, and because experience has shown that votes in national referendums are often driven less by opinions about the new treaties than about the standing of the national governments in referendum states. This problem will only be exacerbated by another debate over a constitution.
Developing new treaties to keep up with the changing needs and personality of the EU is a more complex and time-consuming process than amending a constitution.	
The individual EU member states can no longer be relied on to deal with the pressures of globalization, and a constitution offers the best means of protecting Europe's distinctive features in the face of globalization (Habermas, 2004).	The efforts of the member states and national leaders should be focused on making the existing system work more efficiently, and EU citizens need to time to learn more about how that system works.

And yet calls were already being made in late 2010 by Angela Merkel of Germany and Nikolas Sarkozy of France for an amendment to Lisbon designed to tighten the rules on national debt. Arguing that unsustainable debts posed a major threat to the stability of the euro, they proposed changes that would allow sanctions to be brought against EU member states exceeding the debt ceiling of 60 per cent of GDP set under the stability and growth pact designed to sustain the euro (see Chapter 20). The sanctions would be tightened progressively in the light of failure to act, with the possibility of a recalcitrant eurozone state even losing its voting rights on monetary matters. The proposal met with a mixed response, but what it also helped emphasize was the absence in the treaties of a key mechanism associated with constitutions: the ability to propose and vote upon amendments without having to make wholesale changes.

Other elements of the EU legal order

Discussions about the EU treaties usually focus on the Big Eight (from Paris to Lisbon), and all the similar major agreements reached by the EU member states that might be seen as part of the process of building an EU constitution. Often overlooked have been other treaties and agreements that have had more limited effects, but that have nonetheless resulted in changes to the EU legal order. Among these are the **accession agreements** that are signed each time a new member state joins the EU. The first nine of these were Acts of Accession, signed between the Community and each of the nine states that joined between 1972 and 1994. With eastern enlargement, the EU opted for joint treaties of accession; the first was signed in 2003 with the ten states that joined in 2004, and the second was signed in 2005 with Bulgaria and Romania. As well as outlining the obligations of membership, these joint treaties – unlike the Acts of Accession – had the effect of modifying the EU treaties (for example, changing the number of votes involved in qualified majority voting, and the number of seats in the European Parliament), and had to be ratified in legislative votes by all existing member states before they came into force.

Other European agreements have been more substantial in that they have impacted policy developments in multiple states. Two in particular are noteworthy:

- The Schengen Agreements, signed in 1985 and 1990, allowed a sub-group of Community states to work independently to accelerate the process of bringing down barriers among the member states. Originally signed by France, West Germany and the Benelux countries, Schengen has since expanded to include all EU member states except Britain and Ireland, along with non-EU members Iceland, Norway, and Switzerland. The agreements were made part of the EU legal structure by the Treaty of Amsterdam, although there is no obligation on EU member states to join. A lesser-known treaty, the Prüm Convention (sometimes known as Schengen III), was signed in Germany in May 2005 with the goal of improving cross-border cooperation in the fight against terrorism, cross-border crime, and illegal migration.
- The Social Charter, signed in 1989 with the goal of creating uniform rights for workers throughout the Community. The Conservative government of Britain refused to sign, and blocked later attempts to integrate the Charter into the Maastricht treaty. When the new Labour government of Tony Blair agreed to accept the terms of the Charter in 1997, it was incorporated into the legal framework of the EU by the Treaty of Amsterdam (see Chapter 22).

But arguably most fundamental of all in terms of legal and constitutional implications are two agreements dealing with human rights. As the reach of integration expanded, so the need for an elaboration of these rights became more acute, producing one agreement reached within the framework of the EU, and a second within the framework of the Council of Europe, and each of which is routinely confused with the other.

The first is the **Charter of Fundamental Rights** of the European Union, which was drawn up at the suggestion of the European Council, adopted in 2000, integrated into the treaties by the Treaty of Nice, and came into force with the Treaty of Lisbon. But in spite of concerns about what the Charter might mean in legal terms (concerns that encouraged Britain, Poland and the Czech

● **Accession agreement**: A membership agreement signed between a new member state and the Community or the EU.

● **Charter of Fundamental Rights**: A document adopted in 2000 that collected together statements on human rights outlined in other EU agreements.

DOCUMENT 8.1

Charter of Fundamental Rights of the European Union, Preamble

The peoples of Europe, in creating an ever closer union among them, are resolved to share a peaceful future based on common values.

Conscious of its spiritual and moral heritage, the Union is founded on the indivisible, universal values of human dignity, freedom, equality and solidarity; it is based on the principles of democracy and the rule of law. It places the individual at the heart of its activities, by establishing the citizenship of the Union and by creating an area of freedom, security and justice.

The Union contributes to the preservation and to the development of these common values while respecting the diversity of the cultures and traditions of the peoples of Europe as well as the national identities of the Member States and the organization of their public authorities at national, regional and local levels; it seeks to promote balanced and sustainable development and ensures free movement of persons, services, goods and capital, and the freedom of establishment.

To this end, it is necessary to strengthen the protection of fundamental rights in the light of changes in society, social progress and scientific and technological developments by making those rights more visible in a Charter . . .

Enjoyment of these rights entails responsibilities and duties with regard to other persons, to the human community and to future generations.

Source: European Parliament web site at http://www.europarl.europa.eu/charter/default_en.htm (retrieved July 2010).

Republic to negotiate opt-outs), it was actually no more than a gathering of existing rights already recognized by EU member states into a single document. These include the right to life (confirming the abolition of the death penalty throughout the EU); the right to physical and mental integrity; protection against torture and slavery; respect for private and family life; protection of personal data; freedom of thought and religion; freedom of expression and association; the right to marriage, education, work, property, asylum, equality, health care, social security, free movement and residence; respect for cultural diversity, the right to a fair trial, rights for children, the elderly, the disabled, and workers; and expectations about environmental and consumer protection.

The second document with legal implications for the EU is the **European Convention on Human Rights** (ECHR), drawn up in 1950 by the Council of Europe, and which entered into force in September 1953. Although it directly applies only to members of the Council of Europe, this includes all member states of the EU, and any citizen of the EU who feels that their rights have been limited by EU law can use the Strasbourg-based European Court of Human Rights (see Chapter 13) for redress. Signature of the Convention is a requirement of membership of the Council of Europe, which in 2010 had 47 members: every European state except Belarus and Kosovo, along with Andorra, Lichtenstein, Monaco, San Marino, and Russia. The Convention covers much of the same ground as the Charter of Fundamental Rights, but focuses on civil and political rights, while the Charter ranges across social, economic, cultural and citizenship rights (Greer, 2006, p. 50).

● **European Convention on Human Rights**: An agreement drawn up by the Council of Europe in 1950 that provides the right of petition for citizens, and that has taken on a new life and legal significance since the late 1990s.

For most of its early life, the ECHR had little effect on European integration, the prevailing view in the EEC being that while human rights were important, they were not integral to the project of integration, and anyway they were covered by the Convention. But then the EU began to require respect for human rights as a condition for the entry of new members, issues relating to justice and home affairs moved up the EU agenda, and more effective monitoring of human rights matters were seen as part of the solution to the post-Maastricht backlash against integration (Greer, 2006, pp. 48–9). The first step in bringing human rights more into the mainstream of integration was taken with agreement of the Charter of Fundamental Rights, but while this was a statement of rights it did not provide Europeans with the power to petition the European Court of Justice. It was only when the European Court of Human Rights became a permanent institution in 1998 that the right of petition to the Court became more widely known, changing the nature of the European legal regime.

Interestingly, because Lisbon created a legal personality for the EU, as distinct from each of the member states, it is now in a position to be able to ratify agreements such as the ECHR, with profound potential legal implications for the character of the EU. More issues dealing with rights within the EU are being sent for a hearing before the European Court of Human Rights, thereby increasing the pressure for a rethinking of the relationship between the Charter and the Convention. Meanwhile, negotiations were expected to start in 2010 on the EU becoming a signatory to the Convention. Greer (2006) argues that while the Convention was originally an expression of the identity of western European liberal democracy, emphasizing its contrasts with eastern European communism, the end of the Cold War division of Europe meant that the ECHR evolved into something more like an 'abstract constitutional model' for the whole of Europe, possibly leading to convergence in the operation of public institutions at every level.

SUMMARY

- The EU does not have a constitution as such, but it has a body of treaties that have almost the same role, in the sense that they outline the rules by which the EU functions.
- The process of integration was guided initially by treaties agreed between sovereign states, but through a process of constitutionalization those treaties have since taken on most of the features of a constitution.
- There have been two phases in the development of the treaties: the first lasted until 1986 and was mainly intergovernmental with little public input or interest (influenced by an atmosphere of 'permissive consensus'), while the second has been more open and affected by public debate.
- The process of treaty-drafting has mainly taken place in intergovernmental conferences, the meetings of which have been subject to more public and political pressure since the early 1990s.
- Lisbon may be the last major amendment to the rules of the EU for some time to come, given that most of the rules needed to allow it to function efficiently are now in place, and that 'reform fatigue' has settled in. It has also been argued that a plateau has been reached and that there is a 'constitutional settlement' that obviates the need for additional treaties.
- The major treaties are the foundations of the European legal order, but there have also been other agreements that have contributed to that order: these include accession agreements, agreements among subgroups of member states (such as Schengen and the Social Charter), the Charter of Fundamental Rights of the European Union, and the European Convention on Human Rights.

KEY TERMS AND CONCEPTS

Accession agreement
Charter of Fundamental Rights
Constitution
Constitutionalization
European Convention on Human Rights
Intergovernmental conferences
Permissive consensus
Thin and thick constitutions
Three pillars
Treaty

FURTHER READING

Christiansen, Thomas, and Christine Reh (2009), *Constitutionalizing the European Union* (Basingstoke: Palgrave Macmillan). An assessment of the story of constitution-building in the EU, looking at the mechanics of intergovernmental conferences, the actors involved, and the issues at stake.

Greer, Steven (2006), *The European Convention on Human Rights: Achievements, Problems and Prospects* (Cambridge: Cambridge University Press). A compelling review of the achievements and possible long-term effects on European integration of the European Convention on Human Rights.

Piris, Jean-Claude (2006), *The Constitution for Europe: A Legal Analysis* (Cambridge: Cambridge University Press). An assessment of the background to — and the potential legal, institutional and practical consequences of — the proposed European constitution.

CHAPTER 9

The Member States

Debates about the nature of the relationship between the EU institutions and the member states have heated up as the reach of the EU has expanded, and as more Europeans have come to feel its influence. Within their home states, they know approximately what to expect from the relationship between the whole and the parts, but there is much less understanding about the political status of the member states within the EU. As we saw in Chapter 2, the EU has some qualities that are federal, others that are confederal, and yet others that fit none of the mainstream explanations of how power is shared, divided, or expressed. And even if we could agree on how to characterize the EU, it is – like all systems of government or governance – in a constant state of evolution.

The European Coal and Steel Community was a small institution with limited powers in just two fields of policy. The agenda of the European Economic Community expanded to include the single market, as well as agricultural, transport, and trade policy. Since then, there has been almost no field of national public policy on which the EU has not had some impact, whether direct or indirect, obvious or subtle, deliberate or accidental. And yet the jury is still out on the relative balance of powers and authority in most fields of policy; the EU dominates the making of economic, agricultural and environmental policy, and the member states still have a high degree of control over tax policy, policing, education, and criminal justice, but in most areas of policy there is a wide overlap of powers. Future enlargement of the EU will continue to change the relative roles of the EU and the member states.

- How can we measure the relative levels of policy independence of the member states?
- In which areas of policy does it clearly make the most sense for EU member states to act together, and in which is it better to leave responsibility with individual states?
- Is Europeanization a useful conceptual term?
- What do the four measures used in this chapter (length of membership, economic size, population size, and attitudes towards integration) tell us about the relative powers and influence of different member states?
- Should the EU focus on widening or deepening?

CONCEPT

Competence

A term used to indicate responsibility or authority in an area of public policy. Lisbon (Article 2) points out that exclusive competence in a policy area means that only the EU can legislate or adopt legally binding acts related to that area, and that the member states can only do this themselves if specifically empowered by the EU or in the interests of implementing an act of the EU. The EU has exclusive competence only in five policy areas (competition, customs, fisheries conservation, trade and – within the eurozone – monetary policy), meaning that levels of competence in all other policy areas (except those where the member states have retained their authority) are debatable.

● **Secession**: The act of withdrawing from membership of an association, usually taken to mean some kind of political organization or union.

● **Subsidiarity**: The principle that the EU should limit itself in policy terms to undertaking tasks better dealt with jointly than at the level of the member state.

The place of the member states

The member states of the EU have a peculiar position in international law. On the one hand, they are sovereign actors in the international system, with territory, sovereignty, independence and legitimacy. On the other hand, they have surrendered, pooled or transferred authority to the extent that it is no longer accurate or practical to think of them as independent actors. They are still free to take unilateral action on many issues, and they still have separate votes in the European Council and the Council of Ministers, but in multiple areas of law and policy they are subject to the common rules of the EU. At the same time, though (as we saw in Chapter 2), they have not yet built the kind of legal and political ties that make them members of a European superstate.

In many ways, the European Union still reflects its modest origins in the European Coal and Steel Community: it consists of member states that were each accepted as partners in the club, and which are expected to adhere to its rules as long as they stay. And yet they are free to leave the club any time they wish. If citizens of a region within a state decided to leave and form their own state, their action would be regarded as **secession** and would likely spark legal battles, political resistance, and even perhaps violence of the kind that accompanied the break-up of Yugoslavia in the 1990s. (For a discussion of the implications of secession, see Buchanan, 1991.) But while a decision by a member state to leave the EU would be disappointing to some and welcomed by others, there would be no need for a legal declaration of independence (see Focus on Prospects of the EU losing members).

It is important to be clear about the meaning of the term 'member state'. Bulmer and Lequesne (2005, p. 2) argue that it should not just be thought of as a synonym for the national governments of the member states, but instead as shorthand for all the political actors and institutions within a member state. The nature of the relationship between the member states and the EU institutions is complex and constantly evolving, leaving the precise political role of the member states open to debate, and varying from one policy area to another. The formal division of powers is summarized by four principles contained in the treaties (specifically Article 5):

● **Competence**. This is another term for *authority*, and is used to describe the areas of policy for which the EU is responsible. Hence, for example, it has a high level of competence in the fields of competition and trade, but much less over education and taxation.
● Conferral. This principle holds that the EU can act only where it has been given authority by the member states to achieve objectives set out in the treaties, and that any areas of competence not specifically listed in the treaties default to the member states. (It mirrors the 10th amendment to the US constitution, which declares that powers not delegated to the federal government by the constitution, nor prohibited by it to the states, are reserved to the states or to the people.)
● **Subsidiarity**. By this principle, the EU can only act in areas that do not fall under its exclusive competence if the action needed cannot be better taken by the member states. In other words, the EU should only do what it does best.

- Proportionality. This principle establishes that the EU should not go beyond taking the action needed to achieve the objectives of the treaties. But just where that line is drawn, of course, is a matter for debate.

The challenge of deciding how powers are divided in practice in the EU is heightened by the constantly changing rules of the game: the role of the member states has declined as the competence of the EU institutions has grown, but their powers vary from one set of policies to another. At first, member states gave up only the powers agreed under the terms of the Treaty of Paris, but even in this limited area there was the promise of change to come: the ECSC was allowed to

Focus on . . .
Prospects of the EU losing members

Rarely seriously discussed (but always a theoretical possibility) is the prospect of a member state of the EU leaving the union. This has already happened in the case of a territory, when Greenland in February 1985 became the first and so far only community to leave the EEC. As a colony of Denmark, it had become part of the EEC in January 1973, in spite of its 32,000 residents voting against membership out of concern over loss of control of fishing rights. In May 1979 it was granted self-government by Denmark, clearing the way for a 1982 vote to leave the Community. But no member state of the EU has yet followed the same path (although there was more than passing discussion in 2010 about the possibility of states being expelled from the eurozone).

Article 50 of the Lisbon treaty says that 'any Member State may decide to withdraw from the Union in accordance with its own constitutional requirements', and that all it has to do is notify the European Council, which would then direct the negotiations leading to an agreement 'setting out the arrangements for its withdrawal, taking account of the framework for its future relationship with the Union'. If the state later changed its mind and decided to apply for re-entry, it would have to go through the same steps as a new applicant (see later in this chapter).

Since the EU is not a state, withdrawal of a member would not have the same legal significance or implications as – for example – when Montenegro and Kosovo declared their independence from Serbia in 2006 and 2008. Nor would there be the same violent response as accompanied the secession of Katanga from the Congo in 1960, of Biafra from Nigeria in 1967, or the formation of Eritrea and Timor Leste in 1993 and 2002. Nor would it have the same effect as the secessionist movements in Canada, India, Russia, Spain, and Sri Lanka, all of which have been vigorously resisted, sometimes with violence.

Several EU member states have political parties and movements that campaign for an exit from the EU. In few has the issue been more widely discussed than in Britain, which in 1975 became the first and so far only EEC/EU member state to put membership to a national referendum (see Chapter 16). But while polls reveal that enthusiasm for the EU is lower in Britain than in almost any other member state, they also reveal that the British know less about the EU than the citizens of almost any other EU member state (see Chapter 17). This raises questions about the quality of British public opinion, and makes it difficult to be sure how much the hostility held by many Britons towards the EU is based on a real understanding of the issues. The UK Independence Party was formed in 1993 to campaign for British withdrawal from the EU, but while it won 13 seats in the European Parliament in 2009 it has not fared well in British general elections.

**Illustration 9.1
Conserving North Sea
fisheries**

Fisheries conservation is
one of the few policy areas
in which the EU has
exclusive competence. Here
coastguards and fisheries
inspectors prepare to
control fishing vessels in the
North Sea.

ensure the rational use of coal resources (a precursor to environmental policy),
to promote improved working conditions (a precursor to social policy), and to
promote international trade (a precursor to trade and foreign policy). The EU
institutions have since been given competence over a broadening set of policy
issues, or have accumulated more powers through the pressures of spillover, the
authority of the member states declining along the way. But there has always
been much ambiguity built into the system, the result being that authority in
most areas is divided. Three sets of clues offer us some guidance.

First, we can look at the Treaty of Lisbon, but while Articles 3–6 of the Treaty
on the Functioning of the EU provide what looks like a comprehensive listing of
EU areas of competence (see Figure 9.1), the list is not always as clear as it seems.
Missing, for example, are external relations and immigration. Environmental
policy may be listed as a shared responsibility, but in practice it is now almost
entirely made at the EU level. And while human health is listed as a shared
responsibility, health care is almost entirely a responsibility of the member
states. Even in policy areas where competence is shared, it is not always clear how
far it is shared; in some areas the EU has authority only to support or supplement the work of the member states.

A second set of clues is offered by the existence of policies that are prefaced
with the word 'Common', such as the Common Agricultural Policy (CAP), the
Common Commercial Policy (CCP), the Common Fisheries Policy, the
Common Foreign and Security Policy, and the Common Transport Policy. The
subsidies provided under CAP have impacted the farming communities of every
member state, and it would be hard to find a European farmer or national agricultural department whose work has not been affected in some way. Equally, the
CCP has allowed the European Commission to negotiate trade agreements on
behalf of all the member states (even if national governments have always kept a

Figure 9.1 The division of policy authority

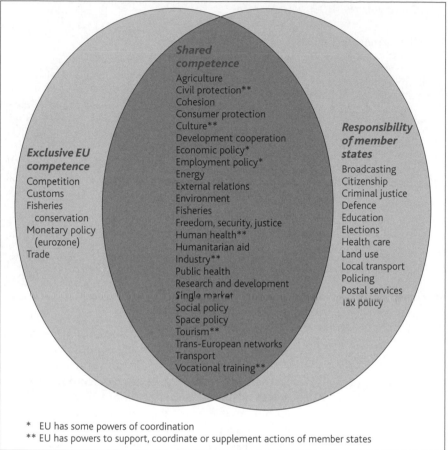

Shared competence
Agriculture
Civil protection**
Cohesion
Consumer protection
Culture**
Development cooperation
Economic policy*
Employment policy*
Energy
External relations
Environment
Fisheries
Freedom, security, justice
Human health**
Humanitarian aid
Industry**
Public health
Research and development
Single market
Social policy
Space policy
Tourism**
Trans-European networks
Transport
Vocational training**

Exclusive EU competence
Competition
Customs
Fisheries
  conservation
Monetary policy
  (eurozone)
Trade

Responsibility of member states
Broadcasting
Citizenship
Criminal justice
Defence
Education
Elections
Health care
Land use
Local transport
Policing
Postal services
Tax policy

*   EU has some powers of coordination
** EU has powers to support, coordinate or supplement actions of member states

close eye on its work), and globalization and policy spillover has helped move the EU into dealing with trade in services and intellectual property, and related fields such as food and product safety, the environment, and labour issues.

On the other hand, authority for the 'common' foreign and security policy is not quite so clear. This is a policy area that was a relatively late addition to the EU agenda, and progress has since been halting. While all the EU states have had approximately similar goals and interests on the trade front, this has not been the case with foreign policy, where – for example – the interests of Britain and France with centuries of imperialism behind them are still quite different from those of smaller states with few political or cultural interests outside Europe, or neutral states such as Austria and Ireland. Meanwhile, progress on the security front has been mixed, partly because of a difference of opinion about priorities and partly because of the lack of a combined European military that would allow words to be backed up by deeds (see Chapter 24).

A final set of clues to the division of policy authority can be found in the body of EU laws, the subjects of which provide insight into areas where the EU is most active and where the member states, by implication, have most thoroughly pooled authority. The data shown in Figure 9.2 reveal the dominance of

Figure 9.2 EU legislation in force, by subject

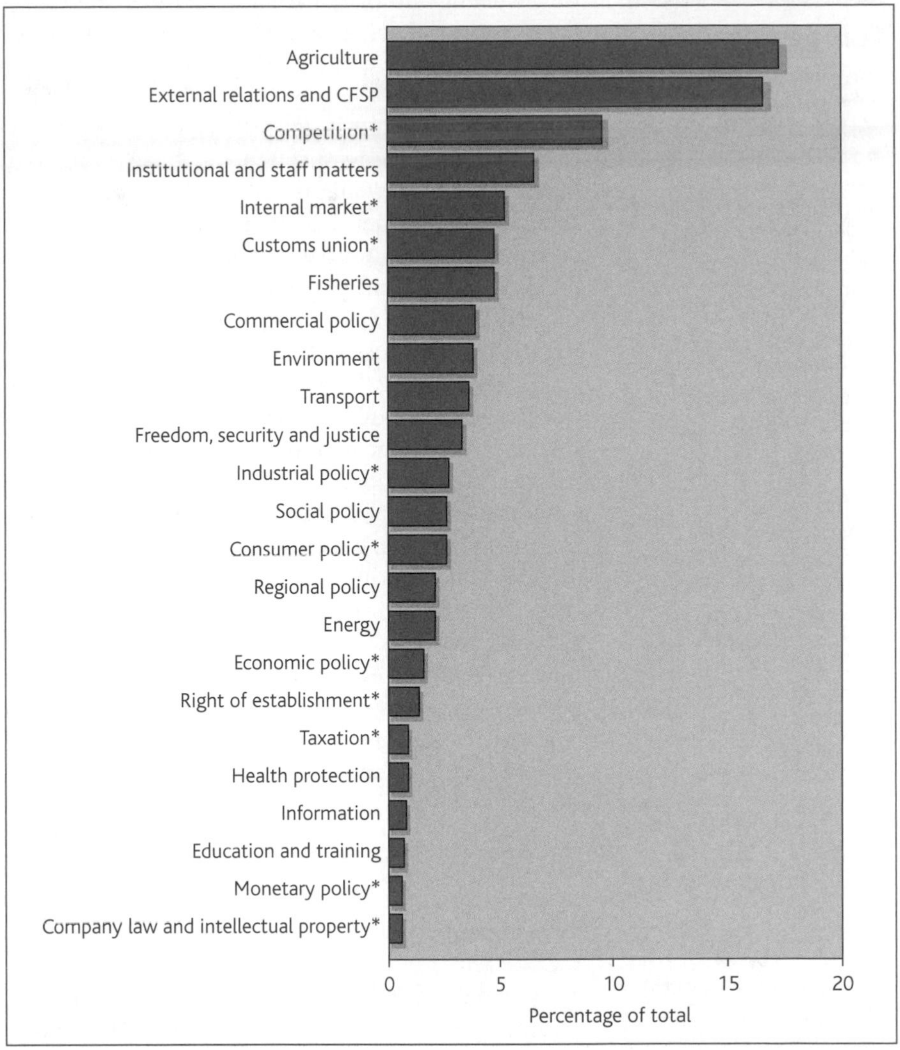

Note: * Economic matters.
Source: Based on data in EUR-Lex web site at http://eur-lex.europa.eu (retrieved February 2010).

economic law (which accounted for nearly one-third of the nearly 18,000 pieces of legislation then in force), agriculture and fisheries (22 per cent), and external relations and commercial policy (20 per cent). But again this source cannot be taken too literally because the reach and significance of laws varies: some cover a large area of ground and have far-reaching policy significance, while others are more focused in both policy and territorial terms. Some areas of policy also demand more technical and finely-tuned pieces of law, hence the volume of laws adopted in a given area may be more an indication of the depth of EU activity rather than its breadth.

In contemplating the EEC/member state dynamic, Jean Monnet was of the opinion that national policies would simply be replaced with European policies in what came to be known as the **Community method**. But this was difficult to

● **Community method**: The process by which policy powers are transferred from the member states to the EU institutions.

CONCEPT

Europeanization

The process by which the policies, laws and institutions of the member states are changed as a result of decision-making at the EU level. Bulmer and Lequesne (2005, p. 12) make a distinction between European integration (concerned with political and policy developments at the supranational level) and Europeanization (concerned with the consequences of integration for the member states). Olsen (2002) lists five aspects of Europeanization: changes in the external boundaries of Europe, the development of European-level institutions, the adaptation of national and sub-national systems of governance to European-wide norms, the export of distinctively European forms of political organization beyond the borders of Europe, and the extent to which Europe is becoming a more unified and stronger political entity.

achieve because it (wrongly) assumed that there would be wholesale agreement on switching authority from the member states to the EU, and a uniform transfer of authority across different policy fields. More recently, attempts to understand the changing place of the member states have focused on the idea of **Europeanization**, a term that has become fashionable among social scientists but whose meaning is contested (see Featherstone, 2003). In brief, it can be defined as the process through which laws and policies in the member states are being brought into alignment with EU law and policy through gradual, incremental, and assymetric adaptation, such that (to paraphrase Ladrech,1994), the political and economic dynamics of the EU become part of the organizational logic of politics and policy making at the national level. Opinion is divided on how far the process has gone, or even how useful it is as a means of understanding the EU policy process (Page, 2003; Graziano and Vink, 2007).

Understanding the place of the member states in the EU is only partly a question of pinning down their powers relative to the EU institutions. It also demands an appreciation of the relative powers and influence of different member states, whose role within the EU is impacted by at least four key factors (suggested by Laffan and Stubb, 2003). First, there is the question of how long each state has been a member, although date of entry can only be taken so far as an analytical tool; in the United States, after all, the founding 13 states long ago ceased to play their original dominating role, having been superseded by larger latecomers such as Florida, Texas and California. And while France and Germany played a critical role in the foundation and early formation of the EEC, and are still key players today, their influence has been diminished by enlargement; where they once had 47 per cent of the votes on the Council of Ministers, today they have only 17 per cent. Meanwhile, the other large founding member state of the EEC – Italy – has rarely lived up to its potential influence, handicapped by political and economic dysfunction, and now by declining population numbers. All this being said, though, the founding members of the ECSC/EEC were able to set many of the rules and principles of integration to their own liking, while newer members had to adapt to pre-existing arrangements on whose formation they had little influence.

The second telling factor in the determination of influence and power is economic wealth, in the sense not just that the biggest or wealthiest economies have had the most political influence, but also in the sense that the poorest economies have been the target of so much political attention, and have occasionally acted as a drag on European growth (consider the implications of the Greek debt crisis of 2010). By economic size, the member states can again be clustered fairly naturally into three groups: large, medium, and small (see Table 9.1). The six founding EEC states were similarly placed in terms of per capita wealth, but enlargement to the UK and Ireland in 1973 opened up the gap between the Community's poorest and wealthiest regions, as did expansion to Greece, Portugal and Spain, and more recently to eastern Europe. Structural funds were created and expanded to invest in the EU's poorer regions, taking up a growing share of the EU budget. The wealthier states took on the burden of helping the poorer states, and problems arising out of preparations for the euro in 1999–2003 complicated the switch to the single currency, while the fallout from the 2007–10 global economic crisis further illustrated the costs and benefits of integrating states with different economic size, structures, and levels of wealth.

The third power factor has been population size: the bigger states have more votes in the Council of Ministers, more members in the European Parliament, louder voices in the European Council, and more prospects of taking policy initiatives and providing leadership on EU issues. By size, the member states can again be clustered fairly naturally into four groups: large, medium, small, and micro (see Table 9.2). Population numbers have repeatedly been a factor in

Table 9.1 EU member states by economic size

Large

Germany	$3.6	trillion
France	$2.8	
UK	$2.8	
Italy	$2.3	
Spain	$1.6	

Medium

Netherlands	$871	billion
Poland	$528	
Belgium	$504	
Sweden	$479	
Austria	$414	
Greece	$356	
Denmark	$341	
Finland	$273	
Ireland	$268	
Portugal	$243	
Czech Republic	$216	
Romania	$200	
Hungary	$155	

Small

Slovakia	$98	billion
Slovenia	$55	
Luxembourg	$53	
Bulgaria	$50	
Lithuania	$47	
Latvia	$34	
Cyprus	$25	
Estonia	$23	
Malta	$7	

Note: Figures refer to gross domestic product.

Source: World Bank data for 2008 at http://web.worldbank.org (retrieved June 2010).

Table 9.2 EU member states by population

Large

Germany	82.1	million
France	62.0	
UK	61.4	
Italy	59.9	
Spain	45.6	
Poland	38.1	

Medium

Romania	21.5	million
Netherlands	16.4	
Greece	11.2	
Belgium	10.7	
Portugal	10.6	
Czech Republic	10.4	
Hungary	10.0	
Sweden	9.2	
Austria	8.3	
Bulgaria	7.6	

Small

Denmark	5.5	million
Slovakia	5.4	
Finland	5.3	
Ireland	4.5	
Croatia	4.4	
Lithuania	3.4	
Latvia	2.3	
Slovenia	2.0	
Estonia	1.3	

Micro

Cyprus	0.9	million
Luxembourg	0.5	
Malta	0.4	

Source: World Bank data for 2008 at http://web.worldbank.org (retrieved June 2010).

debates over voting systems and appointments to key EU offices, with smaller member states worried that they will be outvoted or outsmarted by larger ones. As a result, the large states have not always been able to have their way on policy, and the voting system in the EU has been set up such that – per capita – the smaller states have more influence: while Germany, for example, has one vote in the Council of Ministers per 2.8 million people, Malta has one vote per 80,000 people. Similarly, while each German Member of the European Parliament represents 830,000 people, each Maltese MEP represents 80,000 people.

The final determinant of the influence of member states on the EU has been their contrasting attitudes towards the process of integration (something much less easy to measure than economic or population size). The drivers of integration have been those states whose governments and/or publics have been most enthused about integration (although, given its small size, there is only so far that Luxembourg, the most enthusiastic of EU states, can lead the way). The initial impetus for integration came mainly from Germany and France (although – as we saw – Charles de Gaulle was suspicious of the initiatives being taken by the Community, and worked hard to protect French national interests as he defined them). Britain has since often acted as something of a brake on integration, changing its direction and its priorities in several key ways, but has also been a champion of the single market, trade liberalization, and a common security policy. The possibility even of small states occasionally being the tails that wag the dog of integration was shown by the negative votes in Denmark and Ireland on Maastricht, the Treaty of Nice, and Lisbon, and the negative vote on the constitutional treaty in the Netherlands in 2005.

But to characterize some states as consistently pro-European and others as consistently anti-European is to ignore many of the nuances in the debate about Europe. A pro-European state is not necessarily one that agrees to every initiative, but rather one that works to promote the initiatives it defines as being in the best interests of effective and efficient integration. Equally, resistance is not an

**Illustration 9.2
Austria negotiates EU membership**

Negotiations with the EU over membership have become increasingly complex with time. This February 1991 meeting between Austrian chancellor Franz Vranitsky and Commission President Jacques Delors was only one of many in the relatively trouble-free process of negotiating Austrian membership.

indication of being anti-European, but rather – perhaps – of being more cautious or careful. Also, opinions on Europe vary within member states by social class, age, education, wealth, strength of national identity, time, and even by the policy under consideration. France, for example, has always been more interested in agricultural policy than Germany, poorer EU states are more interested in regional policy than richer states, wealthier states have been more willing to tighten environmental regulations than poorer states, and states with global interests have a clearer stake in how EU foreign policy evolves. Finally, we have to make a distinction between public and political opinion; governments and voters will not always agree on policy towards Europe.

Prospects for future enlargement

Enlargement has been the most telling influence on how the EU has evolved, and on how the role of its member states has changed, and there is little reason to suppose that this will change. If we agree that there are 40 sovereign states in Europe today (see discussion in Chapter 3), and given that 27 are currently members of the EU, then there are at least 13 potential future additional members, containing a total population of about 95 million, or 185 million if Turkey and the Caucasian republics are included. Their membership prospects vary not just in terms of meeting the formal negotiated terms of entry but also in terms of passing an array of political and economic tests. Not least among these are the levels of political support for membership both in aspirant states and within existing states.

In the early years of integration, there were few formal rules on membership; the Treaty of Rome noted that 'any European state' could apply for membership (the term 'European' was never defined), the only conditions being agreement on the terms of membership and the approval of all existing members. But as the EC grew and its rules became more detailed, so the process of applying for membership became more formalized and complex. Articles 2 and 49 of the Maastricht treaty noted that any European state that respected the values of 'human dignity, freedom, democracy, equality, the rule of law . . . [and] human rights' could apply to join. Applicants would also have to meet the **Copenhagen conditions**, agreed at the Copenhagen European Council in 1993 and expanded at the Madrid European Council in 1995:

- Democracy: States must meet the Maastricht terms on freedom, democracy, human rights, and the rule of law.
- Capitalism: States must have viable free market economies and the ability to respond to market forces within the EU.
- The *acquis*: States must be willing and able to assume the obligations of the existing body of EU laws and policies (the *acquis communautaire*).
- Administration: States must have adapted their administrative structures in order to create the necessary conditions for integration.

● **Copenhagen conditions**: The requirements for membership of the EU, including democracy, capitalism, and a willingness and ability to adopt all existing EU laws.

The Lisbon treaty (Article 49) says merely that any European state which respects and promotes the values of respect for human dignity, freedom, democracy, equality, the rule of law, respect for human rights, pluralism and equality can apply. But nothing is that simple, and the formulae provide no hints of the troubling political, economic and social questions that have arisen with every round of enlargement to date, and are likely to continue so to do in future. At the core of the problem is the debate about **widening vs. deepening**, or the respective views of those who argue that continued enlargement is in the best interests of everyone, and of those who argue that deeper and better integration among existing members should be the priority. The questions in the debate have been heightened by the effects of the global economic crisis of 2007–10.

Membership applications are submitted to the European Council, which then consults with the Commission and must have the consent of Parliament before making a decision, which must be unanimous. If an application is approved, the state is considered a **candidate country**, and negotiations open (not necessarily immediately) on the terms of membership and the changes needed in the applicant state to clear the way. Each set of negotiations is tailored to the needs and qualities of the applicant state, and is designed to pin down the adjustments needed by that state to qualify for membership. Discussions are divided into chapters dealing with different aspects of EU policy, within which **benchmarks** (or targets) are set by the Council. The process begins with an assessment by the Commission on where the applicant stands in relation to each chapter, and negotiations end on a given chapter when the Council and Parliament (on the recommendation of the Commission) agree that the applicant has met the benchmarks. In the case of serious and persistent disagreements, negotiations on individual chapters can be suspended and conditions set for their re-opening.

A series of options and steps are made available to help with the transition to membership, including pre-accession strategies to identify the changes needed to smooth the transition, bi-lateral agreements between the EU and the applicant states, participation in EU programmes that allows applicant states to learn more at first hand about how the EU works, and Commission monitoring aimed at outlining the progress (or lack thereof) made by applicants in meeting the terms of membership. Pre-accession aid is also usually made available to help applicants strengthen institutions and improve infrastructure, and improve cross-border cooperation. This habit dates back to the Phare programme set up in 1989 to help the political and economic transition in Poland and Hungary, which was followed by several other programmes, including the Instrument for Pre-Accession Assistance that runs from 2007 to 2013 and distributes financial aid from the EU on the basis of need.

Once all the benchmarks have been met – a process that can take several years – an Accession Treaty is drawn up and signed, which includes the date of entry of the new state into the EU, the changes needed to the EU institutions to accommodate the new member, and a summary of the agreements reached and the conditions set. Assuming that the Accession Treaty is ratified by the applicant state (which may or may not decide to hold a national referendum) and all existing member states, the new member joins the EU on the agreed date. But behind this rather bland formula lies a cornucopia of political, economic and social considerations that leaves the non-EU states at varying levels of readiness for membership:

- **Albania** is considered a potential candidate country, and has been receiving EU development funding since the early 1990s, but is handicapped by corruption and the influence of organized crime. It was part of the

● **Widening vs. deepening**: The competing arguments about whether the EU should continue to expand its membership, or should focus on improving the efficiency of the existing club.

● **Candidate country**: A non-member state of the EU whose application to join has been accepted and with which negotiations on the terms of entry are either planned, under way, or have been agreed.

● **Benchmarks**: Measurable targets set by the Commission in order to provide a focus for applicant states as they work to meet the terms of entry into the EU.

Stabilization and Association Process (SAP) adopted by the EU in 2003 and aimed at building a free trade area and preparing several states for the adoption of EU standards, and it signed a Stabilization and Accession Agreement (SAA) with the EU in June 2006, which entered into force in April 2009, the same month that Albania applied for EU membership.

- **Armenia** is a longer shot for EU membership. It is economically troubled (more than a quarter of its population has left the country since independence in 1991), and has a heavy reliance on Russia from which it imports almost all its natural gas. Armenia also has an unresolved dispute with Turkey over the killing by Ottoman Turks of hundrends of thousands of Armenians during the First World War; Armenia defines this as genocide but Turkey defines it as a result of war.

- **Azerbaijan** is also a long shot. It has the benefit of large oil and natural gas reserves, but has a poor political record, with accusations of vote-rigging and voter intimidation during the 2003 elections that saw Ilham Aliyev succeed his father Heydar as president. Doubts about the country's commitment to democracy undermine its prospects for closer ties with the EU.

- **Belarus** has major political difficulties. Belarussians are regarded ethnically as Europeans, and make up more than 80 per cent of the population, but the dictatorship of Alexander Lukashenko has exerted strong control over Belarus since 1994 (it remains the only European state that has been barred entry to the Council of Europe), and a confederal union between Russia and Belarus has been under discussion since the late 1990s. Relations between the two countries have not always been smooth, however, with particular tensions over Russian energy imports.

- **Bosnia and Herzegovina** is considered a potential candidate country, and has had an SAA with the EU since 2007. It has also been influenced by the EU Police Mission set up in 2003 and by the replacement in 2004 of the NATO peacekeeping mission SFOR with the EU's mission EUFOR. There has been work on visa liberalization with the EU, and the EU accounts for about two-thirds of Bosnia's trade and about half its foreign direct investment. Corruption, organized crime, and ethnic tensions remain barriers to EU membership.

- **Croatia** is the most likely next new member of the EU. In October 2001 it became the second country (after Macedonia) to sign an SAA with the EU, it applied for membership in February 2003, and it was given candidate status in June 2004. Since then negotiations have proceeded relatively smoothly (except for an unresolved border dispute with Slovenia), it has a stable free market economy, and it has recovered relatively quickly from the wars of the 1990s.

- **Georgia** clearly aspires to join the EU but faces many difficulties. After 11 years of corruption and poverty, the Rose Revolution of 2004 saw the replacement of president Eduard Shevardnadze by Mikail Saakashvili, but relations with Russia – upon which Georgia relies for natural gas – have been tense, reaching a new low in 2008 with fighting sparked by the separatist aspirations of Abkhazia and South Ossetia that led to a military intervention by Russia.

- **Iceland** became part of EFTA in 1970, signed a bilateral trade agreement with the EEC in 1972, joined the European Economic Area (EEA) in 1994, and signed the Schengen Agreement in 2000, but kept EU membership at arm's length out of concerns for Icelandic fisheries. Then came the 2007–10 global economic crisis, the near collapse of the Icelandic banking system, and the devaluation of its currency, helping spark an application for EU membership in July 2009; it was given candidate status in June 2010. It faces few major challenges: it is a democratic free market system, it has already adopted many EU laws and policies as a result of being in the EEA, and it has a small and wealthy population. But concerns about the effects of EU membership on Icelandic fisheries have not gone away.

- **Kosovo** is considered a potential candidate country, but its prospects are complicated by its contested legal status. Once part of Serbia, it declared independence in February 2008 and has unofficially adopted the euro, but while nearly 65 UN members have recognized its independence, several EU states (Cyprus, Greece, Romania, Slovakia, and Spain) have not.

- **Macedonia** was the first Balkan country to sign an SAA with the EU (in April 2001). It applied for EU membership in March 2004 and was given candidate status in December 2005, but negotiations had not yet begun as this book went to press. There is an unresolved dispute over its name, which it shares with a northern Greek province (raising concerns in Greece about Macedonia's territorial aspirations), leading to the unfortunate compromise of referring to it as the Former Yugoslav Republic of Macedonia, or FYROM. There have also been some questions about Macedonia's progress on democratic and economic reform, and while it is a small country it is also relatively poor.

- **Moldova** is the poorest country in Europe, and while political leaders have hinted at an interest in EU membership, the country has strong historical and cultural links with Russia. Elections in 2009 led to the communists losing their majority for the first time, cooperation agreements have been signed between the EU and Moldova, and Moldova is part of the European Neighbourhood Policy. There is an unresolved territorial dispute with the region of Transnistria, which declared its independence from Moldova in 1990.

- **Montenegro** has only been a distinct actor in enlargement matters since its declaration of independence from Serbia in June 2006. It adopted the euro in 2002 (although it is not formally part of the eurozone), an SAA was signed with the EU in October 2007, and it applied for EU membership in December 2008, becoming a candidate in December 2010. But unresolved questions hang over its transition to democracy.

- **Norway** has twice applied for EEC/EU membership (in 1970 and again in 1992), has twice been accepted, and has twice turned down membership in national referendums. Like Iceland it is a member of EFTA, the EEA, and the Schengen Agreement, so it has made many of the adjustments needed to be an EU member, the only remaining substantial barrier being domestic public opinion. Past concerns have focused on the impact of membership on Norway's environmental standards and its fishing industry, but these have become less important with time. Opposition to EU membership was strengthened by Norway's relatively unscathed emergence from the 2007–10 global economic crisis.

- **Serbia** is part of the SAP, and after a delay in 2006–07 following concerns that it was not cooperating with the work of the International Criminal

Map 9.1 Prospective members of the EU

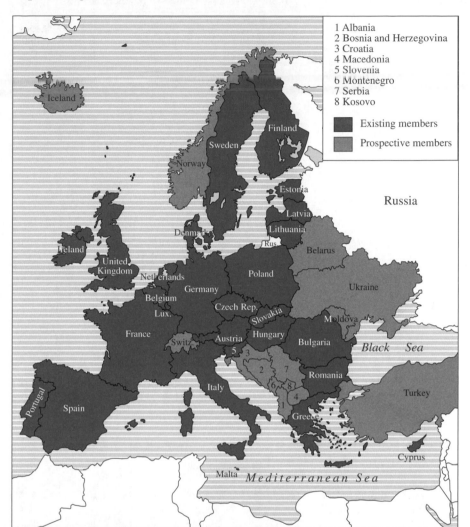

Tribunal for the former Yugoslavia, an SAA was signed with the EU in April 2008, and Serbia applied for EU membership in December 2009. The EU has become its major trading partner and its largest source of foreign direct investment, but unresolved questions remain over Serbia's position on the International Criminal Tribunal for the Former Yugoslavia (which is prosecuting war crimes from the 1990s) and a dispute over the status of EULEX, the EU police and legal mission to Kosovo.

● **Switzerland** signed an EEA membership agreement in May 1992 and also applied to join the EEC, but when EEA membership was turned down in a national referendum in December 1992, the EEC membership application was placed on hold. EU membership was finally turned down in another referendum in 2001, but in 2008 Switzerland became part of the Schengen area. This 'on-again, off-again' approach to the EU reflects Switzerland's concerns about protecting its neutrality and sovereignty.

Table 9.3 Possible future EU members: a summary, 2010

Country	Population (millions)	Per capita Gross National Income	Status
Croatia	4.4	13,580	Candidate (June 2004)
Iceland	0.3	40,450	Candidate (June 2010)
Macedonia	2.0	4,130	Candidate (Dec 2005)
Turkey	73.9	9,020	Candidate (Dec 1999)
Montenegro	0.6	6,660	Candidate (Dec 2010)
Albania	3.1	3,840	Applicant (April 2009)
Serbia	7.3	5,590	Applicant (Dec 2009)
Bosnia & Herzegovina	3.8	4,520	Potential candidate
Kosovo	2.1	2,300	Potential candidate
Armenia	3.0	3,350	Long shot
Azerbaijan	8.7	3,830	Long shot
Belarus	9.7	5,360	Poor prospects
Georgia	4.4	2,500	Mixed prospects
Moldova	3.6	1,500	Mixed prospects
Norway	4.8	87,340	Improving potential
Switzerland	7.6	55,510	Mixed prospects
Ukraine	46.3	3,210	Mixed prospects

Note: Kosovo figures are UN estimates.

Source: Data are for 2008, and come from World Bank at http://www.worldbank.org (retrieved June 2010).

**Illustration 9.3
Turkey and the EU**

Commission president José Manuel Barroso (*centre*), enlargement commissioner Olli Rehn (*left*), and Marc Pierini (head of the Commission delegation to Turkey) look sombre at an April 2008 press conference in Ankara during a visit designed to strengthen ties between the EU and Turkey.

Debating...
Should Turkey be allowed to join the EU?

YES	NO
Turkey is part of the European experience. Unlike many other neighbouring states, it has a long history of political and cultural interaction with Europe (including the rule of the Ottoman Turks over much of southeastern Europe between the sixteenth and nineteenth centuries), and the Turkish middle class has adopted Western secular values. Arguments about its geographical and cultural distance from Brussels have been undermined since Cyprus joined the EU in 2004.	Turkey is not a European state, and its cultural and religious differences with Europe would cause problems with integrating it into mainstream Europe.
In regard to the Copenhagen conditions, Turkey's democratic record has improved (even if it is not yet perfect), it is clearly capitalist, and it has proved willing to make the adjustments needed to fit within the EU legal framework.	Turkey is a poor country, with a per capita GDP less than one-quarter that of Germany, Britain, or France (but bigger than that of Romania or Bulgaria), and so it would likely become a major drain on EU subsidies, development aid, and investments. Many Turks would also likely move to other parts of the EU in search of jobs.
Strategically, accepting Turkey into the EU would send an encouraging message to the EU's Muslim population, and it would also increase the EU's influence in the Muslim world. More democracy for Turkey would raise the prospect of more democracy for its Middle Eastern neighbours.	Europeans may preach social and religious tolerance, but integrating 74 million Turkish Muslims into an EU that is predominantly secular or Christian would be a tall order. (For further discussion, see Morris, 2005.)
Turkey is a large new market with much potential for growth, and would not only offer new opportunities for European corporations but its young labour force would help offset some of the EU's population decline.	Turkey's human rights record has improved, but worrying questions remain about religious tolerance, women's rights, the role of the military in politics, the treatment of Turkey's Kurdish minority, and unresolved questions over the explusion and deaths of numerous Armenians at the hands of the Ottoman Turks in 1915.

- **Turkey** is the troubled outlier on the future enlargement agenda, being both the one remaining non-member with the longest history of aspirations to join the EU, and also the one that has faced the strongest political resistance. Turkey applied for associate membership of the EEC in 1959, and an agreement was signed in 1963 aimed at bringing Turkey into a customs union with the Community, but it only came into force in 1995. Turkey applied for full EEC membership in April 1987 and was given candidate status in December 1999, but negotiations (which opened in 2005) have been rocky; the EU has refused to open several chapters until there is a resolution of the dispute over Cyprus, which is split between a Turkish north and a Greek south. Trade between Turkey and the EU has grown, Turkey has made numerous changes to domestic law and policy to meet EU requirements (including the abolition in 2004 of the death penalty), but still has only a mixed record on democracy and human rights. Turkish membership would mean critical new EU influence in the Middle East, but

Turkey is large (nearly 74 million people), poor (economic integration would pose considerable challenges), and Islamic (raising numerous troubling religious and cultural issues). Public support in Turkey for EU membership has been declining.

● **Ukraine** has had to focus in recent years on stabilizing the democratic changes that came in the wake of its 2004 Orange revolution (sparked by an outcry over rigged elections), while maintaining a balancing act in keeping on good terms with both Russia and the EU. There has been talk of instituting pre-accession arrangements and of setting up a free trade agreement, and major Ukrainian political parties have made public their support for EU membership, but public opinion in Ukraine is mixed, and where many other potential eastern EU members are small and poor, Ukraine is both large (more than 46 million people) and poor.

Just as past rounds of enlargement have changed the personality and reach of integration, and even the meaning of 'Europe', so will future rounds. Enlargement has long been one of the most effective means for the spread of democratic and capitalist ideas (see Chapter 24), and if history is any indication then the promise of enlargement will likely continue to encourage change in the former Soviet republics, and ultimately change the personality of the EU and its relations with Russia. But the question of the EU's absorption capacity remains unanswered: how far can the EU expand while also remaining manageable, true to its core goals, and efficient?

SUMMARY

- The place of the member states of the EU in international law is unusual, because while they are sovereign states they have also transferred unprecedented amounts of authority to the EU.
- Guidance on the relative powers of the member states and the EU institutions can be found in the treaties, common policies, and the body of EU law, but in all three cases there are ambiguities.
- The dynamic of member state/EU relations was once explained by the Community method, but Europeanization has become more popular as an analytical tool, even if there is no agreement on what it means or on its lasting value.
- Understanding the relative powers and influence of the EU member states is partly a function of how long they have been members, of the size and wealth of their national economies, of their population size, and of their attitudes towards the process of integration.
- Where once the process of applying to join the EU was relatively simple, it has become more demanding and complex as the reach and effect of integration has expanded.
- The Copenhagen conditions require that an aspirant member state should be democratic, a free market economy, and willing to adopt the existing body of EU laws and policies and to adapt its administrative structures to fit with the needs of integration.
- Applicant countries in early 2010 included Albania, Croatia, Iceland, Macedonia, Montenegro, Serbia, and Turkey. Countries that face the most challenging barriers to membership include Armenia, Azerbaijan, Belarus, Georgia, Moldova, and Ukraine

KEY TERMS AND CONCEPTS

Benchmarks
Candidate country
Community method
Competence
Copenhagen conditions
Europeanization
Secession
Subsidiarity
Widening v. deepening

FURTHER READING

Bulmer, Simon, and Christian Lequesne (eds) (2005), *The Member States of the European Union* (Oxford: Oxford University Press); Eleanor Zeff and Ellen Pirro (eds) (2006), *The European Union and the Member States*, 2nd edn (Boulder, CO: Lynne Rienner). Two edited collections looking at relations between the EU and the member states, with a survey of analytical approaches, chapters on key states, and a discussion of the effects of Europeanization.

Featherstone, Kevin, and Claudio M. Radaelli (eds) (2003), *The Politics of Europeanization* (Oxford: Oxford University Press). An edited collection dealing with the many facets of the debate over Europeanization.

Nugent, Neill (2004), *European Union Enlargement* (Basingstoke: Palgrave Macmillan). An edited collection of studies of the mechanics and implications of enlargement.

CHAPTER 10

The European Commission

When Europeans think of the major EU institutions, the one that most readily comes to mind is the European Commission. It is the one most often in the news, and the one most often blamed for the excesses of 'Brussels'. And yet despite its visibility, the Commission is both less – and more – than it seems. It is often portrayed as powerful, secretive, expensive, and undemocratic, but in fact has few independent decision-making powers, is one of the most open of all large bureau- cracies found anywhere in the world, and has an institutional budget that is smaller than that of an average mid-sized European city. As for charges that it is undemoc- ratic, it is no better or worse than national bureaucracies, few of whose staff members are held directly accountable to voters or to other institutions.

Headquartered in Brussels, the Commission is both the bureaucratic arm of the EU, responsible for proposing new laws and policies, and its executive, responsible for overseeing their implementation through the member states. It is headed by a president and a 27-member College of Commissioners that functions as something like a European cabinet; beneath them work several thousand career European bureaucrats responsible for the day-to-day work of the Commission, divided up among directorates-general that are the functional equivalent of national govern- ment departments.

The Commission is one of the most supranational of EU institutions, and has long been at the heart of European integration, charged with making sure that EU policies are given substance according to the goals and principles outlined in the treaties. Commissioners and staff members may be citizens of individual states, but they are discouraged from pursuing the interests of those states, and work to promote a policy agenda that focuses on the interests of the EU as a whole.

KEY ISSUES

- Why has the Commission been the target of so much criticism, and is that criticism justified?

- Should Parliament have the right to confirm individual nominees to the College of Commissioners, rather than the College as a whole?

- Should the president of the Commission be directly elected?

- The Commission has been described as the barometer of integration – what is the evidence for this?

- Should the Commission's legislative powers be transferred to Parliament?

- In what ways is the Commission similar to, or different from, national bureaucracies?

How the Commission evolved

The origins of today's European Commission lie in the nine-member High Authority of the ECSC, which was based in Luxembourg, began work in August 1952, and was charged with encouraging the opening of the western European market in coal and steel. Jean Monnet's original hope was that the Authority would be both powerful and independent, but concerns among the Benelux governments that it would be dominated by West Germany and France led to the decision to create also a Special Council of Ministers through which member state governments could offset and balance the work of the Authority (Nugent, 2001, p. 20).

The ECSC High Authority was joined in 1958 by separate commissions for the EEC and Euratom, each headquartered in Brussels and led by nine-member Colleges of Commissioners appointed by national governments for four-year terms. Under the terms of the 1965 Merger treaty, the three commissions were combined in 1967 into a new Commission of the European Communities, which soon became more commonly known as the European Commission. As membership of the Community expanded in the 1970s and 1980s, the number of commissioners grew with two more added for each of the bigger member states and one each for the smaller states. Under the terms of the Treaty of Nice, each member state was given just one commissioner, leaving today's Commission with 27 members.

The Commission has always been a champion of the supranational qualities of the EEC/EU, its powers waxing and waning with changes in the political environment. As we saw in Chapter 5, early attempts to build its powers sparked the 1965 empty chair crisis, from which it emerged both bloodied and weakened. It continued to lose powers with the creation in 1974 of the European Council, and with the introduction in 1979 of direct elections to the European Parliament. After enjoying a newly assertive phase under President Jacques Delors during the late 1980s and early 1990s, the Commission saw its powers declining once again relative to those of the Council of Ministers and the European Parliament. At the same time, though, it also saw its visibility increasing, and exploited its interests in promoting European issues in the face of national priorities.

Under the failed constitution, there was a plan to stop the growth in the number of commissioners, which was becoming unsustainable: with a 12- or 15-member Community there were enough good jobs to go around, but with a 27-member EU the provision of meaningful tasks in the College of Commissioners became difficult to maintain – hence there were commissioners dealing with important policy portfolios like trade and external relations while others were limited to institutional relations and multilingualism. Under Lisbon, the number of commissioners from November 2014 would have been capped at two-thirds of the number of member states (or 18 commissioners in a 27-member EU), but this was not a popular idea with smaller EU states, and one of the concessions made to Ireland as it sought guarantees in the lead-up to its second referendum on Lisbon in October 2009 was a reinstatement of the rule of one commissioner per member state.

How the Commission is structured

The European Commission is headquartered in Brussels, in the European Quarter that lies east of the city centre. It was not given a permanent home until

Illustration 10.1
The European
Commission

The Berlaymont building in Brussels, seat of the European Commission, and the heart of the European Quarter in Brussels.

the building in 1963–67 – on the site of a vacated 300-year old convent run by the Dames de Berlaymont – of a new shared seat for the Commission, the Council of Ministers and the European Parliament. The star-shaped floor plan of the new Berlaymont building provided an architecturally distinctive personality, passed on to the Commission when it eventually took over the entire building. In 1990 asbestos was found in the Berlaymont, so it was emptied and renovated at an estimated cost of more than €800 million. Following the overhaul, senior staff and some of the directorates-general moved back into the building in 2004, but the size of today's Commission makes it impossible to house them all there, so most of its staff have been dispersed to more than 60 buildings scattered around Brussels. In 2009 a master plan was announced aimed at addressing this problem and giving the European Quarter a facelift.

Figure 10.1 Structure of the European Commission

- The bureaucratic-executive arm of the EU
- Headquartered in Brussels
- Headed by a president nominated by the European Council and approved by the European Parliament for renewable five-year terms
- Consists of 27-member College of Commissioners, with one commissioner nominated by each member state, approved by the European Council and the European Parliament, and each given responsibility over a particular policy area
- Divided into directorates-general and services responsible for a combination of internal and external policy areas or administrative functions
- Work supported by a Secretariat General
- Supranational in character

The Commission has five main components: the College of Commissioners, the president of the Commission, the directorates-general and services, a network of advisory and executive committees, and the Secretariat General.

The College of Commissioners

Confusingly, the term 'the Commission' refers both to the entire European Commission with its 38,000 staff, and to the College of 27 commissioners who head the institution. The College is the public face of the Commission, its more influential or active members (particularly the commissioners for trade or competition) being among the few leaders of the EU institutions likely to make much of an impression on the European public. Functioning much like a cabinet in national government, the College consists of commissioners responsible for each of the policy areas in which the EU is active, appointed to serve renewable five-year terms beginning six months after elections to the EP. Commissioners are chosen by the president from lists submitted by the governments of the member states, and a final draft list is submitted to the European Council, which must approve it by a qualified majority vote. Lisbon stipulates that members should be chosen 'on the ground of their general competence and European commitment from persons whose independence is beyond doubt' and that while in office they must refrain from 'any action incompatible with their duties or the performance of their tasks'.

All nominees must attend confirmation hearings before the relevant committees of the European Parliament (EP), which cannot accept or reject them individually, but can only accept or reject the College as a whole. Reservations about an individual nominee can be enough to force a withdrawal (see Spence, 2006a, pp. 34–8, and Nugent, 2002, pp. 82–7), as happened in 2004 when the Italian government nominated Rocco Buttiglione for consideration as justice commissioner. In hearings before the EP, Buttiglione – a committed Catholic – defended comments he had made about homosexuality being a 'sin' and the family existing 'in order to allow women to have children and to have the protection of a male who takes care of them'. He claimed that he would not allow his personal views to impact his work on the Commission, but when it became clear that Parliament would not approve the College with Buttiglione as a member, he was replaced by Franco Frattini. Another rejection came in 2010 when nominee Rumiana Jeleva (the incumbent Bulgarian foreign minister) withdrew her nomination after facing tough questioning about her financial declaration and her ability to be the new commissioner for humanitarian aid, and was replaced by Kristalina Georgieva.

Parliament can also remove the College through a motion of censure, although this has never happened. It came closest in January 1999, when – after charges of fraud, nepotism, and cronyism in the Commission – Parliament tried to dismiss the College. It could not muster the necessary two-thirds majority, but the College dramatically resigned within hours of the publication on 16 March of a report by a committee appointed to investigate the allegations (see Georgakakis, 2004). Individual commissioners can also be asked to resign from office by the president, or can be compulsorily retired by the European Court of Justice in cases of failure to do their job or of engaging in serious misconduct. Commissioners can also retire from office, as several have, often to re-enter

● **College of Commissioners**: The group of 27 commissioners who head the European Commission. They are appointed for five-year renewable terms, one comes from each of the member states, and each is given responsibility over a particular area of policy.

Table 10.1 The European Commissioners, 2009–14

Name	Member State	Portfolio
Party affiliation: social democrat		
José Manuel Barroso*	Portugal	President
Joaquin Almunia*	Spain	VP, Competition
Catherine Ashton	UK	VP, High Representative of the Union for Foreign Affairs and Security Policy
Maros Sefcovic	Slovakia	VP, Inter-Institutional Relations and Administration
László Andor	Hungary	Employment, Social Affairs, and Inclusion
Maria Damanaki	Greece	Maritime Affairs and Fisheries
Stefan Füle	Czech Republic	Enlargement
Party affiliation: centrist		
Siim Kallas*	Estonia	VP, Transport
Neelie Kroes*	Netherlands	VP, Digital Agenda
Karel De Gucht	Belgium	Trade
Máire Geoghegan-Quinn	Ireland	Research and Innovation
Cecilia Malmström	Sweden	Home Affairs
Janez Potocnik*	Slovenia	Environment
Olli Rehn*	Finland	Economic and Monetary Affairs
Androulla Vassiliou	Cyprus	Education, Culture, Multilingualism and Youth
Party affiliation: centre-right		
Viviane Reding*	Luxembourg	VP, Justice, Fundamental Rights and Citizenship
Antonio Tajani	Italy	VP, Industry and Entrepreneurship
Michel Barnier	France	Internal Market and Services
Dacian Ciolos	Romania	Agriculture and Rural Development
John Dalli	Malta	Health and Consumer Policy
Kristalina Georgieva	Bulgaria	International Cooperation, Humanitarian Aid and Crisis Response
Johannes Hahn	Austria	Regional Policy
Connie Hedegaard	Denmark	Climate Action
Janusz Lewandowski	Poland	Budget
Günther Oettinger	Germany	Energy
Andris Piebalgs*	Latvia	Development
Algirdas Semeta	Lithuania	Taxation and Customs Union

* Returning Commissioners.

national politics or to run for the European Parliament. This happened in 2009 when four commissioners were elected to the EP, including Danuta Hübner of Poland and Louis Michel of Belgium.

Despite being nominated by the governments of the member states, commissioners are expected to put Europe first and must swear an oath of office before the European Court of Justice agreeing 'neither to seek nor to take instructions from any Government or body.' Their independence is helped by the fact that they cannot be removed in mid- term by their home governments, although they can be recalled at the end of their terms if there is a change of political leadership at home or a disagreement with their national leaders; hence commissioners hoping to stay in the job will always be keeping a close eye on political opinion at home.

The most famous example of such a disagreement involved one of the British commissioners – Lord Cockfield – and his sponsor, Margaret Thatcher. Cockfield was nominated by Thatcher in 1985 and given responsibility for making preparations for the single market. But he took to the task too enthusiastically for Thatcher, who concluded that he had become – as she put it – 'the prisoner as well as the master of his subject'. Under the circumstances, she concluded, it had become too easy for him 'to go native and to move from deregulating the market to re-regulating it under the rubric of harmonization' (Thatcher, 1993, p. 547). She refused to renominate him in 1989, but his work survived to become the foundations of the Single European Act.

Most commissioners have political reputations in their home states (see MacMullen, 2000), and the pool of potential candidates has grown in quality as the visibility and reach of the EU has grown, as the Commission has become a more significant force in European politics, and as nominations to the College have become more desirable (Nugent, 2001, pp. 88–91). Top-level national government experience is now all but required, and the College usually counts

Illustration 10.2
The College of Commissioners

A meeting of the College of Commissioners, with President José Manuel Barroso in the chair.

among its number former prime ministers, foreign ministers, finance ministers, labour and trade ministers, and former Members of the European Parliament. Although national party affiliation is often a factor in deciding nominations, and party balance has become more of a factor in speculation about the work of the College, most of that work tends to be non-political; the College's policy debates are more technical and administrative in nature than ideological.

At the beginning of each term, all commissioners are assigned policy portfolios, which are distributed at the prerogative of the president. Assignments will be influenced by the abilities, political skills, and experience of individual commissioners, as well as lobbying by national leaders keen to see 'their' commissioner win a good portfolio or one of particular interest to their country. Turnover is high and reassignments common at the end of a term; it is rare that a commissioner will return for a second term, let alone to the same portfolio. In 2009 there were only seven returning commissioners (aside from the president), and all were assigned to new portfolios.

In early Colleges there were few portfolios, but as the reach and the size of the EU grew, so did the number of positions. Just as in national cabinets, there is an internal hierarchy of portfolios, the most powerful being those dealing with the budget, agriculture, trade, and external relations. A new twist was added by Lisbon, which replaced the external relations commissioner with a redesigned High Representative of the Union for Foreign Affairs and Security Policy. The post was created as the latest of a series of steps taken to place responsibility for external relations in one office (there had once been four commissioners dealing with separate parts of the world). The High Representative is appointed by the European Council, with the agreement of the president of the Commission, and not only chairs the Foreign Affairs Council of the Council of Ministers, but is also a vice-president in the Commission, so straddling both institutions. Catherine Ashton was appointed as the first office-holder in 2009 (see Chapter 24).

Although there are similarities between the College of Commissioners and national cabinets when it comes to the management of portfolios, the comparison can only be taken so far; Commissioners do not have the same kind of political responsibilities as national ministers, nor the same control over administrative departments, nor the same responsibility to the public. (In terms of running the departments and services of the Commission, directors-general are actually more like national government ministers than are commissioners.) And while national cabinet ministers usually owe their positions to the national leader of the day, commissioners do not owe their chairs in the College to the president of the Commission.

Each commissioner is supported by a small staff of assistants and advisers known as a **cabinet** (pronounced *cabi-ney*), headed by a *chef de cabinet*. Most members of *cabinets* once came from the same member state and the same national political party as their commissioners, but changes to the rules in 1999 required that *cabinets* should be more nationally diverse. The quality of the *cabinet* staff can have a close bearing on the performance of a commissioner, and the *cabinets* collectively have become a key influence on the operations of the Commission (Spence, 2006a, pp. 60–72). Members keep their commissioners informed, provide policy advice, act as a point of contact for lobbyists, keep in touch with other *cabinets* on Commission business, and provide an essential link between commissioners and the DGs and services (Nugent, 2001, pp. 123–32).

● *Cabinet*: The small group of assistants and advisers that works for each of the commissioners. Headed by a *chef de cabinet*, members provide advice, information and other services to the commissioners.

The President

The dominating figure in the Commission – and the person who is usually the most public face of the EU – is the president. As well as running the Commission, he appears alongside meetings of world leaders, plays an often critical role in negotiations at European Council summits, is expected to make public statements on critical issues, and has bilateral meetings with national leaders ranging from the president of the United States to the leaders of countries receiving EU development aid. Where candidates for the job were once expected to have only modest political experience, and their terms in office were relatively quiet and non-controversial, appointments have become more significant and more hotly contested, and opinions about the performance of presidents in office have become stronger.

Presidents are appointed for renewable five-year terms, taking office – like the commissioners – six months after elections to the European Parliament. The president is expected to give political guidance and direction to the Commission, which also means playing a central role in giving impetus to the direction taken by the EU. Specifically, presidents have the following powers:

- To convene and chair meetings of the College, and approve agendas for College meetings.
- To lay down the guidelines for the work of the Commission, and decide its internal organization.
- To distribute policy portfolios in the College at the beginning of each term, reshuffle portfolios mid-term, and ask members of the College to resign if necessary.
- To assign themselves whatever duties and policy responsibilities interest them.
- To regularly take questions before the European Parliament, on the model of Prime Minister's Question Time in the British House of Commons.
- To represent the Commission in dealings with other EU institutions and at key meetings of national governments and their leaders.

These are the formal aspects of the job, some of which are outlined in the treaties and in the operating rules of the Commission. But as with all major leadership positions, the character of the office changes according to the personality and management style of the office-holder, the agenda each brings to the task, the prevailing political climate, and the ability of a president to work with and command the respect of EU leaders (Spence, 2006a, pp. 27–8). Some presidents (notably Hallstein, Jenkins, and Delors) have been more ambitious and effective, while others (notably Malfatti, Santer and Prodi) have been more low-key in their approach (see Figure 10.2).

The process by which presidents are appointed is technically simple but in reality complex, and has become more so as the powers and significance of the EU have grown. First, the credentials for aspirant presidents have become more demanding: where experience as a national government minister was once enough, experience as a prime minister is now preferred. Second, while the president is formally nominated by the European Council and approved by a majority

● **President of the Commission**: The head of the Commission and the most visible of all the staff members of the EU institutions. Appointed by the European Council for renewable five-year terms, and charged with giving the Commission direction.

Figure 10.2 Past presidents of the European Commission

1958–1967

Walter Hallstein
West Germany
Christian Democrat;
foreign minister

Remembered for helping establish the role of the Commission in Community affairs, for laying the groundwork for the common market and CAP, and for his role in setting off the 1965 empty chair crisis.

1967–1970

Jean Rey
Belgium
Centrist; economics minister

1970–1972

Franco Maria Malfatti
Italy
Christian Democrat;
minister for state industries

The only president so far to have voluntarily resigned from the job, a reflection of how weak the position then was and of the trough into which the Community had sunk.

1972–1973

Sicco Mansholt (interim)
Netherlands
Social democrat;
agriculture minister

1973–1977

François-Xavier Ortoli
France
Conservative; economic affairs
and finance minister

1977–1981

Roy Jenkins
UK
Social democrat; home
secretary and finance minister

Britain's first and so far only Commission president, remembered for his work on the EMS and establishment of the right of Commission presidents to attend world economic summits.

1981–1985

Gaston Thorn
Luxembourg
Socialist; minister of foreign
affairs and trade, and prime
minister 1974–79

1985–1994

Jacques Delors
France
Socialist; economics and
finance minister

The towering figure in the history of the office (Drake, 2000a, pp. 238–44, and Drake, 2000b). Single-minded, hardworking, demanding; and short-tempered, his term was remembered mainly for completion of the single market, the plan for economic and monetary union, the Social Charter and the negotiations leading up to Maastricht.

1995–1999

Jacques Santer
Luxembourg
Christian Democrat;
prime minister 1985–95

Guided the EU towards economic and monetary union, enlargement and the CFSP, but best remembered for charges that he allowed a culture of complacency to go unchallenged, leading to the resignation of the College in March 1999 (Nugent, 2001, pp. 53–5).

1999–2004

Romano Prodi
Italy
Centrist; prime minister
1996–98

Oversaw the launch of the euro, enlargement negotiations, and the draft European constitution, but was widely regarded as disorganized and as a poor communicator.

José Manuel Barroso

José Manuel Barroso (born 1956) was appointed as the eleventh president of the European Commission in December 2004, and confirmed to a second term in late 2009. Born in Lisbon, Barroso studied law at the University of Lisbon and politics at the University of Geneva. While he once embraced far-left Maoist political ideas, he joined the centre-right Portuguese Social Democratic Party in 1980, and was elected to Parliament in 1985, serving six terms as a legislator, and serving as home affairs minister and foreign minister before becoming prime minister in 2002. In that role he supported the war in Iraq, and hosted a meeting between George W. Bush and Tony Blair in the Azores on the eve of the war. His reputation as Commission president has been as a moderate conservative (or a 'centrist reformer' as he likes to describe himself). His first term in office coincided with an era of great change and uncertainty: the euro and eastern enlargement were still new, EU–US relations were in deep trouble, the European constitution collapsed, and the world entered a period of economic crisis. He was welcomed into his second term with the breaking of the Greek debt crisis.

vote in the European Parliament, other political considerations come into play: presidents long had to be acceptable to all the leaders of the EU member states, with the consequence that candidates with well-formed opinions and substantial track records were often dismissed in the search for consensus. The result, argues Spence (2006a, p. 32), was that the strongest candidate was rarely chosen.

This was clear in 2004, as the search began to replace Romano Prodi. Belgian Prime Minister Guy Verhofstadt emerged as the favourite of France and Germany, but was opposed by Britain (just as it had opposed the candidacy of Belgian Prime Minister Jean-Luc Dehaene in 1999) on the grounds that he was too much a European federalist. Austrian Chancellor Wolfgang Schüssel and former NATO chief Javier Solana were also touted, while Britain favoured its own incumbent commissioner Chris Patten, a former Conservative government minister and the last British governor of Hong Kong. French president Jacques Chirac opposed Patten's candidacy, dismissing the prospect of a candidate from 'a country which doesn't take part in all European policies' (a veiled reference to Britain's absence from the eurozone). In the end, the compromise candidate was incumbent Portuguese Prime Minister José Manuel Barroso. He was confirmed relatively quietly to a second term in 2009, despite concerns that he had not been a strong or inspirational leader and that his lack of strong positions made him easier for European leaders to control (Peter, 2009).

Lisbon has changed the rules by requiring that candidates are proposed by the European Council using a qualified majority vote (QMV; see Chapter 11 for explanation), and must be confirmed by a majority vote in the European Parliament. If the first candidate is turned down by the EP, a second must be proposed within a month. The switch to QMV means that no one national leader can any longer veto the choice of president, which will significantly change the dynamics of the process. The first scheduled test of this new process will come in 2014.

Directorates-General and Services

If the College is the cabinet of the European Union, then the body of the EU civil service is found in its **directorates-general** (DGs) and services (see Table 10.2). The DGs are the equivalent of national government departments in the sense that each is responsible for overseeing the development and implementation of laws and policies in specific areas. They are not, however – like most national government departments – executive bodies with direct links to the public (Spence, 2006b). The services, meanwhile, are much as the name implies. Some work externally: the Humanitarian Aid office oversees the provision of EU emergency assistance and relief to victims of natural disasters and civil conflict outside the EU. Others are focused internally: the Legal Service provides in-house legal counsel to the Commission and represents it in cases brought before the European Court of Justice, while the Joint Research Centre provides the Commission with independent scientific and technical advice.

The DGs and services are staffed mainly by a mix of full-time European bureaucrats, known as *fonctionnaires*, and of national experts seconded from the member states on short-term appointments. Permanent jobs in the Commission are both highly sought after and demanding, with thousands of applicants chasing the positions that become available each year, keeping the

Table 10.2 Commission Directorates-general and Services

Directorates-general

Agriculture and Rural Development	Health and Consumers
Budget	Home Affairs
Climate Action	Human Resources and Security
Communication	Informatics
Competition	Information Society and Media
Development	Internal Market and Services
Economic and Financial Affairs	Interpretation
Education and Culture	Justice
Employment, Social Affairs	Maritime Affairs and Fisheries
and Equal Opportunities	Mobility and Transport
Energy	Regional Policy
Enlargement	Research
Enterprise and Industry	Taxation and Customs Union
Environment	Trade
EuropeAid – Cooperation Office	Translation
Eurostat	

Services

Administration and Payment of	Humanitarian Aid
Individual Entitlements	Infrastructure and Logistics
Bureau of European Policy Advisors	Internal Audit Service
Data Protection Officer	Joint Research Centre
European Anti-Fraud Office	Legal Service
External Action Service	Publications Office

● **Directorate-general**: A department within the Commission, headed by a director-general and given responsibility for generating and overseeing the implementation of laws and policies in particular areas.

CONCEPT

Comitology

The process by which executive decisions within the Commission are monitored and influenced by a network of advisory, management and regulatory committees. It traces its roots back to concerns among member states that the Commission might try to change policy in the course of implementing it. Committees were once powerful, feeding charges of the secretive and undemocratic character of the Commission. After years of complaints from the EP, a 2006 decision gave the EP the power to block decisions coming out of the Commission where they were quasi-legislative and adopted using the codecision procedure (see Chapter 12).

Personnel Selection Office busy. Citizenship of an EU member state is usually needed, and the Commission is required to ensure balanced representation by nationality at every level. While it expects all non-support staff applicants to speak at least two languages, multilingualism is increasingly the norm, along with a university degree and professional training in law, business, finance, science, or a related area. Applicants sit entrance exams (the *concours*) and may have to wait as long as three years to find out whether or not they have been accepted. Once appointed, though, they are well paid, and redundancies are rare.

Each DG is headed by a director-general, usually someone who has worked their way up through the bureaucracy of their home state and then through the ranks of the Commission, although the higher the level of appointment the stronger the role that nationality and political affiliation will play in appointments. Directors-general are the main link between the DG and the relevant commissioner, and oversee DGs that vary in size, but not always in relation to the importance of the job they do: the biggest is the DG for Translation with more than 2,300 staff, while the DGs for Agriculture and for Energy each have just under 1,000 staff. The DG for Trade is surprisingly small with less than 500 staff, Budget has just over 400, and Development and Enlargement each employ fewer than 300. Most Commission staff work in Brussels, while several thousand work in Luxembourg and in other parts of the EU, and more than 1,000 work in the Commission's overseas offices.

Committees

The process of implementation is monitored by a network of several hundred committees and sub-committees participating in a phenomenon known as **comitology** (Bergström, 2005). The committees take four different forms:

- Advisory committees look at less politically sensitive issues and provide opinions to the Commission, which must make an effort to take them into account. They have no power to block Commission action.
- Management committees focus on areas such as agricultural and fisheries policy, and have the power to refer Commission measures to the Council of Ministers, which then has the option of overruling the Commission.
- Regulatory committees have the power to refer Commission measures to both the Council and the European Parliament.
- Regulatory committees with scrutiny must allow the Council and Parliament to check proposed measures taken by the Commission before they are adopted, and if either institution objects the Commission cannot proceed.

The Secretariat General

The Commission has its own internal bureaucracy in the form of the Secretariat General, which employs about 700 staff who provide technical services and advice to the Commission, prepare the annual work programme of the Commission, and organize and coordinate the work of the DGs and services (Kassim, 2006). Answering to the president of the Commission, it is headed by a secretary general who chairs the weekly meetings of the *chefs de cabinet*, sits in on meetings of the College of Commissioners, directs Commission relations with other EU institutions, and generally works to makes sure that the Commission runs smoothly. The position was held for nearly 30 years (1958–87) by Emile Noël of France, whose belief in an activist Commission and a leadership role for the Secretariat General influenced its development. In 2005, Catherine Day of Ireland, former director-general for the environment, became the first woman to hold the job.

What the Commission does

The task of the European Commission – according to the Treaty of Lisbon – is to 'promote the general interest of the Union', to 'ensure the application of the Treaties', and to 'oversee the application of Union law'. It does this mainly through its powers of initiation and implementation, its responsibilities for managing the EU budget, and its responsibilities for the external relations of the EU. Thanks to all this work, it has been described as the 'barometer of integration' and the key organization whose activities reflect the patterns of European integration (Dimitrakopoulos, 2004, p. 2).

Most of its work revolves around the development and implementation of EU law, which comes in several different forms (see Figure 10.3).

Powers of initiation

The Commission has a monopoly over the generation of most new European laws, and can also draw up proposals for new policy areas, as it did with the Single European Act and the Delors package for economic and monetary union.

Figure 10.3 The EU's legal tools

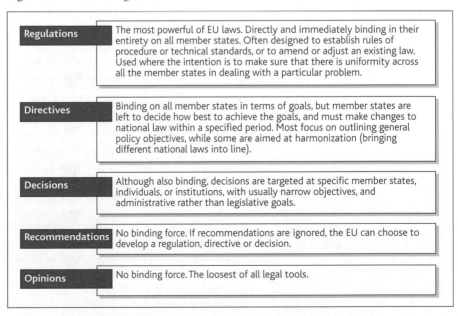

Regulations	The most powerful of EU laws. Directly and immediately binding in their entirety on all member states. Often designed to establish rules of procedure or technical standards, or to amend or adjust an existing law. Used where the intention is to make sure that there is uniformity across all the member states in dealing with a particular problem.
Directives	Binding on all member states in terms of goals, but member states are left to decide how best to achieve the goals, and must make changes to national law within a specified period. Most focus on outlining general policy objectives, while some are aimed at harmonization (bringing different national laws into line).
Decisions	Although also binding, decisions are targeted at specific member states, individuals, or institutions, with usually narrow objectives, and administrative rather than legislative goals.
Recommendations	No binding force. If recommendations are ignored, the EU can choose to develop a regulation, directive or decision.
Opinions	No binding force. The loosest of all legal tools.

Figure 10.4 Powers of the European Commission

- Develops and makes proposals for new EU laws and policies
- Oversees implementation of laws and policies through the member states
- Develops and manages the EU budget
- Represents the EU in international trade negotiations
- Oversees process by which applications for membership of the EU are considered
- Manages a network of more than 130 overseas delegations
- Coordinates the EU's official development assistance and humanitarian aid

Its main guidance comes from the treaties, whose general principles it works to turn into practical laws and policies, but it can also be nudged into action by the European Council, the Council of Ministers, Parliament, a ruling by the Court of Justice, by emergencies and political need, or by pressure from member states, interest groups, and corporations. Proposals for new laws can also come from a commissioner or a staff member of one of the DGs.

A proposal for a new law (or an amendment to an existing law) usually begins as a draft written by middle ranking Eurocrats in the relevant DG. If several DGs have an interest in the topic, then one will be selected as *chef de file*, or lead DG. The proposal then works its way through interested DGs, the Commission's Legal Service, *cabinets* and advisory committees, meetings of interested external policy actors, and the office of the relevant Commissioner. This process can take months or even years to complete. Finished proposals will then be reviewed by the *chefs de cabinet*, meeting together weekly on Mondays, who will decide which proposals need discussion by the College and which do not. The proposals are then reviewed by the College, gathering on Wednesdays

Figure 10.5 Workflow of the European Commission

Focus on . . .
Curved cucumbers and knobbly carrots

Critics of European integration, led by elements of the tabloid press in Britain, like to illustrate their concerns by focusing on examples of laws developed by the Commission that seem to indicate a bureaucracy that has lost touch with reality. A prime example was a new law adopted by the Community in 1989 that classified fruit and vegetables in part by their appearance. The goal was to help consumers compare products across state lines, and the criteria used included the curvature of cucumbers and the smoothness of carrots.

Although well-intentioned, the legislation was seized upon by critics (including governments and supermarket operators) as an example of standardization run amok, and in 2007 the Commission bowed to pressure and agreed to amend the legislation. In 2009, the visual appearance measures were lifted from all but the ten biggest-selling fruits and vegetables (including apples, oranges, lettuce, and tomatoes), while member states were allowed to sell sub-standard products under a special label. The decision, announced then agriculture commissioner Mariann Fischer Boel, meant 'the return to our shelves of the curved cucumber and the knobbly carrot', and an acknowledgement that the regulation of such matters was better left to market operators.

Although relatively trivial, the problem draws attention to the bigger question of just how far the process of integration should go in encouraging standardization and harmonization. There may be an argument that regulating the shape and size of fruit and vegetables can help save space and money, but as well as creating unnecessary waste, this is an example of the kind of micro-management that begs for mockery. And while this is a real example of a real piece of legislation, something of a minor industry has developed over the years in developing Euromyths; the Commission has been (wrongly) credited at various times with legislating that tightrope walkers in circuses must wear hard hats, that lorry drivers should eat healthier breakfasts, that the dimensions of condoms be standardized, and that barmaids must cover their cleavages.

in Brussels, or in Strasbourg if Parliament is in plenary session. Using a majority vote, the College can accept or reject the proposal, send it back for redrafting, or defer making a decision. If accepted, it is sent to the Council of Ministers and the European Parliament for a decision.

Powers of implementation

Once a law has been adopted by the Council of Ministers and Parliament, the Commission is responsible for making sure that it is implemented by the member states. It cannot do this directly but instead must work through national bureaucracies, which leaves it hostage to the abilities, energies and cultures of those bureaucracies, which vary from one member state to another. Every member state is required to report to the Commission on the progress it is making, but this is sometimes easier said than done: the Commission only has a limited number of staff, and while member states may not openly refuse to implement a law, they may drag their feet, or there may be genuine problems with interpreting the meaning and effect of a law. For these reasons, the Commission often relies on less formal means of gathering information, including whistle-blowing by individuals, corporations, and interest groups.

If a member state is slow, the Commission has three options available:

- It can issue a Letter of Formal Notice giving the member state time to comply (usually about two months). Most problems are resolved at this stage.
- If there is still no progress, the Commission can issue a Reasoned Opinion explaining why it feels there may be a violation.
- If there is still no compliance, the Commission can take the member state (or an individual, corporation, or other institution if they are the responsible parties) to the European Court of Justice for failure to fulfil its obligations. The Commission can recommend a fine or a penalty for the member state, but the final decision is left with the Court.

At the same time, the Commission adds pressure by publicizing progress on implementation. Over time, Greece and Italy have been the worst offenders (see Figure 10.6), mainly because their bureaucracies are relatively slow and inefficient. The lead-up to the 2004 eastern enlargement of the EU was a particularly busy time for the Commission, checking that the new incoming members were keeping up with their obligations to implement existing EU law. Just months before the new states joined, the Commission published a report warning of problems in all ten countries, opening them to the risk of fines, export bans, and the loss of EU subsidies. Lithuania and Slovenia had made the most progress, while Poland was singled out for its poor performance in areas as diverse as farm subsidies, inadequate standards at meat and dairy plants, dealing with corruption, and making changes to its fishing industry.

Managing EU finances

Control over the purse-strings is one of the most potent of all political powers, and while the EU budget is relatively small (see Chapter 18), the reach of the Commission is extended by its role in drafting the budget, monitoring its progress through the Council of Ministers and Parliament, and – once the budget is approved – making sure that all revenues are collected and that funds are spent correctly. This means working with national agencies, monitoring the collection of funds, and ensuring that the member states make their required contributions (Nugent, 2001, pp. 287–8).

External relations

Although the process of European integration was inwardly focused in its early years, as the reach of the EEC expanded so its effects were felt outside its member states, and the role of representing the EEC/EU externally largely defaulted to the Commission. The basis of its role lies in the Treaty of Rome, which gave the Commission the authority in areas of exclusive Community competence to negotiate international agreements on behalf of the member states. The EU is now one of the world's dominating political and economic actors (see Chapter 24), and as such the activities and the visibility of the Commission in external relations have grown exponentially (Smith, 2006). Those activities fall into four main categories.

Figure 10.6 Infringements of EU law, 1952–2008

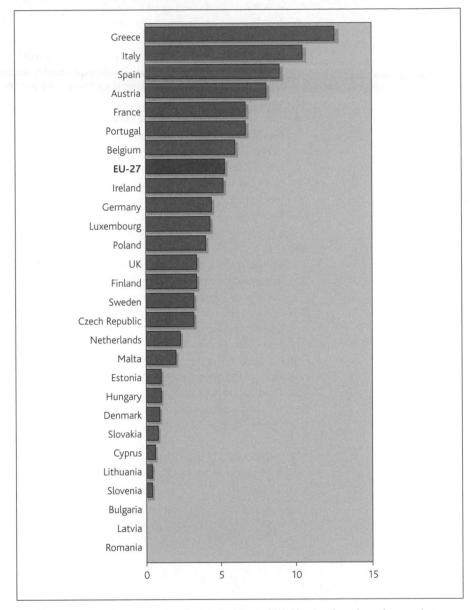

Note: Figures show annual average number of actions for failure to fulfil obligations for each member state since joining EEC/EU.
Source: Figures calculated by author from data in Annual Report of European Court of Justice, http://curia.europa.eu (retrieved January 2010).

● It represents the EU in international trade negotiations. The member states agree common positions and it is left to the Commission to negotiate, whether on bilateral deals or in multilateral negotiations or dispute resolution through the World Trade Organization. Backed by a market of nearly 500 million people, and with the EU's share of world trade standing at 20 per cent (see Chapter 24), the Commission is the representative of an economic and trading behemoth.

- It processes applications for full or associate membership of the EU. This was not the case in the early years of the EEC, but as the number of interested potential members grew, so the Commission helped develop a more strategic approach to the process, evaluating the quality and implications of new applications. If the European Council decides to open negotiations with an applicant country, the Commission manages the process.
- It is a key point of contact between the EU and the rest of the world, and has built a network of more than 130 overseas delegations that are the functional equivalent of EU embassies. They work alongside the national embassies of the individual member states, and foreign countries return the compliment by maintaining offices in Brussels that give them diplomatic ties with the EU, existing separately from their embassies to Belgium. Starting in 2010, the Commission delegations began to be taken over by the new European External Action Service (EEAS) (see Chapter 24).
- It is the EU's coordinator for official development assistance (ODA) and humanitarian aid, a role whose significance has grown as the volume of aid has grown: the EU is now the source of 56 per cent of all ODA provided by the world's wealthiest countries (see Chapter 25).

Unlike trade policy, the lines of responsibility on foreign policy are still unclear. The governments of member states still go their own way on many issues, and the external face of EU foreign policy was divided until Lisbon between the Commissioner for External Relations and the High Representative for the Common Foreign and Security Policy. The precise status of the EU in international forums can also be confusing to the uninitiated; there is no single European Union seat in the United Nations or the North Atlantic Treaty Organization, for example, but the EU is a member of the WTO along with all the individual EU member states, even though the Commission speaks on behalf of all 27 states at most WTO meetings.

SUMMARY

- The European Commission (headquartered in Brussels) is the bureaucratic-executive arm of the EU, responsible mainly for developing proposals for new laws and policies, and then for overseeing implementation in the member states.
- It also manages the EU budget, has responsibilities in external relations, represents the EU in international trade negotiations, processes applications for membership of the EU, and acts as the key point of contact between the EU and foreign governments.
- It is headed by a College of Commissioners, whose members are nominated by the governments of each of the member states to five-year renewable terms and must be confirmed by the European Council and the European Parliament.
- The College is headed by a president, nominated by the European Council to a five-year renewable term and confirmed by a majority vote in the European Parliament. Commission presidents have become the most public face of the EU institutions.
- Most Commission staff work in Brussels-based directorates-general (DGs) and services, but some work in Commission offices in EU member states and abroad.
- The detailed work of the Commission is undertaken by a network of advisory, management and regulatory committees, supported by a Secretariat General.
- The work of the Commission is widely misunderstood, critics claiming that it is too powerful, secretive, and expensive. In fact it can only do what the member states allow it to do, it is no more secretive than national bureaucracies, and its operating budget is quite modest compared to those of national bureaucracies.

KEY TERMS AND CONCEPTS

Cabinet
College of Commissioners
Comitology
Directorate-general
President of the Commission

FURTHER READING

Cini, Michelle (2007), *From Integration to Integrity: Administrative Ethics and Reform in the European Commission* (Manchester: Manchester University Press); Michael W. Bauer (ed.) (2008), *Reforming the European Commission* (London: Routledge). Two books that look at recent reforms to the European Commission and the implications for the EU policy process.

Nugent, Neill (2001), *The European Commission* (Basingstoke: Palgrave Macmillan); David Spence (ed.) (2006), *The European Commission*, 3rd edn (London: John Harper Publishing). The two standard texts on the Commission, covering its structure, powers and responsibilities, the second written by someone with many years of experience working in the Commission.

Smith, Andy (ed.) (2004), *Politics and the European Commission: Actors, Interdependence, Legitimacy* (London: Routledge). A study of the political forces that come to bear on the Commission, arguing that studying the links between politics and technical expertise helps us better understand how it works.

CHAPTER 11

The Councils

PREVIEW

The Council of Ministers and the European Council are often confused with each other, but are quite different. The Council of Ministers consists of national government ministers and shares responsibility with the European Parliament for amending and voting on proposals for new European laws and for approving the EU budget. The European Council, meanwhile, is the meeting place for the heads of government of the member states, in which they make strategic decisions, respond to crises, and discuss pressing economic and foreign policy problems.

Both institutions are primarily intergovernmental. Their members are representatives of the member states, and defend national interests while trying to balance them with the wider European interest. The ministers mainly use a system of qualified majority voting to make decisions, while the European Council relies on consensus, informality, and flexibility. Until Lisbon, both were directed by a presidency, held by a member state for rotating periods of six months. The European Council is now headed by its own president, appointed to limited terms by members of the Council. Meanwhile, the presidency of the Council of Ministers continues to be held by a member state, while its detailed work is undertaken by permanent representatives of the member states based in Brussels.

This chapter looks first at the changing role of the Council of Ministers in the EU decision-making process, and at the implications of qualified majority voting. It then looks at the work of the European Council, with an emphasis on the political dynamics of summitry, and on the effects of the new appointed president of the European Council. It argues that the work of the Council of Ministers has been too often overlooked, thanks mainly to the attention paid to the Commission.

KEY ISSUES

- Is the Council of Ministers primarily intergovernmental or supranational in character?
- Is the work of the Council more legislative or executive in nature?
- Which is more important to the EU decision-making process: the Council of Ministers or Coreper?
- Is summitry an effective and efficient way of reaching decisions, and how does it compare to the often lengthy discussions that take place in committees of the Council of Ministers?
- Should the president of the European Council be a leader or a conductor?

How the Councils evolved

The Council of the European Union, more usually known as the Council of Ministers or just 'the Council', traces its roots back to the Special Council of Ministers that was part of the ECSC. This was created at the insistence of the Benelux governments, which were worried about the dominance of France, West Germany, and Italy (Westlake and Galloway, 2004, p. 6). The agreement reached was that while the High Authority would deal exclusively with matters relating to coal and steel, all other initiatives needed the approval of the Council of Ministers. The Council was designed to be a link between the High Authority and national governments, and to balance the supranational character of the High Authority. It used a majority voting system, with a minor qualification: at least one state that produced at least one-sixth of the total value of coal and steel output had to be in favour, or two such states in the case of a tied vote.

Separate Councils of Ministers were created for the EEC and Euratom in 1958, and national interests moved to the fore as the balance of power shifted from the three Commissions to the three Councils. A qualified majority voting system was created that was designed to protect smaller member states from being overwhelmed by larger states: each Council had only six members, but they were given 17 votes, with four each for the three largest countries, two each for Belgium and the Netherlands, and one for Luxembourg. On some issues a simple majority was enough, but on others a minimum of 12 votes (70 per cent of the total) was needed.

Under the Merger treaty, the three councils were combined in 1967 into a single Council of Ministers, which it was hoped would become less important with time as the Commission initiated, decided, *and* implemented policy. But member states jealously guarded their rights on the Council, and intergovern-mentalism became the byword in Community decision-making. Even so, just how far today's Council of Ministers is intergovernmental or supranational remains a matter of debate. Ministers are national government representatives (giving the Council a distinctly confederal nature), and keep their eyes on public and political opinion at home, tempting them to defend national interests. But Westlake and Galloway (2004, p.8) argue that to portray the Council as intergov-ernmental is misleading, and that it is 'first and foremost a supranational institu-tion' because it acts as a collective body when defending the Council's interests relative to other EU institutions, or the EU's interests to the outside world.

Meanwhile, the broader strategic interests of the Community were discussed in ad hoc summits of leaders of the member states held in 1961 (Paris and Bonn), 1967 (Rome), and 1969 (the Hague), all at the instigation of France and all to address various crises (Werts, 2008, pp. 3–11). As the goals and obligations of the Treaty of Rome became more clear, so it also became clear that the Community lacked a sense of overall direction, and was becoming bogged down by intergovernmental struggles within the Council of Ministers. The inability of the Community to respond quickly and effectively to major international crises was illustrated by the confusion that came in the wake of the end of the Bretton Woods system in 1971 and the energy crisis of 1973, which prompted French foreign minister Michel Jobert to dismiss Europe as a 'nonentity' (Defarges, 1988, pp. 38–9). Clearly, something needed to be done to give the Community a sense of direction.

At a Copenhagen summit in December 1973 it was agreed to arrange more frequent meetings among Community heads of government, and at a summit in Paris in 1974 it was agreed to create a new forum that would (as the summit communiqué put it) take 'an overall approach' to internal and external problems and provide policy progress and consistency (see Document 11.1). The new forum was given neither formal rules nor legal standing nor a separate bureaucracy, and lacked even a fixed name until French president Giscard d'Estaing's announcement at a press conference at the close of the 1974 meeting that 'the European summit is dead, long live the European Council' (Morgan, 1976, p. 5). Given the surfeit of councils in the European system (the European Council, the Council of Ministers, the Council of Europe, and so on), this was an unfortunate choice.

The new body met for the first time as the European Council in Dublin in March 1975, and then triannually until 1985, then biannually (with additional special meetings as needed) until the Treaty of Lisbon, since when it has been committed to four annual meetings. The Council usually convened in the country holding the presidency of the Council of Ministers, but the organization and security needed to set up summits became too onerous, so since 2003 all

DOCUMENT 11.1

Final communiqué of the meeting of heads of Government of the Community, 9 and 10 December 1974 (excerpts)

1. The Heads of Government of the nine States of the Community, the Ministers of Foreign Affairs and the President of the Commission, meeting in Paris at the invitation of the French President, examined the various problems confronting Europe . . .

2. Recognizing the need for an overall approach to the internal problems involved in achieving European unity and the external problems facing Europe, the Heads of Government consider it essential to ensure progress and overall consistency in the activities of the Communities and in the work on political co-operation.

3. The Heads of Government have therefore decided to meet, accompanied by the Ministers of Foreign Affairs, three times a year and, whenever necessary, in the Council of the Communities and in the context of political co-operation . . .

In order to ensure consistency in Community activities and continuity of work, the Ministers of Foreign Affairs, meeting in the Council of the Community, will

act as initiators and co-ordinators. They may hold political cooperation meetings at the same time . . .

4. With a view to progress towards European unity, the Heads of Government reaffirm their determination gradually to adopt common positions and co-ordinate their diplomatic action in all areas of international affairs which affect the interests of the European Community . . .

5. The Heads of Government consider it necessary to increase the solidarity of the Nine both by improving Community procedures and by developing new common policies in areas to be decided on and granting the necessary powers to the Institutions.

6. In order to improve the functioning of the Council of the Community, they consider that it is necessary to renounce the practice which consists of making agreement on all questions conditional on the unanimous consent of the Member States, whatever their respective positions may be regarding the conclusions reached in Luxembourg on 28 January 1966.

routine European Council meetings have been held in Brussels. The European Council was finally given formal recognition as an EU institution with the passage of Lisbon in 2009.

How the Council of Ministers is structured

The Council of Ministers is headquartered in the Justus Lipsius building (also known as the Consilium) in the European Quarter of Brussels, across from the Berlaymont, seat of the European Commission. Named for a little-known sixteenth-century Flemish humanist, the Justus Lipsius is a large, marble-clad building that was opened in 1995 at a cost of €450 million, allowing the Council to move from its old base in the nearby Charlemagne building and a network of rented offices into a single home. But the new building was already too small to account for enlargement of the EU or for the decision to hold all European Council summits from 2003 in Brussels. As the Council spilled over into neighbouring buildings, renovations were made to the Lipsius building to absorb the growth.

The Council of Ministers has five main components: the councils themselves, the presidency of the Council, the Committee of Permanent Representatives, committees and working groups, and the General Secretariat.

The Councils

The different groups of ministers that make up the Council are known either as technical councils, formations or configurations. Where once there were nearly two dozen, there are now just ten (see Table 11.1). Whichever of these groups is meeting, they always act as the Council, and in legal terms their decisions are always taken as the Council. Although equal in terms of their status and powers, some are – in Orwellian terms – more equal than others. The senior council is

Illustration 11.1
The Councils

The Justus Lipsius building in Brussels, seat of the Council of Ministers and the European Council.

Figure 11.1 Structure of the Council of Ministers

- The quasi-legislative arm of the EU
- Headquartered in Brussels
- Member states take turns, in a pre-agreed rotation, at chairing all Council meetings except Foreign Affairs, which is chaired by the High Representative for Foreign Affairs
- Consists of the relevant national government ministers of the member states, membership changing according to the policy area under consideration
- Most negotiations within the Council take place in the Committee of Permanent Representatives, made up of representatives from the member states
- Work supported by a General Secretariat
- Intergovernmental and confederal in character, but with supranational aspects

General Affairs, which prepares and ensures follow-up to meetings of the European Council. Other influential councils include Foreign Affairs (which deals with external relations, trade issues, and development cooperation), Economic and Financial Affairs (Ecofin) (which deals with economic policy coordination and matters relating to the euro), and Agriculture and Fisheries. These four councils meet monthly, while the rest meet between two and four times a year, for a grand total of about 50–60 Council meetings per year. Almost all are held in Brussels, except in April, June, and October when they are held in Luxembourg. Sessions usually last no more than one or two days, depending on how much business they have. Representatives of the Commission and the European Central Bank may also attend, as needed.

Lisbon says that representatives of the member states must be 'at ministerial level', but meetings of the Council do not always attract a matching set of ministers. Some may opt out and send a deputy because they want to avoid political embarrassment on a sensitive issue, or because they may have more important matters to attend to at home, and not all member states divide policy portfolios up the same way; prime ministers, for example, sometimes give themselves key policy portfolios such as foreign or economic affairs, while some of the less important portfolios may be combined with the responsibilities of senior ministers.

Table 11.1 Council of Ministers configurations

Agriculture and Fisheries
Competitiveness
Economic and Financial Affairs
Education, Youth and Culture
Employment, Social Policy, Health and Consumer Affairs
Environment
Foreign Affairs
General Affairs
Justice and Home Affairs
Transport, Telecommunications and Energy

The key to understanding the dynamics of the Council lies in terms such as *compromise*, *bargaining*, and *diplomacy*. The ministers are domestic politicians, so they are driven by national political interests, ideology, the popularity and stability of their home governments, and the attitude of those governments towards European integration. At the same time, they cannot lose sight of broader European issues, and they have increasingly followed the lead of the European Council. As a result they are pulled in several directions, it is difficult always to be sure to whom they are responsible, and the character of the Council remains ambiguous at best (Hayes-Renshaw and Wallace, 2006, pp. 4–5, 27–8).

The Presidency

Until Lisbon, the presidency of both the Council of Ministers and the European Council was held not by a person but by the government of a member state, with each taking turns in a pre-agreed rotation for six months, beginning in January and July each year. All meetings of the Council were organized and chaired by the relevant ministers from the country holding the presidency, giving its government control over the setting of the EU agenda for six months. Lisbon was supposed to clarify and simplify, but ended up muddying the waters by giving the European Council its own president, while arranging for the Foreign Affairs Council to be chaired by the High Representative of the Union for Foreign Affairs and Security Policy. All other meetings of the Council are still chaired by representatives of the member states in a pre-agreed rotation (see Table 11.2).

This arrangement has the advantage of giving each member state the opportunity to guide the direction of the EU. This, in turn, helps make the EU more real to the citizens of the member state in control, allows member states to bring issues of national interest to the top of the agenda, and gives smaller member states an opportunity to counter the influence of bigger states. But while the rotation was viable when there were only six or even 12 member states, it has lengthened as membership has grown, so that with 27 members they must each wait thirteen and a half years for their turn at the helm. The workload that comes with the job has also grown, creating a burden that is especially onerous on

● **Presidency of the Council of Ministers**: The leadership of all meetings of the Council of Ministers except the Foreign Affairs Council. Held by the governments of EU member states in a rotation of six months each.

Table 11.2 Rotation of the Council presidency

	First half	Second half
2010	Spain	Belgium
2011	Hungary	Poland
2012	Denmark	Cyprus
2013	Ireland	Lithuania
2014	Greece	Italy
2015	Latvia	Luxembourg
2016	Netherlands	Slovakia
2017	Malta	UK
2018	Estonia	Bulgaria
2019	Austria	Romania

smaller member states with limited resources and small bureaucracies. The rotation also has the effect of holding the rest of the EU hostage to the different styles, interests and political abilities of the countries in the presidency, and means a constant change of personnel at the top. This is offset to some extent by the use of a *troika* **system** under which each presidency cooperates with its predecessor and successor. With Lisbon, this has evolved into a virtual 18-month three-state team presidency.

The duties of the presidency are as follows (Elgström, 2003, pp. 4–7):

- It prepares and coordinates the work of the Council of Ministers, setting the agendas for several thousand annual meetings of ministers, working parties and committees.
- It arranges and chairs most meetings of the Council of Ministers and Coreper, and represents the Council in dealings with other EU institutions.
- It mediates, bargains, promotes cooperation among member states, and tries to ensure that policy development has consistency and continuity.

It remains to be seen how the new post of president of the European Council will change the dynamic of decision-making, and how the new president will work with the bureaucracy of the Council of Ministers. Over the years the Council of Ministers has increasingly followed the lead of the European Council, opening up the prospect of the president of the European Council making arrangements that will influence the entire structure of the Council.

Permanent Representatives

Although ministers are the most visible and senior members of the Council hierarchy, much of the work of the Council has already been settled before the ministers meet. This is made possible by the Committee of Permanent Representatives, or **Coreper** (*Comité des représentants permanents*). Each member state maintains a Permanent Representation in Brussels, in effect an embassy to the EU that works alongside member state embassies to Belgium. The staffs of the Permanent Representations include experts in each of the policy areas addressed by the EU, and these experts will meet regularly as Coreper (often multiple times each week, and altogether about 2,000 times a year) to go through the proposals for new laws, to argue national positions, and to work out agreements and compromises. All but unknown outside the corridors of Brussels, and the subject of surprisingly little academic study, Coreper is one of the most powerful parts of the EU decision-making structure.

There was no mention of Coreper in the Treaty of Paris, although a Coordinating Committee made up of national civil servants was created in 1953 to help prepare ministerial meetings in the ECSC, and the Committee in turn set up working groups to help with preparatory work. As plans for the EEC evolved in 1955–56, it was decided that the Council needed help, paving the way for the appointment of permanent representatives to the EEC – and supporting staff – in 1958 (Hayes-Renshaw and Wallace, 2006, p. 73). The representatives in turn recruited experts from national ministries to help them work through the increasingly technical and specialized proposals they were reviewing. In 1962 Coreper was subdivided into two parts: Coreper II brings permanent representatives together

● *Troika* **system**: The arrangement under which the member state holding the presidency works closely with its predecessor and successor in order to help encourage policy consistency.

● **Coreper**: The Committee of Permanent Representatives, in which delegates from each of the member states meet to discuss proposals for new laws before they are sent to the Council of Ministers for a final decision.

to discuss the broad issues of integration, dealing with the work of General Affairs, Ecofin, the Justice and Home Affairs Council, and the European Council, while their deputies meet in Coreper I to discuss the work of the other councils.

Thanks to Coreper, as much as 85 per cent of the detailed work of the Council is finished before the ministers even meet (Hayes-Renshaw and Wallace, 2006, p. 77), with only the most politically sensitive and controversial proposals left for the ministers to discuss. This arrangement was described colourfully by Alan Clark, a former British government minister, when he noted in his diaries that 'it makes not the slightest difference to the conclusions of a meeting what Ministers say at it. Everything is decided, and horse-traded off by officials at Coreper. . . The ministers arrive on the scene at the last minute, hot, tired, ill, or drunk (sometimes all of these together), read out their piece and depart' (Clark, 1993).

Working parties and committees

In addition to Coreper, the Council of Ministers has a complex network of working parties and committees (about 250 in all, together meeting more than 4,000 times each year) that support the work of Coreper, and in this sense function as the foundations of the Council edifice. The first port of call for a proposal from the Commission is usually a working party, which reviews the technical details and makes a recommendation to Coreper. The working parties are organized along policy lines, with a variety of charges: some are permanent, some are temporary, some meet weekly, some biannually, and some only once before being disbanded. They bring together policy specialists, national experts, members of the Permanent Representations, and staff from the Commission. The Council also has several standing committees, dealing with economic and financial matters, employment, social protection, security matters, financial services, and other key issues.

The General Secretariat

This is the bureaucracy of the Council, staffed by about 3,000 employees based in Brussels, most of them translators and service staff. It helps prepare Council meetings, provides advice to the presidency, provides legal support to the Council and Coreper, briefs Council meetings on the status of agenda items, keeps records, manages the Council budget, and generally gives the work of the Council some continuity. It was originally focused mainly on secretarial work, but has since become more political, helping manage negotiations, offering counsel to the presidency, and helping with the executive duties of the secretary general (Westlake and Galloway, 2004, pp. 347–9).

The secretary general is appointed by the Council of Ministers to five-year renewable terms. The job was briefly given a new personality and a higher public profile in 1999 when it was combined with the (then) new office of the High Representative for the Common Foreign and Security Policy, a move which had the effect of making the General Secretariat a hub for the development of the EU's foreign and security policies (Christiansen, 2006, pp. 164–7). The first holder of this combined position was Javier Solana, a former minister in the Spanish government and a former secretary general of NATO. With the passage of the Treaty of Lisbon, the job of High Representative was redefined so that the officeholder is now both chair of the Foreign Affairs Council within the Council

Figure 11.2 Powers of the Council of Ministers

- Shares powers with the European Parliament for discussing and passing laws
- Shares powers with Parliament for approving and adopting the EU budget
- Coordinates the economic policies of the member states
- Coordinates justice and home affairs policies of the member states
- Defines and implements the Common Foreign and Security Policy
- Concludes international agreements on behalf of the EU

of Ministers, and also a vice-president of the European Commission. Meanwhile, the job of secretary general reverted back to something more like its pre-1999 character when Solana was succeeded in December 2009 by Pierre de Boissieu, a French diplomat and grand-nephew of Charles de Gaulle.

What the Council of Ministers does

The main job of the Council is to decide – in conjunction with Parliament – which proposals for new European laws and policies will be adopted and which will not. When the College of Commissioners has approved a proposal for a new law, it is sent to the Council, the more complex proposals usually going first to one or more of the Council working parties or committees, which identify points of agreement and disagreement (for more details, see Hayes-Renshaw, Lequesne, and Mayor Lopez, 1989). Proposals are then sent to Coreper, listed as a Roman I item if there is agreement and as a Roman II item if further discussion is needed. Coreper reviews the political implications and tries to clear up as many of the remaining problems as possible. If agreement is reached the

Figure 11.3 Workflow of the Council of Ministers

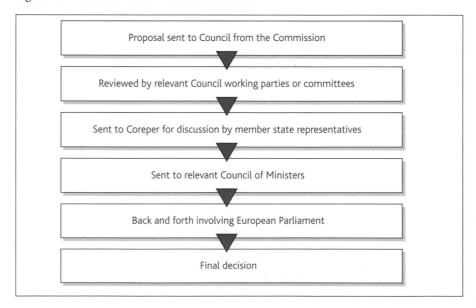

Proposal sent to Council from the Commission

Reviewed by relevant Council working parties or committees

Sent to Coreper for discussion by member state representatives

Sent to relevant Council of Ministers

Back and forth involving European Parliament

Final decision

Focus on . . .
Meetings of the Council of Ministers

On a typical working day, the Justus Lipsius building will be home to dozens of meetings, ranging from working parties and committees up through Coreper to the more infrequent meetings of the ministers themselves. It is not just the ministers or their representatives who attend these meetings, but small teams representing each of the member states, along with representatives of the Commission and the General Secretariat. National delegations are seated in order of the rotation of the presidency, and even if they are limited to five members each, this still means that there will be more than 140 people at a typical Council meeting. If the meeting threatens to become unwieldy, or if sensitive political issues are being debated, the president can clear the room of everyone but 'ministers plus two,' 'ministers plus one', or even just the ministers and the commissioner alone.

In addition to general discussions, there are usually regular postponements and adjournments, huddles of delegates during breaks, regular communication with national capitals, and a constant flow of ministers and officials coming and going. If negotiations become bogged down, the president might use a device known as a *tour de table*, during which the heads of delegations are asked in turn to give a brief summary of their positions on an issue. This can be time-consuming, but it also gives every delegation the chance to take part in discussions, can help focus the discussion, and helps raise possible new points of agreement and compromise.

proposal is sent as an A item to the relevant council, which will usually approve it without debate (this is the case with about two-thirds of council decisions (Westlake and Galloway, 2004, p. 38)). If agreement has not been reached, or if the item was left over from a previous meeting, it is listed as a B item, meaning that it needs further discussion.

The voting system within the Council has changed over the years, the options reflecting changing attitudes towards integration. Where once unanimity was required, it is now all but unknown and ministers mainly have two options. If they are dealing with a procedural issue, or one of a small number of specific policy issues, they can use a simple majority. But formal votes are rarely called, and outcomes are instead determined by silence or the absence of opposition. For all other business, where a vote is needed, the ministers use a **qualified majority vote** (QMV).

Under this arrangement, each minister is given several votes roughly in proportion to the population of his or her member state (see Table 11.3), for a total of 345. To be successful, a proposal must win a triple majority: at least 14 states must be in favour, with a total of at least 255 votes (just under 74 per cent of the total), and the states in favour must be home to at least 311 million people (just under 63 per cent of the population of EU). This arrangement both reduces

● **Qualified majority vote**: A system of voting used in the Council of Ministers, by which proposals must win substantially more than a simple majority.

Table 11.3 Qualified majority voting in the Council of Ministers

Germany	29	Belgium	12	Lithuania	7
UK	29	Hungary	12	Latvia	4
France	29	Portugal	12	Slovenia	4
Italy	29	Austria	10	Estonia	4
Spain	27	Bulgaria	10	Cyprus	4
Poland	27	Sweden	10	Luxembourg	4
Romania	14	Slovakia	7	Malta	3
Netherlands	13	Denmark	7		
Greece	12	Finland	7		
Czech Republic	12	Ireland	7	Total	345

To pass, a proposal must have 255 votes in favour, from a majority of states, which must be home to 63 per cent of the EU population.

the power of big states and encourages states to form coalitions. With effect from November 2014, the qualified majority will be 55 per cent of the votes in the Council, from at least 15 member states that must together be home to 65 per cent of the population of the EU. A blocking minority will also be available, requiring at least four states representing 35 per cent of the population of the EU.

The allocation of votes has long been a bone of contention. Consternation was generated during the debate over the EU constitution when Poland, which had been given 27 votes under the Treaty of Nice, refused to have its quota reduced, even when it was pointed out that Germany – with twice the population and an economy ten times larger – had just 29 votes. Poland also baulked during the debate over Lisbon at the suggestion to change QMV from a triple to a double majority. The then Polish President Lech Kaczynski claimed that such a change would hurt Poland to the benefit of large states such as Germany, and shocked his peers by arguing that Poland would have had a much bigger population had it not been for the ravages of the Second World War; 'Poles like Germans,' he mused, 'while Germans do not like Poles' ('Poles in War of Words Over Voting', *BBC News Online*, 21 June 2007.). He was eventually placated by an agreement to delay switching to the new voting system until 2014, and then to phase it in over three years.

Once the Council has reached a decision, proposals are subject to a complex process of review involving the European Parliament in which – depending on the nature of the topic – they can be discussed and voted upon in each body up to three times. If there is still a failure to agree, proposals are sent to a Conciliation Committee made up of 27 representatives each from Parliament and the Council of Ministers, with representatives of the Commission also in attendance (see Chapter 12 for more details).

The European Council

● **European Council**: The forum in which the heads of government of the member states meet regularly to make strategic decisions on the progress of integration.

The European Council and the Council of Ministers are often confused, and sometimes (wrongly) interchangaeably referred to as 'The Council', but their membership, rules, structure and legal personalities are quite distinct. Among the critical differences:

- Its members are the heads of government of the EU member states (not the ministers).
- It has its own appointed president (and is no longer chaired by a presidency from a member state).
- It discusses broad strategic issues (not proposals for new laws).
- It mainly uses only one means of decision-making (consensus).
- It meets a maximum of four times each year as a rule (not monthly).
- It has no legislative functions and no direct relationship with the European Parliament.

The European Council is the meeting place for the heads of government (or the heads of state in the cases of Cyprus and France) of the EU member states. Until Lisbon, the Council would usually meet every June and December, with additional meetings as needed, but the Council is now committed to meeting four times per year, with additional special meetings as needed. Convening in the Justus Lipsius building in Brussels, the Council usually meets (in closed session) for no more than two days, the heads of government being accompanied by a minister (usually the foreign minister). Also present will be the President of the Council, the President of the Commission (with a deputy commissioner as needed), the High Representative of the Union for Foreign Affairs and Security Policy, and small retinues of staff and advisers, including Permanent Representatives. The President of the Council chairs the meetings, and decisions are taken on the basis of a consensus (except where the treaties provide otherwise).

In spite of its clearly dominating role, the duties of the European Council were long kept deliberately vague and ambiguous, its membership first confirmed by the Single European Act, its role only given a basis in the treaties by Maastricht (Westlake and Galloway, 2004, p. 179), and final confirmation that it was an institution of the EU coming only with the Treaty of Lisbon, which describes its job as follows:

> The European Council shall provide the Union with the necessary impetus for its development and shall define the general political directions and priorities thereof. It shall not exercise legislative functions.

Put another way, the Council rises above the details and focuses on key decisions about the strategic direction of political integration. This includes launch-

Figure 11.4 Structure and powers of the European Council

- The 'board of directors' of the EU, consisting of the heads of government of the member states
- Based in Brussels, where it meets at least four times annually
- Chaired by a president appointed by the European Council for a term of two and a half years, renewable once
- Responsible for taking strategic decisions
- Responsible for making nominations to senior positions, including president of the European Commission, the High Representative of the Union for Foreign Affairs and Security Policy, and president of the European Central Bank

CONCEPT

Summitry

The use of high-level person-to-person negotiations for the discussion and resolution of international issues. This is usual for bilateral or multilateral discussions among the leaders of states, and has been a regular part of the EU decision-making process since the creation of the European Council. Summits by definition are usually short, deal with strategic issues rather than the technical details of policy, and set the tone and character of intergovernmental relations.

ing policy cooperation in new areas, helping drive the EU policy agenda, ensuring policy consistency, and promoting the development of a common EU foreign policy.

Beyond policy-making, the Council also makes appointments to several of the key positions in the EU hierarchy. Aside from the Council's own president, the most important of these is the president of the Commission. The decision to appoint begins with a review of potential candidates in the Council, which makes a decision using QMV, and sends the name of its nominee to the European Parliament, which then votes using a simple majority. If the nominee fails to win a parliamentary majority, the European Council has one month to propose a new nominee. The Council also has a role in confirming the list of new Commissioners, based on suggestions made by the governments of the member states, and is responsible for appointing – again by QMV – the High Representative of the Union for Foreign Affairs and Security Policy.

Its interest in the big picture does not mean that the Council always avoids service in the trenches of political warfare, and in fact many of the most bruising and tiring of all the debates surrounding the process of European integration have taken place in the meeting chambers of the Council. But where the job of the other institutions is to work out the details, the European Council tries to focus on the longer-term needs of the EU, using **summitry** rather than meetings designed to pore over the details of policy.

Because summitry is only loosely institutionalized, if at all, the rules are informal and meetings of the Council take place through a combination of brainstorming, intensive bilateral and multilateral discussions, and bargaining. The outcome is a formal set of Conclusions, whose content depends on a combination of the management skills of the president, the quality of organization and preparation, the negotiating skills of the individual leaders, the personal relationships among those leaders, how they choose to balance their defence of national and European interests, and the prevailing international environment.

Illustration 11.2
The European Council

EU leaders gathering for their traditional family photo at the European Council summit in Brussels in September 2010.

Table 11.4 Key summits of the European Council

Date	Venue	Highlights
March 1975	Dublin	First meeting of the Council
July 1978	Bremen	Creation of European Monetary System
November 1979	Dublin	British budget rebate demand
June 1984	Fontainebleau	British budget rebate agreed
December 1985	Luxembourg	Signature of Single European Act
December 1991	Maastricht	Signature of Treaty on European Union
December 1995	Madrid	Naming of the euro
June 1997	Amsterdam	Signature of Treaty of Amsterdam
March 2000	Lisbon	Agreement of Lisbon Strategy
December 2000	Nice	Signature of Treaty of Nice
February 2003	Brussels	Discussed growing crisis over Iraq
October 2003	Rome	Initiated IGC leading to EU constitutional treaty
December 2007	Lisbon	Signature of Treaty of Lisbon
March 2008	Brussels	Climate change
September 2008	Brussels	Crisis in Georgia
February 2010	Brussels	Informal meeting on Greek debt crisis

Because summits must often deal with crises, decisions are often made in a pressure-cooker environment, with meetings lasting longer than planned, running on into the small hours, and dominated by the expectation of agreements being reached at almost any cost for fear that summits will be declared to be failures.

Much like meetings of the Council of Ministers, national delegations are ranged around a room, their numbers limited in order to keep meetings manageable; typically only the heads of government and their foreign ministers are allowed to be present, along with representatives of the Commission and the Council of Ministers, and no more than one adviser per member state, making a total of about 90 to 100 people. Additional members of national delegations are restricted to nearby suites that they use as a base. Summits combine plenary sessions with breakouts involving different combinations of leaders, officials from the Council of Ministers working hard to draft a set of Conclusions whose content is usually announced at a closing press conference.

Some agenda issues (particularly economic problems) have been perennial, while others have come and gone in response to emergencies, crises, and changes in the international environment. Between 1957 and 2007 there were 130 meetings of European leaders, dealing with a wide variety of needs and problems:

● Launching major new initiatives, including the single market programme during the 1980s, and every new EU treaty.
● Addressing key economic matters, including the steps leading to the launch of the euro, and the EU responses to the 2007–10 global economic crisis and to the 2010 Greek debt crisis.

- Dealing with emergencies and rapidly unfolding events such as developments in eastern Europe in 1989, the crisis in the Exchange Rate Mechanism in 1992, and a February 2003 summit to try and heal rifts over the impending invasion of Iraq.
- Giving momentum to the development of an EU foreign policy.
- Resolving budget disputes.
- Making decisions on new member applications.
- Agreeing critical institutional reforms.

Along the way it has had successes, but it has also had its failures, including a slow response to pressures for agricultural and budgetary reform, and a failure to clear the way to agreements on a common EU response to the two Gulf Wars, the Bosnian conflict, and the crisis in Kosovo in 1998–99. Some of its problems could be traced to the way it was once chaired and managed: with its presidency in the hands of the government of member states, and leadership changing every six months, providing leadership and continuity was always a problem. The dynamics of Council decision-making have also been left hostage to at least five sets of internal pressures:

- The Franco-German axis has often been at heart of the work of the Council, the state of personal relations between the leaders of the two states being a key determinant of the agreements reached. Their role was diminished as eastern enlargement helped change the balance of Council membership, but still crops up occasionally.
- The ideological and personal agendas of individual leaders.
- The levels of experience of individual leaders; membership changes often as elections and political crises bring political change in the member states.
- The levels of support enjoyed at home by individual leaders. Those with a solid base of support are in different negotiating positions from those who are unpopular, or who lead weak or unstable coalition governments, or who are facing a new election that they may lose.
- The different levels of respect and credibility earned by different leaders. Some become (or have tried to become) major players in EU debates, but with enlargement there has been less opportunity for individual leaders to exert themselves in anything more than a passing fashion.

A key change made by Lisbon was to take the position of chair out of the hands of the head of government of the member state holding the presidency of the Council of Ministers, and to give it instead to a president appointed for two and a half years (renewable once) by the European Council. The president is elected using QMV, the incumbent cannot hold national office while serving as president, and he/she can be removed by QMV 'in the event of an impediment or serious misconduct'. It is too early to be sure how the creation of this post will impact the Council's leadership dynamic, particularly as the terms of the job, as outlined in the Treaty of Lisbon, are remarkably vague:

- The president shall chair, 'drive forward' and 'ensure the preparation and continuity' of the work of the Council.
- He shall 'endeavour to facilitate cohesion and consensus' in the Council.

● **President of the European Council**: The head of the European Council, a position created with the passage of the Treaty of Lisbon in 2009. Appointed by the Council for renewable two-and-a-half-year terms, and charged with giving it direction.

Herman van Rompuy

Conseil européen
Bruxelles - 16.09.2010

European Council
Brussels - 16.09.2010

When European leaders opted in November 2009 to appoint Belgian Prime Minister Herman van Rompuy as the first president of the European Council, they chose someone all but unknown outside his home state, and with a modest reputation even there. Born in 1947, he studied philosophy and economics at the Catholic University of Leuven, working as a banker before entering politics in the early 1970s as a government advisor and a member of the Christian Democratic Party. He was elected as a Senator in 1988 and as a member of the House of Representatives in 1995, serving as deputy prime minister and budget minister from 1993 to 1999. In December 2008 he reluctantly agreed to become prime minister following the resignation of Yves Leterme in a financial scandal. He inherited both a fragile coalition government and the job of representing Belgium in the response to the global economic crisis, and developed a reputation as a negotiator and consensus-builder that ultimately helped earn him the job of Council president.

- He shall 'ensure the external representation of the Union on issues concerning its common foreign and security policy, without prejudice to the powers of the High Representative of the Union for Foreign Affairs and Security Policy'.
- He must report to Parliament after each meeting.

History has repeatedly shown that the first holder of a new office can often have a major impact on how the office evolves. As we saw in Chapter 7, the choice of Herman van Rompuy as the first president of the Council was controversial, with some arguing that he was the perfect deal-maker in the sense that he would not rattle the egos of 27 national leaders meeting in committee, while others argued that the appointment of the so-called 'grey mouse' was a missed opportunity to provide the EU with a new sense of leadership. For now, opinion remains split on whether the Council best works as a collective, or whether it still needs the kind of president who can lead from the front.

SUMMARY

- 'The Council of Ministers is where national government ministers make decisions on proposals for new laws, and the European Council is where heads of government discuss broad strategic issues.
- The Council of Ministers is headquartered in Brussels, its membership changing according to the policy area under discussion. It is both intergovernmental and confederal in nature.
- Meetings of the Council are chaired by representatives from the presidency of the Council, which rotates among member states every six months.
- Most of the work of the Council is undertaken by the Committee of Permanent Representatives (Coreper), one of the most influential and most often overlooked institutions in the EU system of governance.
- The main job of the Council is to decide – in conjunction with Parliament – which proposals for new European laws and policies will be adopted and which will not. It also shares powers with Parliament for approving the EU budget.
- Most Council votes are taken using a qualified majority, with each member state given a number of votes roughly in proportion to the size of its population.
- The European Council is much like a board of directors for the EU, meeting at least four times annually in Brussels to address broader issues.
- The European Council uses summitry and bargaining, works on the basis of achieving a consensus, appoints its own president and the High Representative of the Union for Foreign Affairs and Security Policy, and plays a key role in the appointment of members of the College of Commissioners.
- Since Lisbon there has been an appointed president of the European Council, whose job is to provide it with more direction and consistency.

KEY TERMS AND CONCEPTS

Coreper
European Council
Presidency of the Council of Ministers
President of the European Council
Qualified majority vote
Summitry
Troika system

FURTHER READING

Hayes-Renshaw, Fiona, and Helen Wallace (2006), *The Council of Ministers*, 2nd edn (Basingstoke: Palgrave Macmillan). A more analytical text than Westlake and Galloway (below), with more emphasis on the functions of the Council and its relations with other EU bodies.

Werts, Jan (2008), *The European Council* (London: John Harper). Remarkably, the only book-length study of the European Council currently available.

Westlake, Martin, and David Galloway (eds) (2004), *The Council of the European Union*, 3rd edn (London: John Harper). A detailed survey of the workings of the Council, with chapters on key councils, supporting bodies, and procedures.

CHAPTER 12

The European Parliament

PREVIEW   The European Parliament (EP) is the only directly elected European institution, and
has won new powers for itself that have made it a more important actor in
European affairs. Logically, then, the EP should be the one EU institution that has
developed the closest political and psychological ties to ordinary Europeans, particularly those who complain about the EU's democratic deficit. And yet most
European voters remain disengaged, turning out in declining numbers at EP elections, and taking less interest in its work than in the work of national legislatures.

Dividing its time between Brussels and Strasbourg in France (with an administrative secretariat in Luxembourg), Parliament is the legislative arm of the EU, sharing
responsibility with the Council of Ministers for debating, amending and taking the
final vote on proposals for new European laws and the EU budget, and having the
power to confirm or reject senior institutional appointments (such as the president
of the Commission). However, it lacks two of the typical powers of national legislatures: it can neither introduce new laws nor raise revenues. It consists of 736
members elected from the 27 EU member states for fixed and renewable five-year
terms, who sit together not in national blocs but in cross-national party groups.

The EP's structural problems are manifold: it is not part of a European 'government', there is no change of 'government' at stake in EP elections, there are few
prominent personalities in the EP who can fire public imaginations, and the links
between national political parties and party groups in the EP are still not clear (see
Chapter 15). Until European voters can see how the EP impacts their lives, and until
they make choices at European elections on European rather than national issues, it
is unlikely that the EP's situation will improve.

KEY ISSUES

- Is the European Parliament more – or less – than it seems?
- What can be done (if anything) to engage Europe's voters more actively in the work of the EP? Is their disengagement a problem?
- Should the EP have more powers over the legislative process?
- How far has the EP gone to help close the EU's democratic deficit, and what is still missing from the equation?
- Do critics of the procedure by which the EP president is chosen have a point?
- What powers over the other institutions does the EP most obviously lack?

How Parliament evolved

The European Parliament traces its roots back to the first meeting in Strasbourg on 10 September 1952 of the Common Assembly of the ECSC. This consisted of 78 members with a **dual mandate**, serving in both the Assembly and in the national legislatures of the six ECSC member states. It had no power to propose or amend ECSC laws, and although the High Authority was required to answer questions put to it by the Assembly, and could be forced to resign by an Assembly vote of censure, the Assembly ended up being little more than an advisory forum for the discussion of proposals from the High Authority (Gillingham, 1991, p. 282). It could develop its own rules of procedure, however, and used this to good effect by allowing for the formation of cross-national party groups, and by creating standing committees.

The Treaties of Rome created a 142-member European Parliamentary Assembly shared by the ECSC, the EEC and Euratom, which met for the first time in Strasbourg in March 1958 with Robert Schuman as its president. It was given joint powers with the Council of Ministers for approving the Community budget, but its opinions on EEC law and policy remained non-binding. Renamed the European Parliament in 1962, its institutional handicaps were exacerbated by the dual mandate, which encouraged only legislators with an interest in European integration to stand for appointment to the EP. This not only biased their views about the purposes of the EP, but most saw their obligations to the EP as secondary to their role in national parliaments. As the workload of Parliament grew, so the dual mandate became more impractical, and was finally abolished.

The EP crossed a political watershed in 1976 when the European Council agreed to an EP proposal that it should be directly elected. The first elections were held in June 1979, and with MEPs now given a democratic mandate and meeting in public session, they had the moral advantage of being able to argue that they should be given new powers to represent voter interests and to offset and balance the powers of the other EU institutions. Unfortunately, voters have not been quite so ready to back up the EP; few even today know what it does, and turnout at elections has fallen steadily from 63 per cent in 1979 to 43 per cent in 2009 (see Chapter 16).

But as the membership of the EEC/EU grew, so did the size, the powers and the visibility of the EP. Its membership more than tripled between 1973 and 1995 (see Figure 12.1), and it was given shared responsibility with the Council of Ministers over the Community budget; within limits, it could now raise, lower or reallocate spending, and even – if necessary – reject the annual budget altogether (Corbett, Jacobs, and Shackleton, 2005, p. 240). It was given an additional boost in 1980 by a critical decision from the European Court of Justice (*SA Roquette Frères v. Council* (Case 138/79)), which sided with a French company that challenged a Council regulation placing production limits on isoglucose (a starch-based food sweetener), partly on the basis that it had been adopted without an opinion from Parliament. The Court thus established the right of the EP to be consulted on draft legislation, giving it standing to bring cases to the Court (Dehousse, 1998, p. 98).

The EP also used parliamentary questions to hold the other Community institutions more accountable, and steadily won more powers over new policy

● **Dual mandate**: An arrangement under which members of the Common Assembly, and then of the European Parliament, could serve in both the EP and in their national legislatures.

Figure 12.1 Growth of the European Parliament

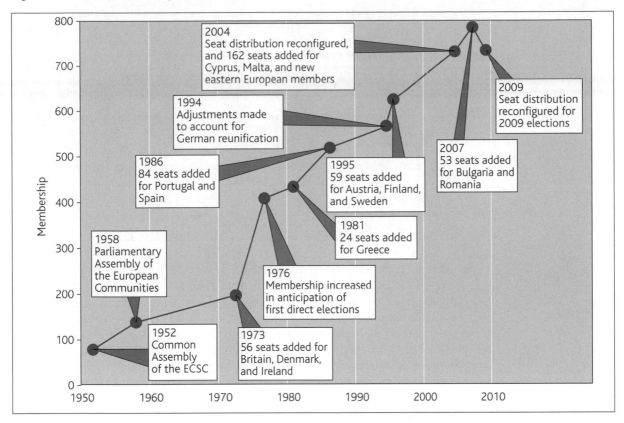

areas and greater input into the lawmaking process (see Rittberger, 2005, Chapters 5 and 6). The Single European Act brought a key change: where the EP's opinions on proposals for new laws had been non-binding (the so-called consultation procedure), the SEA introduced a cooperation procedure under which all laws relating to the single market could be subject to two readings by the EP. Maastricht and Amsterdam introduced the codecision procedure under which a third reading was possible, giving the EP the effective right of veto over most new legislation. With Lisbon, codecision became the ordinary procedure.

How Parliament is structured

The European Parliament is the only directly elected trans-national legislature in the world, and the only directly elected EU institution. It consists of a single chamber with 736 members elected by universal suffrage for fixed, renewable five-year terms. Confusingly, and controversially, it is physically divided among three different locations: plenary sessions (meetings of the whole, or part-sessions) take place in Strasbourg, France, while parliamentary committees meet in Brussels for two weeks every month (except August), and the administrative Secretariat is based in Luxembourg.

Brussels, Strasbourg and Milan had been named as possible homes for the European Parliamentary Assembly in 1958, but the final decision was left to

Figure 12.2 Structure of the European Parliament

- Legislative arm of the EU (but shares powers with Council of Ministers)
- Plenary sessions meet in Strasbourg, committees meet in Brussels, administrative offices in Luxembourg
- Headed by a president elected from among the party groups in Parliament for renewable five-year terms
- Consists of 736 Members of the European Parliament directly elected by voters in the member states for fixed, five-year renewable terms, the number of MEPs being divided among member states approximately on the basis of population
- MEPs organized into cross-national party groups, or may sit as independents
- Detailed work undertaken by 20 standing committees, and by temporary committees and committees of inquiry
- Work supported by a Secretariat
- Character determined by a combination of supranationalism, nationalism, and ideology

national governments. The Assembly meanwhile began holding committee meetings in Brussels, and plenaries in both Luxembourg and Strasbourg, choosing the latter in part because the Council of Europe building was the only one available at the time that was big enough, and in part because many members of the Assembly were also members of the Parliamentary Assembly of the Council of Europe. Since 1981, plenaries have been held in Strasbourg alone, and the split between Strasbourg, Brussels and Luxembourg was confirmed in 1992. The French government went further in 1999 by opening a new €470 million home for the EP in Strasbourg. Named for Louise Weiss, a French feminist, journalist, and MEP, the building was immediately branded a white elephant; because plenary sessions last only three to four days each month (again except August), the building is almost empty for most of the year. Meanwhile, the Espace Léopold complex in Brussels, built for the EP in stages between 1989 and 2009, was big enough to meet all the EP's needs.

**Illustration 12.1
The European Parliament**

The buildings housing the European Parliament: the Louise Weiss plenary chamber in Strasbourg on the left and the Espace Léopold in Brussels on the right.

**Illustration 12.2
A parliamentary plenary**

Members of the European Parliament meeting in a plenary session in Strasbourg.

The EP has long opposed the split and argues that it should have the right to decide for itself where to locate. The division not only forces a tiring and time-consuming travel schedule on MEPs (who must also regularly travel home to meet with their constituents and parties), but inflates the EP's annual budget by an estimated €200 million. Meanwhile, Strasbourg continues to press its demands, laying claim to being symbolic of European unity because it is sited in the French province of Alsace, which was long at the heart of Franco-German hostilities (see discussion in Judge and Earnshaw, 2008, p. 148ff). But this is an increasingly weak argument, and the French government is almost alone in insisting that the EP continues to meet in Strasbourg.

The EP has five main components: Members of the European Parliament, the President of the EP, parliamentary committees, rapporteurs, and the Secretariat.

Members of the European Parliament

Seats in the EP are divided up among the states roughly on the basis of population, so that while Germany today has 99 **Members of the European Parliament** (MEPs), Malta, Luxembourg, Cyprus and Estonia have 5 or 6 each (see Table 12.1). Under Lisbon, the number has been capped at 750, with no more than 96 members from any one state in future, or any less than six. If seats were divided strictly by population, with each MEP representing the same number of people (665,000), then Germany would have 124 MEPs while Cyprus would have one and Malta and Luxembourg would have none. Under the current formula, the Germans, the French and the British have fewer MEPs per capita (about 835,00–845,000 people per MEP), while the Maltese and Luxembourgers have many more MEPs per capita (about 80,000–83,000 people per MEP).

Once elected, most MEPs organize themselves into cross-national political groups based on shared ideology and policy positions (see Chapter 15). Candidates for European elections are chosen according to the rules of their national parties, but once in office they have an independent mandate and cannot always be bound by those parties (Hix and Lord, 1997, pp. 85–90). What

● **Member of the European Parliament**: A representative elected from any of the 27 EU member states to serve in the European Parliament. Elected for fixed, renewable five-year terms.

Table 12.1 Seats in the European Parliament

Germany	99	Portugal	22	Lithuania	12
United Kingdom	72	Czech Republic	22	Latvia	8
France	72	Hungary	22	Slovenia	7
Italy	72	Sweden	18	Estonia	6
Spain	50	Austria	17	Cyprus	6
Poland	50	Bulgaria	17	Luxembourg	6
Romania	33	Slovakia	13	Malta	5
Netherlands	25	Denmark	13		
Greece	22	Finland	13		
Belgium	22	Ireland	12	Total	736

this means for the personality of the EP is debatable. It is often assumed that anyone working within an EU institution will undergo a process of socialization that encourages them to become more pro-European. But the ranks of MEPs include representatives of political parties that are lukewarm and even hostile towards integration, and Scully (2005) has argued that MEPs do not necessarily become more pro-integration, that they often think and act like national politicians, and so to think of the EP as supranational in character is misleading.

MEPs are paid by their home governments, and long received the same as members of their respective national parliaments. This created large income inequalities with the arrival in 2004–07 of new and relatively poorly paid eastern European MEPs. Since the beginning of the 2009 term, all MEPs have been paid the same; in the 2009–2010 term this was €92,000 per year, and they pay their taxes into the EU budget. MEPs are not allowed to hold other significant political offices, whether being a member of a national government or a legislature of a member state, a European Commissioner, a judge on the Court of Justice, or a member of the board of directors of the European Central Bank.

The political experience of MEPs has improved over the years. Where once the EP was seen as something of a haven for 'has-beens' and 'also-rans', and an outlet for politicians who had failed to win office at home or had been temporarily sidelined, its new powers have attracted more seasoned legislators:

● Its ranks have included former chancellors of Germany (Willy Brandt), former presidents of France (Valéry Giscard d'Estaing) and Lithuania (Vytautas Landsbergis), and former prime ministers of Italy (Emilio Colombo, Silvio Berlusconi and Ciriaco de Mita) and Belgium (Leo Tindemans, Jean-Luc Dehaene and Guy Verhofstadt).

● About one-third of MEPs have served as elected representatives in their national legislatures, and a large number (16 per cent in 2004) have also had experience as national government ministers.

● Experience as an MEP has also counted for more, and has appeared on the resumes of several members of the European Commission (including presidents Jacques Delors and Jacques Santer), and several high-ranking members of national governments, including French prime minister Jean-Pierre Raffarin, Polish defence minister Bogdan Klich, and Spanish foreign minister Ana Palacio.

Debating ...
Should the EP have a second chamber?

YES	NO
In almost every large or diverse state (and even most small ones), the national legislature is bicameral, with two chambers providing different levels of representation. The EU is unusual (for its population size) in having a legislature with just one chamber.	The current system works well as it is, and the idea of creating a second chamber has not yet been seriously discussed, suggesting that its absence is not something that much worries most people.
A new upper chamber might represent the member states equally, with the same number of representatives regardless of size, reducing some of the concerns that smaller states have about loss of influence.	While giving states in the United States equal representation in the US Senate regardless of population has its advantages (the biggest state by population, California, is 70 times bigger than the smallest, Wyoming), the population differences in the EU are far greater: Germany has nearly 210 times as many people as Malta.
A new upper chamber could replace the Council of Ministers, which has already to all intents and purposes become something of an upper chamber.	The role and significance of the EP in EU decision-making is overrated, and until such time as it becomes a more substantial body, which generates more interest among EU voters, it is not worth creating a second chamber.
For the sake of efficiency, the legislative authority of the EU should be contained in a single and expanded institution, rather than being shared as it is at present with the Council of Ministers.	Creating a second chamber will be neither desirable nor practical at least until a decision has been made on a single location for the EP.

In economic, gender and social terms, the EP looks much like most national legislatures, with a preponderance of white, middle-aged, middle-class professional men from urban backgrounds. But the proportion of women in the EP has grown from a low of 16 per cent in 1979 to 35 per cent in 2009. This is below the average for the national legislatures of Scandinavian countries (36–47 per cent), but is well above that for Britain (20 per cent), the United States (17 per cent), or Russia (14 per cent) (Inter-Parliamentary Union figures for 2006–09, for lower or single chambers of national legislatures). Turnover for MEPs at elections is higher than is the case in most national legislatures – typically about half the members arriving after an election are newcomers (Corbett, Jacobs, and Shackleton, 2005, p. 48).

The President

The European Parliament is chaired by a president elected by MEPs from among their number for renewable terms of five years, or the span of a parliamentary term. The functional equivalent of the presidents or speakers found in most national European legislatures, the president works with vice-presidents representing the EP's political groups, and has several responsibilities:

Jerzy Buzek

Jerzy Buzek (born 1940) was elected president of the European Parliament in July 2009, becoming the first eastern European to hold the job. A Polish national, he was trained as a chemical engineer, became a government scientist and an academic, and was active in the underground Solidarity labour movement in the 1980s. In 1997 he was elected to the Polish parliament (the Sejm) as a member of the conservative Solidarity Election Action (AWS) coalition, winning barely 1500 votes. He was expected to remain only a junior member of the party, but created shockwaves when he was selected by the coalition leadership to be prime minister. Buzek immediately launched a radical attempt to reform Poland's healthcare, pensions and education systems, making his government so unpopular that in the 2001 elections the AWS lost every one of its seats in the Sejm.

Buzek returned to his career as a professor of chemical engineering. Building upon his status as the first post-cold war Polish prime minister to see out a full four-year term, and exploiting infighting within the AWS to become the right-wing Polish politician of moderation, Buzek was elected to the EP in 2004 where – as a member of the European People's Party – he became a champion of environmental issues and convincingly won re-election in 2009. In line with the political agreement among EP political groups on the rotating presidency of the EP, he was scheduled to step down at the end of 2011 and to be replaced by Martin Schulz of Germany, leader of the Progressive Alliance of Socialists and Democrats.

- To open, chair and close EP debates during plenary sessions.
- To apply the rules of parliamentary procedure.
- To sign the EU budget and all legislative proposals decided by codecision.
- To pass proposals to committees.
- To represent Parliament in legal matters and in its relations with other institutions, including national legislatures. He also addresses meetings of the European Council.
- To preside over meetings of the Conference of Presidents and the Bureau of the EP (see later in this chapter).

In theory, the president is elected in a vote by MEPs choosing from a slate of competing candidates, with the preferred candidate of the biggest political group in the EP having a clear advantage. Also in theory, the president is elected for five-year terms and can remain in office for as long as he or she wants the job and has the support of a majority of MEPs. But because no one political group has yet won a majority of seats in the EP, the president has been chosen since 1989 as a result of bargaining among the leaders of the major groups, particularly the two biggest: the centre-right European People's Party (EPP) and the centre-left Progressive Alliance of Socialists and Democrats (PASD). These groups have taken turns controlling the office for terms of two and a half years (half an EP term), with the smaller liberal democrats occasionally being given a turn (see Table 12.2) (Judge and Earnshaw, 2008, pp. 160–1).

The arrangements made for the election of Jerzy Buzek illustrate how the system works. With EPP president Hans-Gert Pöttering stepping down, British

● **President of the EP**: The leader of the European Parliament, elected by MEPs from among their number, the selection being pre-determined as a result of negotiations among the major party groups.

MEP Graham Watson – leader of the liberal democratic group in the EP – launched a campaign in January 2009 for the presidency, saying that he wanted to end the cycle of back-room deals. He hoped to win the support of Joseph Daul, leader of the EPP, but Daul had no incentive to offer Watson his support, given that the EPP and the socialists had enough votes in the EP to continue with the tradition of the rotating presidency. Italian MEP Mario Mauro announced that he would run against Buzek in an internal EPP contest, but was encouraged by Daul to withdraw his candidacy. Watson then withdrew after a deal was struck by which the liberal democratic group was given its wish for the setting up of a special parliamentary committee to investigate the causes of the 2007–10 global economic crisis. This cleared the way for Buzek – after facing the token opposition of Eva-Britt Svensson, leader of the left-wing GUE-NGL group in the EP – to be elected president in July 2009 (*European Voice*, 6 and 9 July 2009).

Table 12.2 Presidents of the European Parliament

Beginning of Term		Name	Member State	Party Group
Sept	1952	Paul-Henri Spaak	Belgium	Socialist
May	1954	Alcide de Gasperi	Italy	Christian Democrat
Nov	1954	Giuseppe Pella	Italy	Christian Democrat
Nov	1956	Hans Furler	Germany	Christian Democrat
Mar	1958	Robert Schuman	France	Christian Democrat
Mar	1960	Hans Furler	Germany	Christian Democrat
Mar	1962	Gaetano Martino	Italy	Liberal Democrat
Mar	1964	Jean Duvieusart	Belgium	Christian Democrat
Sept	1965	Victor Leemans	Belgium	Christian Democrat
Mar	1966	Alain Poher	France	Christian Democrat
Mar	1969	Mario Scelba	Italy	Christian Democrat
Mar	1971	Walter Behrendt	Germany	Socialist
Mar	1973	Cornelis Berkhouwer	Netherlands	Liberal Democrat
Mar	1975	Georges Spénale	France	Socialist
Mar	1977	Emilio Colombo	Italy	European People's Party (EPP)
July	1979	Simone Veil	France	Liberal Democrat
Jan	1982	Pieter Dankert	Netherlands	Socialist
July	1984	Pierre Pflimlin	France	EPP
Jan	1987	Sir Henry Plumb	UK	Conservative
July	1989	Enrique Barón Crespo	Spain	Socialist
Jan	1992	Egon Klepsch	Germany	EPP
July	1994	Klaus Hänsch	Germany	Socialist
Jan	1997	José Maria Gil-Robles	Spain	EPP
July	1999	Nicole Fontaine	France	EPP
Jan	2002	Pat Cox	Ireland	Liberal Democrat
July	2004	Josep Borrell Fontelles	Spain	Socialist
Jan	2007	Hans-Gert Pöttering	Germany	EPP-European Democrats
July	2009	Jerzy Buzek	Poland	EPP

This system encourages critics to scoff at the EP's claims to be the democratic conscience of the European Union. How can this be so, they ask, unless the EP allows for a free, open and truly competitive contest? Furthermore, the fact that no president has yet served more than a single term makes it difficult for incumbents to come to grips with the job or to become well-known public figures, making it more difficult to draw public attention to the work of the EP. Few presidents were less prepared for the job than the Spanish socialist Josep Borrell Fontelles, who became president in 2004 within the first few weeks of the start of his first term as an MEP. And the fact that the deal on the presidency is worked out between two political groups with dissimilar ideological identities makes it seem all the more artificial and opportunistic. Opposition to the deal-making has been growing within the EP, to be sure, but until one group wins a majority of seats in the EP, or is willing and able to form a coalition with smaller groups, change is unlikely.

The EP is managed by three different committees. The most politically powerful is the **Conference of Presidents**, consisting of the president and the heads of the EP political groups, and responsible for deciding the timetable and agenda for plenary sessions and for managing EP committees. The *Bureau of the EP* functions much like the EP's governing council, and is responsible for administrative, organizational, and staff issues, for monitoring the rules on party groups, for appointing the EP Secretary General, and for administering the EP budget. It consists of the president and the 14 vice-presidents, joined in a non-voting capacity by the six Quaestors of the EP, who are responsible for administrative and financial rules relating to MEPs. Finally, the *Conference of Committee Chairs* discusses organizational issues, watches the progress of legislative proposals and brokers deals between the political groups over the drafting of the parliamentary agenda (Corbett, Jacobs, and Shackleton, 2005, p. 119).

Rapporteurs

One of the most important and influential roles in the EP is that of the rapporteur, an MEP who is appointed to a committee to draft a report on a legislative proposal and to recommend a position or political line to be followed. Appointments are based on a points system, with the different political groups in the EP being given points in relation to their size and essentially bidding against each other for the appointment of rapporteurs to proposals. On recurring proposals such as the annual EU budget, assignment takes place on a rotation. With the help of policy specialists, members of EP committees, and even interest groups, rapporteurs will solicit information on the subject of the proposal and prepare a report to be put before a plenary session of the EP.

Secretariat

● **Conference of Presidents**: The major administrative body of the EP, consisting of the president and the heads of the party groups, and responsible for managing plenary sessions and the EP committee system.

Parliament has its own internal bureaucracy, to match those of the Commission and the Council of Ministers. Based in Luxembourg, the job of the EP Secretariat is to coordinate legislative work and organize plenary sittings and meetings, and to provide MEPs with technical and expert assistance. It employs about 6,000 staff, about one-third of whom work on translation and interpretation, and about 1,000 of whom are employed temporarily by the EP political groups. The balance are permanent EU civil servants, recruited with an eye to ensuring a spread of nationalities; at the higher levels political affiliation is a factor in determining appointments. As with the Secretariat General of the Commission, there has been little turnover in the office of EP Secretary General, so that when Klause Welle of Germany replaced Harald Rømer of Denmark in 2009 he became only the seventh person to hold the job in just over fifty years.

Parliamentary Committees

As with conventional national legislatures, most of the detailed work of the EP is addressed by a network of committees in which MEPs meet to discuss and amend legislative proposals (Neuhold and Sttembri, 2007). Convening monthly or bi-monthly in Brussels, there are now 20 standing (permanent) committees (see Table 12.3), ranging in size between 24 and 76 members, their responsibilities reflecting the priorities of European integration.

Winning appointment to a committee is desirable and competitive, because this is where most of the work of shaping legislation is done. Some committees (particularly Budgets, Environment, and Foreign Affairs) are more influential than others, and national interests also drive MEP choices; so, for example, Polish and Irish MEPs have more interest in agriculture than in foreign and security issues. Membership of committees is determined in part by the seniority of MEPs and in part by the size of political groups in the EP. In most national legislatures, committee chairs are appointed out of the majority party or coalition. But because there is no majority party group in the EP, the chairmanships are worked out through negotiations among political groups and divided up among the groups roughly in proportion to the size of their representation in Parliament. As a result, there is more turnover than is the case with national legislatures.

In addition to standing committees, the EP also has temporary committees set up to examine a variety of politically pressing issues, including (in recent years) human genetics and other medical technologies (2001), the foot-and-mouth crisis (2002), allegations of illegal CIA activities in Europe (2006–07), climate change (2007–08), and the global economic crisis (set up in 2009). The EP can also set up committees of inquiry to investigate breaches or poor appli-

Table 12.3 Committees of the European Parliament

Agriculture and Rural Development	Fisheries
Budgetary Control	Foreign Affairs
Budgets	Industry, Research and Energy
Civil Liberties, Justice and Home Affairs	Internal Market and Consumer
Constitutional Affairs	Protection
Culture and Education	International Trade
Development	Legal Affairs
Economic and Monetary Affairs	Petitions
Employment and Social Affairs	Regional Development
Environment, Public Health and	Transport and Tourism
Food Safety	Women's Rights and Gender Equality

**Illustration 12.3
Committees of the EP**

Most of the detailed work of the European Parliament is undertaken in committees such as this, which meet mainly in Brussels.

cation of EU law, their work designed to assert the EP's rights of scrutiny over other institutions. Finally, there is a Conciliation Committee that meets when the EP and the Council of Ministers have disagreed on the wording of a legislative proposal. There are 27 members from each side, with representatives of the Commission also attending.

What Parliament does

Most conventional national legislatures have four main powers:

● They draft, introduce, discuss, and vote on new legislation.
● They have the final say over the national budget.
● They usually have powers to question and confirm or reject nominees for senior political office.
● Their support is needed (in parliamentary systems, at least) for the formation of the national government.

The European Parliament does not yet have all these powers, but as time has gone on it has become more like a conventional legislature, winning new authority mainly at the cost of the Council of Ministers. It is still a work in progress, and more changes are sure to come. For now, though, the jockeying for power and influence among the EU institutions has left it with powers ranging from the formal to the informal, and from the modest to the significant. These powers fall broadly into three main groups: those over legislation, those over the budget, and those over the other EU institutions.

Powers over Legislation

Although Parliament cannot draft proposals for new laws (a task that is monopolized by the European Commission), there are several ways in which it can play

Figure 12.3 Powers of the European Parliament

- Under the codecision procedure, shares powers with the Council of Ministers over discussion and approval of new legislative proposals, and of the EU budget
- May encourage or pressure the Commission to develop new proposals
- Commission, Council of Ministers, and presidency of Council of Ministers must regularly report to the EP on their activities
- Right to confirm or reject the European Council's nominees for president of the European Commission and High Representative for Foreign Affairs and Security Policy
- Right of approval over appointments to the College of Commissioners, the management team of the European Central Bank, and the Court of Auditors
- May compel removal of the College of Commissioners
- Manages the office of the European Ombudsman

a role in this part of the legislative process. First, it can send representatives to the initial meetings held by the Commission to start the drafting process, helping shape legislation and encouraging the Commission to address issues it thinks are important. Second, it can publish 'own initiative' reports that draw attention to a problem, encouraging the Commission to respond. Finally, it can send a request to the Commission that it submit a proposal on a problem related to the implementation of treaty obligations.

Most of Parliament's legislative work, though, is focused on reviewing proposals received from the Commission, at which point it enters a complex process of bargaining with the Council of Ministers. When proposals are received by the EP, a report is drawn up by a rapporteur and discussed in committee, then sent for a vote in plenary session, the result being the 'position' of the EP. In its early years, Parliament was mainly limited to the **consultation procedure**, by which it could accept, reject, or propose amendments to a proposal. Amended proposals would be sent back to the Council of Ministers, which then decided whether to accept, reject, or further amend the proposal. There was no time limit on how long Parliament could take to give its opinion, so it had the power of delay, but consultation ultimately meant little more than the term implied, and it was the Council that had the final say over adoption.

The Single European Act changed the balance of power by introducing a new **cooperation procedure** giving the EP a second reading for laws in areas relating to the single market, regional policy, the environment, and the European Social Fund. Maastricht changed the balance still further by extending cooperation to cover new policy areas, and – most importantly – introducing a new codecision procedure that allowed for a third reading. Renamed the **ordinary legislative procedure** by Lisbon, this is now the standard approach to law-making, giving the EP virtually equal powers with the Council of Ministers over the adoption of new laws, and making the two bodies 'co-legislatures'.

The last of Parliament's legislative powers is the **consent procedure** (known as the assent procedure until Lisbon), by which the support of the EP is needed in four kinds of decisions: the accession of new member states to the EU and the granting of associate status to others; the withdrawal of a member state from the

● Consultation procedure: The original legislative procedure used in the EP, by which it could comment on proposals from the Commission but had little more than the power of delay.

● Cooperation procedure: A legislative procedure introduced by the Single European Act, giving the EP the right to a second reading on selected proposals. All but eliminated by the Treaty of Amsterdam.

● Ordinary legislative procedure: The most common legislative procedure now used in the EP, under which it has the right to as many as three readings on a legislative proposal, giving it equal powers with the Council of Ministers.

● Consent procedure: A legislative procedure under which the EP has veto rights in selected areas, including the admission of new member states to the EU, and the conclusion by the EU of new international agreements.

Figure 12.4 Workflow of the European Parliament

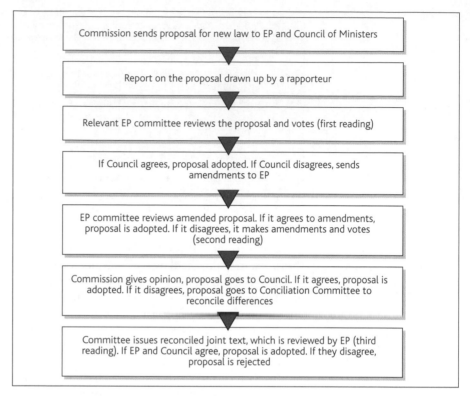

Commission sends proposal for new law to EP and Council of Ministers

Report on the proposal drawn up by a rapporteur

Relevant EP committee reviews the proposal and votes (first reading)

If Council agrees, proposal adopted. If Council disagrees, sends amendments to EP

EP committee reviews amended proposal. If it agrees to amendments, proposal is adopted. If it disagrees, it makes amendments and votes (second reading)

Commission gives opinion, proposal goes to Council. If it agrees, proposal is adopted. If it disagrees, proposal goes to Conciliation Committee to reconcile differences

Committee issues reconciled joint text, which is reviewed by EP (third reading). If EP and Council agree, proposal is adopted. If they disagree, proposal is rejected

EU (although what would happen if the EP did not give its consent is unclear); the conclusion of international agreements, such as those reached by the EU after negotiations under the auspices of the World Trade Organization; and the imposition of penalties by the Council of Ministers on a member state for serious and persistent violations of fundamental rights.

One area in which the EP has won only limited powers is foreign policy, but the EP has creatively used the consent procedure to extend its authority. Maastricht obliged the presidency of the Council of Ministers to consult with the EP on the development of the Common Foreign and Security Policy, for example, and during the 1990s the EP used the consent procedure several times to delay agreements between the EU and third countries. These included an agreement with Russia in protest over Russian policy in Chechnya, with Kazakhstan in protest over that country's poor democratic record, and with Turkey in protest over human rights violations (Pienning, 2001).

Although it is not a legislative power, the EP has also taken a leading role in drawing attention to human rights issues both inside and outside the EU. Debates on human rights problems are held during plenary sessions, the EP participates with the Council of Ministers in agreements to pressure states to release political prisoners, and since 1988 it has awarded the annual Sakharov Prize for Freedom of Thought to individuals or organizations active in the promotion of human rights. Past winners include Nelson Mandela, Burmese democracy leader Aung San Suu Kyi, UN Secretary-General Kofi Annan, and

Sudanese human rights lawyer Salih Mahmoud Osman for his work on the crisis in the Sudanese region of Darfur.

Powers over the budget

Parliament and the Council of Ministers share powers over agreeing the EU budget, making them jointly the budgetary authority of the EU. As with new laws, it is the Commission that drafts the budget, which is then sent to the Council of Ministers (usually in April each year), and then to the EP where it is reviewed by the Committee on Budgetary Control and sent to a plenary session for a first reading. Parliament can accept the draft or propose changes, which are forwarded to the Council of Ministers, which can either accept the changes or add its own, returning the new draft to the EP for a second reading. If there is strong opposition to the budget then the EP – with a two-thirds majority – can reject it, but it has only done this three times so far (in 1979, 1982, and 1984). For the budget to come into force it must be adopted by the EP and signed by the president of the EP.

Powers over other institutions

Parliament has several direct powers over other EU institutions that have helped it develop a modest system of checks and balances, and have given EU citizens more of a role (via the EP) in influencing those institutions. The most compelling relate to the Commission, which must submit regular reports to the EP, including its annual legislative programme and its report on the implementation of the EU budget. The presidency of the Council of Ministers must also report to the EP both on its plans and on its achievements. The EP can submit questions to the Commission and the Council, and can even take the Commission or the Council to the Court of Justice over alleged infringements of the treaties.

The EP's most substantial power over the Commission, often described as the nuclear option because of its deterrent qualities, is to force the resignation of the College of Commissioners through a motion of censure. Several censure motions have been proposed over the years, but all have been defeated or withdrawn because they failed to win the two-thirds majority needed to succeed. As noted in Chapter 10, the closest the EP came to removing the College was during a vote in January 1999 over charges of fraud and corruption. While only 232 MEPs voted in favour, falling far short of the two-thirds majority of 416, the size of the negative vote sparked the creation of a committee of inquiry, whose report ultimately brought down the College.

Parliament also confirms the nominee of the European Council for president of the European Commission. If the nominee fails to win an EP majority, the Council must submit a second nominee within a month. The Council's nominee for High Representative of the Union for Foreign Affairs and Security Policy must also be confirmed by the EP, along with the College of Commissioners as a whole. All nominees to the College must appear before the EP, and while it cannot block individual nominations, its reservations can be enough to lead to the withdrawal of nominations (see Chapter 10). Finally, Parliament has the right to review and confirm the appointment of the president, the vice-president, and the executive board of the European Central Bank; is responsible for

Focus on . . .
The European Ombudsman

One of the institutional changes introduced by Maastricht was the creation of the office of the European Ombudsman, charged with investigating complaints of maladministration by any of the EU institutions except the Court of Justice. The office is something of a branch of the EP, since the ombudsman is appointed by Parliament with no input from the member states, has a term of office that coincides with that of the EP, has an office physically located in the EP buildings in Strasbourg, has a budget that comes out of that of the EP, and can be dismissed by the Court of Justice on a request from the EP. The first ombudsman, Jacob Söderman, was appointed in 1995, and was succeeded in 2003 by Nikiforos Diamandouros, the former national ombudsman of Greece. (For more on the Ombudsman, see Giddings *et al.*, 2002.)

Complaints can be lodged by anyone who is a citizen or a legal resident of the EU, and the ombudsman's office can launch its own investigations if necessary. Complaints can be directed at discrimination, abuse of power, failure to reply, delays in taking action, and administrative irregularities. The ombudsman then informs the institution concerned, tries to find a solution to the problem, and can send a report to the EP if no resolution is achieved. Recent cases have included an attempt by the Commission to blacklist a German non-governmental organization that had raised allegations of maladministration by the Commission, allegations of age discrimination against an Irish language translator employed by the Council of Ministers, and several complaints regarding late payment or non-payment of fees related to contracted work.

● **European Ombudsman**: An official appointed and monitored by the European Parliament and charged with investigating complaints of maladministration by any of the EU institutions except the Court of Justice.

appointing and overseeing the work of the European Ombudsman; and must be consulted on appointments to the Court of Auditors.

The EP's relationship with the Council of Ministers is one of the most important in the EU institutional system. Apart from sharing powers with the Council over the adoption of most new laws, Parliament also closely monitors the work of the Council, regularly submitting oral and written questions on matters of policy. The two institutions work particularly closely together on the Common Foreign and Security Policy, judicial cooperation, asylum and immigration issues, and international crime. The President of the EP also makes an address at the opening of every meeting of the European Council, providing an opportunity for the EP to comment on the Council agenda.

Parliament has also taken the initiative through the years to win new powers for itself over the work of EU institutions. As well as its early campaign to introduce direct elections, it introduced its own Question Time in 1973 – allowing it to demand oral or written replies to questions from commissioners – and initiated the 1992 reconfiguration of the number of seats in Parliament. It has also worked to increase its role in the appointment of the directors and boards of the EU's specialized agencies; an EP campaign led to the creation of the Court of Auditors in 1993, since when it has exerted its moral and legal right to monitor the work of these agencies.

SUMMARY

- The European Parliament is the legislative arm of the EU, sharing powers with the Council of Ministers over the discussion and approval of legislative proposals developed by the European Commission, and over approving the EU budget.
- Plenary meetings of Parliament are held in Strasbourg, its committees meet in Brussels, and its secretariat is based in Luxembourg. Pressure to move Parliament to Brussels has been resisted by France.
- The EP has 736 members elected to renewable five-year terms, the number of seats being divided up among the member states on the basis of population.
- Parliament is headed by a president elected by its members. Since no one party group has yet won a majority in the EP, the presidency is decided by a bargain between the two largest party groups.
- Detailed parliamentary work is undertaken in a network of 20 standing committees.
- Most decisions are made under the codecision procedure, by which the EP and the Council can discuss and amend a proposal up to three times.
- Parliament has the right to confirm nominees to the presidency of the European Commission, to the High Representative for Foreign Affairs, and to the College of Commissioners, and also has powers of scrutiny over the Commission.
- The powers of Parliament have grown, thanks in part to changes in the treaties and in part to Parliament's own initiatives, and yet most EU citizens know little about what it does, and turnout at EP elections has been declining.

KEY TERMS AND CONCEPTS

Conference of Presidents

Consent procedure

Consultation procedure

Cooperation procedure

Dual mandate

European Ombudsman

Member of the European Parliament

Ordinary legislative procedure

President of the EP

FURTHER READING

Corbett, Richard, Francis Jacobs and Michael Shackleton (2007), *The European Parliament*, 7th edn (London: John Harper); and David Judge and David Earnshaw (2008), *The European Parliament*, 2nd edn (Basingstoke: Palgrave Macmillan). The two standard texts on the European Parliament, the former written by insiders with an intimate knowledge of the workings of the EP.

Steunenberg, Bernard, and Jacques Thomassen (eds) (2002), *The European Parliament: Moving Toward Democracy in the EU* (Lanham, MD: Rowman & Littlefield). An edited collection that looks at how the role of the EP has been changing, and speculates on the chances of the EU evolving into a parliamentary democracy.

Whitaker, Richard (2010), *The European Parliament's Committees* (London: Routledge). The first full-length study of the EP's committees, assessing their relationship with political parties.

(For recommended reading on parties and party groups, see Chapter 15.)

CHAPTER 13

The European Court of Justice

PREVIEW

The European Court of Justice does not much make the news, and yet its role in European governance is critical: its task of making sure that the terms of the treaties are respected, understood and applied as accurately as possible has made it essential to the process of integration. As the judicial arm of the EU, it has made decisions that have expanded and clarified the reach and the meaning of the EU, that have established key principles (such as direct effect and the supremacy of EU law), and that have helped transform the treaties into something like a constitution for Europe. It is one of the most clearly supranational of EU institutions.

Headquartered in Luxembourg, the Court has three parts. The Court of Justice works as the final court of appeal on matters of EU law, and is helped by the General Court, created in 1989 to deal with less complex cases, and by the EU Civil Service Tribunal, created in 2004 to deal with staff matters. The two upper courts each have 27 judges while the Tribunal has seven, all of them appointed for six-year renewable terms of office. And while it is an entirely separate institution, the work of the European Court of Human Rights cannot be ignored, because its rulings have had important judicial implications for the EU.

The treaties may not be a constitution as such, and the Court of Justice may not fit the definition of a typical constitutional court (because there is, formally, no EU constitution), but the authority and efficiency of the European institutions has depended heavily on the Court clarifying the meaning and effects of EU law. Its decisions have had an influence on matters as varied as the single market, competition policy, human rights, gender equality, and external trade.

KEY ISSUES

- Can the Court of Justice be a constitutional court without there being an EU constitution?
- Whose interests are represented by the Court of Justice?
- What (if any) is the political role of the Court of Justice?
- Is it possible, as Vassilios Skouris argues, for the Court of Justice to do 'nothing more' than rule on cases? In other words, can judges be objective and neutral?
- Should members of the Court of Justice be elected, or at least subject to approval by the European Parliament?

How the Court evolved

The Court of Justice of the European Union – known more usually as the European Court of Justice (ECJ) – traces its roots back to the founding in 1952 of the Court of Justice of the ECSC. Consisting of seven members (six judges and a representative of the trade unions in the coal and steel industry), its job was to guard the Treaty of Paris by 'ensuring that in the interpretation and application of this Treaty, and of rules laid down for the implementation thereof, the law is observed' (Article 31). In other words, it was to rule on the legality of decisions made by the ECSC High Authority in the event of complaints lodged by member states or by their national coal and steel industries. During its brief existence it reviewed just over 50 cases and issued 16 judgments.

The treaties of Rome created separate courts for the EEC and Euratom, but a subsidiary agreement gave jurisdiction over all three founding treaties to a single seven-member Court of Justice of the European Communities. The new Court had a modest workload, issuing between ten and thirty judgments per year, reaching a new peak of 64 in 1970. Most of the cases were direct actions, or disputes involving EU institutions, member states, individuals, corporations, and occasionally foreign parties. The number of preliminary rulings, where national courts asked the European Court for an opinion on cases under review at the national level, only began to climb in the 1970s. By the early 1980s the expanded reach of integration meant that the Court was taking on hundreds of new cases each year and issuing between 130 and 200 judgments per year (a figure that had risen to about 600 per year by 2004–08).

As the membership of the Community grew, so did the number of judges on the Court, with one more added for each new member state. But with the workload of the Court growing, so grew the backlog of cases and the Court was taking up to two years to issue its more important judgments (Millett, 1990, p. 2). As a result, a new subsidiary Court of First Instance was created in 1989 to review less complicated cases, issuing its first judgment in February 1990. In 2004 the EU Civil Service Tribunal took over responsibility for cases involving disputes between the EU institutions and their staff. A final change came with the Lisbon treaty: the Court of Justice of the European Communities was renamed the Court of Justice, the Court of First Instance was renamed the General Court, and the two together are now formally known as the Court of Justice of the European Union.

Over the years, the ECJ has made numerous judgments that have clarified the meaning of the treaties and expanded the reach of the EU. They have also expanded the authority of the Court itself, just as similar decisions over the years have expanded the authority of the US Supreme Court. Among the most important of the Court's decisions, three in particular stand out.

First, the principle of **direct effect** holds that EU law is directly and uniformly applicable in all member states, and that individuals can invoke EU law regardless of whether or not a relevant national law exists. It was established by the 1963 Court decision *Van Gend en Loos* v. *Nederlandse Administratie der Belastingen* (Case 26/62). The Dutch transport company Van Gend en Loos complained that the Dutch government had increased the duty it charged on a chemical imported from Germany. Its lawyers argued that this was a violation of Article 12 of the EEC Treaty, which prohibited new duties on imports and

● **Direct effect**: The principle that EU law is directly and uniformly applicable in all EU member states, and that challenges can be made to the compatibility of national law with EU law.

exports or increases in existing duties. The Dutch government claimed that the Court had no jurisdiction, but the Court responded that the treaties were more than international agreements and that EC law was 'legally complete . . . and produces direct effects and creates individual rights which national courts must protect'.

Second, the principle of the **supremacy of EU law** holds that EU law trumps national law in policy areas where the EU has responsibility. This was established by the 1964 Court decision *Flaminio Costa* v. *ENEL* (Case 6/64). Costa was an Italian who had owned shares in Edison Volta, an electricity supply company that was nationalized in 1962 and made part of the new National Electricity Board (ENEL). Costa refused to pay his electricity bill, arguing that he had been hurt by nationalization, which was contrary to the spirit of the Treaty of Rome. When the local court in Milan asked the Court of Justice for a preliminary ruling, the Italian government argued that the ECJ had no jurisdiction. The Court disagreed, arguing that by creating 'a Community of unlimited duration ... [with] its own legal capacity' the member states had 'limited their sovereign rights, albeit within limited fields, and have thus created a body of law which binds both their nationals and themselves'.

Third, the principle of **mutual recognition** holds that a product or service provided and sold legally in one member state cannot be barred from another. When West Germany refused to allow imports of Cassis de Dijon (a French blackcurrant liquor) because its wine-spirit content (15–20 per cent) was below the German minimum for fruit liqueurs (25 per cent), the importer charged that this amounted to a restriction on imports, prohibited under the Treaty of Rome. In its 1979 decision *Rewe-Zentral AG* v. *Bundesmonopolverwaltung für Branntwein* (Case 120/78), the ECJ agreed. The issue came up again in the 1984 case *Commission* v. *Federal Republic of Germany* (Case 178/84) over a 1952 German law that prevented beer being imported or sold in Germany that did not meet the *Reinheitsgebot*, a purity law passed in 1516 by the Duke of Bavaria that allows beer to contain only malted barley, hops, yeast, and water. The West German government argued that because German men relied on beer for a quarter of their daily nutritional intake, allowing imports of 'impure' foreign beer would pose a risk to public health. The Court disagreed and ruled in 1987 that Germany had to accept foreign beer imports as long as brewers printed a list of ingredients on their labels.

With the abolition by Lisbon of the three-pillar arrangement, the Court's authority over matters of criminal law has expanded, with criminal sentences for environmental crimes being a valuable test. An attempt to prevent the Commission winning new powers worked its way up to the ECJ, which ruled in 2005 (*Commission of the European Communities* v. *Council* (Case 176/03)) that while criminal law as a general rule did not fall within the scope of the treaties, this did not prevent the Commission from proposing criminal sanctions when they were needed for the effective implementation of EU law (see discussion in Jacobs, 2006). New attention was drawn to the problem in 2006 when toxic waste carried by a European ship was dumped in Côte d'Ivoire, resulting in the deaths of ten people, numerous hospitalizations, and the dismissal of government ministers. With the gates now opened by the Court, the first EU law aimed at harmonizing national criminal law (a directive requiring all member states to consider intentional infringements of intellectual property rights carried out on

● **Supremacy of EU law**: The principle that in areas where the EU has competence (authority), EU law supersedes national law in cases of incompatibility.

● **Mutual recognition**: The principle that a product or service provided legally in one member state cannot be barred from provision in another member state.

a commercial scale a criminal offence) was soon working its way through the legislative process.

How the Court is structured

By definition, a **constitutional court** is one created to issue judgments on questions of whether or not the laws or actions of governments and government officials conflict with the spirit or the letter of constitutionally established powers, rights and freedoms. Not all states have constitutional courts, some choosing to delegate **judicial authority** to supreme courts which deal also with issues of civil law (laws created by legislatures) and common law (laws created and developed through court decisions). Among the EU member states with constitutional courts are Austria, France, Germany, Italy, and Spain, and all the eastern European states; those without constitutional courts include Britain, Denmark, Ireland, Malta, the Netherlands, and Sweden. The European Court of Justice is more purely a constitutional court because it clarifies the meaning and application of the treaties (the functional equivalent of a European constitution), but the idea of a constitutional court is one that a large number of Europeans still find alien.

The ECJ is headquartered in Luxembourg, in the Centre Européen on the Kirchberg Plateau above the city of Luxembourg. When the ECSC was created there was some debate about where its institutions would be based, Luxembourg eventually being chosen as a provisional home. Both the ECSC Court and the single Court for all three Communities that was created in 1958 were housed in temporary buildings until the opening in 1973 of the Court's new black steel and glass Palais de Justice. But with the Court still growing, the Erasmus building was opened in 1988 to house the Court of First Instance, and two more extensions were opened in the early 1990s. It was only in 1992 that Luxembourg was formally confirmed as the home of the ECJ, which now shares the Centre Européen with a cluster of other European institutions that includes the Secretariat of the European Parliament, buildings for the Commission and the Council of Ministers, the seat of the Court of Auditors, and the headquarters of the European Investment Bank.

Figure 13.1 Structure of the European Court of justice

- Judicial arm of the EU
- Headquartered in Luxembourg
- Headed by a president elected from among its judges for renewable three-year terms
- Consists of 27 judges, each appointed for renewable six-year terms of office, with each member state having control over one appointment
- Judges rarely meet as a full court; more often meet as chambers of three or five judges, or as a Grand Chamber of 13 judges
- Assisted by eight advocates-general appointed for renewable six-year terms and charged with reviewing cases, studying arguments, and delivering opinions
- Further assisted by lower 27-member General Court, which hears less complicated cases in selected areas, and by 7-member EU Civil Service Tribunal which hears disputes between the EU institutions and their staff
- Supranational in character

CONCEPT

Judicial authority

The power given to judges to interpret and apply law, and to adjudicate disputes. Judges are expected to consider all aspects of a case and to deliver their opinions impartially, typically being guided by the principles contained in a constitution. But they are only human, and they are subject to biases, ideological leanings, and subjective ideas about the meaning of law and constitutions. This all raises the fundamental question of whether or not their appointments should be subject to public confirmation.

● **Constitutional court**: A court created to deal with matters of constitutional law, and to decide whether or not laws or the actions of elected officials respect the terms of a constitution.

Illustration 13.1
The Court of Justice

Part of the headquarters
complex of the European
Court of Justice in
Luxembourg.

The Court of Justice has five main components: the judges, the President, the advocates general, the General Court, and the EU Civil Service Tribunal.

The judges

The Court of Justice is headed by 27 judges, each appointed for a six-year renewable term of office, the beginnings of their terms staggered so that about half come up for renewal every three years. According to treaty rules, nominees must be 'persons whose independence is beyond doubt and who possess the qualifications required for appointment to the highest judicial offices in their respective countries or who are jurisconsults of recognized competence'. Most judges come to the Court having worked their way up through their national court systems, while some also have experience as government ministers, in elective office, with international organizations, or as lawyers or academics. Unlike the case with the College of Commissioners, the European Parliament has almost no say in the appointment process, although it has argued that there should be confirmation hearings on the model of those used in the United States for appointments to the Supreme Court. The Court of Justice has opposed this idea on the grounds that its deliberations are secret, and confirmation hearings would force nominees to make public their views on judicial issues (Arnull, 2008, p. 21).

Although the judges are appointed by 'common accord' of the governments of the member states, and each member state controls one of the nominations, there is no requirement that the judges come from different member states, nor even from any member state. Theoretically, at least, they could all be Estonian or Polish or Spanish, and the Court could even – in the words of former President Lord McKenzie Stuart – be made up 'entirely of Russians' (Brown and Kennedy, 2000, p. 45). But the desire of member states to control as many appointments to the EU institutions as possible has meant that so far there has never been more than one judge from any member state.

Nominees to the Court must first be vetted by a seven-member panel made up of former members of the ECJ, members of national constitutional courts, and lawyers, of whom one is nominated by the European Parliament. The panel gives its opinion, leaving it to the member states to decide how to proceed. Once confirmed to the Court, judges – like members of the College of Commissioners – must maintain their independence and avoid promoting the national interests of their home states. Upon appointment each takes a short oath: 'I swear that I will perform my duties impartially and conscientiously; I swear that I will preserve the secrecy of the deliberations of the Court.' In order to protect their independence, they are immune from having suits brought against them while they are on the Court and even once they have retired. And while they can resign from the Court, they can only be removed against their will by the other judges and the advocates general (not by the governments of member states or by the other EU institutions), and then only as a result of a unanimous agreement that they are no longer doing their job adequately (Lasok, 2007, pp. 7–8).

Table 13.1 Judges of the European Court of Justice, June 2010

Name	Member State	Year of Birth	Year of Appointment
Vassilios Skouris	Greece	1948	1999
José Narciso Rodrigues	Portugal	1940	2000
Allan Rosas	Finland	1948	2002
Rosario Silva de Lapuerta	Spain	1954	2003
Koen Lenaerts	Belgium	1954	2003
Konrad Schiemann	United Kingdom	1937	2004
Pranas Kuris	Lithuania	1938	2004
Endre Juhász	Hungary	1944	2004
George Arestis	Cyprus	1945	2004
Anthony Barthet	Malta	1947	2004
Marko Ilesic	Slovenia	1947	2004
Jirí Malenovsky	Czech Republic	1950	2004
Uno Lõhmus	Estonia	1952	2004
Egils Levits	Latvia	1955	2004
Aindrias Ó Caoimh	Ireland	1950	2004
Lars Bay Larsen	Denmark	1953	2006
Antonio Tizzano	Italy	1940	2006
Pernilla Lindh	Sweden	1945	2006
Jean-Claude Bonichot	France	1955	2006
Thomas von Danwitz	Germany	1962	2006
Alexander Arabadjiev	Bulgaria	1949	2007
Camelia Toader	Romania	1963	2007
Jean-Jacques Kasel	Luxembourg	1946	2008
Marek Safjan	Poland	1949	2009
Daniel Sváby	Slovakia	1951	2009
Maria Berger	Austria	1956	2009
Alexandra Prechal	Netherlands	1959	2010

Illustration 13.2
European judges

Judges at the European Court of Justice take part in the swearing-in of the new European Commission in 2010.

Although most judges are renewed at least once, the Court has more turnover than the national courts of the United States, the Netherlands, and Belgium, where appointments are for life. Life appointments have the benefit of exploiting the experience of judges and encouraging their independence, but they also restrict the flow of new thinking into the deliberations of a court, and make new appointments more highly contested. The rate of turnover in the Court of Justice means that appointments are relatively frequent; hence in 2010 all but six of the 27 judges were still in their first term in office. In spite of this turnover, the Court has not yet matched other EU institutions on diversity. The first female advocate general (Simone Rozès of France) was appointed in 1981, the first female judge of the General Court (Pernilla Lindh of Sweden) was appointed in 1995, and the first female judge on the Court of Justice (Fidelma Macken of Ireland) was appointed in 1999. In 2010 the Court had only five women judges: Rosario Silva de Lapuerta of Spain, Pernilla Lindh, Camelia Toader of Romania, Maria Berger of Austria and Alexandra Prechal of the Netherlands

For all 27 judges to hear cases together and to meet as a full court would be an inefficient use of time and resources, so meetings of the full court are reserved only for proceedings to dismiss a European commissioner, a member of the Court of Auditors, or the European Ombudsman. All other cases are heard by chambers of three or five judges, or by a Grand Chamber of 13 judges when a member state or another EU institution makes a specific request. To further help manage the workload, each judge has his or her own cabinet of assistants and legal secretaries, equivalent to the *cabinets* of European commissioners and responsible for helping with research and keeping records. The Court also has about 1,500 staff members, most of whom are bureaucrats or translators.

The President

The Court of Justice is headed by a president elected by the judges from among their own number in a secret ballot by majority vote to serve a three-year renew-

Vassilios Skouris

Vassilios Skouris (born 1948) is the president of the European Court of Justice. A lawyer and professor of public law from Greece, he was educated in Germany, earning degrees in constitutional and administrative law from the Free University of Berlin and Hamburg University. He was then a professor of law for several years in German and Greek universities, and served twice in the Greek government as minister of internal affairs. He was first appointed as a Court judge in 1999, was elected as the ninth president of the Court in 2003, elected to a second term in 2006, and to a third (and likely final) term in October 2009.

able term. As well as presiding over meetings of the Court, the president is responsible for organizational matters such as assigning cases to chambers, appointing **judge-rapporteurs** (the Court judges responsible for shepherding a case through the review process), and deciding the dates for hearings. In spite of the growing powers of the Court, presidents are the least known of the senior figures in the EU institutional hierarchy and their work is subject to little public and political scrutiny. When President Skouris was first elected to his position in 2003 it was barely reported by the European media, and his election to a third term in 2009 also passed almost unnoticed.

Table 13.2 Presidents of the European Court of Justice

Term	Name	Member State
1958–1961	A. M. Donner	Netherlands
1961–1964	A. M. Donner	Netherlands
1964–1967	Charles Hammes	Luxembourg
1967–1970	Robert Lecourt	France
1970–1973	Robert Lecourt	France
1973–1976	Robert Lecourt	France
1976–1979	Hans Kutscher	West Germany
1979–1980	Hans Kutscher	West Germany
1980–1984	Josse Mertens de Wilmars	Belgium
1984–1988	Lord McKenzie Stuart	United Kingdom
1988–1991	Ole Due	Denmark
1991–1994	Ole Due	Denmark
1994–1997	Gil Carlos Rodríguez Iglesias	Spain
1997–2000	Gil Carlos Rodríguez Iglesias	Spain
2000–2003	Gil Carlos Rodríguez Iglesias	Spain
2003–2006	Vassilios Skouris	Greece
2006–2009	Vassilios Skouris	Greece
2009–2012	Vassilios Skouris	Greece

● **Judge-Rapporteur**: A judge on the Court of Justice who is appointed to oversee the different stages through which a case is reviewed. Equivalent to rapporteurs in the European Parliament.

Just how political the role of presidents (or even of judges) has become is open to debate. President Skouris was quite clear in 2004 when he argued that while the Commission was 'a political body with the right of initiative', the Court 'has never been and could never be like that. We rule on the cases that are brought before us . . . The importance of the role of the Court is a good subject for conferences and universities but at the end of the day it's a court of justice that carries out a normal task for any court: to rule on the cases, and nothing more' (Skouris, 2004). But is there really 'nothing more'? Even with the best will in the world, judges will bring personal biases (including political views) into their assessments; they are, after all, only human. And the role of politics in court decisions has long been very much a part of the debate in the United States about the work of its Supreme Court, with an ongoing discussion about the merits of constructionists (judges who interpret the US constitution literally, to the extent that this is humanly possible) and activists (those who bring their own views to their judgments).

The Advocates general

Advocates general are court officers whose job is to review cases as they come to the Court of Justice, to study the arguments involved, and to deliver independent opinions in court before the judges decide which laws apply and what action to take. The opinions of the advocates general are not binding on the judges, but they provide a valuable point of reference (Burrows and Greaves, 2007). The Court has eight advocates general appointed to renewable six-year terms. Like the judges, they are theoretically appointed by the 'common accord' of the governments of the member states, but in practice an informal system has developed by which one post is held by nationals of each of the Big Five member states (Germany, Britain, France, Italy and Spain), and the rest are held on a rotating basis by nationals of the smaller states. If needed, the number of positions can be increased by a simple decision of the Council of Ministers. One is appointed First Advocate General on a one-year rotation.

The General Court

With the workload of the Court of Justice growing in the 1980s, a decision was taken under the Single European Act to create a new, lower-level Court of First Instance that could be the first point of decision on less complicated cases. These included actions against EU institutions, actions brought by member states against the Commission, selected actions brought by member states against the Council of Ministers, actions for damage against EU institutions or their staff, actions on trademarks, and appeals from the Civil Service Tribunal. If a case is lost at this level, the parties involved have the right to appeal to the Court of Justice, but only on points of law.

Renamed the General Court by the Treaty of Lisbon, the court has roughly the same institutional structure as the Court of Justice: it has the same number of judges as there are member states of the EU, they are appointed for six-year renewable terms, and its rules of procedure are similar to those of the Court of Justice (although it has no advocates general). The number of judges can be changed by a decision of the Council of Ministers without an amendment to the

● **Advocates general**: Officers of the Court of Justice who review cases as they arrive and deliver preliminary opinions to the Court about which laws apply and what action to take.

● **General Court**: A subsidiary court created in 1989 (as the Court of First Instance) to review less complicated cases coming before the Court of Justice.

treaties. The Court usually sits as a chamber of three judges, but a single judge can hear and decide a case, while there can also be chambers of five judges, a Grand Chamber of 13 judges, and for the most important or complex cases the entire court can sit together. It is overseen by a president elected by the judges for three-year renewable terms. In 2007, Marc Jaeger – a lawyer from Luxembourg and a member of the General Court since 1996 – was elected president. He was confirmed to a second term in 2010.

The General Court has been particularly active in cases dealing with competition, state aid, and intellectual property. In the 2005 case *Laurent Piau* v. *Commission of the European Communities* (Case 193/02), for example, a player's agent named Laurent Piau complained to the European Commission that new rules adopted by FIFA, the international governing body of football, discriminated against agents for football players, amounted to abuse of dominant position and contravened EU competition law. The Commission dropped the case after FIFA changed its rules, but Piau challenged the decision to drop the case, which went to the General Court. In a 2005 judgment, the Court argued that the activities of football clubs and their national associations – as well as FIFA – were economic activities and so were subject to EU competition law, and that while the FIFA rules did not break EU competition rules, those rules could occasionally apply to sport.

The EU Civil Service Tribunal

This is one of the EU's newest institutions, created in 2004 to take over from the General Court any cases involving disputes between the EU institutions and their staff. It began work in 2005 under the jurisdiction of seven judges appointed for six-year renewable terms, with as broad a geographical range as possible, and overseen by a president. Its decisions can be appealed on questions of law to the General Court, and in exceptional situations to the Court of Justice. The Commission has been the target of more than half the cases brought to the Tribunal (a reflection as much as anything of its relative size), and the subjects range from contracts to pensions, job appraisals, promotions, discrimination, salaries, and workplace facilities.

What the Court does

If the Commission is the guardian of the treaties, the Court of Justice is responsible for making sure that in their 'interpretation and application . . . the law is observed', and that EU law is equally, fairly, and uniformly applied throughout the member states. In other words, the Court is the supreme legal body of the EU and the final court of appeal on all matters relating to EU law. In meeting its obligations it has been at the heart of the process of European integration, playing a particularly important role in the late 1970s and 1980s when the Community slipped into a hiatus and the Court kept alive the idea of integration as being something more than the building of a customs union (Shapiro, 1992). It is the most powerful international court in the world, and yet it has no direct powers to enforce its decisions, instead exerting its influence through the work of other actors – institutions, states, and individuals – who support its work (Conant, 2002).

● **EU Civil Service Tribunal**: A subsidiary court created in 2004 to take over from the Court of Justice cases involving complaints by employees of the EU.

Figure 13.2 Powers of the European Court of Justice

- ■ Supreme legal body of the EU and the final court of appeal on all matters relating to EU law.

- ■ Issues preliminary rulings when national courts ask for a ruling on the interpretation or validity of an EU law that arises in a national court case.

- ■ Makes decisions on direct actions when an individual, corporation, member state or EU institution brings proceedings directly before the Court, usually with an EU institution or a member state as defendant.

The Court sits for nine months each year, with a two-month break in the late summer and a one-month break over Christmas. Work on a case begins with a written application made by a lawyer or agent for the party bringing the case, which is filed with the Registrar of the Court and published in its *Official Journal*. This describes the dispute and explains the grounds on which the application is based. The defendant is also notified and given a month to respond. A judge-rapporteur is assigned to the case by the President, and an advocate general by the First Advocate General. These two officials present their preliminary reports to the Court, at which point the case is assigned to a chamber. The Court then decides whether documents need to be provided, witnesses interviewed, or an expert's report commissioned, after which the case is argued by the parties involved at a hearing.

The judges sit in order of seniority, which is determined by how long they have served on the Court, wearing crimson gowns while the lawyers appearing before them wear whatever garb is appropriate in their national courts. Although a case can be heard in any of the official languages of the EU, the main language used by the Court is French. At the end of the oral phase, the advocate general delivers an opinion, and once the chamber has reached a decision, it delivers judgment in open court. Once a judgment has been made, details of the case are published in the *Report of Cases before the Court* (also known as the *European Court Reports*).

Figure 13.3 Workflow of the European Court of Justice

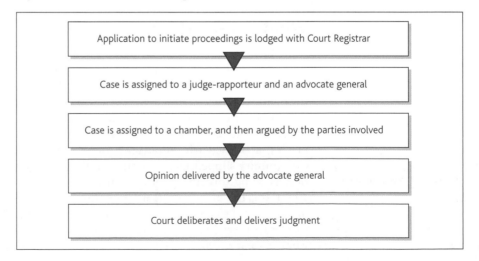

The whole process may take months, or years in more complex disputes; the average time has fallen, though, since the creation of smaller chambers, the General Court and the Civil Service Tribunal. Cases can also be heard on an expedited basis if an urgent decision is needed. Court decisions are technically supposed to be unanimous, but votes are usually taken on a simple majority; all votes are secret, so it is never publicly known who – if anyone – dissented. Judges were not given the right to publicly issue dissenting or concurring opinions, argues Arnull (2008, p. 11), for two main reasons. First, given that they serve short and renewable terms, they might have been tempted to go public in order to curry favour with their home governments in an attempt to be reappointed. Second, there were concerns in the early years of the Court that dissenting opinions might have undermined the Court's authority.

The work of the Court falls into two main parts, preliminary rulings and direct actions.

Preliminary rulings

In order to prevent EU laws being interpreted or applied differently in different situations, national courts can (and sometimes must) ask the Court of Justice for a ruling on the interpretation or validity of an EU law that arises in a national court case. EU institutions can also ask for preliminary rulings, but most are made on behalf of a national court, which is then bound to respect and apply the Court's response. The word *preliminary* is misleading, because the rulings are usually requested and given *during* a case, not before it opens; hence the rulings are actually concurrent rather than preliminary.

Both *Van Gend en Loos* and *Flaminio Costa* are classic examples of preliminary rulings. Another, with important implications for questions of citizenship, came in 2004. The Chens, a Chinese couple living in Britain, moved temporarily to Northern Ireland to have their second child, Catherine, who by virtue of being born there could claim Irish citizenship (she could not have claimed British citi-

Figure 13.4 Cases heard by the European Court of Justice

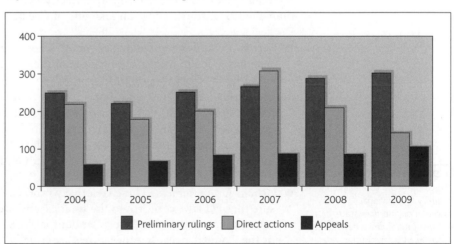

● **Preliminary ruling**: A ruling by the Court of Justice on the interpretation or validity of an EU law that arises in a national court case.

Source: Annual Report of the European Court of Justice, at http://curia.europa.eu (retrieved June 2010).

**Illustration 13.3
The Court in session**

A chamber of the European
Court of Justice in session.

zenship because her parents were only temporary residents). Using the child's
status as a citizen of an EU member state, the Chens hoped to move permanently
back to Britain, but were barred by British authorities. The case went to the
Court of Justice, which ruled in *Zhu and Chen* v. *Secretary of State for the Home
Department* (Case 200/02) that Catherine Chen could live anywhere in the EU,
that denying her parents a similar right would interfere with Catherine's rights,
and that it was not an abuse of EU rights to take advantage of Irish citizenship
laws. Ireland was quick to change its constitution in order to deny automatic citizenship to children born on the island of Ireland unless one of the parents was
an Irish citizen.

Direct actions

These are cases in which one party (which may be an individual, corporation,
member state, or EU institution) brings proceedings against another (often a
member state or an EU institution) directly before the Court of Justice rather
than a national court. They can take one of five main forms.

● *Direct action*: A case in
which there is a complainant
(usually an individual,
corporation, member state, or
EU institution) and a defendant
(usually an EU institution or a
member state).

- *Actions for failure to fulfil an obligation.* These are cases where a member
  state has failed to meet its obligations under EU law, and can be brought
  either by the Commission or by another member state (sometimes at the
  prodding of an interest group or a private company). While most are settled
  before they go to the Court, the defending member state will occasionally
  drag its feet. They are by far the most common of direct actions, accounting
  for all but three of the 210 directs actions heard by the Court in 2008. The
  most common subjects include environment and consumer law, freedom of
  movement, and freedom of establishment.
- *Actions for annulment.* These (relatively rare) cases are aimed at making
  sure that EU laws conform to the treaties, and are brought in an attempt to
  cancel those that do not. The defendant is almost always the Commission
  or the Council, because proceedings are usually brought against an act that
  one of them has adopted (Lasok, 2007, p. 323).

- *Actions for failure to act.* These are cases where an EU institution has failed to act in accordance with the terms of the treaties, and can be brought by other institutions, member states, or individuals. The first such action was brought in 1983 (*European Parliament* v. *Council* (Case 13/83)), when the European Parliament charged the Council of Ministers with failing to agree a Common Transport Policy as required under the Treaty of Rome. The Court ruled that while there was an obligation, because no timetable had been agreed it was up to the member states to decide how to proceed.
- *Actions for damages.* These are cases in which damages are claimed by third parties against EU institutions and their employees. A claim could be made that the institution was acting illegally, or an individual could claim his or her business was being hurt by a piece of EU law. Most of these cases are heard by the General Court.
- *Actions by staff.* These are cases involving litigation brought by staff members against EU institutions as their employers, and are dealt with by the EU Civil Service Tribunal.

Appeals and other cases

In cases where the General Court has issued a judgment, and one of the parties in the case is unhappy with the outcome, an appeal can be lodged with the Court of Justice. The Court can also be asked by the Commission, the Council of Ministers or a member state to rule on the compatibility of draft international agreements with the treaties; if the Court gives an unfavourable ruling, the draft agreement must be changed before the EU can sign it. Finally, the Court can be called in to arbitrate on contracts concluded by or on behalf of the EU (conditional proceedings) and in disputes between member states over issues relating to the treaties.

The European Court of Human Rights

Although it is not part of the EU's network of institutions, and works entirely independently of the EU, no analysis of judicial life in the EU can be complete without addressing the work of the European Court of Human Rights (ECHR). All member states of the EU – and the EU itself – are signatories of the European Convention and members of the ECHR, which means that in decisions dealing with human rights the Court of Justice must refer to precedent created by the decisions of the ECHR. There is another, more minor, link between the two institutions: it is not uncommon to find judges from the ECHR being appointed as judges on the European Court of Justice (but not vice versa).

Founded in 1959 and now headquartered in Strasbourg, the ECHR was established under the terms of the 1950 European Convention on Human Rights, which was in turn adopted under the auspices of the Council of Europe in order to promote the protection of human rights and fundamental freedoms. As we saw in Chapter 8, the Convention covers issues such as right to life, the prohibition of torture and slavery, the right to a fair trial, freedom of thought and expression, freedom of religion, the prohibition of discrimination and of the expulsion of nationals, the right to education, the protection of property, and the abolition of the death penalty.

● **European Court of Human Rights**: A Strasbourg-based court that hears cases and issues judgments related to the 1950 European Convention on Human Rights.

The Court issued its first judgment in 1960, but remained a temporary body until 1998 when it became a permanent institution to which direct access was available to citizens of the 47 member states of the Council of Europe, which are also parties to the European Convention. This new permanence, combined with expanded membership of the Council of Europe, greater media interest in the work of the Court, and simplified procedures, led to a new burst of activity: in its first 30 years the Court was receiving less than 800 applications per year, and had issued less than 70 judgments, but in the ten years after becoming permanent it was receiving an annual average of 45,000 applications and issuing about 800–1,000 judgments per year (Greer, 2006, pp. 34–40). Turkey and Italy have topped the list of violators of human rights (see Figure 13.5); more than half the judgments for the former related to the right to a fair trial and the protection of property, and more than half for the latter related to the excessive length of proceedings.

The Court consists of 47 judges, one for each of the member states of the Council of Europe. As with the European Court of Justice, there is no requirement that each member state should be represented by one of its nationals. Judges are appointed by the Parliamentary Assembly of the Council of Europe for six-year renewable terms of office (with an age limit of 70), and they in turn elect a President and two vice-presidents. The court is divided into five Sections, each balanced by geography, gender, and the different legal systems of the member states, and the membership of which is changed every three years. Each Section selects a Chamber consisting of a Section President and a rotating group of six other judges which deals with the more routine cases brought to the Court.

Figure 13.5 Europe's ten biggest human rights offenders

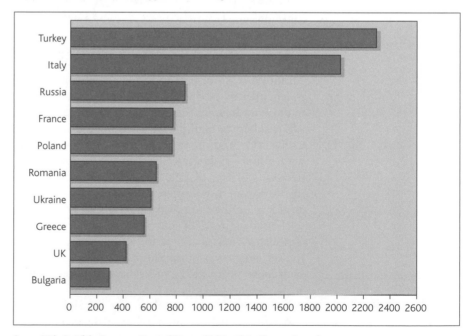

Source: Web site of the European Court of Human Rights at http://www.echr.coe.int (accessed June 2010). Figures are for judgments issued between 1998 and 2009.

**Illustration 13.4
The European Court of
Human Rights**

The headquarters of the
European Court of Human
Rights in Strasbourg.

The more important cases are dealt with by a 17-member Grand Chamber consisting of the President and the two Vice-Presidents (all three of whom are also Section Presidents), the two other Section Presidents, and 12 other judges appointed on a rotating basis.

Any contracting state or any individual who claims to have been harmed by the actions of a contracting state can bring a case to the Court. Most cases are dealt with in writing, a small minority going before a formal hearing. Each case is assigned to a Section, which can either declare it inadmissible or else decide to review it, in which case a decision is made by a simple majority vote. There is a right of appeal to a Grand Chamber, but otherwise a judgment becomes final within three months, and the Committee of Ministers of the Council of Europe is responsible for making sure that the state involved in the case has taken the necessary action to correct the problem.

This chapter would be incomplete without briefly mentioning two other courts with which the European Court of Justice is sometimes confused, but with which there is a much looser judicial relationship. The first of these is the International Court of Justice, the major judicial arm of the United Nations. Founded in 1945, it is based in The Hague, and its job is to settle disputes between UN member states, and to give opinions on legal questions submitted by international organizations and other UN bodies. The second is the International Criminal Court, also headquartered in The Hague, and founded in 2002 to prosecute individuals for crimes against humanity, war crimes, and genocide. All EU member states are members of both courts, and while their rulings can obviously have an impact on judicial matters in the EU, their relationship with the Court of Justice is not as close as that between the Court of Justice and the ECHR.

SUMMARY

● The European Court of Justice (headquartered in Luxembourg) is the judicial arm of the European Union, responsible for clarifying the meaning of the treaties and for issuing judgments in disputes involving EU institutions, member states, and individuals affected by EU law.

● The Court is the least known (and least controversial) of the EU institutions, and yet it has made numerous decisions that have clarified the meaning of integration and have established critical legal principles, such as direct effect, the supremacy of EU law, and mutual recognition.

● The Court consists of 27 judges appointed for six-year renewable terms by 'common accord' of the member states. There is no approval process involving the European Council or the European Parliament.

● The Court is headed by a president elected to three-year renewable terms by the judges from among their number.

● The judges are assisted by eight advocates-general charged with reviewing cases as they come to the Court and with delivering independent opinions.

● Below the Court of Justice there is a General Court that is the first point of decision on less complicated cases, and an EU Civil Service Tribunal that takes cases involving disputes between EU institutions and their staff.

● Court actions are either preliminary rulings (where national courts ask for a ruling on a matter of EU law arising in a national court case) or direct actions (when a dispute between two parties is brought directly before the Court).

● Although it is an independent institution, the work of the Strasbourg-based European Court of Human Rights has an important bearing on EU law.

KEY TERMS AND CONCEPTS

Advocates general

Constitutional court

Direct action

Direct effect

EU Civil Service Tribunal

European Court of Human Rights

General Court

Judge-rapporteur

Judicial authority

Mutual recognition

Preliminary ruling

Supremacy of EU law

FURTHER READING

Alter, Karen J. (2009), *The European Court's Political Power: Selected Essays* (Oxford University Press). A collection of articles on the ECJ written by one of its most active scholars.

Goldhaber, Michael D. (2007), *A People's History of the European Court of Human Rights* (Piscataway, NJ: Rutgers University Press). A compelling and readable survey of the work and effect of the ECHR.

Hartley, T.C. (2007), *The Foundations of European Community Law*, 6th edn (Oxford: Oxford University Press). One of the best of the many guides to EU law, with chapters on institutions, the legal system, legal principles, and the effects on the member states.

CHAPTER 14 Specialized Agencies

PREVIEW

European states have long cooperated on issues as varied as scientific research, patents, telecommunications, sports, higher education, postal services, and standardization, and have set up relevant international organizations. To these have been added more recently a network of specialized EU agencies: financial bodies such as the European Central Bank, regulatory agencies such as Europol and the European Food Safety Authority, executive agencies that manage specific EU programmes, and advisory bodies such as the Committee of the Regions.

There is no template for these agencies: some are part of the EU structure but others are independent, and most have been created only since the 1990s as the policy reach of integration has spread, and the need for better policy coordination has grown. Their size, reach and political role vary enormously: while the European Central Bank (ECB) is responsible for helping manage the euro, has a staff of 1500, and makes decisions that impact business and consumers throughout the eurozone and in much of the rest of the world, the European Training Foundation promotes vocational training in EU neighbouring states and employs just 130 people.

The creation of these agencies has happened mainly below the public radar, and yet their growth has been significant because they have given the EU more of the trappings of a conventional system of government. Their creation has meant adjustments for national government agencies in the member states, better coordination of policy across the EU, and a pooling of policy authority between national governments and the EU institutions. Questions have been asked recently about the lack of a grand plan for agency development, about how they should relate to equivalent national agencies, about how they should be managed and held accountable, and about how they will evolve in future.

KEY ISSUES

- Does the European Central Bank have enough authority?
- Should selected 'regulatory' agencies be converted into full-scale regulatory bodies with greater powers to implement laws and policies?
- Should the EU develop its own European criminal investigation force along the lines of the FBI in the United States?
- Do the EESC and the CoR provide added value, or would the interests of their members be better represented by the European Parliament?
- What role should the EU be playing in space exploration relative to the Americans, the Russians, and the Chinese?

Financial bodies

The economy has long been at the heart of European integration; little surprise, then, that banks should be among the more influential of the specialized European agencies. The oldest is the European Investment Bank, set up under the Treaty of Rome to encourage balanced economic development in the EEC. A newer and more powerful institutional addition is the European Central Bank, which manages monetary policy in the eurozone. Meanwhile, the European Bank for Reconstruction and Development is not part of the EU but has played a critical role in integration by helping eastern European states make the transition to free-market economic policies. Most recently, one of the effects of the 2007–10 global economic crisis was to oblige member states to think long and hard about trans-European financial regulation, which led to the decision to set up several new institutions, including the European Systemic Risk Board and the European System of Financial Supervisors.

European Investment Bank

Headquartered in Luxembourg, the EIB is the world's largest multilateral development bank. An autonomous body that is owned by the EU member states, it was set up in 1958 under the terms of the Treaty of Rome to encourage 'balanced and steady development' within the EEC. Describing itself as the long-term lending bank of the EU, its funds come from subscriptions from EU member states and from borrowing on international capital markets, and it lends on favourable terms to capital projects (long-term projects involving capital assets such as land, buildings, and other structures) that support the policy goals of the EU. It gives priority to investments in poorer parts of the EU, with a focus on transport and communications networks, investments in industry and infrastructure, small and medium-sized companies (those with less than 250 employees), the security of energy supply, and projects that promote environmental sustainability. It also manages a European Investment Fund that provides venture capital, equity and guarantees to small and medium-sized businesses.

Most of its investments have been within the EU, but it also makes loans to neighbouring states, to Russia, and to developing countries. The Bank does not make a profit and deals only in large loans, rarely lending more than half the total investment cost of a project, and often cofinancing projects with other banks. In 2008 it provided almost €60 billion in funding, and because of the global economic crisis increased this during 2009 to nearly €104 billion. Among its recent projects: the upgrading of school infrastructure in Spain, high-speed rail lines in Portugal, the expansion of hospital services in southwest England, new rolling stock for the Madrid metro, and the building of a wind farm in Mexico and a thermal power plant in Slovenia. Its single biggest project was the Eurotunnel that runs under the English Channel between England and France. Opened in 1994 after centuries of speculation and imaginative ideas about what it should look like, the tunnel cost about $15 billion to build (nearly twice the original estimate) and had to wait until 2007 before turning in its first annual profits.

The EIB's shareholders are the member states of the EU, which each subscribe to the Bank's capital of nearly €250 billion, two-thirds of which comes

● **European Investment Bank**: The investment bank of the EU, which supports economic development projects both inside and outside Europe.

**Illustration 14.1
European Central Bank**

The euro sculpture outside the headquarters of the European Central Bank in Frankfurt.

from Germany, Britain, France and Italy. The Bank is managed by a Board of Governors consisting of representatives of the member states (usually their finance ministers), who decide policy and appoint a decision-making Board of Directors (27 members along with a representative from the European Commission) to five-year renewable terms, and a nine-member Management Committee to six-year renewable terms. The latter consists of the president and the eight vice-presidents of the Bank and is its main executive body, overseeing the day-to-day running of the Bank and drafting decisions on spending for the consideration of the Board of Directors. Philippe Maystadt of Belgium was appointed president of the bank in 2000, and renewed for a second term in 2006.

European Central Bank

Although it was created only in 1998, the ECB has quickly become one of the most influential and powerful of all pan-European institutions. Its core task is to help manage the euro by ensuring price stability, setting interest rates, and managing the foreign reserves of the eurozone states. It has been described by Howarth and Loedel (2005, p. xi) as a 'leviathan', and as 'the most important institutional creation in Europe since the institutionalization of the nation state in the seventeenth century'. While this may be something of an overstatement, there is no question that its work has had substantial economic and political consequences. The adoption of the euro was the biggest shift of monetary powers from individual states to a central authority in world history, and as the euro has become more fully integrated into the global financial system, so the stature and the political significance of the ECB has grown. This was true at least, until the Greek debt crisis broke in 2009–10 (see Chapter 20), and it remains to be seen what effect the crisis will have on how the ECB is viewed.

The creation of the ECB was an inevitable part of plans to create a single European currency. First proposed in 1988, the framework of the Bank was described in the Maastricht treaty, and the first step in its eventual creation was

● **European Central Bank**: The central bank of the eurozone, responsible for managing the euro by setting interest rates, encouraging price stability, and managing foreign reserves.

Jean-Claude Trichet

Jean-Claude Trichet (born 1942) served as president of the European Central Bank between 2003 and 2011. Trained as an engineer, he was educated at the Institute of Political Studies in Paris (better known as Sciences Po) and the National School of Administration (ENA). He worked in several positions as a civil servant in the French Treasury and Ministry of Economic Affairs before being appointed a governor of the Bank of France and a governor of the World Bank in 1993. He was appointed to the Governing Council of the ECB in 1998, later becoming president. As such he oversaw many of the start-up challenges of the euro, and helped manage it through the 2007–10 global economic crisis. He developed a strong reputation for political independence, was long critical of eurozone governments and their mounting budget deficits, saw the 2010 bail-out of the euro as doing little more than buying time, and called for urgent and radical action to close deficits and penalize governments that did not take action.

taken in January 1994 with the foundation of the European Monetary Institute (EMI), whose job was to promote cooperation and coordination among national central banks in order to clear the way for the launch of the euro. The ECB was formally established on 1 June 1998, replacing the EMI and becoming part of two new bank networks: the European System of Central Banks (ESCB) consists of the ECB and the central banks of all the EU states, while the **Eurosystem** consists of the ECB and the national banks of member states that have adopted the euro. Self-described as 'the monetary authority of the euro area', the Eurosystem works to promote price and financial stability, to encourage financial integration, and to hold and manage the foreign reserves of the eurozone states.

The ECB got off to a shaky start with an unseemly squabble over the question of who should be its first president. Most member states hoped to see Wim Duisenberg, the Dutch president of the EMI, confirmed in the position, but the government of Jacques Chirac in France preferred to see the job go to Jean-Claude Trichet, governor of the Bank of France. After a lengthy debate at the May 1998 meeting held to mark the launch of the euro, a compromise was reached by which it was agreed that Duisenberg would serve half a term and would then voluntarily relinquish the office in 2002 to Trichet. But the transition was delayed as a result of Trichet's involvement in a court case arising from charges that he had ignored financial mismanagement at the Credit Lyonnais bank while he was an official with the French Treasury. He was cleared in June 2003, and took over as ECB president for an eight-year term in November of that year.

The structure of the ECB is based on the model of the German Bundesbank. Created in 1957, and based in turn on the model of the US Federal Reserve (Kaltenthaler, 2006, pp. 165, 168–9), the Bundesbank was famous for both its competence and its independence. The ECB probably has more independence than the Bundesbank or any existing national central bank; where their powers can be changed by national law, the powers of the ECB are based on a treaty whose terms can only be changed by agreement of all the EU member states

● **Eurosystem**: The monetary authority of the eurozone, made up of the ECB and national central banks, and charged with encouraging financial stability in the eurozone.

Focus on . . .
The European Bank for Reconstruction and Development

The EBRD is not an EU institution, but its work has had an important impact on the economic development policies of the EU. Much like the International Bank for Reconstruction and Development (the World Bank), the EBRD was founded to provide loans, encourage capital investment and promote trade, but its specific focus has been on helping eastern European and former Soviet states make the transition to free-market economies. Suggested by French president François Mitterrand in 1989, it began work in March 1991 and is now the single largest investor in eastern Europe and central Asia. While the World Bank lends mainly to governments, the EBRD makes 60 per cent of its loans to the private sector, and also works with public sector companies to encourage privatization.

Headquartered in London, it is an independent bank that is owned and operated by its 61 shareholder countries and by the EU and the European Investment Bank; the biggest share (€2 billion) is held by the United States, followed by Britain, France, Germany, Italy, and Japan (€1.7 billion each). Like the EIB it has a Board of Governors consisting of a representative from each shareholder country, typically the minister of finance. The Board appoints a president who works with a 23-member Board of Directors to oversee the operations of the Bank; Thomas Mirow of Germany was appointed the Bank's fifth president in 2008. Mirow's predecessor was Jean Lemierre, who in one of his last public speeches before stepping down admitted that perhaps the Bank's work had been completed and that it might be time to shut it down (Lemierre, 2008). It ended its central European operations in 2010, and shifted its focus to Russia, the Ukraine, and the Balkans.

(Hodson, 2010, p. 166). Organizationally, it has a Governing Council charged with making policy and made up of the central bank governors from each state in the eurozone and the Bank's Executive Board. The latter consists of the president, the vice-president, and four other members, all appointed by the governments of the member states to eight-year non-renewable terms, who manage the day-to-day business of the Bank. Finally, a General Council composed of the central bank governors of the 27 member states maintains links to non-eurozone countries. In May 2010, as the maelstrom of the Greek debt crisis swirled, the foundation stone was laid for a new dedicated headquarters for the ECB in Frankfurt, scheduled to open in 2014.

The new financial institutions

In spite of the Eurosystem's responsibility for financial stability, supervision has been left mainly to the member states, guided by the goal of building a single market for financial services. But the 2007–10 global economic crisis emphasized the many problems in the way that European financial markets had been regulated (or, at least, under-regulated). It particularly exposed shortcomings in cross-border supervision, made only too clear by the way that problems in one country quickly spread to other countries. As a result of what they learned, EU finance ministers held discussions in 2009 aimed at developing a new framework for financial supervision in the EU. While care was taken to make sure that EU powers did not stray into national tax policy, it was decided to set up two new institutions, all of which began work in January 2011:

- The European Systemic Risk Board (ESRB) is in charge of the macro-economic supervision of the EU's financial sectors, and responsible for identifying emerging risks in hope of avoiding more financial crises.
- The European System of Financial Supervisors (ESFS) is responsible for ensuring stability in individual financial firms.
- The European Banking Authority (headquartered in London) replaced the advisory Committee of European Banking Supervisors, and has the task of encouraging consistent regulation and supervision in the banking sector with a view to better protecting depositors and investors.
- The European Securities and Markets Authority (headquartered in Paris) oversees the EU market for financial services, and has the power to investigate selected financial products, such as credit default swaps, and ban them if needed.
- The European Insurance and Occupational Pensions Authority (headquartered in Frankfurt, along with the ESRB) encourages closer supervision of the EU insurance and pensions market.

Regulatory and executive agencies

The EU has an expanding body of specialized agencies, including regulatory agencies with mainly technical and managerial responsibilities, executive agencies with powers of implementation (mainly in areas dealing with research funding support), and agencies dealing with specific aspects of the Common Security and Defence Policy. There are now nearly 30 regulatory agencies and a changing number of executive agencies, and the ad hoc nature of the way they have been created has recently sparked a debate over the need for a more structured approach to their management and responsibilities.

Regulatory agencies

What the EU describes as 'Community' or regulatory agencies are in fact rarely involved directly in regulation. They are independent bodies that have been set up under EU law, have their own legal personalities, are mainly funded out of the EU budget, and are given technical, management, or informational responsibilities. They do not have the same executive functions as most of their national equivalents, and are limited to working in their specific areas of expertise. But while they cannot always regulate, they can take decisions on the application of EU standards, and they influence policy-making through the expertise they provide to the Commission. With time they are making more of a mark on policy, and through their coordination work they are bringing the activities of national agencies more into line with one another. The Commission itself considers their main value to lie in helping it focus on its core tasks, helping pool technical and scientific expertise in the interests of better decision-making, and helping add to the visibility of the EU (European Commission, 2008; see also Géradin *et al.*, 2005).

● **Regulatory agencies**: Standing bodies set up under EU law with technical, management and/or informational responsibilities.

The first two regulatory agencies – dealing with vocational training and living and working conditions – were founded in 1975, since when 27 more agencies have been set up, most of them since 1995 (see Table 14.1). (The Euratom Supply Agency is older, but its work relates only to Euratom.) Among them they employ nearly 4,000 staff and have a budget of €1.1 billion. The Commission (2008) divides them into four types:

- Those with the power to adopt decisions legally binding on third parties (such as the European Aviation Safety Agency and the European Chemicals Agency).
- Those that provide scientific and technical advice to the Commission, and to the member states where needed (such as the European Food Safety Authority).
- Those with operational responsibilities (such as the European GNSS Supervisory Authority, which manages Europe's global navigation satellite systems programme).
- Those acting as a clearing house for information.

One example of the latter is the European Environment Agency (EEA), set up in 1990 and headquartered in Copenhagen. It is small, with a staff of just 130 and a €40 million budget, and its main job is to gather and process information from the EU member states, along with Iceland, Norway, Switzerland and Turkey. The idea of creating an inspectorate with powers to monitor national environmental conditions and the application of EU law was opposed by the governments of member states (Collins and Earnshaw, 1993, pp. 238–9), resulting in the much more modest responsibilities of the EEA. It partners with national environmental agencies through the European Information and Observation Network (Eionet) to collect information which is then used to help improve the quality and effectiveness of EU and national environmental policies and to measure the results of those policies.

Majone (1997) argues that in their early years the agencies were denied the powers normally granted to regulatory bodies, and 'seemed to be doomed to play an auxiliary role'. But he also argues that they had the chance to turn their limitations into opportunities given that 'regulation by information' could often be more effective than direct regulation. This would only work, though, if the information was credible, which in turn depended upon the reputation of the agencies for independence and accuracy. Their role has been complicated by concerns in the member states about loss of control by national agencies, and the EU regulatory agencies have found themselves having to manoeuvre carefully between the member states, the Commission and related international organizations. To make sure that they do not become too independent, their management boards consist of national representatives, controls are imposed on their decision-making, and their tasks are narrowly defined. Their role is also impacted by the 1958 ECJ ruling *Meroni v. High Authority* (Case 9/56) in which the Court said that while authority could be delegated to new bodies not mentioned in the Treaty of Rome, such delegation could only happen if that authority was compatible with the regulatory powers of EEC institutions and involved 'clearly defined executive powers' subject to strict review, and no discretionary powers (see Dehousse, 2002).

Table 14.1 EU regulatory agencies

Name	Founded	Headquarters	Responsibilities
Euratom Supply Agency	1960	Luxembourg	Ensures regular and equitable supply of nuclear fuels for EU users
European Centre for the Development of Vocational Training (Cedefop)	1975	Thessaloniki, Greece	As title
European Foundation for the Improvement of Living and Working Conditions (Eurofound)	1975	Dublin	As title
European Environment Agency	1990	Copenhagen	Information clearing house
EU Satellite Centre	1992	Madrid	Analyzes satellite information in support of Common Foreign and Security Policy
European Monitoring Centre for Drugs and Drug Addiction	1993	Lisbon	Information clearing house
European Training Foundation	1994	Turin	Promotes cooperation and vocational education and training in states neighbouring EU
European Agency for Safety and Health at Work (EU-OSHA)	1994	Bilbao, Spain	Information clearing house
Translation Centre for the Bodies of the EU	1994	Luxembourg	Provides translation services for agencies
Community Plant Variety Office	1995	Angers, France	Manages granting of intellectual property rights for new plant varieties
European Medicines Agency	1995	London	Evaluates applications for new medicinal products
Office for Harmonisation in the Internal Market	1996	Alicante, Spain	Oversees registration of trade marks and new designs
Europol	1999	The Hague	Information exchange aimed at helping combat serious international crime
European Aviation Safety Agency	2002	Cologne, Germany	Helps Commission draft new rules
European Maritime Safety Agency	2002	Lisbon	Helps Commission and national authorities

Table 14.1 EU regulatory agencies – *continued*

Name	Founded	Headquarters	Responsibilities
European Food Safety Authority	2002	Parma, Italy	Provides scientific advice
EU Institute for Security Studies	2002	Paris	Think tank
Eurojust	2002	The Hague	Encourages inter-state judicial cooperation
European Railway Agency	2004	Valenciennes, France	Reinforces safety and interoperability of railways as part of EU transport policy
European Agency for the Management of Cooperation at the External Borders (Frontex)	2004	Wroclaw, Poland	Coordinates cooperation on management of the EU's external borders
European Network and Information Security Agency	2004	Heraklion, Greece	Information clearing house
European Defence Agency	2004	Brussels	Encourages systematic approach to European Security and Defence Policy and development of coordinated European defence industry
European Centre for Disease Prevention and Control	2005	Stockholm	Helps strengthen defences against infectious disease
Community Fisheries Policy	2005	Vigo, Spain	Promotes uniformity of Common Fisheries control systems
European Police College	2005	Bramshill, England	Organizes training courses for police officers
European GNSS Supervisory Authority	2007	Brussels	Manages Europe's programme to build global navigation satellite systems, including Galileo
European Chemicals Agency	2007	Helsinki	Coordinates REACH, the programme to manage registration, evaluation, authorization and restriction of chemicals
European Agency for Fundamental Rights	2007	Vienna	Information clearing house
Fusion for Energy	2007	Barcelona	Cooperates with international project to develop fusion energy
European Institute for Gender Equality	2010	Vilnius, Lithuania	Information clearing house

With the growth in their numbers and reach, questions have been asked about the accountability, cost and transparency of the regulatory agencies. Much like the Commission, they are often accused of being too big and of having too many discretionary powers, and yet they are small when compared to many national agencies and it is questionable how much real power they have. Borrás *et al.* (2007) point out that while there have been studies of the driving forces behind the delegation of policy-making powers, and their influence on the design of specialized agencies, there is less understanding of what happens later. They argue the need for increased interaction between agencies and the communities in which they work in order to promote the credibility and the legitimacy of the agencies.

The Commission has recently raised its own questions about the place and the future of the regulatory agencies. In 2002 it proposed setting up an operating framework for the agencies, including details on how they would be set up, their legal basis, and even how decisions would be made on the location of their offices. This idea failed to win support in the Council of Ministers, so in 2008 the Commission issued a white paper (European Commission, 2008) in which it argued that while agencies have a valuable role, they had been set up on an ad hoc basis without a clear idea of their place in the EU system, making it more difficult for them to work effectively. The time was now ripe, argued the report, for an assessment of their purpose and role, and to 'develop a clear and coherent vision on the place of agencies in European governance'. It concluded that the Commission, the Council and Parliament needed to work together to develop more clarity on their different types of functions, along with the development of a standard approach to their management, better regulation, and clearer rules on how agencies were set up and closed.

Executive Agencies

As distinct from the regulatory agencies, which are permanent, executive agencies are created for a fixed period with a specific task in mind. They are created and controlled by the Commission, their staff is appointed by the Commission, and they are almost always based in Brussels. Among those that have come and gone is the European Agency for Reconstruction, set up in 2000 to manage EU aid to Serbia, Kosovo, Montenegro and Macedonia, but whose mandate ended in 2008. In 2010 there were six executive agencies, dealing with issues ranging from competitiveness to transport and the management of EU research funding (see Table 14.2).

The agencies each answer to a directorate-general in the Commission, and much of their work involves dispersing and managing EU research and development funds. One of the projects managed by the Executive Agency for Competitiveness and Innovation is the Marco Polo project which aims to encourage the shift of freight transport from roads to sea, rail and inland waterways, helping reduce some of the congestion on Europe's increasingly busy highways. The Research Executive Agency is central to the EU's research funding programme, providing support for projects under the European Space Policy (see later in this chapter) and the Marie Curie grants that (among other things) encourage Europeans to begin a career in research, and encourage European researchers living overseas to return to Europe.

● **Executive agencies**: Temporary bodies set up by the Commission to help carry out narrow and specific executive tasks.

Table 14.2 EU executive agencies

Name	Founded	Headquarters	Responsibilities
Executive Agency for Health and Consumers	2005	Luxembourg	Supports implementation of EU Public Health Programme
Trans-European Transport Network Executive Agency	2006	Brussels	Manages technical and financial aspects of Trans-European Transport Network
Education, Audiovisual and Culture Executive Agency	2006	Brussels	EU-funded programmes dealing with education, training, AV and culture
European Research Council Executive Agency	2007	Brussels	Funds and promotes European research
Research Executive Agency	2007	Brussels	Research funding body
Executive Agency for Competitiveness and Innovation	2009	Brussels	Programmes related to energy, transport and and the environment

European Police Office (Europol)

With the opening up of the single market in the 1990s it was felt that more direction needed to be given to police cooperation. With this in mind, the Europol Drugs Unit was created in 1994, and in June 1996 the Europol Convention was signed, creating a European Police Office that became fully operational in July 1999. Based in The Hague, Europol describes itself as a 'law enforcement' agency but is in reality a criminal intelligence organization much like Interpol (the French-based international police organization founded in 1923). It has no powers of arrest, and no autonomous powers of investigation, but instead oversees an EU-wide system of information exchange targeted at helping national police forces to combat serious forms of international crime; these include terrorism, organized crime, cyber crime, clandestine immigration networks, and money forging and laundering, and the trafficking of drugs, vehicles, people, child pornography, and radioactive materials. It coordinates operations among the national police forces of the EU, it can ask those forces to launch investigations, and while some see it as the forerunner of a European police force, there is no common EU penal code or police law, making the development of such a force any time soon unlikely. (For a detailed study of Europol, see Occhipinti, 2003.)

Europol is overseen by a Management Board with one representative from each of the member states, and run by a Directorate made up of a director and three deputies each appointed for a maximum of two four-year terms. The appointments are made by the Council of Ministers, and Europol answers to the Justice and Home Affairs Council. As well as its full-time staff, the Europol headquarters are also home to European Liaison Officers seconded from the member states as representatives of national police forces, and whose presence helps build

● **Europol**: The criminal intelligence agency of the EU which works to share information in order to address the most serious forms of international crime.

**Illustration 14.2
Eurojust**

The headquarters of
Eurojust and the
International Criminal
Court in The Hague.

networks and encourage police cooperation. Related to Europol is the European Police College, headquartered at Bramshill in the south of England. This was set up in 2005 and runs training courses that bring together police officers from across Europe.

International terrorism may have moved up the policy agenda since the attacks in the United States in 2001, in Madrid in 2004 and in London in 2005, but terrorism is nothing new to Europe (see Chapter 23). The threats it posed were part of the motivation behind the formation in 1975 of the TREVI group (Terrorism, Radicalism, Extremism, and International Violence) which brought together police officials from EEC states, and paved the way for later EU cooperation. The 9/11 attacks represented a quantum leap in the scale and reach of the problem, but Burich (2008) argues that Europol's role in counter-terrorism activities so far has been no more than 'fledgling'. It has not been granted supranational powers, it has too few staff and too little funding, and its role is not fully trusted by national counter-terrorism agencies that worry about loss of authority and prefer to work through long-standing bilateral and multilateral agreements. But Europol, he contends, could provide added value by helping standardize approaches to terrorism, sharing best practices, and helping outline long-term trends, and has the potential to play an important role if national agencies change their mind.

Examples of recent Europol operations give a sense of where its services are most needed and effective. During 2008–09 there were ram-raids in several continental EU states, where gangs drove stolen vehicles through the main entrances of electrical retailers, bagging as many high-value products as they could before dispersing, each raid usually taking less than 90 seconds. Austrian police discovered that the raiders were from Lithuania, and worked through Europol with the police in Belgium, France, Italy, Lithuania and Sweden to identify several separate criminal groups, and to arrest the 18 leaders in early 2010. At about the same time, another operation – codenamed Diabolo II and involving Europol, Interpol, and police forces in 13 Asian and 27 European countries – led to the seizure of more than 65 million counterfeit cigarettes and nearly 400,000 other counterfeit items (including cameras, toys, shoes, hats and handbags bearing more than 20 different trademarks) brought in to Europe from Asia in shipping containers. Other cases involving Europol have included breaking up a Polish-based counterfeit euro operation, the arrest of child traffickers in Romania, and a six-nation operation to stop credit card fraud.

Another specialized agency related to Europol is **Eurojust** (the Judicial Cooperation Unit), set up in 2002 with headquarters in The Hague to improve investigations and prosecutions involving two or more member states. It has the authority to ask national authorities to launch an investigation or start a prosecution, to coordinate the work of multiple national authorities, to set up joint investigation teams, and to provide supporting information. It is run by a College of 27 national members (most with backgrounds as judges, prosecutors or police officers), who elect one of their number as president and two as vice-presidents. Meanwhile, the work of Europol and Eurojust is complemented by the European Judicial Network, set up in 1998 in order to encourage judicial cooperation in criminal matters (see Chapter 23 for more details).

Advisory bodies

At the heart of the supporting framework of specialized European organizations are two Brussels-based advisory bodies designed to offer key groups input into the making of EU policy. The European Economic and Social Committee (EESC) was set up under the Treaty of Rome as a forum for representatives of employers and workers. It was joined in 1985 by an ad hoc assembly created to channel the opinions of local government into European decision-making, and formalized under Maastricht as the Committee of the Regions (CoR). The value of the two committees is debatable, particularly given that the EESC was created out of unfounded fears that the European Parliament would not represent sectional interests, and also given that neither body has much power. Some would argue that they are more than advisory bodies, and have developed modest political clout, but others would argue that they have not fulfilled the hopes of their founders for a corporatist Europe and a Europe of the regions.

Based in Brussels, the EESC was modelled on parallel bodies that existed in all the founder members of the EEC except West Germany. It has 344 members, divided up among the member states roughly in proportion to population size (see Table 14.3), nominated by national governments, and confirmed for renewable five-year terms by the Council of Ministers. Lisbon placed a cap of 350 on total membership, so future enlargement of the EU will mean a redistribution of seats among the member states. It elects a president and a bureau from among its members for two-and-a-half-year terms, and convenes for two-day meetings in Brussels nine times each year.

The Committee is divided into three groups, with Group I consisting of employers from industry, services, small businesses, chambers of commerce, banking, insurance, and similar areas; Group II consisting of representatives of employees, including national trade unions and cross-national union confeder-

● **Eurojust**: A judicial cooperation unit that works to improve the effectiveness of investigations and prosecutions across EU member states.

Table 14.3 Membership of the EESC and the CoR

Germany	24	Greece	12	Slovakia	9
UK	24	Hungary	12	Estonia	7
France	24	Netherlands	12	Latvia	7
Italy	24	Portugal	12	Slovenia	7
Spain	21	Sweden	12	Cyprus	6
Poland	21	Bulgaria	12	Luxembourg	6
Romania	15	Denmark	9	Malta	5
Austria	12	Finland	9		
Belgium	12	Ireland	9		
Czech Republic	12	Lithuania	9	Total	344

ations; and Group III representing 'various interests', such as agriculture, small businesses, consumer and environmental groups, the academic community, non-governmental organizations, and the professions. The three groups meet separately to discuss matters of common interest, breaking into smaller sections to deal with specific issues, such as agriculture, social policy, transport, energy, regional development, and the environment. Consultation of the EESC by the Commission is mandatory in several policy areas, including agriculture, the movement of workers, social policy, regional policy, and the environment.

As for the Committee of the Regions, its role is to give a voice to the interests of local government, and to help deal with the problem of regional economic disparities (see Chapter 22). Structurally, those problems were first addressed by the launch in 1975 of the European Regional Development Fund, followed ten years later by the creation of an ad hoc Assembly of European Regions, and in 1988 by a Consultative Council of Regional and Local Authorities in 1988. The need for a stronger and more structured arrangement led to the creation under the terms of Maastricht of the Committee of the Regions. As EU spending on regional development has grown so the political role of the CoR has become more significant. And given that so many EU laws are implemented at the local level, the CoR has a more overtly political role than the EESC.

Based in Brussels, the CoR met for the first time in January 1994 and has the same membership structure as the EESC: 344 members chosen by the member states and appointed by the Council of Ministers for five-year renewable terms. Maastricht specified only that members of the Committee should be 'representatives of regional and local bodies', which has been translated in practice to mean elected local government officials, including mayors and members of state, regional, district, provincial, and county councils. It meets in plenary session five times per year and must be consulted by the Commission, the Council of Ministers, and the European Parliament on issues relating to economic and social cohesion, trans-European networks, public health, education, and culture. Being more political than the EESC, its members have formed themselves into party groups along the lines of those found in the European Parliament.

The core weakness of both bodies is that they can only issue opinions. Their role has been further undermined by their being brought into the legislative process only after proposals for new EU laws have reached an advanced stage of agreement by the Council of Ministers and Parliament; Lisbon changed the status of the Committee of Regions, however, by obliging the Commission to consult it as early as the pre-legislative stage, and by giving it the authority to have EU laws reviewed by the Court of Justice if the CoR believes that those laws deal with areas outside the competence of the EU institutions. The two committees provide expert input into EU decision-making and can make the case that they encourage democracy by providing a link between EU institutions and key economic and social sectors.

Other institutions

Alongside the regulatory, executive, and advisory bodies, there are several other EU or European institutions whose work either strengthens that of the major EU institutions, or reflects the new opportunities for Europe-wide cooperation that have grown in recent decades. This section offers examples of three of these bodies, each quite different in terms of goals and structure: the Court of Auditors, Eurocorps, and the European Space Agency.

European Court of Auditors

This is the EU's financial watchdog, founded in 1975 to replace the separate auditing bodies for the ECSC and for the EEC/Euratom. It is difficult to neatly classify because it has been recognized since Maastricht as one of the formal institutions of the EU (along with the Commission, the Council of Ministers, Parliament, the Court of Justice, and – since Lisbon – the European Council), but it has a far more focused remit than any of those bodies. Headquartered in Luxembourg, the Court likes to describe itself as the 'financial conscience' of the EU. It carries out annual audits of the accounts of all EU institutions to ensure that revenue has been raised and expenditure incurred as planned and intended, and to monitor the Union's financial management. The Court reports back to the Commission, the Council of Ministers, and Parliament by the end of November each year. Parliament is supposed to approve the Court's report by the following April, but can use the report to force changes in the Commission's spending and accounting habits.

The Court is headed by 27 auditors, one appointed from each member state for a six-year renewable term. Nominations come from the national governments and must be approved by the Council of Ministers on the advice of the European Parliament. The auditors then elect one of their number to serve as president for three-year renewable terms. Much like the Court of Justice, the members can sit in chambers of between three and six members each. The auditors must be members of an external audit body in their own country or have other appropriate qualifications, but they are expected to act in the interests of the EU and to be completely independent. A regular peer review by a team of international auditors carried out in 2008 confirmed that its record for independence and objectivity was strong.

The Court routinely finds errors in the management of funds, and in 2009 refused to approve the accounts of the EU for the fifteenth year in a row, citing errors in record-keeping and suspected attempts at fraud. Over the years it has issued often scathing criticisms of waste and mismanagement, finding everything from excessive expense claims by European commissioners to fraudulent claims for funds made available under the Common Agricultural Policy. In 2009 it issued a heavily critical report on the Galileo global navigation system (see Chapter 19), which was running several years behind schedule and costing nearly two-thirds more than originally projected. It reserved particular criticism for the lack of policy leadership from the Commission, with which it otherwise has a close working relationship. The Court also has a symbiotic relationship with Parliament; each has helped promote the powers and the profile of the other.

Eurocorps

Offering a prime example of how sub-clusters of EU member states have occasionally taken the initiative to move forward on policy cooperation without their partners, Eurocorps is seen by many as a potential foundation for a future EU military. Tracing its roots back to an experimental Franco-German brigade created in 1991, Eurocorps was formally launched in May 1992 and has been fully operational since November 1995. It today consist of 60,000 troops from its five 'framework' states (Belgium, France, Germany, Luxembourg and Spain), along with staff from several other countries, including Austria, Greece, Poland and Turkey. It made its first significant military commitment in 1998 when nearly 500 Eurocorps personnel joined the NATO Stabilization Force (SFOR) in Bosnia. In 2000, it sent a mission to Kosovo, and in 2004–05 it briefly took over leadership of the NATO-run peacekeeping mission in the Afghan capital of Kabul.

Eurocorps is headquartered in Strasbourg, France. It is overseen by a Common Committee made up of the Chiefs of Defence Staff and political representatives from the five member states, who meet annually. Day-to-day operations are overseen by the Eurocorps Committee, made up of representatives from the national ministries of defence, and by a commander appointed from one of the member states: Hans-Lothar Domröse of Germany took over in 2009. Although participation in Eurocorps is open to all EU member states, the response to date has been disappointing to those who favour the building of an EU military capacity. Supporters of Eurocorps point to its role in bringing France and Germany into European defence matters, but critics note that it relies almost entirely on non-Eurocorps assets such as intelligence, advanced weapons, and transportation.

European Space Agency

The ESA is not part of the network of EU agencies, but its creation and its work impact policy in the EU, and it provides an example of the expanding variety of cooperative ventures in which Europeans have become engaged. Headquartered in Paris, ESA has 18 member states: all 15 pre-2003 western European EU member states, along with the Czech Republic, Norway, and Switzerland. It has a staff of nearly 2,000, and had a budget in 2009 of nearly €3.6 billion. It also operates a launch facility at Korou in French Guiana, and an astronaut training facility in Cologne, Germany. ESA focuses on space exploration and research, working mainly with the French commercial satellite company Arianespace (founded in 1980), and on human space flight through its participation in the International Space Station, in which 11 ESA member states cooperate with the United States, Russia, Japan and Canada.

● **Eurocorps**: A multinational military force set up among several EU states, outside EU structures, that some see as the seed of a common European military.

The ESA traces its roots back to the 1950s, when a combination of the 'brain drain' of European scientists to the United States and the early ventures in space exploration prompted a group of western European scientists to meet to talk about the need for coordination and cooperation among their peers. Two new bodies – the European Launch Development Organization and the European Space Research Organization – were founded in 1964, and made their first modest contributions with research satellites launched on American rockets. In 1975 the two organizations were merged to form the European Space Agency, and that same year ESA launched its first major mission, gathering information on gamma-ray emissions in the universe. It worked with NASA of the United States in 1978 to launch the world's first high-orbit telescope, and in 1986 launched the Giotto deep space mission to study the Halley and Grigg-Skelljerup comets. In 1983, Ulf Merbold of West Germany became the first ESA astronaut to go into space, as a member of the NASA space shuttle *Columbia* mission. By 2010 the European Astronaut Corps had sent nearly two dozen astronauts into space aboard either US space shuttle or Russian Soyuz missions to the International Space Station.

The ESA cooperates closely with the EU on policy (particularly on projects such as the Galileo satellite navigation system) and there has been talk of integrating the ESA more fully into EU institutional structures. In 2007 the EU adopted a European Space Policy emphasizing the importance of maintaining an independent launch capacity, the on-going European commitment to the International Space Station, and the development of technologies that would allow Europe to be competitive in space policy. Ten mainly eastern European countries have applied to join ESA, so an expansion in its size and activities is on the cards.

SUMMARY

- As the policy reach and responsibilities of the EU have grown, so a network of specialized agencies has grown, including financial bodies, advisory bodies, executive agencies, and a mix of EU and independent bodies whose work relates to that of the main EU institutions.
- Financial institutions include the European Investment Bank, the European Central Bank, and the independent European Bank for Reconstruction and Development. New regulatory institutions have been proposed as part of the EU response to the 2007–10 global economic crisis.
- Other agencies have varying technical, managerial and executive responsibilities, dealing with such issues as vocational training, gathering environmental information, monitoring drug use, evaluating new medicinal products, and improving aviation, maritime, and food safety.
- Executive agencies are set up for a fixed period of time with a specific task in mind, such as trans-European transport networks, education and training, and research.
- Police and judicial cooperation have been encouraged and promoted by Europol and Eurojust, which are active in helping deal with serious forms of cross-border crime.
- The two major advisory bodies are the European Economic and Social Committee, a policy forum for key economic and social groups, and the Committee of the Regions, which gives voice to the interests of local government.
- The European Court of Auditors is the EU's financial watchdog, charged with making sure that the EU accounts are correct. It usually finds that they are not.
- Eurocorps maintains a multinational European military force for use mainly in humanitarian and peacekeeping operations, and the European Space Agency undertakes space research and manages Europe's astronaut programme

KEY TERMS AND CONCEPTS

Eurocorps
Eurojust
European Central Bank
European Investment Bank
Europol
Eurosystem
Executive agencies
Regulatory agencies

FURTHER READING

Géradin, Damien, Rodolphe Muñoz, and Nicolas Petit (eds) (2005), *Regulation Through Agencies in the EU: A New Paradigm of European Governance* (London: Edward Elgar). An edited collection of studies of the motives behind setting up specialized agencies and the potential effects.

Howarth, David, and Peter Loedel (2005), *The European Central Bank: The New European Leviathan?* 2d edn (Basingstoke: Palgrave Macmillan); Karl Kaltenthaler (2006), *Policy-making in the European Central Bank: The Masters of Europe's Money* (Lanham, MD: Rowman & Littlefield). Two studies of the work of the ECB.

Occhipinti, John D. (2003), *The Politics of EU Police Cooperation: Toward a European FBI?* (Boulder, CO: Lynne Rienner). The only full-length study to date of EU police cooperation.

CHAPTER 15

Parties and Interest Groups

PREVIEW The EEC was designed and long run by bureaucrats and politicians, who referred little – if at all – to public opinion. But as the reach of integration expanded, so more Europeans became interested in expressing their views. For some this was a positive interest, driven by a belief that European institutions deserved, even demanded, their attention and input. For others it was a critical interest, driven by concerns that the European institutions were undemocratic, too powerful, and a threat to national sovereignty. For both groups, political parties and interest groups have been key channels of engagement.

While political parties are at the heart of political life in the member states, we have yet to see transnational political parties fighting European election campaigns on European issues. Instead, elections to the European Parliament are contested by national political parties running in separate national contests. MEPs organize themselves into European party groups, or clusters of national parties based on alliances among like-minded legislators. But change is in the air, generated by the growth of a network of European party organizations through which national parties work together and coordinate policy.

If parties have not yet fully exploited what Europe has to offer, interest groups have made more progress. National groups have paid more attention to Brussels, opening European offices and building transnational networks designed to capitalize on the strength of their numbers. They have been encouraged by the Commission, which uses groups as a source of expertise and to report on the implementation of EU law by the member states. The input of groups, even if they promote the interests of their members rather than working for the broader European interest, has helped strengthen the legitimacy and responsiveness of the EU decision-making system.

KEY ISSUES
- Should national political parties work through Europarties to replace political groups in the EP, or is the current system sufficient?
- What would be the effect on the EP if one of the party groups were to win a majority of seats?
- Given the numerous parties represented in the EP, is there a problem in the EU of too much democracy?
- What does the relative weakness of party activity at the EU level mean for the character and quality of interest group activity?
- How are interest groups and their lobbying activities likely to affect levels of support for European integration?

European political groups

Political parties lie at the heart of democratic government, playing several critical roles in the way that national political systems are ordered.

- They represent the views and interests of voters and party members.
- They recruit and provide a training ground for political leaders, who in turn become the personalities that drive politics and put a human face on government.
- They offer voters competing sets of public policy options.
- They help articulate and aggregate the collective goals of different interests in society.
- They mobilize and engage voters in the political process.
- They provide the labels by which the philosophies of candidates for office can be better understood.
- They form governments and oppositions.

Although EU member states are replete with political parties, covering every ideological taste from the far left to the far right, party activity at the European level has been rather different in character from that at the national level. When the Common Assembly of the European Coal and Steel Community first met in Strasbourg in 1953, its members were arranged in alphabetical order by name, but they were also members of national parliaments and political parties, and they naturally gravitated towards like-minded peers from other countries. Within months the Assembly had changed its own rules of procedure to allow for the formation of cross-national **political groups**, for each of which at least nine members were needed. The tradition of MEPs sitting not in national blocs, as some might expect, but in ideological groups has continued since.

● **Political groups**: Groups formed within the European Parliament that bring together MEPs from like-minded political parties from the different member states.

Illustration 15.1
European political groups

A meeting of the Progressive Alliance of Socialists and Democrats, one of the major party groups in the European Parliament.

Although these groups are not formally political parties, they are not much different in terms of goals and structures: they consist of MEPs with common ideologies and policy preferences, their members tend to vote together on issues before Parliament, and they have their own budgets, leadership structures, operating rules, and committees. One key difference between EP political groups and national political parties is that the groups do not campaign together across member states; EP elections are fought in 27 separate national contests by national parties that then form groups during the term of the EP. Another difference is that while parties in the member states form governments, and are intimately linked to executives, groups in the EP do not. Except for the EP's role in confirming and monitoring the Commission, there are few formal political links between the two institutions. For it to function more like its national equivalents, the membership of the College of Commissioners would have to come out of Parliament, and to be determined by the balance of parliamentary political groups.

In order for parties to form a group they must have at least 25 members from at least one quarter of member states, and no MEP is allowed to belong to more than one group. Participating MEPs must have a common 'political affinity', must inform the president of the EP of their plans, and must publish a statement in the *Official Journal of the European Union* (Rule 29, European Parliament Rules of Procedure, 16th ed., 2008). Groups then elect their own chairs (or cochairs where the groups are confederal) and appoint governing bureaux and supporting secretariats.

The number and membership of EP political groups has changed as the balance of their constituent parties has changed, as new parties have come and gone, and as political philosophies, circumstances and opportunities have evolved. This has created a confusing game of musical chairs, made all the more difficult to follow by the ever-changing names of the party groups (few of which trip easily off the tongue). Some have been little more than marriages of convenience, bringing together MEPs with sometimes quite different philosophies, but others have built more focus and consistency over time, and have become part of the permanent structure of Parliament. (For a history of EU party groups, see Bardi, 2002. For an overview of the groups, see Corbett, Jacobs and Shackleton, 2005, Chapter 5. For the dynamics behind transnational party cooperation, see Hanley, 2007.)

The greatest consistency has been in the mainstream left, centre right, and right of the political spectrum, where three groups – the socialists, the liberals, and the European People's Party – have a history dating back to the beginnings of the EP and have consistently won the largest share of seats in EP elections. They have been joined since the mid-1980s by green parties whose numbers in the EP have grown but which have not yet achieved as much influence. Meanwhile, conservative, nationalist and eurosceptic groups on the margins have had a more chequered history, their memberships and labels changing more frequently according to the changing numbers and interests of their members. Figure 15.1 illustrates not just the changing fortunes of the three largest groups, but also the declining support for smaller groups, whose share of the vote since 1979 has been cut almost in half. No one political group has yet won enough seats to form a majority, and while it might be logical for likeminded groups to try and form a majority coalition, multi-partisanship has been the normal order of business.

Figure 15.1 EP political groups

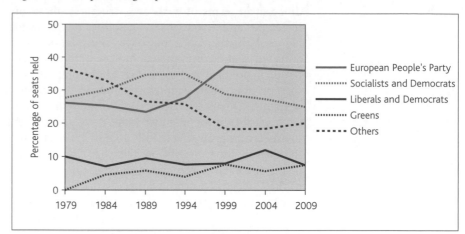

Although there is no formal obligation for MEPs to vote with their political group, greater discipline gives groups greater impact, and research has revealed greater voting cohesion within parties: as the main groups have grown, and as the powers of the EP have expanded, their policy distinctions have become more clear and group cohesion has grown (Hix, Noury, and Roland, 2007). (For details on the positions on Europe of the major party families, see Marks, Wilson and Ray, 2002.) Ringe (2009) argues that because MEPs lack the resources to be able to make informed decisions in every policy area, they often fall back on the positions taken by their party groups and the EP committees of which they are members. In spite of the structural weakness of party groups, the result of this reliance is more group cohesion and consistency.

Although the most visible arena of party activity in the EU is the European Parliament, party affiliations also factor into the work of the Councils and the European Commission. In the former, every minister and head of government is a member of a domestic political party, and both ideology and party platforms influence their decisions. While Parliament has seen a steady rise of centre-right parties at the expense of centre-left parties, there has been more volatility in the Councils, reflecting the ebb and flow of party fortunes in national elections. The right dominated in the 1980s, lost ground to the left in the 1990s, and was back in the early 2000s. As for the Commission, party politics are less openly on display, reflecting the bureaucratic qualities of the institution, but nominations are made by the national governments of the day, commissioners are typically members of national parties, and more attention is now paid to their affiliations. In spite of trends in national politics, however, there has been a shift to the left in the Commission in recent years.

After the 2009 EP elections there were seven political groups in place. Running from left to right on the ideological spectrum, they were as follows:

European United Left–Nordic Green Left (GUE–NGL)

This is the main left-wing group in the EP, and the product of complex changes that have taken place at this end of the spectrum since the mid-1980s. Less a full-

Figure 15.2 The EP political groups

	NAME	ACRONYM	PHILOSOPHY	ASSOCIATED EUROPARTY
GUE/NGL	European United Left-Nordic Green Left	GUE-NGL	Left	Party of the European Left
S&D	Progressive Alliance of Socialists and Democrats	PASD	Social democrat	Party of European Socialists
The Greens | EFA	The Greens–European Free Alliance	Greens-EFA	Green/regionalist	European Green Party
	Alliance of Liberals and Democrats for Europe	ALDE	Centre-left	European Democratic Party
	European People's Party	EPP	Centre-right	European People's Party
ECR	European Conservatives and Reformists	ECR	Conservative	Movement for European Reform
EFD	Europe of Freedom and Democracy	EFD	Eurosceptic	None

fledged group than a confederation of two others, it traces its origins to a Communist Group formed in 1973. This broke up after the collapse of the Soviet Union in 1989, with Italian and Spanish communists forming the European United Left (GUE) while French, Greek, and Portuguese communists formed Left Unity. GUE fell apart in 1993, was resurrected in 1994, and in 1995 teamed up with the Nordic Green Left, consisting of newly-arrived leftist MEPs from Finland and Sweden. After the 2009 elections the group had 35 members from 13 EU states, the biggest national delegations coming from Germany, France, Portugal, and the Czech Republic. The group is critical of the elitist qualities of the EU, campaigns for more direct democracy and enforcement of human rights, and opposes the 'radically market-oriented logic' of European economic policy.

Progressive Alliance of Socialists and Democrats (PASD)

The PASD is the main left-wing group in the EP, tracing its origins back to the creation in the ECSC Common Assembly of the Socialist Group. This went on to become the largest group in Parliament, its size adding to the concerns of conservative eurosceptics about the interventionist tendencies of European economic policies. At the first direct elections in 1979 it won a plurality of seats (113 to the 107 won by the European People's Party (EPP)), picking up even bigger shares in the next three elections. A Confederation of Socialist Parties of the European Community had been created in 1973, and when in 1992 it renamed itself the Party of European Socialists, the EP political group followed suit by renaming itself the Group of the Party of European Socialists (PES) (see Lightfoot, 2005).

Focus on . . .
The rise of Europarties

Party activity at the European level has been encouraged in recent years by a growth in the number and variety of pan-European party organizations and confederations. While these Europarties are not yet well-known to the EU electorate and do not make much of a mark on national politics in the EU member states, their work promises to help improve coordination among like-minded national parties, and to help give party groups in the EP greater stability and cohesion. They may even evolve into the pan-European parties that are today so patently missing from EP election campaigns.

The first Europarties were founded in the 1970s in the lead-up to the first EP elections: the Confederation of Socialist Parties of the European Community was founded in 1973 (and was renamed the Party of European Socialists in 1992). It was followed by the moderately conservative European People's Party and the centre-left European Liberal Democratic and Reform Party in 1976, and by a group of regional parties that created the European Free Alliance in 1981. But it has only been since 2002 that the real growth in Europarty activity has taken place (see Figure 15.3).

Europarties are still evolving, and have yet to run EU-wide campaigns for EP elections, but they have become more adept at coordinating policy and at building links between party leaders at the national and European levels (Hix, 2005, p. 192). One attempt to run a truly European campaign in 2009 was organized by an Irish businessman named Declan Ganley. In 2006 he formed a party named Libertas to campaign against the Treaty of Lisbon in the Irish referendum; this ran in the 2009 EP elections on a platform of greater democracy and transparency within the EU, but while it fielded several hundred candidates, only one (in France) was elected.

During the late 1990s PES felt the effects of a rightward shift within the European electorate, including a reaction in Britain against the governing Labour Party. In the 1999 elections the EPP for the first time beat it into second place in the EP, where it has since remained. It became the Socialist Group in 2004, and in 2009 became the Progressive Alliance of Socialists and Democrats (PASD). After the 2009 elections it had members from every EU member state, the biggest national blocs coming from Germany, Italy, Spain, France, Britain and Romania. It contains many shades of opinion ranging from former communists on the left to more moderate social democrats towards the centre, but along with the EPP is the most firmly pro-European of the political groups in the EP.

The Greens–European Free Alliance (Greens–EFA)

This is another of the confederal marriages of convenience in the EP, bringing together national parties with approximately similar aims, but allowing each a high degree of independence. The Greens trace their roots back to the Rainbow Group formed in 1984 as a coalition of green parties (then making their first early mark on national politics in western Europe), regional parties, and left-wing parties unaffiliated with other political groups. **Green politics** is popularly associated with environmental issues, but greens in fact pursue a wider variety

● **Europarties**: Pan-European party organizations or confederations that coordinate policy and build links among national political parties in Europe.

● **Green politics**: A political philosophy based on ecological wisdom, sustainability, social justice, grassroots democracy, and non-violence.

Figure 15.3 Europarties

NAME	YEAR FORMED	PHILOSOPHY
Party of European Socialists	1973	Social democratic
European Liberal Democratic and Reform Party	1976	Liberal
European People's Party	1976	Christian democratic
European Free Alliance	1981	Regionalist
Europe of the Nations	2002	Conservative, eurosceptic
Party of the European Left	2004	Socialist/communist
European Green Party	2004	Green
European Democratic Party	2004	Centrist
EU Democrats	2005	Eurosceptic

of interests related to social justice, and refuse to be placed on the traditional ideological spectrum. In 1989 the greens formed their own Green Group, which in 1999 entered into its current alliance with the European Free Alliance. The latter describes itself as the representative of stateless peoples and national minorities, and argues that regions should have more power. After the 2009 elections the group had 55 members from 14 EU states, the biggest national blocs coming from Germany and France.

Alliance of Liberals and Democrats for Europe (ALDE)

ALDE is the main centrist political group in the EP, although it has long come a distant third in elections behind the socialists and the EPP. It began life as the Liberal Group in the ECSC Common Assembly, changing both its name and its positions during the 1970s and 1980s as parties from new member states joined its ranks. Most of its MEPs now fall in or around the centre, with a wide range of opinions on the EU, and the group has suffered over the years from defections to the EPP. Its current name was agreed after the 2004 EP elections, and reflects its association with two Europarties: the European Liberal Democratic and Reform Party, and the European Democratic Party. It is the only political group except the socialists and the EPP to have garnered enough support in the EP to have one of its members elected as president; this has happened four times so far, the last time being in 2002 when the conservatives and the socialists were unable to agree on whom to appoint as president, and chose Irish liberal democrat Pat Cox as a compromise. Following the 2009 elections the group had 84 members from 19 EU member states, the biggest national blocs coming from Germany and the UK.

European People's Party (EPP)

● **Christian Democracy**: A political philosophy associated mainly with continental western Europe that applies Christian principles to public policy; moderately conservative on social and moral issues, and progressive on economic issues.

The EPP is the major political group on the centre-right and has been the biggest of the groups in the EP since 1999. It traces its origins to the formation in the ECSC Common Assembly in 1953 of the Christian Democrat Group, which identified with the moderately conservative principles of **Christian Democracy**, including social conservatism, liberal democracy, a mixed economy, European federalism, and a rejection of secularism. But the group's policies began to change as it incorporated centre-right parties from other member states that

Table 15.1 Party representation in the European Parliament, 2009

	EPP	PASD	ALDE	Greens EFA	ECR	GUE NGL	EFD	NA	Total
Germany	42	23	12	14	-	8	-	-	99
France	29	14	6	14	-	5	1	3	72
Italy	35	21	7	-	-	-	9	-	72
UK	-	13	11	5	25	1	13	4	72
Poland	28	7	-	-	15	-	-	-	50
Spain	23	21	2	2	-	1	-	1	50
Romania	14	11	5	-	-	-	-	3	33
Netherlands	5	3	6	3	1	2	1	4	25
Belgium	5	5	5	4	1	-	-	2	22
Czech Rep.	2	7	-	-	9	4	-	-	22
Greece	8	8	-	1	-	3	2	-	22
Hungary	14	4	-	-	1	-	-	3	22
Portugal	10	7	-	-	-	5	-	-	22
Sweden	5	5	4	3	-	1	-	-	18
Austria	6	4	-	2	-	-	-	5	17
Bulgaria	6	4	5	-	-	-	-	2	17
Denmark	1	4	3	2	-	1	2	-	13
Finland	4	2	4	2	-	-	1	-	13
Slovakia	6	5	1	-	-	-	1	-	13
Ireland	4	3	4	-	-	1	-	-	12
Lithuania	4	3	2	-	1	-	2	-	12
Latvia	3	1	1	1	1	1	-	-	8
Slovenia	3	2	2	-	-	-	-	-	7
Cyprus	2	2	-	-	-	2	-	-	6
Estonia	1	1	3	1	-	-	-	-	6
Luxembourg	3	1	1	1	-	-	-	-	6
Malta	2	3	-	-	-	-	-	-	5
	265	184	84	55	54	35	32	27	736

subscribed neither to Christian Democracy nor to European federalism (Judge and Earnshaw, 2008, p. 137). In 1976, in line with the creation that year of the European People's Party, it changed its name to the European People's Party Group.

The EPP might have been a natural fit for British and Danish conservatives, but their euroscepticism kept them functioning separately as the European Democrats (ED) until 1992, when they joined forces with the EPP. The new coalition contested the 1999 EP elections as the EPP–ED, and benefited from growing anti-European and anti-immigrant sentiment in several EU states to overtake the socialists and win a plurality of seats in the EP for the first time. The political shift to the right continued in 2004, giving the group nearly 37 per cent of the seats in the EP. In spite of the defection of British conservatives, it held on to that share in 2009, with members from 26 member states, the biggest national blocs coming from Germany, Italy, France, Poland and Spain. The priorities of the EPP include a 'pragmatic' response to the global economic crisis (including better coordination of economic policies), reform of financing for the EU, the development of a joint EU immigration policy, and 'effective transatlantic solidarity'.

European conservatives

European conservatives – further to the right than the EPP, and more eurosceptic – have not had a stable history in the EP, but have been part of its group network since the early 1970s, working along two main strands. One traces its origins to the 1965 formation of the European Democratic Union, which became the European Democratic Alliance after the 1979 elections, and in 1999 became the anti-Maastricht Union for Europe of the Nations (UEN). The second revolves around the British Conservative party and its internal divisions over Europe. They were at the core of the European Democrats (ED), which suffered from defections to the EPP during the 1980s, and in 1992 – on the brink of collapse – formed a coalition with the EPP, in spite of differences over the direction of European integration. The UEN was wound up after the 2009 elections, and British conservatives joined up with Polish conservatives to form the new European Conservatives and Reformists Group, whose policies included 'opposition to EU federalism and a renewed respect for true subsidiarity' as well as 'controlled immigration and an end to abuse of asylum procedures'. It had 54 members from 8 member states, more than half of them from Britain and Poland.

Eurosceptics

Political groups on this side of the EP have been the most unstable of all, repeatedly changing their name and structure, and united mainly by their hostility to the EU. They date back to the 1994 formation of the Europe of Nations group led by the Anglo-French financier Sir James Goldsmith. This evolved in 1999 into Europe of Democracies and Diversities, which was reconstituted after the 2004 elections as the Independence/Democracy (Ind/Dem) group, bringing together – in its own words – a cluster of 'EU critics, eurosceptics, and eurorealists'. In 2009, Ind/Dem was reformed as Europe of Freedom and Democracy (EFD), with 32 members from nine member states. At the heart of the new group were 13 MEPs from the United Kingdom Independence Party (UKIP), which supports Britain's withdrawal from the EU. EFD is more conservative than its predecessors, noting on its web site that it opposes further European integration 'that would exacerbate ... the centralist political structure of the EU', demanding referendums on any new European treaties, and believing that member states 'have the right to protect their borders and strengthen their own historical, traditional and cultural values'. Outside its core issues, members of the group are free to vote as they wish.

Nationalists

Suffering similar levels of instability to the eurosceptics, the nationalists in the EP trace their origins back to the formation in 1984 of the European Right, consisting mainly of French and Italian right-wingers, notably the far-right

French politician Jean-Marie Le Pen. It was disbanded in 1994, and was briefly reformed in January 2007 as Identity, Tradition and Sovereignty (ITS) when the accession of Bulgaria and Romania gave it enough MEPs to apply for group status. Its members spoke of the need to defend 'Christian values, the family and European civilization', and included Le Pen and Allesandra Mussolini, granddaughter of the former Italian dictator. The group lasted less than a year before infighting tore it apart.

Non-attached members

The EP has always had a small cluster of non-attached members, who have either been elected as members of parties that have not been able to reach agreement to join a political group, or who have deliberately chosen to remain outside the group structure. Their numbers have waxed and waned as the membership of groups has changed, but they have rarely numbered more than two or three dozen at a time.

Interest groups

Every EU member state has a diverse and active community of interest groups that works to influence government on a wide variety of issues. They use multiple methods, including political lobbying, support for election campaigns, and the provision of expertise and information. When public policy in Europe was made primarily at the national or local level, these groups naturally focused most of their efforts on national and local government. But as more decisions were made at the level of the EEC/EU, more groups began to pay more attention to European-level policy making, with a particular interest in trying to influence the European Commission and the European Parliament (Mazey and Richardson, 2003 and 2006). Many either opened offices in Brussels or became part of Brussels-based umbrella organizations, contributing to the steady rise of a European lobbying industry. Counting only Eurogroups (those organized to work at the European level), there were estimated to be about 500 in 1985, rising to 700 in 1996, and to 851 in 2006 (Philip, 1985; Aspinwall and Greenwood, 1998; Balme and Chabanet, 2008). Overall, the number of groups with offices in Brussels now runs well into the thousands, the majority representing business interests, while the balance represent mainly public interests and the professions.

Interest groups have benefited from two structural problems within the EU decision-making system. First there has been the relative weakness of party activity in the EP, which has left Europe without the same degree of voter mobilization and engagement witnessed at the level of the member states, and has in turn helped lift the political profile of interest groups. Second, the small size of the European Commission has worked to the benefit of interest groups by allowing them to fill a structural need. With too few staff to manage both the drafting of new laws and the monitoring of implementation by the member states, the Commission has come to rely on interest groups for the provision of expertise at the drafting phase and to act as watchdogs at the implementation phase. Interest groups also benefit from the different points of contact and influence made available by the multi-level character of the EU.

● **Interest group**: An organization that represents and promotes the political, economic or social interests of its members, which may be individuals, cultural or social groups, professions, or industries.

**Illustration 15.2
Interest groups**

Periodic European Business Summits bring together representatives of business and consumer interest groups, European corporations and the EU institutions

The Commission has occasionally gone further than simply engaging groups for the support they might be able to offer, and has also funded the work of groups, and set up formal channels through which groups can work directly with the Commission. This immediately raises the question, of course, of how far such groups can remain objective in their dealings with the Commission. On the environmental front, for example, the Commission has funded since its creation in 1974 the European Environmental Bureau, a Brussels-based umbrella organization for local, national, and regional environmental groups. Between 1993 and 2001 it also sponsored the Consultative Forum on the Environment and Sustainable Development (otherwise known as the European Green Forum), through which representatives of interest groups, industry, business, local authorities, trade unions and academia could advise the Commission on policy development.

The Commission is not alone in attracting the attention of interest groups, which will also make sure to work with the national delegations of the member states in Brussels (because of their participation in the Committee of Permanent Representatives), the working parties and committees of the Council of Ministers, and the committees of the European Parliament. As we saw in Chapter 14, they also have direct representation in the European Economic and Social Committee, which in spite of its limited influence is another platform for the open discussion of the kinds of issues that interest groups deal with. The EESC has been instrumental in changes to laws dealing with a variety of issues, and also has a number of technical experts among its members and sets up its own working groups to which additional experts are invited to give evidence, so it can provide useful specialist comments on a proposal.

Reflecting the long emphasis of European integration on economic matters, business and labour groups have long been the most active and visible at the EU level. Individual corporations are represented either directly or through lobbying firms in Brussels, and several cross-sectoral and multi-state federations have been created to represent wider economic interests (see Figure 15.4). More numerous, but smaller, are the many groups representing special interests, such

Figure 15.4 Business and labour groups represented in Brussels

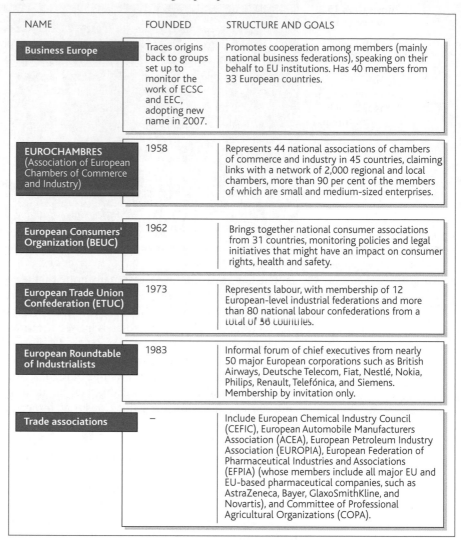

NAME	FOUNDED	STRUCTURE AND GOALS
Business Europe	Traces origins back to groups set up to monitor the work of ECSC and EEC, adopting new name in 2007.	Promotes cooperation among members (mainly national business federations), speaking on their behalf to EU institutions. Has 40 members from 33 European countries.
EUROCHAMBRES (Association of European Chambers of Commerce and Industry)	1958	Represents 44 national associations of chambers of commerce and industry in 45 countries, claiming links with a network of 2,000 regional and local chambers, more than 90 per cent of the members of which are small and medium-sized enterprises.
European Consumers' Organization (BEUC)	1962	Brings together national consumer associations from 31 countries, monitoring policies and legal initiatives that might have an impact on consumer rights, health and safety.
European Trade Union Confederation (ETUC)	1973	Represents labour, with membership of 12 European-level industrial federations and more than 80 national labour confederations from a total of 38 countries.
European Roundtable of Industrialists	1983	Informal forum of chief executives from nearly 50 major European corporations such as British Airways, Deutsche Telecom, Fiat, Nestlé, Nokia, Philips, Renault, Telefónica, and Siemens. Membership by invitation only.
Trade associations	–	Include European Chemical Industry Council (CEFIC), European Automobile Manufacturers Association (ACEA), European Petroleum Industry Association (EUROPIA), European Federation of Pharmaceutical Industries and Associations (EFPIA) (whose members include all major EU and EU-based pharmaceutical companies, such as AstraZeneca, Bayer, GlaxoSmithKline, and Novartis), and Committee of Professional Agricultural Organizations (COPA).

as the European Environmental Bureau, the European Platform for Social NGOs, Amnesty International, the European Youth Forum, and the European Women's Lobby. They often lack the resources or the expertise to compete with industry or with business federations, and the compartmentalized nature of EU decision-making works to their disadvantage because it demands that groups be able to monitor and respond to policy developments in multiple different institutions. They will occasionally work to address these handicaps by building pan-European coalitions of national groups that are adept at mobilizing the interest and resources of millions of individual members.

One of the sub-species of interest groups that typically plays a critical role in the national capitals of liberal democracies is the **think tank** (or policy institute). These are private organizations set up to undertake research, to organize conferences and seminars, to sustain a public and political debate over the issues in

● **Think tank**: An organization that conducts research into a given area of policy with the goal of fostering public debate and political change.

Civil society

A key indicator of a healthy political society is the willingness and ability of its individual members to organize themselves in order to address problems and provide services without the nudging or the support of government or the marketplace. This is the essence of a civil society, whose existence and functioning is also indicative of the willingness of government to entertain competing views about the sources and effects of societal problems. But citizen action can also be a sign that government is not responding adequately to the needs of society, thereby encouraging citizens to take matters into their own hands.

which it is interested, and to influence decision-makers either directly or indirectly. Most are privately funded, but some are supported by governments, political parties, or corporations, and have a clear national or ideological agenda. In the United States, Washington DC is well-known as the home of several hundred think tanks of many different persuasions, but Brussels is beginning to develop a similar reputation in Europe. Among the organizations based in Brussels with an EU focus are the following:

- The Centre for European Policy Studies (CEPS), which focuses on generating research and debate on pressing EU issues and on managing a network of corporate and institutional partners.
- The European Policy Centre, dedicated to 'making European integration work' by developing recommendations to improve the way in which the EU operates and relates to ordinary Europeans.
- The European Enterprise Institute, which encourages debate on issues relating to entrepreneurship and competitiveness.
- The European Trade Union Institute, which promotes research and education on issues relating to labour in Europe.
- The International Crisis Group, set up in 1995 in response to criticisms of the failure of the international community to respond effectively to the tragedies in Bosnia, Rwanda, and Somalia, and which now has its international headquarters in Brussels.

The work of interest groups has helped offset the national and intergovernmental influences in EU policy-making by reaching across state borders to promote the common sectional interests of groups of people in multiple member states. More of those interests are now part of European policy calculations, Eurogroups have helped promote a European consciousness in policymaking, and along the way they have become protagonists; where once they focused mainly on monitoring policy, they now try to change it using increasingly sophisticated means (Aspinwall and Greenwood, 1998). The work of interest groups has also helped offset concerns about the European democratic deficit, by offering a channel through which Europeans can lobby and influence the content of EU law and policy. This has in turn helped to focus the attention of ordinary Europeans on how the EU influences the policies that affect their lives, helping draw them more actively into the process by which the EU makes its decisions, and encouraging them to bypass their national governments and to focus their attention on European responses to shared and common problems.

To be sure, interest groups represent only the particular views of their members, and their leaderships are not elected and are therefore rarely accountable to any group bigger than the board of trustees. But most rely on the active support and input of their members, claim to speak on behalf of those members, and the competition among hundreds of interest groups can help provide some balance to policy debates. In this sense, interest groups are a critical part of a healthy **civil society**, or the arena that exists outside the state or the marketplace and within which individuals take collective action on shared interests. They will usually organize themselves into non-governmental organizations (NGOs) in the form of charities, community groups, professional associations, cultural

Figure 15.5 Comparing lobbying rules in Brussels and Washington, DC

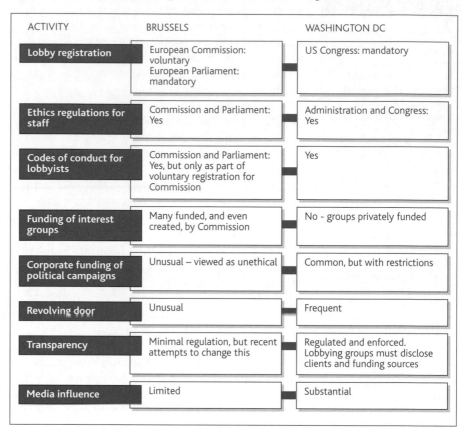

ACTIVITY	BRUSSELS	WASHINGTON DC
Lobby registration	European Commission: voluntary European Parliament: mandatory	US Congress: mandatory
Ethics regulations for staff	Commission and Parliament: Yes	Administration and Congress: Yes
Codes of conduct for lobbyists	Commission and Parliament: Yes, but only as part of voluntary registration for Commission	Yes
Funding of interest groups	Many funded, and even created, by Commission	No - groups privately funded
Corporate funding of political campaigns	Unusual – viewed as unethical	Common, but with restrictions
Revolving door	Unusual	Frequent
Transparency	Minimal regulation, but recent attempts to change this	Regulated and enforced. Lobbying groups must disclose clients and funding sources
Media influence	Limited	Substantial

Source: Based on *Delegation of the European Commission to the United States, Lobbying in the EU: An Overview* (2008). At http://www.eurunion.org/EUInsight (retrieved July 2010).

groups, and trade unions, and take action outside government to deal with problems or provide services that have not been addressed by government.

If enough such organizations are working and cooperating on the same issues, the creation of these groups can coalesce into social movements. The existence of a diverse civil society is confirmation both that individuals are engaging with their communities, and that government is willing to tolerate public discourse; civil societies barely exist in totalitarian regimes. Where each of the member states of the EU has a well-developed civil society of its own, however, the broader EU is only just catching up. Balme and Chabanet (2008) note the irony in the fact that as support for integration has declined, or has at least run into greater resistance, so social movements have flourished in the EU, addressing everything from unemployment and poverty to women's rights, migration policy, and environmental protection.

One of the core functions of most interest groups is **lobbying**, or attempts to influence the decision-making process. This has long been part of political life at the national level in liberal democracies, although it is less developed in Europe than in the United States, and its political role is quite different (see McGrath, 2005). Lobbying in the United States is a major industry, with estimates of the

● **Lobbying**: Efforts made to influence the decisions made by elected officials or bureaucrats on behalf of individuals, groups, or organizations.

number of lobbyists in Washington DC alone standing in the range of 20,000 or more – compared to Commission estimates of about 15,000 in Brussels (Delegation of the European Commission to the United States, 2008). Washington lobbyists are professional and aggressive, are often generously funded, and long ago became part of the national political scene in the United States. Americans, also, are more than familiar with the phenomenon of the revolving door, where former members of Congress, of the White House staff, or of government departments are employed by lobbying organizations and paid large fees to exploit their insider knowledge and contacts in order to wield influence.

The lobbying world in Brussels is quite different, in part because of political realities and in part because of political culture. The political reality is that EU institutions have far less power than their American equivalents, so lobbyists have been less drawn to Brussels and still focus much of their attention on national government. Money also plays a smaller role in European politics, whereas campaigning in the United States can be enormously expensive, and candidates rely heavily on corporate and interest group donations to support their efforts. As for political culture, Europeans are both less used to lobbying than Americans and more sceptical about its role in the democratic process. The differences are reflected in the extent to which lobbying is regulated in the two cities (see Figure 15.5). In Washington DC, lobbyists are required to register, and there is a federal law (the Lobbying Disclosure Act) which obliges lobbying groups to list their clients and their sources of funding. In Brussels, registration is voluntary for dealings with the Commission (although mandatory for Parliament), and it was only in 2005 that the Commission launched the European Transparency Initiative in an attempt to make the lobbying process more open. This led to the creation in 2008 of a voluntary Register of Interest Representatives, but while the pressure to impose more control over the lobbying process has grown, the rules have not yet been agreed.

SUMMARY

● MEPs organize themselves into like-minded political groups, which must have at least 25 members from at least one-quarter of member states.

● Groups have developed more consistency and cohesion with time, the most stability being found among the socialists, the liberals, and the centre-right European People's Party (EPP). The socialists had the biggest bloc of seats in the EP until 1999, since when the EPP has had the biggest bloc. But no one political group has yet won a majority.

● Political groups have common ideologies and policy preferences, and their own leadership structures and operating rules, but do not campaign across member states during EP elections. There are no formal links between the political make-up of Parliament and the European Commission.

● The consistency of political groups has been encouraged by the creation of several Europarties that bring together like-minded parties in different EU member states.

● National interest groups have increasingly turned their attention to the EU, with a particular focus on influencing the Commission, the Council of Ministers, and the European Parliament.

● Group activity has helped offset the relative weakness of party activity at the European level, and groups have exploited the shortage of staff in the Commission to play a key role in the drafting and the implementation of law and policy.

● Business and labour groups have long been the most active at the EU level, but the number of special interest groups and Brussels-based think tanks has grown.

● Lobbying is a growth industry in Brussels, although the opportunities have so far been fewer than those available at the national level, and the rules looser.

KEY TERMS AND CONCEPTS

Christian Democracy

Civil society

Europarties

Green politics

Interest group

Lobbying

Political groups

Think tank

FURTHER READING

Arvanitopoulos, Constantine (ed.) (2010), *Reforming Europe: The Role of the Centre-Right* (New York: Springer); Simon Lightfoot, *Europeanizing Social Democracy? The Rise of the Party of European Socialists* (London: Routledge, 2005). Studies of the two major party groups in the European Parliament.

Coen, David, and Jeremy Richardson (eds), *Lobbying the European Union: Institutions, Actors, and Issues* (Oxford: Oxford University Press, 2009); and Robin Pedler, *European Union Lobbying: Changes in the Arena* (Basingstoke: Palgrave Macmillan, 2002). Two studies of lobbying in the EU, including chapters on different EU institutions, key lobbies, and major campaigns.

Lindberg, Bjorn, Anne Rasmussen, and Andreas Warntjen (eds), *The Role of Political Parties in the European Union* (London: Routledge, 2009). An edited collection of studies of the mechanics and role of political parties in the European and national arenas.

CHAPTER 16

Elections and Referendums

PREVIEW

European integration has been criticized over the decades for its weak democratic qualities. The treaties have too often been negotiated behind closed doors, argue the critics, and member states have had to surrender sovereignty with too little reference to the views of European voters. This has undermined enthusiasm for the European project, which has often seemed elitist and distant from the needs and interests of ordinary Europeans. And yet there are two key channels through which they can influence the direction taken by EU policy.

First, elections to the European Parliament are held every five years, and give voters the opportunity to elect representatives to the EP, which has become more powerful in recent years. But European voters have not taken full advantage of EP elections: turnout has fallen from a high of 63 per cent in 1979 to a low of 43 per cent in 2009, and many of those who cast their votes make their choices more on the basis of national issues than of European issues; elections are often polls on the job being done by incumbent governments, with the result that the bigger mainstream parties often do less well than smaller parties.

Second, national referendums on European issues have been held with growing frequency. There is no consistency as to when and where they will be held: thus Ireland must hold referendums on amendments to its national constitution, and political pressures have led to several votes on European issues in Denmark and France, but most EU member states have avoided them. Nonetheless, the pressures to hold referendums on the adoption of new treaties have grown, and even a single national vote has occasionally been enough to spark a Europe-wide debate about the progress of integration.

KEY ISSUES

- How far does the arithmetic of proportional representation account for the difficulties of the EP?
- Which explanation for low voter turnout at EP elections is most compelling?
- What changes would be needed in order to elevate EP elections from second order to first order?
- What could or should be done to improve turnout at EP elections?
- Have referendums improved the quality of the democratic debate over Europe?
- Should national referendums become a more structured and regular part of the European political calendar?

CONCEPT

Proportional representation

An electoral system in which seats in a legislature are distributed among parties in proportion to the share of the vote each receives. For some, PR is a more democratic method for choosing candidates than SMP, because it allows for a more accurate reflection of voter preferences, while SMP tends to result in over-representation of fewer parties. But by sending so many parties to national legislatures, or to the European Parliament, PR makes it difficult for any one party to win a majority, creating often unstable coalition governments.

● **Coalition government**: A government made up of representatives from more than one political party, demanding compromises among the participating parties.

European elections

Direct elections to the EP have been held every five years since 1979 (in years ending with a four or a nine), but they have yet to earn a firm place in the European political consciousness. Theoretically, they should have been widely welcomed, because they give European voters a direct link with the work of the EU and help address concerns about the EU's democratic deficit: the EP is the only EU institution directly elected by voters, has won growing powers over the EU policy process, and should logically have attracted the interest and input of EU voters. But turnout at EP elections has been falling, and neither the EP nor the parties that contest its elections have been able to make the necessary psychological connection with voters on European issues.

The logistics of the elections are impressive: there were about 375 million eligible voters in 2009, making the EP elections the second largest democratic elections in the world after those held in India. Voters must be 18 years of age, must be citizens of one of the EU member states, and can vote in whichever EU member state they are legally resident; all they need to do is make a declaration to the electoral authority of the member state in which they are living, meet local registration qualifications, and meet the terms of rules set by their home state. Member states have different rules on the minimum age for candidates, ranging from 18 in Germany, Spain, Sweden and several other countries to 23 in France and 25 in Italy and Cyprus. They also have different rules on how candidates qualify: some states do not allow independent candidates, some require candidates to pay deposits, others require them to collect signatures, and so on.

For EP elections – and, in most cases, for national elections – every EU member state uses variations on the theme of **proportional representation** (PR). This contrasts with the single-member plurality (SMP) system used in national elections in Britain, Canada, and the United States, where each legislative district is contested by multiple candidates and the winner is the candidate who wins the most votes (a plurality). PR typically involves bigger and multi-member districts, with competing parties publishing lists of candidates for each district, and seats being distributed among parties according to the share of the vote each receives. While most EU member states structure their entire territory as a single electoral district and parties run with national lists of candidates, five states (Belgium, France, Ireland, Italy and the UK) are divided into between three and twelve Euro-constituencies, and their parties publish constituency lists of candidates.

All liberal democracies are representative democracies, which are – by definition – systems in which the votes of the public determine the make-up of legislatures, whose members are expected to represent the interests of voters. But no electoral system has yet been invented that is truly reflective of the balance of voter support for different political parties, and both PR and SMP have their advantages and disadvantages (see Figure 16.1). For better or for worse, PR has become the normal order of political business throughout Europe. The result is that politics in national legislatures and in the European Parliament have come to be coloured by two main characteristics: **coalition governments** made up of two or more political parties, and the representation of a wide range of political opinion. This stands in contrast to the United States, for example, which has only two parties that have any real chance of winning control (the Democrats and the Republicans), thereby almost always guaranteeing legislative majorities for one or the other.

Figure 16.1 Comparing electoral systems

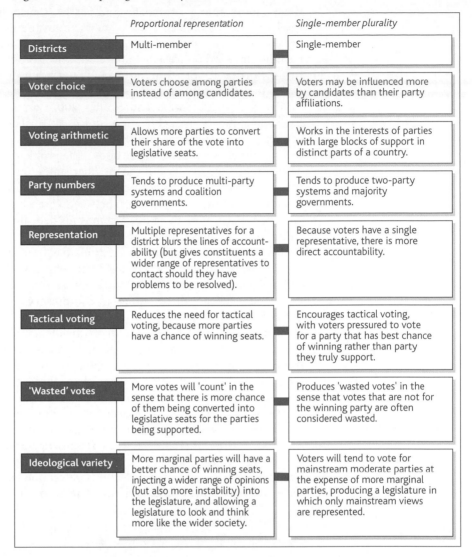

	Proportional representation	Single-member plurality
Districts	Multi-member	Single-member
Voter choice	Voters choose among parties instead of among candidates.	Voters may be influenced more by candidates than their party affiliations.
Voting arithmetic	Allows more parties to convert their share of the vote into legislative seats.	Works in the interests of parties with large blocks of support in distinct parts of a country.
Party numbers	Tends to produce multi-party systems and coalition governments.	Tends to produce two-party systems and majority governments.
Representation	Multiple representatives for a district blurs the lines of accountability (but gives constituents a wider range of representatives to contact should they have problems to be resolved).	Because voters have a single representative, there is more direct accountability.
Tactical voting	Reduces the need for tactical voting, because more parties have a chance of winning seats.	Encourages tactical voting, with voters pressured to vote for a party that has best chance of winning rather than party they truly support.
'Wasted' votes	More votes will 'count' in the sense that there is more chance of them being converted into legislative seats for the parties being supported.	Produces 'wasted votes' in the sense that votes that are not for the winning party are often considered wasted.
Ideological variety	More marginal parties will have a better chance of winning seats, injecting a wider range of opinions (but also more instability) into the legislature, and allowing a legislature to look and think more like the wider society.	Voters will tend to vote for mainstream moderate parties at the expense of more marginal parties, producing a legislature in which only mainstream views are represented.

Coalitions oblige political parties to work together, and oblige party leaders to consider the views and interests of more than those who elected them. The result is a moderation of policies, except in those cases where the balance of power in a coalition is held by small parties whose influence can be out of all proportion to their size, and which end up becoming the tails that wag the dog. But moderation and consensus may not always be what is needed, and the energy generated by trying to reach agreement among the parties in the coalition can result in hamstrung leadership and an inability to take the sometimes unpopular steps needed to address pressing problems. (For a study of coalition governments in western Europe, see Müller and Strøm, 2003.)

There has been a long debate about the efficiency and efficacy of European elections in providing voters with real choices and providing the EU institutions with legitimacy. Van der Eijk and Franklin (1996, p. 6) argue that voters have never been encouraged to develop preferences for EU policies that would help them choose among candidates and parties, that policy differences on Europe rarely figure in media coverage of news about the EU, and that candidates and parties rarely offer policies that provide real choices on Europe, and often do not even put forward policies that are relevant to EU affairs. As a result, the opportunity to educate voters on European issues has been missed, as has the opportunity to generate public enthusiasm about EP elections.

For their part, Farrell and Scully (2007) argue that while the European Parliament has been highly successful as an institution in terms of winning greater powers and establishing increasingly efficient working practices, it has been 'a failure as a representative body'. The problem lies in the manner in which MEPs are elected in many of the member states: most want to work in a powerful EP but find that European elections fail to result in a visible style of representation that offers a connection between voters and the EU. Farrell and Scully conclude that a more open list system is needed, along with a regionalization of electoral procedures for large member states.

One issue of concern in EP elections has been declining voter turnout, the number falling from a respectable 63 per cent in 1979 to a disappointing 43 per cent in 2009 (see Figure 16.2). Rates are highest in Luxembourg, Belgium, Malta, Italy, and Greece, where voting is compulsory (although the laws are not enforced), but compulsory turnout has made little difference in Greece, and in most states in 2009 fewer than half of voters turned out (see Figure 16.3). Expectations that turnout might be high in eastern European states still in the flush of young democracy and new membership of the EU came to nothing; fewer than one in three voters turned out in six of those states in 2009. Even in the two stalwarts of European integration – France and Germany – turnout has fallen to less than 50 per cent. (For an analysis of turnout, see Franklin, 2006, pp. 233–7.)

There are several explanations for these trends, perhaps the most compelling of which is the difference between **first-order and second-order elections**. These were distinguished by Reiff and Schmitt (1980) according to how much was at stake: because national elections determine who controls national executives and legislatures, which in turn make the decisions that have the most

● **First-order and second-order elections**: Elections with different stakes, the former for government institutions (such as national executives and legislatures) with significant powers, and the latter for institutions (such as local government and the European Parliament) with fewer powers.

Figure 16.2 Turnout trends at European elections

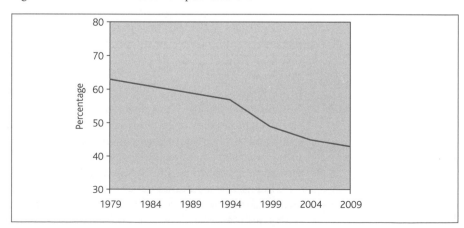

Figure 16.3 Turnout at the 2009 European Parliament election

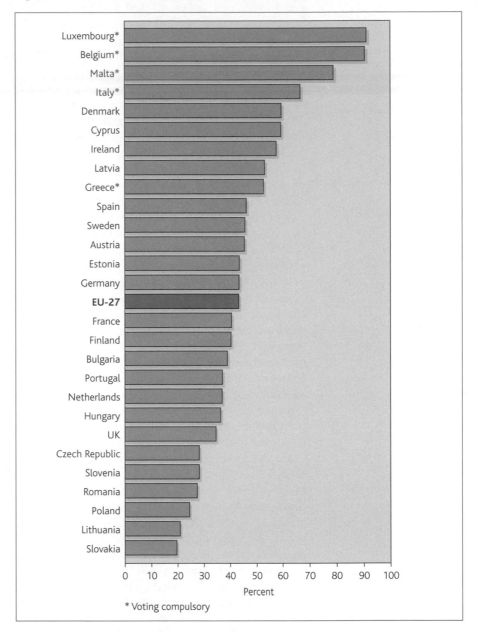

* Voting compulsory

immediate impact on the lives of voters, they also attract the most media attention, they are more hard fought, and voters find it easier to engage with the issues (because they are more immediate), and hence are more likely to turn out on election day. By contrast, second-order elections, such as by-elections and local government elections, have lower stakes and attract less voter interest. EP elections are more clearly second-order: there is no change of government at stake, voters find it more difficult to engage with European issues than with national issues, and the result is that they are less inclined to turn out.

Low turnout is also related to several other factors (see discussion in Judge and Earnshaw, 2008, pp. 77–80). First, there is the simple problem of the fuzzy shape of the EP on the European political radar: few Europeans much know or care what it does, which is in turn a function of generally low voter knowledge on European integration (see Chapter 17). This makes them less inclined to make the effort to vote. Second, there are few well-known figures in the European Parliament who might act as a catalyst for higher turnout. Turnover among MEPs is relatively high, as are changes in the leadership of party groups, and no president has yet served more than one term, all of which reduces the opportunities for individual MEPs to rise above the pack and energize voters. Third, as we saw in Chapter 15, there are (as yet) no Europe-wide political parties running in EP elections, which means that there is less opportunity to mobilize voters and to inject energy into election campaigns. Finally, most voters still see EP elections very much in national terms, a problem exacerbated by the lack of Europe-wide parties and by the focus in national media on the horse-race between national parties, and on what the elections mean for the country rather than what they mean for Europe.

Falling turnout is also related to trends in national elections, where there have been signs of declining overall turnout in several EU member states over recent decades (although rates vary from one country to another, and from one election to another). Explaining voter turnout has been described as one of the great puzzles of political science, whether trying to understand trends in turnout, or which variables best explain voter turnout, or even why anyone bothers to vote at all (Franklin, 2005, p. xi). One explanation for falling turnout comes out of modernization theory, which argues that while it might be logical to think that political participation in general is a function of the amount of information and education available to voters, and the amounts of both have increased dramatically, there are at least two reasons why this has actually led to falling turnout (Thomassen, 2005, pp. 6–7). First, voters with more resources are more likely to become directly involved in political decision-making, will be less likely to see political parties as intermediaries between citizens and the state, and may opt for less conventional means of influencing policy. Second, voters are more likely to turn out in elections only when faced with real choices and when it is clear that real change will follow according to which party or coalition is in power. With party identification declining, voters will be motivated more by the changing stakes in each election, which means that they will decide from one election to another whether or not to vote.

The concept of second-order elections not only helps explain low voter turnout, but also helps explain the choices made by those who *do* vote:

- Voters will often treat EP elections less as an opportunity to determine the make-up and work of the EP than to comment on the national government of the day and on its performance in dealing with domestic issues (Heath *et al*, 1999). In that sense, then, they are less European elections than subsidiary national elections. This has also been true of some of the referendums held on new EU treaties, where the result has been at least in part a reflection of the popularity or unpopularity of the national government and its position on the treaty under review (see later in this chapter).

Debating . . .
Does low voter turnout hurt democracy?

YES	NO
Without an engaged citizenry there can be no political accountability.	Low voter turnout is not necessarily a sign of declining faith in politics: research has found that Europeans are shifting away from indirect participation in politics through their elected representatives in favour of direct participation through joining interest groups, voting in referendums, signing petitions, or taking direct political action. There has, in other words, been a shift away from representative democracy to participatory democracy (Almond, Dalton, and Powell, 2002, p. 42ff.).
Low voter turnout may reflect declining faith in the political process, a sense of disconnection with (and disengagement from) politics, and a belief among voters that the stakes are not high enough or important enough to merit setting aside time to go to the polls.	
Voting is at the heart of the democratic process. Regardless of their wealth, position, race, gender or educational background, all members of society are politically equalized by the right to vote. A failure to vote is a form of voluntary disenfranchisement that gives more influence to those who do vote.	While many people do not vote because they feel disconnected from politics, there is another group of voters who are content as they are, and who feel that whoever is in office it will not make much difference to their lives.
	Lower turnout may be less an indication of declining faith in the political process than of declining faith in political parties.
Government often looks like – and pays more attention to – the people who vote: turnout is highest among older, better educated and wealthier Europeans, while it is lowest among the young, the poor, and racial minorities, whose interests are often lower down the list of national political priorities.	Low voter turnout might suggest that politics has become marginal to the lives of many, which may be no bad thing. Politics sometimes come to matter too much, and if disengagement with elections means devoting more time and attention to family, education, recreation, and community service, society may benefit.

● Given that the political stakes in EP elections are seen as relatively low, there is an inclination for participating voters to make their choices with their hearts rather than their heads. In other words, they are more likely to express their feelings than to make hard-headed political choices. The result is that smaller parties which normally do not win much support in national elections will often do well in EP elections. This in turn means that true voter preferences are not reflected in the party make-up of the European Parliament.

The effects of these two phenomena have been particularly clear in the UK, where the governing party has typically done poorly at EP elections, and small parties have done well. For example, it took until 2010 for the Greens to win their first seat in the British Parliament, but they surprised even themselves by winning nearly 15 per cent of the national vote in the 1989 EP elections, which converted into 12 seats in the European Parliament. Meanwhile, the often very different results of European and national elections in Britain were clearly illustrated by the outcomes of the June 2009 EP election and the May 2010 general election (see Figure 16.4). The unpopular governing Labour party was beaten

Figure 16.4 The contrasting results of recent British general and European elections

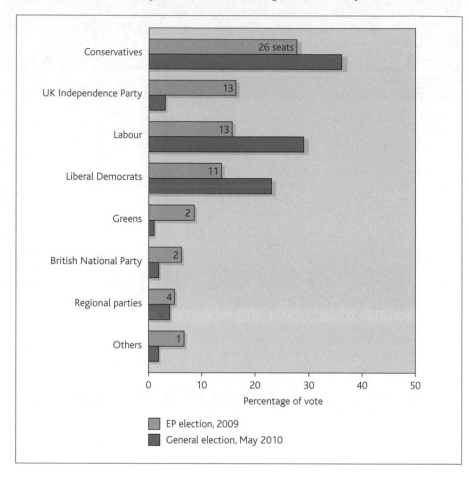

into third place in the EP election by the UK Independence Party (UKIP), which won 16.5 per cent of the vote (and 13 seats in the EP). But Labour almost doubled its share of the vote in the 2010 general election, while UKIP won just 3.1 per cent of the vote (and no seats). Similarly, the right-wing British National Party won a share of the vote in the EP election that was three times its usual share of the vote in general elections.

As noted earlier, there has been much conjecture that declining voter turnout in Europe may be a function of a switch to alternative or less 'conventional' forms of political participation. The most telling of these has been support for the work of interest groups, which – as we saw in Chapter 15 – are becoming more active at the European level. Europeans, like the residents of all democratic societies, also have the following options:

- Running for public office.
- Organizing or taking part in public demonstrations.
- Signing a petition.
- Contacting elected officials.

Illustration 16.1
European elections

Posters encourage Italian voters to take part in the 2009 European Parliament elections. While about two-thirds of Italians went to the polls, the turnout for the EU as a whole reached a record low.

- Volunteering for a local community organization.
- Attending political rallies and speeches.
- Setting up a web site or a blog.
- Civil disobedience or passive resistance.

One new channel for the expression of citizen interests in the EU, introduced by the Treaty of Lisbon, is the petition or the **citizen initiative**. In Article 11 of the treaty, it states that 'Not less than one million citizens who are nationals of a significant number of Member States may take the initiative of inviting the European Commission, within the framework of its powers, to submit any appropriate proposal on matters where citizens consider that a legal act of the Union is required for the purpose of implementing the Treaties'. But Lisbon neither defined what would constitute a 'significant' number of member states, nor is it clear how the details of the one million citizens would be recorded and confirmed as genuine, nor is it specified to whom in the Commission such initiatives should be submitted, nor is it clear what the obligations of the Commission would be upon receiving an initiative. Until it is tested in practice, it will be difficult to assess the significance of this option.

● **Citizen initiative**: An option introduced by Lisbon that allows a petition (signed by at least a million people) to be submitted to the Commission.

● **Referendum**: A form of direct democracy (otherwise known as a plebiscite, a ballot question, or a proposition) in which the affected electorate is asked to vote on whether or not to accept a specific proposal.

National referendums

Less scholarly attention has been paid to the study of national referendums in the EU than to the study of elections, and yet they have been held with increased frequency, and they are the subject of often intense short-term public and political attention; at few times is voter attention drawn more actively to European issues than when one of the member states organizes a referendum. They have occasionally resulted in dramatic changes of political direction, and the EU's democratic deficit is rarely more apparent than when national governments refuse to put major European questions to a public test. In many cases they have done this out of fear of negative outcomes, usually explaining their decisions with questionable political and constitutional reasoning. Such avoidance tactics reflect well neither on the process of European integration nor on the style of national politicians, and the pressures to hold referendums on European issues have been growing, while the opportunities to avoid a vote have been declining.

The use of national referendums varies from one country to another. At one end of the spectrum is Ireland, which has a constitutional requirement that all international treaties (including EU treaties) likely to impact national sovereignty need constitutional amendments, which in turn require a national referendum; hence there were 22 amendments to the Irish constitution between 1972 and 2008, of which six dealt with European issues. In the middle of the spectrum lies Italy, whose voters since 1974 have often gone to the polls to express opinions on domestic issues as diverse as nuclear power, hunting, electoral reform, divorce and abortion. (They also voted in 1989 on whether the European Parliament should be given the power to adopt a treaty on European union developed at the prompting of Italian politician Altiero Spinelli.) Meanwhile, Denmark has had referendums on the rules of royal succession and changes to the minimum voting age, France has had several votes on changes to the constitution, and the UK has had several regional referendums on questions related to devolution. For most EU states, though, their experience with national votes on European matters has been something of a political novelty.

So far more than 40 referendums have been held dealing with European issues (see Table 16.1), making Europe – in the view of de Vreese and Semetko (2004, p.4) – the single most voted-on issue in the world. More than half of the referendums have been held since 1998, and more than one-third of them in just two countries: Denmark and Ireland. In only seven EU member states – Belgium, Bulgaria, Cyprus, Germany, Greece, Portugal, and Romania – has there never been a referendum on a European issue. Where there have been such votes, most have fallen into one of two major categories.

Membership of the EC, the EU or the euro

In none of the six founding states of the three European Communities was it considered politically or constitutionally necessary to put membership to a national vote. This was a reflection in part of the way that their creation was negotiated and planned by political leaders, and in part of the modest goals of the Communities, each of which was considered – at the time – little more than a conventional international organization. It was only later, as membership of the EEC and then the EU involved both a bigger political commitment and significant changes to national law and policy, and generated more public debate, that national referendums began to appear more regularly on the political calendar. Even so, of today's 27 member states, referendums on joining the EEC/EU have been held in only 14, all but two of which joined after 1995.

The first four membership referendums were held in 1972 in France, Denmark, Ireland, and Norway. The French vote was unique in the sense that it asked not whether the French wanted to be part of the EC but whether they favoured the enlargement of the Community to include Britain, Denmark,

Table 16.1 National referendums on EU issues

Year	Country	Issue	Outcome
1972	France	Enlarging the EEC	Yes
	Ireland	Join EEC	Yes
	Norway	Join EEC	No
	Denmark	Join EEC	Yes
1975	UK	Continued membership of EEC	Yes
1982	Greenland	Continued membership of EEC	No
1986	Denmark	Single European Act	Yes
1987	Ireland	Single European Act	Yes
1989	Italy	Mandate for Spinelli Treaty	Yes
1992	Denmark I	Maastricht treaty	No
	Ireland	Maastricht treaty	Yes
	France	Maastricht treaty	Yes
	Switzerland	Join European Economic Area	No
1993	Denmark II	Maastricht treaty	Yes
1994	Austria	Join EU	Yes
	Finland	Join EU	Yes
	Sweden	Join EU	Yes
	Norway	Join EU	No
1998	Ireland	Treaty of Amsterdam	Yes
	Denmark	Treaty of Amsterdam	Yes
2000	Denmark	Adopt euro	No
2001	Ireland I	Treaty of Nice	No
	Switzerland	Negotiate EU membership	No
2002	Ireland II	Treaty of Nice	Yes
2003	Malta	Join EU	Yes
	Slovenia	Join EU	Yes
	Hungary	Join EU	Yes
	Lithuania	Join EU	Yes
	Slovakia	Join EU	Yes
	Poland	Join EU	Yes
	Czech Republic	Join EU	Yes
	Estonia	Join EU	Yes
	Latvia	Join EU	Yes
	Sweden	Adopt euro	No
2005	Spain	Constitutional treaty	Yes
	France	Constitutional treaty	No
	Netherlands	Constitutional treaty	No
	Switzerland	Join Schengen Agreement	Yes
	Luxembourg	Constitutional treaty	Yes
2008	Ireland I	Treaty of Lisbon	No
2009	Switzerland	Freedom of worker movement to Bulgaria and Romania	Yes
	Ireland II	Treaty of Lisbon	Yes

Ireland, and Norway. With 60 per cent turnout, 68 per cent voted in favour. For Denmark, Ireland, and Norway, meanwhile, it was a simple question of whether or not to accept membership of the EEC. In the Irish and Danish cases there was little controversy, high turnout, and strong support for joining (83 per cent and 63 per cent respectively). But in Norway there was a debate generated by concerns over fishing, the environment, and national sovereignty. In the event, just over 53 per cent voted against Community membership, as a result of which prime minister Trygve Bratteli resigned from office. Norway was again accepted for EU membership in 1994, again put the issue to a national vote (in November of that year), and again opted to stay out, this time by the slightly smaller figure of just over 52 per cent.

In 1975, Britain held a referendum that was not only unusual in both its timing and its objectives, but was also the first (and so far only) national referendum in British history. There had been no vote before Britain joined the EEC on 1 January 1973, on terms negotiated by the Conservative government of Edward Heath. But when a new Labour government won power in 1974 under Harold Wilson, opponents of Europe within Labour pushed for a referendum on membership. A split emerged within the government, at which point the vote was called – most senior members of the government and the opposition were in favour, while those opposed came mainly from the left, from the far right, and from the Scottish and Welsh nationalist movements. On referendum day in June, 64 per cent turned out and more than 67 per cent voted Yes (see Broad and Geiger, 1996). This should have put the matter to rest, but the debate over Britain's membership of the EU has never entirely gone away.

In 1982 there was another vote on whether or not to stay in the EEC, this time in a region of a member state, resulting in the first and so far only defection from the EEC/EU. The vote was held in Greenland, a sparsely populated autonomous region of Denmark whose 32,000 residents had voted heavily against Danish membership of the EEC in 1972. Following home rule in 1979 and the election in 1981 of an anti-European government, a decision was taken to hold a referendum, the major issue being protection of fishing rights. The 1982 vote resulted in 54 per cent opting to leave the Community, which Greenland eventually did three years later. (In 2008, Greenland voted for self-rule in another referendum, opening the possibility of independence, but during the fallout from the 2007–10 global economic crisis – which hit neighbouring Iceland particularly hard – there was speculation that Greenland might apply to rejoin the EU.)

The rising political pressure to put EU membership to a national vote resulted in national referendums in all three of the countries that joined in 1995 (Austria, Finland and Sweden), and in nine of the 12 countries that joined in 2004–07 (the exceptions being Bulgaria, Cyprus and Romania). For the 1995 applicants, the results ranged from 52 to 67 per cent in favour, while for the 2004–07 applicants they were in the range of 54 per cent in favour (Malta) to 92 per cent in favour (Slovakia), with turnout rates ranging between 46 per cent in Hungary and 91 per cent in Malta.

In connection with only one other membership issue – adoption of the euro – have national referendums been held, and here the significance has been less with those countries that have held votes than with the large number that have not. Only in two countries – Denmark and Sweden – were referendums held, and in both cases the result was negative (53 per cent opposed in Denmark and by 58 per cent in Sweden). Discussions were held in several other member states about the political desirability of a vote, but pro-euro governments often feared the outcome. The Blair administration was in favour of Britain joining the euro and regularly spoke of the possibilities of a referendum, but opinion polls found British opposition running high and the vote was indefinitely delayed. In the Netherlands there was also hostility to the euro, but no referendum; this led to speculation that at least one reason why Dutch voters rejected the European constitution in 2005 was because they had been denied a vote on the euro (Aarts and van der Kolke, 2006).

Adoption of a new treaty

As with membership of the EEC, it was long assumed by most leaders of the member states that no public votes were needed on the adoption of new treaties, ostensibly because they were amendments only to the terms of membership of an international organization. But again, as the impact and reach of the EU expanded, the stakes were raised and public opinion on the treaties took on a new significance. The first treaty vote was taken in February 1986 in Denmark on the Single European Act. Since the terms of the treaty were relatively non-controversial, it was accepted by more than 65 per cent of voters, and by nearly 70 per cent of voters in a referendum in Ireland in 1987. But then came the Maastricht treaty, containing more controversial proposals about foreign and monetary policy, and this time three member states put the treaty to a vote and it fell to Denmark in June 1992 to become the first EEC/EU member state ever to reject a treaty in a referendum. Ireland and France followed with votes in favour, clearing the way for Denmark to achieve another first: negotiating opt-outs from a treaty and putting it to a second national vote (this it did in May 1993 when a sizeable majority voted Yes).

The Treaty of Amsterdam was again relatively non-controversial and was put to a national referendum only in Ireland and Denmark, passing by 62 per cent and 55 per cent. Much the same relative peace was expected with the Treaty of Nice, but the Irish Supreme Court had ruled in 1987 that changes to the terms of EU membership required an amendment to the Irish constitution, and all such amendments required a referendum. Expecting no problems, the Irish government did little to promote Nice, and was shocked when voters rejected it in a June 2001 referendum (with just 34 per cent turnout). A second attempt was made in October 2002 after a more organized government information campaign, and Nice was this time approved by a large majority.

Undoubtedly the most important of public referendums on a treaty were those held in 2005 on the proposed European constitutional treaty. The stakes had been raised, because – for the first time – ratification by all member states was required in order for the treaty to come into force. Plans were made in 10 of the 25 member states to hold such referendums, and this time there were much stronger doubts that it would pass every test, the general assumption being that the spoiler would be Britain, where hostility was clear and substantial. But it was to be two of the Community's founding members – France and the Netherlands – which were to reject the constitution in votes held within days of each other in May and June. With no renegotiation or opt-outs available, the effect of the votes was – for the first time – to stop a treaty dead in its tracks. Ireland captured the

Illustration 16.2
The 2005 French
referendum

French newspaper headlines
on 30 May 2005 declare the
result of the referendum in
which voters rejected the
proposed EU constitutional
treaty.

headlines again in 2009 when voters rejected the Treaty of Lisbon. Once again the Irish government was obliged to negotiate written assurances, and in an October 2009 re-vote the treaty was approved.

The rules on referendums vary from one state to another, with two key distinctions. The first of these is between referendums that are mandatory (usually required under the terms of a national constitution) and those that are facultative (that is, they can be initiated by a political leader or by public demand). In some EU member states, such as Denmark and Ireland, changes to the national constitution require a referendum, but Ireland is the only member state where a new EU treaty – because of its impact on national sovereignty – requires a constitutional amendment and therefore a referendum. (Non-member Switzerland has a requirement that a referendum must be held on joining an international organization if at least 50,000 people or eight cantons support a petition in favour.) There has been no acknowledgement in Denmark that new treaties need changes to the constitution, so its referendums have been facultative rather than mandatory.

The second distinction is between referendums that are binding (mandatory referendums are almost always binding) and those that are advisory or consultative (and so, by definition, non-binding). The Netherlands offers a curious example of the distinction: the law does not allow for referendums, but between 2002 and 2005 there was a Temporary Referendum Law on the statute books, allowing for non-binding referendums on laws passed by the House of

Representatives. The law had lapsed by the time the May 2005 referendum was held on the EU constitutional treaty, the way for which was paved by another temporary law, allowing for the first national referendum (on any topic) in Dutch history (see Nijebore, 2005).

As a means of allowing citizens input into decision-making, referendums have their advantages and disadvantages. The main advantage is that they are a form of direct democracy that engage the electorate directly with key political issues. They can also encourage intensive debate about those issues that can help offset some of the problems of voter apathy that have plagued elections. Finally, they can be a way of bypassing an impasse in government; if government itself is undecided over what action to take, it can defer the issue to the electorate. On the other side of the ledger, however, referendums have many disadvantages:

- The fact that so many are either facultative and/or non-binding raises the question of why they should be held in the first place; legislative elections, after all, are entirely binding in their results (at least in liberal democracies).
- Even though voters are usually asked to vote Yes or No on a contained proposition, the issues and debates behind the proposition are often too complex to be reduced to a single statement. The wording of the proposition can raise problems, potentially defining the issue too narrowly or not defining it narrowly enough and offering governments a means of wriggling out of an unfavourable result. (There was a long debate in Britain, for example, over the precise wording of the proposition for the stillborn referendum on the euro.)
- Referendums have been criticized as a means of bypassing representative democracy, potentially handing decision-making to the most motivated and best-informed groups in a society, and opening the way for voters to be influenced by propaganda and expensive advertising campaigns.
- Referendums can be used to defer public debate on an issue, with political leaders claiming that knotty questions should be delayed until the holding of a referendum that may never actually happen.

One problem with referendums that has been particularly obvious in the case of the EU has been the tendency of some member states to repeat their votes until the voters 'get it right'. This happened with the double vote in Denmark on Maastricht, and again with the double votes in Ireland on Nice and Lisbon. To be sure, the initial negative votes left governments with no option but to think again about the content of the treaties, and the terms for Denmark and Ireland were amended slightly in order to placate opponents. But why arrange for voters who had initially said No to vote again following the negotiation of opt-outs and the preparation of better planned government information programmes? And what would have happened if any of the second votes had also been negative? Would the treaties have died, as in the case of the constitutional treaty, or would the other member states have gone ahead without the state that voted No?

There are questions, too, about the importance and political significance of Europe's referendums. As with EP elections, there is evidence to suggest that the results are often driven less by attitudes towards the EU and more by prevailing levels of support for governing and opposition parties at home. In the case of the Maastricht treaty votes, for example, support was high in France but voters used the referendum to punish the unpopular Mitterand government, while in Denmark the Yes vote was in large part a function of the popularity of the country's new social democratic government (Franklin, Marsh and Wlezien, 1994). Much also depends, though, on what kind of job political parties and interest groups do in mobilizing supporters for their positions. In votes on new treaties, a critical problem has been the complexity of the treaties and the failure of many voters to read the treaties or to understand the issues involved. This makes them more vulnerable to manipulation, and also plays into the hands of usually better organized and more motivated opponents. But there is also evidence to suggest that voter opinions are better developed in states that have had referendums, because more effort is usually made to debate and explain the issues than is the case with EP elections (Christin and Hug, 2002).

In spite of the many concerns about referendums, they have become increasingly common in the EU. Several member states have had a long history of local referendums that have now apparently expanded into new support for national votes, several states have broken the habits of centuries by holding their first national referendums, and public support for votes on new EU treaties has grown. As resistance to European integration has expanded, so the arguments that legislative votes on new treaties are enough has come to ring increasingly hollow. The challenge now, though, is to develop a more methodical and consistent approach to organizing referendums, and to deciding how to respond to the results.

SUMMARY

● Direct elections to the European Parliament have been held every five years since 1979, using proportional representation (PR).

● Among the consequences of PR is the return of numerous political parties to power, resulting in most EU states in a tradition of coalition governments.

● Since the introduction of direct elections to the EP in 1979, turnout has fallen from a high of 63 per cent to a low of 43 per cent in 2009. Among the explanations for this trend is the difference between first-order and second-order elections.

● While turnout at EP elections has fallen, support for non-conventional forms of political participation has grown.

● Voters in some states have been offered national referendums, although there is no consistency on when and where they will be held. In terms of referendums, Europe has become the single most voted-on issue in the world.

● The subject of most referendums has been membership of the EEC/EU or the euro, or approval of a new treaty.

● Denmark and Ireland have had the most referendums on European issues, and only seven EU member states – Belgium, Bulgaria, Cyprus, Germany, Greece, Portugal, and Romania – have had none.

● A distinction must be made between referendums that are mandatory or facultative (initiated by public or political demand), and between those that are binding and non-binding.

● The outcome of EP elections and of national referendums is often influenced by the popularity of governing and opposition parties in different member states.

KEY TERMS AND CONCEPTS

Citizen initiative
Coalition government
First-order and second-order elections
Proportional representation
Referendum

FURTHER READING

Déloye, Yves, and Michael Bruter (eds) (2007), *Encyclopaedia of European Elections* (Basingstoke: Palgrave Macmillan). A useful source of reference on matters relating to European elections.

Hobolt, Sara Binzer (2009), *Europe in Question: Referendums on European integration* (Oxford University Press); Aleks Szczerbiak and Paul Taggart (eds) (2005), *EU Enlargement and Referendums* (Abingdon: Routledge, 2005). Two contributions to the growing academic literature on referendums on EU issues.

Lodge, Juliet (ed.) (2001 and 2005), *The 1999 Elections to the European Parliament* and *The 2004 Elections to the European Parliament* (Basingstoke: Palgrave Macmillan). Valuable surveys of two recent EP elections.

CHAPTER **17** | # Public Opinion

PREVIEW In a perfect democratic world, the values, views and concerns of citizens should be routinely on the minds of elected leaders, who are – after all – the representatives of the citizens. But there are at least two flaws with this proposition. First, it is diffi-cult always to know what the citizens want, either because they may not know themselves, or because of the pitfalls in measuring public opinion. Second, opinion is typically divided on almost every public issue, leaving elected officials to decide whether to side with the majority or to be concerned only with those who elected them.

These are problems that exist at the national and local level within the member states, but they are magnified at the European level by the mixed feelings of most Europeans about the exercise of integration, coupled with their often low levels of knowledge about the structure and work of the EU. Attitudes can be summed up as follows: sometimes supportive, sometimes hostile, and often badly-informed. Most Europeans do not know what to make of the EU, neither understand how it works nor fully understand its implications, and have opinions about European integration that could at best be described as 'soft'; neither strongly opposing nor supporting what it is being done in their name.

This chapter looks at public opinion in the EU as it relates to integration and an understanding of what 'Europe' represents. It focuses on euroscepticism (hostility to integration, or to the direction being taken by the European project), the knowledge deficit (the gap between the responsibilities of the EU and what Europeans know and understand about how it works), and Europeanism (the values that Europeans have in common, and that exist independently of the experience of regional integration).

KEY ISSUES
- What are the political implications of euroscepticism?
- Given the knowledge deficit, how far can we be sure about public opinion on European integration?
- Why do so few Europeans understand the structure and effects of the EU, and what can be done about this?
- What are the prospects for a European public sphere?
- Is Europeanism a useful analytical concept?
- Is it fair to think of Europe as a multicultural society, or has hostility to immigration from outside Europe indicated otherwise?
- Are Europeans cosmopolitans?

Attitudes towards integration

Overall, European public opinion is at best equivocal about the EU and the process of integration. Some Europeans embrace it with enthusiasm, and are disappointed that it has not gone further and moved more quickly towards the achievement of a federal United States of Europe. Others think it has already gone too far, and that withdrawal of their country from the EU would be no bad thing. But as with so much in the world of public opinion, most Europeans fall somewhere between the two poles, supporting what has been achieved but being unsure about how much further they would like the process to go.

We know this mainly from the results of the Commission-sponsored **Eurobarometer** polling service, which carries out biannual surveys of opinion in all the member states. When asked, for example, what they think about the costs and benefits to their home state of membership in the EU, between 48 and 58 per cent of those asked in surveys between 1995 and 2009 agreed that it had been 'a good thing', while only 10–17 per cent considered it 'a bad thing', and 25–31 per cent considered it neither good nor bad (Eurobarometer 72, First Results, December 2009, p. 30). Levels of support and opposition remained stable during this period in spite of the growth in EU membership. But these are the average figures for all the member states, within each of which polls reflect a wide range of opinions (see Figure 17.1) with few easily discernible patterns:

- There is not much of a correlation, for example, between support for the EU and length of membership. In some of the founding states (particularly Luxembourg, the Netherlands and Belgium), positives were high, but in France and Italy only half of respondents thought membership had been a good thing. In some of the new eastern European states there are strong majorities in favour (particularly Romania, Slovakia, and Poland), but others sit at the other end of the rankings (notably the Czech Republic, Hungary and Latvia).

- Similarly, there is only a weak correlation between public opinion and relative wealth or poverty. On a per capita GDP basis, the EU's five wealthiest states are Luxembourg, Denmark, the Netherlands, Ireland, and Finland, and yet positive views about EU membership ranged in these countries between 79 per cent and 52 per cent. The five poorest member states are Bulgaria, Romania, Latvia, Lithuania, and Poland, where positive views ranged from 66 per cent to 25 per cent.

Fligstein (2008) concludes that attitudes towards integration are driven more by association and identity; hence those who have benefited most from integration (including business owners, managers, professionals, white-collar workers, the educated, and the young) have had more to do with their counterparts in other societies and so think of themselves more as Europeans, while older, poorer, less educated, and blue-collar Europeans have benefited less, fear the effects of integration on national sovereignty, worry that its pro-business orientation will overwhelm national welfare states, and retain a stronger sense of national identity. Meanwhile, a third group of mainly middle-class Europeans sees the EU in mostly positive terms but could go either way.

● **Eurobarometer**: The EU's public opinion polling service, which carries out two major surveys every year, along with 'flash' surveys on more discrete issues.

Figure 17.1 What Europeans think: EU membership

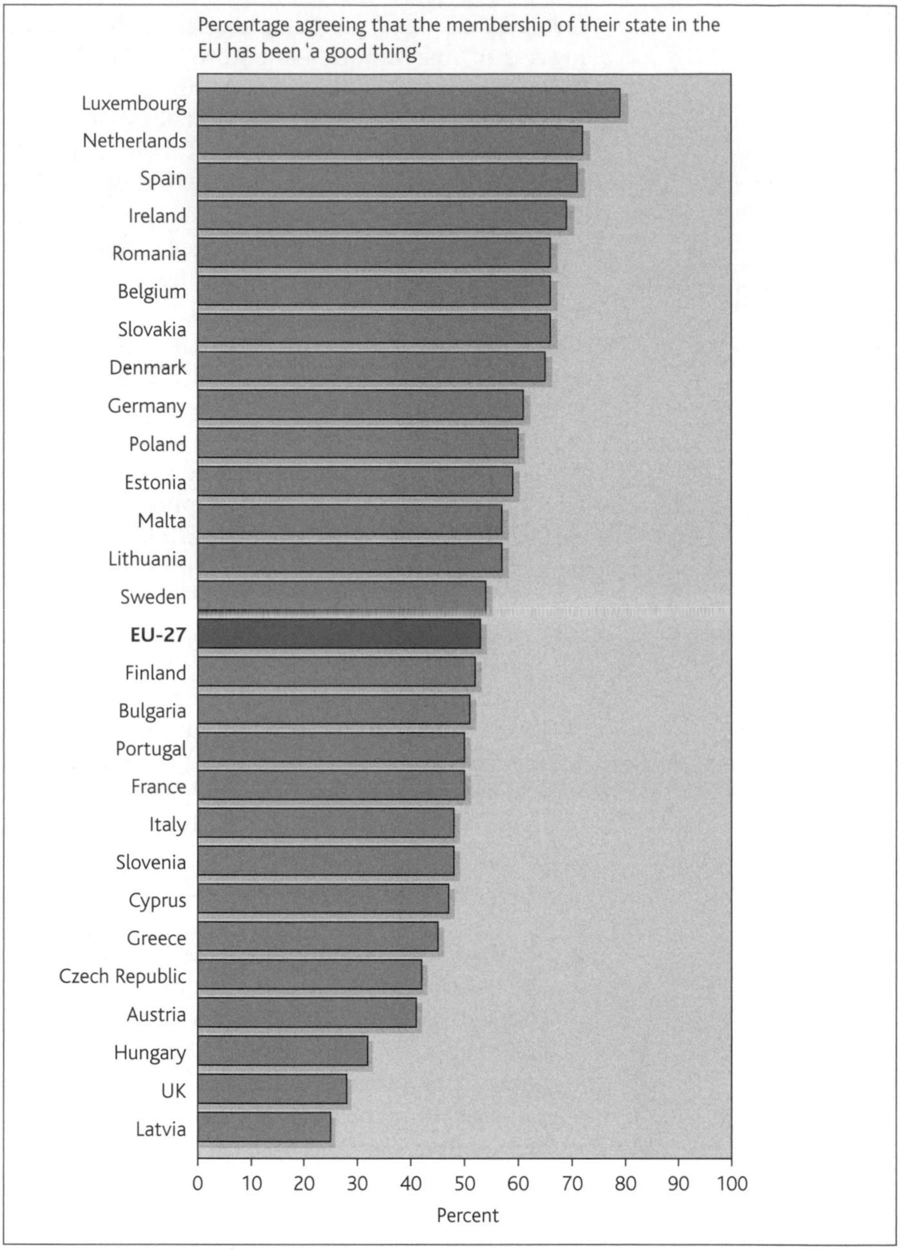

Percentage agreeing that the membership of their state in the EU has been 'a good thing'

Source: European Commission, *Eurobarometer* 71, September 2009.

When asked what the EU means to them personally, most respondents opt for the practical changes brought by the single market and the availability of the euro (see Figure 17.2). This is no surprise given that these are among the European initiatives most likely to have had a direct impact on the lives and choices of Europeans. About 20–25 per cent of respondents identified the more nebulous role of integration in promoting peace and democracy, while about

CONCEPT

Euroscepticism

Opposition to the process of European integration, or doubts about the direction in which it is moving, based mainly on concerns about the loss of state sovereignty and about the undemocratic or elitist manner in which decisions on integration have been taken. There are many shades of eurosceptic opinion: some eurosceptics argue that integration should go no further, others that the process should either be reformed or reversed, and some that their state should leave the EU altogether.

Figure 17.2 What Europeans think: integration

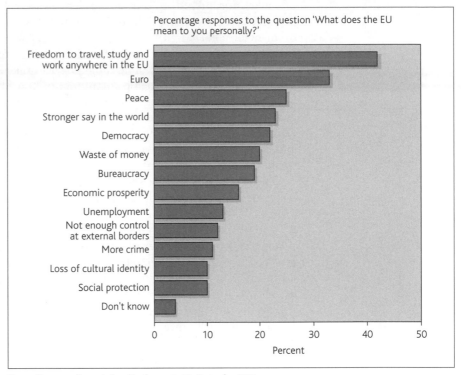

Source: European Commission, *Eurobarometer* 71, September 2009.

one in five associated the EU with more bureaucracy and wasted money. The latter is a problem with which the EC/EU has long had to wrestle, the media interest in cases of fraud, excessive agricultural spending, and expense claims by European officials contrasting with the reality that the EU budget is actually quite small (see Chapter 18). Few misconceptions are held more actively by more Europeans than the idea that the EU spends and wastes large sums of money.

It is difficult always to know why these polls produce the results that they do, because there has been relatively little specific study of the reasoning behind support for the EU. This, presumably, is because such support is taken as the benchmark or the reference point for understanding the process of integration; Europe has, after all, been working to cooperate rather than to disintegrate. We do not even have a label to describe supporters of integration; they may be euro-believers, euroenthusiasts, federalists, or europhiles. By contrast, hostility to integration has attracted much new attention in recent years on the back of negative votes in national referendums and controversy over the writing of new treaties, such that the phenomenon of **euroscepticism** has been the subject of growing study and public debate. In short, we have a better understanding of why people oppose the EU than of why they support it.

When integration was a relatively quiet and modest exercise, as it was until the early 1980s, euroscepticism was so marginal as to be barely measurable, certainly in the public arena. Efforts to complete the single market in the 1980s and 1990s were met with generally positive responses, or at least an absence of significant opposition. But as we saw in Chapter 6, as the speed and the breadth of integration picked up during the debates over Maastricht, and the process began to reach into more parts of European life, so euroscepticism entered its era of growth. The year 1992 was a watershed, with the Danish vote against Maastricht in June and the crisis in the Exchange Rate Mechanism in September, the first revealing that the public could be encouraged to vote against a European initiative, and the second being a reminder of how far European economies had become invested in the process of integration. Euroscepticism began to play a greater role both in domestic politics – with the rise of minor parties opposed to European integration, and splits within mainstream parties between Europeans and anti-Europeans – and in European politics, where it influenced thinking on treaty reforms, enlargement, and new policy initiatives.

The arguments put forward by eurosceptics vary by member state and by issue, ideology and time, but they have included the following:

- The EU is on its way to becoming a federalized European superstate at the expense of the self-determination of its member states.
- The EU institutions are undemocratic, elitist, bureaucratic, inefficient and insufficiently accountable to the citizens of the member states.
- The EU is promoting policies that are unpopular both with the political left (it puts too much emphasis on free markets) and with the political right (it puts too much power in the hands of workers).
- Too many decisions are taken by national leaders without reference to their citizens, who are too often denied national referendums on such crucial developments as treaty revisions. There have even been charges of a conspiracy among European leaders to move ahead without reference to citizens (see, for example, Booker and North, 2005).
- Attempts to build common policies do not take enough account of national differences; this is true of the Common Foreign and Security Policy, for example, which is seen to threaten the neutrality of member states such as Ireland and Finland.

Euroscepticism first came to prominence in Britain, where the Thatcher government made clear its hostility to many aspects of integration in the 1980s, and where segments of public opinion began to follow suit in the 1990s. Britain had dragged its feet on applying to the EEC in the 1950s, in 1975 it became the only member state ever to hold a national referendum on whether or not to stay in the EU, the term *eurosceptism* first began to appear in the British media in the mid-1980s (Harmsen and Spiering, 2005), Britain resisted numerous EU initiatives ranging from the Schengen Agreement to adoption of the euro, and it has overall attracted the most media and public attention for its unwillingness to be a 'good' European. (Unfortunately, this ignores the many occasions when Britain has not just cooperated but has provided leadership on European issues, particularly on foreign, trade and defence policy.)

Euroscepticism has spread more widely since the 1990s, becoming particularly clear in the actions and opinions of many eastern European political leaders and citizens. As it has spread, so it has become clear that it is far from monolithic, and is less a well-defined ideology than a set of related positions based on opposition to European integration. For Taggart and Szczerbiak (2001), for example, there is a difference between its soft and hard forms. Where the former is based

**Illustration 17.1
Euroscepticism**

Eurosceptic members of the European Parliament call on the EU to respect the outcome of the negative Irish vote on the Lisbon treaty in June 2008.

on qualified opposition to the direction being taken by the EU and a further expansion of its powers, the latter (which is less widepread but easier to see) implies outright rejection of the entire project of European political and economic integration. It is most obvious in the case of single issue political parties that argue for the withdrawal of their countries from the EU (such as the People's Movement in Denmark, several communist parties, and the UK Independence Party in Britain), or more broad-based parties that resist European integration in its current form (such as the Democratic Socialists and the Free Democrats in Germany, the Greens in Portugal and the Netherlands, and the British Conservative Party). Kopecky and Mudde (2002) make even finer distinctions, their study of euroscepticism in east central Europe helping them identify four shades of opinion that distinguish between diffuse opposition to the core principle of European integration and specific opposition to the way the EU is evolving (see Figure 17.3).

Figure 17.3 Shades of euroscepticism

		EUROPEAN INTEGRATION	
		Support	Oppose
EUROPEAN UNION	Support	**Euroenthusiasts** Support European integration and the EU	**Europragmatists** Support the EU, but neither oppose nor support European integration
	Oppose	**Eurosceptics** Support European integration but worry about the extent to which the EU reflects the goals of integration	**Eurorejects** Oppose both the EU and European integration

Source: Based on Petr Kopecký and Cas Mudde, 'The Two Sides of Euroscepticism: Party Positions on European Integration in East Central Europe', in *European Union Politics* 3:3, September 2002, 297–326.

The long-term significance of euroscepticism is hard to determine. It has certainly grown in both breadth and depth since the 1990s, and has been a factor in the calculations of governments as they consider new steps in the process of integration. But while Eurobarometer polls have shown support for the EU running at about 3:1 over opposition since the mid-1990s, much of that support remains soft in the sense that strong feelings about Europe (whether for or against) are harder to find. The majority of Europeans lie somewhere in the middle, occasionally expressing strong views about some aspect of integration but otherwise generally accepting what has been done in their name since the 1950s. Fligstein (2008) argues that it is this swing group that is most critical for the future of European integration; if they favour more cooperation, then politicians will oblige, but if they remain focused on the member states to which they belong then the European project will be more likely to stall.

The knowledge deficit

As we will see in Chapter 18, the democratic deficit (the gap between the powers of the EU institutions and the ability of EU citizens directly to influence the work of those institutions) has long been at the heart of the debate about Europe. Much more rarely discussed, but with equally important implications for the political character of the EU, is what we might call the **knowledge deficit**. This can be defined as the gap between the powers of the EU institutions and the ability of EU citizens to make informed judgements about the exercise of European integration. It affects their ability to understand the decisions taken by the EU and the governments of its member states, to sort through the claims of pro- and anti-Europeans, and to understand how to make use of the channels through which those decisions can be influenced.

The size and reach of the deficit is clearly reflected in the results of recent Eurobarometer surveys. In the late 1990s and early 2000s, respondents were asked to rate themselves on a scale of 1 to 10, giving themselves a 1 if they knew nothing at all about the EU, its policies, and institutions, a 10 if they knew a great deal, and something in between according to how much or how little they knew. In a 2005 survey, about one in five gave themselves a rating of 1 or 2, while about half gave themselves a rating of between 3 and 5, and only about 2 per cent gave themselves a rating of 9 or 10 (Eurobarometer 63, September 2005, p. 75). In other words, more than two-thirds of respondents gave themselves a failing score.

The 2009 poll was structured differently – asking people to respond to the statement 'I understand how the EU works' – but the result was much the same: only 44 per cent of respondents said that they knew how the EU worked, while the rest said that they did not (see Figure 17.4). Men claimed to be better informed than women, higher levels of education correlated (unsurprisingly) with better knowledge, and younger Europeans were better informed than their seniors. By state, the 2009 poll had several interesting results:

● **Knowledge deficit**: The gap between how the EU works and what ordinary Europeans know about that process.

Figure 17.4 What Europeans think: understanding the EU

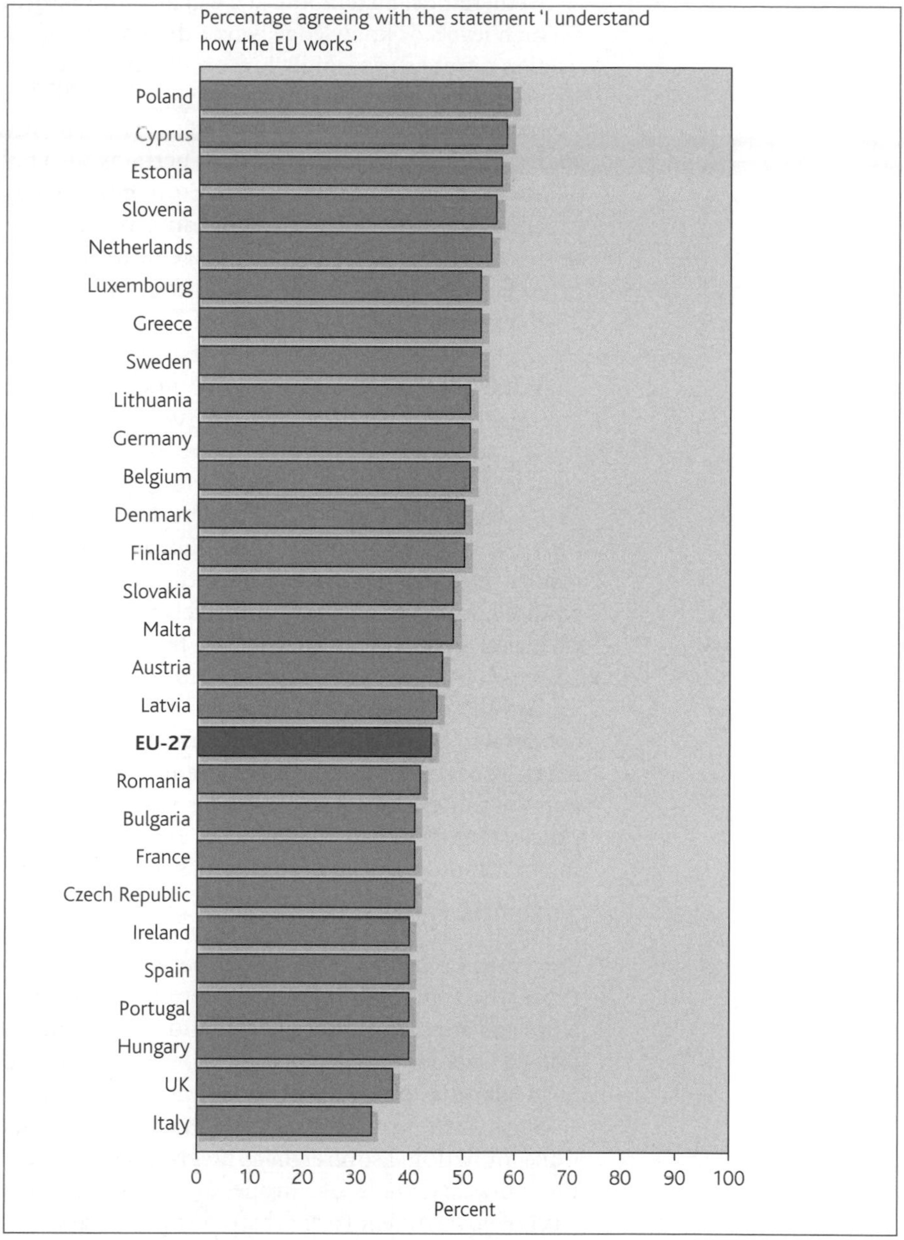

Percentage agreeing with the statement 'I understand how the EU works'

Poland	
Cyprus	
Estonia	
Slovenia	
Netherlands	
Luxembourg	
Greece	
Sweden	
Lithuania	
Germany	
Belgium	
Denmark	
Finland	
Slovakia	
Malta	
Austria	
Latvia	
EU-27	
Romania	
Bulgaria	
France	
Czech Republic	
Ireland	
Spain	
Portugal	
Hungary	
UK	
Italy	

Percent: 0 10 20 30 40 50 60 70 80 90 100

Source: European Commission, *Eurobarometer* 71, September 2009.

● Respondents in some of the newer member states (especially Poland, Cyprus, Estonia, and Slovakia) considered themselves better informed than those of older member states, a difference that is probably explained by the sheer novelty of membership, which meant fresher debates about the EU and higher levels of attention paid in national media to the implications of membership. (In older states, meanwhile, membership was less newsworthy and the debates had often staled.)

- Among the six founding members, citizens of four countries (the Netherlands, Luxembourg, Germany and Belgium) still claimed relatively high levels of knowledge, while the French – long the champions of integration – were surprisingly low on the list, and the Italians (less surprisingly, given their historically lower levels of attachment to the EU) were at the bottom.
- Ireland was also low on the list, perhaps surprisingly given how much attention had been devoted to Europe in the votes on the treaties of Nice and Lisbon in 2001 and 2008 respectively.
- Less surprising was Britain's place near the bottom of the scale, the hostility to Europe among many Britons translating into relatively low levels of interest in how the EU works.

While these data measure how much people *think* they know (and we can reasonably ask ourselves how the survey subjects were able to determine how much they knew or did not know), other more specific questions have occasionally put that knowledge to the test by measuring how much people *actually* know. These focus on details about the European Parliament, the presidency of the Council of Ministers, the EU budget, and other issues (see Figure 17.5). The results once again paint a rather dismal picture, although they fit with what studies have revealed about low levels of political knowledge among the citizens of liberal democracies in general, few of whom keep up with politics in any sustained manner, and many of whom are easily swayed by partisan appeals.

Are these numbers a cause for concern? Much depends on how we think about civic duty, or the belief that in return for rights we have responsibilities. In other words, if government is there to protect our interests through democracy and the rule of law, then we are responsible for participating in the democratic process, which in turn means being at least reasonably informed. 'To take no part in the running of the community's affairs', argued Aristotle, 'is to be either a beast or a god.' On the other hand, perhaps it is a fundamental right of all those living in a democracy to ignore or disengage themselves from public affairs if they so choose. But if we subscribe to the view that knowledge is power, then those who remain uninformed open themselves up to manipulation by political elites and special interest groups, and their ignorance contributes to the centralization and potential abuse of power. The European knowledge deficit is a particular matter of concern for several reasons.

First, the debate over Europe involves decisions with fundamental implications for national sovereignty. Integration is at heart about changes in the role of the individual states of Europe, and about the potential construction of a new level of government (or perhaps just governance) that is changing the nature of political power in Europe. The trend is for state governments to lose power, and for the development of a network of European institutions, and a body of European laws and policies, all of which impact the lives of every European. For this to be happening without the understanding and input of many ordinary Europeans is a matter of deep concern.

Second, ignorance encourages detachment in the sense that Europeans are less likely to understand what is at stake in EU decision-making, are less likely to understand what options they have available to make their views heard, and are less likely to make use of elections, referendums, or public debates in order to

Figure 17.5 What Europeans think: misconceptions about the EU

In polls taken between 2005 and 2009 . . .

50% of respondents knew that a different member state held the presidency of the Council of Ministers every six months (2008).

45% knew that Members of the European Parliament were directly elected (2007).

45% knew that the statement 'The EU currently consists of 15 member states' was wrong (2007).

36% knew that the EU had an official anthem (2005).

33% asked in 2005 knew that the last EP elections (held in 2004) had not been held in 2002.

33% said they 'sometimes' or 'often' looked for information on the EU (2007).

28% considered themselves 'very well' or 'fairly well' informed about European political affairs (2007).

27% thought that agricultural spending was the biggest item on the EU budget (regional spending had overtaken it several years before (2007).

27% thought that the biggest item on the EU budget was administrative costs (2007). (They actually accounted for just 5 per cent of the EU budget.)

23% was the average estimate among Britons in 2009 of the size of the UK contribution to the EU budget as a percentage of gross national income. The true figure was 0.2 per cent.

16% knew that they had the right to request access to non-published EU documents (2007).

Sources: European Commission, *Eurobarometer* 63, September 2005, 78–9; *Eurobarometer* 66, September 2007, 152–60; *Eurobarometer* 67, November 2007, 125, 131; *Eurobarometer* 69, November 2008, 71; *Flash Eurobarometer: Attitudes towards the EU in the United Kingdom*, July 2009.

influence politics at the level of the EU. The European Parliament is the institution that suffers most from this dilemma; it is the only directly elected EU institution, it has worked hard to accumulate more influence over decision-making, and yet more than half of EU citizens apparently do not realize that it is directly elected, and turnout at EP elections (as we saw in Chapter 16) has fallen steadily.

Third, there can be no real accountability without the existence of an informed citizenry, the absence of which will encourage and perpetuate the kind of **elitism** that has long been the chief concern of critics of the EU. If Europeans fail to engage in the work of the EU, then decision-making will inevitably be left in the hands of national leaders, bureaucrats, and interest groups. When the EEC was more obviously an international organization, and when few Europeans either understood or much cared about its impact on their lives, negotiations on the terms of integration took place among national government representatives in smoke-filled rooms. But as the reach of integration expanded in the 1980s and 1990s, so more ordinary Europeans demanded the right to be heard, and expressed their disquiet through negative votes on treaties and by paying closer attention to the European policies of national political parties. And yet there was still a high degree of political manipulation at work, exemplified in the manner in which several governments refused to put the constitutional treaty to a national referendum, and then sidestepped public opinion by repackaging most of the failed constitution as the Treaty of Lisbon.

● **Elitism**: The view that decision-making is focused in the hands of elites, meaning – in the case of the EU – elected officials, bureaucrats, and interest groups.

Fourth, their failure to arm themselves with independent information makes Europeans more susceptible to the appeals of pro- and anti-Europeans, who will often use scare tactics, misinformation, or a selective use of facts to state their case and to characterize the opportunities offered or the threats posed by integration. This problem has worsened as more people have turned away from mainstream sources of political news to internet sites that cater to their more particular interests and that reinforce their biases and predispositions. These trends undermine the quality of the debate about the EU, which is less likely to move in creative and constructive directions unless participants can make informed decisions. There is also a danger that this problem will translate into the success of candidates for office with the same limited views as voters. A knowledgeable and demanding electorate is more likely to elect knowledgeable candidates because they will be better placed to assess the competence of those running for office.

In few places has anti-European feeling grown more widely in the face of a prevailing ignorance than in the UK. The benefits of membership are constantly questioned in public debates, political parties that question or oppose EU membership have won significant voter support, there is a cottage industry of anti-EU publishing that generates books with titles such as *The Last Days of Britain* (Jenkins, 2000) and *The Great European Rip-off* (Craig and Elliott, 2009), and turnout at European Parliament elections is among the lowest in the EU (just over one-third in 2009). And yet polls routinely find low levels of knowledge and interest among Britons in the EU, raising the obvious question of how far we can value the findings of polls in Britain on the EU when so few Britons appear able to make informed judgements about European issues. Their opinions might not change significantly were they better informed, but at least those opinions would be based on a better grasp of core facts and well-reasoned analysis, and the British people would be less easily manipulated by either side in the debate over Europe.

Ireland presents another example of the dilemma. Irish voters in June 2001 stopped the Treaty of Nice in its tracks by voting against adoption (then changed their minds in a 2002 vote), and in June 2008 stopped the Treay of Lisbon in its tracks with a negative vote (once again changing their minds in a 2009 vote). It is interesting that two-thirds of Irish residents feel that membership of the EU has been good for their country (see Figure 17.1), and yet only 40 per cent admit that they understand how it works (Figure 17.3). What, then, can we make of the referendum results? At least part of the problem was low voter turnout: just 35 per cent in 2001, rising to 48 per cent in 2002, 53 per cent in 2008, and 58 per cent in 2009. To describe the 2008 result as 'decisive' (as some media observers did) was an overstatement given that 72 per cent of voters either voted Yes or did not vote at all. Analysis suggests that while some of those who voted No were motivated by genuine and well-thought out opposition, some were motivated either by confusion about the terms of Lisbon, fears about loss of sovereignty, and misplaced fears that Lisbon posed a threat to Ireland's neutrality or might mean the loss of its special low capital tax status.

Why is it that so few Europeans understand the EU, and what can be done to close the knowledge deficit? The core source of the problem is the simple challenge of getting to grips with the rules and procedures of the EU, which is not only a unique entity in organizational terms but regularly changes its own oper-

Europeanism

The political, economic and social values that Europeans have in common, that are most clearly supported and promoted by Europeans, and that give distinctive qualities and personality to the European experience. The view that there might be such values has long been obscured by nationalism, war, conflict, and divisions over the merits of integration. Among ordinary Europeans, though, there has been a growing confluence of opinion on universal ideas such as democracy and free markets, as well as more specific issues such as welfare, the definition of the family, attitudes towards work and leisure, capital punishment, the place of force in international relations, and the role of religion in public life.

ational rules. It would help if there was a (preferably brief) constitution to which Europeans could refer for clarification of those rules, but instead they have been offered a series of treaties, each of which has amended those that came before, each of which has been longer than its predecessor, and most of which have contained rules that have even occasionally baffled constitutional experts. The Treaty of Lisbon exemplifies the problem: the consolidated version is nearly 500 pages long, could use the eye of a good editor to take out repetition and obfuscation, and contains numerous titles, chapters, sections, protocols, and declarations.

In spite of the well-meaning efforts of the European Commission to provide information on the EU and its work, at the end of the day there are three critical barriers to better public understanding. First, many Europeans are just not interested in public affairs. National polls and the results of educational surveys find high levels of apathy towards politics and government among Europeans from many different backgrounds. Second, most Europeans still identify most closely with their home states and take a closer interest in domestic politics than in European politics. Finally, most Europeans still do not fully understand the significance of Europe for their states or for themselves. When we pay attention to the political environment in which we live, we care more for the issues that most immediately and clearly bear on our daily lives. Until Europeans choose to agree that they have a stake in integration, they are unlikely to take much interest in it.

Europeanism

Studies of public opinion on European integration rarely venture much further than asking how people feel about the wisdom of the EU and the place of their member state within the EU. Less frequently discussed has been the broader and more fundamental question of how far Europeans agree (or disagree) on core political, economic, and social values. In other words, behind the debate over Europe, how much evidence is there that the balance of European public opinion is moving in the same direction? Is there a growing sense that Europeans think along similar lines and have similar values? The short answer is Yes. While many may have their doubts about integration, most agree not just on the basic principles of democracy and capitalism, but much more. As a result, we can identify the phenomenon of **Europeanism**, or the political, economic and social values that Europeans have in common, and that help strengthen the sense of identity discussed in Chapter 3. This may not always be entirely obvious at first, until European public opinion is compared with that in other parts of the world, when the distinctions start to become more clear.

The study of Europeanist ideas was given a boost by public opposition to the 2003 US-led invasion of Iraq, reflected in the massive anti-war demonstrations held on 15 February in almost every major European city, from London to Berlin, Paris, Rome, Dublin, and Madrid (see Chapter 7). Inspired by what they saw, the philosophers Jürgen Habermas and Jacques Derrida wrote an article for the German newspaper *Frankfurter Allgemeine Zeitung* in which they described 15 February as marking the birth of a 'European public sphere', and argued that the opportunity had been created for the construction of a 'core Europe' that might become a counterweight to the international influence of the United

Focus on . . .
Prospects for a European public sphere

In a world dominated by states, and where human society is often divided by history, language, and culture, it is hard to conceive of multi-state communities or identity. This has certainly been true of the European Union, where analysts are quicker to point to the strength of state and national identities than to the idea that there is much of a sense of trans-European identity or consciousness. There has been growing debate about the idea of a European public sphere, defined by Fossum and Schlesinger (2007, p. 1) as 'a communicative space (or spaces) in which relatively unconstrained debate, analysis and criticism of the political order can take place'. Such a sphere might help foster a sense of European identity and encourage more association with Europe than with states and nations. But its existence and prospects are questioned, and Eriksen (2005) asks whether it can exist without a collective European identity.

The idea that millions of people speaking different languages, administered by separate governments, and living under different cultures could feel a bond with each other, and could have broadly similar values and aspirations may instead be little more than the kind of 'imagined community' described by Benedict Anderson (1991) in his study of nations. Anderson refers back to the argument made by Seton-Watson (1977, p. 5) that a nation exists 'when a significant number of people in a community consider themselves to form a nation, or behave as if they formed one'. Anderson replaces 'consider' with 'imagine' on the basis that few of the members of a nation will know or meet each other, 'yet in the minds of each lives the image of their communion' (Anderson, 1991, p. 6). He may have been writing about nations, but his core idea can be applied to other situations, one of those being the European Union. As we saw in Chapter 3, few Europeans consider themselves primarily as such, but the majority feel some sense of affinity with Europe, which raises the question of what Europe signifies and why they feel this sense of identity with it.

States. Looking to explain what Europe represented, they listed several features of what they described as a common European 'political mentality', including secularization, trust in the 'organizational capacities of the state', welfarism, and a preference for multilateralism and a peaceful means to the resolution of international problems (Habermas and Derrida, 2003).

This was an interesting start to the discussion about what Europeans might have in common, but it was limited in its perspective, and overlooked the growing number of studies of the core political, economic and social ideas and goals on which Europeans agree – much of it, ironically, written by American observers of Europe. In his book *The European Dream*, for example, Rifkin (2004, p. 3) contrasts the American emphasis on personal material advancement with the European concern with broader human welfare, noting how Europeans give preference to 'community relationships over individual autonomy, cultural diversity over assimilation, . . . sustainable development over unlimited material growth, deep play over unrelenting toil, universal human rights and the rights of nature over property rights, and global cooperation over the unilateral exercise of power'.

Sifting through the data and the analyses, it is possible to identify a substantial list of issues on which European generally agree, and where European public

● **Public sphere**: A communicative space within which the members of a community (such as a state, or the European Union), can talk with one another about shared concerns.

opinion is distinctive. First, Europeans have an instinctive preference for collective ideas and the welfare state. They understand that social divisions will occur in spite of efforts to address them, but where Americans (for example) emphasize self-reliance and are uncomfortable with large public programmes, Europeans generally support the role of the state as an economic manager and as a guarantor of societal welfare. They welcome and encourage individual endeavour, but they also believe that the community is responsible for working to make sure that economic and social handicaps are minimized. They are more ready to criticize capitalism as the source of many social ills, they believe that individual rights extend to education, health care, and social security, and they believe that equality of results is more important than equality of opportunity (Prestowitz, 2003, pp. 236–7).

Along these lines, Europeans – although they might not be familiar with the term – have an instinctive sympathy for **communitarianism**. It has been defined as a preference for collective ideas over individual independence (Selznick, 2002, p. 4), or a balance 'between community and autonomy, between the common good and liberty, between individual rights and social responsibilities' (Etzioni, 1995). Tony Blair summed up the core of communitarian ideas when he argued (with more than a hint of idealism) that in contrast to the 'crude individualism' of Britain in the 1980s, there was by the 1990s more of a focus on addressing problems collectively, and the view that 'It's up to me' was being replaced by 'It's up to us' (Blair, 1998). Most Europeans (unlike Americans) would argue that society can sometimes be a better judge of what is good for individuals rather than vice versa, and that there may sometimes be reason for the state limiting individual rights for the greater good of the community (anti-smoking laws being one example that comes to mind). Critics respond by arguing that this attitude courts the danger of encouraging authoritarianism.

Second, we saw in Chapter 3 that Europeans are changing their views about political identification. They agree that the state has an important role to play in ordering society, but as for what defines their identity, they are increasingly torn between nation, state, and Europe, which is encouraging them in turn to rethink their views about patriotism. Although the modern state was born in Europe, it is now being remodelled there more actively than probably anywhere else in the world, squeezed as it is between a revival of identification with nations and the growing reach of Europe. When asked what they are, most Europeans will still call themselves French or German or Latvian or Hungarian, but among those who are members of national minorities, national identity is increasingly important, and a small but growing minority think of themselves first and foremost as Europeans (see Figure 3.1 p. 52).

More than is true of many other parts of the world, except diverse societies such as India and China, Europeans have a strong tradition of **multiculturalism**. Complex patterns of immigration and invasion dating back centuries have exposed them to different cultures and to people speaking different languages, and they have regularly adopted and integrated values from the new groups with which they have come into contact. This has happened so often that it is often difficult to be sure what constitutes a feature of the home culture and what does not, raising challenging questions about the meaning of national identity. There is a limit to European tolerance, however, and it does not always extend to religion or race; the arrival in Europe of new ethnic, racial and religious groups in

● **Communitarianism**: The view that individual rights should be balanced with those of the community, and that community interests can sometimes outweigh those of individuals.

● **Multiculturalism**: The recognition and promotion of multiple different cultures, without promoting the interests or values of a dominant culture. Contrasts with attempts at assimilation and cultural integration, or the 'melting pot' philosophy.

**Illustration 17.2
Secular Europe**

The historical role of Christianity in European public life is symbolized by St Peter's basilica in the Vatican, but the growing hold of secularism means that tourists routinely outnumber worshippers in all Europe's great cathedrals.

the postwar era has had the unfortunate effect of heightening the racism and religious tensions that have long been part of the European experience. But it is important to remember that multiculturalism is not the same thing as multiracialism; when German Chancellor Angela Merkel declared in October 2010 that her country's efforts to create a multicultural society had 'utterly failed' (*The Guardian*, 17 October 2010), she was referring to the pressures arising from rising numbers of Muslim and non-European immigrants.

As associations with the state and the nation have been redefined, so more Europeans have turned to the idea that some values and ideas might be universal, and that all Europeans, certainly, and possibly even all humans, may belong to a single moral community above and beyond state boundaries or national identities. In this sense, Europeans have championed **cosmopolitanism**, or the idea that local and global concerns cannot be divorced, and that rather than Europe or the world being separate from the community or state in which each of us lives, the importance of the universal trumps that of the local. The study of this idea is still in its early stages (see Rumford, 2007, and Beck and Grande, 2007), and much of the literature is heavily theoretical, but evidence of European cosmopolitanism can be found – for example – in European attitudes towards international affairs, which are generally more inclusive and less exceptionalist than those found in the United States.

Third, if there is one quality that unites and distinguishes European attitudes and values more clearly than any other it is **secularism**. Religion is growing almost everywhere in the world except Europe, where its role in political and social life has been declining: church attendance has fallen, public expressions of

● **Cosmopolitanism**: The view that all humans belong to a single community based on a shared morality, and that they should rise above more narrow identities based on race, religion, nationality, or state.

● **Secularism**: The belief that government should exist independently from religion, and that political or social organizations should not be based on religious beliefs.

faith have become more unusual, Europeans have turned away from organized religion, agnosticism and atheism are more openly and widely admitted, and the role of relgion in political and public life has been marginalized. In contrast to the United States, where political leaders – especially candidates for the presidency – are expected to wear their faith on their sleeves, and where religion plays a role (either directly or indirectly) in issues as varied as abortion, euthanasia, and same-sex marriage, it has all but disappeared from public debate in Europe. This is particularly true of western, northern and non-Catholic Europe, where large majorities say that religion does not play an important role in their lives (see Figure 17.6).

Finally, European views about inter-state relations have undergone a metamorphosis since the end of the Second World War. Where the larger European states were once engaged in competition for power and influence that frequently dragged in smaller states and led to regional conflict and war, the more popular view today is that disputes should be settled peacefully wherever possible, that military power should only be used as a residual safeguard and that its role should be limited to peacekeeping rather than peacemaking, and that state interests should be set aside in the interests of international cooperation and the

Figure 17.6 What Europeans think: religion

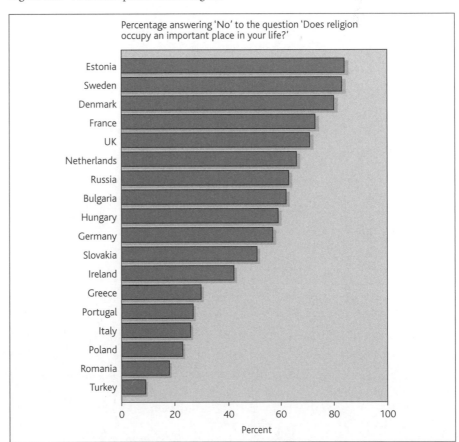

Source: Gallup poll taken in 2007–08, available at https://worldview.gallup.com (retrieved March 2010).

pursuit of problem-solving through multilateralism (see Chapter 24 for more discussion). So far has European aversion to military force gone that US Defence Secretary Robert Gates was moved in a February 2010 speech to talk of a crisis in NATO because of a failure by European governments to invest in weapons and equipment. The achievement of peace in Europe after 'ages of ruinous warfare' had been a great achievement, he argued, but the trend had now 'gone too far', and might lead to a perception of weakness among hostile states (Associated Press, 23 February 2010).

SUMMARY

- Polls find that most EU citizens feel that membership of the EU has been good for their state, and that they identify with the EU, but they also reveal a high degree of equivocation in attitudes towards integration.
- Particularly since the early 1990s, there has been a growth in levels of euroscepticism, but there are many different shades of opinion, varying by time and place.
- Polls reveal that levels of knowledge about the EU among Europeans are low.
- Political ignorance is not unusual, and is found to varying degrees throughout the democratic world.
- While domestic government can work around the knowledge deficit, at the level of the EU this becomes a problem because it encourages detachment from the process of integration, and makes the publicmore susceptible to the appeals of pro- and anti-Europeans.
- Closing the knowledge deficit is difficult because many Europeans are not interested in public affairs, and because most identify most closely with their home states and take a closer interest in domestic politics.
- The debate about Europe has overlooked the broader question of how far Europeans agree (or disagree) on core political, economic and social values.
- Most Europeans agree not just on universal ideas such as democracy and free markets, but also subscribe to concepts such as communitarianism, multiculturalism, cosmopolitanism and secularism, and agree on a wide range of specific issues such as the definition of the family, attitudes towards work and leisure, capital punishment and the role of military force.

KEY TERMS AND CONCEPTS

Communitarianism
Cosmopolitanism
Elitism
Eurobarometer
Europeanism
Euroscepticism
Knowledge deficit
Multiculturalism
Public sphere
Secularism

FURTHER READING

Fossum, John Erik, and Philip Schlesinger (eds) (2007), *The European Union and the Public Sphere: A Communicative Space in the Making?* (Abingdon: Routledge). An edited collection of studies of the prospects for a European public sphere.

McCormick, John, *Europeanism* (Oxford: Oxford University Press, 2010). The last section of this chapter is drawn from arguments made in this book, where more detail can be found on the supporting data and analysis.

Taggart, Paul, and Aleks Szczerbiak (eds), *Opposing Europe? The Comparative Party Politics of Euroscepticism, Vols 1 and 2* (Oxford: Oxford University Press, 2008). The most thorough study yet of euroscepticism.

CHAPTER 18

Public Policy in the EU

PREVIEW

So far in this book we have looked at the history, principles, and the political character, institutions and processes of the European Union, and at how it relates to those who live under its jurisdiction. In this final section of the book we examine what the EU has meant in terms of the policies it has pursued. We will see where the EU has been most active, what influences bear on the policy process and key policy makers, and what difference integration has made in practical terms to the lives of Europeans and to the place of Europe in the world.

Public policy can be defined as whatever governments do (or avoid doing) to address the needs and problems of society. It takes the form of public statements, government programmes, laws, and actions, as well as inertia and avoidance. If it was limited to the formal powers of government and its published objectives then it might be relatively easy to understand and measure, but government and governance are also influenced by informal activities, opportunism, the ebb and flow of political and public interest in policy issues, and simply responding to needs and problems as they present themselves.

Understanding the policy process at the national level is not easy, because of unresolved debates about the personality of government institutions, and about the many pressures that come to bear on the process. At the European level, the challenges are compounded by the failure of political scientists to agree on the character and powers of the EU institutions, by the debates about how those institutions relate to the governments of the member states, and by the competing influences of intergovernmentalism and supranationalism. Matters are further complicated by changes in the rules, membership, powers, priorities, and policy agenda of the EU.

KEY ISSUES

- What are the key legal sources of EU policy?
- Is the policy cycle a realistic and helpful way of understanding policy?
- Is incremental change desirable and/or inevitable, or does it stifle policy?
- What are the costs and benefits of multispeed integration?
- Is there a European democratic deficit, and – if so – does it matter?
- Should the EU institutions be given more of their own budgetary resources, and thus greater policy freedom?

Public policy

The actions taken (or avoided) by governments as they address the needs of society. Policy takes the form of platforms, programmes, public statements, and laws, but is often also driven by crises and opportunities. Its content is influenced by values and ideology, and its development and implementation in the EU is driven by a complex and ever-changing balance between EU institutions, state and local governments, independent agencies, interest groups, the media, public opinion and the international policy environment.

The legal basis of policy

Public policy is a collective term for the actions of government. It describes their approaches to the problems and needs of the societies they govern, and the actions they take to address those problems and needs. When parties or candidates run for office, or when administrators are appointed to manage public programmes, they will typically have a shopping list of issues they plan to address, along with proposals for how to address them. Once in office, they will (theoretically) set out to make the changes they proposed. But they do not always succeed: they may be diverted by other more urgent problems jostling for attention, or find that their proposals lack adequate political support, or find that implementing their policies is more difficult then they anticipated. But whatever the outcome, the courses of action they follow or avoid are collectively and individually understood as their policies. These policies become the defining qualities of governments and their leaders, the reference points by which they are assessed, and the key deciding factor in whether or not they will be returned to another term in office.

Even though there is no European 'government' as such, the EU institutions – as we have seen – are active in designing and implementing approaches to the problems and needs of Europeans in areas ranging from agriculture to competition, trade, the environment, regional policy, and social policy. We know this because the treaties outline their responsibilities, and the institutions publish statements, agendas, action programmes, and policy papers that spell out their goals, interests, positions, and opinions. But having an agenda or a platform is one thing; having the authority to act is quite another, and to pin down the policy responsibilities of the EU, we must first look at its rules. These are found in three main places.

Primary rules

These are found in the treaties, meaning not just the major agreements such as Rome, Maastricht and Lisbon, but also the more minor housekeeping treaties and the treaties of accession signed by incoming member states. As we saw in Chapter 8, these collectively function as something like the constitution of the EU, outlining its general goals and organization, giving insight into the relative powers and responsibilities of the EU institutions and the member states, and providing the framework upon which the development of EU law and policy is based. If this was the end of the story, then life might be relatively simple. But the treaties – like most state constitutions – contain ambiguities, and often lack the detail needed to allow us to be certain about how powers and responsibilities are defined or should be implemented. We saw in Chapter 9 how competence in some areas (including competition, trade and monetary policy in the eurozone) lies almost exclusively with the EU institutions, but how in all other cases there is a division of responsibilities between the EU institutions and the member states.

Secondary rules

These consist of all the laws adopted by the EU, and related judgements handed down by the European Court of Justice, all of them growing out of the framework provided by the treaties. EU law (which was, strictly speaking, Community law until the three-pillar system was abolished by the Lisbon treaty) gives substance to the treaties by converting general goals into particular and more measurable objectives, while Court judgements have helped offset some of the ambiguities in the treaties and in EU law. Another source of secondary rules is the body of international agreements signed by the EU. Until Lisbon, the EU had no legal personality and so could not enter into legal agreements with third parties (only the European Community could do that), but it now has a legal personality (Article 47) so it can sign agreements with international organizations or with non-EU states, although only in policy areas where it has competence, such as trade.

Tertiary rules

Described as such because they are not legally binding (and so are not actually rules at all), these include Recommendations and Opinions issued by the EU, as well as the action programmes, strategies, and declarations of the EU institutions. They also include **green papers and white papers** published by the Commission. The former are exploratory policy documents that make suggestions and invite feedback, while the latter often follow green papers and outline proposals for new EU laws and policies. Recent green papers have dealt with reform of the Common Fisheries Policy, the management of bio-waste, a tobacco-free Europe, diplomatic protection for EU citizens in third countries, public access to EU documents, and mental health. Recent white papers have included proposals for a European climate change policy, a European communication policy (designed to improve the way in which the Commission projects the EU to its citizens), and a European space policy.

These, then, are the formal sources of EU policy. But government and governance both contain heavy doses of informality and unpredictability, nicely summed up in the comment of British Prime Minister Harold Macmillan; when asked by a journalist about the greatest challenge facing a statesman, he replied 'Events, dear boy, events'. Leaders must always expect to have to deal with emergencies and change their policies accordingly. A prime example was offered in April 2010 when a volcano in Iceland erupted, producing clouds of ash that covered most of northern Europe and prompting a decision to close the airspace over most of the EU and cancel thousands of scheduled flights, leaving hundreds of thousands of passengers stranded. Numerous questions were raised after the event about how far the EU was ready to deal with major disruptions to air travel, and there were complaints that the Commission and national transport ministers had been too slow to act, and that air traffic control in Europe was too fragmented. The result included calls to accelerate a pre-existing plan (Single European Sky II) to replace the 27 separate air traffic zones with nine 'airspace blocks', to upgrade and harmonize air traffic control systems across Europe, and to reduce the number of air traffic control centres. These changes might eventually lead to the transfer of air traffic control powers away from the member states to the EU.

● **Green papers and white papers**: Documents published by the EU that test the waters by making suggestions for new policies, the latter being more detailed and specific than the former.

The policy cycle

Understanding public policy is as much an art as a craft, and while numerous models of the process have been proposed (institutional, rational, incremental, elite, public choice and so on), none has won general support. But everyone agrees that policy making is a complex process, and that the EU case has many similarities with national policy systems. In other words, says Richardson (2006), it is 'ugly but familiar'. The most common way of trying to understand policy is to see it in terms of a cycle; while this imposes unrealistic simplicity and logic on a process that is anything but (see Young, 2010), it offers us a guide through the maze. There are five stages in that cycle (see Figure 18.1).

Agenda setting

New laws and policies cannot be adopted without agreement that a need or a problem exists, which in turn means 'deciding what to decide' (Young, 2010, p. 52) and placing the issue on the public agenda. The content of that agenda will be driven by numerous forces and pressures, including economic and social conditions, political leadership, the competing perspectives of political parties and governments, understanding of the causes and effects of problems, changing levels of public interest, and the competing sub-agendas of all the actors involved in EU decision making. Some issues are perpetual – like taxes and employment – because they affect most people most of the time, while others are more transient and will come and go according to changing levels of urgency and public interest. But understanding the dynamics of the EU agenda is critical, because it has a close relationship with the character and reach of European integration (Princen, 2009, p. 5).

The European Council sets the broad agenda by looking at strategic issues relating to the direction of European integration. The Commission is then charged with working to turn general goals into more specific plans of action. Formally, both are influenced and limited by treaty obligations, by the pressures to harmonize national laws and policies in the interests of integration, and by

Figure 18.1 The EU policy cycle

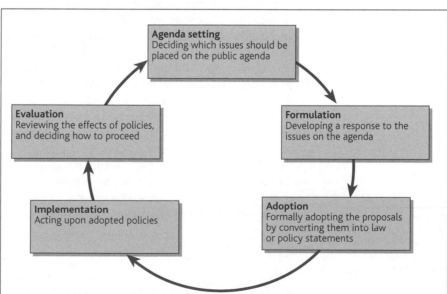

● **Agenda setting**: The process by which the list of problems and issues that require a public response is developed and agreed.

legislative pressures that spark new laws out of requirements or assumptions built into existing laws. Informally, they will be influenced by **policy evolution** (the redefinition of policy responses in light of changing levels of support and understanding), by demands and pressures from other EU institutions (including efforts by the European Parliament to encourage the Commission to launch new initiatives), by political and public opinion in the member states, by the need to respond to emergencies and crises (such as the 2007–10 global economic crisis, or Greece's debt problems in 2009–10), or by the obligations of international law.

The Council and the Commission are driven by quite different sets of pressures. First, while elected national leaders in the Council are driven by ideology and public opinion, and constantly have their eye on the next election, bureaucrats in the Commission are driven more by treaty and legislative obligations. For national leaders, policy success or failure can make the difference between winning or losing office, but, for the career bureaucrats who shape the details of new EU laws and policies, success or failure has quite different implications. Second, identifying and implementing solutions at the national level is less difficult than at the European level, where the sheer variety of the needs, values, priorities, and opinions of different member states makes it harder to reach agreement on the existence or causes of problems, or the potential effects of different policy alternatives.

Formulation

Assuming that there is agreement on the existence of a problem or a need, a response must be developed. This will involve launching studies, drawing up new laws, publishing plans of action, announcing new policy initiatives, or – looking at the bigger picture – making changes to the treaties. In most cases it will also involve more public spending, which presents its own set of challenges. Conversely, policy makers may be unable to decide how to respond, or may drag their feet, swayed by the sheer complexity of a problem, by doubts about its cause and the best response, or by the lack of political and public agreement or support. This has long been a problem with climate change, for example; supporters of action argue that the science is clear, the problem is pressing, and immediate action is needed, but opponents argue that the science is inconclusive, that action may cause undesirable economic or social side-effects, and that there is no point in wealthy industrialized countries taking action without China, India and other newly industrializing powers going along.

Logically, it would make sense to study and understand the causes and dimensions of a problem, and to list all possible options with their relative costs and benefits before taking action. But while policy makers will often make heroic efforts in this direction, they will always disagree over cause and response because of their different biases and values. What, for example, causes poverty, and what is the best way of addressing it? Are poor people just lazy and unambitious, or are they the victims of structural economic and societal problems? Policy makers will also often be faced with emergencies that make it difficult always to give much thought to the best responses, and will often be unsure about the consequences of following a particular path of action. The result is that policymaking is often driven by intuition, opportunism, or – in the famous

● **Policy evolution**: The process by which the goals of public policy change according to new political and economic pressures, improved understanding, and new levels of public support and interest.

Figure 18.2 The EU policy structure

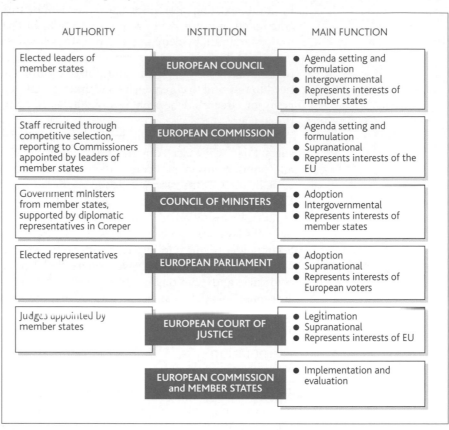

words of the American scholar Charles Lindblom (1959) – simply 'muddling through'.

Responsibility for policy formulation at the European level lies mainly with the Commission, because of its monopoly over the process of drafting proposals for new laws and policies. But the Commission does not work in a vacuum, and engages with numerous external actors in the design of law and policy, and has its choices limited by the extent of its authority. A phenomenon it has championed since the early 1990s is the **open method of coordination**. Endorsed by the European Council in 2000, this contrasts with the 'hard' setting of binding legal norms by basing policymaking on a 'soft' combination of cooperation, reciprocal learning, and the voluntary participation of member states (see Heidenreich and Bischoff, 2008). It is used mainly in policy areas such as health care, education and pensions where the EU has limited competence, and has also been at the heart of the efforts since 1997 to promote a European Employment Strategy (see Rhodes, 2010).

Adoption

Once a new law or policy has been drafted, it must be formally adopted (or rejected). The focus here is on the Council of Ministers and the European

● **Open method of coordination**: A procedure by which EU member states are encouraged to cooperate and agree on voluntary action in policy areas where the EU institutions have limited formal competence.

Illustration 18.1
The Policymakers

Three of the leading players in the EU policy process: the president of the European Parliament (Jurzy Buzak), the president of the European Commission (José Manuel Barroso), and the president of the European Council (Herman van Rompuy).

Parliament, and their role under the ordinary legislative procedure as the joint institutions of decision. Once again, though, they do not work in a vacuum; the Council will be driven by the opinions of member state governments, and Parliament cannot ignore the views of voters. The member state holding the presidency of the Council of Ministers also plays a role, because it wants to make sure that as much business as possible is successfully concluded during its term. This in turn depends on the resources the presidency is prepared to bring to bear, as well as the backlog of unfinished business it inherits from its predecessor, and on the prevailing political climate.

The distinction between formulation and adoption is not clear, because numerous changes to law and policy can be made as proposals go back and forth between the Council and Parliament. Here, the negotiating styles of the representatives of each member state come into play, which depend in turn on the attitude of the home government towards European integration. For example, while Britain has a reputation as a lukewarm European, it also takes its obligations to international agreements seriously, and its negotiators will work hard to mould laws and policies that they believe Britain can implement. By contrast, Greek and Italian negotiators are well-known for often taking a less focused approach. Combined with the relative slowness and inefficiency of their national bureaucracies, this helps explain why – as we saw in Chapter 10 – the Greek and Italian governments have the worst record in the EU when it comes to being taken to the European Court of Justice for infringements of EU law.

Implementation

It is tempting to assume that once a new law or policy has been adopted, it will be translated into practical change on the ground in relatively short and painless order. But even at this late stage there may be political or bureaucratic resistance, and policies can be reinterpreted and redefined (Knill, 2006). Unanticipated problems may arise, including a lack of political agreement or will, difficulties within the institutions responsible for implementation, resistance from the subjects of policy (people, corporations, public agencies, and governments), bureaucratic lethargy or inefficiency, inadequate funding, a redefinition of priorities as a result of changed circumstances or new data, and conflicting interpretations of the content and goals of policies.

The Commission is responsible for overseeing implementation, but it must work through national bureaucracies, whose efficiency and commitment varies from one member state to another, and from one national department to another. Because the Commission has neither the staff nor the resources to follow progress on every piece of legislation, it relies heavily on individuals and interest groups to keep an eye on their home governments and to draw public attention to any foot-dragging, as well as on the European Court of Justice to issue favourable judgements where the Commission decides to take legal action against a member state. The quality of implementation (and of policymaking in general) has also been helped by the creation of the specialized agencies reviewed in Chapter 14, which generate data and are in a strong position to monitor the effects of policy.

Evaluation

Continuing to think systematically (which is not always a reflection of reality in the policy world), the final stage in the policy cycle involves deciding whether or not a law or policy has worked. If the root causes of a problem are clear, if the problem is relatively contained and visible, if targets and dates were included in the policy response, and if independent assessments are available (a series of big 'ifs'), then the link between cause and effect might be measurable. But in most cases it is impossible to be certain of the causes of a problem, or to be sure which actions result in which consequences. Take, for example, attempts to reform EU economic performance under the failed Lisbon Strategy of 2000, which was replaced in 2010 by the Europe 2020 Strategy (see Chapter 19). The problem (sluggish economic growth) was fairly clear, but opinion was divided on the causes (was it too much regulation, too few efforts to open up the marketplace, or too little investment in research and development?), on why the Lisbon Strategy failed, and on how far those failures might be addressed under the Europe 2020 Strategy.

The most immediate responsibility for evaluation lies with the member states and the Commission, but the European Parliament, the member states, interest groups, the media, and ordinary Europeans will often want their say. And, given that success has a thousand fathers while failure is an orphan, and that government institutions will rarely admit their mistakes for fear of losing funding and influence, evaluation is far from a value-neutral process. The final decision on whether laws and policies should be continued, adjusted, or abandoned, is – as a result – more often about changes in levels of political support and limits on spending as it is of a well-considered assessment of how a particular policy option has worked out. Since 2002 the Commission has been pursuing a Better Regulation initiative designed to simplify and improve law-making by better assessing the impact of regulations, by reducing red tape, and by looking more closely at alternatives to regulation.

The qualities of EU policy

All policy systems, whether at the local, state, or international level, have their own distinctive qualities. These are based on a combination of the powers and responsibilities of the institutions involved, and of the political, economic, and social environment in the communities for which the policies are being developed. For example, policy in a progressive and democratic state such as Sweden will be quite different in character from policy in an authoritarian state such as North Korea.

The clues to such qualities can be found in a combination of the formal and the informal. Formally, policy is driven by institutional rules: what the policy actors are allowed to do, and not allowed to do, according to the existing body of constitutions (or treaties), laws, and policies. It will also be influenced by the relative powers of the institutions involved, and their different bases of power (the Commission is a European bureaucracy, the Council of Ministers is driven by national interests, the EP represents the voters, and so on). Informally, policy is driven by circumstances, by changing needs and opportunities, by crisis, and by the balance of pressures brought to bear by all the parties interested in policy, including (in the case of the EU) the member states, the EU institutions, interest groups, corporations, political parties, foreign governments, and ordinary citizens. With these thoughts in mind, we can identify at least six main features of the EU policy process.

Compromise and bargaining

Democratic politics is driven by compromise, or the need to blend multiple competing opinions into a decision on a course of action. No-one will ever have entirely their own way, because policymaking demands discussion and the striking of bargains, and the parties involved will bring their own priorities, preferences, perspectives, and biases to the table. This is particularly true of the coalition governments found in most EU states, where participating parties will routinely be forced into compromises, and of federal systems such as Austria, Belgium and Germany, where powers are divided between national and subnational government. In the case of the EU – where power is not always clearly defined, and where the 'government' is effectively a coalition of member states – the challenges of achieving compromise are that much greater.

Political games

Politics is all about struggles for power and influence, with each of the actors involved trying to press its views on the others and win maximum advantage. In many senses it is a game, or even a sport, with individuals or teams vying against one another for victory. Just as there are many different agendas at work in the EU, so there are many different games constantly under way. Peters (1992, pp. 106–7) describes three sets of interconnected games – those between the member states, the EU institutions, and the directorates-general within the Commission – but there are many more, including those played by groups of member states pursuing shared interests, by interest groups within the member states playing off the EU institutions against their own national governments, by party groups within the European Parliament, and by the EU and the member states as they try to define their changing relative positions in the international system.

Incrementalism

Policymaking rarely involves dramatic departures, which is why (in describing the actions of leaders) *brave* and *radical* are often seen as code words for *risky* and *foolhardy*. Instead, policy is usually based on **incrementalism**, where new initiatives build on what came before, the only distinction being just how much of a change of direction is involved. Political leaders routinely promise change and new approaches when running for office, but they inherit pre-existing laws and policies, and while they may amend or overturn them, or let them fade away through inattention, they will usually take a cautious approach to change. Few systems of governance are slower or more cautious than the EU; even the most substantial policy initiatives – new treaties, enlargement, or the agreements to develop common foreign and defence policies – build on what has come before. The intergovernmental qualities of the EU mean that member states and EU institutions can rarely take the initiative without wide conferral. So long does it sometimes take to reach agreement that the EU policy process has often been accused of inertia.

Another dimension of incrementalism is path dependence, or the idea that policy decisions on new problems will be influenced to some extent by decisions taken in the past. The Commission faces a particular form of such dependence in the sense that many 'new' EU laws are not really all that new, but are simply a recasting of existing legislation, or so-called daughter directives designed to add more specific goals to earlier framework directives. (A 2000 framework directive on water quality, for example, outlined the general need to improve water quality; later daughter directives went into more detail on how this would happen.)

Multispeed integration

Ideally, all the partners in a shared enterprise will move ahead at the same pace and in the same direction. But while this is usually true of states (although in federations the partners will sometimes adopt different policies in areas where they have authority), it is not always true of the EU, which has seen many instances of **multispeed integration**. The assumption in the six-member EEC was that nothing would be done without the agreement of all member states, but as membership expanded so the dynamic changed; not all states always found themselves with the same goals in mind. As a result, initiatives were taken among sub-groups of states, while individual states negotiated opt-outs in areas where the majority wanted to move ahead. For example: Britain at first opted out of the Social Charter, Britain and Ireland have not joined the Schengen Agreement, several EU member states have not adopted the euro, and only those states with large militaries and no concerns about neutrality have been active in developing a common defence policy.

At a more focused level, an important feature of policy in the EU is **derogation**. This is an arrangement by which a member state is excused from imple-

● **Incrementalism**: A method of developing policy through small and often unplanned changes rather than through more radical or wholesale change.

● **Multispeed integration**: Integration pursued by groups of member states with common or shared interests, as distinct from the idea that all member states should move together with the same goals.

● **Derogation**: A partial repeal or abrogation of a law, allowing an EU member state to apply a law differently, or giving it longer to meet a deadline.

menting a specific part of a law or a treaty, or is allowed to apply it differently, or is given longer to achieve implementation. Derogations are usually allowed where a group of people affected by a new law or policy have unique needs, or where there are economic or political problems that call for flexibility. For example, Cyprus, Malta and several eastern European countries were given extensions to meet some of the targets on free movement of people, goods and services, and to meet some of the requirements of EU competition law. Another example: in 2010 Bulgaria asked for a derogation from the target under the Europe 2020 Strategy calling on member states to spend three per cent of their GDP on research and development. Bulgaria was spending just 0.15 per cent of its GDP on research and felt it could probably achieve a target of no more than two per cent at most (EurActiv.com, 28 May 2010).

Spillover

This has been a central part of the process of policymaking in the EU from the beginning. It might be also be described – borrowing from descriptions of American military ventures – as 'mission creep', where a project goes beyond its original goals as new needs and opportunities arise. Where the European Coal and Steel Community had limited and precise interests, and the European Economic Community focused on the common market, competition, agriculture, trade and fisheries, a combination of practical need, economic realities, opportunism, and political pressure saw the policy responsibilities of the EEC and then the EU expand into numerous new areas – a process that continues today. As the American scholar Aaron Wildavsky once put it, policy can become its own cause in the sense that the actions of organizations can often lead to ever larger numbers of unanticipated consequences (Wildavsky, 1979, p. 62). This has been at the heart of eurosceptic complaints about the reach of integration.

Elitism and the democratic deficit

The EU has long been criticized as elitist, with too many decisions being taken by 'unaccountable' European bureaucrats and by the leaders of the member states, without sufficient reference to public opinion. The use of national referendums, the growing powers of the European Parliament, and the rise of interest group lobbying have all helped make the policy process more open, but the **democratic deficit** (the lack of institutional openness and direct accountability in EU institutions) remains a problem and a topic of debate. This led to the famous quip that if the European Community applied for membership of itself, it would not be admitted on the grounds that it did not conform to the democratic principles outlined in the Treaty of Rome (reported in British House of Commons debates, 29 November 1990).

How far the deficit exists, however, and how much it poses a problem, depends on how we understand the EU (see Debate on the democratic deficit). Although its critics often describe the EU with terms such as 'elitist', 'secretive' and 'remote', and while the lack of democratic accountability was once considered to be a 'crisis of legitimacy' (Franklin, 1996, p. 197), others are not so sure. Moravcsik (2002), for one, argues that concern for the deficit is misplaced, because the EU institutions are constrained by constitutional checks and

● **Democratic deficit**: The gap between the powers transferred to the EU institutions and the ability of European citizens to influence the decisions they take.

Debating . . .
Does the democratic deficit matter?

YES	NO
Other than through the European Parliament, European citizens as a whole have no direct representation in the meeting rooms and corridors of the EU institutions, many of whose meetings are not open to the public.	The EU is a confederation, which means it is a union of states in which the governments of the states work together to make decisions, representing the interests of their citizens. There is no need for direct representation of citizens within the EU institutions.
If the EU is to be taken more seriously by its citizens, and its work better understood, then they must have a better idea of their stakes in the process of integration. This is less likely to happen so long as they are not given more direct influence over the membership and decisions of the EU institutions.	The interests of European voters are adequately represented in the European Parliament, whose powers over law-making offset and balance the Council of Ministers. The EP can also place pressure on the Commission to launch policy initiatives.
As long as European leaders feel that they have only limited direct accountability to the European citizenry as a whole, rather than their own national constituencies, they will continue to be driven by national rather than European interests, are likely to continue to often disagree over key issues, and the EU will have less credibility and influence as a global actor.	The governments of the member states are elected, and they either send representatives to the EU institutions (European Council, Council of Ministers) or appoint the leaders of those institutions (European Commission, European Court of Justice). So EU citizens have both direct and indirect representation.
	Public interests are also represented through the work of the European Court of Justice and the European Court of Human Rights, through national referendums (several of which have resulted in changes to policy goals), through the work of interest groups, through the work of the European Ombudsman, and through the (as yet untested) option of citizen's initiatives.

balances, including 'narrow mandates, fiscal limits, super–majoritarian and concurrent voting requirements and separation of powers'. On balance, he concludes, 'EU policy-making is, in nearly all cases, clean, transparent, effective and politically responsive to the demands of European citizens', and 'the EU redresses rather than creates biases in political representation, deliberation and output'. Follesdal and Hix (2006) disagree, arguing that opposition to the leadership elites and policy status quos is an essential feature of the practice of democracy, that political competition is an essential vehicle for opinion formation, and that what is missing from the EU is an electoral contest for political leadership at the European level.

The EU budget

There are few influences on the public policy process quite so important as the budget. Most government action costs money, and the impact of policies will often depend on where funds are raised (particularly the balance between taxes

Figure 18.3 The EU budget, 2011

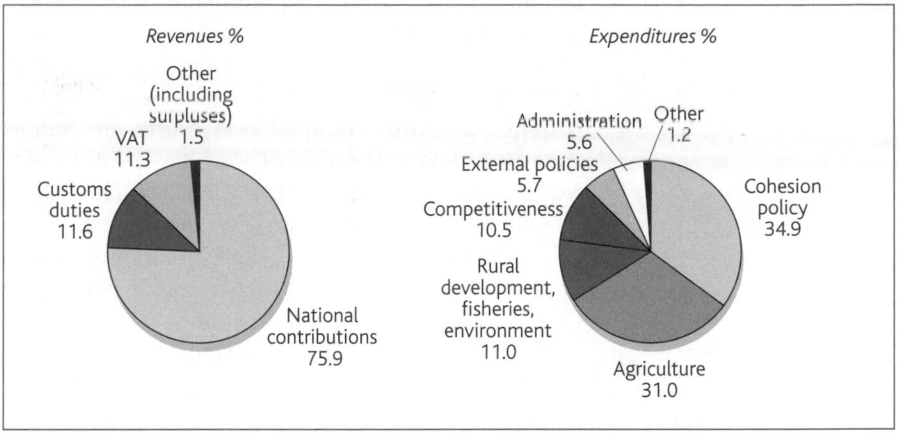

Source: European Commission at http://ec.europa.eu/budget (retrieved August 2010).

and borrowing), the kinds of activities that are taxed, where funds are spent, the efficiency of spending, and the relative amounts spent on different activities. Take, for example, the Common Agricultural Policy: for decades, more Community funds were spent on agricultural subsidies than on any other area of policy (the CAP share was as high as 75 per cent of Community spending in the late 1970s). This not only had important consequences for European farming, and for the relative influence of farming and non-farming communities, but also diverted spending away from other activities, such as regional development.

There are two major defining features of the EU budget.

- It is surprisingly small. In spite of popular misconceptions about large and wasteful EU spending, the budget in 2011 was just under €143 billion, based on a limit of 1.24 per cent of the combined gross national income of the 27 member states. This worked out at about €290 per person in the EU, and was slightly less than the amount budgeted that year for just one government department in just one EU member state: Britain's Department of Work and Pensions.

- It must be balanced. There is no EU debt, so the EU is spared the problems that normally accompany debts (such as interest payments). In this regard the EU stands in contrast to many of its member states, which have long carried national budget deficits, most of which were made worse by increased borrowing and spending during the 2007–10 global economic crisis.

● **National contributions**: The typical method for funding international organizations, based on financial contributions by their member states. In the case of the EU, these are calculated according to gross national income.

● **Own resources**: Independent sources of income for the EU, generated mainly out of policy areas controlled by the EU rather than the member states.

In spite of its modesty and relative orderliness, the EU budget has long been at the heart of political conflict, much of it driven by the core question of monetary independence: how much should the EU depend on **national contributions** from the member states (which give the states leverage over the European institutions) and how far should the EU be allowed to have its **own resources** (independent sources of revenue, which would give the European institutions greater freedom of action)? (For a survey of EU budgetary battles, see Laffan and Lindner, 2010, p. 214ff.) To this debate have been added questions over the relative role of EU institutions in the budgetary process, and problems generated by efforts in some member states to give as little as possible while taking back as much as possible.

The European Coal and Steel Community had its own (very limited) income, raised by a levy on producers. With the creation of the EEC, the budgetary structure shifted to national contributions, which were calculated roughly on the basis of size, so that France, Germany, and Italy each contributed 28 per cent of the EEC budget, Belgium and the Netherlands just under 8 per cent each, and Luxembourg 0.2 per cent. The first major political battle broke out in 1965 when the Commission and Parliament both tried to win more control over the budget but came up against Charles de Gaulle's concerns about national sovereignty and protecting French farmers; the result was the 1965 empty chair crisis (see Chapter 5). But the pressures for reform did not go away, and agreements reached between 1970 and 1975 led to a switch to revenues raised from own resources: customs duties, agricultural levies, sugar contributions, a fixed-rate portion of value added tax (VAT) receipts, and a fixed-rate levy on gross national income.

The new structure created several dilemmas: two-thirds of spending went on agricultural subsidies (which grew as European farmers produced more), revenue from customs duties was falling in tandem with reductions in the Community's external tariffs, revenue from agricultural levies fell as the Community became more self-sufficient in food production, and income from VAT slowed because consumption was falling as a percentage of the Community's GDP (Shackleton, 1990, pp. 10–11). At the same time, several member states were unwilling to raise the limit on the EC's own resources, and the Community could not make up any shortfalls by running a deficit or borrowing. Matters were brought to a head in the early 1980s by one of the most famous political conflicts in the history of the European Community: the campaign by British Prime Minister Margaret Thatcher to renegotiate British contributions to the Community budget.

With its relatively small farming sector and its relatively large import bill, the UK paid more into the EC budget through tariffs and received less back than most other member states. A 1970 agreement reflecting the interests of the six founder states (Laffan and Lindner, 2010, p. 215) had fixed the budgetary rules before Britain became a member, but few could have anticipated Thatcher's position. She saw CAP as a wasteful distortion of free markets based on a Franco-German compromise, and as an example of profligate spending that flew in the face of her attempts to cut public spending at home. Determined to shake things up, she demanded change at her first European Council meeting in June 1979 (in a statement wrongly but colourfully quoted as 'I want my money back'), but it would be June 1984 before a settlement was reached that won a rebate for Britain while also marking a step forward in reforming Community spending on agriculture (Dinan, 2004, pp. 181–3, 186–9).

With the Community on the brink of insolvency, its was decided to raise the ceiling on own resources to 1.4 per cent of VAT, and more reforms agreed by the European Council in February 1988 resulted in a shift away from annual (and often politically bruising) debates about the budget to the more orderly agreement of multi-year packages known as 'financial perspectives'.

**Illustration 18.2
Thatcher demands her
money back**

Meetings of the European
Council in the early 1980s
had to wrestle with
demands by Margaret
Thatcher (*pictured centre*)
for a renegotiation of
British contributions to the
Community budget.

Decision-making follows roughly the same path as EU law, with the proposed budget being developed by the Commission, debated and amended by the Council of Ministers and Parliament, and then implemented by the Commission under the watchful eyes of the Court of Auditors. Behind this simplified outline there is intensive bargaining and literally thousands of management decisions are taken involving EU institutions and every layer of government in the member states from the national to the local. The last round led to the fourth package, running from 2007 to 2013, in which revenues come from three main sources:

● Nearly 76 per cent come from member states according to national levels of economic productivity (up from 43 per cent of revenues in 2003, and 70 per cent in 2007). Each member state makes a contribution that is roughly in proportion to its GDP (see Figure 18.4).
● Nearly 12 per cent come from duties collected on imports from non-member states under the common external tariff, and from agricultural levies.
● Revenues from VAT account for just over 11 per cent, down from 38 per cent in 2003 and 15 per cent in 2007.

In terms of where the funds are spent, the EU once broke spending down by area, so that (in 2006, for example) nearly 47 per cent of spending went on agriculture, 30 per cent on the structural funds, nearly 9 per cent on 'internal policies', 5 per cent on external actions, and 6 per cent on administration. Since then, the listing has been changed to take the focus away from potentially controversial policy areas (mainly agricultural spending) to policy goals. EU expenses (like those of almost all budgets) consist of a combination of mandatory payments for which it is committed (agricultural subsidies, for example) and discretionary payments where there is more flexibility (such as spending on regional or energy policy). In 2010, spending was broken down as follows:

● 42 per cent (€59.5 billion) went to the 'preservation and management of natural resources', a new collective concept for spending on agriculture (nearly €44 billion), rural development, fisheries, and the environment.

Figure 18.4 National contributioms to the EU budget

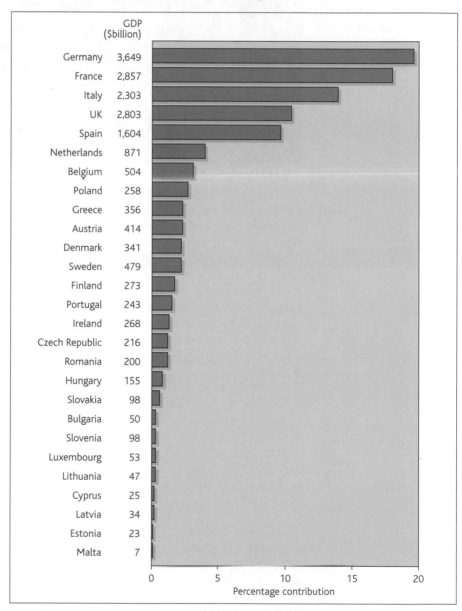

Source: Budget data from European Commission at http://ec.europa.eu/budget (retrieved February 2010). GDP data (for 2008) from World Bank at http://www.worldbank.org (retrieved June 2010).

- 35 per cent (nearly €50 billion) went on cohesion policy, a new term for the old structural funds aimed at encouraging development in the poorer parts of the EU (see Chapter 22). The proportion of EU spending in this area has almost tripled since the mid-1970s.
- 10.5 per cent (nearly €15 billion) went on promoting 'competitiveness for growth and employment', meaning mainly research and development, trans-European energy and transport networks, and education.
- 5.7 per cent (just over €8 billion) was spent on activities promoting the EU 'as a global player', including development aid, spending under the Common Foreign and Security Policy, and €1.6 billion in pre-accession assistance to eastern European states with aspirations to EU membership.
- 5.6 per cent (€7.9 billion) was spent on administration, including salaries and pensions for EU staff, buildings, and infrastructure. Just under half of that went to the European Commission. One of the most common misconceptions about the EU among ordinary Europeans is that spending in this area is much higher than it is.
- 0.7 per cent (about €1 billion) was spent on 'freedom security and justice' (police cooperation, drug control, crime prevention, and asylum policies), and a further 0.5 per cent (about €700 million) was spent on 'citizenship' (culture, identity, health, consumer safety, and civil protection).

Most notably, the share of spending on cohesion that went to the twelve newest members of the EU crossed the 50 per cent barrier for the first time in 2010 (much of it in the form of agricultural spending). The budget was also impacted by the European Economic Recovery Plan, a stimulus package put together in response to the global economic crisis and involving a transfer of EU spending into infrastructure projects.

SUMMARY

- Public policy is whatever governments do (or avoid doing) to address society's needs. It takes the form of platforms, programmes, public statements, and laws, but is often also driven by crises, emergencies and opportunities.
- Formally, policymaking in the EU is driven by primary rules found in the treaties, secondary rules in the form of laws adopted by the EU and judgements handed down by the European Court of Justice, and tertiary 'rules' in the form of action programmes, strategies, declarations and other activities.
- Informally, there are numerous influences on policy, and numerous models have been developed to help understand the system.
- One approach is to see policy as a cycle, beginning with the setting of agendas and moving through formulation, adoption, implementation, and evaluation.
- EU policy, like all democratic policymaking, is driven by bargaining and the search for compromise, by political games among interested parties, by elitism, and by incremental rather than radical change.
- Policymaking in the EU also has several unique features, including multispeed integration, spillover, and the democratic deficit. But opinion on the significance of the latter is divided.
- The EU budget is small and yet it has been the subject of repeated political squabbles over the years. These have abated since a 1988 agreement to replace annual budgets with five-year budget packages.
- Most revenues come from national contributions from the member states, and most spending goes to agriculture and regional development.

KEY TERMS AND CONCEPTS

Agenda setting

Democratic deficit

Derogation

Green papers and white papers

Incrementalism

Multispeed integration

National contributions

Open method of coordination

Own resources

Policy evolution

Public policy

FURTHER READING

Lindner, Johannes (2006), *Conflict and Change in EU Budgetary Politics* (Abingdon: Routledge). One of the more recent of the surprisingly few full-length studies of the EU budget.

Richardson, Jeremy (ed.) (2006), *European Union: Power and Policy-Making*, 3rd edn (Abingdon: Routledge). An edited collection of studies of EU policy-making process, including chapters on the role of different EU institutions in the process.

Wallace, Helen, Mark A. Pollack, and Alasdair R. Young (eds) (2010), *Policy-Making in the European Union*, 6th edn (Oxford: Oxford University Press). Another edited collection, this one focusing on specific policy areas, including agriculture, the single market, competition, and social policy.

CHAPTER 19

Economic Policy

PREVIEW

European integration has long focused on economic matters. The core goal of the Treaty of Rome was the construction of a single market, the Single European Act and the Maastricht treaty were attempts to complete the single market and to prepare for a single currency, and many of the most taxing European political struggles have been about subsidies to agriculture, building common trade and competition policies, dealing with unemployment and labour immobility, and (more recently) how to respond to the global economic crisis and pressures on the euro.

Economic integration was intended to generate wealth and opportunity in order to help Europe recover from the ravages of war, while also building enough ties of mutual interest and dependence to make future war unthinkable. In this sense, it succeeded: Europe today is more peaceful and prosperous than at any time in its history, and the EU is the world's biggest and wealthiest capitalist marketplace, its biggest trading power, its biggest market for corporate mergers and acquisitions, and its biggest source of foreign direct investment. Meanwhile, the euro has become one of the world's three leading international currencies, leading to speculation about what it might mean for the balance of global monetary power.

But many problems remain. These include persistent unemployment, slow economic growth, too little progress on the liberalization of labour markets, the impact of a declining and aging population, EU dependence on imported oil and natural gas, and claims that Europe's economic possibilities have sometimes been more rhetorical than real. An attempt under the 2000 Lisbon Strategy to make the EU the world's most competitive and dynamic economy within ten years fell flat, forcing an extension to 2020, with critics charging that too few EU governments were prepared to make the necessary reforms.

KEY ISSUES

- Is Europe's poor economic reputation deserved?
- How do the changes achieved as a result of the single market programme weigh up with the problems that remain?
- What are the remaining barriers (political, legal, economic and social) to the completion of the single market?
- How wise was the EU response to the global economic crisis?
- Is the rise of European multinationals as impressive as it sounds?
- Is the EU fulfilling its expected role as an economic superpower?

The outlines and limits of economic policy

Economic policy is typically at the top of the public policy agenda in every free market system, and is often the deciding factor in determining which governments are elected to office and how they fare in public opinion. And yet the dynamics and principles of economic policy are poorly understood, even by professional economists; hence the quip by Laurence J. Peter (author of the 'Peter Principle') that an economist is an expert who will know tomorrow why the things he predicted yesterday didn't happen today. If economists truly understood how economies functioned, then they would be able to predict, correct for, and explain downturns in the marketplace. But the 2007–10 global economic crisis caught most unawares, and even today there is no final agreement on either its causes or on what long-term impact the corrective action taken by governments will have. As for ordinary Europeans, they react instinctively to problems such as unemployment, inflation and higher taxes, but are rarely equipped to place them in a wider context.

Broadly defined, **economic policy** deals with the production, distribution, and consumption of goods and services. Although it deals mainly with matters relating to money, markets, production, supply, costs, and efficiency, it has implications for almost every other sector of policy. It can have an effect on environmental quality, crime rates, education, national security, public health, tourism, scientific research, land use, transport, housing, and every kind of public service. More specifically, it can be divided into four key sub-fields: trade policy (covered in Chapter 24), competition policy (covered later in this chapter), and fiscal and monetary policy.

Fiscal policy is concerned with budgets: how government raises revenues, how it spends that money, and what effect this has on deficits, taxes, and the broader fortunes of the economy. Governments raise revenues mainly through taxation, borrowing (by issuing bonds, for example), drawing on reserves, or selling assets such as land and licences to minerals. Governments can take one of three main stances on fiscal policy: an expansionary stance means that spending exceeds revenue (which has the effect of building debt), a contractionary stance means that revenue exceeds spending, and a neutral stance keeps spending and revenue in balance. Fiscal policy is ultimately concerned with how governments use the balance between income and spending to manipulate the economy, for example by encouraging growth and creating jobs. Keynesian economists argue that increased spending and lowered tax rates are the best ways to stimulate demand, while classical economists argue that budget deficits increase demand for credit in the financial markets, lowering demand.

For its part, monetary policy (see Chapter 20 for more details) is also concerned with the growth and stability of an economy, but from the perspective of money supply: how government controls the value of a currency and deals with problems such as inflation by raising or lowering interest rates (the cost at which money can be borrowed). Policy can again be expansionary or contractionary, depending on the supply of money; the former involves lowering interest rates during a recession in an effort to encourage job creation, while the latter involves reducing the money supply or taking on inflation by raising interest rates. Where fiscal policy tends to be managed by executives in national

● **Economic policy**: Policy dealing with the management of goods and services, including productivity, consumption, money supply, and competition.

● **Fiscal policy**: Policy dealing with budgets: how and where government revenues are raised and how and where public funds are spent.

CONCEPT

Customs union

An arrangement under which all tariffs, duties and other restrictions on trade among participating countries are removed, and a common external tariff is agreed so that all goods coming into the union from third parties are subject to the same costs. Theoretically it leads to trade creation among members of the union, because costs are lower than those on imported goods subject to tariffs. The European customs union was declared complete in 1968, but routine customs checks at internal borders remained until 1993.

systems of government, monetary policy is usually managed by central banks with often independent powers.

One of the structural problems faced by the EU, which became all too clear during the Greek debt crisis in 2010, was that while the European Central Bank (ECB) has a high degree of control over monetary policy in the eurozone, the EU institutions have little direct control over fiscal policy. And because the EU budget must be balanced, the Commission cannot use revenues and spending to help it deal with EU-wide economic problems. In other words, responsibility for fiscal and monetary policy – on which there is usually a high degree of coordination at the national level – is divided at the EU level, with fiscal policy resting with the member states, monetary policy divided between the ECB and the central banks of states outside the eurozone, and the one obvious coordinating body (the European Commission) left with few powers beyond its limited options as a mediator and confidence builder. The Greek debt crisis underlined the importance of EU leaders working together on core economic issues and giving financial markets a better idea of who is in charge. Achieving this, though, will be no easy task.

The single market

The building of a single European market – an area within which there is free movement of people, money, goods, and services (see Chapter 5) – has long been at the heart of European integration, has absorbed more political energy than any other item on the European agenda, and has been one of the few EU programmes on which supporters and opponents of integration have been able to agree. It has also probably meant more in real, practical terms to Europeans than almost anything else the EU has achieved (except perhaps adoption of the euro). Certainly it has had a more easily measurable effect on their personal choices than, say, policies on foreign relations, agriculture, cohesion, or the environment. At the same time, the pressures of spillover have moved the EU in often unexpected directions, the full implications of the single market having often been learnt on the fly.

The single market project was founded on economic priorities and has had its greatest impact on policies in the areas of trade, competition, and employment. It was the core goal of the Treaty of Rome, but although there was progress in the 1960s and 1970s, it was uneven; tariffs and trade quotas ended in 1968 with completion of the **customs union**, but non-tariff barriers remained a problem, many of them being neither immediately obvious nor visible; they included discriminatory regulations and taxes, efforts by governments to protect national industries, border controls that increased transport costs, and limits on bidding for public contracts (Neal, 2007, p. 129). The 1985 Commission White Paper on the single market (Commission, 1985) identified three main sets of barriers that needed to be removed:

● *Physical barriers* in the form of internal customs and border checks which required that almost everyone had to travel with a passport and sometimes even a visa, and demanded additional paperwork (involving additional time and cost) for the movement of goods across borders. These checks were the most visible and obvious reminders of Europe's internal economic divi-

Economic liberalization

The process of opening up markets through reduced regulation and a removal of other restrictions on competition. This poses universal problems because of the ongoing debate about how much regulation is enough – the fact that there was too little was one of the causes of the 2007–10 global economic crisis. As for the EU, leaders and parties are divided over the extent to which the state should manage the economy, and the long-held desire to protect national corporations and control the movement of migrants has taken a long time to diminish.

sions, and the reason for removing them, noted the White Paper, was 'not one of theology or appearance, but the hard practical fact that the maintenance of any internal frontier controls will perpetuate the costs and disadvantages of a divided market'.

● *Technical barriers* created by concerns about safety, health, environmental, and consumer protection, by different requirements for educational and professional qualifications, and by problems as routine as different electrical currents and designs for electrical plugs. As many as 100,000 different technical regulations and standards may have been in place in the member states before 1986 (Neal, 2007, p. 131). Subject to some conditions, argued the White Paper, there should be a principle of mutual recognition: 'if a product is lawfully manufactured and marketed in one Member State there is no reason why it should not be sold freely throughout the Community' (see Chapter 13).

● *Fiscal barriers* in the form mainly of indirect taxation that caused distortions of competition and artificial price differences. Notable examples included excise duties on petroleum products, tobacco and alcohol, and different rates of value added tax (VAT, a consumption tax assessed on the value added to goods and services as they move through the production process). Consumers noticed the differences as they moved from one member state to another and compared prices. Wine was much cheaper in France than in Britain, and as late as 2002 VAT and duties on beer varied from a low of 12 cents per litre in Germany and Spain to a high of €1.16 in Britain and €1.74 in Finland (Commission, 2002).

As we saw in Chapter 6, mounting economic problems in the 1970s increased the pressure for reform. The EEC's national economies were too fragmented, European companies were losing ground to their American and Japanese competitors, there were mounting trade deficits, levels of inflation and unemployment were too high, and the European marketplace was unable to generate enough new jobs, leading to the coining in 1985 of the term 'Eurosclerosis' (which was borrowed to describe also the lack of political leadership). New ideas and approaches now converged to spark the 'relaunch' of Europe contained in the Single European Act (SEA). Progress on implementing the changes required by the SEA was initially rapid, with cross-border checks coming down, and restrictions on free movement being eased. Decisions by the European Court of Justice also helped, notably the 1974 Dassonville ruling that allowed for challenges to be mounted to national laws that introduced new technical barriers to trade, and the 1979 Cassis de Dijon decision which meant that almost any products accepted in one member state should be accepted in all others.

But while **economic liberalization** has been at the heart of work on the single market, all has not been well. The market for services has opened up more slowly than the market for goods, for example, and breaking down national markets in financial services and transport has been relatively slow; it is easier for consumers to use credit and debit cards in other countries, and to transfer money across borders, but some restrictions remain. Barriers also continue to be created by national tax systems, and by the slowness with which the market for postal services has been opened up (although the latter is increasingly a moot point given the rise of the internet and e-mail). There are also still some restrictions on free movement, particularly from the newer (and poorer) eastern European states to their western neighbours.

The failures were reflected in the outcome of a much-trumpeted launch in 2000 of the Lisbon Strategy (see Chapter 7), aimed at making the EU 'the most dynamic and competitive knowledge-based economy in the world' within ten years. But it was already clear by 2004 that governments were not moving quickly enough, that the single market programme was beginning to show signs of its age, and that there was insufficient political will to deal with too much regulation, too many protections for workers against dismissal, and too few efforts to open up markets. The EU has also fallen behind in research and development, with expenditure as a percentage of GDP stagnant since the mid-1990s, in contrast to high or growing levels of investment in the United States, Japan, China and South Korea. And there has been an ongoing tension between two models of economic management, pitting the Anglo-Saxon preference for open markets with the continental or Rhenish preference for government intervention.

As a result, the Lisbon Strategy was transformed into the **Europe 2020 Strategy**, which moved the Lisbon deadline to 2020 and focused on innovation, education, sustainable growth, a low-carbon economy, and job creation. Its goals include jobs for at least 75 per cent of the working age population, the investment of at least three per cent of GDP in research and development, the meeting of targets on climate change, a reduction in levels of poverty, and an increase in the number of Europeans completing their high school education and the number completing a degree or a diploma.

Meanwhile, European economies were hard hit by the breaking in 2007 of a global financial crisis that would last into 2010 and has since been dubbed (by Americans if not always by Europeans) the **Great Recession**. European political leaders were quick to blame the United States for sparking the crisis by allowing too much credit to be offered to those unable to pay, and by not providing for enough government regulation of the financial sector. They charged that this was an American problem that did not call for an American-style rescue plan in Europe, and yet many European financial institutions suffered because they had bought American 'toxic assets'. After some indecision, EU governments generally moved in the same direction, bailing out banks and other financial institutions whose collapse might have posed systemic risks to the EU financial system, working to recapitalize the banking system and to protect savers' deposits, raising the minimum guarantee for individual bank deposits, and supporting a stimulus package proposed by the European Commission.

Then came the debt crisis in Greece in early 2010, which again saw EU disagreement over what to do. The Greek government had been borrowing heavily since adopting the euro in 2001, building a budget deficit that left it susceptible to the effects of the Great Recession. With concerns that Greece might default on its debt, or perhaps even leave the euro altogether (or be asked to leave), confidence in the euro fell in early 2010, obliging the Greek government to impose unpopular austerity measures, and EU leaders to think about how far they would be prepared to go to rescue troubled national economies. Other EU states were also struggling to keep their budget deficits under control in 2010: EU rules set a target of three per cent, but Britain, Spain and Ireland were all in the range of 10–12 per cent, and Italy was running at 5 per cent. A

● **Europe 2020 Strategy**: A long-term economic strategy aimed at job creation, improved educational attainment, and sustainable growth.

● **Great Recession**: The international financial crisis that broke in 2007, bringing recession to most advanced economies in 2008–10, and challenging the ability of EU leaders to work together on broad economic problems.

failure to resolve the Greek problem would have left other troubled economies vulnerable. In the event, it was agreed to offer a combination of eurozone and International Monetary Fund loans as a last resort if Greece was unable to raise loans in the open market (see Chapter 20 for more details).

Europe's regional and national economies have been counted out numerous times over the last few decades, earning the continent a reputation – as *The Economist* lamented in March 2010 – for being one 'whose economy is rigid and sclerotic, whose people are work-shy and welfare-dependent, and whose industrial base is antiquated and declining – the broken cogs and levers that condemn the old world to a gloomy future'. Europe's particular needs, it went on, included more open labour markets, more limits on public spending, fewer regulations, reforms to welfare and public education, and more incentives to encourage more women into the workplace. While the US economy (often praised as a model of openness and innovation by *The Economist*) has also been suffering, and emerging states such as Brazil, India and China emerged relatively unscathed from the recession, the EU clearly has much work to do to shake off its unfortunate reputation.

Effects of the single market

For ordinary Europeans, the most practical effect of the single market is freedom of movement. Forty years ago, travelling from one European country to another meant the production of passports and even sometimes visas, and waiting in lines for customs and immigration checks, with limits on how much in the way of goods and money could be taken from one country to another. Forty years before that, borders were often rigorously defended for fear of military invasion. Today, customs and immigration checks are almost entirely gone, and there is little to remind road travellers of state borders beyond signs indicating that they are about to leave one country and enter another. Perhaps nothing is more remarkable than driving across the border between Germany and its four immediate western neighbours; where those borders once had deep military and political significance, and France did all it could to protect itself from German invasion, now there are simply signs indicating passage from one state to another.

Today, with some relatively minor restrictions, a citizen or legal resident of any EU member state has the right to move across borders and to live and work in other member states. They may need to show an identity card or passport, they might have to register with the local authorities, or show that they will not become a burden on the social services of the new country, but they no longer need visas or residence permits, they mainly have the right to be treated the same as a national of the member state, and they can only be expelled on grounds of public policy, public security or public health, and not on economic grounds.

Concerns about the movement of workers from the east to the west following enlargement in 2004–07 led to an agreement that the EU-15 states could temporarily restrict entry of eastern European workers, but on a voluntary basis. Most opted to impose the limits, the most notable exception being the UK, which left its borders open, expecting perhaps no more than 20,000 new arrivals per year after enlargement; it was astonished when it received nearly 450,000

Illustration 19.1
The single market

This sign at the border between Germany and Luxembourg symbolizes one of the most remarkable achievements of European integration: the removal of almost all internal border controls among EU member states.

work permit applications from eastern Europe in the period 2004–06 (Home Office, 2006). The influx gave rise to the creation of the iconic 'Polish plumber' (actually a 2005 invention of French nationalists), representing the influx of cheap labour from the east. But almost all restrictions in the EU-15 have now gone, and by 2008 many of the migrants to Britain had returned home, motivated by recession in the west and improved wages and job opportunities in the east (Pollard *et al.*, 2008).

Not only have the rules on movement across borders changed, but so have the economic and sociological dynamics of migration. Where it was once driven mainly by economic need, with people moving to other countries in search of jobs or better opportunities, and the major flows being from north to south, Europeans are increasingly moving not because they must but because they choose to. Migrants may be looking for a different cultural environment, looking to be educated in a different country, retiring to warmer parts of the EU, being posted by their employer, or looking for a new start in a new country. And where once it was mainly poorer Europeans who were looking to move, today it is as often students, professionals, managers, and retirees.

The binding of the European marketplace has not just meant removing or harmonizing physical, technical and fiscal barriers, but has demanded the building of the infrastructure needed to encourage the flow of people, goods, and services. Recognizing this need, the Commission in 1990 adopted an action plan on the building of **trans-European networks** (TENs) that would encourage the integration of transport, energy supply, and telecommunications systems across the EU. Since then, a list of priority projects has been developed, and changes have come out of a combination of deliberate government policy and incidental economic pressures.

Developments include a Europe-wide transport network based around a set of 30 'priority axes' focused mainly on revitalizing rail transport as a more efficient and environmentally friendly alternative to road and air travel. These axes

● **Trans-European networks**: Construction projects aimed at building an integrated European transport, energy supply, and telecommunications system.

include the Paris–Brussels–Cologne–Amsterdam–London high speed rail system, the Nordic triangle railway/road system, the so-called 'motorways of the sea' (shipping lanes around the coasts of the EU), the completion of an inland waterway system from the North Sea to the Black Sea, a UK/Ireland/Benelux road axis, and high speed rail links through southwest and eastern Europe. A European high-speed train network has also been under construction to connect Europe's major cities, with critical links provided by the 1994 opening of the Eurotunnel under the channel between Britain and France, the 1998 opening of a bridge between Sjaelland and Fyn in Denmark, and the 2000 opening of the Øresund Bridge between Denmark and Sweden.

In conjunction with the European Space Agency, the EU is also developing – so far with mixed results – a global navigation satellite system known as Galileo and intended to be an alternative to (although compatible with) the US-operated Global Positioning System (GPS). GPS was developed by the Americans in the 1970s for military purposes (civilian applications came later), and because the US reserves the right to limit its signal strength, and even to close public GPS access during times of conflict, there are clear incentives for the EU to develop an alternative. Several non-EU countries have joined the Galileo project, including China, India, and South Korea, and there has been talk of Australia, Brazil, Canada, Japan, Mexico, Russia and others joining in the future. The Galileo project was agreed in 2003, but completion has been delayed and the first of 22 satellites needed are not now expected to be completed and launched until 2012 at the earliest. Galileo has also caused concerns in the United States, which worries that enemies could use it for military strikes against the US, and is unsettled by the participation of China.

Meanwhile, the pressure for energy supply networks has grown out of plans for a better integrated and interconnected internal market for gas and electricity supply, for greater liberalization of that market, and for securing the supply of natural gas from Russia. About a quarter of the EU's demand for gas is met by imports from Russia, and much of it comes via pipelines that run through Ukraine. In 2005–06 and again in 2008 disputes broke out when Russia accused Ukraine of falling behind on its payments for gas, and diverting some of the gas intended for the EU. When Russia cut the supply, it meant a reduction in supply also to more than a dozen European countries. The disputes accelerated plans to build a supply pipeline direct from Russia to Germany via the Baltic Sea, and another from Russia to the Balkans via the Black Sea.

The rise of corporate Europe

Before the Second World War, the capitalist world was dominated by European corporations, their successes often based on preferential access to imperial markets. But the postwar years saw European companies losing market share to competition, first from the United States and then from Japan. The new multinationals were more dynamic, invested more in research and development, and had the advantage of large and increasingly wealthy home markets. European business, meanwhile, was typically focused on its own home markets, leading to criticisms that it was nationalistic, hierarchical, conservative, and driven less by quantity than by quality. (For a view from the early 1970s, see Brooke and Remmers, 1972, Chapter 6.)

Focus on . . .
Open skies over the Atlantic

One of the most visible effects of the European single market on business has been the dramatic change that has come to the airline market in recent decades. Where once every European state felt the need to protect and promote its own national flag carrier – Lufthansa in Germany, Iberia in Spain, KLM in the Netherlands, and British Airways and Air France, for example – a combination of economic pressures and privatization has led to a liberalization of the airline market, with loss-making airlines either closing or being taken over, air fares falling, and changes to landing rights under open skies agreements.

In 1992 the Netherlands signed a bilateral agreement with the United States by which each country provided the other with unrestricted landing rights. Although there was initial political resistance in the EU, the pressures for wider agreements grew, and in 2007 the EU–US Open Skies Agreement was signed allowing an EU airline and any US airline to fly between any point within the territory of the other, rather than being limited to the usual major hubs, such as New York, Chicago, Los Angeles, London, Frankfurt, and Paris. EU airlines are also allowed to offer flights between the US and non-EU countries, but while US airlines are allowed to offer flights between EU cities, the same is not allowed for EU airlines in the US – a source of some resentment among EU airline operators.

The agreement came into effect in 2008, the expectation being that it would offer passengers more choices for points of departure and arrival; that it would open up access to airports such as London Heathrow that had previously limited the number of airlines given access; that it might bring down air fares; that it might encourage more competition from economy airlines such as Ireland's Ryanair; and that it might lead to a new round of airline mergers. But progress has been interrupted by the slowdown in the international travel market in the wake of the global economic downturn.

European companies were also discouraged from pursuing **corporate mergers** or takeovers across state borders by capital gains taxes, double taxation on company profits, different legal systems, differences in regulations and standards, and slow progress on building the common market. Among the mergers that took place in the Community in 1966–69, 59 per cent were between or among companies in the same country, 26 per cent were international (and most of those involved American firms), and just 8 per cent involved companies in two or more Community states (European Commission figures quoted by Layton, 1971, p. 3).

With competitiveness and liberalization moving up the EC agenda in the 1980s, the Commission tried to overcome market fragmentation and to wean national governments off their focus on often state-owned 'national champions'. Changes to company laws and regulations made cross-border mergers easier, and the dynamics of the single market increased the pressures for European companies to work harder to profit from new opportunities. They were further encouraged by EC programmes aimed at promoting research in information technology and advanced communications. As a result, there was a surge of takeovers and mergers across European borders (see Figure 19.1), such that the European mergers and acquisitions market is now the biggest in the

● **Corporate merger**: An arrangement by which two or more independent companies fuse their assets and liabilities so as to create a single new company. This should be distinguished from a takeover, where the companies involved continue to exist as separate legal entities.

world. Where once European consumers bought most of their goods and services from companies that were either national, American, or Japanese, they now see more businesses coming into their local community from other European states, and many of those businesses have identities that are increasingly European or international. Among the more notable examples of recent mergers and acquisitions:

- The string of mergers among British, American and Canadian companies since 1989 that has created GlaxoSmithKline, by 2010 the fourth biggest pharmaceuticals company in the world.
- The rise of the Dutch company ING, which by 2009 had become the biggest commercial and savings bank in the world.
- The rise of the Royal Bank of Scotland to become (by 2005) the sixth biggest bank in the world (its position slipping only slightly in the wake of its problems during the global economic crisis).
- A string of mergers and cooperative ventures in the energy market, revolving around EDF and GDF Suez in France and E.ON and RWE in Germany, which has raised concerns about competition because these corporations are vertically integrated in the sense that they both generate and transmit energy, helping them keep prices high.
- A string of changes in the airline industry. Although the closure of Swissair in 2002, the 2003 merger of Air France and KLM, and the 2005 merger of Lufthansa and SWISS generated speculation of more mergers and bankruptcies to come, little actually happened. But the rise of competitive low-cost airlines was only too clear, and by 2009–10 there was more talk of mergers generated by the worsening economics of the airline industry, by growing pressures on national governments not to prop up loss-making flag carriers, and by greater competition from foreign airlines.

One of the more dramatic examples of the building of a pan-European corporation with global reach has been the story of the European Aeronautic Defence and Space Company (EADS). Where Britain, France, Germany and

Figure 19.1 Corporate mergers across European borders

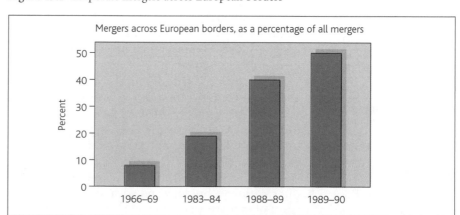

Sources: Based on figures in Owen and Dynes (1989), p. 222; Amin *et al.* (1992); European Commission (1994).

**Illustration 19.2
Airbus**

The European single market has helped encourage the rise of European corporate giants such as Airbus, whose biggest foray into the global aviation market has been the construction of the A380 super-jumbo.

other European states long had a history of national success in aircraft manufacture, economic pressures and competition from the Americans forced a string of mergers, takeovers and closures after the Second World War. National manufacturers realized the need to cooperate, and the result was the creation in 1970 of Airbus Industrie. France, Germany and Britain were the major shareholders, joined in 1971 by Spain. The success of Airbus helped force two major US civilian aircraft manufacturers (Lockheed and McDonnell-Douglas) out of the market, leaving a virtual global duopoly today between Airbus and Boeing. EADS was created in 2000 as a result of a merger between Aérospatiale of France, Daimler-Chrysler Aerospace of Germany, BAE Systems of Britain (which left the consortium in 2006), and CASA of Spain. As well as being the parent company for Airbus, it also develops and markets military aircraft, communications systems, missiles, and – through its 30 per cent share in Arianespace – space rockets and satellites.

One of the effects of the recent history of mergers, most of which were encouraged by the pressures and opportunities created by the single market, has been reclamation of some of the dominant global positions once held by European companies, and lost after the Second World War. In 1969, the *Fortune* magazine list of the world's biggest 400 corporations showed that 238 (nearly 60 per cent) were American while just 108 (27 per cent) were European. By contrast, the 2010 *Fortune* Global 500 list of the world's 500 biggest corporations (by revenues) showed that 159 (32 per cent) were based in the EU and 139 (28 per cent) were from the United States (see Figure 19.2). The 25 biggest corporations in the world in 2010 included Royal Dutch Shell, BP, AXA, ING, Total, Volkswagen, BNP Paribas, Allianz, Carrefour, and ENI. The sheer size and reach of many European companies has helped them benefit from globalization (Hamilton and Quinlan, 2008).

Figure 19.2 The world's biggest corporations, by region

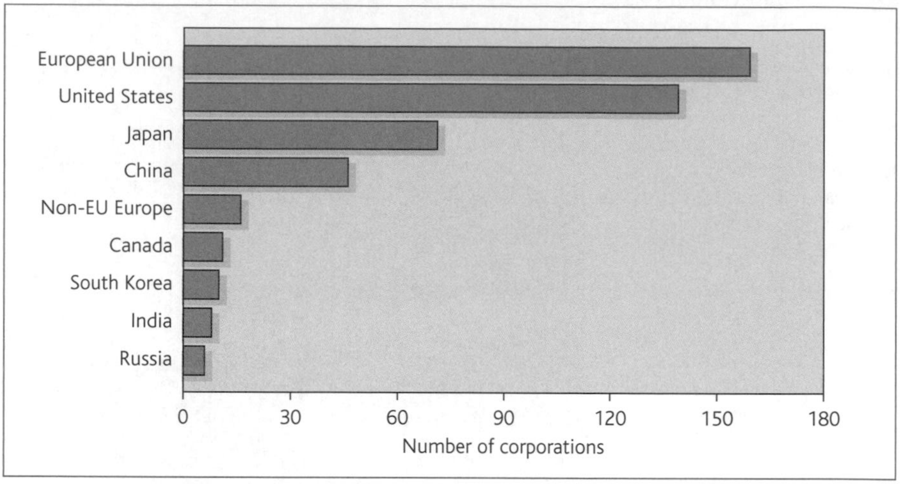

Source: *Fortune* magazine data at CNNMoney.com, http://money.cnn.com/magazines/fortune/global500/2010 (retrieved August 2010).

Competition policy

Adam Smith, the father of capitalism, once warned that although they seldom met together, people working in the same trade had an inclination to conspire against the public and raise prices. There can never be such a thing as a perfectly free and open market, because there will always be unintentional distortions that give one business or industry advantages over another. But other distortions are more deliberate. A group of businesses may form a cartel to corner and control the market, or reach agreements not to compete with one another. Near-monopolies might try to gain an even larger market share by abusing their dominant position to undermine competitors. A business might monopolize the market altogether, in which case it would be able to raise prices, and invest less in product development or good service. And it is not only dominant market share that can lead to distortions; government subsidies, too, can give producers an unfair advantage, and lead to skewed patterns of international trade.

Recognizing these problems, the EU – and, more specifically, the European Commission – has long been engaged in efforts to identify and remove barriers to open market competition. For Cini and McGowan (2009, p. 1), its competition policy, while not perfect, has become perhaps the most supranational of all EU policies and something of a flagship for the EU. And unlike many other policy areas, the Commission not only has the power to fine recalcitrant companies, but also has a global reach and can block mergers or impose fines on foreign companies where there are concerns about wider threats to competition.

It took some time for all this to happen, even though the Treaty of Paris included a lengthy outline of the details of ECSC competition policy, the principles of which were carried over in the Treaty of Rome. The Commission focused initially on restrictive practices, then paid more attention to monopoly control in the 1970s, finally adding a focus on state aids and merger control as the single

● **Competition policy**: Policy aimed at limiting the marketplace distortions created by monopolies, cartels, price-fixing, abuse of dominant position, and market-sharing.

market took hold in the 1980s and 1990s. Changes in the political climate combined with greater institutional confidence in the European Commission to see renewed efforts to promote the liberalization of the single market by preventing abuses such as price fixing and illegal market-sharing, monitoring state subsidies to corporations, and guarding against abuses of dominant position by bigger companies (Wilks, 2005; Cini and McGowan, 2009).

Ironically, the prospects for such abuses were to grow in large part because of the single market. As we saw earlier in this chapter, it took a while for European corporations to take advantage of the single market, but once they did, and began building ever bigger multinationals through mergers and acquisitions, so the opportunities for abuse accelerated. The Commission's directorate-general for competition, once a backwater of Community administration (Büthe, 2007), has since been active in seeking out and ending attempts to dominate the market, making many controversial decisions but also becoming one of the most respected and powerful of all DGs, enjoying a high degree of discretion. It has also become one of the more well-known DGs, helped by the media coverage that mergers often attract, surrounded by what Wilks (2005, p. 120) describes as sometimes 'frenzied political lobbying' that generate 'theatrical shows of Shakespearean proportions'.

As Harrop (2002) suggests, it is rare to find markets dominated by monopolies, the more common reality being duopolies (where two large corporations have the biggest shares, such as Airbus and Boeing) or oligopolies (where three or more corporations are dominant). The degree of the problems created mounts with the share of the market taken by the biggest corporations, as in the pharmaceuticals, aerospace, motor vehicle, and computer markets. Against this background, the three most important aspects of EU competition policy have been the reduction of restrictive practices, the control of mergers, and monitoring the impact of state aid.

Restrictive practices

The Treaty of Rome prohibited business agreements that might interfere with trade between member states by having 'as their object or effect the prevention, restriction, or distortion of competition', and gave the Commission the power to intervene against any abuse of dominant position (Articles 81 and 82). With the completion of the customs union in 1968, cases involving conflict of interest started arriving at the European Court of Justice, which made judgments that helped expand the authority of the Commission, whose case load grew. It took on IBM in 1980–84 for abuse of dominant position in the computer market, then challenged a wide array of industries for market-sharing agreements, fixing prices, and exclusive purchasing and distribution agreements (Büthe, 2007, pp. 183–4). Among the more prominent of its decisions are:

- In 2001 the Commission imposed an €800 million fine on eight companies (including Hoffmann-La Roche) accused of running a global cartel aimed at trying to eliminate competition in the market for 12 vitamins.
- In 2003 it charged Japanese electronics company Nintendo with operating an agreement between 1991 and 1998 with seven of its distributors in Europe to maintain high prices for its games consoles and cartridges.

- In 2009, the Commission fined energy giants E.ON of Germany and Gaz de France (GDF) Suez €553 million for a long-standing secret agreement not to compete in the European natural gas market.

The most notable of the Commission's attempts to deal with allegations of abuse of dominant position relates to Microsoft, which has an estimated 90–92 per cent share of the world market for computer operating systems. After complaints from competitors that Microsoft was packaging its Media Player brand with Windows, squeezing out rivals, the Commission ordered Microsoft to offer a version of Windows without Media Player and to provide its rivals with information that would allow them to write programmes that would work more smoothly on Windows. In March 2004 it imposed a fine of €497 million ($794 million) on Microsoft for abuse of dominant market position.

Microsoft paid the fine, and made a version of Windows available without Media Player, but it did not release the necessary information to its rivals. The Commission then imposed a daily fine of €2 million on Microsoft, which responded by appealing the original 2004 decision. In 2006 the Commission imposed another fine of €281 million ($449 million) for continued non-compliance. Microsoft finally capitulated in 2007, but the Commission then fined it an additional €899 million in 2008 for failing to comply with the original 2004 ruling, and in 2009 announced that it planned to investigate Microsoft's bundling of its Internet Explorer with Windows.

Mergers

Relatively little was done by the EC in regard to mergers until the effects of the single market began to be more widely felt in the late 1980s, and in 1989 the European Merger Control regulation was adopted. If a merger is proposed that exceeds a set sales turnover level, the Commission will investigate and decide whether an opinion is needed. At least in the early years, most mergers were allowed to proceed (only 11 of 140 proposals between 1990 and 1993 were overturned (Harrop, 2002)), but as the number and the size of the proposed mergers grew, so did the number of Commission objections.

- While the Commission approved the 1999 merger of US oil giants Exxon and Mobil, it approved the 2000 merger of French petroleum giants TotalFina and Elf Aquitaine only on condition that they sold many of their highway service stations, which would otherwise have made up 60 per cent of the market.
- The merger in 2003 of pharmaceutical companies Pfizer and Pharmacia was allowed only on condition that they sold or licensed some of their patents, which would otherwise have controlled large segments of the market.
- A planned 2006 merger between E.ON of Germany and Endesa of Spain was complicated by conditions imposed by the Spanish government designed to create a national champion in the energy sector. The Commission argued that Spain had illegally usurped the Commission's powers to impose conditions on mergers, and that the conditions contravened the free movement of capital. The case went to the Court of Justice,

and while E.ON dropped its takeover bid after the Italian company Enel bought a stake in Endesa, the case – argue Cini and McGowan (2009, p. 153) – served as warning to any member state that 'might be tempted to prevent flagship companies from falling into foreign hands'.

● The proposed takeover in 2007 by low-cost airline Ryanair of the Irish national airline Aer Lingus was blocked on the grounds that the new airline would have had a near-monopoly of flights in and out of Dublin.

Emphasizing the impact of globalization, the Commission can even try to block mergers involving companies based outside the EU, as it did most famously in the case of Boeing and McDonnell Douglas in 1997. This move so upset the US government that then vice president Al Gore threatened a trade war, to which European competition commissioner Karel van Miert responded by threatening heavy fines and the impounding of any Boeing aircraft that entered EU airspace (Cini and McGowan, 2009, p. 158). A compromise was worked out and the merger went ahead, but not so the planned takeover of Honeywell by General Electric in 2001. It was approved by the US government, but the Commission argued that it would have created dominant positions in the markets for the supply of avionics and non-avionics equipment, particularly jet engines. In spite of an angry response from US politicians and media, the takeover was shelved (Reid, 2004, 88–91, 94–105).

State aid

The Treaty of Paris included the argument that subsidies or other aids provided by states were incompatible with the common market for coal and steel, but allowed them in some situations in the interests of promoting economic openness. Ironically, the EEC was to become complicit in one of the most expensive and controversial of all postwar arrangements for state aid: the Common Agricultural Policy. Dealing with the issue of state aid has also been the one area of competition policy where Commission authority has been the weakest, mainly because it comes up against the governments of the member states, making the issue more politically sensitive (Büthe, 2007, p. 189); by contrast, mergers and restrictive practices usually pit the Commission against private companies.

State aid includes subsidies, tax and interest breaks, guarantees, government stakes in companies, grants, contracts, and any other agreement or arrangement that gives a company or an industry special advantages. Governments are required to notify the Commission of plans to provide aid, but in most cases the complaints have come from competing firms or other governments (Cini and McGowan, 2009, pp. 170–2). The provision, measurement, and effects of state aid present a different set of challenges to those posed by investigations into restrictive practices and mergers. How far, for example, can regional development policy be considered a distortion of markets when every member state has its own such policies, and cohesion policy is so much a part of the EU agenda? The issue of state aid has also been vastly complicated by the response of EU governments to the global economic crisis, which included bail-outs and assistance to troubled companies (although the Commission did play a moderating role in resisting some of the more extreme suggestions for bail-outs).

SUMMARY

● Economic cooperation has long been at the heart of the process of European integration.

● The key elements of economic policy are fiscal and monetary policy, but while member states control the former, they have mainly transferred control of the latter to EU institutions.

● Early progress on the building of the single market was hampered by the persistence of non-tariff barriers, mainly of a physical, technical, or fiscal nature.

● While there has been progress since the Single European Act, economic liberalization remains patchy, and the EU was embarrassed by its failure to achieve the goals of the Lisbon Strategy.

● The long-term effects of the EU response to the 2007–10 global economic crisis remain unknowable.

● One of the effects of the single market has been an acceleration of corporate mergers and acquisitions across European borders, which has helped European corporations regain some of their pre-war global dominance.

● In order to guard against abuse of dominant position, the EU has long had a competition policy focused on the reduction of restrictive practices, the control of mergers, and monitoring the effects of state aid.

● EU competition policy is among the most visible, effective, and respected of all policies pursued by the European Commission, and has had implications far beyond the borders of the EU, most notably in the United States, where mergers have been blocked and corporations punished for restrictive practices.

KEY TERMS AND CONCEPTS

Competition policy
Corporate merger
Customs union
Economic liberalization
Economic policy
Europe 2020 Strategy
Fiscal policy
Great Recession
Trans-European networks

FURTHER READING

Cini, Michelle, and Lee McGowan (2009), *Competition Policy in the European Union*, 2nd edn (Basingstoke: Palgrave Macmillan). The standard survey of EU competition policy, with chapters on its development, the responsible policy actors, and key activities.

McDonald, Frank, and Stephen Dearden (eds) (2005), *European Economic Integration*, 4th edn (New York and Harlow: Prentice-Hall/Financial Times). An introduction to EU economic integration, with separate chapters on related policy areas, ranging from agriculture to the environment.

Neal, Larry (2007), *The Economics of Europe and the European Union* (Cambridge and New York: Cambridge University Press). A useful single-author survey of economic policy in the EU, including chapters on the single market, the euro, and the economies of key member states.

CHAPTER 20

Inside the Eurozone

PREVIEW

Nothing has had quite so clear an effect on the idea of European integration as the euro: it has changed the daily lives of everyone living in the eurozone states, and is immediately obvious to anyone travelling in those states. While the primary motive behind its launch in 1999 was economic, there were also political considerations: it was designed to extend European integration not just into the pockets and bank accounts of Europeans, but also into global financial markets.

Prospects for the single market were always bound to be limited as long as any person or company moving across borders had to deal with different currencies. Exchange rates fluctuated, costs and profits could never be firmly predicted, and currency conversion meant additional layers of bureaucracy and planning. For ordinary Europeans, foreign currencies emphasized the psychological challenges of travel, and made it more difficult to compare prices with those at home. The euro not only stands as a visible reminder that Europeans are engaged in a common project, but has also re-emphasized the strengths and weaknesses of the EU as an international economic actor.

Seventeen EU member states now use the euro, and adoption in most of the others (even Britain, Denmark, and Sweden, where resistance is strongest) is on the political agenda. There was an unmistakable pause for thought following the stern consecutive tests of the 2007–10 global economic crisis and of the 2009–10 Greek debt crisis, but the former impacted every international currency, and the latter was less a euro problem than a home-grown problem sparked by bad political and economic decisions. The future of the euro now depends mainly on how soon – and with what effects – post-crisis policy adjustments make themselves felt.

KEY ISSUES

- Was moving ahead with the euro a wise choice?
- Are British, Danish and Swedish doubts about the euro justified?
- To what extent have the problems of the euro been the result of bad decisions, and to what extent has it been the victim of circumstance?
- Will the euro survive? And if so, will it replace the dollar as the world's leading currency?
- What are the long-term implications of the Greek debt crisis?

Monetary policy

As we saw in Chapter 19, monetary policy is concerned mainly with money supply: with the value of a currency, with confidence in that currency, and with the control of inflation and interest rates. But where it is normally managed at a national level, with states having a monopoly over the creation and management of currencies, Europeans are now dealing with the world's biggest multi-national currency. Because not all EU states have yet adopted the euro, and because fiscal policy is still mainly controlled by the member states, the euro finds itself not only working its way through uncharted territory, but also faced with policy-making procedures that implicate the member states, the European Central Bank, and the European Commission. To complicate matters, there is a difference of opinion between the euro's two major powers – France and Germany – over who should be in charge of the euro, France preferring elected politicians and Germany preferring central bankers. And as if all this was not enough, the EU bent the rules on which states could adopt the euro, and eurozone states have since been lax in meeting their own standards designed to provide the euro with underlying stability.

Since its launch in 1999 as an electronic currency, and in 2002 as a cash currency, the euro has changed the daily lives of millions of European consumers and of businesses in the eurozone. It has also changed the dynamics of international financial and foreign exchange markets, where it has taken its place alongside the US dollar, the Japanese yen, the British pound, and other major international currencies. Its introduction was remarkable, because never before in history had such a large group of sovereign states voluntarily replaced their national currencies with a common currency, thereby surrendering a large measure of economic independence. Many of those currencies were deeply entrenched in the histories of their states: the Greek drachma, for example, dated back to classical Greece and more recently to the establishment of the modern Greek state in 1832, the Dutch guilder dated back to the seventeenth century, and the Italian lira dated back to national unification in 1861. The German deutschmark – created in 1948 to replace the Reichsmark – may have been much younger but had become a symbol of West Germany's postwar renaissance, the West German Bundesbank (created in 1957) developing a reputation for independence and for helping West Germany to become the region's dominant economy.

Although the creation of the euro was an economic project, and the logical partner of the construction of the single market, its significance went further: its introduction, noted German foreign minister Joschka Fischer (2000), 'was not only the crowning-point of economic integration, it was also a profoundly political act, because a currency is not just another economic factor but also symbolizes the power of the sovereign who guarantees it'. As well as offering eurozone states a world-class currency that would expand the international financial and political reach of the EU, it also represented the first serious threat to the global leadership of the US dollar since the latter had taken over from the British pound in the 1950s.

As we saw in Chapter 5, stable exchange rates had long been considered an essential prelude to the building of the European single market, most of the early concerns of western European governments being addressed by the Bretton

● **Monetary policy**: Policy aimed at encouraging economic growth and stability by controlling the supply of money and its cost through the setting of interest rates.

Woods system. Its stabilizing effects through the 1950s and 1960s were reflected in the numbers: the British pound remained steady at a value of about $2.80 between 1950 and 1967, while the West German deutschmark ranged modestly between 3.90 and 4.20 to the dollar. Meanwhile, steps were taken towards European monetary cooperation with the signature in 1958 of the European Monetary Agreement, the convening in 1964 of the Committee of Central Bank Governors, and the 1969 agreement among Community leaders to work towards economic and monetary union (EMU). The Werner committee report in 1970 recommended monetary union within ten years, beginning with reduced exchange rate fluctuations, to which end the 'snake in the tunnel' was launched in 1972.

The viability of the snake was undermined by the 1971 US decision to end convertibility between gold and the US dollar and the energy crises of the 1970s, and to complicate matters, there was a philosophical split among EEC governments on how to proceed: 'monetarists' such as Belgium, France and Luxembourg wanted to fix exchange rates as a means to economic convergence, while 'economists' such as the Netherlands and West Germany saw economic convergence leading to the fixing of exchange rates (for details see Hosli, 2005, pp. 18–21). The monetarist view won out, paving the way for the launch of the European Monetary System (EMS) in 1979, based on an Exchange Rate Mechanism (ERM) intended to encourage exchange rate stability. Several states had problems meeting the terms, but the EMS encouraged a new focus on monetary policy, paving the way for the introduction of the three-stage Delors plan of 1989, which was confirmed by Maastricht. As we saw in Chapter 6, this set a target of January 1997 for monetary union (later changed to January 1999), and outlined several 'convergence criteria' for states wanting to adopt the currency, including limits on budget deficits, public debt, inflation, interest rates, and exchange rate fluctuations.

In 1995 the European Council named the new currency the euro, and in 1997 it was decided that 11 member states were ready to begin Stage III of the Delors Plan in January 1999, the exceptions being Britain, Denmark, and Sweden (which did not want to participate), and Greece (which was not ready). In 1997, at the insistence mainly of Germany, and prompted by concerns about the mixed record of member states in meeting the terms of the convergence criteria, EU leaders signed the **Stability and Growth Pact**. This obliged them to keep their budget deficits to less than 3 per cent of gross domestic product, placed a 60 per cent limit on government borrowing (Hosli, 2005, pp. 67–9), and allowed the Commission to fine any state in breach of the pact. While supported by most EU leaders in principle, the pact was criticized for being too inflexible, and was described undiplomatically in 2002 by Commission president Romano Prodi as 'stupid'. But the costs of a failure to impose the rules were made only too clear by the case of Greece, which was allowed to adopt the euro in 2001 in spite of the fact that it did not meet the budget deficit target, and went on to so mismanage its economy that it set off a 2009–10 debt crisis that rocked the euro to its core – see pp. 352–3.

Stage III of the Delors Plan was completed on 1 January 1999 when exchange rates among the participating currencies were permanently locked in place, the ECB took over responsibility for monetary policy in the eurozone, and the euro became available electronically (people could open euro bank accounts, make

● **Stability and Growth Pact**: An agreement reached in 1997 by which eurozone governments undertook to control their budget deficits in the interests of currency stability.

The creation of the euro was acclaimed by some as one of the most important achievements of integration, from both an economic and a political perspective, but was met by others with scepticism bordering on outright opposition.

transfers to other accounts, and so on). It became a cash currency in January 2002 when euro coins and banknotes finally replaced national currencies in 12 states (all the EU-15 except Britain, Denmark and Sweden). The eurozone expanded to Slovenia in January 2007, to Cyprus and Malta in January 2008, to Slovakia in January 2009 and to Estonia in January 2011. The euro has also been adopted unofficially in Kosovo and Montenegro, several African countries have pegged their currencies to the euro, and it is increasingly widely accepted in those parts of the world that rely most heavily on European tourism.

Following the launch of the euro in 1999, the Exchange Rate Mechanism (ERM) was transformed from one designed to keep EU member states within a band of exchange rate fluctuations to one designed to link other EU currencies to the euro. The goal of this **ERM II** is to improve the stability of those currencies and to provide a better sense of how potential euro members are faring. With Greece joining the euro in 2001, only Denmark remained within ERM II, but it was later joined by Cyprus, Malta, Slovakia, and Slovenia (now all euro members), and by the three Baltic states. Members of ERM II are allowed to let their currencies fluctuate within a wide band of ±15 per cent relative to the euro, but can choose to follow narrower bands. Any EU member state can adopt the euro once it has met the convergence criteria and stayed within ERM II for at least two years, but it will take a while before the impact of the jitters created by the Greek debt crisis is better understood.

In Britain, opposition to the euro has been clear and constant. British doubts were deeply influenced by the events of Black Wednesday (16 September 1992) when Britain left the ERM following speculation on the pound (see Chapter 6). The Blair government was in favour of joining, but only with a supporting vote in a national referendum that it kept postponing for fear that it would lose. Gordon Brown – then Britain's finance minister – developed his own set of

● **ERM II:** A reformed Exchange Rate Mechanism designed to help improve the stability relative to the euro of currencies in EU states outside the eurozone.

Map 20.1 The eurozone

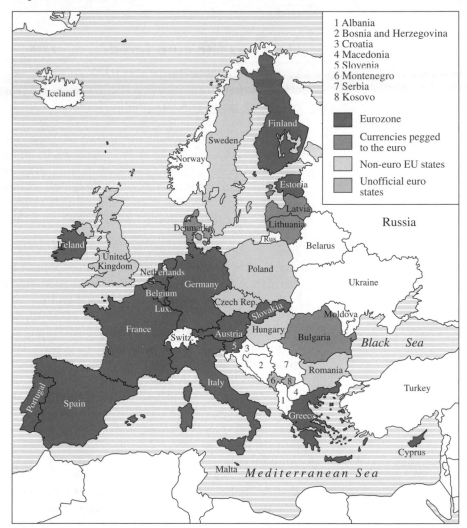

domestic tests of British readiness to join, including convergence between the British and eurozone economies, and the flexibility of business and the work-force. When Brown became prime minister in 2007 he drew unflattering comparisons between growth and unemployment rates in the eurozone and Britain, arguing that domestic policy had helped Britain achieve financial stability and avoid the economic downturn that hit some eurozone states (Buller and Gamble, 2008) (an argument whose ironies became that much more clear as the British economy suffered a downturn during the global economic crisis). But the most fundamental source of British opposition lies in public opinion: polls have shown opposition to adoption running at 50–60 per cent and support running at about 25–30 per cent, although (at least before the Greek debt crisis) they also suggested that many Britons might change their mind if the government favoured adoption. The Cameron-led coalition government that took office in

May 2010 declared that Britain would not join the euro during its parliamentary term.

How has the euro fared?

Economic and monetary union has been described by Dyson (2008, p. 3) as 'a classic example' of elite-driven integration, relying on the principle of permissive consensus, being driven by political leadership coming mainly out of France and Germany, and having the paradoxical twin effect of promoting European unification while also unleashing new debates about how decisions on integration are taken. It has also been one of the most complex of all EU policy areas, contrasting the technical opinions of policy-making elites and professional economists with the instinctive reactions of a bemused European public, for which the advent of the euro has meant more direct changes in their daily lives than perhaps any other European initiative. Although the preparations for the switch had been carefully made, and can be dated back at least to the launch of the snake in the tunnel in 1972 (but perhaps arguably to the adoption of the 1958 European Monetary Agreement), the final launch of the euro was still a leap into the dark. And attempts to understand its economic impact have been muddied by the global economic crisis, predicted and understood only by a minority of experts, and by the Greek debt crisis of 2009–10, more easily predicted but still not well understood in terms of its long-term implications.

On foreign exchange markets, the euro set out at a sturdy $1.18, but fell quickly to a low of 82.5 cents in October 2000, regaining ground to a new high of nearly $1.60 in July 2008 before falling back to $1.19 in June 2010 as a result of the Greek crisis (see Figure 20.1). Although its higher value against the dollar may have seemed like a cause for celebration, it hurt EU economies by making their exports more expensive, and by making visits to Europe more expensive for tourists. As far as ordinary Europeans are concerned, opinion on the euro was doubtful at first, but then solidified in most EU states.

- In early 1997 there were majorities in favour of the euro in only 8 of the eleven potential member states: the Italians were most enthusiastic with 74 per cent in favour, while the Dutch were split 52:42. Opponents outnumbered supporters in Austria by 47 to 41, and in Finland by 62 to 29. Most worryingly of all, because of its leadership of the eurozone, opponents in Germany outnumbered supporters by 54 to 32. For the EU-15 as a whole, supporters outnumbered opponents by the modest margin of 47 to 40 (Eurobarometer 47, October 1997, p. 28).
- A year later, favourable opinions had generally strengthened, with supporters outnumbering opponents by 60 to 28 in the EU-15, and a notable change of opinion in Germany, where 51 per cent were in favour compared to 36 per cent opposed (Eurobarometer 49, September 1998, p. 45).
- By the time euro coins and notes went into circulation in 2002, not much had changed overall, with supporters outweighing opponents by 67 to 25 in the EU-15. But strong majorities favoured the euro throughout the eurozone, and Britain remained the only country where opponents outnumbered supporters (by 50 to 31) (Eurobarometer 57, Spring 2002, p. 76).

Figure 20.1 The fluctuating value of the euro

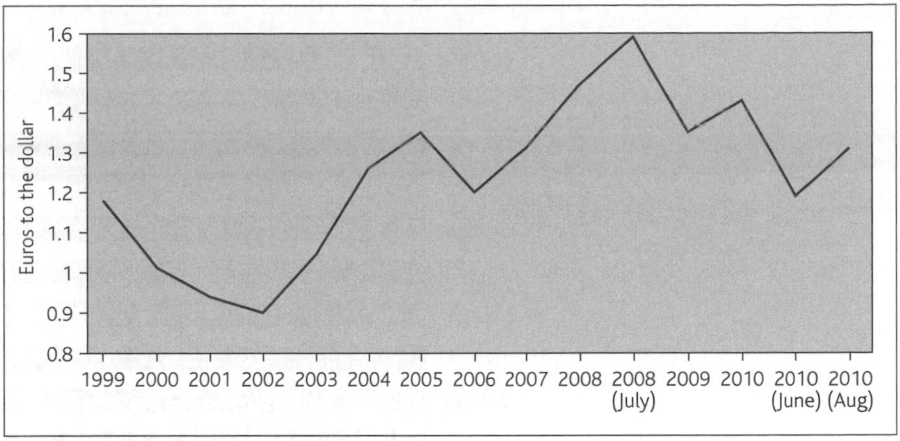

Exchange rate against US dollar as of the first week of January each year.
Source: European Central Bank at http://www.ecb.int/stats/exchange (retrieved August 2010).

By 2009, at the height of the global economic crisis, it appeared that most Europeans had become used to the euro. Overall the poll figures had not changed much from 2002, with supporters outnumbering opponents by 61 to 33, but the numbers remained stable even with EU enlargement, and even against a background of declining support in Italy, and large numbers of opponents (one-third or more of the population) in Greece, Estonia, Denmark, Lithuania, Sweden, the Czech Republic, Latvia, and Poland. At least three out of five Europeans were in favour in every eurozone state except Portugal, in several states the opponents were thin on the ground, and Britain remained the one clear anomaly with 66 per cent opposed and 27 per cent in favour (see Figure 20.2). Interestingly, the only country where everyone had an opinion was Greece, with 62 per cent in favour, 38 per cent opposed, and no Don't Knows.

The political calculations surrounding the euro – based on a set of often opaquely technical economic and financial considerations – are more complex than the personal calculations of ordinary Europeans, most of whom respond to the euro almost entirely from the perspective of convenience. The most immediate benefit of the euro to consumers is that they can travel to multiple countries without having to exchange currencies or pay fees, and they can more clearly see how prices compare without having to translate them back into their home currency. The existence of the euro has also had an important psychological effect on Europeans, making the foreign seem more familiar, and removing one of the most persistent reminders of the differences among European states. It has also given the eurozone states more of a clearly vested interest in the economic development of the others. Finally, the existence of the euro helps businesses, whose transactions are easier to undertake, and who do not have to be concerned about fluctuations in exchange rates.

But there are disadvantages as well, the biggest concern being loss of policy independence. A national currency gives a government (or central banks, at least) a powerful means of managing its economy through adjusting interest rates, which in turn have an effect on inflation and on rates of spending and

Figure 20.2 What Europeans think: The euro

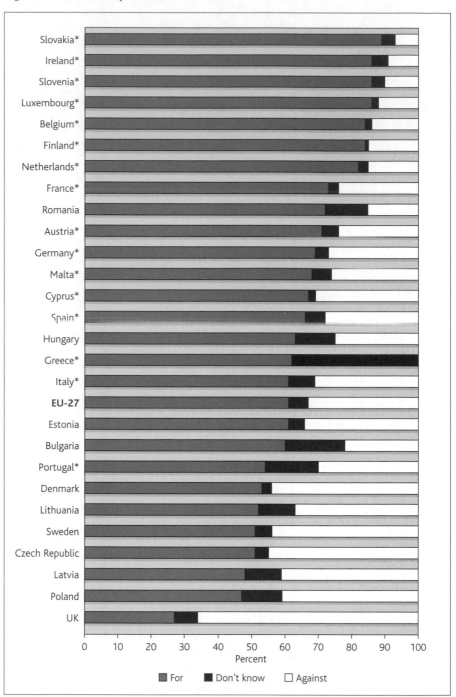

* eurozone states
Source: Eurobarometer 71, September 2009, p. 157.

saving. Independent decisions that were once made by the central banks of the eurozone states are now made jointly by those states working within the European Central Bank. And where different countries that had different economic cycles, economic structures, and levels of wealth and poverty could once borrow, adjust interest rates, and if necessary devalue their currencies in response to changed economic circumstances, now they must move in concert with their neighbours. An economic downturn in one (particularly a crisis as dramatic as those that came to Greece and Ireland in 2010) has implications not just for all the other euro states, but even for the global economy.

States adopting the euro must also give up a powerful symbol of national identity and independence. This is true for smaller EU states that have seen their currencies as the last means of exerting some real control over national economies, and is especially true for bigger and wealthier European states with world-class currencies. Consider the case of Germany, where the success of the deutschmark was central to the country's postwar renaissance. Consider also Britain, where national pride explains much of the reticence towards giving up the pound; it is the world's oldest currency still in use (dating back to Anglo-Saxon times), once circulated through much of the British Empire, and for decades was the world's leading international currency. For many Britons, giving up the pound is not just about a loss of economic independence, but would further confirm the decline of Britain's world role. (Some might argue, however, that participation in the euro would actually help increase Britain's global economic influence.)

Not surprisingly for such a monumental project, the euro has had many troubles, the greatest difficulties coming from the challenge that several states have faced with keeping within the terms of the Stability and Growth Pact. When recession hit most industrialized countries in 2002–03, France, Germany, Italy, and Portugal either breached the budget deficit limit or came close, and were soon joined by most other eurozone states, thereby undermining the prospects for economic growth. In November 2003 the two biggest eurozone economies – France and Germany – breached the limits and blocked attempts by EU finance ministers to impose large fines on the two countries. They instead argued (with British support) that the rules of the pact were too rigid and needed to be applied more flexibly. By December the pact had all but collapsed, and in 2005 the rules were relaxed in order to make it more achievable and enforceable.

Then came the global economic crisis of 2007–10. The implications of an economic downturn had been anticipated and warned against by some economists, but politics overrode economics, and the recession revealed some of the advantages and disadvantages of monetary union. It particularly showed how far EU states – like almost all others – were part of a globalized financial system where problems in one part could have immediate and sometimes surprising knock-on effects in others. At the same time, the contrasts between Ireland and Iceland gave pause for thought; while the former could take some comfort from its membership of the EU and the euro, sharing the costs but also the opportunities, the isolation and vulnerability of Iceland was made clear by a banking crisis in 2008 that sent shockwaves through the Icelandic community and undermined its national currency, the krona. Parties and political leaders that had been lukewarm on EU membership now changed their positions, seeking a

Focus on . . .
The Greek debt crisis

The debt crisis that broke in Greece in October 2009 was to some extent predictable, caused many a sleepless nights for EU leaders as they wrestled with the terms of their response, and generated a new round of assertions about crisis in Europe. It was remarkable that a country with just over two per cent of the EU's population and less than two per cent of its GDP could have caused shockwaves around the EU, which in turn impacted financial markets all over the world.

After being allowed to join the euro in spite of its failure to meet the budget deficit terms of entry, Greece failed to respect eurozone rules on spending, failed to address the more obvious problems in its economy, went on a spending spree fuelled by borrowing, manipulated statistics to exaggerate its levels of economic growth, ran a budget deficit that – at nearly 13 per cent – was far above the 3 per cent limit set by the stability and growth pact, and accumulated a national debt that was ultimately bigger than its national economy. Meanwhile, the government was not bringing in enough revenue, thanks in part to widespread tax evasion.

When the global economic crisis began to take hold in 2007–8, the Greek economy was weak and exposed, and Greece's credit rating was downgraded, reducing the prospect of badly needed foreign investment. The government was obliged to implement drastic and politically unpopular spending cuts; to raise taxes on fuel, tobacco, and alcohol; and to extend the retirement age by two years. More broadly, its problems raised fears of problems in other eurozone countries facing budgetary pressures, such as Ireland, Italy, Portugal and Spain. There was even speculation that countries like Ireland and Greece might have to leave the euro, but just how this would have been arranged was not made clear.

Unable to grow its way out of the problem because of its small economy, and unable to devalue its currency (which it would have been able to do if it still had the drachma), Greece faced a severe test. But it was also a wake-up call for the entire eurozone, and a learning experience for the implications of having a common currency. It was clear that urgent action was needed to ensure that eurozone governments lived within the rules that had been set for membership, and for anyone who was paying attention, it also contained lessons for the United States: the national debt there in mid-2010 stood at 90 per cent of GDP, and was fast catching up to the level of 120 per cent of GDP in Greece.

haven in European integration, and Iceland lodged its formal application for EU membership in July 2009.

After some initial indications of independent national responses to the crisis, EU governments improved their policy coordination. On the monetary front the ECB made interest rate cuts, while calls were made for a complete overhaul of the EU financial system. Then in late 2009 came the most severe test ever faced by the euro: the debt crisis in Greece. This was not just a problem for Greece, brought on by profligate spending and economic mismanagement, but threatened to spread to other eurozone states with similar deficit and debt problems, posed a severe test of the abilities of eurozone leaders to make policy, and threatened to undermine the international credibility of the euro. Is Greece's debt 'trashing the euro', asked *The New York Times* in February 2010? Could Greece 'kill off the euro', asked the host of an influential BBC radio news show in May 2010? 'The experiment of a monetary union without political union has failed',

**Illustration 20.2
The Greek debt crisis**

Greek demonstrators protest against austerity measures imposed by their government in the wake of the Greek debt crisis, which posed the most severe challenge yet to the stability of the euro.

argued a commentator in *The Financial Times*. 'The EU is thus about to confront a historic choice between integration and disintegration.'

Eurozone leaders met in early 2010 to discuss their response, with additional worries posed by the prospect that it might involve the humiliation of seeking help from the International Monetary Fund, thereby further damaging the standing of the euro and its value in foreign exchange markets. Citing eurozone rules, German Chancellor Angela Merkel at first refused to support a bailout for Greece, and eurozone leaders instead agreed that if Greece was unable to attract loans from the financial markets, a last resort package of bilateral loans from inside the eurozone (mainly Germany and France) would be arranged, along with funds and technical assistance from the IMF, assuming all eurozone states were in favour. Merkel also warned that states which regularly cheated on their public finances might in future be expelled from the eurozone. (She later shocked other EU leaders by proposing (along with French President Nikolas Sarkozy) a change to the treaties designed to tighten the rules on national debt. At its October 2010 meeting the European Council headed off the prospect of yet more bruising battles involving national referendums by deciding that the changes could be agreed through votes in national legislatures.)

The key challenge with the Greek crisis, as is so often the case in financial matters, was to restore investor confidence, which meant sending a clear message that Greece would be helped through the crisis. But the initial eurozone offer at the end of April of a €45 billion ($60 billion) EU-IMF rescue package did not impress the markets, and within three weeks the amount had more than doubled to €110 billion ($145 billion), offered on condition that Greece cut public spending and boost tax revenue. This sparked riots in the streets of Athens, during which three people died, and encouraged little improvement in investor confidence. Barely a week later, a loan guarantee package worth €750 billion (nearly $1 trillion) was announced, taking many by surprise and this time sparking a jump in share prices on both sides of the Atlantic. The aura of crisis ultimately dissipated, but troubling questions remained about the significance of the circumstances that had led to the crisis, and how the euro would look once it was over. *The Economist* reflected wider concerns when it asked its readers in May 2010 whether the euro would still exist in ten years, and undoubtedly there were many troubling questions that demanded a response.

Writing before the Greek crisis, Chang (2008, p. 251) felt that there was 'reason to be optimistic' for the euro. Business and household confidence had improved, unemployment was down, external demand was solid, and member states had made reforms to their labour markets. But she also noted the need to finally complete the single market, to open up protected services, and to better integrate the financial market. Writing at about the same time, Cohen (2008) argued that the euro had failed to live up to expectations. While it had removed the problem of exchange rate disturbances within Europe, the eurozone – before the global economic crisis – was mainly a passive participant in global monetary affairs, leaving it vulnerable to fluctuations in the value of the euro relative to the dollar and other major currencies. It had also failed to mount a significant challenge to the US dollar. The main problem, he argued, was that the euro was 'a currency without a country' and its power to deal with external challenges was limited by the absence of a single voice to speak on its behalf. Interestingly, neither Chang nor Cohen had much to say about the dangers posed by Greek economic policy, an indication of just how much of a surprise the debt crisis was when it finally broke.

The euro as an international currency

Long before Greece, and even before the launch of the euro, speculation had begun to grow in some quarters that the euro had a bright future in store as an international currency, and might pose the first real challenge to the global dominance of the US dollar. For Nobel laureate Robert Mundell (2000, p. 57), the euro promised to 'challenge the status of the dollar and alter the power configuration of the international system'. A 2005 study predicted that if the eurozone continued to expand in size and if US economic policies continued to undermine confidence in the dollar, then the euro could supplant the dollar as the world's leading reserve currency by 2022 (Chinn and Frankel, 2005). In September 2007, no less a giant of banking than Alan Greenspan, the chairman of the US Federal Reserve System, was quoted by the German news weekly *Stern* as believing it possible that the euro could replace the dollar as the primary reserve currency, and that the European Central Bank had 'developed into a global economic force to be taken seriously'.

The stability and credibility of a currency depends mainly on how much value is placed on that currency as a medium of exchange (meaning that it can be used to settle international financial transactions), as a unit of account (it can be used to invoice foreign trade, anchor exchange rate regimes, or denominate international commodities), and as a store of value (investors hold deposits and loans in the currency, governments use it as a reserve, and its purchasing power remains reasonably steady over time) (see Chang, 2009, p. 193). Government and consumer confidence also plays a role: the bigger, wealthier and more open a national economy, the more likely that its currency will circulate internationally, and that consumers and businesses will trust and use that currency.

In all senses, the currencies of most advanced capitalist societies are stable and credible, in contrast to those of weaker states whose currencies are often overvalued, have not developed much long-term stability or credibility, and in extreme cases are almost worthless (a problem, for example, that encouraged Zimbabwe in 2009, following years of hyperinflation, to abandon the Zimbabwe dollar and replace it with credible international currencies such as the US dollar and the euro). Having a world-leading currency offers many benefits to the state that owns and controls that currency.

- It means political leadership, because the government that controls that currency will inevitably play a major role in international monetary policy decisions, which can be turned to the benefit of its home state.
- Other countries are more likely to hold more of their foreign reserves in that currency, helping it maintain its value.
- There is more chance that key internationally traded commodities such as oil, gold, and silver will be denominated in that currency, which means fewer problems for the home state when it comes to buying those commodities; if they are denominated in another currency then the price will fluctuate according to the relative values of the two currencies.
- It makes it easier for a country to run foreign trade deficits, and gives a country the advantage of borrowing in its own currency, making it less hostage to fluctuations in the value of its currency relative to others.

The most telling measure of global monetary influence is the extent to which a currency is used as an anchor or **reserve currency**, or one in which governments hold a significant amount of their foreign exchange reserves, and one in which products traded in the international marketplace (such as oil and gold) are denominated. During the eighteenth and nineteenth centuries, the British pound was the world's primary reserve currency, its strength underpinned by the size of the British economy and by the trade network linking Britain to its empire. But the costs of fighting two world wars, combined with the rise of the United States as an economic power, put paid to the dominance of the pound. Underpinned by the size and reach of the US economy, and encouraged by the US role as anchor of the Bretton Woods system, the dollar during the 1950s became the world's dominating and most respected currency. Its global leadership continue to be unquestioned until the 1990s, its share of international foreign exchange reserves far exceeding those of the German deutschmark, the British pound, or the Japanese yen.

The launch of the euro changed the nature of the game. Even though two-thirds of international foreign reserves were held in US dollars at the time, the euro took over nearly one-fifth of foreign reserves (thanks mainly to a switch from the deutschmark), since when its share has grown to more than one-quarter (see Figure 20.3). It did this even while holdings in foreign currencies were growing, from $1.4 billion in 1999 to $2.7 billion in 2004 and $4.5 billion in 2009. But after its initial burst of speed, the euro settled onto something of a plateau, holding at about 25–27 per cent of the share of reserves in the period

Figure 20.3 The euro as a reserve currency

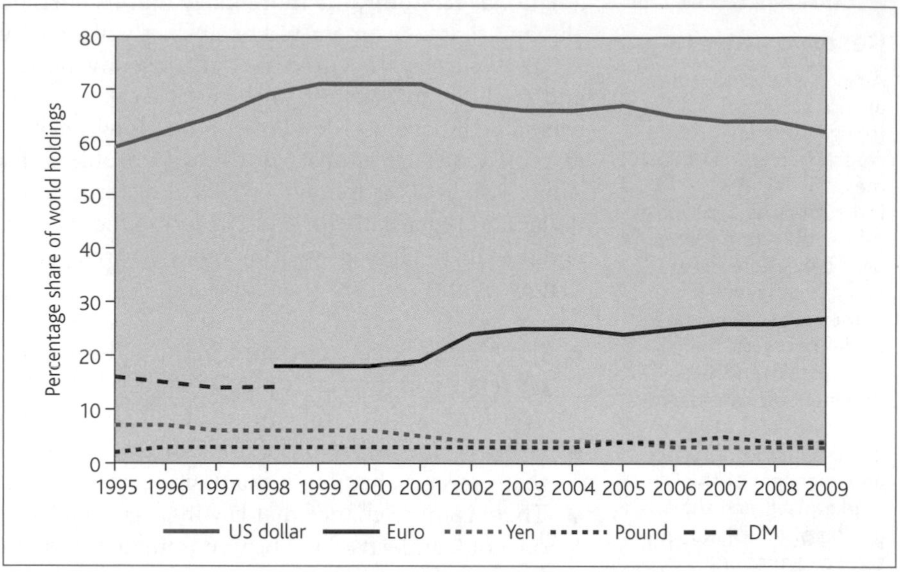

Source: International Monetary Fund at http://www.imf.org/external/np/sta/cofer/eng/index.htm (retrieved August 2010).

2003–09. The role of the dollar continued almost unchanged in spite of the global economic crisis, when the reputation of the United States as the home of high quality and dependable financial assets took a drubbing. And it also held in spite of the rapidly growing US national debt.

Several developments meanwhile suggested that there was new international interest in seeking an alternative to the US dollar, even if it was not necessarily the euro. Many of the concerns were driven by the level of influence the United States has over international economic policies, but also by the risks that countries such as China were taking in holding large dollar reserves against a background of the escalating US national debt. Also, as countries traded more with the EU, ran the argument, so they would want to switch more of their foreign reserves into euros. (Again, this was before Greece.) Several countries – including Russia, China and Saudi Arabia – switched from holding all their foreign reserves in US dollars to using a basket of currencies. There was also talk in Russia and China of using the Special Drawing Rights made available by the International Monetary Fund since 1969 as an alternative to the US dollar – but these cannot be traded and cannot be used to pay bills. Finally, there was talk of the possible development of an Asian currency unit, and even conjecture that China might allow the yuan to trade freely on international markets and become a new reserve currency and a lynchpin of world currency markets along with the dollar and the euro (O'Neill, 2010).

Cohen (2008) argues that the euro suffers several handicaps, the most difficult of which is the lack of clear leadership within the European Central Bank, where decisions are made communally by the Governing Council and the Executive Board, and members may be inclined to think more in terms of national interests than of European interests. It is telling that the president of the

Debating...
Will the euro survive?

YES

The stakes are too great. If the euro fails, or if any of its member states decide to leave, it will undermine the single market and cast unprecedented levels of doubt over the entire exercise of European integration.

The problems experienced by eurozone states in 2009–10 were less a result of problems with the euro than they were of policy choices made by national governments and financial institutions.

Regional integration has always been an exercise in improvisation, driven by frequent crises, but national governments have proved adept at learning from (most of) their mistakes. The problems of 2009–10 led to structural changes in regulatory and financial systems that will leave the euro much stronger.

The costs for a state opting out of the euro are too great. As well as the immediate expense of converting to a new national currency, there will be numerous potential costs in the form of reduced investor confidence and currency revaluation. Also, switching to a new currency takes time, long enough for a state considering such a switch to be persuaded otherwise by an upturn in economic fortunes.

NO

The euro had critical design flaws from the beginning, the most notable being the decision to leave fiscal policy in the hands of the member states. Efforts were made to fix these problems in 2010, but the crises of 2009–10 shook the entire structure of monetary integration, against which must be set the mixed feelings of many ordinary Europeans about the euro.

There is not enough confidence in the ability of eurozone leaders to agree policy or to fully understand the implications of the euro's structural faults. The kinds of reforms needed to bolster the euro are too politically troubling to be accepted by all EU governments and their voters.

The eurozone states continue to have different economic cycles and sometimes different sets of economic policies and priorities. There can be no 'one size fits all' policies for the eurozone, and national leaders need to have their independent policy options restored to them.

A middle-range option is for selected states to leave the euro and for the remainder to reformulate themselves as a smaller, deeper, and better managed eurozone. So while the old eurozone may not survive in its current form, it could be replaced by a new and sleeker version.

ECB has so far failed to win the same kind of international status and exposure as the chairman of the US Federal Reserve. This is particularly ironic given that – according to Martin and Ross (2004) – the ECB was given more autonomy than any other EU institution, and greater independence than any other central bank in the world. The failure of the euro to live up to expectations was meanwhile helped by the continuing dominance of the US dollar, helped in turn by the large size and relative stability of the US economy, the established role of the dollar in international markets, and the fact that commodities such as oil and gold are still priced in dollars (Goldberg, 2010). Then came the Greek debt crisis.

SUMMARY

- The euro was launched in 1999 as an electronic currency, and in 2002 as a cash currency. Its creation was not only an economic act, but also a political act designed to help expand the international financial and political reach of the EU.

- Twelve EU states adopted the euro in 2002, and were later joined by five more, with expectations that most of the rest (opposition being strongest in Britain, Denmark, and Sweden) would eventually follow.

- The euro started out well, with optimistic speculation that it would quickly become a world-class currency. Then came the 2007–10 global economic crisis, when eurozone leaders at first appeared undecided about how to act, before taking ameliorative action. This was followed by the challenge of the Greek debt crisis of 2009–10.

- The Greek crisis not only revealed the dangers to the eurozone of mismanagement and incompetence in even a single member state, but once again found eurozone leaders failing to agree on how to respond. They eventually offered a large loan guarantee package to Greece, but many questions were raised about the future of the euro.

- Immediately upon its creation the euro became the world's second largest reserve currency, leading to speculation that it might pose a serious challenge to the US dollar. But after its share of reserves grew to just over 25 per cent it appeared to have settled onto something of a plateau, lagging well behind the 60–65 per cent share of the US dollar.

- Many questions remain about the long-term prospects of the euro. How will it be impacted by the crises of 2007–10? Will eurozone leaders learn from their mistakes? How will its weaknesses compare with those of the United States, where doubts are growing about the underlying economic stability of the US dollar?

KEY TERMS AND CONCEPTS

ERM II
Monetary policy
Reserve currency
Stability and Growth Pact

FURTHER READING

Chang, Michelle (2008), *Monetary Integration in the European Union* (Basingstoke: Palgrave Macmillan). A textbook survey of the history behind the euro, monetary policy-making in the EU, and the effects of the euro.

Hosli, Madeleine O. (2005), *The Euro: A Concise Introduction to European Monetary Integration* (Boulder, CO: Lynne Rienner). A brief survey of the history behind the euro, the structure of the European Central Bank, and the workings of the eurozone.

Marsh, David (2008), *The Euro: The Politics of the New Global Currency* (New Haven, CT: Yale University Press). A highly readable study of the history and politics of the euro, based on interviews with an impressive cast of characters.

CHAPTER 21

Managing Resources

PREVIEW Agriculture was long a headline issue in EU politics. It was one of the few policies listed in the Treaty of Rome, and the Common Agricultural Policy (CAP) for decades topped the EC/EU budget. Spending on agriculture helped encourage greater production, contributing to the end of food shortages and providing essential investments in western Europe's rural communities. But it also distorted markets, diverted resources away from other arguably more important priorities, and created tensions with the EU's trading partners. Attempts to reform agricultural policies were long resisted by western European farmers, but enlargement combined with the pressures of international trade regimes to force changes to CAP, which has since moved down the EU agenda.

The contrasts offered by environmental policy could not be more clear. Environmental issues did not begin to appear on the European policy agenda until the late 1960s, and even then the response was not particularly strategic. It was only as public and political support for environmental management began to build in the late 1970s and early 1980s that environmental policy drew more attention, since when the focus of policy-making in the EU has shifted away from the member states. The underlying logic was twofold: different environmental standards stood as a barrier to the single market, and most environmental problems – particularly those relating to air pollution, water pollution, and the disposal of waste – are better addressed by states working together rather than in isolation. EU policy has helped transform Europe from a region that once lagged behind the United States to one that in many respects has set global standards for environmental management. On the headline problem of climate change, though, while the EU has a well-developed climate change programme, it has failed to take as much international leadership as it might.

KEY ISSUES

- Why has agriculture traditionally been so prominent a part of the EU policy agenda?

- What does the approach to reforming CAP say about the nature of policy-making in the EU more generally?

- What is the most effective potential response to dealing with the problem of overfishing?

- What are the costs and benefits of addressing environmental policy needs at the European level rather than at the level of the member states?

- Has the EU become a global environmental leader? If so, what explains its new role?

Agricultural policy

Agriculture is one of the most fundamental of all areas of public policy, because without guaranteed supplies of adequate nutrition, much else about life is moot. But in liberal democracies, where agriculture was long ago superseded as the base of the economy by industry and services, it contributes little to jobs and wealth, and is not often a leading political issue (although this is more true today in western European states than in eastern states such as Poland, Romania, and Bulgaria, with their relatively large agricultural populations). And yet despite its marginal role in national politics, agricultural policy continues to be placed high up the agenda of European integration, a result mainly of history.

Farming played a key role in western European economies after the Second World War, accounting in 1950 for 12–15 per cent of the GDP of West Germany, France and the Netherlands, and nearly 30 per cent of the GDP of Italy. It was also a large employer, with 18 per cent of the Dutch workforce active in agriculture, 23 per cent of that in West Germany, 31 per cent in France, and more than 44 per cent in Italy (see Figure 21.1). The memories of postwar food shortages and rationing were still fresh in the minds of many Europeans, and there were concerns that because food prices fluctuated so much on the international market, and because these fluctuations could have a knock-on effect on inflation (if prices went up) or on jobs and debt (if they went down), subsidies would be needed to offset the problems and to encourage people to stay in the rural areas.

It was against this background that representatives of the six EEC founding states met in Stresa, Italy, in July 1958, and negotiated the details of what would become the **Common Agricultural Policy** (CAP) of the EEC. They agreed three principles: a single market in agricultural produce, 'Community preference' (a coded term for protectionism aimed at giving Community produce priority over imported produce), and joint financing (meaning that the costs of CAP would be met by the Community rather than by individual member states). So strong were the interests of the member states that agriculture became one of only five policies listed in the Treaty of Rome (the others being trade, transport, competition, and the single market).

CAP was born against a background of concern for food supplies in western Europe, and had several goals: to increase agricultural productivity and thereby encourage a 'fair' standard of living for those working in agriculture, to stabilize markets, to assure supplies, and to ensure reasonable prices for consumers (Article 39). These goals would be achieved mainly through guaranteed minimum prices for EEC farmers, regardless of how much they produced and how much the market could bear. In other words, while much of what the EEC was to achieve on the economic front would be based on encouraging competition and free trade, on the agricultural front it pursued policies that were protectionist, interventionist, and anti-market, and that insulated a critical economic sector from competitive forces.

The long-term result of CAP was a dramatic growth in agricultural productivity (although much of this would probably have happened anyway because of technological breakthroughs and growing efficiency). But this came at the cost of soaking up much EEC spending, and drew criticism not just from the member states but also from major trading partners such as the United States, and the governments of developing countries whose farmers could not compete.

● **Agricultural policy**: Policy dealing with the production and distribution of food, with a focus on supply, prices, quality, land use, trade and employment.

● **Common Agricultural Policy**: One of the oldest and most controversial of EU policies, based at first on a system of price supports for farmers, but later reformed.

Figure 21.1 Europe's changing farming population

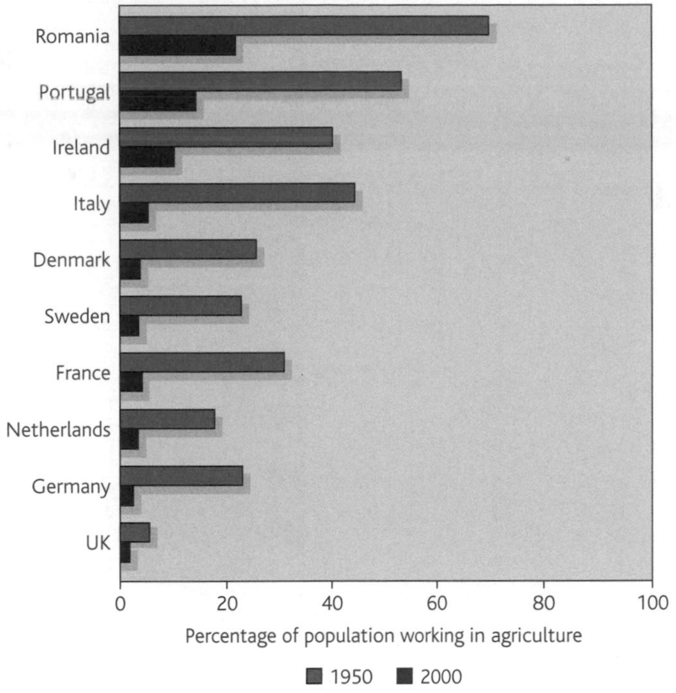

Percentage of population working in agriculture

■ 1950 ■ 2000

Source: Figures calculated by Rieger, 2005, p. 163.

And the system persisted even as agriculture played a declining role in European economies (down by 2000 to less than three per cent of GDP in almost every European state – the exceptions being Bulgaria, Greece, Hungary, Poland, Lithuania, Romania, and Spain – and accounting for about 2 to 6 per cent of jobs) (see Figure 21.2). By 1990, *The Economist* spoke for many of the critics of CAP when it described EU agricultural policy as 'the single most idiotic system of economic mismanagement' ever devised by rich western countries (*The Economist*, 29 September 1990).

How was this system sustained? At the heart of any discussion of CAP lie the peculiar interests of France, where agriculture was a bigger postwar employer and producer of economic wealth than in any of the EEC Six but Italy. Although the French government was a critical actor in the early agreements on European integration, domestic political and public support was thin, and in order to win that support it had to be shown that integration offered France clear benefits. It had its own system of national subsidies to farmers, which by the late 1950s was helping generate large surpluses, for which export markets were needed. For its part, West Germany had food shortages, but was importing from other countries than France because prices were lower. The Germans resisted a protectionist CAP, and were more interested in the customs union because of the benefits it promised to German industry, but Charles de Gaulle made progress on the customs union conditional on his having his way with CAP, and was able to

Figure 21.2 The changing economic role of European farming

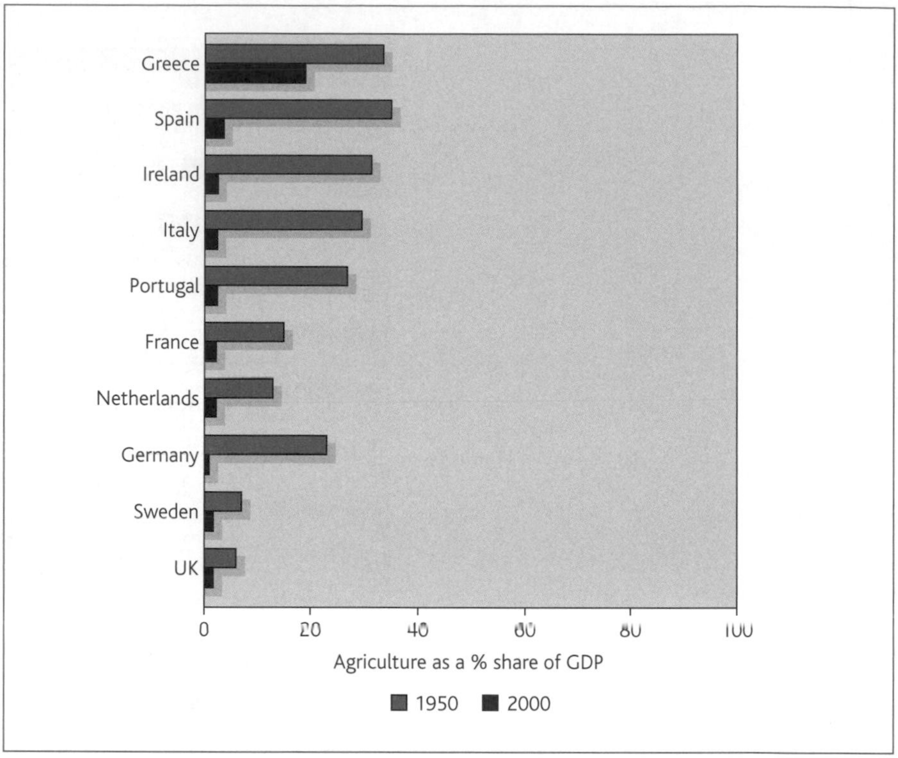

Source: Figures calculated by Rieger, 2005, p. 163.

wrest an agreement from the Germans in early 1962 on its key principles (Dinan, 2004, pp. 94–7).

France continued to be the driving force in EU agricultural policy even after the terms of CAP were agreed. The French farming population fell between 1950 and 2000 from nearly 31 per cent to just 3.4 per cent, while the share of agriculture in GDP fell over the same period from 15 per cent to just over 2 per cent. But French farmers had a strong domestic political role, enhanced by the number of people who live in the rural areas of France (and are thus economically impacted by farming), and by the semi-mythical role that the rural areas play in the French national psyche. More than one-fifth of EU agricultural production comes from France, which also takes the biggest share of EU farm spending (about one-sixth in 2010). The French government lobbies the EU on behalf of its farmers, and any threats to French farming interests are likely to bring farmers out in organized protests ranging from mass demonstrations to letting cattle loose in local government buildings, blocking highways with tractors, and dumping farm waste on Parisian avenues. But the political influence of farmers has been declining: many small farmers are living in poverty, thousands leave the land every year to look for other work, and the French farm lobby has been unable to stop reforms to EU agricultural policy.

For its first quarter century, CAP was a system of agricultural price supports (Burrell, 2009). Every year, representatives of the Commission, the Council of

Ministers, and farmers unions negotiated three kinds of prices for agricultural products: a target price that they hoped farmers would receive on the open market as a fair return on their investments, a threshold price to which EU imports would be raised to make sure that target prices were not undercut, and a guaranteed price that would be paid as a last resort to take produce off the market if it was not meeting the target price (Grant, 1997, p. 67). For example, in 1990 the target price for wheat was 234 ecus per tonne, the threshold price was 229 ecus, and the guaranteed price was 172 ecus (Swinbank, 2002, p. 166). The costs were borne by the European Agricultural Guidance and Guarantee Fund (EAGGF), which was created in 1962 and rapidly became the single biggest item on the Community budget; by 1970, agriculture was soaking up 75 per cent of Community spending. The Guidance section was used to improve agriculture by investing in new equipment and technology, while the Guarantee section (which accounted for most of the spending) protected markets and prices by buying and storing surplus produce and encouraging agricultural exports.

In some respects, CAP was a success. Western European agricultural production grew in leaps and bounds, and not only did the Community become self-sufficient in almost every product it could grow or produce in its climate (including wheat, barley, wine, meat, vegetables, and dairy products), but today's EU is a global agricultural trading powerhouse; it accounted in 2008 for 42 per cent of the world's agricultural exports (worth nearly $567 billion) and 42 per cent of its imports (although only about a quarter of its trade was with states outside the EU) (see Figure 21.3). Duplication was reduced as member states specialized in different products, CAP helped make most farmers wealthier and their livelihoods more predictable and stable, and the bad old days of food shortages disappeared. But in other respects CAP was less successful.

**Illustration 21.1
Demonstrating French farmers**

Agriculture has long been a core public issue in France, such that attempts to reform the Common Agricultural Policy will often spark demonstrations by French farmers.

Figure 21.3 The world's biggest agricultural exporters

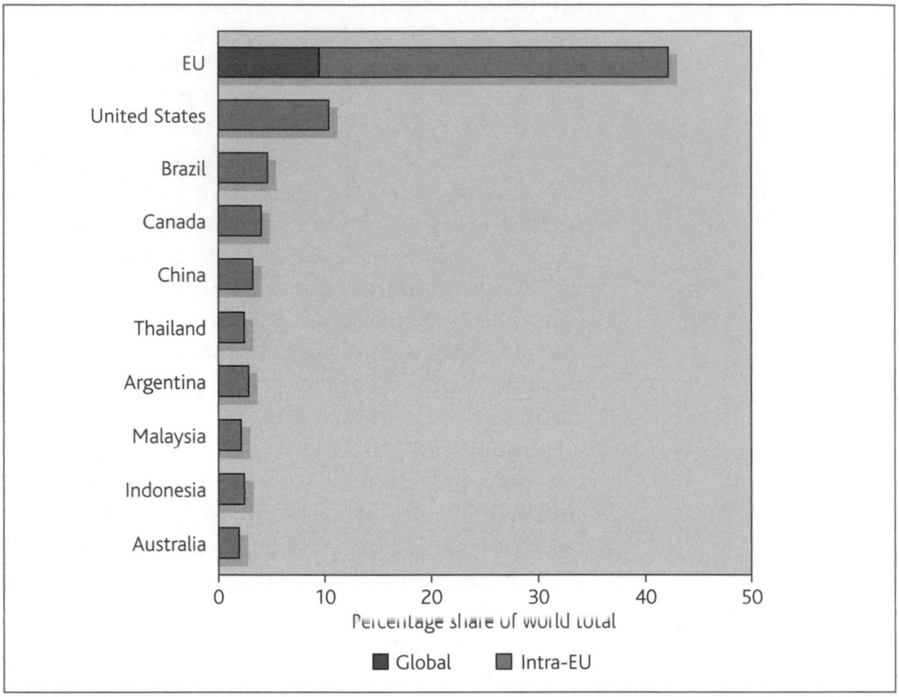

Source: World Trade Organization figures for 2008 at http://www.wto.org (retrieved May 2010).

First, spending grew as improvements in agricultural technology helped farmers produce more food from less land, with the result that the supply of commodities such as butter, cereals, beef, and sugar exceeded demand. The Community was obliged to buy the surplus, some of which was stored in warehouses, prompting jibes in the media about butter mountains and wine lakes (and jokes about visitors to Brussels stepping off the train and asking for directions to these mountains and lakes). Some of the excess was destroyed or converted (hence wine might be turned into spirits or even into heating fuel), but the rest was sold cheaply outside the Community or given away ('dumped') as food aid to poorer countries. This undercut local farmers, distorted the international marketplace, and soured Community relations with the United States (even though it also subsidized its farmers, and engaged in similar dumping). At the same time, the rules of the EAGGF were so convoluted that they were easy to exploit, encouraging farmers and suppliers to inflate their production figures and make fraudulent claims (Laffan, 1997, pp. 207–10).

As if these problems were not enough, environmentalists complained that the artificially high prices encouraged farmers to increase production by using chemical fertilizers and herbicides, and to cut down hedges and trees and 'reclaim' ecologically important wetlands so as to make their farms bigger and more efficient. The price of food for consumers was inflated, and the sight of excess production and increased spending on CAP did little to encourage public support for European integration. CAP also failed to close the income gap between rich and poor farmers: about 70 per cent of spending went to 20 per cent of farms, which were typically the biggest and wealthiest farms in northern Europe, while small farms – accounting for 40 per cent of the Community total, and often in the south – received only 8 per cent of funds. Under the circumstances, the case for reform was clear, but most suggestions came up against the resistance of farming lobbies and the governments over which they had the most influence (Dinan and Camhis, 2004).

The first major attempt to reform CAP came in 1968 with the Mansholt Plan, named for incumbent European agriculture commissioner Sicco Mansholt. The idea here was to amalgamate farms into bigger and more efficient units, and to encourage smaller farmers to leave the land. Both ideas met vehement opposition in France and West Germany, and agricultural reform was sidelined until Margaret Thatcher's campaign in the early 1980s to renegotiate British contributions to the Community budget, which coincidentally drew new attention to the problem of agricultural overproduction. The pressure for reform grew with international criticism generated by the pressures to reduce trade tariffs under the Uruguay Round of negotiations within the General Agreement on Trade and Tariffs (GATT). In 1991 agriculture commissioner Ray MacSharry suggested replacing guaranteed prices with a system of direct payments to farmers if prices fell below a certain level, and using the 'set-aside' system to encourage farmers to take land out of production as a condition of receiving CAP funding (Lewis, 1993, p. 337). His proposals (which earned him the nickname 'Mack the Knife' in British tabloids) were accepted in spite of opposition from farmers and their unions.

The pressures for reform continued as the EU began to make plans for eastern enlargement, which promised to increase CAP spending (see Jensen *et al.*, 2009). In 1998, agriculture commissioner Franz Fischler made several new proposals: that the EU move away from compensating farmers when prices fell below a certain level; that the set-aside scheme be ended; that prices for beef, cereals, and milk be cut; that more environmental management conditions be attached to payments to farmers; and that there should be more investment in developing the EU's rural areas. The core idea behind the reforms was 'decoupling', or breaking the link between subsidies and production, and encouraging farmers to produce for the market rather than for EU subsidies. The result of these and other changes, argued Fischler, would be to leave CAP 'virtually unrecognizable from the days of old' (Fischler, 2003). The link between subsidies to farmers and the amount they produce has indeed been broken, the prices paid for a wide range of agricultural products have fallen, direct payments for bigger farms have been cut, CAP has become less trade-distorting and more market-oriented, and the share of EU spending on agriculture has fallen from 75 per cent in 1970 to 31 per cent today.

Western European farmers were concerned that because so many of their eastern counterparts (relatively speaking) still worked in agriculture, and because so many operated small and relatively unproductive farms, enlargement would soak up most spending under CAP. At the same time, it was important to make sure that eastern European governments and their farmers did not feel that they were being treated as second-class citizens. The compromise ultimately agreed (without much enthusiasm) was to allow eastern European farmers a small but growing proportion of agricultural payments. Under a 2000–06 programme named Sapard (the special accession programme for agriculture and rural development), which was designed to help applicant countries prepare for

CAP, €22 billion was invested in eastern European agriculture, a rural development package worth €5.1 billion was made available for 2004–06, and agreement was reached that direct aids would be phased in over ten years, starting at 25 per cent in 2004 and moving up in annual increments of 5 per cent.

In 2008, EU leaders carried out a 'health check' of agricultural policy, and introduced changes that simplified CAP and allowed it to better respond to changes in the market. Direct payments to farmers have since fallen, funds have been transferred into rural development, and guaranteed prices are now seen mainly as a safety net to be used only when prices are unsustainably low. As this book went to press, more discussions about reform were in the pipeline, with an eye to controlling the EU budget while increasing spending in areas outside agriculture. There was talk of less spending but more regulation. Incoming agriculture commissioner Dacian Ciolos was from Romania, and as such was particularly concerned about the imbalance of payments between western and eastern Europe, and also spoke of the need to compensate farmers for 'public goods' such as land management. There was also a revival of an ongoing debate about the need to renationalize agricultural policy by returning powers to the member states (see Niemi and Kola, 2005), the argument being that climate and geography make it difficult to have a 'one size fits all' policy.

Overall, CAP today looks very different from the system designed in the 1960s. Then, the focus was on ensuring regular food supplies; today, the focus is on helping farmers survive and compete in the European and global markets. 'EU agricultural policy making', argues Burrell (2009), 'can no longer be described as an inward looking process seeking a compromise among different national interests.' Structurally, the main change has been a switch from price supports to direct payments, which now account for most agricultural spending in the EU budget, and overall agricultural spending has fallen as a percentage of total EU spending. There is more of a focus today on quality rather than quantity, driven mainly by changing consumer demands and rising concerns about the state of the environment. CAP payments have conditions attached, linked to food safety, animal health and welfare, sustainable development and the management of rural landscapes. Consumers are helped by more attention being paid to indicating the origin of agricultural produce and to encouraging organic production.

Fisheries policy

Although it has not been nearly as controversial or as expensive as agricultural policy, fisheries policy has been the target of an equally sustained programme of political attention, and has been one of the policy areas in which a truly EU-wide approach has been agreed (but with mixed results). (For a survey of EU fisheries policy, see Lequesne, 2004.) Fishing today employs only about 400,000 Europeans, but the EU fishing industry is the world's third biggest (after China and Japan), and the health of that industry has implications for large numbers of Europeans: almost every EU member state has a coastline (the exceptions being Austria, the Czech Republic, Hungary, Luxembourg, and Slovakia), the EU has the world's largest maritime territory (it has more sea than land), about 60 per cent of the EU population lives within a few kilometres of the sea, and they account for more than 40 per cent of EU gross domestic product. The structure

Figure 21.4 The EU's ten biggest fishing fleets

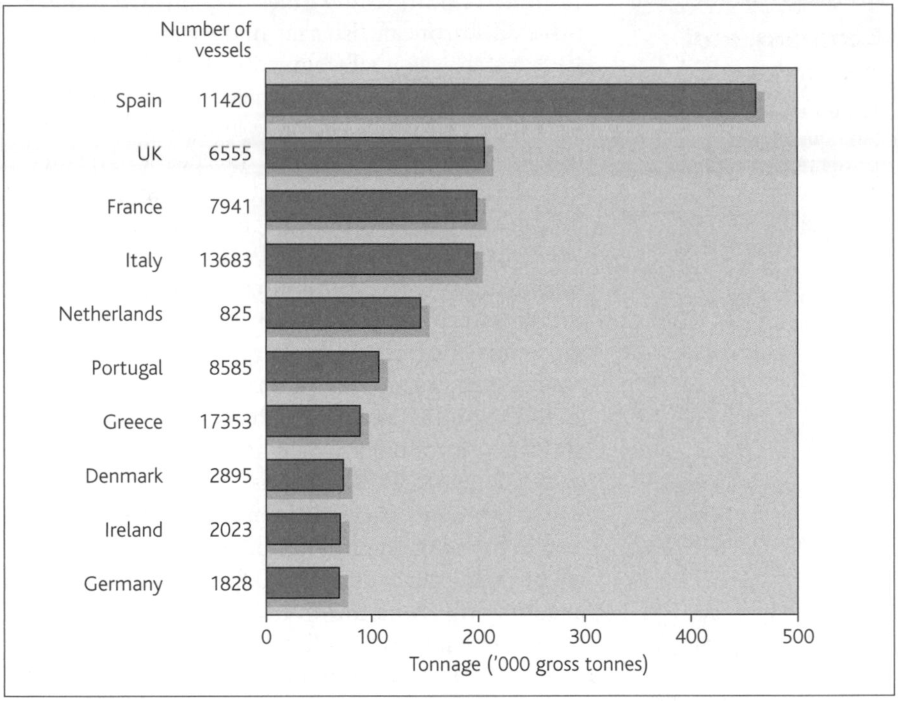

	Number of vessels
Spain	11420
UK	6555
France	7941
Italy	13683
Netherlands	825
Portugal	8585
Greece	17353
Denmark	2895
Ireland	2023
Germany	1828

Tonnage ('000 gross tonnes)

Figures are for 2008.
Source: European Commission at http://ec.europa.eu/fisheries/fleetstatistics (retrieved August 2010).

of fishing fleets varies from one member state to another, so – for example – while Greece has by far the biggest fleet in the EU by number of vessels, it ranks low on the list when measured by tonnage. Spain's fleet is third largest by number but is by far the biggest by tonnage (see Figure 21.4).

The main (theoretical) goal of the **Common Fisheries Policy** (CFP) has been to help support a competitive fishing industry while also preventing overfishing and ensuring sustainability. It does this mainly through conservation, imposing national quotas (Total Allowable Catches, or TACs) on the take of Atlantic and North Sea fish; setting rules on fishing gear and mesh sizes for fishing nets, and requiring accurate reporting of catches and landings. It also sets rules on the protection of marine mammals, birds, and vulnerable species of fish; requires that all EU fishing boats are licensed; has a fleet management policy that limits the size of EU fishing fleets; manages the market in order to monitor prices, quality, marketing, and competition; and reaches agreements with third countries on access to their fishing grounds.

At the heart of fishing policy has been access to – and management of – resources. Before 1970 each European coastal state had control over its own fishing grounds, but this did not stop the occasional dispute breaking out, such as the famous cod wars of the 1950s and 1970s between Britain and Iceland over access to North Sea fisheries. In 1970 it was agreed that Community fishing boats could have access to all fishing grounds with the exception of those closest to the coast, and a common market for fisheries products was created. In 1976, in line

● **Common Fisheries Policy**: A joint EU policy aimed at managing fish stocks and regulating the EU fishing industry.

CONCEPT

Common pool resources

Resources that do not come under the jurisdiction of a single state, authority, or government, and are open to unregulated exploitation. They include the air, oceans, rivers, lakes, fisheries, grazing land, and groundwater basins. Those motivated by maximum profit and minimum cost will be tempted to extract as much as they can from such resources, leaving the costs to be borne by all other parties interested in the resources. The failure of EU fisheries policy is an example of the difficulties of managing common pool resources.

with changes in international law, access to marine resources was expanded from 12 miles (19km) to 200 miles (322km) from the coastline, and it was decided to place all European fisheries under Community jurisdiction and to develop the CFP, which was finally agreed in 1983. Not all states were happy about opening up their fishing grounds; hence French patrol boats fired on Spanish trawlers operating inside the 200-mile limit in 1984, and more than two dozen Spanish trawlers were intercepted off the coast of Ireland. The Spanish fishing fleet was bigger at the time than the EC fleet combined, and fishing rights were high on the agenda during Spain's negotiations to join the EC.

Reforms came to the CFP in 2002, aimed at placing a greater emphasis on sustainability and on minimizing the impact of fishing on marine ecosystems. Problems with enforcement led to the creation in 2005 of the Community Fisheries Control Agency, charged with enforcing the rules and with training fisheries inspectors. Another discussion about reform of the CFP in 2009–10 emphasized the problems of fleets that were too large, catches that were unsustainable, and the unprofitability of most fisheries operations. Under the 2007–13 budget package, nearly €4 billion was set aside for the European Fisheries Fund, under which payments are made to member states, which can decide for themselves how best to invest the money; it might be used for developing sea and inland fisheries, encouraging aquaculture (fish farms), supporting processing and marketing, and encouraging economic diversification in fishing communities.

The challenges faced by EU fisheries are not unique to Europe; overfishing is a global problem, researchers estimating that as much as one-fifth of the worldwide fish catch is unregulated and illegal, and that overfishing has left major fish stocks depleted. Combined with the effects of pollution, this threatens sustainability and the future of marine ecosystems (see Clover, 2005). Fisheries are a classic example of the dilemma of **common pool resources**, where a large resource exists that is difficult to effectively manage, and where rational self-interest encourages all those who have access to the resource to extract as much of it as possible, maximizing their benefits at the cost of others. The CFP, then, cannot function in isolation, but must be part of a global regime to manage fisheries. The record so far of the EU on managing its fisheries has not been a good one, and the pressures for radical reform have been growing.

Environmental policy

In contrast to agricultural policy, which was high on the EEC agenda from the beginning, environmental policy has only crept on to that agenda more recently, a function of changing public and political interest in environmental issues. The environment was not something to which national governments paid much attention in the 1950s, and there was no mention of the environment in the Treaty of Rome, although its references to 'a harmonious development of economic activities, a continuous and balanced expansion, [and] . . . an accelerated raising of the standard of living' could all be interpreted in retrospect as setting the stage for what followed. A few laws were agreed in the early years of the Community dealing with radiation in the workplace and the management of dangerous chemicals, but they were prompted less by concerns for the environment than by the drive to build a single market (Hildebrand, 1993). It was only in the late 1960s and early 1970s that Community governments began to pay much attention to environmental issues, encouraged heightened public concerns driven by a combination of new scientific understanding, several headline-making environmental disasters (such as oil spills), and growing concerns among the affluent Western middle classes about quality of life issues (McCormick, 1995, Chapter 3).

The landmark United Nations Conference on the Human Environment, held in Stockholm in July 1972, drew wider political and public attention to the problems of the environment for the first time, encouraging governments to create new environmental agencies, to develop broad-ranging environmental policies, and to pass new laws. Three months later, the EEC heads of government meeting in Paris agreed the need for an environmental policy, and the European Commission adopted its first Environment Action Programme (EAP) in late 1973. New EAPs came into force in 1977, 1982, 1987, 1993, and 2002, the latter running until 2012. Meanwhile, in an attempt to improve the quality of the data upon which policy was based, the European Environment Agency was created in 1993 (see Chapter 14).

The first two EAPs emphasized preventive action and the need to guard against different national policies becoming barriers to the single market. The third EAP switched the focus by factoring environmental considerations in to other policy areas – notably agriculture, industry, energy, and transport – so that the environment was no longer secondary to the single market (Hildebrand, 1993). But these changes took place outside the treaties, and a new sense of urgency was created by enlargement to Greece, Portugal, and Spain, none of which had strong environmental standards. The Single European Act finally gave a legal basis to Community environmental policy and made environmental protection a component of all EC policies. Most importantly, the SEA began a process by which **sustainable development** was moved to the heart of European policy. The SEA noted the importance of 'prudent and rational utilization of natural resources', Maastricht called for 'sustainable and non-inflationary growth respecting the environment', and Amsterdam confirmed the need for a 'balanced and sustainable development of economic activities'. Sustainable development is now one of the core policy objectives of the EU, applying to everything that it does.

In contrast to many other areas of EU public policy, where (in spite of concerns about the elitism of the EU policy process) the average European engages little, opinion polls have found that support for action at the EU level is overwhelmingly preferred to action at the level of the member states. Environmental concerns have also translated into the rise of numerous and often politically influential national public interest groups, the green consumer lifestyle has become thoroughly mainstream since the mid-1990s, and environmental consciousness has translated into support for green politics. Green political parties have had members elected to the European Parliament and the national legislatures of most EU member states, and have been part of coalition governments in Belgium, Finland, France, Germany, Italy, and several other countries.

If the breadth and depth of the EU's activities in the environmental field have not always attracted much attention, in two areas at least there has been a different record. On chemicals policy the EU has now become a world leader, changes in the way chemicals are tested and recorded at home leading to pressures for changes in the United States and more generally in the international regime (see

● **Environmental policy**: Policy dealing with the management of renewable natural resources (such as air, water, land and forests) and with limiting the harmful impact of human activity.

● **Sustainable development**: Development that recognizes natural limits and does not result in permanent and harmful environmental change or natural resource depletion.

Figure 21.5 Main areas of EU environmental policy

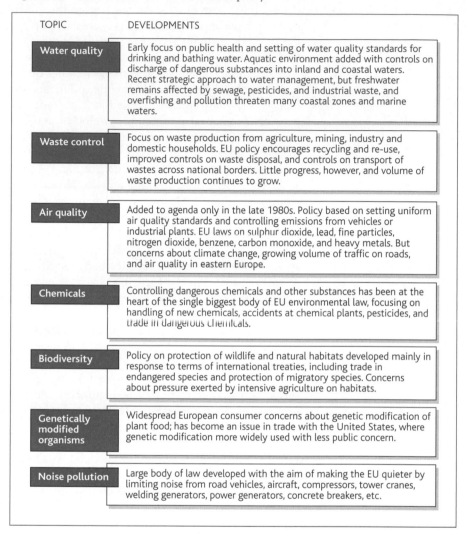

TOPIC	DEVELOPMENTS
Water quality	Early focus on public health and setting of water quality standards for drinking and bathing water. Aquatic environment added with controls on discharge of dangerous substances into inland and coastal waters. Recent strategic approach to water management, but freshwater remains affected by sewage, pesticides, and industrial waste, and overfishing and pollution threaten many coastal zones and marine waters.
Waste control	Focus on waste production from agriculture, mining, industry and domestic households. EU policy encourages recycling and re-use, improved controls on waste disposal, and controls on transport of wastes across national borders. Little progress, however, and volume of waste production continues to grow.
Air quality	Added to agenda only in the late 1980s. Policy based on setting uniform air quality standards and controlling emissions from vehicles or industrial plants. EU laws on sulphur dioxide, lead, fine particles, nitrogen dioxide, benzene, carbon monoxide, and heavy metals. But concerns about climate change, growing volume of traffic on roads, and air quality in eastern Europe.
Chemicals	Controlling dangerous chemicals and other substances has been at the heart of the single biggest body of EU environmental law, focusing on handling of new chemicals, accidents at chemical plants, pesticides, and trade in dangerous chemicals.
Biodiversity	Policy on protection of wildlife and natural habitats developed mainly in response to terms of international treaties, including trade in endangered species and protection of migratory species. Concerns about pressure exerted by intensive agriculture on habitats.
Genetically modified organisms	Widespread European consumer concerns about genetic modification of plant food; has become an issue in trade with the United States, where genetic modification more widely used with less public concern.
Noise pollution	Large body of law developed with the aim of making the EU quieter by limiting noise from road vehicles, aircraft, compressors, tower cranes, welding generators, power generators, concrete breakers, etc.

Focus). But undoubtedly the biggest volume of political attention (if not necessarily the most effective policy results) has been drawn by climate change, where the EU is one of the world's four major policy players, along with the United States, China, and India, and has been at the heart of efforts to achieve international agreement (see Jordan *et al.*, 2010, and Wurzel and Connelly, 2010).

The science of the greenhouse effect was established in the nineteenth century, and the problem of climate change was well known to scientists as long ago as the early 1980s, but it has only been since the late 1990s – thanks to increasingly dire warnings of its possible effects – that it has become a headline issue. So firm is its new place on the public policy agenda that it even survived the economic downturns of 2007–10; history has shown that environmental issues tend to rise and fall on the public agenda in inverse relationship to the state of the economy, but this has not applied to climate change. However, putting it on the agenda has been relatively easy compared to the search for

Focus on . . .
Europe's leadership on chemicals

The control and handling of chemicals has long been at the top of the EU environmental agenda, with a large body of laws designed to control the release of new chemicals onto the market, to prevent accidents at chemical plants, to control the use of pesticides, and to regulate trade in dangerous chemicals. The earliest EU chemicals legislation dates from 1967, and was motivated by the desire to remove obstacles posed to the common market by different sets of national regulations. During the 1970s, the desire to protect consumers led to measures to ban or limit the commercialization of dangerous substances and preparations. Since the 1980s the focus has been on efforts to minimize the impact of chemicals on the environment (McCormick, 2001, chapter 6).

All these initiatives were capped in 2006 with the adoption of the REACH regulation (Registration, Evaluation, Authorization and Restriction of Chemical substances), which entered into force in June 2007. Prompted by concerns that thousands of new chemical compounds (many of them synthetic) had been placed on the market with little information about their potential threats to human health and the environment, REACH requires that manufacturers and importers gather information on the properties of the chemicals that are produced or imported and submit that information to the European Chemicals Agency. This manages a database through which all that information is made available to consumers and industry, the goal being to make clear any known risks associated with those chemicals. The regulation also encourages manufacturers to develop alternatives to the most dangerous chemicals.

The US government initially lobbied hard against REACH, because US laws on chemicals have traditionally been lax, making it difficult to ban or restrict chemicals, and manufacturers have been resistant to releasing information for fear of losing competitive advantage. But the US ultimately had to concede not only to its passage, but to the new reality that US chemical manufacturers would have to follow the EU lead or else potentially lose access to the lucrative European market for many of their products (Layton, 2008). Where the United States had long been the leader on environmental regulation, with Europeans having to make adjustments, the record on chemicals suggests that the roles may be in the process of being reversed.

viable solutions to the problem (Jordan *et al.*, 2010, p. 3), and it has also been argued that much of what the EU has so far achieved has been as a fortuitous result of changes in economic conditions rather than of deliberate pollution control policies (Kerr, 2007).

Climate changes as a result of natural causes, but evidence suggests that warming of the climate has been accelerated by emissions of greenhouse gases such as carbon dioxide (CO_2), which trap more solar radiation, warming the atmosphere, and causing a wide range of climatic and environmental effects. While this is often described as the ultimate global environmental issue, national governments have been reluctant to take unilateral action for fear of losing comparative economic advantage. The vast majority of scientists around the world argue that our understanding of the causes and effects of climate change is complete, but enough have expressed doubt to offer a way out for those opposed to action.

Illustration 21.2
Air pollution

Improving the quality of European air has been a core focus of EU environmental policy, which has helped make scenes such as this increasingly rare on the European landscape.

The EU both supported and signed the core international agreement – the 1992 UN Framework Convention on Climate Change – and a 1997 protocol to the convention that was signed in Kyoto, Japan, with the goal of giving the convention some substance. In 2000 the Commission launched the European Climate Change Programme, listing measures that could be taken to reduce emissions (including greater use of renewable energy), and in 2002 the EU-15 ratified Kyoto, committing them to cutting CO_2 emissions by 8 per cent on 1990 levels by 2008–12. This would be done with an **Emissions Trading Scheme**, launched in 2005. Under this arrangement (also known as cap and trade), member states set limits on CO_2 emissions from industrial plants (more than 10,000 are involved), which are given emission allowances. Those that use less than their allowance can sell the balance to companies that are having trouble meeting the limits.

The results of EU climate change policy have been mixed. By 2004, the EU-25 had reduced their CO_2 emissions by 7.3 per cent compared to 1990 levels, while the US saw a rise in emissions over the same period of 15.8 per cent. By 2007, EU emissions were down only 4.3 per cent, and while most EU member states were in negative territory, and making greater progress than the United States or Japan, they were not down far enough to meet targets, and the achievements of member states such as Germany and Britain were offset by increases in Italy, Portugal and Spain (see Figure 21.6). According to the International Energy Agency (http://www.iea.org, figures retrieved May 2010), the EU accounted in 2007 for just over 13 per cent of global emissions (or 7.9 tonnes per person), while the United States accounted for 20 per cent of emissions (or 19 tonnes per person). In March 2007, the EU announced its 20-20-20 Strategy aimed at cutting CO_2 emissions by 20 per cent (on 1990 levels) and generating 20 per cent of its energy from renewable sources by 2020. The agreement included all 27

● **Emissions Trading Scheme**: A free-market mechanism for reducing greenhouse gases, using emission caps and tradable emission allowances.

Figure 21.6 Changes in greenhouse gas emissions

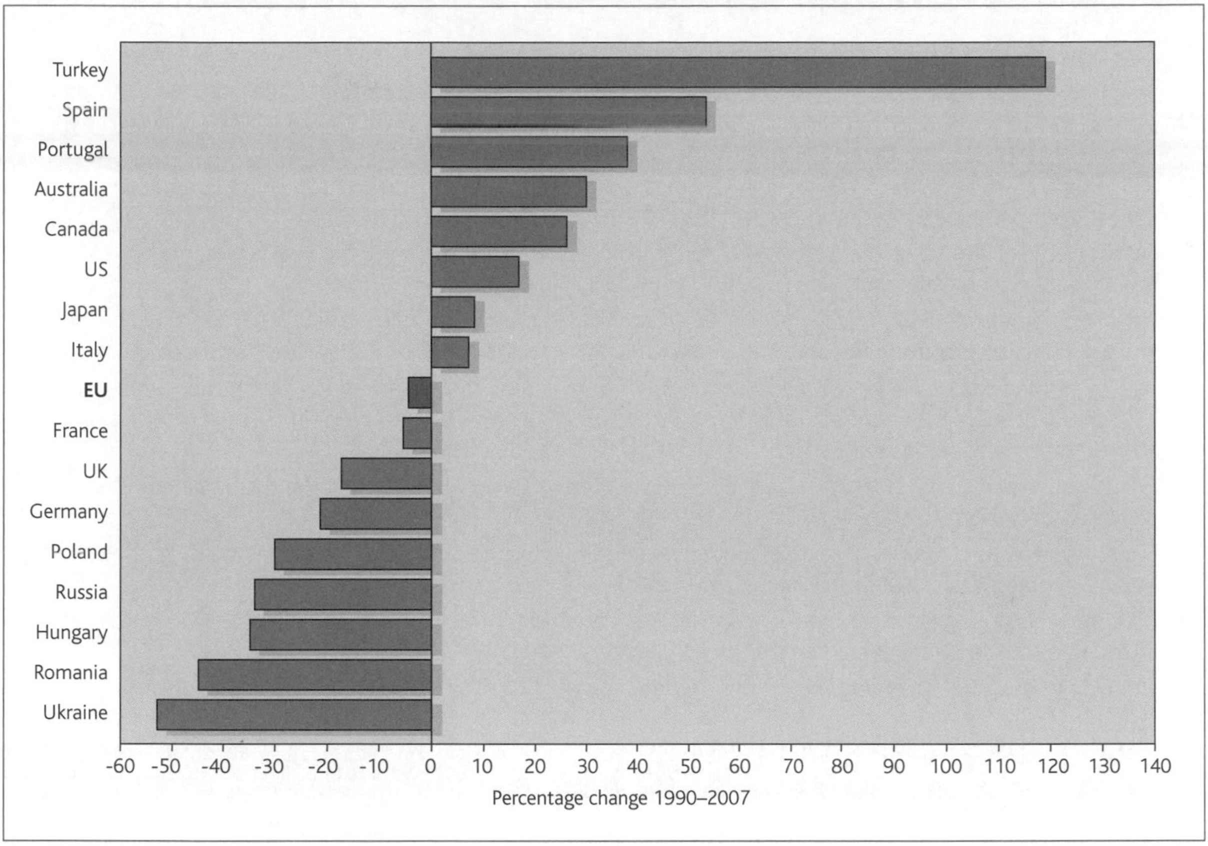

Source: United Nations Framework Convention on Climate Change at http://unfccc.int (retrieved May 2010).

member states, and was intended to be a bargaining position as preparations were made for a replacement to the Kyoto protocol, set to expire in 2012. But whatever the trends in industrialized countries, the greatest growth in emissions continues to be in industrializing states such as China (up 172 per cent between 1990 and 2007) and India (up 125 per cent).

In December 2009, the parties to the climate change convention and the Kyoto protocol met in Copenhagen to try and give climate change policy more teeth, but the conference ended in failure. Although an accord was agreed acknowledging that climate change is one of the greatest challenges facing the world today, and that action should be taken to keep temperature increases below 2°C, it was not legally binding, and included no commitments for specific cuts in CO_2 emissions. The EU had come into the negotiations on something of a moral high ground, having said that it would go ahead with its emissions trading scheme whatever was agreed at Copenhagen, but was later criticized for its failure to take a leadership position by increasing its CO_2 reduction commitments and providing the kind of example that many observers felt that the conference needed. In the end, however, it was mainly the failure of the US to make real commitments and of China and India to cooperate that led to an absence of agreement.

SUMMARY

- Agriculture has been a far more prominent issue on the EU agenda than it is on the agendas of most economically developed states.
- At the heart of EU activities has been the Common Agricultural Policy, which began as a system of price supports designed to prevent food shortages.
- CAP encouraged greater production, but also swallowed large amounts of spending, skewed European and global markets, and raised the ire of environmentalists.
- Reforms to CAP have switched the focus from quantity to quality, breaking the link between payments and the amount that farmers produce.
- Fishing employs relatively few people in Europe, but has economic knock-on effects for coastal communities and for all EU coastal member states.
- The Common Fisheries Policy was adopted in 1983, focusing on managing fishing fleets and catches, along with the welfare of the marine environment. But overfishing remains a problem in European waters as it does all over the world, and a more effective global regime is clearly needed.
- The environment was a latecomer to the European policy agenda, drawing sustained political and public attention only from the late 1960s.
- EU policy focuses on sustainable development, and EU activities have focused on air and water quality, waste control, chemicals, and the protection of biodiversity.
- EU chemicals policy has tightened up controls and management at home and has had global implications by affecting all states that seek access to the European market.
- The EU has set itself ambitious targets on climate change, but has failed to build a global leadership position.

KEY TERMS AND CONCEPTS

Agricultural policy

Common Agricultural Policy

Common Fisheries Policy

Common pool resources

Emissions Trading Scheme

Environmental policy

Sustainable development

FURTHER READING

Ackrill, Robert (2000), *The Common Agricultural Policy* (London: Continuum); Wyn Grant (1997), *The Common Agricultural Policy* (Basingstoke: Macmillan). Despite all the fuss and expense surrounding CAP, these are two of the few full-length published studies of this critical topic.

Knill, Christoph, and Duncan Liefferink (2007), *Environmental Politics in the European Union: Policy-making, Implementation and Patterns of Multi-level Governance* (Manchester: Manchester University Press); Andrew Jordan (2005), *Environmental Policy in the European Union: Actors, Institutions and Processes* (London: Earthscan). Two studies of EU environmental policy, including chapters on the policy process and on specific policy areas, including air and water pollution.

Skogstad, Grace, and Amy Verdun (eds) (2009), 'The Common Agricultural Policy: Policy Dynamics in a Changing Context', in *Journal of European Integration* 31:3. A special issue of this journal, with several useful contributions on the background, dynamics, and future of CAP.

CHAPTER 22

Cohesion Policy

Social and economic inequalities are a fact of life, if for no other reason than because humans have different aspirations and abilities, and because economies vary by time and place in the opportunities they provide . Differences in wealth, income and aptitude skew the dynamics of open markets, benefiting some at the cost of others and reducing the free flow of people, money, goods and services. As a result, efforts to remove those differences have long been at the heart of European integration.

Cohesion policy focuses on promoting the single market by creating new economic opportunities in the poorer parts of the EU: the GDP of the wealthiest EU states is several times that of the poorest, and urban areas are generally wealthier than rural areas, creating economic pressures that interfere with balanced development. Meanwhile, social policy focuses on encouraging free movement of labour, improving living and working conditions, and protecting the rights and benefits of workers. At the core of EU concerns have been the curiously persistent high rates of unemployment in parts of the EU, made worse since 2007 by the effects of the global economic crisis.

Improved social mobility and a more open labour market are, in turn, a function of the portability of educational qualifications. Education policy is still very much the responsibility of the member states, and this is unlikely to change, but the Council of Europe and the EU have been behind programmes to establish equivalencies across national borders and to encourage Europeans to complete at least part of their education in another member state.

KEY ISSUES

- In the face of globalization, how much can the EU hope to achieve in terms of reducing economic inequalities among its member states?

- Is cohesion better promoted collectively or should there be more emphasis on the use of national resources?

- Is there such a thing as a European Social Model?

- Why are rates of unemployment as high as they are in parts of the EU but not in others, and what role does integration have in addressing this problem?

- What are the implications of the rise of the Erasmus generation?

The quest for economic equality

Europeans are among the wealthiest people in the world, living in advanced post-industrial societies with diverse economies, a wide array of generous public services, well-developed infrastructure, and a high standard of living when measured by access to education, jobs, housing, and disposable income. But economic inequality persists, and levels of income and opportunity vary both within EU member states and from one state to another.

Overall, the wealthiest parts of the EU are in the economic heartland running from London to Milan, while the poorest parts are in the eastern, southern, and western peripheries. Wealth tends to go hand in hand with education and services, which is partly why Luxembourg – whose economy is based almost entirely on banking and financial services – is the wealthiest country in the world when measured by per capita GDP. Meanwhile, the tribulations of the EU's marginal areas have different causes: some are depressed agricultural areas; some are declining industrial areas; some are geographically isolated from the opportunities offered by bigger markets; and most suffer lower levels of education and health care, as well as underdeveloped infrastructure.

The data illustrate the dimensions of the problem. Using the comparative measure of per capita GDP adjusted to account for purchasing power (how much can be bought with a unit of currency in each member state), Map 22.1 shows that most western European states are at the higher end of the range, and most eastern European states at the lower end. If we take the figure for the whole EU as 100, the per capita GDP of Luxembourg – at 267 in 2009 – is nearly seven times that of Bulgaria and Romania (41–42) with their larger rural and agricultural populations. The contrasts are even greater when we look at the regions of the member states: the figure for central London in 2009 was 303 (but it was also the most expensive city in the world in which to live) and for Brussels was 248, while at the other end of the scale lay Severozapaden in Bulgaria (26) and Nord-Est Romania (24). A related picture is painted by the data for unemployment (see Map 22.2, p. 386).

With such problems in mind, the EU has worked on trying to broaden the provision of economic opportunity. Through what was once known as regional policy, but is now known more generally as **cohesion policy**, it tries to strengthen the internal bonds of the European marketplace by supplementing national efforts to reduce regional economic disparities, bringing down the remaining barriers to the single market, and improving the global competitiveness of the EU. In addition to the obvious economic and social benefits of greater opportunity, there is an important psychological element to this: the benefits of integration are made more clear to poorer states benefiting from the new opportunities created by redistribution of wealth and to the richer states capitalizing on the opportunities created by the building of new markets (European Commission, 2007).

The origins of cohesion policy can be traced back to grants made available by the European Coal and Steel Community to help revitalize depressed industrial areas. The Treaty of Rome emphasized the need for the member states to 'strengthen the unity of their economies and to ensure their harmonious development by reducing the differences existing among the various regions and the backwardness of the less favoured regions'. It also set up a European Social Fund designed to help promote worker mobility by supporting retraining and job

● **Cohesion policy**: Policy aimed at redistributing wealth and creating new opportunities in poorer parts of the EU with the goal of closing the income gap.

Map 22.1 Economic wealth in the EU

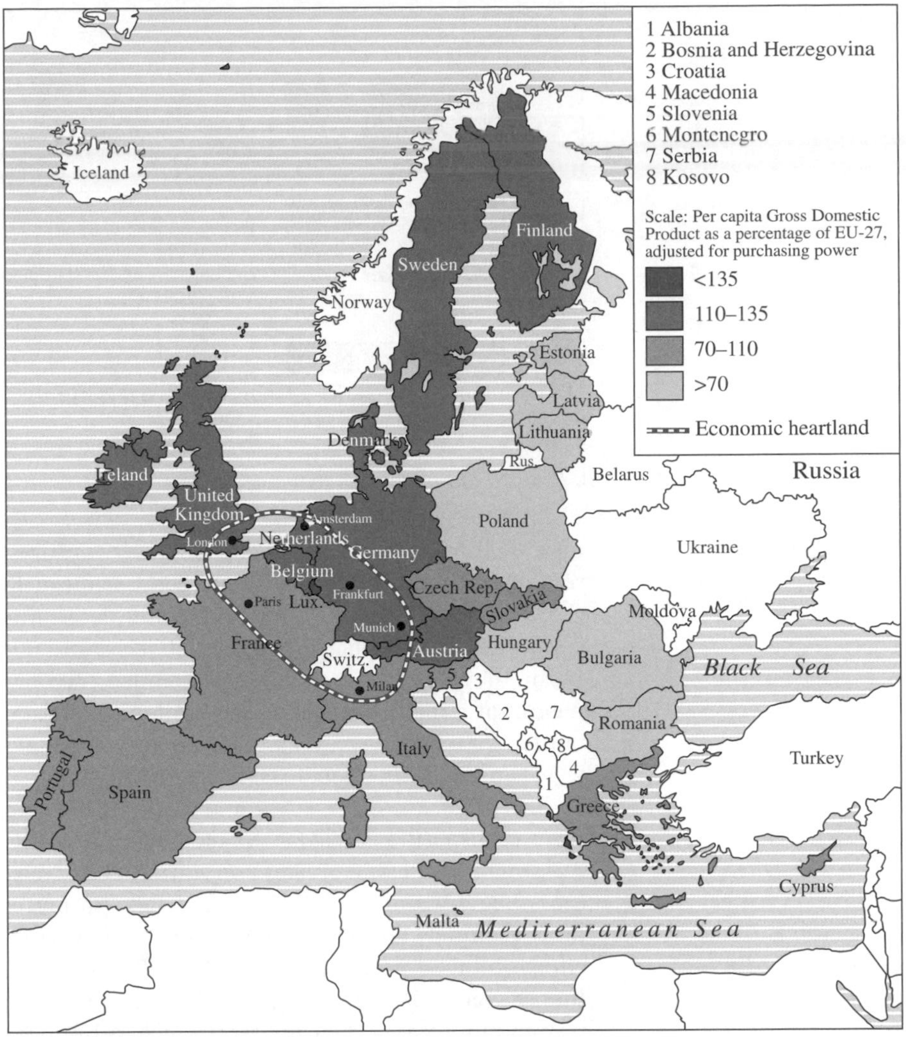

All figures for 2009 except Bulgaria (2008) and Romania (2007). Highest: Luxembourg, 267. Lowest: Bulgaria, 41. Figure for United States is 146 and for Japan is 109.
Source: Based on Eurostat figures at http://epp.eurostat.ec.europa.eu (retrieved August 2010).

creation. But because economic disparities among the founding six member states were relatively limited (with the notable exception of southern Italy), there was a less than enthusiastic response when the Commission in 1969 proposed a common regional policy, including the creation of a regional development fund. Dealing with the problems of CAP and controlling the Community budget were higher priorities, certainly for France and Germany.

It was only with the 1973 accession of Britain and Ireland, which widened the economic disparities within the Community, that there was a change of heart. A 1973 Commission-sponsored study (the Thomson Report) pointed out that regional differences would be a barrier to a balanced expansion, that they threatened to undermine plans for economic and monetary union, and that they could

Figure 22.1 The structural funds

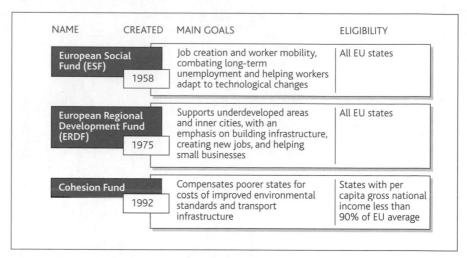

NAME	CREATED	MAIN GOALS	ELIGIBILITY
European Social Fund (ESF)	1958	Job creation and worker mobility, combating long-term unemployment and helping workers adapt to technological changes	All EU states
European Regional Development Fund (ERDF)	1975	Supports underdeveloped areas and inner cities, with an emphasis on building infrastructure, creating new jobs, and helping small businesses	All EU states
Cohesion Fund	1992	Compensates poorer states for costs of improved environmental standards and transport infrastructure	States with per capita gross national income less than 90% of EU average

pose a threat to the common market (European Commission, 1973). In response, it was decided to set up the European Regional Development Fund (ERDF) in 1975. Because member states determined which projects would be supported on their home territory, it was more a 'national' policy than a joint European project (Bachtler and Mendez, 2007), and the relatively wealthy regions of richer Community states often received funds when poorer regions in poorer states were in greater obvious need. Britain, Ireland, France, and Italy were the biggest net beneficiaries.

The accession of Portugal and Spain in 1986 meant a further widening of regional disparities, added to which there were concerns that the Single European Act would result in a greater concentration of wealth in the Community's core economies (McAleavey, 1993, p. 92). These prompted reforms which generated a more genuinely European cohesion policy, with a doubling of spending and more efforts to invest in those parts of the EU most obviously in need. The SEA listed the key goal of strengthening the 'economic and social cohesion' of the Community, since when the term *cohesion* has been used interchangeably with regional and structural policy to describe efforts to bridge economic differences within the EU. Another initiative came in 1993 during the negotiations over Maastricht when Spain, worried that it would become a net contributor to Community funds, pushed for the creation of a new Cohesion Fund that would compensate poorer EU states for the costs of tightening their environmental quality standards and investing in improvement of infrastructure.

Eastern enlargement once again changed the nature of the game, bringing in states still suffering from the stultifying effects of decades of Soviet-style central planning and under-development, and widening the gap between rich and poor even further. Whatever the case for investments in the relatively wealthy western states, the influx of far poorer eastern states changed the entire economic and political balance. Another round of reforms and adjustments led to the creation of the system that exists today, which is based around three principal **structural funds**: the European Social Fund, the European Regional Development Fund, and the Cohesion Fund (see Figure 22.1). Through each, resources are trans-

● **Structural funds**: Funds managed by the EU and designed to invest in economic development and job creation in poorer parts of the EU.

ferred to those parts of the EU most clearly in need of help. Each fund has a different target – whether job creation in inner cities, the retraining of workers, or helping meet the costs of tighter environmental regulation – and eligibility for spending varies according to need.

The EU has also made investments in economic growth through four other funds that, unlike the multi-annual, long-term, and strategic qualities of the structural funds, are focused on particular market sectors or specific problems, such as addressing the effects of job losses generated by increased international competition.

- The *Solidarity Fund* (created 2002) supports responses to natural disasters by restoring infrastructure, providing temporary accommodation, funding rescue services and protecting cultural heritage.
- Sparked by changes to the Common Agricultural Policy, the *European Agricultural Fund for Rural Development* was set up in 2006 to help modernize farming and forestry, help offset the costs of EU agricultural law, encourage better food quality, and support improvements to the rural environment and diversification of the rural economy.
- The *Globalization Adjustment Fund* (created 2007) helps workers who have lost their jobs as a result of trade liberalization to find new jobs. Most of the help so far has gone to people once employed in the vehicle, mobile phone, furniture, textile and clothing industries.
- The *European Fisheries Fund* (2007–13) helps fishermen and fishing vessel owners affected by efforts to control overfishing, and encourages sustainable development of coastal fishing areas.

In the period 2007–13 a total of nearly €350 billion (or €700 per resident of the EU) was budgeted for the structural funds. As Figure 22.2 shows, the biggest recipients in per capita and/or absolute terms were the eastern member states, along with Portugal, Greece and Spain; Estonia received the most in per capita terms (€2658 per person) while Poland received the most in absolute terms (nearly €67.3 billion, or nearly 20 per cent of all structural fund spending). Western European states received the least in per capita and absolute terms, the only clear anomalies being Portugal and Greece.

Where once policy priorities were based on dividing the regions of the EU into three categories known as Objectives 1, 2 and 3, they now have different labels but approximately similar goals.

- The Convergence Objective targets regions with a per capita GDP that is less than 75 per cent of the EU average, the goal here being to encourage more investment, new jobs, and improved infrastructure. Before eastern enlargement, the then Objective 1 regions were mainly on the margins of the EU-15: Greece, southern Italy, Sardinia and Corsica, Spain, Portugal, Ireland, western Scotland, northern Finland, and eastern Germany. Except for a few under-populated areas in Scandinavia, the focus has since moved east, where almost all of eastern Europe now qualifies. The biggest recipients in 2007–13 were, in order, Poland, Spain, the Czech Republic, Hungary, and Italy. Spending comes out of all three structural funds, and accounts for more than 80 per cent of all EU regional spending.

- The Regional Competitiveness and Employment Objective covers parts of the EU not already covered by the Convergence Objective, and its goal is to make these areas more competitive and more attractive for investment. Funds come from the ERDF and the ESF, and the biggest recipients in 2007–13 were France, Germany, the UK and Italy.

Figure 22.2 Spending under the structural funds

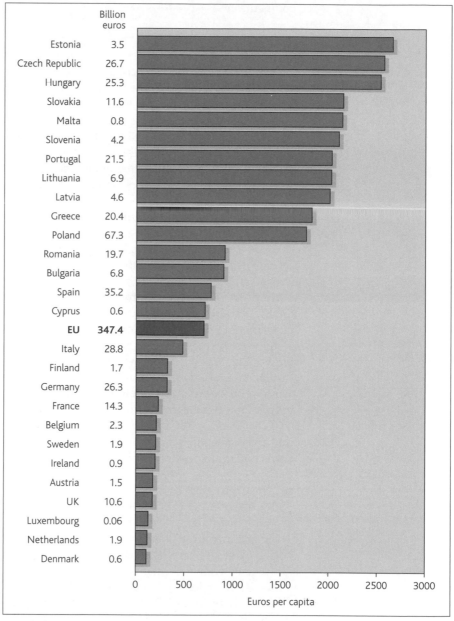

Per capita figures calculated by author.

Source: Spending totals (for 2007–13) from European Commission at http://ec.europa.eu/regional_policy/policy/fonds/index_en.htm (retrieved August 2010).

● The Territorial Cooperation Objective focuses on encouraging cooperation between European regions, and the development of common solutions to the challenges of urban, rural and coastal development. Financed out of the ERDF, it accounted for less than three per cent of structural fund spending in 2007–13.

Opinion on the effectiveness of spending under the structural funds is divided, mainly because the link between cause and effect in economic matters is so difficult to determine. Reducing gaps in wealth and opportunity is as much a function of effective economic policies and changes in the wider economic environment as it is of the redistribution of wealth, making it hard to pick out the particular effects of EU spending. In a 2001 review, Pastor (2001, pp. 59–62) argued that EU policy benefited from a clearly defined set of goals, and that it had helped reduce the income gap between rich and poor states, but that there were too many structural funds (creating duplication), that it had tended to generate greater inequalities within poorer states where more prosperous regions had progressed more quickly than less prosperous regions, that too big a share of funding had gone to the poorer regions of wealthy states, and that while poorer states outperformed richer states during periods of economic growth, they did worse than the EU average during times of recession

More recently, the effect of the global economic crisis has been to pull EU states in different directions: while the need for more development investment in poorer parts of the EU remains clear, the desire to control spending and budgets has made wealthier governments look more closely at the efficiency of

Illustration 22.1
Cohesion policy

European regional development funds made possible the building of Lisbon's Estação do Oriente as a combined railway/metro/bus station, shopping complex, and exhibition site.

spending patterns. EU funding is intended to complement national spending, but one study (Hagen and Mohl, 2009) suggests that in poorer states in particular it does not result in an increase in national public spending. Questions remain about whether cohesion is better promoted collectively or whether there should be a 'renationalization' of policy through which member states whose GDP is 90 per cent or more of the EU average should use national resources rather than relying on EU assistance, receiving a corresponding reduction in the amount they pay into the EU budget. Not surprisingly, poorer states oppose this idea, along with the Commission and the European Parliament.

Social policy

The quest for economic equality has also meant a debate at the EU level about **social policy**, covering issues such as improved working and living conditions, and the rights of workers, women, and the disabled. The EU's interest in this area is a logical outcome of the postwar histories of welfare promotion in most northern and western European states, and has been part of the single market programme because of the need to ensure equal opportunities and working conditions. At the same time, its efforts have been controversial, pitting supporters in labour unions, the Commission, and Parliament (at least when it was dominated by social democrats) against opponents in European business and among conservative political parties. Supporters argue that the opportunities of the single market need to be more equitably spread, while opponents argue that social policy runs the danger of making European companies less competitive in the global market. Questions have also been raised about whether these issues are best dealt with at the national or EU level. The result, concludes Hantrais (2007, pp. 21–2) is that EU activities in the field of social policy have been extended progressively but cautiously.

The Treaty of Rome was based on the hopeful but naive assumption that the single market would help encourage better distribution of resources, allowing the kind of economic growth that would improve life for all European workers. The treaty made note of the need to address working conditions, equal pay for equal work, and social security for migrant workers, and made provision for the creation of the European Social Fund (ESF). But with the political focus in the 1960s on completing the single market and resolving battles over agricultural policy, the movement of workers remained heavily restricted, and market forces failed to address problems such as gender and age discrimination, different wage levels, different levels of unemployment, and improvements in safety and health in the workplace.

The widened economic gap brought on by enlargement in 1973 not only sparked new efforts on regional policy but also pushed social issues back up the agenda (although in a reserved and conditional fashion). In 1974 the first in a series of four-year Social Action Programmes was launched, based on the ambitious goals of achieving full employment, improved living and working conditions, and gender equality. But although there was increased spending under the ESF, with a focus on helping combat long-term unemployment and creating jobs and training schemes for young people, a combination of economic recession and resistance from several Community leaders ensured that words failed to be translated into deeds (Brine, 2002).

● **Social policy**: Efforts made by the EU to promote equal pay, equal working conditions, gender equality, worker training, and workers' rights.

Focus on . . .
The European Social Model

There has been much speculation among policymakers and academics about the qualities and implications of the European Social Model (ESM), the features of which (see Giddens 2006) include support for a developed and interventionist state, a robust welfare system that provides protection for all, efforts to contain inequality, and a key role for unions and related agencies in promoting workers' rights. As well as welfare and pensions, the model includes employment policy, worker training, and rules and policies on labour markets, equality, and benefits, and it has the twin policy goals of sustainable economic growth and improved living and working conditions.

Greece, Portugal and Spain had very different approaches to welfare when they joined the Community, their reliance on family, community and church contrasting with the more universal and tax-funded approaches taken by northern European states. Eastern enlargement later brought in states still wrestling to move away from the effects of centralized communist government (Hantrais, 2007, pp. 26–7). The contrasting tensions of harmonization and respect for

national diversity have since complicated efforts to build a single ESM.

In the early 1990s the Commission was arguing that while the EU had been unable to achieve many of the goals of the ESM, it could be 'fairly claimed' that nowhere else in the world had so much progress been made (European Commission, 1994). Modernizing the ESM was part of the 2000 Lisbon Strategy to make the EU the most competitive and dynamic knowledge-based economy in the world within a decade. But this target failed to be met, and those who now question the meaning and prospects of the ESM are harder to find than those who think it is realistic . Marlier *et al.* (2007) argue that in spite of social spending in the EU, the ESM has been unable to withstand the challenges posed by globalization, and point to the problems posed by high public debts in the member states and the EU's aging population, high unemployment, and low productivity; the ESM, they argue, is unsustainable, and the EU needs to cut social spending and ease business regulation.

The idea of a European social space was championed by President François Mitterrand of France in the early 1980s, the cause being taken up by Jacques Delors when he became president of the Commission in 1985 (Hantrais, 2007, p. 5). Social policy cropped up again in the discussions leading up to the Single European Act, when concerns were raised about worker mobility and about 'social dumping': money, services, and businesses moving to those parts of the EU with the lowest wages and social security costs. The Commission tried to focus the attention of national governments on these problems, but further recession ensured more political resistance. In 1987 a new direction was taken when the Belgian presidency of the Council of Ministers suggested that the Community consider developing a charter of basic social rights modelled on Belgium's own new national charter. (It also had links with the often overlooked European Social Charter, which was drafted by the Council of Europe, opened for signature in 1961, and which addressed many of the same issues.)

Hoping to draw more attention to the social consequences of the single market, Delors took up the cause of what became known as the Community Charter of the Fundamental Social Rights of Workers (or, more simply, the

● **European Social Model**: The notion of a common European approach to social issues, based on an interventionist state, welfare, workers' rights, and efforts to address inequality.

Social Charter). But while the moderate conservative West German government of Helmut Kohl was supportive, as were states with socialist governments (such as Greece and Spain), conservative British Prime Minister Margaret Thatcher was enthusiastically opposed. Arguing that it was 'quite inappropriate' for laws on working regulations and welfare benefits to be set at the Community level, she described the document as 'a socialist charter – devised by socialists in the Commission and favoured predominantly by socialist member states' (Thatcher, 1993, p. 750). Undeterred, the other 11 member states adopted the Charter at the 1989 Strasbourg summit of the European Council, heralding it as the social dimension of the Single European Act.

The Social Charter brought together all of the social policy goals that had been developed by the Community, including the right to freedom of movement, to fair remuneration for employment, to social protection, to freedom of association and collective bargaining, to equal treatment, to health and safety in the workplace, to the protection of children and the handicapped, and to a retirement income that allowed a reasonable standard of living (see Document 22.1). Plans to incorporate the charter into Maastricht were blocked by the government of John Major in Britain, so a compromise was reached whereby it was attached to Maastricht as a protocol (known as the social chapter, and often confused with the Social Charter). Britain was excluded from voting in the Council on social issues while the other member states formed their own ad hoc Social Community. This textbook example of multi-speed integration ended in 1997 when the new government of Tony Blair committed Britain to the goals of the social protocol, and it was incorporated into the treaties by the Treaty of Amsterdam.

Social policy up to this point was more talk than action, Hantrais (2007, p. 13) arguing that neither the Charter nor the chapter (the Maastricht protocol) signalled 'a strong commitment to social affairs as an objective in its own right, or on a par with economic union'. On the specific matters of policy, family issues have been almost entirely excluded, opinion is divided about the impact that EU policy has had on women's rights (particularly equal access to employment), the work of the EU has focused more on awareness-raising than hard policy initiatives, and poverty remains a problem across the EU in spite of the opportunities that were supposed to have been created by the single market.

If one issue has dominated the debate on social policy it has been the failure of the European marketplace to help reverse the often high rates of unemployment in the EU. Employment levels were high in the 1960s, but then came the recession and energy shocks of the 1970s, causing a steady loss of jobs. . By the late 1990s, while the number of unemployed in the United States hovered around 5 per cent, and in Japan about 4 per cent, it ranged from a low of 4–6 per cent in the Netherlands, Britain, and Sweden, to 11–12 per cent in Germany, France, and Italy, and a high of nearly 19 per cent in Spain (*The Economist*, various issues, late 1998). By 2007 the European figures had improved slightly, but were still not impressive: Poland and Belgium were in double digits, France and Germany were at 8–9 per cent, and the eurozone was running at 7.1 per cent, compared to a healthy 4.5 per cent in the United States (*The Economist*, various issues, late 1998).

Then came the 2007–10 global economic crisis, which led to job losses throughout the liberal democratic world, moving the EU-27 and the United

● **Social Charter**: A charter of the social rights of workers, adopted by 11 Community states in 1989 and merged into the treaties by Amsterdam in 1997.

DOCUMENT 22.1

Selected articles from the Community Charter of the Fundamental Social Rights of Workers

1. Every worker of the European Community shall have the right to freedom of movement throughout the territory of the Community, subject to restrictions justified on grounds of public order, public safety or public health.
2. The right to freedom of movement shall enable any worker to engage in any occupation or profession in the Community in accordance with the principles of equal treatment as regards access to employment, working conditions and social protection in the host country...
4. Every individual shall be free to choose and engage in an occupation according to the regulations governing each occupation.
5. All employment shall be fairly remunerated . . .
8. Every worker of the European Community shall have a right to a weekly rest period and to annual paid leave, the duration of which must be harmonised in accordance with national practices while the improvement is being maintained.
10. Every worker of the European Community shall have a right to adequate social protection and shall, whatever his status and whatever the size of the undertaking in which he is employed, enjoy an adequate level of social security benefits . . .

11. Employers and workers of the European Community shall have the right of association in order to constitute professional organisations or trade unions of their choice for the defence of their economic and social interests...
13. The right to resort to collective action in the event of a conflict of interests shall include the right to strike, subject to the obligations arising under national regulations and collective agreements . . .
16. Equal treatment for men and women must be assured . . .
19. Every worker must enjoy satisfactory health and safety conditions in his working environment . . .
21. Young people who are in gainful employment must receive equitable remuneration in accordance with national practice . . .
24. Every worker of the European Community must, at the time of retirement, be able to enjoy resources affording him or her a decent standard of living . . .
26. All disabled persons, whatever the origin and nature of their disablement, must be entitled to additional concrete measures aimed at improving their social and professional integration.

Source: Europa web site at http://eur-lex.europa.eu/en/treaties/index.htm#founding (retrieved July 2010).

States alike up to about to 10 per cent (see Map 22.2). Today, eastern European states generally have higher levels of unemployment, as would be expected given the time it is taking to make the transition from Cold War-era central planning and economic inefficiency, but several western European states are also suffering, notably Spain, Ireland (not so long ago famous for its dramatic economic transformation), and France. In the case of Spain, much of the problem in 2008–10 stemmed from the collapse of the housing market, many of the newly jobless having worked in the construction industry. Job protection also makes it difficult to move workers from one market sector to another.

Why EU rates have been so high is debatable (the effects of the global economic crisis notwithstanding), and numerous explanatory factors have been suggested. One is the large number of European workers (about one-third of the workforce, by some estimates) who lack skills and have few or no formal qualifications, making them less employable. Another is that while millions of new

Map 22.2 Unemployment in the EU

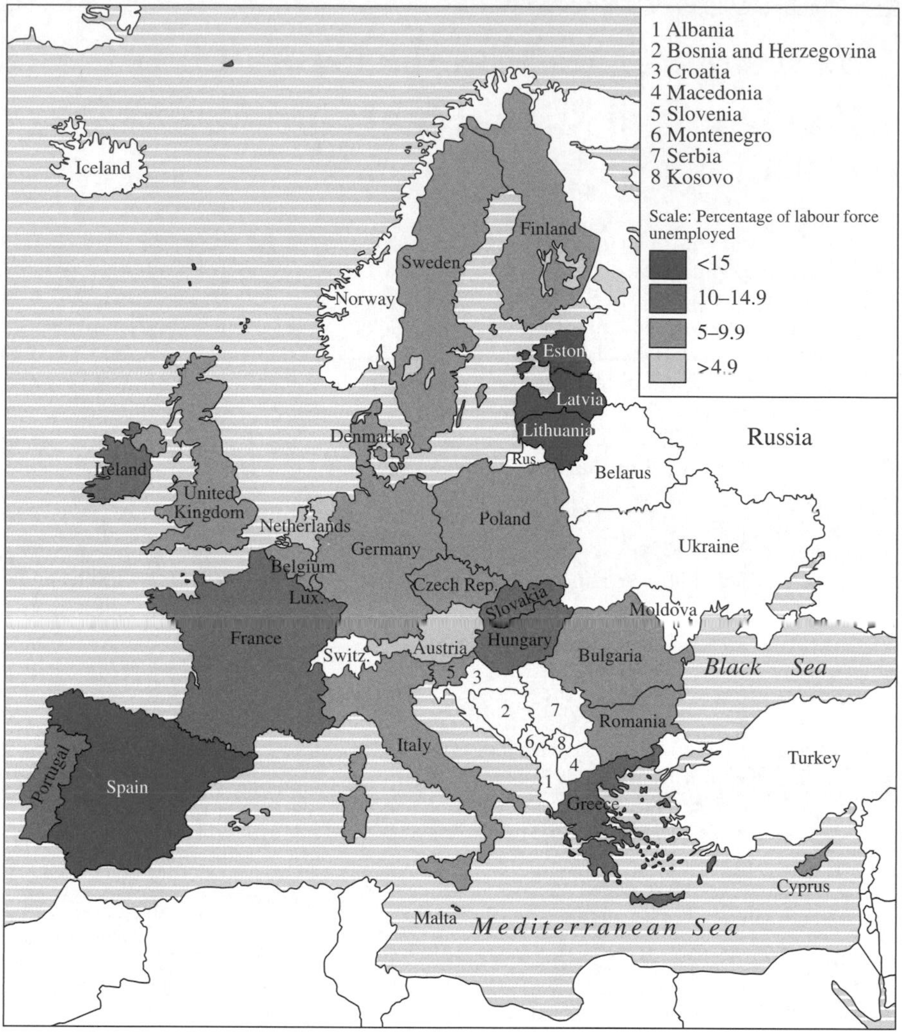

1 Albania
2 Bosnia and Herzegovina
3 Croatia
4 Macedonia
5 Slovenia
6 Montenegro
7 Serbia
8 Kosovo

Scale: Percentage of labour force unemployed

<15
10–14.9
5–9.9
>4.9

All figures for June 2010. Highest: Latvia, 22.5. Lowest: Netherlands, 4.1. Average for EU-27: 9.7. Figure for United States was 9.9 and for Japan 5.0.
Source: Based on Eurostat figures at http://epp.eurostat.ec.europa.eu (retrieved August 2010).

jobs have been created in the EU in the last two decades, nearly half have been temporary or part-time jobs, and many are in the service sector. Because men and women new to the job market are filling many of these jobs, their creation has done little to help ease long-term unemployment. Another problem is that while EU laws have given workers stronger protection against dismissal than is the case in the United States, they have also slowed down the creation of new jobs. Short-term trends have made the problem worse, including the erosion of exports and investments in the wake of the global economic crisis, and job cuts in industries that have suffered the effects of the economic downturn.

The Treaty of Amsterdam introduced a new employment chapter that left competence for employment policy in the hands of member states but also called on them to develop a coordinated employment strategy. Amsterdam acknowledged that employment was a matter of shared concern for all member states, and set up a system under which information on national employment policies could be shared. It also obliged the EU and member states to work toward a coordinated strategic approach to employment, and when the European Council met in Luxembourg in November 1997, employment was the sole item on the agenda. The outcome was the launch of a European Employment Strategy (EES, also known as the Luxembourg process) designed to encourage cooperation on national employment policies through the open method of coordination. Full employment was one of the core goals of the Lisbon Strategy, but a mid-term review of the EES in 2005 was side-lined by growing doubts over the efficacy of Lisbon; these were, it later turned out, but a preview of the disorder into which EU economic and employment policies were thrown by the effects of the global economic crisis.

Education policy

It was understood from the early days of the EEC that a true single market demanded an open labour market, but although the Treaty of Rome set the goal of free movement of people, this was subject 'to limitations justified on grounds of public policy, public security or public health'. Because the movement of workers was initially seen in terms of filling economic need, free movement was available only to those who were economically active, and governments discouraged skilled workers from leaving for other countries. As part of the package, education was mentioned in the Treaty of Rome only in connection with the need to develop principles for a common policy on vocational training. These were agreed in 1963, and an Education Committee was set up in 1974 to bring together national ministers of education to develop an action plan (Ertl, 2006). It would not be until the era of the Single European Act in the 1980s, however, when the issue of free movement moved to the top of the political agenda, that new attention would be paid to the importance of educational mobility. Although there is today still no formal EU education policy as such, Walkenhorst (2008) argues that EU initiatives amount to a *de facto* European policy.

The Community's first programmatic steps were taken in 1987 with the launch of Comett, a programme designed to encourage contacts and exchanges between universities and industry, and wound up in 1995. This was accompanied by Erasmus, designed to encourage inter-university cooperation, and followed in 1995 by Socrates, designed to encourage students in higher education to study in different countries, to promote cooperation among European universities, and to support the recognition of diplomas and courses across borders. This ran for four years, was succeeded in 2000 by Socrates II, which was in turn succeeded in 2007 by the Lifelong Learning Programme (LLP), which brought together four pre-existing EU educational programmes: Comenius, Erasmus, Leonardo da Vinci, and Grundtvig (see Figure 22.3). The EU is also interested in education in other parts of the world: Tempus was launched in 1990 to provide support to higher education in eastern Europe (and has since expanded to Central Asia, North Africa, and the Middle East), while Erasmus Mundus was launched in 2003 to help bring foreign students and faculty to Europe and to support partnerships between European and non-European universities.

● **Education policy:** Policy focused on encouraging cross-border mobility of students and staff, and educational cooperation among the member states.

Figure 22.3 The Lifelong Learning Programme

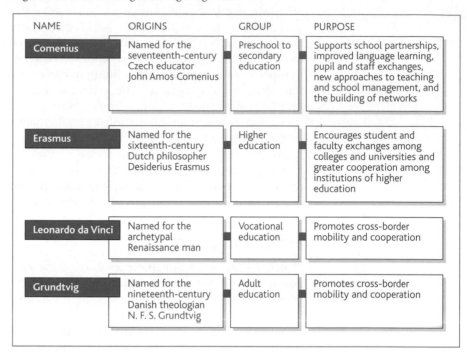

At the heart of recent changes in the substance and direction of EU education policy have been the Lisbon Strategy (see Chapter 7) and the **Bologna Process**. Lisbon gave a boost to the EU's educational activities, with efforts to recycle or update old initiatives and to launch new ones, all with the object of helping promote competitiveness, and encouraged in part by the globalization of education (Walkenhorst, 2008). As a result, students and faculty are more mobile than ever before, encouraged by increased opportunities for study abroad and educational exchanges. Within the OECD, EU states such as Britain, Germany and France are among the most popular destinations in the world for foreign students (see Figure 22.4).

In 2002 the education ministers of the member states agreed a ten-year work programme based on the open method of coordination. For Walkenhorst (2008), the approach reflects 'a general tendency in EU politics towards more flexibility and away from formal supranational regulation', and has the effect of moving 'the locus of policy co-ordination away from Brussels to national capitals and EU summits, thereby returning member states to the centre of policy-shaping'. This approach carried over into the Europe 2020 Strategy (see Chapter 19), which listed education as one of its five major priorities, and was guided by a strategic framework on education agreed in 2009 based on five benchmarks, including reducing the number of pupils leaving school early, increasing the number of graduates in maths and science, and increasing the participation of adults in lifelong learning.

As for the Bologna Process, the focus here has been on the transferability of educational qualifications across borders. The Commission at first tried plodding through one profession at a time, generating – after years of debate – about

● **Bologna Process**: An agreement among European states (not limited to the EU) under which requirements for higher education qualifications have been standardized, increasing their transferability.

60 separate pieces of Community law dealing with doctors, nurses, dentists, vets, midwives, lawyers, architects and pharmacists (Hantrais, 2007, pp. 55–6). (It took 17 years of negotiations to reach agreement on standards for architects alone.) Mutual recognition has since taken over as the guiding principle, and the only remaining distinction is between the freedom to provide services and the freedom of establishment: any EU national who legally provides services in one state can do so temporarily or occasionally in another without having to apply for recognition of their qualifications, although they may be asked to provide proof of the qualifications, and show language ability. Where someone wants to live and work permanently in another state, they must show proof that their training is at a level equivalent to that required in the new state.

Another problem was created by different ideas in different states about the requirements for higher education: qualifications came in many different guises, with different names, and requiring varying amounts of time and different courses of study. For example, while the equivalent of a bachelor's degree could be earned in Britain and Ireland in three years, on the continent this could once take as long as five to eight years. Not only did this place greater pressures on continental students, but there was little agreement among different states on how qualifications from one would be translated or understood in another.

With this dilemma in mind, the Lisbon Recognition Convention was drafted by the Council of Europe and signed in 1997, establishing that university degrees and related qualifications must be recognized by members unless substantial differences could be identified and proven. Two years later, a declaration was signed in Bologna by education ministers from 29 countries proposing a European Higher Education Area within which university education would be comparable and transferable, where students and faculty could move freely in order either to pursue a job or to undertake more study, and that would help

**Illustration 22.2
Education policy**

Thanks to efforts by the Commission to promote educational exchanges, European students now find it easier to study at universities outside their home state, and to have their qualifications recognized across state borders.

Figure 22.4 Top ten destinations for foreign students

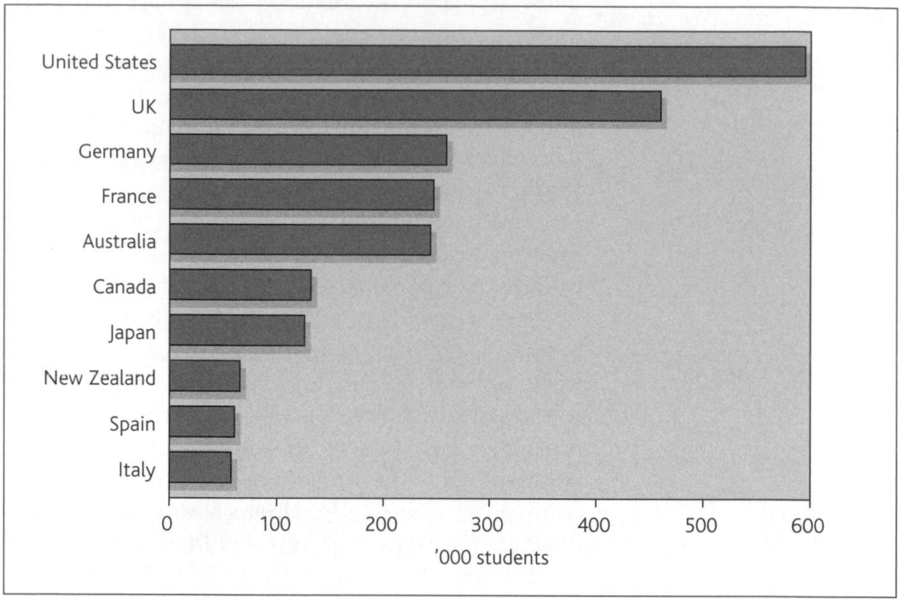

Figures are for 2007, and are for non-citizen students in the reporting country, except the United States where the figure is for non-resident students.
Source: OECD at http://stats.oecd.org (retrieved August 2010).

make European higher education more attractive and internationally competitive.

Although Bologna was born as a means of standardizing credits, it has expanded to make sweeping changes to curricula in Europe. And although it is more a pan-European agreement than an EU initiative, reaching now to nearly 50 countries, it has become a core part of EU education policy. Its major effect has been agreement on three cycles of higher education qualifications, based on comparable numbers of credits under the European Credit Transfer and Accumulation System, or ECTS. One year of study equates to 60 ECTS credits, or about 1500 to 1800 hours of study, and university degrees are organized according to the 3–2–3 cycle:

● The first cycle of 180–240 ECTS will usually lead to the award of a bachelor's degree, or equivalent, over three years.
● The second cycle of 90–120 ECTS will usually lead to the award of a master's degree, or equivalent, over two years.
● The third cycle, for which there is no specific ECTS range, will lead to the award of a doctoral degree, over three years.

The ECTS system, which was launched as a six-year pilot programme in 1992 under the EC's Eramus programme, has since evolved from a credit transfer to a credit accumulation system. Although degrees can still retain their different names, most EU member states have switched to a system based on equivalents of the bachelor's degree: so, for example, Italy has converted its 4- to 6-year *laurea* into a 3-year undergraduate *laurea triennale* and a postgraduate *laurea magistrale*, and Austria's *Magister* and *Diplom* have been replaced with a *Bakkalaureus*. The ECTS system has not only encouraged curricular changes in the EU member states, thereby helping build a European higher education area, but has also had an impact internationally: non-European students find it easier and more attractive to study in Europe, and the United States has had to pay closer attention to European developments because of the large transatlantic traffic in students (Roper, 2007).

One of the effects of EU policy has been the rise of the **Erasmus generation**. Erasmus has allowed students and faculty to study and work in universities outside their home countries, has encouraged cooperation between European institutions of higher education, and has been joined by Erasmus Mundus, aimed at helping encourage the globalization of European education. Under Erasmus, about 200,000 European students per year can live and study in other European countries for periods of at least three months, encouraging them to learn new languages but also to learn more about the culture of other European countries. An estimated two million students had taken advantage of Erasmus by 2008 (Eurostat, 2009, p. 189), spearheading the development of a new kind of European – mainly younger, better-educated, and more cosmopolitan – with a heightened sense of European identity. Members of the Erasmus generation travel, they are multilingual, they make friends across borders and marry citizens of other European states, and they take a more inclusive view of themselves in their political and social environment.

Among the most telling practical and psychological barriers to free movement across borders is language: monolingualism not only discourages migration but also poses a handicap to multi-national businesses by making it more difficult to build exports, and stands as a potent reminder to Europeans of their differences, making it more difficult to understand the way other European societies think and work. The EU has not just its 23 official languages (see Chapter 3), but also many local languages, dozens of dialects, languages spoken by new immigrants from outside Europe, and languages spoken by non-EU European states.

Language training has improved, with almost all secondary school pupils in the EU now required to learn at least one foreign language, and more states requiring two languages, but the record in real language ability is patchy and skills vary substantially from one language to another and from one state to another. English is by far the preferred language of study, being taught to nearly 85 per cent of pupils in the EU-27 compared to the 24 per cent learning German and the 22 per cent learning French. Less than 10 per cent of Estonians, Greeks, Poles or Czechs are being taught French, and less than two per cent of Spanish and Portuguese pupils are being taught German (Eurostat, 2009, pp. 187–8). English has become all but a second national language in the Netherlands and the Scandinavian states, and its role as the lingua franca of Europe is being strengthened by its steady rise as the international language of diplomacy, commerce and entertainment. This unfortunately encourages the linguistic laziness of the British, and worries the French and increasingly the Germans as they work to stop the infiltration of English words and phrases into their languages.

● **Erasmus generation:**
Students who have participated in the EU's Erasmus educational exchange programme since 1987, and who are seen as leaders in the effort to build a sense of European identity.

SUMMARY

- Levels of income and economic opportunity vary both within EU member states and from one state to another.
- EU cohesion policy works to strengthen the internal bonds of the European marketplace by supplementing national efforts to reduce economic disparities, mainly through the use of three structural funds that redistribute wealth from richer to poorer parts of the EU.
- The effects of cohesion policy have been hard to measure, in part because the links between cause, effect, and response are so difficult to measure.
- EU social policy addresses issues such as improved working and living conditions, and the rights of workers, women, and the disabled.
- Although the Treaty of Rome referred to the need to improve working conditions and to raise the standard of living, most early Community initiatives in this area were more rhetorical than practical.
- The idea of a European Social Model has been more aspirational than actual, although the approaches of north-western, southern, and eastern states have achieved closer uniformity with time.
- One problem that European policy has so far been unable to address has been the persistence of high levels of unemployment in many parts of the EU, a problem made much worse by the effects of the global economic crisis.
- At least initially in the interests of promoting the free movement of workers, the EU since the late 1980s has been increasingly active in efforts to promote mobility in education.
- One of the effects has been the rise of the Erasmus generation, a group of mainly younger, better-educated, and more cosmopolitan Europeans with a heightened sense of pan-European identity.

KEY TERMS AND CONCEPTS

Bologna process	European Social Model
Cohesion policy	Social Charter
Education policy	Social policy
Erasmus generation	Structural funds

FURTHER READING

Baun, Michael, and Dan Marek (eds) (2008), *EU Cohesion Policy after Enlargement* (Basingstoke: Palgrave Macmillan). A comparative study of the effects of cohesion policy, with cases from western and eastern Europe.

Hantrais, Linda (2007), *Social Policy in the European Union*, 3rd edn(Basingstoke: Palgrave Macmillan). A look at social policy in the EU, its role in setting a European social policy agenda, and its impact on national welfare systems.

Kleinman, Mark (2001), *A European Welfare State: European Union Social Policy in Context* (Basingstoke: Palgrave Macmillan). A study of the relationship between social policy and economic integration, and the role of EU social policy in the development of a European welfare state.

CHAPTER 23

Justice and Home Affairs

PREVIEW

Justice and home affairs (JHA) is one of the newer areas of EU policy, encapsulating efforts to develop a coordinated approach to international crime and terrorism, to manage immigration, and to improve security and the protection of rights through police and judicial cooperation. The pressure for action grew with the final effort to complete the single market in the late 1980s, which increased the political demand for common internal policies while also managing external borders. The goals of JHA were established by Maastricht; it has at heart been an effort to create an 'area of freedom, security and justice' within the EU, a controversial notion because it has touched on many issues deeply entrenched in national political and judicial systems, and comes up against concerns about the protection of state sovereignty (Lavenex, 2010).

The policies dealt with under JHA combine matters that are both internal and external to the EU, including free movement of people within the EU and control of the EU's external borders. Among other things, there have been efforts to standardize the processing of applications for asylum, to manage immigration by skilled workers while controlling illegal immigration, to develop policies on visas and personal data protection, and to encourage cooperation among police forces and judicial authorities in order to control terrorism, organized crime, drugs, and trafficking in humans. With time, these efforts have developed more consistency, moving from a loose collection of intergovernmental initiatives to a more coordinated supranational approach. The new dynamic is reflected most clearly in the creation of European arrest and evidence warrants, confirming the trend towards mutual recognition on judicial matters.

KEY ISSUES

- Why have EU member states been so resistant to pressures to cooperate on justice and home affairs?

- Does immigration from outside the EU represent a threat or an opportunity?

- Is immigration the only (or best) response to the economic problems posed by Europe's declining and aging population?

- Should Europe fear, welcome, or only selectively admit immigrants?

- How far do the self-proclaimed progressive qualities of European society extend, given the response to non-white and non-Christian immigration?

- Can the threat of terrorism ever be fully expunged?

The evolution of cooperation

As with so many other areas of policy, the need for cooperation on **justice and home affairs** was something to which EU governments turned their attention more by accident than by design. When they did so, they did so relatively quickly, and Monar (2001) argues that no other field of endeavour has made its way so rapidly or so comprehensively to the centre of the treaties or to the top of the EU policy agenda. He notes the importance of several 'laboratories' in which policies were early developed and working practices established (including the Council of Europe, the TREVI group set up to respond to international terrorism, and the Schengen agreement). He also notes several driving factors behind the development of policy, including transnational challenges such as a sharp rise in the number of asylum applications, the threats posed by Russian organized crime in the 1990s, and the emerging problem of cyber crime.

There was no reference to JHA in the Treaty of Rome, and such cooperation as existed among western European states in the early years of the Community was piecemeal and uncoordinated, lacking either goals or institutional and legal arrangements (Monar, 2001). More active than the Community was the Council of Europe, which addressed issues related to criminal matters and human rights, championed international conventions on extradition and the transfer of sentenced criminals, and hosted meetings which had the effect of encouraging national government ministers dealing with internal affairs to take a more multinational approach to their tasks. But the Community itself took economic integration literally and there was no effort to develop coordinated policies on JHA.

In 1967 the Naples Convention on cooperation between the customs authorities of Community states was signed, although it was not specifically a Community initiative (Hobbing, 2003, p. 8). This provided for the cross-border surveillance of criminal suspects by national police and customs authorities, its key contribution being to encourage exchanges and cooperation between national governments. (It was superseded in 1997 by the convention on mutual assistance and cooperation between customs administrations of the EU, otherwise known as Naples II.)

In 1971 the Pompidou group, named for French President Georges Pompidou, was set up to share experience on the combatting of drug use and trafficking (it was later incorporated into the Council of Europe). This was followed in 1975 by the creation of the TREVI group (see Chapter 14), set up to coordinate anti-terrorist activities, its mandate expanding after 1985 to include drug trafficking and organized crime. Another impetus for cooperation on JHA came from the 1985 Schengen agreement, the implementation of which helped begin the process of harmonizing policies on visas, illegal immigration, asylum, extradition, and police and judicial cooperation. It also spawned the computerized Schengen Information System, providing police and customs officials with a database of undesirables whose entry into the Schengen area they wished to control. In 1990, the Dublin Convention on Asylum was signed by the then 12 EC member states as part of an effort to decide which member state was responsible for reviewing applications for asylum from a third country national (preventing asylum-seekers from shopping around among member states for the best deal). It was superseded in 2003 by the Dublin Regulation; with some exceptions, asylum-seekers must now apply to the member state through which they first enter the EU.

● **Justice and home affairs**: Policy dealing with issues such as international crime and terrorism, asylum, immigration, and police and judicial cooperation.

Community member states learned from these early exercises in cooperation, so that when the pressures for a more focused and structured approach to policy began to grow in the 1990s, there was already something of a track record in place. But each member state still had its own domestic system of justice and home affairs. It was only as completion of the single market caused several member states (including Belgium, the Netherlands and Portugal) to lose their land borders with non-Community states – obliging them in essence to pass responsibility for the control of those borders to their Community neighbours – that reform, cooperation and the need for burden-sharing became more pressing. Further need was generated by the activities of Russian criminal gangs in the wake of the collapse of communism, by the sharp increase in the number of visa applications in the wake of the Balkan civil wars, and by the more inclusive and structured approach to international terrorism that was sparked by the September 2001 attacks in the United States.

The formal inclusion of JHA in the work of the Community arose for the first time in the discussions leading up to Maastricht, when an attempt was made to integrate JHA and the Common Foreign and Security Policy into a single structure. But a difference of opinion emerged between states, cutting to the heart of questions about national sovereignty: security has been central to the definition of state powers since the start of the Westphalian era, and continues to raise challenging questions even today about democracy, civil liberties and the appropriate role of government in the lives of citizens. The messy compromise reached with Maastricht was to make police and judicial cooperation one of three 'pillars' in the European Union (the others being the European Community and the Common Foreign and Security Policy), which meant that cooperation on JHA matters was intergovernmental and that all decisions had to be unanimous. This did not discourage the rapid growth of cross-border police cooperation, however, with the new European Police Office (Europol, which became fully operational in 1999) helping lead the way.

Constitutional change was brought by the Treaty of Amsterdam, which – reflecting the growing dissatisfaction with intergovernmental approaches and a desire to make European integration more relevant for ordinary Euorpeans – established 'an area of freedom, security and justice', incorporated Schengen into the *acquis* (with opt-outs for Britain, Denmark and Ireland), and made asylum, immigration and judicial cooperation EU responsibilities. At the Tampere European Council in October 1999, a programme of action was agreed to address the problems created by free movement across borders, including a list of about 60 initiatives needed to be taken by 2004 on issues such as asylum, immigration, and cross-border crime.

The 9/11 attacks in the United States forced the hands of EU governments, heightening the urgency of dealing with potential threats arising out of the dismantling of the EU's internal borders; as movement inside the EU became easier, so the need to strengthen external borders became more obvious (see Wolff *et al.*, 2009). In 2004 the European Council adopted the Hague Programme, which listed ten priorities for EU policy, including the strengthening of fundamental rights and citizenship, a comprehensive response to terrorism, the development of a balanced approach to dealing with legal and illegal immigration, the integrated management of the EU's external borders, the creation of a common asylum procedure, efforts to better integrate immigrant communities, and the need for a strategic approach to tackling organized crime.

With the Treaty of Lisbon and the demise of the pillar system, JHA was finally incorporated into the mainstream of EU policy concerns and ceased to be a matter for intergovernmental decision-making. This does not mean, however, that there is today a single European policy in this area. Britain and Ireland, for example, maintain their opt-outs from Schengen, while the picture is complicated by the involvement of non-EU members Iceland and Norway in Schengen and the Dublin Convention. Efforts on the JHA front have reflected all the core notions of spillover, incrementalism, and compromise, and overall there has been more of a focus on cooperation rather than harmonization, resulting in a pattern of shared competences involving European, state, and sub-state levels of governance (Lavenex, 2010, p. 458).

Institutional developments have paralleled those on policy. Europol has grown to be one of the most prominent of the EU's specialized agencies, joined along the way by Eurojust and the European Police College (see Chapter 14 for more details). Specific elements of the JHA agenda are addressed by the European Monitoring Centre for Drugs and Drug Addiction, by the European Fundamental Rights Agency, and by Frontex (which is responsible for coordination of EU efforts to manage its external borders). Within the Commission, a new directorate-general on JHA was created in 1999, which was later renamed Justice, Liberty and Security, and in 2010 split into two new DGs: the Justice DG is responsible for the development and consolidation of the EU area of freedom, security and justice, while the Home Affairs DG focuses on security and migration. Along the way, JHA has also become central to the agendas of the European Council and the European Parliament.

Asylum and immigration

Migration has long been part of the European demographic landscape, although the issue has taken on new complexity since the Second World War. The scale has also changed: Europe is now home to nearly 70 million migrants, or one-third of the world total, according to UN estimates (see later in this chapter). Where migration flows were once mainly internal to Europe, they have since the 1950s also become an external matter, a new and more difficult dimension added by the arrival of newcomers of different ethnicities and religions. As long as migration was limited to white Christians it generated relatively little political or social resistance, but as the ranks of immigrants have included more Africans, Middle Easterners, South Asians, and Muslims, so racial and religious discrimination have entered the equation; controlling immigration (for which read, mainly non-white immigration) has become a hot-button issue (in the EU as in the United States), generating a more coordinated policy response and also feeding in to the rise of right-wing anti-immigrant political parties.

The attraction of life in a wealthy and democratic country – either for the economic opportunities it offers or as a haven from war, persecution or natural disasters at home – is often irresistible to the citizens of states facing hardship, and just as many Latin Americans have sought to move to the United States in search of work, so many Russians, Middle Easterners and North Africans have sought to move to the EU. For the wealthy and educated the challenges are far

Illustration 23.1
Europe's aging population

Immigration from outside the EU has sparked political and social controversy, but some see it as one answer to the problem of Europe's declining and aging population.

less than for the poor and the unskilled, who may be welcome as sources of cheap and seasonal labour but are not expected to stay indefinitely.

Asylum – involving efforts by individuals to be admitted to the protection of a country other than their home state, usually for political reasons – has moved up the policy agenda since the 1980s in the wake of a sharp increase in asylum applications. Many of these were generated by the outbreak of small wars and ethnic conflicts following the end of the Cold War, in which civilians were often targeted. One of the challenges has been to distinguish genuine asylum-seekers from economic migrants, questions about which caused several EU states in the 1990s (in the wake of the Balkan civil wars) to tighten their previously liberal asylum laws.

Asylum-seekers are only a small part of the global refugee problem, but one that matters a great deal to the EU; according to the UN High Commissioner for Refugees (UNHCR), the EU received about 75 per cent of the approximately 380,000 asylum claims lodged with industrialized countries in 2007–09, or about two and a half times as many as those made to the US and Canada. Among EU states, France, Britain and Germany accounted for the greatest number of applications, and most asylum-seekers came from the Middle East, Kosovo, and troubled African states (see Figure 23.1).

All EU member states are signatories to the 1950 Geneva Convention, which commits them to protecting refugees by making sure that they are not sent back to a state where they face the risk of death, torture, or other inhuman or degrading treatment. Policy remained focused on the national level until the completion of the single market, at which point there was a clear need for a coordinated approach. But EU policy to date has not gone much further than developing minimum standards and procedures for asylum seekers, and agreeing how applications should be processed and what kinds of cases merit the granting of asylum.

● **Asylum**: An effort by an individual to win residence in a state in order to achieve protection from threats of death, torture or persecution in their home state.

Figure 23.1 Asylum applications to the EU

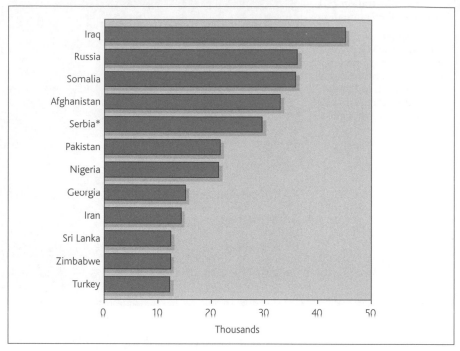

Figures are for 2008–09 combined. * Mainly from Kosovo.
Source: United Nations High Commissioner for Refugees at http://www.unhcr.org (retrieved August 2010).

The Tampere European Council in 1999 supported the idea of moving beyond a loose intergovernmental approach and called for the establishment of a common European asylum system. Lavenex (2001) notes that this thinking was based in part on addressing criticisms of 'fortress Europe', and in part on the hope of avoiding a repeat of the 'embarassing' European response to the 1999 Kosovo refugee crisis when more than 800,000 ethnic Albanians fled their homes in the face of attacks by Serb security forces; the EU response was found wanting in both policy and structural terms. The Hague Programme included the target of agreeing a Common European Asylum Policy by 2010, to which end Frontex was created in 2005, a European Refugee Fund was opened in 2008, an EU Blue Card (a single work and residence permit for skilled migrants) was adopted in 2009, and a European Asylum Support Office was set up in 2010. But Hague expired without agreement of a common policy, and it was replaced by the Stockholm Programme for 2009–14, containing similar plans for increased cooperation.

As regards immigration, major changes are taking place in Europe, of an order that Craig and Smeeding (2006, p. 1) describe as amounting to an 'historic transformation'. Where once Europeans were focused on demographic change within their borders, they are now increasingly focused on the movement of people across borders, with particular concern about inflows of non-Europeans and how to manage those inflows. This is not an issue unique to the EU, because almost all industrialized countries must respond to their magnetic qualities as

**Illustration 23.2
The EU's external borders**

Confidence in the effect of opening up internal EU borders has depended heavily on confidence in protecting its external borders. Here border guards keep an eye on movements across the Slovak-Ukrainian border.

sources of jobs and opportunities for the residents of poorer and less stable societies. But demographic and economic trends in an already crowded Europe mean that managing numbers poses a particular challenge, and the issue has also become one of critical electoral salience.

According to UN data, the number of international migrants worldwide grew between 1990 and 2010 by more than 37 per cent, reaching a total of 214 million. Of those, nearly 70 million (or nearly one-third) were in Europe, where they accounted for just under ten per cent of the population of the region (United Nations, 2009). These numbers include all those born in another country, whether or not they have adopted the citizenship of their new home state. A different picture is offered by Eurostat data, which include only non-nationals living in the EU; in 2009, there were nearly 32 million, making up 6.4 per cent of the population of the EU. Of these, more than one-third (or 11.9 million) were citizens of another EU member state (Vasileva, 2010).

Luxembourg tops the list with more than a third of its population foreign-born, a reflection of how its long vibrant economy and liberal immigration laws have attracted workers from many parts of mainly Catholic Europe (the Portuguese today making up the largest immigrant minority in Luxembourg). Eastern European states sit at the other end of the scale; there was little migration in the region during the Cold War era, and most of these states are today exporters rather than importers of labour (see Figure 23.2). But their situation could change if the record of several western European states is any indication: Ireland, long a source of emigrants, now has one of the largest per capita immigrant populations of any European state, and where Greece, Italy, Portugal and Spain were once also sources of emigrants, economic growth has made them a magnet for immigrants coming from as far afield as Albania, Bulgaria, Egypt, Morocco, Poland, Russia, Ukraine, and Latin America.

Immigration

Human populations have never been static, their movements encouraged over the centuries by a changing variety of geographical, economic, political and cultural pressures. At no time have people been so mobile as they are today, encouraged by a combination of 'push factors' (including poverty, war, political instability, discrimination, natural disasters, and environmental degradation) and 'pull factors' (including labour shortages, strong economies, political and social stability, historical or cultural links, and the presence of large communities from the source country) (Europol, 2009). The political response to immigration cuts to the heart of the economic and cultural priorities of states.

Figure 23.2 Immigrants as a percentage of the population

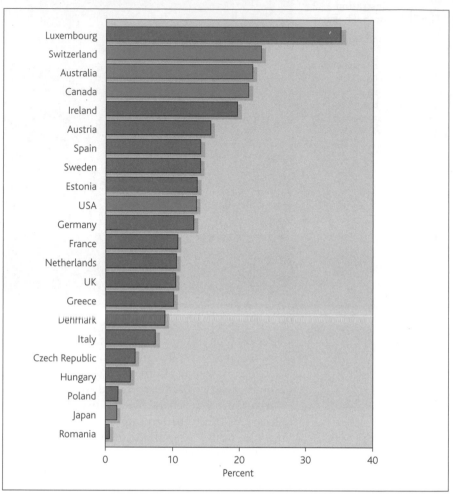

Figures are estimates for 2010.

Source: United Nations, Department of Economic and Social Affairs, Population Division (2009), *Trends in International Migrant Stock: The 2008 Revision* (United Nations database, POP/DB/MIG/Stock/Rev.2008).

National identity of the kind discussed in Chapter 3 has long involved an attitude of 'us' and 'them' in Europe, but the legal and political response to immigration has been far from uniform. European borders were mainly quite open in the decades leading up to the First World War (passports were not required by most travellers), but then few Europeans had either the means or the opportunity to move to another country, and so there were relatively few 'foreigners'. Regulations were tightened before and after the First World War, but it was only with the rise of cheap and mass international travel in the 1950s and 1960s that immigration moved higher up the policy agenda. Even then, European governments were less concerned about the movements of other Europeans than they were with managing inflows of non-Europeans, such as Algerians to France, Turkish guest workers to Germany, and West Indians and South Asians to Britain.

Focus on . . .
France and the Roma

A relatively small but troubling aspect of European immigration policy captured international media headlines in July 2010 when France expelled more than 1,000 Roma (gypsies), closing down their camps and despatching them to their home states of Bulgaria and Romania. The French government claimed that the camps encouraged the exploitation of children for begging, prostitution and crime, and that living standards in the camps were unacceptable. In fact, domestic political considerations may have been a large part of the equation: President Nikolas Sarkozy had low public approval ratings, and the expulsions may have been part of an attempt to head off growing support for the anti-immigrant National Front. It was by no means the first time that France had taken such action, having closed down camps many times before, and deporting an estimated 10,000 Roma in 2009 alone. About 400,000 of Europe's estimated 10–12 million Roma are thought to live in France, including about 12,000 from Bulgaria and Romania.

The political outcry over the 2010 deportations was immediate and extensive. The European Commission reminded France of the requirements of the 2004 directive on freedom of movement, which establishes the rules for deportation cases, and threatened the possibility of legal proceedings. It also began investigations into whether other EU states were breaking EU rules on the treatment of the Roma. Viviane Reding, the commissioner responsible for justice and fundamental rights, described the deportations as a 'disgrace'and reflected that 'this is a situation I had thought Europe would not have to witness again after the Second World War'. The French action was also condemned by many MEPs, who criticized the French government for targeting the Roma.

However, EU law holds that EU states can deport foreigners considered to be a public security risk or a burden on the welfare system, and while the citizens of Bulgaria and Romania have the right to enter France without a visa, they must have a work or residence permit if they plan to stay for more than three months. From 2014 they will have full freedom of movement in the EU, like citizens of other EU states. Majority public opinion in France was behind the deportations, which fits with a long history of discrimination against the Roma. But the EU has been criticized for taking too long to develop policies on the Roma, and even critics of French actions admitted that they might finally concentrate political minds (Peter, 2010).

Policy continued to be made mainly at the national level, but although national policies in the EU have long been restrictive, this has not prevented growing numbers of migrants from making their way into the EU; by 2008, the EU-25 had become the second most popular target for legal immigration after the United States (see Figure 23.3). While legal immigration can be managed, in terms of the numbers allowed to enter, the states from which they come, and the jobs that they fill, illegal immigration poses an entirely different set of challenges. Illegal immigrants have different motives for moving, are usually unskilled, and will sometimes use desperate measures to achieve their goals, risking injury and even death to move to another country. Their efforts overlap with the generation of fake identity and travel documents, with the trafficking or smuggling of humans, and with prostitution, in all of which organized crime is often involved. Once they have reached their target country illegal immigrants often live on the

Figure 23.3 Legal immigration flows in the OECD

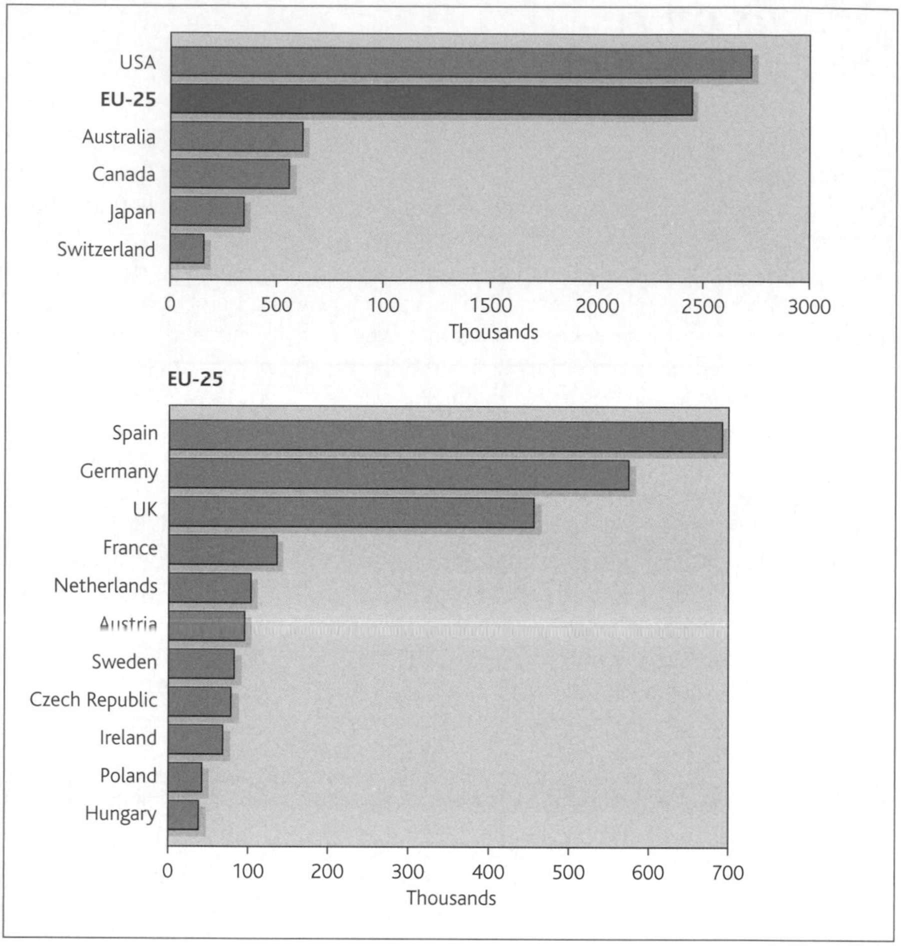

Figures are for 2008.
Source: OECD at http://www.oecd.org (retrieved September 2010).

margins of society, finding it much harder than legal immigrants to adapt and integrate.

By its very nature it is impossible to be sure about the scale of illegal immigration, and most statistics are no more than educated guesses. Some estimates place the number of illegal immigrants arriving in the EU each year at about half a million, but Frontex recorded in its general report for 2009 (see Frontex web site) that just over 140,000 illegal immigrants were caught trying to enter the EU in 2008, and another 106,000 in 2009 (the sharp decrease being ascribed to a combination of tighter border controls and the global economic crisis). Meanwhile, estimates of the total number of illegal residents of the EU range as high as three million.

As to where the EU's illegal immigrants come from, Frontex notes that the nationalities most often detected crossing external EU borders illegally in 2008 were (in order) Albanians, Afghans, Moroccans, Somalis, Iraqis, Tunisians,

Nigerians, Eritreans, Palestinians and Algerians. Most of the illegal immigrants from Africa arrive in Italy, while others enter through Spain and the Canary Islands. Those arriving from the Middle East and South Asia mainly use land routes across Turkey and arrive in Greece, and the western Balkans have become a key transit point for immigrants from all over the world (Europol, 2009). Meanwhile, non-EU eastern European states are both a source of illegal immigrants and a point of transit for arrivals from other parts of the world.

There was some early talk of the need to coordinate immigration policy across the Community in the 1970s, but it was only with the acceleration of the single market programme in the 1980s that the focus shifted away from states and towards the development of an EU approach (Luedtke, 2006); even so, rhetoric has long outweighed substantial policy change, and the waters have been muddied by the emotive qualities of the immigration debate, which is regularly sidetracked by myths, stereotypes, and discrimination. The Tampere European Council agreed on the need for a common EU policy, arguing that it should be based on a comprehensive approach with a balance between humanitarian and economic admission, fair treatment for third-country nationals, and the development of agreements with countries of origin.

Agreement has since been reached on contained issues such as family reunification, the long-term status of third-country nationals legally resident in the EU for at least five years, and the status of students and researchers. There has also been work on improving the management of the EU's external borders, and encouraging improved cooperation among police forces and border officials. But there is still no common EU immigration policy. At least part of the explanation for this lies in the extent to which immigration sparks public controversy at the national level, limiting the amount of political support for a harmonized EU policy that may be either more liberal or more restrictive than national policy (Givens and Luedtke, 2004). There is also widespread support for the view that the member states should have the right to decide how many immigrants they will accept, and a belief that Europe already has enough people, and that the EU should be tightening rather than loosening its borders.

In 2008 a pact on immigration and asylum was adopted, its main goal being to reduce illegal immigration while better managing the arrival in the EU of skilled workers. It had political rather than legal force, and included calls on member states not to offer mass amnesties to illegal immigrants (as Italy and Spain have done in the past), and to remove undocumented foreigners found on their territory. It also cleared the way for the adoption in 2009 of the EU Blue Card, designed to mirror the US Green Card by making it easier to attract skilled workers to the European Union. But disagreements remain over which forms of immigration to classify as legal (Lavenex, 2010) – should the right to family reunification be extended to children over the age of 12, for example? – and eastern European states argued that the Blue Card should only be agreed once there was full free movement for citizens of all EU states.

Meanwhile, the debate over immigration has touched on the debate about Europe's aging and declining population. With the balance between retired and working-age Europeans changing in favour of the former, and concerns that economic growth and the costs of social security cannot be sustained with current trends, the argument has been made that Europe's best hope lies in replenishing numbers through immigration; most of the population growth in the EU in recent decades – about 90 per cent to be precise (Craig and Smeeding, 2006, p. 2) – has been met by immigration. But many new immigrants are non-white and non-Christian, posing a severe test of the self-proclaimed progressive qualities of European society. New tensions have been born out of racial and religious intolerance, which in turn has fed into support for right-wing anti-immigrant political parties. They have done particularly well in national elections in Austria (where the Freedom Party won enough seats to enter a coalition government in 1999), in Belgium, Denmark, France, the Netherlands and Sweden, and in local and European elections in several other countries.

Police and judicial cooperation

If immigration is mainly an issue related to the EU's external borders, police and judicial cooperation focuses on how to manage crime, security and migration within the EU. This involves not just improving responses to serious crime, such as drug trafficking, money laundering, child pornography, terrorism, and corruption, but also encouraging the mutual recognition of judicial decisions on civil proceedings involving divorce, child custody, bankruptcy, and related issues. Civil liberties are also at the heart of this cooperation, including personal data protection, the rights of minorities, the rights of children, the right of free movement, a level playing field for consumers and businesses, and improved harmonization of consumer and contract law.

The work of the European Police Office (Europol) and of the Judicial Cooperation Unit (Eurojust) was addressed in Chapter 14. The former is a criminal intelligence agency that has eased information exchange among national police forces dealing with serious forms of cross-border crime, while the latter has helped improve investigations and prosecutions involving two or more member states. The EU has also created a **European Judicial Network** responsible for improving judicial cooperation on civil and commercial matters among the member states, complementing the work of Europol and Eurojust. Set up in 1998, it links contact points designated by the member states, drawn from local and state authorities in charge of international judicial cooperation; more than 300 were in place by 2009, managed by a small secretariat within the offices of Eurojust in The Hague.

One of the most substantial results of European cooperation has been the extension of the principle of mutual recognition to judicial matters, seen most clearly in the agreement of the **European arrest warrant**. First proposed by the European Council in 2001, it was introduced in January 2004 and had been adopted by all member states by July 2005. Once issued, it requires a member state to arrest and transfer a suspect or criminal back to the state issuing the warrant within 90 days, and replaces the lengthy extradition process that was once involved in European cross-border criminal actions. It applies only to cases carrying a potential penalty of more than 12 months in jail, or an agreed sentence of at least 4 months, and can be used only for prosecution, not for investigations. It also prevents EU states from refusing to surrender their own nationals, and is based on the idea that EU citizens can be held responsible for their actions wherever they are in the EU. It was first used in January 2004 to transfer a suspect in a crime in Sweden back home from Spain, since when it has been used with increasing frequency: about 14,000 warrants are now issued

● **European Judicial Network**: A network of contact points created in 1998 in order to help improve cross-border cooperation within the EU on civil and commercial matters.

● **European arrest warrant**: A warrant by which member states can request the transfer of suspects or criminals from another member state.

annually in the EU. One of the early high profile cases involved a suspect in the July 2005 London bombings, who was arrested in Rome a week after the bombings and extradited to Britain in September; in 2007 he was found guilty of conspiracy to murder and sentenced to 40 years in jail.

The EU has also had in place since 2008 a European evidence warrant, standardizing methods for obtaining documents, data and other evidence in cross-border cases. Warrants can be issued in the event of criminal proceedings brought before a court in any member state as long as the evidence requested is 'necessary and proportionate' for the proceedings, and it must already exist and be readily available; in other words, the warrant cannot ask police forces in other states to find new evidence. Warrants can either be sent direct to the second state or transmitted via the European Judicial Network. Before the creation of the warrant, it was left to courts or the justice ministry in each member state to decide whether or not to meet a request for evidence; under the terms of the warrant the grounds for refusal have been greatly limited (it can be refused, for example, in cases where immunity exists or national security is potentially harmed). One effect of the new warrant is that fewer cases are likely to collapse for lack of evidence.

The struggle against terrorism

The push for European police and judicial cooperation has been given new meaning since the 2001 terrorist attacks in the United States. However, **terrorism** is nothing new to Europeans, who have long had to deal with individuals who feel that the only way to achieve their objectives is to generate fear by attacks on political, military, and civilian targets. Terrorism was part of the western European landscape in the 1960s and 1970s with the activities of groups campaigning for recognition of Palestine (one of which was behind the murder of 11 Israeli athletes at the 1972 Munich Olympics), and the disputes in the Basque Country and Northern Ireland (which became particularly violent in the latter after 1968–69). There were also the anti-capitalist activities of the West German Red Army Faction (better known as the Baader-Meinhof gang, which was active mainly between 1970 and 1977) and – in Italy – of the Red Brigades (allegedly behind the kidnap and murder in 1978 of former Italian prime minister Aldo Moro) and of the Armed Revolutionary Nuclei (implicated in a bombing at Bologna railway station in August 1980 that killed 85 people).

Agreeing the meaning of the terms *terrorism* and *terrorist* is fraught with difficulty, and no standard definition has yet been agreed under international law. For some, terrorists are criminals and murderers who have chosen to target non-combatants in their immoral efforts to pursue an ideological, political, or religious agenda, while for others they are freedom fighters for whom almost any target associated with oppression is legitimate. What they have in common is an effort to generate fear and terror in the hope that this will bring about political change. For Hoffman (2006, p. 41), terrorism is political in its aims and motives, is based on the use or threat of violence, is designed to have an impact far beyond its immediate target, is conducted by an organization with an identifiable chain of command or cell structure, and is not perpetrated by a state (although it can be sponsored by a state).

● **Terrorism**: Efforts to achieve political change by creating public fear and insecurity, mainly through attacks on civilian targets.

**Illustration 23.3
Terrorism**

A poster in Rome expresses
solidarity with Londoners
following the July 2005
terrorist bombings. Echoing
the famous headline of a
French newspaper after the
9/11 attacks, it declares 'We
are all Londoners.'

The 2001 attacks in New York and Washington DC may have been directed against US foreign policy, but European states – particularly those like Britain and Spain whose governments had supported the US-led invasion of Iraq – also became the targets of Islamic militants. The threats exemplifed by 9/11 were brought much closer to home with a coordinated attack on the Madrid railway system on 11 March 2004 (timed to impact the general election that was held three days later). It resulted in the deaths of 191 people and injuries to nearly 2,000, and was a factor in the defeat of the incumbent conservative government of José María Aznar. On 7 July 2005, a similarly coordinated attack on the London public transport system by suicide bombers resulted in 52 deaths and more than 700 injuries. There have been many other failed or foiled attacks related to Islamic extremism as well, mainly in western European states. These events have fed into growing Islamophobia in Europe, although it must always be stressed that many Muslims are second- or even third-generation Europeans, and that only a very small minority are in sympathy with the kind of militancy or extremism that so often captures the headlines.

While the threat of militant Islamic terrorism tends to capture most of the headlines and generate most public concern, there are other sources as well. According to Europol, for example, there were more than 1,300 successful or attempted terrorist attacks in ten EU member states in 2007–09, only one of which involved Islamic extremists. By rank, the states most often targeted were Spain, France, Greece, Italy, Germany, Austria, Hungary, Ireland, Denmark and Portugal, with France and Spain alone accounting for nearly 93 per cent of the total. In the same period, nearly 2,200 individuals were arrested for terrorism-related offences in eighteen member states. (The numbers exclude the UK, for which data were not provided.) The greatest number of attacks were planned or carried out by nationalist and separatist movements such as the Basque ETA, the

Corsican FLNC, and Irish republican splinter groups. Threats were also posed (and attacks often carried out) by left-wing and anarchist groups critical of capitalism, militarism, and fascism (they were most active in Spain, Greece and Italy), by right-wing groups mainly targeting racial minorities, and by single-issue groups such as animal rights extremists (Europol, 2010).

In 2001, just ten days after the US attacks, the European Council adopted a rushed Action Plan on Combating Terrorism, which was revised after the London and Madrid bombings, and has been revised several more times since. Its seven goals included efforts to deepen the international consensus and enhance international efforts to combat terrorism, reducing the access of terrorists to financial and economic resources, improving the capacity of EU states to detect and prosecute terrorists and to prevent terrorist attacks, to enhance the ability of the EU and its member states to deal with the consequences of a terrorist attack, and to address the factors that contributed to support for terrorism.

In 2004 the new post of EU Counter-Terrorism Coordinator was created, but its first holder, former Dutch interior minister Gijs de Vries, stepped down in 2007 in protest at his lack of operational powers and at the unwillingness of member states to either provide information on their anti-terror activities or to give the action plan some substance (Lavenex, 2010). (He was replaced by Gilles de Kerchove, the Belgian Director for Justice and Home Affairs at the EU Council Secretariat.) In 2005 a Counter-Terrorism Strategy was agreed with four goals: *protect* Europeans by reducing Europe's vulnerability to attacks, *prevent* people from turning to terrorism by addressing the root causes of radicalization, *pursue* terrorists across borders and globally, and better prepare European authorities to *respond* to attacks.

Bossong (2008) argues that while the EU agreed an impressive list of anti-terrorism measures after 9/11, the original EU Action Plan did not improve the credibility of the EU's efforts. It was drawn up rapidly, the Commission using it as a window of opportunity to push for large-scale agenda change, but the result was an overload of the EU's decision-making and implementation capacity. By making several controversial proposals and setting tight deadlines for agreeing them, it heightened doubts about the legitimacy and appropriateness of EU efforts, and ultimately raised troubling questions about the right balance between security and liberty.

Following the London bombings the Council of Ministers decided that all anti-terrorism measures agreed to that point should be adopted immediately: these included the European arrest and evidence warrants discussed earlier, the strengthening of Schengen and visa information systems, the inclusion of barometric details on passports (and eventually in visas), efforts to combat terrorist financing (including tighter controls on money laundering), efforts to discourage the recruitment of terrorists (a policy given new urgency by the discovery that three of the London bombers were British nationals), and new controls over the trade, storage and transport of explosives.

SUMMARY

- It was only with efforts to complete the single market in the late 1980s and early 1990s that the pressures grew to coordinate policy on asylum, immigration, cross-border crime, and managing the EU's external borders. Policy initiatives were intergovernmental at first, and JHA was eventually incorporated into the mainstream of EU policy concerns by Lisbon.
- Immigration has long been part of the European demographic landscape, but it has been complicated by the rising numbers of migrants from outside Europe.
- The EU receives more applications for asylum than any other part of the world, but policy has not progressed much beyond agreeing standards and procedures.
- About one-third of all international migrants in the world live in Europe. Illegal immigration has been a rising problem for the EU since the end of the Cold War.
- Immigration may be the only viable response to problems arising from Europe's aging and declining population, but the new racial and religious diversity of immigrants has sparked controversial anti-immigrant sentiment.
- Police and judicial cooperation has been encouraged by Europol, Eurojust, and the European Judicial Network, spawning the introduction of European arrest and evidence warrants.
- Terrorism has long been a problem in Europe, but efforts to take an EU-wide approach were accelerated by the 9/11 attacks in the United States and the 2004/05 bombings in Madrid and London.
- The vast majority of successful or attempted terrorist attacks in the EU in recent years have involved not Islamic extremists, but nationalist and separatist movements, left-wing and anarchist groups, right-wing racist groups, and single-issue groups.

KEY TERMS AND CONCEPTS

Asylum
European Arrest Warrant
European Judicial Network
Immigration
Justice and home affairs
Terrorism

FURTHER READING

Geddes, Anthony (2008), *Immigration and European Integration: Towards Fortress Europe?* 2nd edn (Manchester: Manchester University Press). An assessment of the EU role in the management of immigration and asylum.

Mitsilegas, Valsamis, Jörg Monar, and Wyn Rees (2003), *The European Union and Internal Security: Guardian of the People?* (Basingstoke: Palgrave Macmillan, 2003).

von Hippel, Karin (ed.) (2005), *Europe Confronts Terrorism* (Basingstoke: Palgrave Macmillan). A review of the EU response to 9/11, with country case studies and chapters on transatlantic cooperation.

CHAPTER 24

The EU as a Global Actor

PREVIEW The great powers of the nineteenth century were European, and exerted global influence mainly through their empires and trading interests. But the toll of two world wars left behind a relatively tame and introspective Europe, and the EEC in its early years was too focused on internal challenges to much think about its global role; western Europe followed the lead of the United States, while its eastern states were dominated by the Soviet Union, and a few holdouts tried to remain neutral.

By the 1970s, the logic of Community members working together on a broader range of foreign policy issues was becoming more clear, but it was only with the end of the Cold War that all began to change. Eastern Europe was freed from Soviet control, the divide between east and west began to close, the borders of the European marketplace expanded, and enlargement took the EU first to the Russian border and then into the former Soviet Union. The end of the Cold War also meant a change in the nature of security issues, the soft power preferences of the Europeans becoming more distinct from the hard power abilities of the United States.

Red faces were generated by the weak and divided EU response to the 1990–91 Gulf war and the Balkan crises of the 1990s, few really believing that the EU had the means to be much of a global actor (mainly because it lacked a combined military or a common defence policy), and European leaders regularly reiterated the need for the US and the EU to work in concert. And yet there was mounting evidence that the EU voice was being finally heard on pressing international issues, that its global economic power mattered , and that its global role was changing.

KEY ISSUES
- Is the EU a new kind of global actor? If so, what are its features?
- Do the EU's relative military weaknesses matter in the age of globalization?
- Has Europe achieved Kant's state of perpetual peace?
- Should the EU be working to achieve security policy independence of the United States, or should it continue to place NATO policy at the top of its agenda?
- Why is the EU's trade power so often overlooked in discussions about its global role, while so much attention is focused on its lack of combined military power?

Understanding the global role of the EU

Until the First World War, the international system was dominated by Europe's great powers (Britain, France, Germany, and Russia), which were distinguished by four key qualities: they had large militaries and the ability to project power beyond their borders; their interests were continental or even global in scope; they were willing to defend their interests aggressively; and their status was acknowledged by other powers (Levy, 1983, pp. 16–18). No other states had such far-reaching influence and interests, the great powers of the future – the United States, China, India, and Japan – being either marginalized, isolated or under colonial control.

But the two world wars brought a close to the age of the great European powers, ushering in the new Cold War tensions between the United States and the Soviet Union. By virtue of the size, destructive abilities, and global reach of their militaries, backed up by large nuclear arsenals, the US and the USSR earned a new label: **superpower**. The United States also became an economic and even a cultural superpower, its resources giving it an unprecedented level of global political influence. In this new **bipolar system**, most other states either sided with the Americans or the Soviets, or tried (usually without much success) to remain non-aligned.

With the break-up of the Soviet Union in December 1991, many commentators, particularly in the United States, began to argue first that the world had entered a new unipolar era in which the United States was the only superpower, unchallenged on the military front but also perhaps even on the economic and political fronts. Some described it as a hyperpower (Védrine and Moïsi, 2001, p. 2), a global hegemon, and even as a new kind of global empire (Ferguson, 2004). But even as this new analysis was getting into its stride, there was talk of the emergence of new global powers in the form of the BRIC states: Brazil, Russia, India, and China (Wilson and Purushothaman, 2003). There were suggestions that the unipolar system was being replaced by a **multipolar system**: the US would remain pre-eminent but would face new competition from China and India. Some even suggested that a mix of domestic problems and foreign competition might be early signs of the decline of America (Mason, 2008).

Overlooked in much of this debate was the European Union. There were a few suggestions that it had great power potential (see Reid, 2004; Haseler, 2004; Leonard, 2005; McCormick, 2007), but it drew curiously little academic and media attention, in spite of its growing economic presence. There were several possible reasons for this.

- Great power is still popularly equated with military power, and since the EU has neither a combined military nor a clear common defence policy (or, at least, a policy based on the idea of maintaining a large military with global reach), few consider it a superpower in the same league as the US or the old USSR.
- Great power is still popularly associated with states, the assumption being that only states have the ability to achieve global influence (mainly because only states maintain militaries). Taken individually, even the larger EU states have only a modest international reach, while the EU itself, say the cynics, is not sufficiently coordinated to express its collective power at a global level.

● **Superpower**: An actor that has the ability to project power globally, and that enjoys a high level of autonomy and self-sufficiency in international relations (Fox, 1944, pp. 20–1).

● **Bipolar system**: An arrangement in international relations in which power is divided, shared and controlled by two dominant actors.

● **Multipolar system**: An arrangement in international relations in which power is divided, shared and controlled by more than two dominant actors.

- Power is more impressive when it is expressed visibly, and nothing is more visible than the sight of massive American ordinance raining down on a rogue regime, or of American aircraft carriers being despatched for a show of force. The EU has little to match this kind of raw power, its influence being subtle and latent rather than obvious and assertive.
- Cynics like to point to the regular failure of the EU to provide leadership. They quote its military embarrassments in the Balkans in the 1990s, the often public disagreements among its leaders (the divisions over Iraq in 2003 being a prime example), and evidence that the United States is taken more seriously by problem states such as North Korea, Iran, or Israel.

And yet there is reason to both question the efficacy and reach of American power, and to take a closer look at the reach of the EU. Military power did not prevail in Vietnam (and has been struggling in Afghanistan), it is expensive in human and financial terms, and it has little to offer the resolution of problems such as terrorism, poverty, or climate change. Meanwhile, the limits of American economic power were reflected in the US role in sparking the 2007–10 global economic crisis, and its inability to respond to that crisis in isolation.

As for claims that China and India are great powers, these overlook several troubling facts: neither state has the ability to commit its military all over the world, both countries are still remarkably poor (the per capita gross national income of the United States in 2008 was 16 times greater than that of China and 44 times greater than that of India), their political influence is still mainly regional rather than global, neither has a world-class currency, the global reach of their corporations is still quite modest, China's human rights record and lack of economic transparency severely limit its global influence, and India must deal with massive poverty and pressing domestic social and religious divisions before it will be able to have much global influence.

As we saw in Chapter 19, the evidence of the EU's economic power is compelling, and in economic terms it is incontestably a superpower. As a military actor, however, the EU does not measure up so well. If the military forces of the 27 member states are added together, they are substantial (see later in this chapter), and individual EU states – particularly Britain and France – have been active in military operations in many different parts of the world since 1945. But it projects nothing like the kind of power or presence that the United States can project. But does this matter? It does if we still believe that security threats can only be met with force, but perhaps this is no longer true. It may be that we are entering a new era of multipolarity based not on military but on economic power, and in which the EU may act as a new kind of international actor, based less on power (a term suggesting a desire to encourage others to change) than on influence (a term suggesting a desire to provide an example). There are four key qualities to the EU as a new model of global power.

First, it has mainly rejected the realist argument that states pursue self-interest in an anarchic international system, with little trust in long-term cooperation or alliances (see Chapter 1) and instead more clearly reflects the arguments of **idealism**. This is a philosophy that was a product mainly of the First World War, suffered reduced credibility in the years leading up to the Second World War (although it is reflected in the work of David Mitrany), and was supplanted during the Cold War by realism. For Hedley Bull, it meant a belief in the possi-

● **Idealism**: A view of international relations that emphasizes the possibilities of peace through international cooperation and the role of international law.

Focus on . . .
The Kagan thesis

In his book *Of Paradise and Power* (Kagan, 2003), the American public intellectual Robert Kagan contrasted the worldviews of the United States and Europe, arguing that the former was still mired in a Cold War view of a world divided into good and evil, while the latter saw a more complex picture, and was 'moving beyond power into a self-contained world of laws and rules and transnational negotiation and cooperation'. He went on:

- Europeans and Americans no longer share a common view of the world.
- The differences come from a disparity of power; when the US was weak, it practised the strategies of weakness, but now that it is strong it behaves as all powerful states do.
- Americans prefer military force, coercion, unilateralism; Europeans prefer negotiation, diplomacy, persuasion.
- While European integration has produced economic and political miracles, it has not made the EU into a superpower, because it remains militarily weak.
- The European inability to respond to threats leads not only to tolerance of those threats but also to denial.
- While Americans seek finality in international affairs, and have a tendency to act unilaterally, Europeans are more patient, quicker to appeal to international law, and prefer negotiation and persuasion to coercion.

But Kagan defined power mainly in military terms. And while he may have been right to argue that states with 'great military power are more likely to consider force a useful tool of international relations than those who have less military power' (Kagan, 2003, p. 27), there is new reason to question the dynamics of power:

- Military power is expensive in human and financial terms, has little value in the resolution of problems such as terrorism and poverty, does not always prevail, and can create international tensions where none might otherwise exist.
- The era of globalization has made economic power more important than military power; in other words, control of the means of production has become more important than control of the means of destruction.
- The European preference for diplomacy and negotiation is not so much a strategy of weakness as one that recognizes the new realities of the international system. It has been argued that Europe is not a continent of pacifists, but one where the 'just' causes of war are actively debated and where there are different opinions about the role of military force (Menon *et al.*, 2004).

---

bilities of a 'fundamentally more peaceful and just world order' generated by 'the awakening of democracy, the growth of "the international mind", ... [and] the good works of men of peace or the enlightenment' (Bull, 1972). Idealism emphasizes the importance of international organizations and international law, a prime example being democratic peace theory, which holds that democracies are unlikely to go to war with one another, a view given substance in the case of the EU.

Second, Europeans have a clear preference for **multilateralism** over unilateralism. If the latter is understood as a willingness by a state to go it alone and to rely on its own resources to achieve change, then multilateralism means a belief in approaching problems in concert and cooperation with other states. Europeans have long been used to forming political and security coalitions,

● **Multilateralism**: A belief that problems should be addressed by states working together, perhaps through international organizations, rather than in isolation.

Power

Power is the ability of one actor (whether a person or a state) to encourage others to act in a certain way. In the debate about the EU, three aspects of power feature centrally. **Civilian power** encapsulates efforts to focus on non-military rather than military means of achieving objectives. **Hard power** implies attempts to exert influence through the use of threats, coercion, and force. (Although hard power is usually associated with military force, it can also apply to economic means, as in the use of sanctions.) **Soft power** implies attempts to exert influence through the use of encouragement and incentives, such as diplomacy, negotiation and the offer of economic investment and rewards. The deft balancing of hard and soft tools is sometimes described as smart power.

and with multilateralism now clearly part of the DNA of the European Union, they have had decades of experience of working together to agree new laws and policies, and of making efforts to be inclusive. Supporting multilateral cooperation, declared the European Commission in 2003, is 'a basic principle' of EU foreign policy, and the EU should consider itself a 'driving force' in pursuing UN initiatives on sustainable development, poverty reduction and international security (Communication from the European Commission, 2003).

Third, the EU is more interested in the use of **civilian power** than in the use of military power. This is an idea suggested as early as 1972 by François Duchêne, when he argued that the lack of military power was not the handicap that it once was, and that western Europe might become 'the first major area of the Old World where the age-old process of war and indirect violence could be translated into something more in tune with the twentieth-century citizen's notion of civilized politics' (Duchêne, 1972). The EU-27 may have a large military establishment, and many EU states have actively engaged in military actions over the last few decades, but most Europeans instinctively prefer the peaceful resolution of problems. Europe's global power today is expressed more through trade, investment and the reach of European multinational corporations than through conflict and the reach of European militaries. Overall, the EU is less interested in **hard power** (threats, coercion, and force) than in **soft power** (opportunities, encouragement, and incentives).

Finally, and perhaps most importantly, the EU may be a compelling case of the possibilities of Immanuel Kant's notion of **perpetual peace**. Writing in 1795, Kant argued that the natural state of humans living side by side was one of war (open hostilities or the threat of war) rather than peace, and outlined the necessary conditions for the achievement of a lasting peace (see discussion in Bohman and Lutz-Bachmann, 1997):

- No peace treaties should be signed that hold out prospects for future war.
- No states should come under the dominion of others.
- Standing armies should be abolished.
- National debts should not be built with a view to war.
- No states should interfere with the governments of other states.
- States should not permit acts of hostility during war which would undermine confidence in the subsequent peace.
- State constitutions should be republican (that is, based on freedom and equality for all, and respect for the rule of law).
- States should live under a league of peace (seeking to end all wars forever) as distinct from a treaty of peace (seeking to end only one war).
- Peaceful strangers should not be treated as enemies.

The EU record in almost all these qualities (except the abolition of standing armies) has been strong. The natural state of today's Europe is one of peace rather than war, and while Europeans face the external (and to some extent internal) threat of terrorism, they no longer threaten one another, nor do they pose a threat to others.

Perpetual peace

The conditions needed to end state-sponsored violence and to achieve a lasting peace. The idea traces its intellectual heritage to Jeremy Bentham with his *Plan for an Universal and Perpetual Peace* published in 1789, which was followed six years later by Immanuel Kant's *Thoughts on Perpetual Peace*. Among Kant's conditions, the most relevant to understanding the EU is that of living under a league of peace in which the partners seek to end all wars forever. Kant's ideas were directed at achieving world peace rather than regional peace in Europe, but the EU has arguably come closest to fulfilling those ideas.

● **Foreign policy**: Policy governing the relations between a state and other states, dealing with issues such as security, trade, immigration, and economic relations.

● **Mixed system**: An arrangement in which state policies and common multi-state policies co-exist, as was long the case with the example of EU foreign policy.

● **Common Foreign and Security Policy**: An attempt made under the Maastricht treaty to develop common foreign policy principles and positions among EU states.

Foreign policy

In its early years, European integration focused almost entirely on economic cooperation, and was inward-looking to the point of almost entirely excluding attention to the place of the EEC in the world. The building of large militaries had been at the heart of Europe's historical squabbles, and while there was a stillborn attempt to build a European military with the European Defence Community, the political focus during the 1950s and 1960s was on rebuilding rather than rearming. Besides, the west was under the military shield of the Americans, and the east under that of the Soviets, so – other than contributing to NATO and Warsaw Pact forces – the military initiative had been mainly taken out of European hands. The only part of the Treaty of Rome that had a clear international component was the Common Commercial Policy, under which the member states agreed to develop shared policies on trade.

But as the reach of integration expanded in the 1960s, it became clear that the EEC needed to think more actively about its place in the world, and a modest first step was taken in 1970 with agreement of European Political Cooperation (EPC), an informal process that brought Community foreign ministers together at regular meetings to discuss international issues. EPC took place outside the EU institutional structure, but had the effect of encouraging Community leaders to negotiate common positions. This trend continued when the Single European Act committed member states to 'endeavour jointly to formulate and implement a European foreign policy'. But rather than developing a single overall policy – or even a set of common targeted policies – the Community remained what Groux and Manin (1985) called a **mixed system**, or one in which national and common policies co-existed.

The tumultuous international changes of the late 1980s and early 1990s found the Community unprepared to respond to major foreign policy challenges, but the thinking of its leaders was given new focus. Under Maastricht, the EU agreed to 'define and implement' a **Common Foreign and Security Policy** (CFSP) with the goals of strengthening the security of the EU, promoting peace and international security in accordance with the principles of the UN Charter, promoting international cooperation, and promoting democracy, the rule of law, and respect for human rights. Member states were expected to do nothing that would run counter to EU interests, to inform and consult each other on matters of shared interest, and to coordinate their actions in international forums. The CFSP also created three organizational tools:

● *Common strategies* have been agreed where member states have important interests in common, as in their dealings with Russia, the Ukraine and the Mediterranean.
● *Joint actions* bring states together on issues such as support for the Middle East peace process, observing elections in Russia and South Africa, and sending a naval force to discourage piracy off the coast of Somalia.
● *Common positions* have been agreed on approaches to the Balkans, the Middle East, Myanmar, Zimbabwe, and the International Criminal Court, and on policy issues such as terrorism.

But there still remains a lack of policy focus and leadership, and there are differences of opinion among the member states. Some have their own national agendas (Britain and France, for example, have special interests in their former colonies, while Austria, Finland, Ireland, and Sweden want to maintain their neutrality), and there has long been a fundamental strategic division between **Atlanticists** who favour close ties with the United States (among them Britain, the Netherlands, Portugal, and several eastern European states), and **Europeanists** (led by France and Germany) who want greater EU policy independence.

Institutionally, outsiders dealing with the EU have been faced with the problem neatly summed up in the apocryphal question credited to former US Secretary of State Henry Kissinger: 'Who do I call if I want to speak to Europe?'. Of all the EU institutions, the most logical to represent EU interests was the Commission, but in the 1990s it divided the world up among four different commissioners, only establishing more focus in 1999 when a single commissioner for external relations was created. But the waters were muddied when a new position – the High Representative (HR) for the CFSP – was also created within the Council of Ministers. The HR was intended to be the EU spokesman on foreign affairs, the first officeholder being Javier Solana, former secretary-general of NATO, who served two terms between 1999 and 2009. Matters were further complicated by the habit of rotating the presidency of the Council of Ministers among member states, obliging foreign governments to deal with a new set of policy leaders every six months.

Lisbon brought more change by combining the posts of HR and external relations Commissioner into a single High Representative of the Union for Foreign Affairs and Security Policy. Appointed by the European Council (using a qualified majority) and confirmed by the president of the Commission, the new HR (Catherine Ashton became the first office-holder in 2009) is charged under Lisbon with 'conducting' the CFSP and ensuring the consistency of the EU's external action. Where the old HR was combined with the post of secretary-general of the Council of Ministers, the new HR not only chairs the Foreign Affairs Council but is also a vice-president of the European Commission, and heads the new 5,000-member European External Action Service (EEAS), the EU's diplomatic corps. This was due to begin work in April 2010, but was delayed by a struggle between the Commission (which wanted to retain as many of its powers over external relations as possible) and Parliament (which wanted the power of oversight over the EEAS).

But while the existence of a newly powerful HR gives new focus to EU foreign policy, the co-existence of the president of the Commission and the president of the European Council (not to mention commissioners responsible for enlargement, development, trade, and international cooperation) still leaves the waters muddied. Kissinger's apocryphal question has still not been clearly answered, and this does not help strengthen the place of the EU in the international system.

Just how far the EU has travelled along the path to a common foreign policy is debatable. It has made much progress since the 1970s, both on agreeing common positions and on improving its institutional machinery. But another more fundamental question remains: how much have the states with which the EU interacts noticed or cared? The United States is still the world's biggest national economy, controls the world's leading international currency, and has

● **Atlanticists** and **Europeanists**: The division of opinion between those who continue to support close security ties with the United States and those favouring greater European policy independence.

Catherine Ashton

The first person appointed to the redesigned post of High Representative of the Union for Foreign Affairs and Security Policy was Catherine Ashton, the incumbent EU trade commissioner from Britain. Born in 1956, she had a background working in interest groups and business, was appointed to the British House of Lords by Tony Blair in 1999, served for several years in government, and in 2008 replaced Peter Mandelson as the European trade commissioner. Her lack of trade experience raised eyebrows then, as did her lack of foreign policy experience when she was nominated to the new HR post in 2009. She did not start well in confirmation hearings before the European Parliament, her performance being described by one report as 'uninspired and uninspiring', and as 'rich in subjunctives and poor on specifics' (*European Voice*, 11 January 2010). But supporters argued that she had often been underestimated, and expected her to grow into her new office, particularly once the new EEAS was in place.

by far the world's largest military; for these reasons alone, its voice is much louder and is listened to more intently when it comes to resolving international economic problems or dealing with the world's hottest trouble spots, from Iran to Iraq, Afghanistan, North Korea, Israel–Palestine, Sudan and Somalia. The EU has a growing presence on economic issues, underpinned by the size of the European marketplace, by its dominating position in global trade, and by the growing visibility of the euro, but great power is still defined by most people in military terms, and as long as there is no joint EU military, or until we rethink how we understand power and influence in the world, the impact of the EU is likely to be constrained.

Security and defence policy

The European Union is a more impressive military force than most people realize. If the budgets, the numbers of uniformed personnel, and the armaments of the 27 member states are combined, the EU has the second biggest military in the world after that of the US. It has more personnel than the United States, its combined defence budget – while still far short of that of the United States – is greater than that of Russia, China, India, and Brazil combined, it has more non-nuclear submarines and surface naval combat vessels (aircraft carriers excepted) than the United States, and its air force of nearly 3,500 combat aircraft is second only to that of the United States (International Institute for Strategic Studies, 2007).

But as a security actor, argues Howorth (2007, p.3), the EU is still in its 'early infancy'. Although several defence agreements were signed or discussed, western European security until the end of the Cold War fell squarely under the remit of the North Atlantic Treaty Organization (NATO). A different track might have been followed after 1955, when the Western European Union (WEU) was created in the wake of the collapse of the European Defence Community. But the WEU was always marginalized, and it was eventually wound up in 2011. Its most lasting contribution was the agreement reached in 1992 among its foreign and

● **Security policy**: Policy dealing with national defence, with identifying and offsetting military and other threats to national interests.

**Illustration 24.1
Security policy**

A German naval vessel participating in Operation Atalanta, designed to help protect shipping from the threat of piracy off the coast of Somalia.

defence ministers – meeting at the Hotel Petersberg, near Bonn – on the **Petersberg tasks**. Assuming that the WEU might become the European arm of NATO or the military wing of the EU, the ministers agreed that military units of WEU states, acting under the authority of the WEU, could include humanitarian, rescue, peacekeeping, and other crisis management operations, including peacemaking. These tasks were incorporated into the goals of the EU by the 1997 Treaty of Amsterdam.

The end of the Cold War meant the beginning of a change in the political relationship between the United States and the EU: the limits of EU military abilities were revealed in the 1990–91 Gulf war and the crises in the Balkans, while its desire to reduce its reliance on the United States has grown (Jones, 2007). The birth of the EU as a security actor, argues Howorth (2007, p. 4) can be dated from a December 1998 meeting in St. Malo, France, between Tony Blair – who, as the still new prime minister of Britain, wanted to see his country play a more central role in EU defence matters – and French president Jacques Chirac. The resulting declaration argued that the EU should be in a position to play 'its full role on the international stage', and should have 'the capacity for autonomous action, backed up by credible military forces, the means to decide to use them, and the readiness to do so' (an idea that might be read as code for independence from the United States).

France and Germany had already taken the initiative to set up a joint military force outside formal EC/EU structures when they created Eurocorps in 1992 (see Chapter 14). In 1996, a NATO ministerial meeting agreed that the WEU would be responsible for the development of a European Security and Defence Identity

● **Petersberg tasks**: The priorities set in 1992 by the Western European Union (humanitarian, rescue, peacekeeping, and other crisis management operations), and later adopted by the EU.

Debating . . .
Does the EU need a common military?

YES	NO
Whatever we say and think about economic power, military power is still regarded as the trump card in international relations. The EU may be the world's biggest capitalist marketplace and the world's biggest trading power, but until it can back up its global presence with a combined military and a common defence policy, it will be able neither to defend itself effectively from security threats, nor to exert much influence over responses to security problems in other parts of the world.	Military competition has often been a source of Europe's most difficult internal tensions.
	The maintenance of large militaries is financially expensive, and draws resources away from other needs, such as education, health care, the alleviation of poverty, and the building and maintenance of infrastructure.
Whatever hopes more idealistic Europeans may have about soft approaches to dealing with international problems, militaries will always be needed as a last resort to deal with security threats.	History is replete with examples of military power failing to achieve its objectives, and even of causing problems by creating a threat to which other actors must respond by building their own militaries.
Without a common military, the EU will have to continue relying either on its individual member states or on the United States. Either way, its freedom of independent action will be limited as a result.	The EU member states have shown that they cannot agree on military matters, so it is best to leave them the freedom to go their own way, and to come together on an ad hoc basis as needed.

(ESDI); this would allow European NATO members to act independently where NATO did not wish to, and would be run politically by the WEU. But the ESDI turned out to be a false start, and – encouraged by the idea that the EU should take responsibility for the development of a European policy outside NATO – it was replaced in 1999 by the **European Security and Defence Policy** (ESDP). This set the 'headline goal' of the EU states being able to deploy a 60,000-member Rapid Reaction Force (RRF) into the field at 60 days' notice, and being able to sustain it for at least one year. Organizational committees and a military staff were set up, and the ESDP was given new impetus by the 9/11 attacks in the United States and the realization that international terrorism constituted a new kind of threat that would not quickly go away.

In December 2003, the European Council adopted the **European Security Strategy**, the first ever joint declaration by EU member states of their strategic goals. The Strategy declared that the EU was 'inevitably a global player', and 'should be ready to share in the responsibility for global security'. It listed the key threats facing the EU as terrorism, weapons of mass destruction, regional conflicts, failing states, and organized crime. Having found that the RRF idea was too ambitious, EU defence ministers agreed in May 2004 to the formation of as many as 15 'battle groups' made up of 1,500 personnel each, and capable of being deployed at 15 days' notice and sustained for between 30 and 120 days. Also in 2004, a European Defence Agency was created within which national defence ministers meet to promote planning and research in the interests of the ESDP.

● **European Security and Defence Policy**: A critical step in the development of a European security policy outside NATO, based on the Petersberg tasks and the maintenance of 'battle groups' capable of short-notice military action.

● **European Security Strategy**: The first comprehensive outline of the EU's security priorities, identifying threats and outlining key objectives.

Map 24.1 NATO's European members

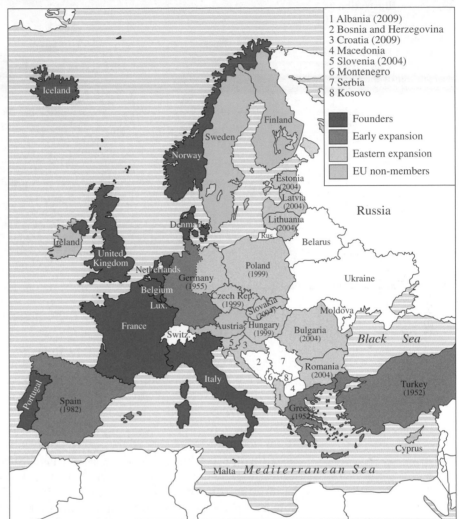

1 Albania (2009)
2 Bosnia and Herzegovina
3 Croatia (2009)
4 Macedonia
5 Slovenia (2004)
6 Montenegro
7 Serbia
8 Kosovo

Founders
Early expansion
Eastern expansion
EU non-members

In spite of the many doubts and questions that surround EU aspirations on security and defence policy, its achievements on the ground have grown: it deployed peacekeeping troops in 2003 in Macedonia (Operation Concordia) and in the Democratic Republic of Congo (Operation Artemis); it took over peace-keeping operations from NATO in Bosnia in 2004; it has had police and other missions in Afghanistan, the Central African Republic, Chad, Georgia, Guinea-Bissau, Indonesia, Moldova, Macedonia, Palestine, Ukraine, and Kosovo; in 2008 the EU launched Operation Atalanta in the Indian Ocean, aimed at combating piracy off the coast of Somalia; EU personnel accounted at the beginning of 2010 for nearly 40 per cent of the forces in Afghanistan, and a significant number of those in Kosovo and Lebanon; and along the way, individual EU states have engaged in military operations such as Britain's mission in Sierra Leone in 2000 (establishing order after a UN force had failed) and France's contributions to peacekeeping in Haiti, Côte d'Ivoire, and Lebanon.

Illustration 24.2
Trade policy

A container ship heads out to sea, a reminder of the remarkable global trading power of the European Union.

After stagnating between 1989 and 1999, Howorth notes (2007, p. 115), EU security and defence policy has come a long way in a few short years; but he also concludes that the EU 'still has a long way to go before it can overcome all its short-comings and emerge as a fully credible coordinated military actor able to carry out the full range of Petersberg tasks'. British foreign secretary David Miliband was critical during a speech in November 2007 when he noted that 'It's frankly embar-rassing . . . when European nations – with almost two million men and women under arms – are only able, at a stretch, to deploy around one hundred thousand at any one time' (Miliband, 2007). And yet questions remain about what the EU *should* be able to achieve: its heritage as a civilian power remains strong, it does not aspire to become a major military actor on a par with the United States, and the nature of security threats has changed in recent years. Meanwhile, the question of how far it should develop policy independence from the United States, and how far it should continue to be driven by the needs of NATO, remains unanswered.

Trade policy

● **Trade policy**: Policy dealing with the exchange of goods and services across borders, and including issues such as tariffs, quotas, and protectionism.

● **Common Commercial Policy**: The common trade policy of the EU, included in the Treaty of Rome and under which the EU has effectively used its power to deal and negotiate with third parties on trade issues.

While questions linger about the global impact of the EU's foreign and security policies, on matters of trade there are few remaining doubts: the EU is the world's largest trading power (a trading hyperpower, even), and trade – argues Orbie (2008) – has become the EU's 'most powerful external policy domain'. At its core has been the **Common Commercial Policy** (CCP), in place since the Treaty of Rome. Intended formally to contribute 'to the harmonious develop-ment of world trade, the progressive abolition of restrictions on international trade, and the lowering of customs barriers', the CCP was in fact designed to protect the EU's trading interests. Although a comprehensive EU trade policy took many years to develop, the CCP early helped establish strong EU positions on global trade negotiations, and underpinned the growing global presence of the EU as a trading powerhouse: it accounts for approximately one-sixth of trade

Table 24.1 The world's five biggest trading powers

	% Share imports			% Share exports	
Merchandise					
	EU-27	18.3		EU-27	15.9
	United States	17.4		China	11.8
	China	9.4		United States	10.6
	Japan	6.1		Japan	6.5
	South Korea	3.5		Russia	3.9
Commercial services					
	EU-27	23.9		EU-27	26.9
	United States	14.2		United States	18.8
	Japan	6.4		China	5.3
	China	6.4		Japan	5.3
	South Korea	3.5		India	3.7

Source: World Trade Organization, *International Trade Statistics 2009*, at http://www.wto.org (retrieved August 2010). Figures are for trade in 2008, and exclude intra-EU trade.k.org (retrieved June 2010).

in merchandise and about a quarter of trade in commercial services (see Table 24.1). Related data build a compelling case:

● The EU is the world's wealthiest marketplace, with a population of nearly half a billion predominantly middle-class consumers with plenty of disposable income.
● It accounts for nearly one-third of global economic output, its combined gross domestic product being bigger than that of the United States, more than four times bigger than that of China, and nearly 16 times bigger than that of India (see Figure 24.1).
● The euro sits alongside the US dollar and the Japanese yen as one of the three most important currencies in the world. The Chinese and the Indians have nothing to compare.
● It is the biggest source and target of foreign direct investment in the world, accounting in 2007 (before the global economic crisis) for about two-thirds of investment inflows into (and outflows from) OECD member states (OECD figures at http://www.oecd.org; retrieved January 2010).
● As we saw in Chapter 19, it is the biggest market in the world for mergers and acquisitions, and the global presence of European multinationals has grown accordingly in strength and reach.

The most obvious developments on the trade front have been closest to home, where almost all the barriers that once divided EU states have disappeared. As late as the 1960s and 1970s it was relatively unusual to find items for sale (or services on offer) in western European states that were not domestically produced, grown or generated, and consumers were supplied mainly either by domestic corporations or by the big US multinationals such as Ford, Kodak, IBM and Esso). As the single market encouraged mergers and acquisitions across

Figure 24.1 The EU in the global economy

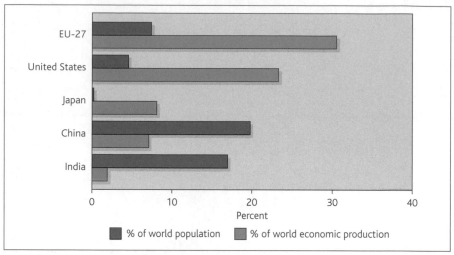

Figures are for 2008.
Source: Calculated from figures generated by World Bank, http://www.worldbank.org (retrieved June 2010).

European borders, and opened up domestic trading opportunities, so European consumers saw more products and services coming from neighbouring states. The result is that about 60–67 per cent of all EU trade is now generated within the EU (see Figure 24.2). From this base the EU has in turn become a global trading power, selling goods and services around the world, and being a market to which foreign countries and corporations want access.

Figure 24.2 The EU and world trade

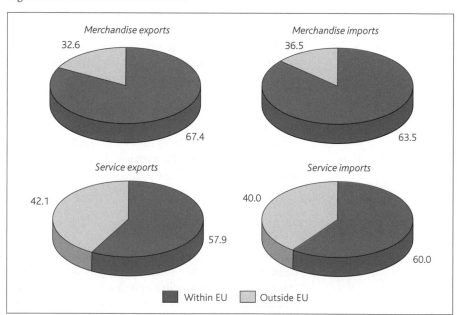

Figures are percentages for 2007.
Source: World Trade Organization at http://www.wto.org (retrieved April 2010).

Figure 24.3 Disputes before the World Trade Organization

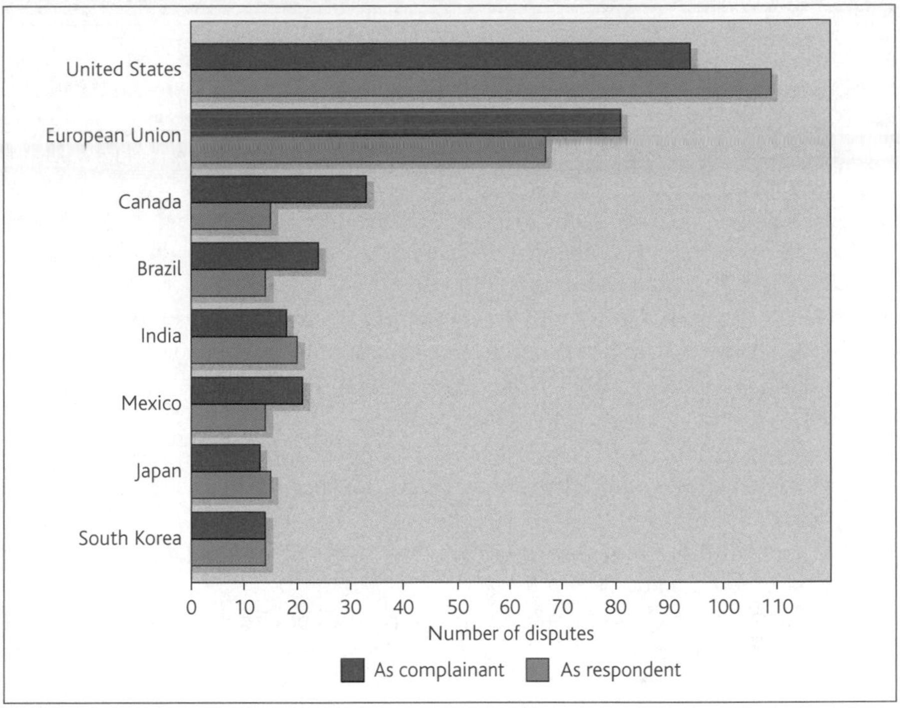

Figures are for 1995-2010.
Source: World Trade Organization at http://www.wto.org (retrieved May 2010).

The role of the EU as a trading power is reflected in the number of times it has been involved in cases brought before the World Trade Organization (WTO). Since the creation of the WTO with its dispute resolution process in 1995, any member state that has a trade dispute with another can take their case to the WTO, which will investigate and issue a judgement that is binding upon the parties involved. Given that they are the world's two biggest trading powers, it is not surprising that the EU and the United States have brought more cases before the WTO than any other members (see Figure 24.3). In many instances the disputes have been between the EU and the US (which have tussled over hormone-treated beef, agricultural imports from Latin America, tariffs on steel imports, and subsidies to aircraft manufacturers). The EU has even gone beyond issues dealing with trade in goods and moved into areas outside its legal competence, including intellectual property rights, trade in services, and the tax regimes of third countries (Billiet, 2005).

The EU has not always had its way on trade negotiations, to be sure, and Meunier (2005) finds a mismatch between the institutional unity of the EU on trade issues and its external bargaining power. But the statistics make a compelling case, and whatever doubts there may be about the internal economic policies of the EU (see Chapter 19), its global economic presence is uncontested. We may never be able to do without military power to deal with the most serious international security problems, but in a world of globalization, new technology, new patterns of migration, and greater market freedom, control of the means of production is more important than control of the means of destruction. On the economic front at least, the EU is in a commanding position.

SUMMARY

● Understanding the global role of the EU depends on how we understand power in the international system, long conventionally associated with military power and with states.

● Talk of a Cold War bipolar system was briefly replaced after the collapse of the Soviet Union by talk of a unipolar system based on US hegemony, but this has since been replaced with talk of a multipolar system bringing in new powers such as China and India, but curiously often overlooking the EU.

● Depending on how we understand the international system, there is evidence of the EU emerging as a new kind of power based on idealist principles, with a preference for the use of multilateralism, civilian power, and soft rather than hard instruments of influence.

● The EU's Common Foreign and Security Policy has been less a common policy than a means to setting shared positions, and it has suffered from a lack of leadership and focus.

● The EU is a more impressive military power than most people realize, but it has made only limited progress along the path to a common security policy.

● Questions remain about what the EU *should* be able to achieve in security policy, how far it should develop policy independence from the United States, and how much it should continue to be driven by the needs of NATO.

● Buoyed by the size of the single market and by the near-completion of a Common Commercial Policy, the EU has become a trading superpower.

● Its trading power is clearly reflected in the number of disputes in which it has been involved within the World Trade Organization.

KEY TERMS AND CONCEPTS

Atlanticists	Europeanists	Perpetual peace
Bipolar system	Foreign policy	Petersberg tasks
Civilian power	Hard power	Power
Common Commercial Policy	Idealism	Superpower
Common Foreign and Security Policy	Mixed system	Security policy
European Security and Defence Policy	Multilateralism	Soft power
European Security Strategy	Multipolar system	Trade policy

FURTHER READING

Howorth, Jolyon (2007), *Security and Defence Policy in the European Union* (Basingstoke: Palgrave Macmillan). An overview of the trials and tribulations of the EU in this critical policy area.

Kagan, Robert (2003), *Of Paradise and Power: America and Europe in the New World Order* (New York: Knopf). Required reading (in spite of the criticism directed at Kagan's arguments) for what it says about Europe's global role.

Keukeleire, Stephan, and Jennifer MacNaughtan (2008), *The Foreign Policy of the European Union* (Basingstoke: Palgrave Macmillan); Orbie, Jan. (ed.) (2008), *Europe's Global Role: External Policies of the European Union* (Aldershot: Ashgate); Smith, Karen E. (2008), *European Union Foreign Policy in a Changing World*, 2nd edn (Cambridge: Polity). Just three of the numerous studies that have been published on the foreign policies of the EU.

CHAPTER 25

The EU and the World

PREVIEW

In Chapter 24 we looked at how the EU's foreign, security and trade policies have shaped its role as a global actor. In this chapter, those policies are examined more closely by looking at the EU's relations with different parts of the world. We begin with an assessment of the most important political and economic relationship in the world, between the EU and the United States. This has not always been an easy relationship, the differences that lurked under the surface during the Cold War having become more visible since the collapse of the Soviet Union removed the one project that the two most clearly had in common.

The chapter then looks at the EU's relations with its immediate neighbours: the Mediterranean, the Middle East and Russia. Beyond the inner rim of potential future members of the EU there is a 'circle of friends' consisting of countries that have no realistic prospect of EU membership, but with which the EU is building close political and economic ties. Particularly important is Russia, by far the biggest of its neighbours but the one over whom the greatest doubts continue to linger.

Further afield, there are fascinating developments in the EU's relations with China, for many the most convincing candidate for the world's next superpower. Ties between the two have improved, and yet uncertainties remain and the EU is wary about China's human rights record and foreign policy. Finally, Europe's former African, Caribbean and Pacific colonies have long played a part in the definition of the EU's global interests, and the EU has become by far the biggest source of official development assistance in the world. But the jury is still out on the efficacy of European development assistance policy.

KEY ISSUES

- Can Europeans and Americans ever see the world in the same way?
- What does the European model have to offer its near neighbours as a means to the promotion of capitalism and democracy?
- How are the driving forces behind EU relations with Russia and China different, and what are the likely results?
- What impact is the tripartite relationship between the EU, the United States and China likely to have on international politics and economics?
- Does fair trade hold out better prospects for developing countries than development aid?

The EU and the United States

The bilateral relationship between the United States and the European Union is the most important (and the most thoroughly studied) in the world. The two actors are economic superpowers, accounting between them for nearly 54 per cent of global economic production, more than a quarter of global trade in merchandise, and more than one-third of global trade in services. They also control the two key international currencies, the dollar and the euro, and as homes to the world's largest multinational corporations they dominate international commerce, controlling millions of jobs around the world and being the major sources (and targets) of foreign direct investment, as well as being among each other's biggest trading partners. They also maintain the biggest and most powerful military forces in the world, accounting between them for 75 per cent of global spending on defence. Finally, this combination of economic and military power translates into global political influence; the US and the EU dominate the world's major international organizations, and what one says and does matters a great deal not only to the other but to much of the rest of the world.

In spite of this, the transatlantic relationship has not always been an easy one (see Lundestad, 2003, and McGuire and Smith, 2008, Chapter 1). Before the Second World War, Americans kept their distance, wary of being drawn into European conflicts and critical of European colonialism. Meanwhile, Europeans kept a worried eye on rising American political, economic, and cultural influence. After the Second World War, western Europeans fell into an often reluctant subservience to American leadership; they had little choice but to rely on American economic investments and American security guarantees, even if they often disputed the American interpretation of Cold War threats and the solutions the United States pursued. But while western European governments might have privately railed against US policy, in public they mainly went along, recognizing the importance of the **Atlantic Alliance**.

The United States has always been a supporter of European integration, and it is unlikely that the EEC would have been created or would have evolved into today's EU without that support. It made critical early contributions through the Marshall Plan and by providing a security umbrella in the form of NATO, guarantees which helped western Europe concentrate on internal reorganization and reconstruction. But American generosity was not entirely charitable: peace and economic reconstruction in western Europe suited American interests, reinforcing the region's abilities to resist and offset Soviet influence, building an important market for American exports, and establishing western Europe as a critical political and economic partner of the United States.

While there were deliberate US policies that helped pave the way for European integration, the United States also contributed unconsciously in two other ways. First, it pursued policies that helped unite Europeans either in support of US policy or in opposition (but mainly the latter). The war in Vietnam (which peaked in 1965–75) strained the Alliance, western European governments refusing to provide either military or political support to the United States, and the European anti-war movement directing sustained criticism at American policy. The unilateral decision of the United States in 1971 to end dollar convertibility with gold brought political and economic strain, and the growing transatlantic gap in Middle East policy became clear in 1973 as

● **Atlantic Alliance**: The military and political alliance between the United States and western Europe, resting mainly on their Cold War opposition to the Soviet bloc.

western European governments parted company with the Americans over military assistance to Israel during the Yom Kippur War. The litany of differences grew: over West German policy towards East Germany, over US policy in central America, over the 1979 Soviet invasion of Afghanistan, and over the deployment by the Reagan administration of nuclear weapons in Europe.

Second, American policy has often helped the EU identify its weaknesses. It was competition from US corporations in the 1960s that helped western Europeans realize how little progress they were making on rebuilding their own industries, the US decision on the dollar and gold led to exchange rate volatility that helped concentrate European minds on how to build the groundwork for monetary union, and then came the serial security embarrassments of the 1990s: the 1990–91 Gulf war, the outbreak of fighting in the Balkans in 1991, and the crisis in Kosovo in 1999. These revealed just how much European governments still disagreed among themselves on foreign policy, and showed how poorly prepared the EU was to deal with major international security problems. The EU continues to be unfavourably compared with the United States as a global actor that punches below its weight, and that has so far failed to be taken as seriously as it would like by American policy makers.

Formal attempts by the two sides to build links have had mixed results. In November 1990 the Transatlantic Declaration committed them to regular high-level contacts and called for cooperation in policy areas such as combating terrorism, drug trafficking and international crime (European Commission, 1991). In late 1995 the New Transatlantic Agenda committed them to work together on promoting peace and democracy around the world. Under the 1995 Transatlantic Business Dialogue, European and American business leaders began meeting at regular conferences, and the 1998 launch of the Transatlantic Economic Partnership was designed to encourage more discussions on trade issues; the US is the EU's major trade partner (see Table 25.1).

Table 25.1 The EU's five biggest external trading partners

	% Share imports		**% Share exports**	
Merchandise				
Asia (excl. China)	18.3	**United States**	18.7
China	15.9	Non-EU Europe	17.5
Non-EU Europe	14.2	Asia (excl. China)	17.1
United States	11.8	Africa	8.9
Africa	9.3	Russia	8.0
Commercial services				
United States	31.0	**United States**	28.0
Non-EU Europe	16.3	Non-EU Europe	16.9
China	3.2	Japan	4.0
Japan	3.2	Russia	3.8
Russia	3.1	Japan	3.6

Source: World Trade Organization at http://www.wto.org (retrieved April 2010).
Figures are for 2007 (services) and 2008 (merchandise) for the EU-27, and refer to percentage share of trade outside the EU.

But behind the diplomatic smiles, the nature of the game had changed with the end of the Cold War. The one truly common transatlantic project – opposing and outwitting the Soviets – was gone, shedding new light on the pre-existing differences between the two sides. They disagreed on approaches towards international trouble spots such as Cuba, Iran, Iraq, and Libya (Haass, 1999), and the US was disappointed by the inability or unwillingness of the Europeans to step up and take their share of responsibility for international security. But the EU played a critical role in capitalizing on the end of the Cold War by reaching out to the east, and began building the foundations of its common foreign and security policies. Its trading power also became more clear, and the cases it took to the new World Trade Organization often targeted the United States. Public support for common EU foreign policies has since grown, and is particularly strong on the question of policy independence from the US, favoured by almost four out of five Europeans (see Figure 25.1).

The September 2001 terrorist attacks in the United States might have been an opportunity to redefine the transatlantic relationship, but they ended up having the opposite effect. There was an initial massive outpouring of political and public sympathy in the EU, and a hope among European leaders that both sides could work together on a response. But while they agreed on the threats posed by terrorism and weapons of mass destruction, and on the invasion of Afghanistan, Europeans were shocked when the administration of President George W. Bush adopted a belligerent tone of unilateralism, arguing that states were either for or against the US in the war on terrorism, categorizing Iran, Iraq, and North Korea as part of an 'axis of evil', and rejecting multilateralism in favour of the right of the United States to act alone. It was also clear that Americans and Europeans disagreed over the causes of terrorism: Bush argued that terrorists 'hated America' and were envious of its democratic principles, while Europeans preferred to look at the root causes of militant resentment, including criticism of US policy on the Arab–Israeli problem, and the stationing of US troops in Saudi Arabia.

When the Bush administration started making plans for an invasion of Iraq in 2002, the tensions between the United States and the EU broke into the open. Led by France and Germany, several European governments openly opposed and criticized US policy, while American critics of the EU accused it of dithering and raised the spectre of 1930s-style appeasement. US defence secretary Donald Rumsfeld bewildered many with his off-the-cuff remarks at a January 2003 press conference, dismissing Germany and France as 'old Europe' and as problems in the alliance, while arguing that the centre of gravity in NATO Europe had shifted eastwards to its new members. Europeans responded by using unflattering Wild West metaphors to describe President Bush. In an October 2003 poll, 53 per cent of Europeans ranked the United States as a threat to world peace on a par with North Korea and Iran.

The fallout over Iraq sparked a flood of academic and media analyses of the state of the transatlantic relationship (see, for example, Mowle, 2004, and Kopstein and Steinmo, 2008). Optimists argue that it was a short-term squabble and that both sides can and must overcome their differences because it is in their interests to work together. Pessimists argue that the rift was inevitable, was indicative of deeper problems, and that the relationship can never be the same again. But whatever happens, Iraq showed that the Europeans – buoyed by their

Figure 25.1 What Europeans think: policy independence from the United States

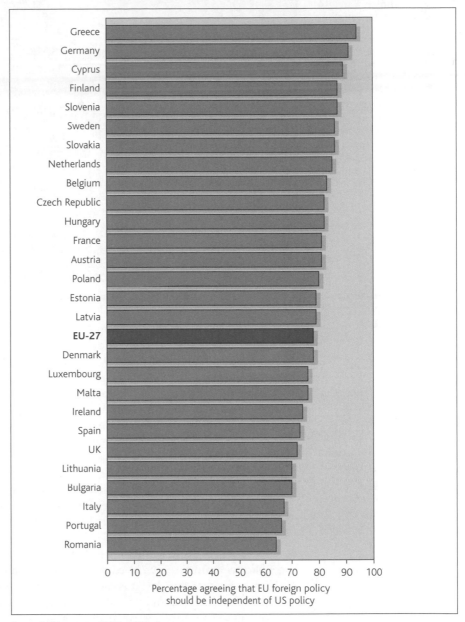

Percentage agreeing that EU foreign policy
should be independent of US policy

Source: Eurobarometer 68, May 2008.

economic power and by their reduced dependence on American security with
the end of the Cold War – had become more assertive, and more aware of how
they differed from the Americans on many key issues, whether climate change,
the role and purposes of the United Nations, the Middle East peace process, or
the International Criminal Court (the United States is one of a small and not
very select group of countries that has refused to ratify the 1998 treaty creating
the court; others include China, Iraq, Iran, Israel, and Russia).

Illustration 25.1
Transatlantic relations

The US-EU bilateral relationship is the most important in the world, but also one that is fraught with difficulties. Here President Obama, who had shown little interest in EU affairs, meets with Commission president Barroso and other European leaders at the 2009 US–EU Summit.

What are the prospects for continued strong relations between the EU and the United States? On the one hand, both parties agree on the general goals of promoting democracy, free markets, human rights, and the rule of law. They can also, when it suits them, usually set aside their differences to address pressing international problems. They are also deeply invested in each other economically, as reflected in their trade relationship, their mutual flows of foreign direct investment, and the manner in which economic problems in one quickly spill over into the other. On the other hand, both sides are ambitious and assertive, and they have quite different styles and values on a wide range of issues.

- Europeans take a more progressive and liberal position than Americans on a host of social issues, including abortion, capital punishment, same-sex marriage, and euthanasia, in part because religion plays a less prominent role in European calculations.
- Europeans are more willing to support the role of government in providing public programmes such as education, health care and welfare. Whereas most Americans feel that it is more important for government to provide them with the freedom to pursue other goals, most Europeans feel that it is more important for government to guarantee that no one is in need (see, for example, discussion in Russell, 2006, pp. 48–9).
- On security policy, Europeans (as we saw in Chapter 24) favour the use of soft power and peacekeeping, while Americans have fewer concerns about hard power.
- On foreign policy, Europeans favour multilateralism while Americans are more amenable to unilateralism.

Americans and Europeans are bound tightly by history, culture, politics and economic principles, but they have long kept their distance from one another,

Debating...
Can Europeans and Americans ever really agree?

YES	NO
The two sides have long agreed on the core ideas of democracy and capitalism, and whatever their differences they will continue to work together on their promotion of both.	The two sides have quite different ideas about their places in the world, and often disagree about the means of dealing with critical international problems. The United States is influenced by its view of itself as an exceptional society, and by realist self-interest, while the EU takes a more universal and cosmopolitan view of the world.
Beneath the occasional political differences the two sides are tied by massive flows of foreign direct investment, by substantial trade flows, by shared concerns about critical international issues, by close cultural and historical ties, and by cooperation in numerous areas of policy, from intelligence-gathering and sharing to the technical management of everything from civil aviation to education.	Europeans and Americans have quite different sets of values. Europeans (for example) favour approaches to foreign policy based on economic opportunity and free trade while the United States continues to maintain and deploy massive military power.
Both sides bring complementary interests, skills and circles of influence to the resolution of international problems, and mainly realize that working together (and matching their relative advantages) is preferable to being at odds.	The cold war transatlantic alliance was a marriage of convenience, and so long as the two sides lack a mutual enemy of the size and reach of the old Soviet Union their differing worldviews will be more obvious and problematic. Radical Islam might be a candidate for bringing them together, but Europeans and Americans disagree on many of the fundamentals of the best approach.

and the rise of a more assertive Europe suggests that – assuming Europeans can build the necessary level of agreement on foreign policy – the transatlantic relationship, while never static in the past, is likely to undergo further substantial change in the future. One multi-author study (Kopstein and Steinmo, 2008, p. 4) agrees on the many differences between the two sides, leaving open only the question of where they will lead; while Europeans and Americans may be growing apart in many respects, they may also find enough common ground to continue to work together.

Looking to the neighbourhood

We saw in Chapters 5 to 7 how enlargement has influenced developments in new member states of the EU, and changed the character of the EU itself. We also saw in Chapter 9 that as many as 17 countries have prospects of eventually becoming members of the EU, if we extend the definition of Europe to include the Caucasus and Turkey. Just outside that ring of potential future members is another group of states that sit on the EU's borders, that do not qualify for membership as the terms are currently defined, and yet which mainly want a strong bond with the EU, and which the EU is willing to court in the interests of creating a 'circle of friends'. This circle takes in most of North Africa and the Middle East, along with the rather different challenge of how to deal with Russia.

November 1995 saw the launch of the Euro-Mediterranean Partnership – otherwise known as the **Barcelona Process** – with the goal of strengthening political, economic and social ties between the EU and all North African and Middle Eastern states bordering the Mediterranean; these included Algeria, Egypt, Israel, Jordan, the Palestinian Authority, Turkey, and – until they joined the EU – Cyprus and Malta. The programme included goals such as agreeing shared values, promoting democracy, developing policies that complemented those of the US in the Mediterranean, and establishing a free trade area in the Middle East by 2010. Although the partnership encouraged economic and cultural ties, it was tripped up by the lack of progress on the Middle East peace process, by concerns among some partner countries about the dominant role of the EU, and by the focus on the Mediterranean being distracted by the inclusion of the many EU states that do not border the Mediterranean.

In 2008, on an initiative mainly from French President Nikolas Sarkozy, the Barcelona Process evolved into the **Union for the Mediterranean**. This was originally to have focused only on Mediterranean states (but would have used EU funds), was to have included a Mediterranean Investment Bank, and was proposed (in the case of Turkey) as an alternative to membership of the EU. But in the face of criticism from other EU states it was expanded to all EU states, and was portrayed to Turkey as a stepping stone to EU membership rather than an alternative. It has many of the same policy goals as the Barcelona Process, has an institutional headquarters in Barcelona, has a rotating co-presidency (one EU state and one non-EU state), and consists of 43 members: the 27 EU member states along with 16 neighbouring states (see Map 25.1).

Meanwhile, the **European Neighbourhood Policy** (ENP) was adopted in 2004 with the goal of avoiding the emergence of dividing lines between an enlarged EU and its immediate neighbours, promoting a relationship that the EU describes as 'privileged'. It targets 16 of those neighbours and is based on developing action plans with each of these countries intended to define how relations between the parties will develop, and the interests they share. The EU agenda includes plans to encourage democracy, human rights, the rule of law, market economics, and good governance in the ENP countries, and cooperation on measures against terrorism.

Although discussions about the EU's relationship with its neighbours is often couched in terms of often rather dry and technical projects and programmes, it has a bigger and wider significance; in a world where debates about how to promote peace and democracy never end, the European soft power model has come to offer a contrast to the American hard power model. Arguably, the promise of access to the European marketplace has become the single most effective means for the promotion of democracy and capitalism. This is partly why Mark Leonard believes that 'Europe will run the 21st century'. It has a transformative power, he argues, that 'comes from its ability to reward reformers and withhold benefits from laggards', and it functions as 'a club with rules and benefits to hand out. By couching their relations in terms of creating a neighbourhood club . . . [Europeans] can create the incentives to drive reform without being imperial' (Leonard, 2005, pp. 56, 103–4).

The EU's relationship with the Middle East has long been difficult, made worse in recent decades by tensions with Iran, Iraq and Israel. Europe's interests in achieving Middle East peace are far greater than those of the United States, the

● **Barcelona Process**: A programme launched in 1995 and aimed at strengthening ties between the EU and most of its North African and Middle Eastern neighbours.

● **Union for the Mediterranean**: A project by which the Barcelona Process was relaunched in 2008, with a focus on security cooperation, immigration, the environment, transport and education.

● **European Neighbourhood Policy**: A policy aimed at encouraging democracy and capitalism in 16 eastern European and North African neighbours of the EU.

Map 25.1 The European neighbourhood

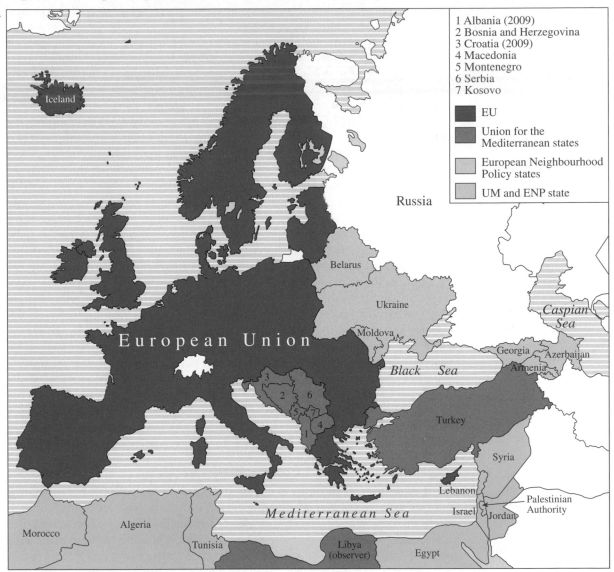

1 Albania (2009)
2 Bosnia and Herzegovina
3 Croatia (2009)
4 Macedonia
5 Montenegro
6 Serbia
7 Kosovo

▉ EU

▉ Union for the Mediterranean states

▉ European Neighbourhood Policy states

▉ UM and ENP state

major foreign player in the region, for at least four major reasons. First, the EU (which has few domestic oil supplies, unlike the United States) relies on the Middle East for about 40 per cent of its oil needs, or about twice as big a proportion as the United States. Second, it has a bigger trading relationship with many Middle Eastern countries than does the United States. Third, Europe attracts many more immigrants from the Middle East than does the United States. Finally, Europe faces a more immediate threat from Islamic militancy and terrorism than does the United States, being home to a far greater number of Muslims, having to live more immediately with the prospect of home-grown terrorism, and being easier to reach should Iran ever develop nuclear weapons and the ability to use them. But in spite of this, the EU has played only a supporting role so far to the United States, benefiting (or suffering, depending on your point of view) from the US political-military role in the region while often being critical of US policy (Nitze and Hadar, 2009).

Few problems have been more central to the EU's Middle Eastern policy (and yet, oddly, less closely studied) than Israel. Where Israeli–western European relations were generally strong in the 1950s, they have soured since the 1967 Six Day War and the Israeli occupation of the West Bank and Gaza that has persisted ever since. The Community fell out with the United States on arms supplies to Israel during the 1973 Yom Kippur war, Greece and Spain did not establish diplomatic relations with Israel until the 1980s, and the EU has made the creation of a Palestinian homeland a condition of Middle Eastern peace. Perhaps most (in)famously, an October 2003 Eurobarometer Flash Poll in the (then) 15 member states of the EU found that more Europeans (59 per cent) regarded Israel as a greater threat to world peace than any other country, including Iran, North Korea, and Iraq. More recently, the EU described Israeli attacks on Lebanon in 2006 as 'a disproportionate use of force', and it continues today to be more openly critical than the United States of the building of Israeli settlements in the occupied territories of the West Bank, particularly in East Jerusalem.

But how much EU opinion matters to Israel is debatable. The United States has long been the political champion of Israel, and its major supplier of military aid. The Israeli lobby in Washington DC is strong, and Israeli leaders generally care far more what the United States has to say than what the European Union has to say. European criticism of Israeli policy has spawned analyses suggesting that anti-Semitism is alive and well in many parts of Europe. Israel meanwhile criticizes what it regards as the EU's pro-Arab policies in the Middle East, while many Europeans abhor the militarism that influences Israeli policy and the strong role played by religious fundamentalism in Israeli justifications for continued occupation of Palestinian territory. At the same time, Israel has a heavy dependence on the European market for its exports, and so cannot afford to allow relations to deteriorate too much. In short, it is at best a love-hate relationship. (For more details see Pardo and Peters, 2009.)

Troubles also loom to the east, where the EU–Russia relationship has blown hot and cold since the end of the Cold War (Antonenko and Pinnick, 2005). Relations were at first positive, with Russia seeking the kind of respectability and economic opportunities that the EU could offer, while the EU sought Russian support for eastern enlargement. In 1994 a Partnership and Cooperation Agreement was signed between the EU and Russia, coming into effect in 1997 and aimed at encouraging cooperation, establishing the conditions for a possible future free trade area, and expressing EU hopes for 'a stable, democratic and prosperous Russia, firmly anchored in a united Europe free of new dividing lines'. There has been talk since the late 1990s of building a Common European Economic Space that would give Russia new access to the European single market in return for the necessary changes in Russian law, and in 2003 the Putin administration sided with Germany and France in opposing the US-led invasion of Iraq.

But then Russia began to worry about its economic imbalance with the EU, and looked askance at the applications for EU membership from three former Soviet republics (Estonia, Latvia, and Lithuania). The EU became critical of the authoritarian tendencies of the Putin administration, and at Russian policy in Chechnya. The two sides disagreed over climate change and over illegal immigration from Russia, and new attention was paid to EU–Russian relations in early 2004 when Russia insisted that its pre-existing trade agreements with future eastern European members of the EU should stay in place after they joined the EU. The EU responded that Russia would have to deal with them in future as it dealt with any other EU member state, and threatened to impose trade sanctions on Russia and to block its application to the World Trade Organization if it persisted with its demands (Johnson and Robinson, 2005, p. 1). Tensions grew as NATO membership expanded into the former Soviet bloc (nine former Soviet or eastern bloc states are now members), and as Russia expressed displeasure with the leading role of the EU in criticizing the fraudulent October 2004 Ukrainian presidential elections, feeding in to the 'orange revolution' that led to a new vote in December.

The EU–Russia relationship today remains tense. Both sides need each other but do not entirely trust the motives of the other. At the heart of the tensions are economic considerations, particularly energy: the EU relies on Russia for about one-fifth of its oil needs and one-quarter of its gas needs. For its part, Russia is only too aware that the EU not only accounts for 70 per cent of its exports but is also the biggest source of foreign investment in Russian industry and infrastructure. Curiously, opinion polls have indicated that as many as 60 per cent of Russians would be willing to see their country join the EU (Allen and Smith, 2002), and yet most Russians still give more weight to relations with the US; this is changing, though, as the memories of the Cold War fade and younger Russians take over the reins of government and business.

The EU and China: New discoveries

The Western world has a new fascination with the rising global role of China, whose large population and rapidly transforming economy have already led many to jump to the conclusion that China will soon be (if it is not already) a superpower. But this depends on how we define a superpower (see Chapter 24), and it also rather overlooks China's crushing poverty, its lack of a currency with global credibility or a military with global reach, and its poor record on human rights. None of this has been enough to stand in the way of a growing speculative literature on the global role of China, and another more specifically on EU–Chinese relations, assessing the bilateral links between these two economic giants from multiple angles (see, for example, Casarini, 2009; Ross *et al.*, 2009; Shambaugh *et al.*, 2008; and Kerr and Fei, 2007). China is now the EU's second biggest trading partner (after the United States), and the EU is China's biggest export market.

In spite of this, the EU–China relationship is not yet well understood. Europe and China have for centuries had trade links that have impacted both sides, and yet their physical distance from each other has led to a high degree of mutual misunderstanding (Yahuda, 2008), and it has only been since the mid-1990s that there have been efforts to build closer relations between the two. But even today the story is not a simple one, complicated by questions about China's long-term plans, and by the dynamics of the tripartite relationship between the EU, the United States, and China. The latter promises not only to change the nature of the international system, but will also inevitably impact the way that other states, such as Japan, India and Russia, relate to China (Kerr and Fei, 2007).

Ties between China and the Community were established in 1975 with the first visit to China by a European Commissioner. A trade agreement was signed in 1978, an agreement on trade and economic cooperation in 1985, and the Commission opened a Delegation in Beijing in 1988. Relations soured following the June 1989 crackdown in Tiananmen Square, which resulted in the imposition of Community sanctions on China. Within three years relations were back on a stronger footing, although an arms embargo remained in place. A series of EU–China summits were held between 1998 and 2002, supported by policy papers from the Commission that included reference to 'a maturing partnership' between the two sides. An agreement was signed in 2003 bringing China into the Galileo navigation satellite programme (much to the chagrin of the United States), and numerous China–EU meetings addressed issues such as human rights, maritime transport, technology, climate change, and intellectual property.

The EU has remained critical of China's poor human rights record, and there have been disagreements on climate change and other issues, but where the two sides had rarely spoken to each other at the diplomatic level, by the early 2000s joint meetings had become almost routine. Negotiations began in 2007 aimed at upgrading the 1985 trade agreement to a Partnership and Cooperation Agreement. The strengthening of ties has been helped by the removal of the restrictions of the Cold War, the fact that Taiwan is not an issue in Europe as it is in the United States (where there is an active Taiwan lobby), the fact that the Europe (unlike the United States) has no military presence in East Asia, the clearly shared commercial and economic interests of the two actors, and the role of the Commission in developing policy proposals that have 'offered a benign view of China's rise and identified a range of areas for collaboration' (Shambaugh *et al.*, 2008, pp. 304–5) .

For Casarini (2009, p. 15), the EU–China relationship has gone through three phases: a period of constructive engagement from the mid-1990s, moving to a strategic partnership between the two sides in 2003–5 (marked by cooperation on technology, notably space and satellite navigation), followed more recently by 'pragmatic restraint' in light of US concerns about how the relationship has been evolving. Along the way, she argues, the EU has been unable to define a clear position on China, and its leaders have been unable to agree what kind of power China has become. The result has in turn been a challenge to the emergence of the EU as a global actor. Much depends on how the implications of new Chinese power in the world are understood, and on the political impact of critics of China's human rights record and military aspirations. Unlike the Europe–US relationship, where communication has always been strong (even if the two do not always agree) and where neither actor has much reason to worry about the global aspirations of the other, the Europe–China relationship is influenced by questions and doubts about the implications of rapid economic change in China, and about what China's new wealth and commercial demands will mean for international relations.

The EU and development cooperation

The age of European imperialism is long dead, but its effects are still felt in the heritage of political and economic ties between EU states and former European

CONCEPT

Development policy

Since the end of the colonial era there has been political and moral pressure on wealthy industrialized states to provide aid to developing countries, many of which were once colonized by the major European powers. The effects of this aid have been controversial; critics charge that it has been targeted for the wrong uses, that it has created dependence rather than independence, and that too little has been made available. Meanwhile, the leaders of many developing countries have been accused of failing to ensure the equitable distribution of that aid, of lining their own pockets, and of spending on non-essential showcase projects such as new airports and conference centres rather than schools and hospitals.

colonies. Existing colonies were given associate membership of the EEC when it was created in 1958, and former French colonies that are now overseas departments of France – French Guiana, Guadeloupe, Martinique, and Réunion – are integrated into the EU. For others, EU **development policy** has had three main components (Bourdet *et al.*, 2007, pp. 1–3): trade agreements with different groups of countries aimed at helping them boost exports and economic growth, official development assistance (ODA) in the form of grants and technical aid, and policies aimed at specific economic sectors with the goal of helping boost long-term development. But in spite of the long history of EU development policy, it has (like trade policy) been remarkably little studied, and the relative role of the member states and the European Commission is not yet well under-

Table 25.2 The ACP states

AFRICA (48)

Angola	Gabon	Nigeria
Benin	Gambia	Rwanda
Botswana	Ghana	São Tomé and
Burkina Faso	Guinea	Principe
Burundi	Guinea Bissau	Senegal
Cameroon	Ivory Coast	Seychelles
Cape Verde	Kenya	Sierra Leone
Central African	Lesotho	Somalia
Republic	Liberia	South Africa
Chad	Madagascar	Sudan
Comoros	Malawi	Swaziland
Congo (Brazzaville)	Mali	Tanzania
Congo (Kinshasa)	Mauritania	Togo
Djibouti	Mauritius	Uganda
Equatorial Guinea	Mozambique	Zambia
Eritrea	Namibia	Zimbabwe
Ethiopia	Niger	

CARIBBEAN (16)

Antigua and Barbuda	Dominican Republic	St Lucia
Bahamas	Grenada	St Vincent and the
Barbados	Guyana	Grenadines
Belize	Haiti	Suriname
Cuba	Jamaica	Trinidad and Tobago
Dominica	St Kitts and Nevis	

PACIFIC (15)

Cook Islands	Nauru	Solomon Islands
Fiji	Niue	Timor-Leste
Kiribati	Palau	Tonga
Marshall Islands	Papua New Guinea	Tuvalu
Micronesia	Samoa	Vanuatu

**Illustration 25.2
Development policy**

Members of a team from the EU's Humanitarian Aid and Civil Protection department (ECHO) help clear away the ruins after the 2010 Haitian earthquake.

stood (Carbone, 2007), nor are the overall effects of EU policy on helping address global poverty and underdevelopment.

Under the **Africa Caribbean Pacific** (ACP) programme, trade agreements have been signed with selected former colonies, mainly those of Belgium, Britain, France, and Portugal. These began with the 1963 and 1969 Yaoundé Conventions (named for the capital of Cameroon, where they were signed) by which 18 former colonies of the original six EEC member states were given preferential access to Community markets. In return, the 18 states allowed the Community limited duty-free or quota-free access to their markets. With Britain joining the EEC in 1973, many former British colonies were added to the equation, so the Lomé Convention (named for the capital of Togo) was signed in 1975, raising the number of ACP states to 46, and offering them the opportunity of duty-free exports to the Community. An insurance fund called Stabex was also set up to compensate these states for declines in the value of 50 specified agricultural exports, including coffee, tea, and cocoa, and a fund called Sysmin was created to help mineral-producing ACP countries diversify their economies.

A second Lomé Convention was signed in 1980, increasing EEC aid and investment spending. Lomé III (1985–90) shifted the focus to self-sufficiency and food security, while Lomé IV (1990–2000) added a structural adjustment element to ACP aid by encouraging economic diversification in the ACP states rather than simply providing project aid. It also banned exports of toxic wastes between the EU and ACP countries, and included clauses aimed at promoting human rights and protecting tropical forests in ACP countries. But while these agreements may have generated closer commercial ties between the EU and the ACP states, and encouraged an increase in ACP exports to Europe, there were many problems as well. Economic growth in most ACP states was sluggish, imports to the EU from the ACP grew more slowly than those from other parts

● **Africa Caribbean Pacific**: A programme under which former colonies of EU member states have been targeted for preferential trade agreements.

Figure 25.2 Europe's development aid

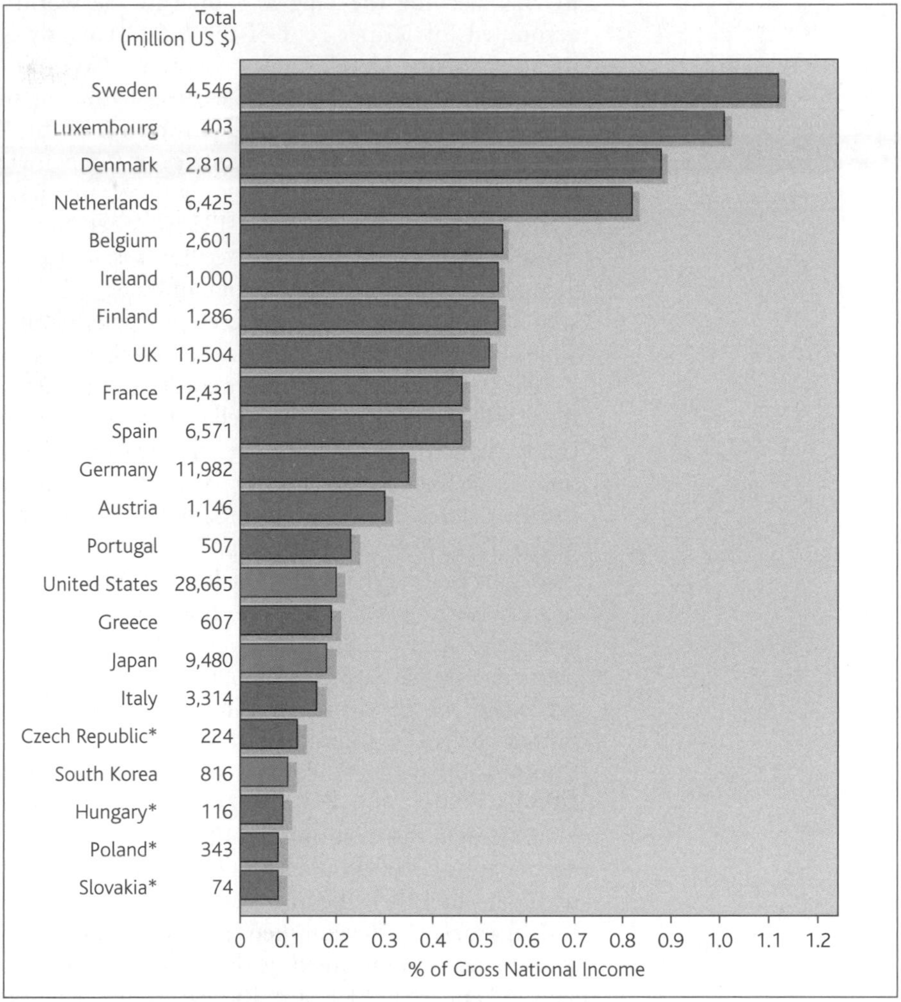

Country	Total (million US $)
Sweden	4,546
Luxembourg	403
Denmark	2,810
Netherlands	6,425
Belgium	2,601
Ireland	1,000
Finland	1,286
UK	11,504
France	12,431
Spain	6,571
Germany	11,982
Austria	1,146
Portugal	507
United States	28,665
Greece	607
Japan	9,480
Italy	3,314
Czech Republic*	224
South Korea	816
Hungary*	116
Poland*	343
Slovakia*	74

% of Gross National Income

Figures are for 2009 for Development Assistance Committee (DAC) of OECD, except * non-DAC members.
Source: OECD at http://www.oecd.org (retrieved April 2010).

of the world; development aid funds took too long to be disbursed; not enough attention was paid to the environmental implications of the focus on cash crops for export; and the programme did not much change the EU–ACP relationship.

In 1996 an intensive review of the ACP programme was launched (see Holland, 2000), and negotiations opened in 1998 between the EU and the ACP states aimed at replacing the Lomé Convention with a more flexible structure based around a series of interregional free trade agreements between groups of ACP countries and the EU. The result was the Cotonou Agreement (named for the capital of Benin), which was signed in 2000 to cover a period of 20 years. In spite of the changes it brought, critics are still not impressed, charging that it is less innovative than it might have been, and that EU development aid policy today is less the model that it once was, and has become more symbolic (Arts and Dickson, 2004).

The second element of EU development policy has been ODA, for which the EU has become the biggest source in the world: its member states in 2009 accounted for 56 per cent of the total of nearly $120 billion given by the 24 members of the Development Assistance Committee of the OECD (see Figure 25.2). Although the United States gives by far the most ODA in absolute terms, the EU states have the advantage in relative terms; the UN General Assembly in 1970 set a target for donor countries of 0.7 per cent of gross national income, which has to date been met by only five countries: Denmark, Luxembourg, the Netherlands, Sweden and non-EU member Norway. Donor countries in 2005 made a commitment to increase their assistance, the EU members of the DAC pledging to reach a collective total of 0.56% of GNI by 2010. But they fell short, some having made little general progress towards that target, and most in 2009–10 feeling the financial pressures arising out of the global economic crisis.

EU states work both multilaterally and bilaterally on overseas aid. Much of their collective ODA is channelled through the European Development Fund (EDF), which was set up under the Treaty of Rome to provide technical and financial assistance to former or existing colonies of the original six EEC member states. It is funded directly by the member states rather than coming under the EU general budget, and is managed by its own committee operating according to its own set of rules. It is organized in five-year packages, the amount in each having risen steadily to the nearly €23 billion ($17.5 billion) budgeted under the Tenth EDF (2008–13). At the same time, each member state has its own bilateral development policies, but this parallel existence of 28 policies has prevented the EU from agreeing focused development goals, and has undermined the EU's international influence. This is changing, though, as the Commission in particular has set targets and standards (Orbie and Versluys, 2008).

Although the amounts spent by the EU on development are impressive, money is not everything. The real impact of aid depends on how resources are used, and how well they are used. ODA is widely criticized for taking a 'Band-Aid' approach to development problems, for being invested in the wrong kinds of activities, and for breeding dependence rather than independence (see discussion in Lancaster, 2006, and Riddell, 2007). There is also the argument that fair trade can do more to help with development than aid, and many questions have been raised about how much political influence aid provides, and what role it plays in promoting better governance.

SUMMARY

- The relationship between the EU and the United States is the most important in the world, and yet it has not always been a happy one.
- The United States has provided direct support to European integration, as well as indirect support by pursuing policies that have united the Europeans in support or in opposition, and by helping the EU identify its weaknesses.
- Both sides agree on the general goals of promoting democracy and capitalism, but they also have quite different styles and values on a wide range of issues, raising questions about how the transatlantic relationship will evolve.
- The EU has been active in reaching out to its neighbours with the goal of creating a 'circle of friends' and of promoting democracy and free markets in the region.
- The Barcelona Process had the goal of strengthening political, economic and social ties between the EU and all non-EU Mediterranean states, and was relaunched in 2008 as the Union for the Mediterranean.
- The European Neighbourhood Policy has the goal of avoiding the emergence of dividing lines between an enlarged EU and its immediate neighbours.
- The EU relationship with the Middle East has been troubled, while that with Russia has blown hot and cold, in spite of the fact that both need each other.
- The EU–China relationship has undergone much change in recent decades, although it is not yet fully understood.
- Their shared history has placed Africa, the Caribbean and the Pacific at the top of the EU development policy agenda. But the jury is still out on the effects of that policy.

KEY TERMS AND CONCEPTS

Africa Caribbean Pacific

Atlantic Alliance

Barcelona Process

Development policy

European Neighbourhood Policy

Union for the Mediterranean

FURTHER READING

Kerr, David, and Liu Fei (eds) (2007), *The International Politics of EU-China Relations* (Oxford: Oxford University Press). One of the growing number of studies of EU–China relations, this one looking at their global implications.

McGuire, Steven, and Michael Smith (2008), *The European Union and the United States* (Basingstoke: Palgrave Macmillan); Jeffrey Kopstein and Sven Steinmo (2008) (eds), *Growing Apart? America and Europe in the Twenty-First Century* (New York: Cambridge University Press). Two assessments of the history, character and prospects of the transatlantic relationship.

Mold, Andrew (ed.) (2007), *EU Development Policy in a Changing World: Challenges for the 21st Century* (Amsterdam: Amsterdam University Press). An edited collection of studies of the past and the future prospects of EU development policy.

Weber, Katja, Michael Smith, and Michael Baun (eds) (2007), *Governing Europe's Neighbourhood: Partners or Periphery?* (Manchester: Manchester University Press). An assessment of the European Neighbourhood Policy and its possibilities.

Conclusions:
Where Now for the EU?

This has been a book about the politics and policies of the European Union. Its purpose has been to explain how the EU works, where it came from, how it evolved, the context within which it has functioned, and its impact on Europe and Europeans. In the preceding 25 chapters, we have:

- Looked at the underlying theoretical explanations of European integration, and have seen how the EU has evolved from being primarily an international organization to becoming a political system in its own right, with qualities that sit somewhere on a spectrum between intergovernmental and supranational, and between federal and confederal.
- Reviewed the personality and character of Europe and its inhabitants, attempting to pin down the region's geographical and cultural limits, to understand what the terms *Europe* and *European* mean, and to identify the norms and values that make the EU and its inhabitants distinctive.
- Surveyed the colourful and controversial history of the EU, tracing events from the signature of the Treaty of Paris in April 1951 through to today's European Union, containing 27 member states and nearly 500 million people, with many other European states considering the prospects of membership.
- Examined the structure and work of the major European institutions, seeking to understand how they function relative to each other and to the member states, and reviewing what their work has meant for the decisions taken by Europe's national leaders and for the lives of ordinary Europeans.
- Assessed the impact of integration on policies in fields as diverse as agriculture, asylum, commerce, competition, corporate mergers and acquisitions, defence, economic development, education, employment, the environment, fisheries, foreign affairs, immigration, monetary affairs, police and judicial cooperation, security, the single market, trade, and workers rights.

The book began with the assertion that the story of European integration has been one of an ongoing tension between success and failure, between swagger and humility, and between optimism and pessimism. We have seen how the process of integration has routinely been made up on the fly, and how the story of the EU has often been one of responses to crises rather than of well-considered strategic initiatives. We have seen how Europeans and their political leaders have often been carried along on a tidal surge of political and economic pressures that they have neither always anticipated nor entirely understood. Opinion is divided on the cumulative results.

On the one hand, supporters of integration point out that Europe has enjoyed the longest spell of generalized peace in its recorded history, that the EU has become the world's wealthiest marketplace, the world's biggest trading power, the world's biggest market for corporate mergers and acquisitions, and the world's biggest source of and target for foreign direct investment. They also argue that the EU has helped promote a new and helpful sense of European identity, encouraged greater policy efficiency by reducing duplication and contradictory goals, transformed the global role of Europe, and given birth to a new model of power that relies on civilian rather than military means to project itself. But detractors charge that integration has undermined national sovereignty, has often proceeded in the face of public hostility, has lacked sufficient accountability or transparency, has failed to take enough account of the differences within European society, and has created a new level of elitist and technocratic government above the level of the member states.

Against this contradictory background, what can we now expect of the European Union? Making predictions is always difficult, not least because so many of us see only what we want to see, and ignore or dismiss evidence that disproves our preferences. Many of us are also the captives of history, routinely projecting the future on the basis of the past. But while an observer contemplating the new European Coal and Steel Community in 1952 might have made some brave forecasts about its likely long-term effects, it is unlikely that they could have foreseen the end of centuries of on-again, off-again war and conflict in Europe, the dismantling of Europe's borders, the abolition of many of its currencies, the advent of a new Europe less constrained by state structures, the upheavals that would transform European society, and the revolutions in international trade and communications that would fundamentally alter the global connections among states and people alike.

Given today's rapid pace of political, economic, social and technological change, the ongoing controversy about the implications of European integration, and the problem of the sheer number of people who either know little about how the EU works or do not fully grasp what it means, forecasting the future for Europe is even more difficult now than it was in 1952. Undaunted, I will end this book with some general thoughts on how the process of integration may unfold, and what the future might hold for Europe and the European Union.

First, European integration – in one form or another - is here to stay. This may seem to be stating the obvious, but it is worth some emphasis. The European Union will always have its champions and its critics, but even if the treaties and their accompanying laws could all be magically revoked tomorrow, and all the EU institutions closed down, the ties that have bound Europeans and their states since 1945 would not only remain but would continue to tighten through an invisible hand of political, economic and social cooperation. But there will be no such revocation; the institutions of the EU will continue to function, new laws will continue to be made, the treaties will continue to be finetuned, and the attempt to agree a constitution for Europe will almost certainly be revisited, later rather than sooner.

Second, the process of integration will continue to be marked by crisis and controversy. Europe's leaders will continue to be obliged to react to events at least as often as they are able to concentrate on making long-term plans, ordinary Europeans will continue to be puzzled by the EU and divided over its merits, and the process of integration will continue to be periodically described as dead or dying (certainly, at least, as long as *The Economist* continues to publish). Partly in response, the rules of the EU will continue to change, driven by the key priority of making the EU institutions more transparent and accountable. The effect will be to continue to push the EU along the path towards a federal future (I can hear the protests even as I write these words) but the result will almost certainly be a quite different variation on the theme of federation than any we have yet seen; it may even stop at confederation. But there will be no clearly discernible end state; as with all polities that have ever existed, the EU will continue indefinitely to be a work in progress. All that will change will be the pace of change, and – hopefully – the quality of the debate about the nature and effects of such change.

Third, the membership of the EU will continue to change. There are more than a dozen potential future members waiting on the sidelines, the state lines of a few existing members could change as the pressures of separatist movements grow, and it is not impossible (although it is highly unlikely) that some member states may even opt to leave the EU. As a result, the internal dynamics of the EU will change; the days of Franco-German dominance have long gone, the effects of eastern enlargement are still being played out, and future realignments will continue to add new priorities to the mix of European integration, obliging changes of perspective, new policy initiatives, and some hard thinking about how best to manage the related demands of widening and deepening. The multi-speed option will remain on the table, but Europeans will continue to find themselves subject to the same sets of political, economic and social pressures, and will continue to move in the same broad direction, with or without the EU.

Fourth, the European state will continue its steady decline. The Westphalian system may have been born in Europe, but in no other part of the world has its retreat been more evident than in Europe. There have been many causes behind that retreat, but regional integration has been a key part of the mix, represented most forcefully in Europe by the pressures of the single market, but also by the thinking of Europeans. Just as more of them have more actively contemplated their European identity, so more have also rediscovered their national identities, and the state has found itself squeezed between the two. In spite of the rearguard actions fought in the name of intergovernmentalism, the supranational qualities of Europe will continue to grow and the role of the state in European public and political life will continue to decline.

Fifth, the advent of the European Union will continue to force a reappraisal of the dynamics of the international system. The era of the great European powers is long gone, as is the bipolar era of the Cold War, while the unipolar era of American hegemony is increasingly difficult to discern through the fog of change brought by globalization and the rise of China and India. The EU is routinely overlooked in discussions about the great new powers of the future (or even of the present), and yet as we better understand the increasing advantages of economic and normative power over military power, and as we rethink the nature of the connections among societies, so more people will likely come to appreciate better the impact of the EU on global politics and economics. In one field particularly – the declining value of the military as a primary tool of statecraft – the EU will continue to lead the way, even if its efforts are not always conscious, deliberate, or always entirely understood. Wealthy democratic states do not go to war with one another, and in no other part of the world has this idea taken a firmer grip than in Europe; that grip will continue to tighten, and the EU will continue to be the leading champion of the use of soft power.

Finally, the EU will continue to face major challenges, and many of these will force European governments and societies into a fundamental rethinking of some long-cherished assumptions. The EU will continue to need to adjust to the flaws in its rules and policies, not all of which have been entirely predictable, and many of which have only been revealed by crisis. The EU will also have to continue working on more effective responses to the problems of unsustainable growth, underperforming economies, climate change, unemployment and underemployment, terrorism, poverty, and social exclusion. More generally, the EU will have to address the critical effects of demographic change: Europeans are living longer and getting older, they are having fewer children, and they are witnessing new patterns of immigration resulting in greater racial, cultural, and religious diversity.

Whatever happens, the European Union deserves closer and better-informed attention. In the Preface to this book I quoted the appeal made in February 2010 by Commission president José Manuel Barroso in a speech to the European Parliament, in which he called on Europeans to deny the 'intellectual glamour of pessimism and constant denigration' that was doing so much harm to the EU and to Europe's image. He went on to argue that 'what Europe needs to succeed is policies focused on results, better governance structures and confidence in our own ability to solve the problems we face.' The European Union is a human construct, and like all such constructs it is imperfect, and always will be. The real test it has always faced, and will long continue to face, is to address its imperfections. Winston Churchill once famously argued that democracy was the worst form of government – except for all the rest. The European Union may be imperfect, but it might also be argued that – in terms of what history suggests about how Europeans might otherwise manage themselves - it is better than the alternatives.

Bibliography

Aarts, Kees, and Henk van der Kolk (2006), 'Understanding the Dutch "no": The Euro, the East and the Elite', *PS: Political Science & Politics*, April, pp. 243–6.

Acheson, Dean (1969), *Present at the Creation: My Years in the State Department* (New York: W. W. Norton).

Allen, David, and Michael Smith (2002), 'External Policy Developments,' in Geoffrey Edwards and Georg Wiessala (eds), *The European Union: Annual Review of the EU 2001/2002* (Oxford: Blackwell).

Almond, Gabriel A. (1966), 'Political Theory and Political Science', *American Political Science Review*, 60:4, December, pp. 869–79.

Almond, Gabriel A., Russell J. Dalton, and G. Bingham Powell (eds) (2002), *European Politics Today*, 2nd edn (New York: Longman).

Alter, Karen J. (2009), 'The European Court and Legal Integration: An Exceptional Story or Harbinger of the Future?', in Karen J. Alter, *The European Court's Political Power: Selected Essays* (Oxford: Oxford University Press).

Amin, Ash, D. R. Charles and Jeremy Howells (1992), 'Corporate Restructuring and Cohesion in the New Europe', *Regional Studies*, 26:4, January, pp. 319–31.

Anderson, Benedict (1991), *Imagined Communities*, revised edition (London: Verso).

Anderson, Benedict (2006), *Imagined Communities: Reflections on the Origins and Spread of Nationalism* (London and New York: Verso).

Anderson, Scott (1992), 'Western Europe and the Gulf War,' in Reinhardt Rummel (ed.), *Toward Political Union: Planning a Common Foreign and Security Policy in the European Community* (Boulder: Westview Press).

Antonenko, Oksana, and Kathryn Pinnick (eds) (2005), *Russia and the European Union* (Abingdon: Routledge).

Armstrong, Kenneth A., and Simon J. Bulmer (1998), *The Governance of the Single European Market* (Manchester and New York: Manchester University Press).

Arnull, Anthony (2008), *The European Union and its Court of Justice*, 2nd edn (Oxford: Oxford University Press).

Arts, Karin, and Anna K. Dickson (2004), *EU Development Cooperation: From Model to Symbol* (Manchester: Manchester University Press).

Aspinwall, Mark, and Justin Greenwood (1998), 'Conceptualising Collective Action in the European Union: An Introduction', in Justin Greenwood and Mark Aspinwall (eds), *Collective Action in the European Union* (London: Routledge).

Bachtler, John, and Carlos Mendez (2007), 'Who Governs EU Cohesion Policy? Deconstructing the Reforms of the Structural Funds', *Journal of Common Market Studies*, 45:3, September, pp. 535–64.

Balibar, Ötienne (2004), *We, the People of Europe? Reflections on Transnational Citizenship* (Princeton, NJ: Princeton University Press).

Balme, Richard, and Didier Chabanet (2008), *European Governance and Democracy: Power and Protest in the EU* (Lanham, MD: Rowman & Littlefield).

Bardi, Luciano (2002), 'Transnational Trends: The Evolution of the European Party System', in Bernard Steunenberg and Jacques Thomassen (eds), *The European Parliament: Moving Toward Democracy in the EU* (Lanham, MD: Rowman & Littlefield).

Barnet, Richard J. (1983), *The Alliance: America, Europe, Japan; Makers of the Post-war World* (New York: Simon & Schuster).

Beck, Ulrich, and Edgar Grande (2007), *Cosmopolitan Europe* (Cambridge: Polity Press).

Bergström, Carl Fredrik (2005), *Comitology: Delegation of Power in the European Union and the Committee System* (Oxford: Oxford University Press).

Bernstein, Barton J. (1980), 'The Cuban Missile Crisis: Trading the Jupiters in Turkey?', *Political Science Quarterly* 95:1, Spring, pp. 97–125.

Billiet, Stijn (2005), 'The EC and WTO Dispute Settlement: The Initiation of Trade Disputes by the EC', *European Foreign Affairs Review*, 10:2, Summer, pp. 197–214.

Birch, Anthony (1966), 'Approaches to the Study of Federalism', *Political Studies* XIV:1, February.

Black, Jeremy (2000), *Modern British History Since 1900* (Basingstoke: Macmillan).

Blair, Tony (1998), in speech to the Labour Party Conference, Blackpool.

Blankart, Charles B. (2007), 'The European Union: Confederation, Federation or Association of Compound States?', *Constitutional Political Economy* 18:2, June, pp. 99–106.

Bohman, James, and Matthias Lutz-Bachmann (eds) (1997), *Perpetual Peace: Essays on Kant's Cosmopolitan Ideal* (Boston, MA: MIT Press).

Booker, Christopher, and Richard North (2005), *The Great Deception: Can the European Union Survive?* revised edn (London: Continuum).

Borrás, Susana, Charalampos Koutalakis, and Frank Wendler (2007), 'European Agencies and Input Legitimacy: EFSA, EMeA and EPO in the Post-Delegation Phase', *Journal of European Integration* 29:5, December, pp. 583–600.

Börzel, Tanja (2005), 'What Can Federalism Teach Us About the European Union? The German Experience', *Regional and Federal Studies* 15:2, June, pp. 245–57.

Bourdet, Yves, Joakim Gullstrand and Karin Olofsdotter (eds) (2007), *The European Union and Developing Countries: Trade, Aid and Growth in an Integrating World* (Cheltenham: Edward Elgar).

Bossong, Raphael (2008), 'The Action Plan on Combating Terrorism: A Flawed Instrument of EU Security Governance', *Journal of Common Market Studies* 46:1, January, pp. 27–48.

Breslin, Shaun, Richard Higgott, and Ben Rosamond (2002), 'Regions in Comparative Perspective' in Shaun Breslin, Christopher W. Hughes, Nicola Phillips and Ben Rosamond (eds), *New Regionalisms in the Global Political Economy: Theories and Cases* (Abingdon: Routledge).

Briand, Aristide (1997), 'Memorandum on the Organization of a Regime of a European Federal Union Addressed to Twenty-Six Governments of Europe', in Trevor Salmon and Sir William Nicoll (eds), *Building European Union: A Documentary History and Analysis* (Manchester: Manchester University Press).

Brine, Jacqueline (2002), *The European Social Fund and the EU: Flexibility, Growth, Stability* (London: Continuum).

British Home Office (2006), *Accession Monitoring Report May 2006–June 2006* (published online 22 August).

Broad, Roger, and Tim Geiger (eds) (1996), 'The 1975 British Referendum on Europe' *Contemporary British History* 10:3, Autumn, pp. 82–105.

Brooke, Michael Z., and H. Lee Remmers (eds) (1972), *The Multinational Company in Europe: Some Key Problems* (London: Longman),

Brown, L. Neville, and Tom Kennedy (2000), *The Court of Justice of the European Communities*, 5th edn (London: Sweet & Maxwell).

Brunkhorst, Hauke (2004), 'A Polity Without a State? European Constitutionalism Between Evolution and Revolution', in Erik Oddvar Eriksen, John Erik Fossum, and Agustín José Menéndez (eds), *Developing a Constitution for Europe* (London: Routledge).

Buchanan, Allen (1991), *Secession: The Morality of Political Divorce From Fort Sumter to Lithuania and Quebec* (Boulder, CO: Westview).

Bull, Hedley (1972), 'The Theory of International Politics, 1919–1969', in Brian Porter (ed.), *The Aberystwyth Papers: International Politics, 1919–1969* (Oxford: Oxford University Press), pp. 33–4.

Buller, Jim, and Andrew Gamble (2008), 'Britain: The Political Economy of Retrenchment', in Kenneth Dyson (ed.), *The Euro at 10: Europeanization, Power, and Convergence* (Oxford: Oxford University Press).

Bulmer, Simon, and Christian Lequesne (eds) (2005), in Introduction to *The Member States of the European Union* (Oxford: Oxford University Press).

Bures, Oldrich (2008), 'Europol's Fledgling Counterterrorism Role', *Terrorism and Political Violence*, 20:4, October, pp. 498–517.

Burgess, Michael (1996), 'Introduction: Federalism and Building the European Union', *Publius* 26:4, Autumn, pp. 1–15.

Burgess, Michael (2000), *Federalism and European Union: The Building of Europe, 1950–2000* (London: Routledge).

Burgess, Michael (2006), *Comparative Federalism: Theory and Practice* (London: Routledge).

Burgess, Michael (2009), 'Federalism', in Antje Wiener and Thomas Diez (eds), *European Integration Theory*, 2nd edn (Oxford: Oxford University Press).

Burrell, Alison (2009), 'The CAP: Looking Back, Looking Ahead', *Journal of European Integration* 31:3, May, pp. 271–89.

Burrows, Noreen, and Rosa Greaves (2007), *The Advocate General and EC Law* (Oxford: Oxford University Press).

Büthe, Tim (2007), 'The Politics of Competition and Institutional Change in the European Union: The First Fifty Years', in Sophie Meunier and Kathleen R. McNamara (eds), *The State of the European Union, Vol. 8* (Oxford: Oxford University Press).

Cafruny, Alan W., and J. Magnus Ryner (2007), *Europe at Bay: In the Shadow of US Hegemony* (Boulder, CO: Lynne Rienner).

Camilleri, Joseph A., and Jim Falk (1992), *The End of Sovereignty?* (Aldershot: Edward Elgar).

Caporaso, James (ed.) (2000), *Continuity and Change in the Westphalian Order* (Malden, MA: Blackwell).

Carbone, Maurizio (2007), *The European Union and International Development: The Politics of Foreign Aid* (Abingdon: Routledge).

Carubba, Clifford J. (2001), 'The Electoral Connection in European Union Politics', *Journal of Politics* 63:1, February, pp. 141–58.

Casarini, Nicola (2009), *Remaking Global Order: The Evolution of Europe–China Relations and its Implications for East Asia and the United States* (Oxford: Oxford University Press).

Cerutti, Furio, and Sonia Lucarelli (eds) (2008), *The Search for a European Identity* (Abingdon: Routledge).

Chang, Michelle (2009), *Monetary Integration in the European Union* (Basingstoke: Palgrave Macmillan).

Chinn, Menzie, and Jeffery Frankel (2005), 'Will the Euro Eventually Surpass the Dollar as the Leading International Reserve Currency?', National Bureau of Economic Research Working Paper 11510.

Christiansen, Thomas (2006), 'The Council of Ministers: Facilitating Interaction and Developing Actorness in the EU', in Jeremy Richardson (ed.), *European Union: Power and Policy-Making*, 3rd edn (Oxford and New York: Routledge).

Christiansen, Thomas, and Christine Reh (2009), *Constitutionalizing the European Union* (Basingstoke: Palgrave Macmillan).

Christin, Thomas, and Simon Hug (2002), 'Referendums and Citizen Support for European Integration', *Comparative Political Studies* 35:5, June, pp. 586–617.

Cini, Michelle, and Lee McGowan (2009), *Competition Policy in the European Union*, 2nd edn (London: Palgrave Macmillan).

Clark, Alan (1993), *Diaries* (London: Farrar, Straus & Giroux).

Clover, Charles,(2005), *The End of the Line: How Overfishing is Changing the World and What We Eat* (London: Ebury Press).

Cohen, Benjamin, J. (2008), 'The Europe in a Global Context: Challenges and Capacities', in Kenneth Dyson (ed.), *The Euro at 10: Europeanization, Power, and Convergence* (Oxford: Oxford University Press).

Collins, Ken, and David Earnshaw (1993), 'The Implementation and Enforcement of European Community Environment Legislation', in David Judge (ed.), *A Green Dimension for the European Community* (London: Frank Cass).

Commission of the European Communities (1970), 'Economic and Monetary Union in the Community' (the Werner Report), *Bulletin of the European Communities*, Supplement 11.

Commission of the European Communities (1973), *Report on the Regional Problems of the Enlarged Community* (the Thomson Report), COM(73)550 (Brussels: CEC).

Commission of the European Communities (1985), *Completing the Internal Market: The White Paper* (the Cockfield Report), COM(85)310 final, 14 June (Brussels: CEC).

Commission of the European Communities (1989), *Report of the Committee for the Study of Economic and Monetary Union* (Luxembourg. Office of Official Publications).

Commission of the European Communities (1990), *Transatlantic Declaration on EC–US Relations*, 23 November (Brussels: European Commission).

Commission of the European Communities (1994a), 'Competition and Integration: Community Merger Control Policy', *European Economy*, 57.

Commission of the European Communities (1994b), 'European Social Policy: A Way Forward for the Union'. White Paper COMM(94) 333 final, 27 July.

Commission of the European Communities (2002), *Update on the Internal Market: Scoreboard No. 10* (Luxembourg: CEC).

Commission of the European Communities (2003), Communication to the Council and the European Parliament, of 10 September, 'The European Union and the United Nations: The Choice of Multilateralism', COM (2003) 526 final.

Commission of the European Communities (2007), *Growing Regions, Growing Europe: Fourth Report on Economic and Social Cohesion* (Luxembourg: Office for Official Publications of the European Communities).

Commission of the European Communities (2008), *European Agencies: The Way Forward* (Luxembourg: CEC).

Conant, Lisa (2002), *Justice Contained: Law and Politics in the European Union* (Ithaca: Cornell University Press).

Corbett, Richard, Francis Jacobs, and Michael Shackleton (2005), *The European Parliament*, 6th edn (London: John Harper).

Costello, Cathryn (2005), 'Ireland's Nice Referenda', *European Constitutional Law Review* 1:3, October, pp. 357–82.

Coudenhove-Kalergi, Richard N. (1926), *Pan-Europa* (New York: A.A. Knopf).

Craig, David, and Matthew Elliott (2009), *The Great European Rip-off: How the Corrupt, Wasteful EU is Taking Control of Our Lives* (London: Arrow Books).

Criddle, Byron (1993), 'The French Referendum on the Maastricht Treaty, September 1992', *Parliamentary Affairs* 46:2, April, pp. 228–39.

Crystal, David (2003), *English as a Global Language*, 2nd edn (Cambridge: Cambridge University Press).

de Rougemont, Denis (1966), *The Idea of Europe* (London: Macmillan).

de Vreese, Claes H, and Holli A. Semetko (2004), *Political Campaigning in Referendums: Framing the Referendum Issue* (Abingdon: Routledge).

Defarges, Philippe Moreau (1988), 'Twelve Years of European Council History (1974–1986): The Crystallizing Forum,' in Jean-Marc Hoscheit and Wolfgang Wessels (eds), *The European Council 1974–1986: Evaluation and Prospects* (Maastricht: European Institute of Public Administration).

Dehousse, Renaud (1998), *The European Court of Justice* (New York: St Martin's Press).

Dehousse, Renaud (2002), *Misfits: EU Law and the Transformation of European Governance*. Working Paper No. 2/02, Jean Monnet Center for International and Regional Economic Law and Justice, New York University School of Law.

Delegation of the European Commission to the United States (2008), *Lobbying in the EU: An Overview*. At http://www.eurunion.org/EUInsight.

Dell, Edmund (1995), *The Schuman Plan and the British Abdication of Leadership in Europe* (Oxford: Oxford University Press).

Delors, Jacques (1991), 'European Integration and Security,' *Survival* 33:2, Spring, pp. 99–109.

Dimitrakopoulos, Dionyssis (2004), *The Changing European Commission* (Manchester: Manchester University Press).

Dinan, Desmond (2004), *Europe Recast: A History of European Union* (Basingstoke: Palgrave Macmillan).

Dinan, Desmond (2004a), 'Reconstituting Europe', in Maria Green Cowles and Desmond Dinan (eds), *Developments in the European Union 2* (Basingstoke and New York: Palgrave Macmillan).

Dinan, Desmond, and Marios Camhis (2004), 'The Common Agricultural Policy and Cohesion', in Maria Green Cowles and Desmond Dinan (eds), *Developments in the European Union 2* (Basingstoke: Palgrave Macmillan).

Dinan, Desmond (2005), *Ever Closer Union: An Introduction to European Integration*, 3rd edn (Basingstoke: Palgrave Macmillan).

Drake, Helen (2000a), 'The European Commission and the Politics of Legitimacy in the European Union,' in Neill Nugent (ed.), *At the Heart of the Union: Studies of the European Commission*, 2nd edn (New York: St Martin's Press).

Drake, Helen (2000b), *Jacques Delors: Perspectives on a European Leader* (London: Routledge).

Duchêne, Francois (1972), 'Europe's Role in World Peace', in Richard Mayne (ed.), *Europe Tomorrow: Sixteen Europeans Look Ahead* (London: Fontana), pp. 43, 47.

Duff, Andrew (2008), *True Guide to the Treaty of Lisbon* (Brussels: Alliance of Liberals and Democrats for Europe).

Dunkerley, David, Lesley Hodgson, Stanislaw Konopacki, Tony Spybey, and Andrew Thompson (2002), *Changing Europe: Identities, Nations and Citizens* (Abingdon: Routledge).

Dyson, Kenneth, and Kevin Featherstone (1999), *The Road to Maastricht: Negotiating Economic and Monetary Union* (Oxford: Oxford University Press).

Dyson, Kenneth (2008), Introduction to *The Euro at 10: Europeanization, Power, and Convergence* (Oxford: Oxford University Press).

Eden, Sir Anthony (1960), *Memoirs: Full Circle* (London: Cassell).

Eichengreen, Barry (2007), *The European Economy Since 1945: Coordinated Capitalism and Beyond* (Princeton: Princeton University Press).

Elgström, Ole (2003), 'Introduction', in Ole Elgström (ed.), *European Union Council Presidencies: A Comparative Perspective* (London: Routledge).

Eriksen, Erik Oddvar, John Erik Fossum, and Agustín José Menéndez (eds) (2004), in their introduction to *Developing a Constitution for Europe* (London: Routledge).

Eriksen, Erik Oddvar (2005), 'An Emerging European Public Sphere', *European Journal of Social Theory* 8:3, August, pp. 341–63.

Ertl, Hubert (2006), 'European Union Policies in Education and Training: The Lisbon Agenda as a Turning Point?', *Comparative Education* 42:1, February, pp. 5–27.

Etzioni, Amitai (1995), *The Spirit of Community: Rights, Responsibilities and the Communitarian Agenda* (London: Fontana Press).

Europol (2009), 'Facilitated Illegal Immigration into the European Union' Report available at http://www.europol.europa.eu/publications (retrieved September 2010).

Europol (2010), *EU Terrorism Situation and Trend Report 2009* (The Hague: Europol).

Eurostat (2009), *Europe in Figures: Eurostat Yearbook 2009* (Luxembourg: Office for Official Publications of the European Communities).

Farrell, David M., and Roger Scully (2007), *Representing Europe's Citizens? Electoral Institutions and the Failure of Parliamentary Representation* (Oxford: Oxford University Press).

Farrell, Mary, Björn Hettne, and Luk Van Langenhove (eds) (2005), *Global Politics of Regionalism: Theory and Practice* (London: Pluto Press).

Favell, Adrian (2008), *Eurostars and Eurocities: Free Movement and Mobility in an Integrating Europe* (Oxford: Blackwell).

Fawcett, Louise and Andrew Hurrell (eds) (1992), *Regionalism in World Politics: Regional Organization and International Order* (Oxford: Oxford University Press).

Featherstone, Kevin (2003), 'Introduction: In the Name of "Europe"', in Kevin Featherstone and Claudio M. Radaelli (eds), *The Politics of Europeanization* (Oxford: Oxford University Press).

Ferguson, Niall (2004), *Colossus: The Price of America's Empire* (New York: Penguin).

Fischer, Joschka (2000), 'From Confederacy to Federation: Thoughts on the Finality of European Integration', speech given at Humboldt University, Berlin, 12 May.

Fischler, Franz (2003). Speech before First European Parliamentary Symposium on Agriculture, Brussels, 16 October.

Fitzmaurice, John (1988), 'An Analysis of the European Community's Cooperation Procedure', *Journal of Common Market Studies* 26:4, June, pp. 389–400.

Follesdal, Andreas, and Simon Hix (2006), 'Why There is a Democratic Deficit in the EU: A Response to Majone and Moravcsik', *Journal of Common Market Studies* 44:3, September, pp. 533–62.

Forsyth, Murray (1981), *Unions of States: The Theory and Practice of Confederation* (Leicester: Leicester University Press).

Fossum, John Erik, and Philip Schlesinger (eds) (2007), *The European Union and the Public Sphere: A Communicative Space in the Making?* (Abingdon: Routledge).

Fox, W. T. R. (1944), *The Super-Powers: The United States, Britain and the Soviet Union – Their Responsibility for Peace* (New York: Harcourt Brace).

Franklin, Mark, Michael Marsh and Christopher Wlezien (1994), 'Attitudes Toward Europe and Referendum Votes: A Response to Siune and Svensson', *Electoral Studies* 13:2, June, pp. 117–21.

Franklin, Mark (1996), 'European Elections and the European Voter', in Jeremy Richardson (ed.) *European Union: Power and Policy-Making* (London: Routledge).

Franklin, Mark. N. (2005), *Voter Turnout and the Dynamics of Electoral Competition in Established Democracies Since 1945* (Cambridge: Cambridge University Press).

Franklin, Mark (2006), 'European Elections and the European Voter', in Jeremy Richardson (ed.), *European Union: Power and Policy-Making*, 3rd edn (Abingdon: Routledge),

Gabel, Matthew J. (1998), 'The Endurance of Supranational Governance: A Consociational Interpretation of the European Union', *Comparative Politics* 30:4, July, pp. 463–475.

Georgakakis, Didier (2004), 'Was it really just poor communication? A socio-political reading of the Santer Commission's resignation', in Andy Smith (ed.), *Politics and the European Commission: Actors, Interdependence, Legitimacy* (London: Routledge).

Géradin, Damien, Rodolphe Muñoz, and Nicolas Petit (eds) (2005), *Regulation Through Agencies in the EU: A New Paradigm of European Governance* (London: Edward Elgar).

Giddens, Anthony (2006), *Europe in the Global Age* (Cambridge: Polity Press).

Giddings, Philip, Roy Gregory and Anthea Harris (2002), 'The European Union Ombudsman', in Alex Warleigh (ed.), *Understanding European Union Institutions* (London: Routledge).

Giersch, Herbert (1985), *Eurosclerosis* (Kiel: Institut für Weltwirtschaft).

Gilbert, Mark (2003), *Surpassing Realism: The Politics of European Integration since 1945* (Lanham, MD: Rowman & Littlefield).

Gillingham, John (1991), *Coal, Steel, and the Rebirth of Europe, 1945–55* (New York: Cambridge University Press).

Gillingham, John (2003), *European Integration 1950–2003: Superstate or New Market Economy?* (Cambridge: Cambridge University Press).

Givens, Terri, and Adam Luedtke (2004), 'The Politics of European Union Immigration Policy: Institutions, Salience, and Harmonization', *Policy Studies Journal* 32:1, February, pp. 145–65.

Goldberg, Linda S. (2010), 'Is the International Role of the Dollar Changing?', *Current Issues in Economics and Finance* 16:1, January, pp. 1–7.

Gorst, Anthony, and Lewis Johnman (1997), *The Suez Crisis* (London: Routledge).

Grant, Wyn (1997), *The Common Agricultural Policy* (Basingstoke: Macmillan).

Graziano, Paolo, and Maarten P. Vink (eds) (2007), *Europeanization: New Research Agendas* (Basingstoke: Palgrave Macmillan).

Greer, Steven (2006), *The European Convention on Human Rights: Achievements, Problems and Prospects* (Cambridge: Cambridge University Press).

Griffiths, Martin (1999), 'David Mitrany', in *Fifty Key Thinkers in International Relations* (London: Routledge).

Griffiths, Richard T. (2000), *Europe's First Constitution: The European Political Community, 1952–1954* (London: Kogan Page).

Groux, Jean, and Philippe Manin (1985), *The European Communities in the International Order* (Brussels: Commission of the European Communities).

Guild, Elspeth (1997), 'The Legal Framework of Citizenship of the European Union', in David Cesarani and Mary Fulbrook (eds), *Citizenship, Nationality, and Migration in Europe* (London: Routledge).

Haas, Ernst B. (1958), *The Uniting of Europe: Political, Social, and Economic Forces, 1950–1957* (Stanford: Stanford University Press).

Haas, Ernst B. (1964), 'Technocracy, Pluralism and the New Europe', in Stephen R. Graubard (ed.), *A New Europe?* (Boston: Houghton Mifflin).

Haas, Ernst B. (1970), 'The Study of Regional Integration: Reflections on the Joy and Anguish of Pretheorizing', *International Organization* 24, Autumn, pp. 607–46.

Haas, Ernst B. (1975), *The Obsolescence of Regional Integration Theory* (Berkeley: Institute of International Studies, University of California).

Haas, Ernst B., and Philippe C. Schmitter (1964), 'Economics and Differential Patterns of Political Integration: Projections about Unity in Latin America' *International Organization*, 18:4, Autumn, pp. 705–37.

Haass, Richard (ed.) (1999), *Transatlantic Tensions: The United States, Europe, and Problem Countries* (Washington, DC: Brookings Institution).

Habermas, Jürgen, and Jacques Derrida (2003), 'February 15, or What Binds Europe Together: Plea for a Common Foreign Policy, Beginning in Core Europe', *Frankfurter Allgemeine Zeitung*, 31 May. Reproduced in Daniel Levy, Max Pensky and John Torpey (eds) (2005), *Old Europe, New Europe, Core Europe* (London: Verso).

Habermas, Jürgen (2004), 'Why Europe Needs a Constitution', in Erik Oddvar Eriksen, John Erik Fossum, and Augustín José Menéndez (eds), *Developing a Constitution for Europe* (London: Routledge).

Hagen, Tobias, and Philipp Mohl (2009), 'How does EU cohesion policy work? Evaluating its effects on fiscal outcome variables'. Discussion paper 09–051, Centre for European Economic Research, Mannheim.

Haltern, Ulrich (2003), 'Pathos and patina: the failure and promise of constitutionalism in the European imagination', *European Law Journal*, 9:11, February, pp. 14–44.

Hamilton, Daniel S., and Joseph P. Quinlan (2008), *Globalization and Europe: Prospering in the New Whirled Order* (Baltimore: Center for Transatlantic Relations).

Hanley, David (2008), *Beyond the Nation State: Parties in the Era of European Integration* (Basingstoke: Palgrave Macmillan).

Harmsen, Robert, and Menno Spiering (2005), 'Introduction: Euroscepticism and the Evolution of European Political Debate', in Robert Harmsen and Menno Spiering (eds), *Euroscepticism: Party Politics, National Identity and European Integration* (Amsterdam: Rodopi).

Harrop, Jeffrey (2002), 'Competition Policy', in Jackie Gower (ed.), *The European Union Handbook*, 2nd edn (London and Chicago: Fitzroy Dearborn).

Hartley, Emma, *Did David Hassselhof End the Cold War? 50 Facts You Need to Know: Europe* (Cambridge: Icon Books, 2006).

Haseler, Stephen (2004), *Super-State: The New Europe and its Challenge to America* (London: I B Taurus).

Hayes-Renshaw, Fiona, Christian Lequesne, and Pedro Mayor Lopez (1989), 'The Permanent Representations of the Member States of the European Communities,' *Journal of Common Market Studies* 28:2, December, pp. 119–37.

Hayes-Renshaw, Fiona, and Helen Wallace (2006), *The Council of Ministers*, 2nd edn (Basingstoke: Palgrave Macmillan).

Heater, Derek (1992), *The Idea of European Unity* (New York: St Martin's Press).

Heater, Derek (2004), *Citizenship: The Civic Ideal in World History, Politics and Education,* 3rd edn (Manchester: Manchester University Press).

Heath, Anthony, Iain McLean, Bridget Taylor, and John Curticel (1999), 'Between First and Second Order: A Comparison of Voting Behaviour in European and Local Elections in Britain', *European Journal of Political Research* 35:3, May, pp. 389–414.

Heidenreich, Martin, and Gabriele Bischoff (2008), 'The Open Method of Co-ordination: A Way to the Europeanization of Social and Employment Policies?', *Journal of Common Market Studies* 46:3, June, pp. 497–532.

Hitchcock, William I. (2004), *The Struggle for Europe: The Turbulent History of a Divided Continent* (New York: Anchor Books).

Hildebrand, Philipp M. (1993), 'The European Community's Environmental Policy, 1957 to 1992: From Incidental Measures to an International Regime?' in David Judge (ed.), *A Green Dimension for the European Community: Political Issues and Processes* (London: Frank Cass).

Hix, Simon (1994), 'The Study of the European Community: The Challenge to Comparative Politics', *West European Politics*, 17:1, January, pp. 1–30.

Hix, Simon, and Christopher Lord (1997), *Political Parties in the European Union* (New York: St Martin's Press).

Hix, Simon (2005), *The Political System of the European Union*, 2nd edn (Basingstoke: Palgrave Macmillan).

Hix, Simon, Abdul G. Noury, and Gerard Roland (2007), *Democratic Politics in the European Parliament* (Cambridge: Cambridge University Press).

Hobbing, Peter (2003), 'Management of External EU Borders: Enlargement and the European Border Guard Issue'. Paper presented at the Workshop 'Managing International and Inter-Agency Cooperation at the Border', Geneva, 13–15 March. Available at http://www.dcaf.ch/border/bs_genevaconf_030313Hobbing.pdf.

Hodson, Dermot (2010), 'Economic and Monetary Union', in Helen Wallace, Mark A. Pollack, and Alasdair R. Young (eds), *Policy-Making in the European Union*, 6th edn (Oxford: Oxford University Press).

Hoffman, Bruce (2006), *Inside Terrorism,* 2nd edn (New York: Columbia University Press).

Hoffmann, Stanley (1965), 'The European Process at Atlantic Crosspurposes', *Journal of Common Market Studies*, 3:2, pp. 85–101.

Hoffmann, Stanley (1966), 'Obstinate or Obsolete? The Fate of the Nation State and the Case of Western Europe', *Daedelus*, vol. 95, pp. 863–4, 908–11.

Hoffmann, Stanley (1982), 'Reflections on the Nation-State in Western Europe Today', *Journal of Common Market Studies*, 21:1/2, September/December, pp. 21–37.

Holland, Martin (2000), 'Resisting Reform or Risking Revival? Renegotiating the Lomé Convention,' in Maria Green Cowles and Michael Smith (eds), *The State of the European Union: Risks, Reform, Resistance, and Revival* (Oxford: Oxford University Press).

Hooghe, Liesbet, and Gary Marks (2001), *Multi-Level Governance and European Integration* (Lanham, MD: Rowman & Littlefield).

Hosli, Madeleine O. (2005), *The Euro: A Concise Introduction to European Monetary Integration* (Boulder, CO: Lynne Rienner).

Hourani, Albert (1989), 'Conclusions', in William Roger Louis and Roger Owen (eds), *Suez 1956: The Crisis and Its Consequences* (Oxford: Clarendon Press).

Howarth, David, and Peter Loedel (2005), *The European Central Bank: The New European Leviathan?* 2nd edn (Basingstoke: Palgrave Macmillan).

Howorth, Jolyon (2007), *Security and Defence Policy in the European Union* (Basingstoke: Palgrave Macmillan).

International Institute for Strategic Studies (2007), *The Military Balance 2007* (London: Routledge).

Ionescu, Ghita (1975), *Centripetal Politics: Government and the New Centres of Power* (London: Hart-Davis McGibbon).

Jacobs, Francis (2006), 'The Role of the European Court of Justice in the Protection of the Environment' *Journal of Environmental Law*, 18:2, May, pp. 185–205.

James, Robert Rhodes (ed.), *Winston S. Churchill: His Complete Speeches, 1897–1963: Vol III, 1943–49* (London Chelsea House Publishers, 1974).

Jenkins, Lindsay (2000), *The Last Days of Britain: The Final Betrayal* (Forest Hills, NY: Orange State Press).

Jenkins, Roy (1989), *European Diary, 1977–1981* (London: Collins).

Jensen, Maria Skovager, Kim Martin Lind, and Henrik Zobbe (2009), 'Enlargement of the European Union and Agricultural Policy Reform', *Journal of European Integration*, 31:3, May, pp. 329–48.

Johnson, Debra, and Paul Robinson (eds) (2005), *Perspectives on EU–Russia Relations* (Abingdon: Routledge).

Jones, Seth G. (2007), *The Rise of European Security Cooperation* (Cambridge: Cambridge University Press).

Jordan, Andrew, Dave Huitma, Harro van Asselt, and Frans Berkhout (eds) (2010),*Climate Change Policy in the European Union: Confronting the Dilemmas of Mitigation and Adaptation?* (Cambridge: Cambridge University Press).

Judge, David, and David Earnshaw (2008), *The European Parliament*, 2nd edn (Basingstoke: Palgrave Macmillan).

Judt, Tony (2005), *Postwar: A History of Europe since 1945* (New York: Penguin).

Kagan, Robert (2003), *Of Paradise and Power: America and Europe in the New World Order* (New York: Knopf).

Kaltenthaler, Karl (2006), *Policy-making in the European Central Bank: The Masters of Europe's Money* (Lanham, MD: Rowman & Littlefield).

Kassim, Hussein (2006), 'The Secretariat General of the European Commission', in David Spence (ed.), *The European Commission*, 3rd edn (London: John Harper).

Keleman, R. Daniel (2006), 'Shaming the Shameless? The constitutionalization of the European Union', in *Journal of European Public Policy* 13:8, December, pp. 1302–7.

Keohane, Robert O., and Stanley Hoffmann (1990), 'Conclusions: Community Politics and Institutional Change', in William Wallace (ed.), *The Dynamics of European Integration* (London: Royal Institute for International Affairs).

Kerr, David, and Liu Fei (eds) (2007), *The International Politics of EU-China Relations* (Oxford: Oxford University Press).

Kerr, Richard A. (2007), 'Global Warming: How Urgent Is Climate Change?' *Science*, 318:5854, 23 November, pp. 1230–1.

Knill, Christoph (2006), 'Implementation', in Jeremy Richardson (ed.), *European Union: Power and Policy-Making* (Abingdon: Routledge).

Kopstein, Jeffrey and Sven Steinmo (eds) (2008), *Growing Apart? America and Europe in the Twenty-First Century* (New York: Cambridge University Press).

Kowalski, Krzysztof (2009), Lecture on the History and Origins of the EU Flag, Indiana University, September.

Laffan, Brigid (1997), *The Finances of the European Union* (Basingstoke: Macmillan).

Laffan, Brigid, and Alexander Stubb (2003), 'Member States' in Elizabeth Bomberg and Alexander Stubb (eds), *The European Union: How Does it Work?* (Oxford: Oxford University Press).

Laffan, Brigid, and Johannes Lindner (2010), 'The Budget: Who Gets What, When and How?' in Helen Wallace, Mark A. Pollack, and Alasdair R. Young (eds), *Policy-Making in the European Union*, 6th edn (Oxford: Oxford University Press).

Lancaster, Carol (2006), *Foreign Aid: Diplomacy, Development, Domestic Politics* (Chicago: University of Chicago Press).

Landman, Todd Landman (2003), *Issues and Methods in Comparative Politics: An Introduction*, 2nd edn (London and New York: Routledge).

Lasok, K. P. E. (2007), *European Court Practice and Procedure*, 3rd edn (Haywards Heath: Tottel Publishing).

Lasswell, Harold D. (1968), 'The Future of the Comparative Method', *Comparative Politics*, 1:1, October, pp. 3–18.

Laursen, Finn (ed.) (2003), *Comparative Regional Integration: Theoretical Perspectives* (Aldershot: Ashgate).

Lavenex, Sandra (2001), 'The Europeanisation of Refugee Policies: Normative Challenges and Institutional Legacies', *Journal of Common Market Studies*, 39:5, December, pp. 851–74.

Lavenex, Sandra (2010), 'Justice and Home Affairs: Communitarization with Hesitation', in Helen Wallace, Mark A. Pollack, and Alasdair R. Young (eds), *Policy-Making in the European Union*, 6th edn (Oxford: Oxford University Press).

Layton, Christopher (1971), *Cross-Frontier Mergers in Europe* (Bath: Bath University Press).

Layton, Lyndsey (2008), 'Chemical Law Has Global Impact', *Washington Post*, 12 June.

Lemierre, Jean (2008), interview with the Atlantic Council at http://www.acus.org (retrieved June 2009).

Leonard, Mark (2005), *Why Europe will Run the 21st Century* (London: Fourth Estate).

Lequesne, Christian (2004), *The Politics of Fisheries in the European Union* (Manchester: Manchester University Press).

Levy, Jack S. (1983), *War in the Modern Great Power System, 1495–1975* (Lexington, KY: University Press of Kentucky).

Lewis, David P. (1993), *The Road to Europe: History, Institutions and Prospects of European Integration 1945–1993* (New York: Peter Lang).

Lightfoot, Simon (2005), *Europeanizing Social Democracy? The Rise of the Party of European Socialists* (London: Routledge).

Lijphart, Arend (1971), 'Comparative Politics and the Comparative Method', *American Political Science Review*, 65:3, September, pp. 682–93.

Lijphart, Arend (1977), *Democracy in Plural Societies: A Comparative Exploration* (New Haven, CT: Yale University Press).

Lijphart, Arend (1999), *Patterns of Democracy* (New Haven, CT: Yale University Press).

Lindberg, Leon N. (1963), *The Political Dynamics of European Economic Integration* (Stanford: Stanford University Press).

Lindblom, Charles (1959), 'The Science of "Muddling Through"', *Public Administration Review*, 19:2, pp. 79–88.

Lipset, Seymour Martin (1990), *Continental Divide: The Values and Institutions of the United States and Canada* (London: Routledge).

Lim, Timothy C. (2006), *Doing Comparative Politics* (Boulder, CO: Lynne Rienner).

Lister, Frederick K. (1996), *The European Union, the United Nations, and the Revival of Confederal Governance* (Westport, CT: Greenwood).

Luedtke, Adam (2006), 'The European Union Dimension: Supranational Integration, Free Movement of Persons, and Immigration Politics', in Craig Parsons and Timothy M. Smeeding (eds), *Immigration and the Transformation of Europe* (Cambridge: Cambridge University Press).

Lundestad, Geir (2003), *The United States and Western Europe Since 1945* (Oxford: Oxford University Press).

MacMullen, Andrew (2000), 'European Commissioners: National Routes to a European Elite,' in Neill Nugent (ed.), *At the Heart of the Union: Studies of the European Commission*, 2nd edn (New York: St Martin's Press).

Maas, Willem (2007), *Creating European Citizens* (Lanham, MD: Rowman & Littlefield).

Macmillan, Harold (1971), *Riding the Storm 1956–59* (New York: Harper & Row).

Majone, Giandomenico (1997), 'The New European Agencies: Regulation by Information', *Journal of European Public Policy*, 4:2, June, pp. 262–75.

Majone, Giandomenico (2006), 'Federation, Confederation, and Mixed Government: An EU-US Comparison', in Anand Menon and Martin Schain (eds), *Comparative Federalism: The European Union and the United States in Comparative Perspective* (Oxford: Oxford University Press).

Marks, Gary (1993), 'Structural Policy and Multi-level Governance in the EC', in Alan Cafruny and Glenda Rosenthal (eds), *The State of the European Community*, Vol. 2 (Boulder, CO: Lynne Rienner).

Marks, Gary, Carole J. Wilson and Leonard Ray (2002), 'National Political Parties and European Integration' *American Journal of Political Science*, 46:3, July, pp. 585–94.

Marks, Sally (2003), *The Illusion of Peace: International Relations in Europe, 1918–23*, 2nd edn (Basingstoke: Palgrave Macmillan).

Marlier, Eric, A. B. Atkinson, Bea Cantillon and Brian Nolan (2007), *The EU and Social Inclusion: Facing the Challenges* (Bristol: Policy Press).

Martin, Andrew and George Ross (eds) (2004), *Euros and Europeans: Monetary Integration and the European Model of Society* (Cambridge: Cambridge University Press).

Mason, David S. (2008), *The End of the American Century* (Lanham, MD: Rowman & Littlefield).

Mattli, Walter (1999), *The Logic of Regional Integration: Europe and Beyond* (Cambridge: Cambridge University Press).

Mazey, Sonia, and Jeremy Richardson (2003), 'Interest Groups and the Brussels Bureaucracy', in Jack Hayward and Anand Menon (eds), *Governing Europe* (Oxford: Oxford University Press).

Mazey, Sonia, and Jeremy Richardson (2006), 'Interest Groups and EU Policy-Making', in Jeremy Richardson (ed.), *European Union: Power and Policy-Making*, 3rd edn (Abingdon: Routledge).

McAleavey, P. (1993), 'The Politics of European Regional Development Policy: Additionality in the Scottish Coalfields', *Regional Politics and Policy*, 3:2, pp. 88–107.

McCormick, John (1995), *The Global Environmental Movement* (London: John Wiley).

McCormick, John (2001), *Environmental Policy in the European Union* (Basingstoke: Palgrave Macmillan).

McCormick, John (2007), *The European Superpower* (Basingstoke: Palgrave Macmillan).

McGrath, Conor (2005), *Lobbying in Washington, London, and Brussels: The Persuasive Communication of Political Issues* (New York: Edwin Mellen Press).

McGuire, Steven, and Michael Smith (2008), *The European Union and the United States* (Basingstoke: Palgrave Macmillan).

McKay, David (2001), *Designing Europe: Comparative Lessons from the Federal Experience* (Oxford: Oxford University Press).

Menon, Anand, Kalypso Nicolaidis and Jennifer Welsh (2004), 'In Defence of Europe – A Response to Kagan', *Journal of European Affairs*, 2:3, August, pp. 5–14.

Meunier, Sophie (2005), *Trading Voices: The European Union in International Commercial Negotiations* (Princeton: Princeton University Press).

Miliband, David (2007), Speech at the College of Europe, Bruges, 15 November, available at http://www.coleurop.be/events/909.

Millett, Timothy (1990), *The Court of First Instance of the European Communities* (London: Butterworth).

Milward, Alan S. (1984), *The Reconstruction of Western Europe 1945–51* (Berkeley: University of California Press).

Minahan, James B. (2000), *One Europe, Many Nations: A Historical Dictionary of European National Groups* (Westport, CT: Greenwood).

Mitrany, David (1966), *A Working Peace System* (Chicago: Quadrangle).

Mitrany, David (1970), 'The Functional Approach to World Organisation', in Carol A. Cosgrove and Kenneth J. Twitchett (eds), *The New International Actors: The UN and the EEC* (London: Macmillan).

Monar, Jörg (2001), 'The Dynamics of Justice and Home Affairs: Laboratories, Driving Factors and Costs', *Journal of Common Market Studies*, 39:4, November, pp. 747–64.

Monnet, Jean (1978), *Memoirs* (Garden City, NY: Doubleday).

Moravcsik, Andrew (1993), 'Preferences and Power in the European Community: A Liberal Intergovernmentalist Approach', *Journal of Common Market Studies*, 31:4, December, pp. 473–524.

Moravcsik, Andrew (1998), *The Choice for Europe* (Ithaca, NY: Cornell University Press).

Moravcsik, Andrew (2001), 'Federalism in the European Union: Rhetoric and Reality' in Kalypso Nicolaidis and Robert Howse (eds), *The Federal Vision: Legitimacy and Levels of Governance in the United States and the European Union* (Oxford: Oxford University Press).

Moravcsik, Andrew (2002), 'In Defence of the 'Democratic Deficit': Reassessing Legitimacy in the European Union', *Journal of Common Market Studies*, 40:4, November, pp. 603–24.

Moravcsik, Andrew (2007), 'The European Constitutional Settlement', in Sophie Meunier and Kathleen R. McNamara (eds), *Making History: European Integration and Institutional Change at Fifty* (Oxford: Oxford University Press).

Morgan, Annette (1976), *From Summit to Council: Evolution in the EEC* (London: Chatham House).

Morgan, Iwan W. and Philip J. Davies (eds) (2008), *The Federal Nation: Perspectives on American Federalism* (New York: Palgrave Macmillan).

Morris, Chris (2005), *The New Turkey: The Quiet Revolution on the Edge of Europe* (London: Granta).

Mowle, Thomas S. (2004), *Allies at Odds? The United States and the European Union* (New York: Palgrave Macmillan).

Müller, Wolfgang C. and Kaare Strøm (eds) (2003), *Coalition Governments in Western Europe* (Oxford: Oxford University Press).

Mundell, Robert (2000), 'The euro and the stability of the international monetary system', in Robert Mundell and Armand Clesse (eds), *The Euro as a Stabilizer in the International Economic System* (Dordrecht: Kluwer).

Neuhold, Christine, and Pierpaolo Sttembri (2007), 'The role of European Parliament committees in the EU policy-making process', in Thomas Christiansen and Torbjörn Larsson (eds), *The Role of Committees in the Policy-Process of the European Union* (Cheltenham: Edward Elgar).

Niemi, Jyrki, and Jukka Kola (2005), 'Renationalization of the Common Agricultural Policy: Mission Impossible?', *International Food and Agribusiness Management Review*, 8:4, pp. 23–41.

Nijeboer, Arjen (2005), 'The Dutch Referendum', *European Constitutional Law Review*, 1:3, October, pp. 393–405.

Nitze, William, and Leon Hadar (2009), 'EU could bring peace to Middle East', *The Guardian*, 4 December.

Nugent, Neill (2001), *The European Commission* (Basingstoke: Palgrave Macmillan).

Nye, Joseph S. (1970), 'Comparing Common Markets: A Revised Neofunctionalist Model', *International Organization*, 24:4, Autumn, pp. 796–835.

Occhipinti, John D. (2003), *The Politics of EU Police Cooperation: Toward a European FBI?* (Boulder, CO: Lynne Rienner).

Ohmae, Kenichi (1995), *The End of the Nation State: The Rise of Regional Economies* (New York: The Free Press).

Ohmae, Kenichi (2005), *The Next Global Stage: Challenges and Opportunities in our Borderless World* (Upper Saddle River, NJ: Wharton School Publishing).

Olsen, Johan P. (2002), 'The Many Faces of Europeanization' *Journal of Common Market Studies*, 40:5, December, pp. 921–52.

O'Neill, Jim (2010), 'A Twenty-first Century International Monetary System: Two Scenarios', in Paola Subacchi and John Driffill (eds), *Beyond the Dollar: Rethinking the International Monetary System* (London: Chatham House).

Orbie, Jan (2008), 'The European Union's Role in World Trade: Harnessing Globalisation?', in Jan Orbie (ed.), *Europe's Global Role: External Policies of the European Union* (Aldershot: Ashgate).

Orbie, Jan, and Helen Versluys (2008) 'The European Union's International Development Policy: Leading and Benevolent?, in Jan Orbie (ed.), *Europe's Global Role: External Policies of the European Union* (Aldershot: Ashgate).

Owen, Richard, and Michael Dynes (1989), *The Times Guide to 1992: Britain in a Europe Without Frontiers* (London: Times Publications).

Page, Edward C. (2003), 'Europeanization and the Persistence of Administrative Systems', in Jack Hayward and Anand Menon (eds), *Governing Europe* (Oxford: Oxford University Press).

Palayret, Jean-Marie, Helen Wallace and Pascaline Wynand (eds) (2006), *Visions, Votes And Vetoes: The Empty Chair Crisis And the Luxembourg Compromise Forty Years On* (Brussels: Peter Lang).

Palmer, Michael, and John Lambert (eds) (1968), *European Unity: A Survey of European Organizations* (London: George Allen & Unwin).

Pan, Christoph, and Beate Sibylle Pfeil (2004), *National Minorities in Europe* (West Lafayette, IN: Purdue University Press).

Panayi, Panikos (2000), *An Ethnic History of Europe Since 1945: Nations, States and Minorities* (Harlow: Longman).

Pardo, Sharon, and Joel Peters (2009), *Uneasy Neighbors: Israel and the European Union* (Lanham, MD: Lexington Books).

Parsons, Craig A., and Timothy M. Smeeding (eds) (2006a), *Immigration and the Transformation of Europe* (Cambridge: Cambridge University Press).

Parsons, Craig, and Timothy M. Smeeding (2006b), 'What's Unique about Immigration in Europe?', in Craig Parsons and Timothy M. Smeeding (eds), *Immigration and the Transformation of Europe* (Cambridge: Cambridge University Press).

Pastor, Robert A. (2001), *Toward a North American Community: Lessons from the Old World for the New* (Washington, DC: Institute for International Economics).

Pearce, David, and Francois-Carlos Bovagnet (2005), 'The Demographic Situation in the European Union' *Population Trends*, No. 119 (London: Office for National Statistics, Spring).

Peter, Laurence (2009), 'Profile: EU Commission Chief Barroso', *BBC News Online*, 8 July.

Peter, Laurence (2010), 'Delays Bedevil EU Help for Roma', on BBC News Online at http://www.bbc.co.uk, 16 September.

Peters, B. Guy (1992), 'Bureaucratic Politics and the Institutions of the European Community,' in Alberta Sbragia (ed.), *Euro-Politics: Institutions and Policymaking in the 'New' European Community* (Washington, DC: Brookings Institution).

Peters, B. Guy, and Jon Pierre (2004), 'Multi-level Governance and Democracy: A Faustian Bargain?', in Ian Bache and Matthew Flinders (eds), *Multi-Level Governance* (Oxford: Oxford University Press).

Philip, Alan Butt (1985), *Pressure Groups in the European Community* (London: University Association for Contemporary European Studies).

Pienning, Christopher (2001), 'The EP Since 1994: Making Its Mark on the World Stage', in Juliet Lodge (ed.), *The 1999 Elections to the European Parliament* (Basingstoke: Palgrave Macmillan).

Pijpers, Alfred (1998), entry on 'Intergovernmental Conferences', in Desmond Dinan (ed.), *Encyclopedia of the European Union* (Basingstoke: Macmillan).

Pinder, John (1991), *European Community: The Building of a Union* (Oxford: Oxford University Press).

Pollard, Naomi, Maria Latorre and Dhananjayan Sriskandarajah (2008), *Floodgates or Turnstiles? Post-EU Enlargement Migration Flows to (and from) the UK* (London: Institute for Public Policy Research).

Prestowitz, Clyde (2003), *Rogue Nation: American Unilateralism and the Failure of Good Intentions* (New York: Basic Books).

Princen, Sebastiaan (2009), *Agenda-Setting in the European Union* (Basingstoke: Palgrave Macmillan).

Puchala, Donald J. (1975), 'Domestic Politics and Regional Harmonization in the European Communities', *World Politics*, 27:4, July, pp. 496–520.

Raz, Joseph (1998), 'On the Authority and Interpretation of Constitutions: Some Preliminaries', in Larry Alexander (ed.), *Constitutionalism: Philosophical Foundations* (Cambridge: Cambridge University Press).

Reid, T.R. (2004), *The United States of Europe: The New Superpower and the End of American Supremacy* (New York: Penguin).

Reiff, Karlheinz, and Hermann Schmitt (1980), 'Nine Second-Order National Elections: A Conceptual Framework for the Analysis of European Election Results,' *European Journal of Political Research*, 8:1, March, pp. 3–44.

Renan, Ernest (1882), in speech titled 'What is a Nation?' Given at the Sorbonne in March, translated by and quoted in Timothy Baycroft, *Nationalism in Europe 1789–1945* (Cambridge: Cambridge University Press, 1998).

Rhodes, Martin (2010), 'Employment Policy: Between Efficacy and Experimentation', in Helen Wallace, Mark A. Pollack, and Alasdair R. Young (eds), *Policy-Making in the European Union*, 6th edn (Oxford: Oxford University Press).

Richardson, Jeremy (2006), 'Policy-making in the EU: Interests, ideas and garbage cans of primeval soup', in Jeremy Richardson (ed), *European Union: Power and Policy-Making*, 3rd edn (Abingdon: Routledge).

Riddell, Roger (2007), *Does Foreign Aid Really Work?* (New York: Oxford University Press).

Rieger, Elmar (2005), 'Agricultural Policy: Constrained Reforms', in Helen Wallace, William Wallace and Mark A. Pollack (eds), *Policy-Making in the European Union*, 5th edn (Oxford: Oxford University Press).

Rifkin, Jeremy (2004), *The European Dream: How Europe's Vision of the Future is Quietly Eclipsing the American Dream* (New York: Jeremy Tarcher/Penguin).

Ringe, Nils (2009), *Who Decides, and How? Preferences, Uncertainty, and Policy Choice in the European Parliament* (Oxford: Oxford University Press).

Rittberger, Berthold (2005), *Building Europe's Parliament: Democratic Representation Beyond the Nation-State* (Oxford: Oxford University Press).

Robyn, Richard (ed.) (2005), *The Changing Face of European Identity* (Abingdon: Routledge).

Roper, Steven (2007), 'European Education Reform and Its Impact on Curriculum and Admissions: Implications of the Bologna Process on United States Education', *Journal of Political Science Education*, 3:1, January, pp. 51–60.

Rosamond, Ben (2000), *Theories of European Integration* (Basingstoke: Macmillan).

Ross, George (1995), *Jacques Delors and European Integration* (New York: Oxford University Press).

Ross, Robert, Øystein Tunsjø, and Zhang Tuosheng (eds) (2009), *US–China–EU Relations* (Abingdon: Routledge).

Ruggie, John Gerard, Peter J. Katzenstein, Robert O. Keohane, and Philippe C. Schmitter (2005), 'Transformations in World Politics: The Intellectual Contribution of Ernst B. Haas', *Annual Review of Political Science*, vol. 8, pp. 271–96.

Rüland, Jürgen, Heiner Hänggi, and Ralf Roloff (eds) (2008), *Interregionalism and International Relations: A Stepping Stone to Global Governance?* (Abingdon: Routledge).

Rumford, Chris (2007), 'Introduction' to *Cosmopolitanism and Europe* (Liverpool: Liverpool University Press).

Russell, James W. (2006), *Double Standard: Social Policy in Europe and the United States* (Lanham, MD: Rowman & Littlefield).

Salmon, Trevor, and Sir William Nicoll (eds) (1997), *Building European Union: A Documentary History and Analysis* (Manchester: Manchester University Press).

Sbragia, Alberta (1992), 'Introduction' and 'Thinking about the European Future: The Uses of Comparison', in Alberta Sbragia (ed.), *Euro-Politics: Institutions and Policymaking in the 'New' European Community* (Washington, DC: Brookings Institution).

Scully, Roger (2005), *Becoming Europeans? Attitudes, Behaviour, and Socialization in the European Parliament* (Oxford: Oxford University Press).

Selznick, Philip (2002), *The Communitarian Persuasion* (Baltimore, MD: Johns Hopkins University Press).

Seton-Watson, Hugh (1977), *Nations and States: An Inquiry Into the Origins of Nations and the Politics of Nationalism* (London: Methuen).

Shackleton, Michael (1990), *Financing the European Community* (New York: Council on Foreign Relations Press).

Shambaugh, David, Eberhard Sandschneider, and Zhou Hong (eds) (2008), *China-Europe Relations: Perceptions, Policies and Prospects* (Abingdon: Routledge).

Shapiro, Martin (1992), 'The European Court of Justice', in Alberta Sbragia (ed.), *Euro-Politics: Institutions and Policymaking in the "New" European Community* (Washington, DC: Brookings Institution).

Sherrington, Philippa (2000), *The Council of Ministers: Political Authority in the European Union* (London: Pinter).

Simpson, A. W. Brian (2001), *Human Rights and the End of Empire: Britain and the Genesis of the European Convention* (Oxford: Oxford University Press).

Skouris, Vassilios (2004), Interview with the *Financial Times* (London), 30 June. Available at http://www.open-europe.org.uk.

Smith, Anthony D. (ed.) (2001), *Nationalism* (Cambridge: Polity Press).

Smith, Graham (1999), *The Post-Soviet States: Mapping the Politics of Transition* (London: Edward Arnold).

Smith, Michael (2006), 'The Commission and External Relations,' in David Spence (ed.), *The European Commission*, 3rd edn (London: John Harper).

Snyder, Francis (2003), 'The Unfinished Constitution of the European Union: Principles, Processes and Culture' in J. H. H. Weiler and Marlene Wind (eds), *European Constitutionalism Beyond the State* (Cambridge: Cambridge University Press).

Sørensen, Georg (2004), *The Transformation of the State: Beyond the Myth of Retreat* (Basingstoke: Palgrave Macmillan).

Sørensen, Georg (2006), 'The Transformation of the State' in Colin Hay, Michael Lister and David Marsh (eds), *The State: Theories and Issues* (Basingstoke: Palgrave Macmillan).

Spaak, Paul-Henri (1971), *The Continuing Battle: Memoirs of a European 1933–66* (Boston: Little, Brown).

Spence, David (2006a), 'The President, the College and the Cabinets', in David Spence (ed.), *The European Commission*, 3rd edn (London: John Harper).

Spence, David (2006b), 'The Directorates-General and the Services: Structures, Functions and Procedures', in David Spence (ed.), *The European Commission*, 3rd edn (London: John Harper).

Spero, Joan E., and Jeffrey A. Hart (2003), *The Politics of International Economic Relations* (Belmont, CA: Wadsworth).

Spinelli, Altiero (1972), 'The Growth of the European Movement Since the Second World War', in Michael Hodges (ed.), *Europe Integration: Selected Readings* (Harmondsworth: Penguin).

Stirk, Peter M. R., and David Weigall (eds) (1999), *The Origins and Development of European Integration: A Reader and Commentary* (London and New York: Pinter).

Strange, Susan (1996), *The Retreat of the State: The Diffusion of Power in the World Economy* (Cambridge: Cambridge University Press).

Swinbank, Alan (2002), 'The Common Agricultural Policy' in Jackie Gower (ed), *The European Union Handbook*, 2nd edn (London: Fitzroy Dearborn).

Taggart, Paul, and Aleks Szczerbiak (2001), 'Parties, Positions and Europe: Euroscepticism in the Candidate States of Central and Eastern Europe', Paper presented at the Annual Meeting of the Political Studies Association, Manchester, April.

Talbot, Strobe (1992), 'America Abroad: The Birth of the Global Nation', *Time*, 20 July, p. 70.

Thatcher, Margaret (1993), *The Downing Street Years* (New York: HarperCollins).

Thomassen, Jacques (2005), 'Introduction', in Jacques Thomassen (ed.), *The European Voter: A Comparative Study of Modern Democracies* (Oxford: Oxford University Press).

Tsoukalis, Loukas (2003), 'Monetary Policy and the Euro', in Jack Hayward and Anand Menon (eds), *Governing Europe* (Oxford and New York: Oxford University Press).

Tushnet, Mark V. (2000), *Taking the Constitution Away From the Courts* (Princeton: Princeton University Press).

Union of International Associations Homepage (retrieved July 2010), at www.uia.org.

United Nations, Department of Economic and Social Affairs, Population Division (2009), *Trends in International Migrant Stock: The 2008 Revision* (United Nations database, POP/DB/MIG/Stock/Rev.2008).

United Nations Department of Economic and Social Affairs, Population Division (2009), *World Population Prospects, the 2008 Revision* (Geneva: United Nations).

Urwin, Derek W. (1995), *The Community of Europe*, 2nd edn (London: Longman).

van Creveld, Martin (1999), *The Rise and Decline of the State* (Cambridge: Cambridge University Press).

van der Eijk, Cees, and Mark N. Franklin (eds) (1996), *Choosing Europe? The European Electorate and National Politics in the Face of Union* (Ann Arbor: University of Michigan Press).

van Dormael, Armand (1978), *Bretton Woods: Birth of a Monetary System* (New York: Holmes & Meier).

van Eekelen, Willem (1990), 'WEU and the Gulf Crisis,' *Survival*, 32:6, pp. 519–32.

Vasileva, Katya (2010), 'Foreigners living in the EU are diverse and largely younger than the nationals of the EU Member States', *Eurostat Statistics in Focus*, 45/2010 (Brussels: Eurostat).

Védrine, Hubert, with Dominique Moïsi (2001), *France in an Age of Globalization* (Washington, DC: Brookings Institution).

Walkenhorst, Heiko (2008), 'Explaining change in EU education policy' *Journal of European Public Policy*, 15:4, June, 567–87.

Wallace, Anthony (2004), 'Completing the Single Market: The Lisbon Strategy', in Maria Green Cowles and Desmond Dinan (eds), *Developments in the European Union 2* (Basingstoke: Palgrave Macmillan).

Wallace, William (1983), 'Less than a Federation, More than a Regime: The Community as a Political System', in Helen Wallace, William Wallace and Carole Webb (eds), *Policy-Making in the European Community*, 2nd edn (Chichester: Wiley).

Wallace, William (2005), 'Foreign and Security Policy', in Helen Wallace, William Wallace, and

Mark A. Pollack (eds), *Policy-Making in the European Union*, 5th edn (Oxford: Oxford University Press).

Ward, Ian (1996), *A Critical Introduction to European Law* (London: Butterworth).

Watts, Ronald J. (2008), *Comparing Federal Systems*, 3rd edn (Montreal: Institute of Intergovernmental Relations).

Weigall, David, and Peter Stirk (eds) (1992), *The Origins and Development of the European Community* (Leicester: Leicester University Press).

Werts, Jan (2008), *The European Council* (London: John Harper).

Westlake, Martin, and David Galloway (eds) (2004), *The Council of the European Union*, 3rd edn (London: John Harper).

Wexler, Immanuel (1983), *The Marshall Plan Revisited: The European Recovery Program in Economic Perspective* (Westport, CT: Greenwood Press).

White, Brian (2001), *Understanding European Foreign Policy* (Basingstoke: Palgrave Macmillan).

Wildavsky, Aaron (1979), *Speaking Truth to Power* (New York: John Wiley).

Wilks, Stephen (2005), 'Competition Policy: Challenge and Reform', in Helen Wallace, William Wallace, and Mark A. Pollack (eds), *Policy-Making in the European Union*, 5th edn (Oxford: Oxford University Press).

Wilson, Dominic, and Roopa Purushothaman (2003), 'Dreaming With BRICs: The Path to 2050', Global Economics Paper No. 99, Goldman Sachs, 1 October.

Windrow, Martin (2004), *The Last Valley: Dien Bien Phu and the French Defeat in Vietnam* (London: Weidenfeld & Nicolson).

Wolff, Sarah, Nicole Wichmann, and Gregory Mounier (eds) (2009), *The External Dimension of Justice and Home Affairs: A Different Security Agenda for the European Union?* (Abingdon: Routledge).

Wurzel, Rüdiger, and James Connelly (eds) (2010), *The European Union as a Leader in International Climate Change Politics* (Abingdon: Routledge).

Yahuda, Michael (2008), 'The Sino-European Encounter: Historical Influences on Contemporary Encounters', in David Shambaugh, Eberhard Sandschneider and Zhou Hong (eds), *China–Europe Relations: Perceptions, Policies and Prospects* (Abingdon: Routledge).

Young, Alasdair R. (2010), 'The European Policy Process in Comparative Perspective', in Helen Wallace, Mark A. Pollack, and Alasdair R. Young (eds), *Policy-Making in the European Union*, 6th edn (Oxford: Oxford University Press).

Younger, Kenneth (1959), in a review of Ernst Haas, *The Uniting of Europe*, International Affairs 35:1, January.

Zimmerman, Joseph F. (2008), *Contemporary American Federalism: The Growth of National Power* (Albany, NY: State University of New York Press).

Zurcher, Arnold J. (1958), *The Struggle to Unite Europe 1940–58* (New York: New York University Press).

Index

Note: key entries (usually with definitions) indicated in **boldface**.